COOKING WITH SPICES

SPICE	Bread, Rolls and Sweet Buns	Soups, Casseroles and Gravies	Salads, Dressings and Dips	Desserts and Sweets	Pickles and Preserves
ALLSPICE Strong flavor; tastes like a blend of cinnamon, cloves and nutmeg. Sold whole as dried berries or ground.	Use sparingly in yeast or baking-powder doughs.	Add a pinch to beef, pork, veal or lamb dishes.	Gives pizzazz to ham salad. Sprinkle a little in dressing for fruit salads.	Delicious in applesauce cookies, fruit bars and fruit pies. Stir a pinch into holiday fruitcake. Sprinkle into hard sauce for Christmas plum pudding.	Use whole spicy berry for making tiny pickled cucumbers.
CHILI POWDER Rich blend of spices such as cumin, garlic powder, oregano and chili peppers.	Brings a dash of spicy flavor to cornbread and corn muffins.	A must for Mexican-style dishes. Adds zip to bean or tomato soup. Sprinkle into spaghetti sauce.	Mix in dressings for potato and macaroni salad. Good in dips.	Not recommended.	Gives a hot touch to tomato and other relishes and chutneys.
CINNAMON Warm, sweet, pungent spice. Actually a tree bark. Sold as rolled dried sticks or ground.	Popular in coffee cakes, breakfast rolls, muffins and sweet yeast breads.	Essential for Greek and Middle Eastern savory meat dishes and stews, especially lamb. Use in pork marinades, tomato sauce and fruit soups.	Sprinkle into fruit salads. Especially good with carrots, spinach, peas, squash and onions.	A must for pumpkin and apple pie—good in all fruit pies. Add to cookies. Delicious in cakes with dried fruit, gingerbread, bread pudding and custard.	Imparts a nice note to chutneys, jams and pickles.
CORIANDER Bold flavor. Reminiscent of sage, citrus and caraway. Coriander seeds are from the cilantro plant.	Add to coffee cakes, Danish pastries, and banana and carrot breads, and sprinkle over a variety of baked goods.	Enhances pea soup, fruit soups, lentil stews, curries, rice pilaf and Mediterranean stews.	Try a little in creamy fruit salad dressings, marinated mushrooms and tomato salads. Nice touch in sandwich spreads, marinades and stuffings.	A hint is good in gingersnap cookies and cookies with dried fruit. A pinch can enliven a fruit cake.	Well received in pickling brines.
CUMIN Very aromatic and nutty flavor. Sold as seed or ground.	Sprinkle ground cumin into savory bread dough or cumin seeds over top of unbaked loaf.	Frequently used in chili and other Southwestern dishes, carrot soup, curries, and Middle Eastern and Mediterranean lamb dishes.	Adds subtle touch to dressings for chicken salad and fruit salads. Stir a pinch into yogurt dips.	Try in oatmeal and spice cookies, and in apple pie. Excellent in gingerbread and holiday cakes with dried fruit.	An all-purpose spice for pickled vegetables, vegetable relishes, chutneys and curried preserves.
CURRY POWDER Blend of spices such as turmeric, fenugreek, cumin, coriander, ginger and ground hot red pepper.	Add a large pinch to bread dough or cornmeal muffins.	Use sparingly as flavor enhancer; add more for a real curry bite.	Use to make curried chicken salad. Sprinkle a bit into seafood and vegetable dips, and into spreads.	Not recommended.	Pickled carrots and green beans are good with curry. Use sparingly.
FENNEL Flavor similar to anise or licorice but milder. Sold as seed, whole or ground.	Use to flavor sweet rolls and savory yeast or quick breads.	Excellent in fish stews, borscht, minestrone, lamb casseroles, duck stew, sausage and cabbage dishes, and in pasta sauces.	Goes well in salad dressings, cheese spreads and meat and fish marinades.	Popular in Scandinavian cookies and pastries. Try in rice pudding and scones.	Good in pickled cucumbers and other vegetables and in green tomato relish.
GINGER Pungent underground stem, or rhizome. Sold fresh, dried, candied or ground.	A pinch of ground or a tablespoon of chopped candied ginger imparts great flavor to bread or rolls.	Enhances chicken broth. Stir into gravies for beef, pork and veal, and into vegetable mixtures.	A good seasoning for fruit salad, and in salad dressings for piquancy. Use sparingly.	Stir large pinch of ground ginger into cookie doughs for extra zip. Use fresh or ground in rice pudding, gingerbread and applesauce cake.	An all-round spice for jams, jellies, and pickled fruits.

IMPORTANT INFORMATION

Dear Reader:

WELCOME TO **THE FAMILY CIRCLE COOKBOOK.**

We have grouped the tabbed dividers at the back of this book. You will need to insert each tabbed divider in place before its chapter. Simply open the rings and insert each tabbed divider as follows:

Enjoy **THE FAMILY CIRCLE COOKBOOK:** *New Tastes for New Times.*

The Editors

Title page: Chicken Breasts in Orange Sauce (237).

Front cover: Cornish Hens (288); Green Beans, Rice with Sweet Peppers, Cranberry Fool (530); Vegetarian Four-Bean Chili (225); Warm Spinach and Pear Salad with Bacon Dressing (177).

Back cover: Melon and Shrimp with Cilantro-Lime Dressing (170); Baked Ziti with Vegetables (191); Tropical Fruit Salad with Ginger-Yogurt Dressing (174).

THE FAMILY CIRCLE COOKBOOK

New Tastes for New Times

BY THE EDITORS OF FAMILY CIRCLE
AND DAVID RICKETTS
Photographs by Steven Mark Needham

SIMON & SCHUSTER

NEW YORK LONDON TORONTO SYDNEY TOKYO SINGAPORE

SIMON & SCHUSTER
Simon & Schuster Building
Rockefeller Center
1230 Avenue of the Americas
New York, New York 10020

Copyright © 1992 by NYT
Women's Magazines.
Family Circle is a registered trade-
mark of The Family Circle, Inc.

DESIGNED BY BARBARA MARKS
Manufactured in the United States
of America

10 9 8 7 6 5 4 3 2

**Library of Congress
Cataloging-in-Publication Data**

The Family circle cookbook : new
  tastes for new times / by the
  editors of Family Circle and
  David Ricketts ; photographs by
  Steven Mark Needham.
      p. cm.
  Includes index.
  1. Cookery. I. Ricketts,
David. II. Family circle
(New York, N.Y.)
TX651.F34   1992
641.5—dc20   92-1146
                          CIP
ISBN: 0-671-73572-1

FAMILY CIRCLE MAGAZINE

EDITOR IN CHIEF: *Jacqueline Leo*
CREATIVE DIRECTOR: *Douglas Turshen*
FOOD EDITOR: *Jean Hewitt*
ASSOCIATE EDITOR: *Diane Mogelever*
HOME ECONOMIST: *Regina C. Ragone*
ADMINISTRATIVE ASSOCIATE: *Sheena
  K. Gonzalez*
TEST KITCHEN ASSISTANTS:
*Ruth Deep   Frantiska Sliva
Constanta Ionesco*

THE FAMILY CIRCLE COOKBOOK: NEW TASTES FOR NEW TIMES

COOKBOOK DIRECTOR AND EDITOR:
  David Ricketts
NUTRITION EDITOR AND RESEARCH
  DIRECTOR: *Susan McQuillan*
MICROWAVE EDITOR: *Beatrice Cihak*
TEST KITCHEN MANAGERS:
Jo Ann Brett   Paul E. Piccuito
TEST KITCHEN ASSOCIATES:
*Georgia Chan Downard
Jim Fobel
Chris Gibson
Sandra Rose Gluck
Dora Jonassen
Michael Krondl
Perla Meyers
Catherine Paukner
Veronica Petta
Sarah Reynolds
Marie Simmons
Nina Simonds
Isabelle Vita
Marianne Zanzarella*
RESEARCH ASSOCIATES:
*Marjorie Cubisino
Ceri E. Hadda   Lyn Stallworth*
NUTRITION ANALYSIS:
Hill Nutrition Associates, Inc.

PHOTOGRAPHER AND PHOTOGRAPHY
  DIRECTOR: *Steven Mark Needham*
FOOD STYLISTS:
*Anne Disrude   Sandra Robishaw
Dora Jonassen   Polly Talbott
Paul E. Piccuito   Diane Simone Vezza*
ASSISTANTS:
Christopher Holt   Katarina Mesarovich
PROP STYLISTS:
*Betty Alfenito   Petra Henttonen
Bette Blau*
PHOTOGRAPH, PAGE 7, *by Gary Denys*

FAMILY CIRCLE BOOKS

DIRECTOR: *Margie Chan*
EDITORIAL DIRECTOR: *Carol A. Guasti*
ASSOCIATE EDITOR: *Kim Gayton Elliott*
ASSOCIATE BUSINESS MANAGER:
  Carrie Meyerhoff
PROJECT COORDINATOR:
  Laura Berkowitz

PRODUCTION DEPARTMENT

MANAGER: *Wendy Allen*
SUPERVISOR: *Helen Russell*
TYPESETTERS:
Cheryl Aden   Maureen Harrington

DAVID RICKETTS is currently a
Contributing Editor for *Family
Circle* magazine and serves as
Project Editor for many Family
Circle cookbooks. Formerly an
editor at *Food & Wine* and *Cuisine*
magazines, Mr. Ricketts also held
the position of Senior Associate
Food Editor and Test Kitchen
Director of *Family Circle* magazine.
He was a collaborator on the
cookbook *Cooking Great Meals
Every Day* (Random House, 1983)
and continues to consult with food
companies, advertising agencies,
public relations firms and marketing
companies concerning food issues
and trends for the 1990s.

ACKNOWLEDGMENTS

*We would like to thank all the
individuals at Simon & Schuster
who worked with us on this project.
Their expertise, diligence and
patience is very much appreciated.
Specifically, we would like to thank
Jack McKeown, Linda
Cunningham, Toula Polygalaktos,
Eve Metz and Toni Rachiele. A
special thank-you also goes to
Barbara Marks and Dolores Simon.
Finally, we would like to thank the
following individuals, companies
and organizations for generously
supplying valuable information for
this book: American Dairy
Association; American Dairy
Council; Butterball Turkey;
Dannon Yogurt Company; The
Edleman Agency; Fleischman's
Yeast; Fleishman-Hiller; General
Electric Company; King Arthur
Flour; Lewis and Neale; Fishery
Council, Richard Lord; National
Broiler Council, Dot Tringali;
National Fish and Seafood Council;
National Fisheries Institute, Emily
Holt; National Lamb Council;
National Live Stock and Meat
Board; National Pork Council;
National Seafood Educators;
National Turkey Federation; North
Atlantic Seafood, Jayne Whelan;
Ra. C. Auletta & Co.; Rice
Council; Specialty Brands; United
Fresh Fruit and Vegetable
Association, Laura A. Kinkle;
U.S.D.A., Kate Alfriend.*

CONTENTS

This page, from top: Mushroom and Green Onion Soup (127);
Warm Spinach and Pear Salad with Bacon Dressing (177); Baked Ziti
with Vegetables (191); Swordfish with Orange-Ginger Marinade (319);
Fig Thumbprints (516) and Maple Nut Rugelach (515).

PREFACE

As we tasted, refined and retasted the seven hundred plus recipes in this book, there was real excitement generated in the Family Circle Test Kitchens. "I want the book *now!*" was heard many times during these months and we knew we were on to something. "Healthy" and "quick" aren't just food guidewords for the 90's, they're the soul of this book. Home cooking has taken a turn for the better—with more variety, newer flavors and better nutrition than ever before. And *that's* what this book is all about.

The Family Circle Cookbook has recipes and helpful information for the busy person looking to serve quick, easy and healthful meals. There are also more challenging projects for the weekend chef, or the experienced culinary whiz. You'll find updated versions of traditional recipes, and many innovative combinations relying on readily available ingredients. The flavors, colors and textures of the dishes, vividly captured in over five hundred new photographs, are made possible by the abundance of good, natural foods found in supermarkets, at farm stands, at green markets and in our gardens.

Today's markets feature an incredible assortment of quality foods, available year-round. We urge you to take advantage of them: fruits such as strawberries, peaches, plums, kiwifruit and grapes; fresh herbs; and vegetables like broccoli and squash. If you haven't checked out "exotic" and ethnic ingredients such as jícama, tofu, shiitake mushrooms, pita bread and couscous, now's the time to do so. Although we're not saying "goodbye, ketchup" and "hello, salsa," the joy of cooking in the 90's owes itself in part to using both familiar and new ingredients—and our delicious recipes are the forum for trying wonderful new culinary combinations.

To assist you in the kitchen, ingredient primers and how-to techniques are clearly illustrated for quick reference. There are microwave recipes and adaptations to speed up preparation and cooking times. And easy-to-read charts and tips provide a helping hand.

More healthful eating is a top priority in this decade, so each recipe has counts for calories and major nutrients and tags to indicate whether it is low in calories, fat, sodium and/or cholesterol. Menus alongside the recipes help you plan everyday meals, weekend entertaining, holidays and special events.

Appreciating the dimensions of this book is a little like learning to swim . . . you won't understand what it can do for you until you dive in and make something to share.

Happy cooking!

Jean Hewitt, Food Editor
Family Circle Magazine

CHAPTER 1

WHAT YOU NEED TO KNOW

Whether you cook every day for yourself or your family, or only once in a while for holidays and special occasions, *The Family Circle Cookbook: New Tastes for New Times* will help you get the best possible results. In this chapter we provide the basics of good cooking and good eating—everything you need to know to prepare successfully any of the hundreds of recipes in the chapters that follow.

If you're an inexperienced cook, familiarize yourself with this chapter before you begin. Learn the basics of buying, preparing and storing foods, as well as what kind of kitchen equipment you need and how to use it. If you're an old hand, refer back to this chapter for tips on ingredient or baking pan substitutions, food equivalents, freezer storage times, shopping and safety tips or a refresher course in good nutrition.

Quick Recipes: To meet the needs of busy cooks, recipes that can be completed in 30 minutes or less are flagged *quick*. Throughout Chapter 1 we refer you to other sections of the book that provide useful tips and information on speedy food preparation.

Healthful Recipes: Today's cook is, above all, health-conscious, so we've included up-to-date dietary guidelines and information on essential nutrients. In this book, you'll find:

■ Nutritional analysis for all recipes. Those recipes that meet specific criteria are flagged *low-calorie, low-fat, low-cholesterol* and/or *low-sodium* (see *Flagged Recipes, page 10*).

■ An aisle-by-aisle shopping guide introduces you to the abundance of new and nutritionally modified products available in supermarkets today and tells you how to choose the freshest, most nutritious foods.

■ A list of fat-fighting cooking techniques helps you keep added fat out of foods once you get them home.

New Tastes: We know that good food is only good for you if you eat it, so we place equal emphasis on great flavor, sound nu-

trition and easy preparation. In developing recipes for this cookbook, we took advantage of the number-one rule for good eating—*eat a variety of foods*—and used it to introduce newly available fresh foods and food products. We make your job in the kitchen easier by giving you clearly written recipes to guide you through each dish. On pages to come, you'll find an exciting mixture of old favorites and new ideas—an array of all-American classics seasoned with ethnic influences and updated with modern cooking techniques.

A RECIPE FOR SUCCESS

■ Always read through the *entire* recipe before you start to cook to be sure you have all ingredients on hand and to familiarize yourself with the steps.

■ Ingredients are listed in the order in which they are used. Gather all ingredients at one time and arrange on work surface in order of use.

■ Measure and prepare ingredients as indicated in ingredient list *before* moving on to directions.

■ All measurements are *level*.

■ Follow directions in step-by-step order.

■ When a recipe calls for eggs, use *large* eggs unless otherwise indicated.

■ If a recipe calls for room-temperature eggs, remove them from the refrigerator 30 minutes before using, or run them under warm tap water.

■ Check the Ingredient Substitutes chart in this chapter before substituting one ingredient for another in any recipe.

■ Recipes in this book have been developed for cooking at sea level. At altitudes higher than 3,000 feet, some adjustments in ingredients, cooking time and temperatures may be necessary. Check with a county cooperative extension office or the home economics department of a local university for cooking directions and modifications specific to your area.

■ Preheating directions are included in recipes. Allow at least 15 minutes for the oven to reach the temperature you've set.

MEASURING UP

Successful recipes depend on accurate measuring of ingredients. See the *Kitchen Equipment* section of this chapter *(page 32)* for information on basic measuring equipment.

▪ Measure flour, sugar and other dry or solid ingredients in graduated metal or plastic measuring cups that can be filled to the top and leveled with the dull straight edge of a knife or a metal spatula.

▪ Measure liquid ingredients in spouted clear glass or plastic measuring cups that allow extra room at the top to prevent spillage. Place cup on a level surface and pour in liquid to desired line, reading the measure at eye level.

▪ Measure small, level amounts of dry and liquid ingredients in graduated measuring spoons. Measure *away* from the mixing bowl to avoid spilling extra ingredients into the bowl.

▪ To measure flour, stir flour in package or canister, then lightly spoon into dry measuring cup or spoon. Level with a straight edge. Do not pack flour into measuring cup.

▪ To measure granulated white and brown sugars, spoon into measuring cup and level with straight edge. Gently or firmly pack light or dark brown sugar into dry measure according to recipe direction; level with straight edge. Brown sugar should hold its shape when emptied from cup.

HOW TO MEASURE PANS

Be sure your pans are the kind and size specified in the recipe. The size of some cookware is expressed in liquid measure at its level full capacity.

Measure the top inside of bakeware for length, width or diameter; take a perpendicular measurement inside for depth.

Sizes for skillets and griddles are taken from the top outside dimensions, exclusive of handles.

See *Baking Dish and Pan Substitutes, page 13,* if you do not have the specific-size pan called for in a recipe.

CASSEROLE MEASUREMENT CHART

Casserole recipes are imported from all over the world, as are casserole dishes, and each country has its own system of measurements. The chart below will help you to convert your casserole's measurements from one system to another, so you can be assured your recipe will turn out perfectly.

Cups	=	Pints	=	Quarts	=	Liters
1		½		¼		0.237
2		1*		½*		0.473
4		2*		1*		0.946
6		3		1½		1.419
8		4		2		1.892
10		5		2½		2.365
12		6		3		2.838

* *In Canada, 1 pint = 2½ cups;*
1 quart = 5 cups.

IMPORTANT MEASURES

Dash or pinch	under ⅛ teaspoon
½ tablespoon	1½ teaspoons
1 tablespoon	3 teaspoons
1 ounce liquid	2 tablespoons
1 jigger	1½ ounces
¼ cup	4 tablespoons
⅓ cup	5 tablespoons plus 1 teaspoon
½ cup	8 tablespoons
⅔ cup	10 tablespoons plus 2 teaspoons
¾ cup	12 tablespoons
1 cup	16 tablespoons
1 pint	2 cups
1 quart	2 pints
1 gallon	4 quarts
1 pound	16 ounces

OVEN TEMPERATURES

Use an oven thermometer periodically to check the accuracy of your oven thermostat.

Very Slow	250°–275°
Slow	300°–325°
Moderate	350°–375°
Hot	400°–425°
Very Hot	450°–475°
Extremely Hot	500°+

FLAGGED RECIPES

Where appropriate, recipes are flagged *low-calorie, low-fat, low-cholesterol, low-sodium* and/or *quick*.

The criteria used for flagging are as follows (the limit goes up to and includes the number):

LOW-CALORIE*

Main dish	350 cal.
Side dish	100 cal.
Snack	100 cal.
Condiment	25 cal.
Dessert	150 cal.

Recipes that meet the criteria for low-calorie but contribute more than 50% calories from fat are not flagged.

LOW-CHOLESTEROL*

Main dish	75 mg
Side dish	15 mg
Snack	7 mg
Condiment	5 mg
Dessert	25 mg

Recipes that meet the criteria for low-cholesterol do not necessarily meet the criteria for low-fat.

LOW-SODIUM

Main dish	140 mg
Side dish	100 mg
Snack	65 mg
Condiment	50 mg
Dessert	50 mg

- Recipes flagged *low-fat* contribute no more than 30% calories from fat (see *Fat: The 30% Solution*, page 15).
- Recipes flagged *quick* can be prepared from start to finish in 30 minutes or less.

SERVING SIZES

Our recipes are analyzed for nutrient values per serving. The number of servings in a recipe is generally based on standard portion sizes for individual foods; for example, 3 to 3½ ounces for cooked meat, poultry or fish, or ½ cup for vegetables. A recipe that yields 6 servings may feed 6 people or only 4 or 5, depending on the appetites of your family or guests.

DAILY NUTRITION INFORMATION

Refer to the nutritive content listings of our recipes, then use these guidelines to check that daily menus are well balanced and healthful.

	Average Healthy Adult (Age 25+)	
	Women	Men
Calories[1]	2,000	2,700
Protein[2]	50 g (200 cal)	63 g (252 cal)
Fat[3]	66 g (594 cal)	90 g (810 cal)
Sodium[4]	1,100-3,300 mg	1,100-3,300 mg
Cholesterol[5]	300 mg	300 mg

Calories (cal) that do not come from protein or fat should be derived from complex carbohydrates, which are found in whole grains, fresh fruits, vegetables, pasta, etc.

[1] RDA [2] (8%–12% of calories) RDA [3] (30% of calories) Amer. Heart Assn. and Nat'l Acad. of Science [4] USDA [5] Amer. Heart Assn.

FOOD EQUIVALENTS

Berries

1 pint	1¾ cups

Bread

Crumbs, soft, 1 cup	2 slices
Cubes, 1 cup	2 slices
1 pound, sliced	22 slices

Broth

Beef or Chicken, 1 cup	1 teaspoon instant bouillon, 1 envelope bouillon, 1 cube bouillon, dissolved in 1 cup boiling water

Butter or Margarine

½ stick	¼ cup or 4 tablespoons
1 pound	4 sticks or 2 cups

Cream and Milk

Cream, heavy, 1 cup	2 cups, whipped
Milk, evaporated, small can	⅔ cup
Milk, sweetened condensed, 14-ounce can	1⅔ cups
Milk, nonfat dry, 1 pound	5 quarts liquid skim

Cheese

Cream, 8-ounce package	1 cup
Cottage, 8 ounce	1 cup
Cheddar or Swiss, 1 pound, shredded	4 cups
Blue, crumbled, 4 ounces	1 cup
Parmesan or Romano, ¼ pound grated	1¼ cups

Chocolate

Unsweetened, 1 ounce	1 square
Semisweet pieces, 6-ounce package	1 cup

Coconut

Flaked, 3½-ounce can	1⅓ cups
Shredded, 4-ounce can	1⅓ cups

Cookies

Chocolate wafers, 1 cup crumbs	19 wafers
Vanilla wafers, 1 cup fine crumbs	22 wafers
Graham crackers, 1 cup fine crumbs	14 square crackers

Dried Beans and Peas

1 cup	2¼ cups, cooked

Eggs (large)

Whole, 1 cup	5 to 6
Yolks, 1 cup	13 to 14
Whites, 1 cup	7 to 8

Flour

All-purpose, sifted, 1 pound	4 cups
Cake, sifted, 1 pound	4¾ to 5 cups

Gelatin

Unflavored, 1 envelope	1 tablespoon

Nuts

Almonds, 1 pound, shelled	3½ cups
Peanuts, 1 pound, shelled	3 cups
Pecans, 1 pound, shelled	4 cups
Walnuts, 1 pound, shelled	4 cups

Pasta

Macaroni, elbow, uncooked, 8 ounces	4 cups, cooked
Noodles, medium width, 8 ounces, uncooked	3¾ cups, cooked
Noodles, fine width, 8 ounces, uncooked	5½ cups, cooked
Spaghetti, 8 ounces, uncooked	4 cups, cooked

Rice

Long-grain white rice, uncooked, 1 cup	3 cups, cooked
Enriched precooked rice, uncooked, 1 cup	2 cups, cooked
Brown rice, uncooked, 1 cup	3 to 4 cups, cooked

Sugar

Granulated, 1 pound	2 cups
Brown, firmly packed, 1 pound	2¼ cups
10X (confectioners', or powdered), sifted, 1 pound	3⅓ to 4 cups

FOOD EQUIVALENTS

Vegetables and Fruits

Apples, 1 pound	3 medium-size	Orange, 1 medium-size, squeezed	1/3 to 1/2 cup juice
Bananas, 1 pound	3 medium-size	Onions, yellow cooking, 1 pound	5 to 6 medium-size
Cabbage, 1 pound, shredded	4 cups	Onions, small white silverskins, 1 pound	12 to 14
Carrots, 1 pound, sliced	2½ cups	Peaches, 1 pound	4 medium-size
Herbs, chopped fresh, 1 tablespoon	1 teaspoon dried	Mushrooms, 1 pound, sliced	3 cups
Lemon, 1 medium-size, grated	2 teaspoons rind	Potatoes, all-purpose, 1 pound	3 medium-size
Lemon, 1 medium-size, squeezed	2 tablespoons juice	Tomatoes, 1 pound:	
Lime, 1 medium-size, squeezed	1 tablespoon juice	Large	2
Orange, 1 medium-size, grated	2 tablespoons rind	Medium-size	3
		Small	4

INGREDIENT SUBSTITUTES

When the Recipe Calls for	You May Substitute
1 square unsweetened chocolate	3 tablespoons unsweetened cocoa powder plus 1 tablespoon butter, margarine or vegetable shortening
1 cup *sifted* cake flour	7/8 cup *sifted* all-purpose flour (1 cup less 2 tablespoons)
2 tablespoons flour (for thickening)	1 tablespoon cornstarch
1 teaspoon baking powder	1/4 teaspoon baking soda plus 5/8 teaspoon cream of tartar
1 cup corn syrup	1 cup sugar and 1/4 cup liquid used in recipe
1 cup honey	1¼ cups sugar and 1/4 cup liquid used in recipe
1 cup sweet milk	1/2 cup evaporated milk plus 1/2 cup water
1 cup buttermilk	1 tablespoon vinegar plus enough sweet milk to make 1 cup
1 cup sour cream (in baking)	7/8 cup buttermilk or sour milk plus 3 tablespoons butter
1 egg (for custards)	2 egg yolks plus 1 tablespoon water
1 cup brown sugar (packed)	1 cup granulated sugar OR 1 cup sugar plus 2 tablespoons molasses
1 teaspoon lemon juice	1/4 teaspoon vinegar
1/4 cup chopped onion	1 tablespoon instant minced onion
1 clove garlic	1/8 teaspoon garlic powder
1 cup tomato juice	1/2 cup tomato sauce plus 1/2 cup water
2 cups tomato sauce	3/4 cup tomato paste plus 1 cup water
1 tablespoon fresh snipped herbs	1 teaspoon dried herbs
1 tablespoon prepared mustard	1 teaspoon dry mustard
1/2 cup (1 stick) butter or margarine	7 tablespoons vegetable shortening

BAKING DISH AND PAN SUBSTITUTES

If you do not have the specific-size baking pan or mold called for in a recipe, substitute a pan of *equal volume* from the list below.
- If the pan you are substituting is made of glass, reduce the baking temperature by 25°.
- If you are substituting a pan that is shallower than the pan in the recipe, reduce the baking time by about one-quarter.
- If you are substituting a pan that is deeper than the pan in the recipe, increase the baking time by one-quarter.

Common Kitchen Pan Substitutes

4-cup baking dish:
9-inch pie plate
8 × 1¼-inch round layer-cake pan—C
7⅜ × 3⅝ × 2⅝-inch loaf pan—A

6-cup baking dish:
10-inch pie plate
8 or 9 × 1½-inch round layer-cake pan—C
8½ × 3⅝ × 2⅝-inch loaf pan—A

8-cup baking dish:
8 × 8 × 2-inch square pan—D
11 × 7 × 1½-inch baking pan
9 × 5 × 3-inch loaf pan—A

10-cup baking dish:
9 × 9 × 2-inch square pan—D
11¾ × 7½ × 1¾-inch baking pan
15½ × 10½ × 1-inch jelly-roll pan

12-cup baking dish:
13½ × 8½ × 2-inch glass baking dish (12 cups)
13 × 9 × 2-inch metal baking pan (15 cups)
14 × 10½ × 2½-inch roasting pan (19 cups)

Three 8-inch-round pans:
two 9 × 9 × 2-inch square cake pans

Two 9-inch-round layer-cake pans:
two 8 × 8 × 2-inch square cake pans,
13 × 9 × 2-inch pan

9 × 5 × 3-inch loaf pan:
9 × 9 × 2-inch square cake pan

9-inch angel-cake tube pan:
10 × 3¾-inch Bundt pan—J
9 × 3½-inch fancy tube pan—I

Total Volume of Various Special Baking Pans

Tube pans:

7½ × 3-inch Bundt tube pan—J	6 cups
9 × 3½-inch fancy tube or Bundt pan—I or J	9 cups
9 × 3½-inch angel-cake or tube pan—H	12 cups
10 × 3¾-inch Bundt or Crownburst pan—J	12 cups
9 × 3½-inch fancy tube mold—I	12 cups
10 × 4-inch fancy tube mold (Kugelhopf)—I	16 cups
10 × 4-inch angel-cake or tube pan—H	18 cups

Springform pans:

8 × 3-inch pan—B	12 cups
9 × 3-inch pan—B	16 cups

Ring molds:

8½ × 2¼-inch mold—E	4½ cups
9¼ × 2¾-inch mold—E	8 cups

Charlotte mold:

6 × 4¼-inch mold—G	7½ cups

Brioche pan:

9½ × 3¼-inch pan—F	8 cups

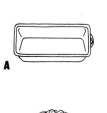
A

B

C

D

E

F

G

H

I

J

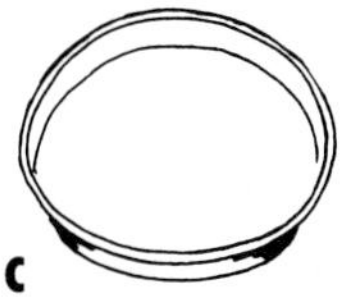

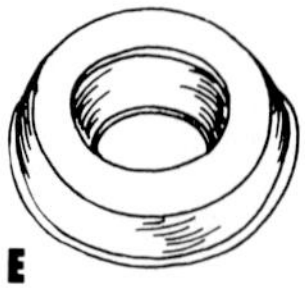

GOOD EATING

Healthful eating today means eating in moderation and eating different kinds of foods to give you an overall diet plan that's low in fat and high in complex carbohydrates and contributes sufficient amounts of essential proteins, vitamins and minerals. A well-rounded diet for healthy people doesn't require tedious calculations or strict modifications that take the fun out of eating. But it does require some understanding of sound nutrition principles to help you make sensible choices in the supermarket, in restaurants, and even at fast-food stands. What follows is a brief overview of current dietary recommendations and a primer on essential nutrients to provide you with the basic information you need to plan an adequate diet.

The Committee on Dietary Allowances of the National Academy of Sciences National Research Council publishes the Recommended Dietary Allowances (RDA), which sets standards for the daily nutritional needs of healthy males and females at various stages of their lives. In addition to the RDA, the U.S. Department of Agriculture (USDA) and the U.S. Department of Health and Human Services, as well as medical authorities such as the American Heart Association and American Cancer Society, also offer guidelines for sensible eating. As research continues and we come to know more about the relationship between nutrition and health, these guidelines are subject to change. The best defense is a well-informed attack: keep up-to-date on the latest medical and nutritional findings. If you have specific dietary problems, or are taking any prescription medication, consult a physician or registered dietitian before planning your diet.

USDA DIETARY GUIDELINES FOR AMERICANS

Eat a variety of foods to get the energy, protein, vitamins, minerals and fiber you need for good health.

Maintain healthy weight to reduce your chances of having high blood pressure, heart disease, a stroke, certain cancers and the most common form of diabetes.

Choose a diet low in fat, saturated fat and cholesterol to reduce your risk of heart attack and certain types of cancer. Because fat contains over twice the calories of an equal amount of carbohydrates or protein, a diet low in fat can help you maintain a healthy weight.

Choose a diet with plenty of vegetables, fruits and grain products, which provide needed vitamins, minerals, fiber and complex carbohydrates and can help lower your intake of fat.

Use sugars only in moderation. A diet with lots of sugars has too many calories and too few nutrients for most people and can contribute to tooth decay.

Use salt and sodium only in moderation to help reduce your risk of high blood pressure.

If you drink alcoholic beverages, do so in moderation. Alcoholic beverages supply calories but little or no nutrients. Drinking alcohol is also the cause of many health problems and accidents and can lead to addiction.

To follow these dietary guidelines, choose wisely from the basic food groups. Breads, cereals, rice and pasta represent the grain group, from which you should choose the most servings (6 to 11) every day. Choose 3 to 5 servings of vegetables and 2 to 4 servings of fruit each day. Choose 2 to 3 servings each from the dairy group and the protein group, which consists of meat, poultry, fish, eggs, beans and nuts. Foods such as solid fats, oils and sweets provide little nutritional value other than calories and should be used sparingly.

For more information on eating right

from USDA, *write to* U.S. Dept. of Agriculture, Human Nutrition Information Service, 6505 Belcrest Road, Hyattsville, MD 20782. *Ask for their list of available publications.*

FAT: THE 30% SOLUTION

Nutrition authorities agree that an overall healthful diet for Americans is one that derives no more than 30% of total calories from fat. To figure out how many grams of fat are recommended for the amount of calories your daily diet provides:

Multiply your total calories for the day by 0.30 (30%) to get your calories from fat. Divide calories from fat by 9 (1 gram fat = 9 calories) to get grams of fat per day. For example:

2,000 (calories/day) x 0.30
= 600 (calories from fat)
600 ÷ 9 = 67 gm fat

Add up grams of fat in food choices for the day to see if you're on target. If not, choose more lower-fat foods.

The 30% solution is meant as a guideline for your *overall* diet, but it may be helpful to analyze individual foods and recipes to find out how they fit into your eating plan. To do this:

Multiply grams of fat by 9. Divide this number by the total calories in the dish. Multiply this number by 100 to get the percentage of calories from fat. For example, let's say a serving of lasagne provides 425 calories and 19 grams of fat.

19 x 9 = 171
171 ÷ 425 = 0.40
0.40 x 100 = 40

(percent calories from fat)

Although this dish provides well over 30% calories from fat, it still fits into the 30% solution when you serve it with lower-fat side dishes, such as steamed vegetables with herbs and unbuttered bread. Round out the menu with fresh fruit or another lowfat dessert.

While it's not necessary to calculate your percentage of calories from fat on a daily basis, it's a good idea to give yourself a check-up every so often to make sure you're on the right track.

KNOW YOUR NUTRIENTS

Calories The term "calorie" is used to describe the amount of energy derived from carbohydrates, proteins and fats in the foods we eat. When the number of calories consumed exceeds the amount needed by the body, excess calories are stored as fat. In a well-balanced diet, 8% to 12% of the calorie count should come from protein, no more than 30% from fat and the remainder from complex carbohydrates.

Protein Essential for the growth, repair and maintenance of all body cells, protein is a component of antibodies, enzymes and hormones that fight disease and regulate body processes. There are thousands of different types of human proteins, made up of chemical building blocks called amino acids. Complete proteins, found in animal and dairy foods, contain all the amino acids necessary in human nutrition. Incomplete proteins from plant sources provide only some of the essential amino acids and so it is particularly important for vegetarians and those on meat-restricted diets to eat a wide variety of foods in order to provide all the amino acids necessary to build complete proteins.

Carbohydrates All carbohydrates are composed of sugars. Simple carbohydrates, found in table sugar and honey, for example, provide energy but lack other nutrients and so should be eaten in moderation. Complex carbohydrates, found in fruits, vegetables, legumes and grain products, provide vitamins, minerals and fiber (*see Fiber Facts, page 397*), as well as sugar for energy.

Cholesterol is a fat-like substance that is produced by our bodies to help manufacture hormones and maintain cell membranes. Dietary cholesterol is found in

15

meat, poultry, fish, eggs and dairy products. Excessive consumption of dietary cholesterol and saturated fat may result in elevated levels of cholesterol in the blood. High blood cholesterol levels have been linked with heart disease, clogged arteries and stroke.

Fat Despite bad press, not all fat is bad. Fat provides energy, helps the body maintain normal temperature, is a component of all body cells and carries the fat-soluble vitamins A, D, E and K through the body. However, excessive amounts of saturated fat and *total* fat in the diet have been linked to a variety of diseases and certainly play a role in the problem of obesity in our society.

The building blocks of dietary fat are called fatty acids. All fat is made up of three types of fatty acids:

■ SATURATED FATTY ACIDS are predominant in animal foods and tropical oils made from palm kernel and coconut. Most solid fats contain a high proportion of saturated fatty acids. Saturated fat has been shown to increase cholesterol levels in the blood.

■ POLYUNSATURATED FATTY ACIDS are high in most vegetable oils, including corn, safflower, sesame, cottonseed and soybean oils, and some seafood (*see Fatty Fish Facts, page 296*). Polyunsaturated fats have been shown to decrease cholesterol levels in the blood. The process of hydrogenation, which converts liquid oils to solid fats (for instance, corn oil to corn oil margarine), also converts some of the polyunsaturated fatty acids to saturated fatty acids.

■ MONOUNSATURATED FATTY ACIDS are primarily from plant sources and particularly high in olive, canola (rapeseed), avocado and peanut oils. Monounsaturated fats have been shown to decrease cholesterol levels in the blood.

For more information on dietary fat and cholesterol, contact your local office of the American Heart Association.

Sodium is necessary to regulate water balance in the body and is active in muscle contraction. It also helps maintain normal blood pressure in healthy people. But as crucial as sodium is, we need surprisingly little of it to function. Indeed, excess sodium in the diet may be a contributing cause of high blood pressure in salt-sensitive individuals.

VITAMINS AND MINERALS

Essential to your body's metabolism, vitamins and minerals help proteins, fats and carbohydrates produce energy. Vitamins and minerals work interactively to ensure the continuance of all body processes and each also has specific functions in disease prevention and body maintenance. (*See background information on fruits and vegetables, throughout pages 393 to 486, for good sources of specific vitamins and minerals.*)

Vitamin A promotes bone and tooth formation, maintains night vision, helps fight infection and protects the lining of the mouth, nose, throat and digestive tract. Beta-carotene, a plant pigment that is used to make vitamin A in the human body, may play a role in the prevention of certain types of heart disease and cancer.

Vitamin B-Complex includes thiamin, riboflavin, niacin, vitamin B_6, pantothenic acid, folic acid, biotin, and vitamin B_{12}. Overall, the B vitamins are essential to energy-production, maintenance of healthy skin and mucous membranes in the mouth, nose, throat and digestive system and the functioning of the nervous system. Vitamins B_6, B_{12} and folic acid aid in preventing certain types of anemia.

Vitamin C helps fight infection, aids in wound healing, helps build strong blood vessels, bones and teeth, and is essential to maintenance of a healthy nervous system. Vitamin C improves the absorption of dietary iron from nonmeat sources.

Vitamin D helps maintain healthy bones and teeth and promotes normal growth by aiding the absorption of dietary calcium and phosphorus.

Vitamin E protects cell membranes from toxic substances, particularly in the lungs.

Vitamin K is necessary for normal blood clotting and regulation of calcium levels in the blood.

Calcium is necessary for healthy bones, teeth, nerves, muscles and heart tissue; aids in the healing process of wounds and broken bones.

Iron helps carry oxygen from the lungs to all body cells; prevents anemia.

Magnesium is important for protein synthesis and energy production.

Phosphorus works with calcium to maintain healthy bones and teeth; aids in normal muscle function; activates enzymes necessary for energy production.

Potassium controls the volume of fluids in body cells and, along with sodium, is active in nerve transmission and muscle contraction.

Zinc plays important roles in protein and fatty acid metabolism, immune system protection, vitamin activation and reproductive function.

LOWFAT SUBSTITUTES

Choose among these more healthful options as substitutes for some of the higher-fat foods we use every day.

INSTEAD OF	USE
Whole Eggs	two egg whites for each whole egg in omelets, egg dishes and most baked goods
Sour Cream	lowfat plain yogurt or pureed cottage cheese with lemon juice; reduced-fat sour cream products
Ricotta Cheese	a mixture of half part-skim ricotta cheese and half lowfat cottage cheese
Heavy Cream	half-and-half as a liquid; chilled, whipped evaporated milk or nondairy whipped topping made from polyunsaturated fats
Whole Milk	skim milk or 1% fat
Mayonnaise	reduced-fat mayonnaise or a mixture of half pureed lowfat cottage cheese and half plain yogurt
High-Fat Cheeses	lowfat or skim-milk cheeses with less than 5 grams fat per ounce
Ice Cream	ice milk, lowfat frozen yogurt, frozen fruit juice bars, sorbet or fruit ice

FAT-FIGHTING COOKING TECHNIQUES

MOIST-HEAT COOKING

Moist-heat cooking helps tenderize food and keep it juicy, and reduces the need for extra fat. Techniques include:

Poaching: Poached foods cook immersed in liquid—e.g., water, defatted chicken stock, wine—in a covered pan, usually on the stove top. Herbs or spices can add flavor to the poaching liquid with no added fat. For maximum food tenderness, the liquid should simmer gently, not boil. As the food cooks, it adds flavor to the poaching liquid, which can be served as a broth after the food is removed. Or, after removing the poached food from the pan, you can reduce the liquid (by evaporating the water to concentrate the flavor) and stir in pureed vegetables or fruit to make a light sauce.

Steaming: This easy, healthful method is very speedy—most vegetables and fish steam in under 10 minutes. Steaming involves cooking food in a covered saucepan over a small amount of boiling water, usually in a colander or steamer basket. Steamed foods retain much of their original flavors, vitamins, minerals, colors and shapes, and the liquid can be saved for soups and stews.

Braising: Braised foods are usually pan-browned, in a minimal amount of fat or nonstick cooking spray. Then, a small amount of liquid is added and the food is covered, and slowly oven-baked or simmered on the stove top. This helps food retain its moisture, allows flavors to meld and creates a tasty sauce. Braising is ideal for less tender cuts of meat that tend to be lower in fat. If the dish is made ahead of time and refrigerated, any fat in the sauce will rise to the top and can be skimmed away before reheating.

DRY-HEAT COOKING

Grilling, broiling, baking and roasting are all methods of dry-heat cooking that don't require added fat. Ideally, dry heat sears food on the outside and leaves it juicy on the inside. However, dry-heat cooking does not reduce toughness, so it's best used with relatively tender foods, or foods that have been marinated first. Be careful not to overcook foods with dry-heat methods.

Grilling: The backyard barbecue provides its own delicious taste, but you can use a lowfat sauce or marinade to add extra flavor. Try pureed vegetable sauces or a low-calorie topping of lemon juice spiked with a mixture of fresh or dried herbs.

Broiling: Broiling can be considered an indoor version of grilling, but without the smoky flavor. Broiled foods also must be turned and watched carefully so they don't burn. Broil meats on a rack in a broiler pan so the fat drains off.

Baking and roasting: Set meats or poultry to be baked or roasted on a rack in a baking or roasting pan so the fat drains off. Or use a gravy separator to isolate the fat and use the meat juices as a light sauce. Turning food during cooking is not necessary, although basting with pan juices or other liquids helps keep the food moist inside, crisp outside. If you wish, bake poultry or fish on a bed of vegetables, such as chopped celery, carrot and onion, to add flavor and retain moisture.

LOWFAT FRYING

Strictly speaking, "frying" means cooking food in fat. The fat provides flavor as well as prevents food from sticking to the pan. Two techniques provide alternatives to frying in large quantities of fat:

Nonstick sautéing: Traditionally, sautéing means cooking food in a small amount of fat or oil. Nonstick pans, which minimize or eliminate the need for fat, are a boon for the health-conscious cook. With a good nonstick pan, you can scramble an egg without butter or sauté chicken, fish or vegetables in just a few drops of oil.

Stir-frying: Food cut into uniformly small pieces and stirred constantly in a very hot wok, deep sauté pan or skillet cooks quickly with little oil. You can even "stir-fry" with small amounts of chicken or beef broth instead of oil.

MICROWAVE COOKING

Using your microwave oven is ideal for healthful cooking because it can yield moist results without any added calories from fat since foods cook in their own juices. Vegetables are especially suited to the microwave oven because they retain maximum flavor, color and nutrients. Even eggplant, a vegetable notorious for soaking up oil, microwaves to juiciness with no added fat.

KITCHEN STAPLES (KNOW YOUR INGREDIENTS)

STOCKING THE PANTRY

Pantry or cupboard items are those staple foodstuffs that don't require refrigeration. Most have a relatively long shelf life when sealed and stored properly, but all should be checked periodically and used up or replaced. Typical pantry items are:

Baking powder is a common leavener in cakes, cookies, batter breads and muffins. *Double-acting baking powder* acts twice: first when it is combined with liquids in a recipe and then in the oven when it is exposed to heat. Once opened, baking powder begins to lose its potency after about 6 months.

Baking soda is a leavening agent that is activated by and used with acidic ingredients such as buttermilk, sour cream, yogurt, molasses and citrus juices. Use 1 teaspoon of baking soda, mixed in with dry ingredients, for each cup of liquid in a recipe. Baking soda begins to act as soon as it combines with liquid, so batter should be baked as soon as possible.

Bread crumbs or cracker crumbs should be stored tightly sealed on a cool pantry shelf or in the freezer; refrigeration may cause mold. Homemade crumbs should be made from fresh bread to avoid a stale taste and stored, tightly sealed, in the freezer.

Chocolate keeps better on a cool shelf than in the refrigerator. A harmless white bloom and crumbly texture may develop with time; this is simply fat rising to the surface and will disappear in cooking. Sweet, unsweetened and semisweet baking chocolates are most commonly available in bars that are divided into 1-ounce squares. Semisweet chocolate chips can be substituted, ounce for ounce, for semisweet squares.

Cocoa powder is chocolate with much of the cocoa butter removed. Dutch-process cocoa contains more fat than regular unsweetened cocoa powder. Instant cocoa contains sugar and emulsifiers for easy dissolving; it is used for making hot chocolate beverages and is generally unsuitable as a substitute in baking.

Corn syrup is available in light and dark forms which are usually interchangeable in cooking. Corn syrup is only about half as sweet as granulated sugar. Like all liquid sweeteners, corn syrup cannot be substituted directly for sugar in baking.

Cornstarch (or corn flour) is a tasteless starch that contains no gluten and therefore resists forming lumps, which makes it an excellent thickener.

Dried fruits, including raisins, currants and prunes, should be stored out of direct light in covered jars or tins for up to several months.

Flours, common The most common flour is a blend of hard and soft wheats known as white *all-purpose flour*, which can be used for a variety of baking and thickening purposes. Bleached all-purpose flour has been whitened by a chemical agent to achieve a color favored by some bakers. Unbleached flour is light yellow. Although there is no detectable difference between bleached and unbleached flours in terms of taste and texture in baked goods, bleaching does destroy small amounts of vitamin E. Enriched all-purpose flour has had some of the nutrients removed in milling (particularly the B vitamins) replaced. *Whole-wheat flour* contains much of the grain's nutritional germ oil and fibrous bran but as a result becomes rancid more quickly than refined flour. Store in an airtight container for no longer than 2 months or refrigerate to extend shelf life. To use in baking, substitute up to one-third whole-wheat flour for the all-purpose flour called for in a recipe. *Bread flour* is made from hard winter wheat, which is high in gluten, the protein that provides a firm, elastic structure to baked goods and allows yeast-raised products to rise and expand. *Cake flour* is made from soft wheat, with less expansive gluten. This flour bakes to the light, crumbly texture desirable in fine cakes. *Self-rising flour* contains salt and leaveners and should be used only in recipes that are modified for its self-rising properties. Store at cool room temperature for no longer than 3 months. *Semolina flour* is coarsely ground from protein-rich, hard durum wheat. It lacks rising properties and so is ideal for pasta and noodles. Small amounts may be substituted for all-purpose flour in baking. *Instant-blend flour* is formulated to dissolve immediately in fat or liquid and so is excellent for thickening sauces and gravies but unsuitable for baking.

Flours, other *Barley flour* is often used in combination with wheat flour in Scottish baking. *Buckwheat* is botanically classified as a fruit, belonging to the same family as rhubarb, but it is treated as a grain in the form of groats and flour. Buckwheat flour is most often used in noodles and pancakes and can be substituted in small amounts for some of the all-purpose flour called for in a recipe. *Cornmeal* comes in colors—yellow, white and blue—each of which can be substituted for the others in cooking. *Potato flour* can be used as a thickener for soups, gravies, sauces and cheese fondues. To avoid lumping, mix with sugar or blend with fat before adding liquid. *Rye flour* lacks elasticity, so is usually combined with other flours in baking. *Soy flour* has both a high protein and high fat content, which makes it less shelf-stable than other flours. Mainly used in commercial products, soy flour can be substituted only in very small amounts for all-purpose flour in baking.

Honey has almost twice the sweetening power of sugar and a distinct flavor of its own, depending on the variety.

Maple syrup must contain a minimum of 35% pure maple syrup in order to carry the label. Less expensive maple syrups are a mixture of maple and other syrups. The most prized pure syrups are light in color and delicate in flavor. To inhibit mold growth, store in the refrigerator after opening.

Molasses is a by-product of sugar refining with powerful flavor but less sweetening power. Unsulfured molasses is pure, unrefined molasses treated with preservatives. Blackstrap molasses is also unrefined, but rarely used because of its powerful bitter flavor.

Oatmeal can be used in baking but must be combined with wheat flour in yeast breads in order for the dough to rise.

Salt enhances the flavor of all foods and adds a distinct flavor of its own. *Table salt* is finely ground and contains stabilizers to keep it free-flowing. Iodine is added to table salt in geographic areas where deficiency in the diet may be a concern. *Kosher, rock* and *sea salts* are large crystals of coarsely textured salts with few or no additives. Coarse salts are used in cooking, for sprinkling on baked goods and roast meats, and can be ground in a salt grinder for fresher-tasting table salt. *Pickling salt* is an additive-free salt prized for pickling because it doesn't cloud the brine.

Sugar is a common sweetener that comes in many forms. *Granulated* or *table* sugar, made from sugar cane or beets, is neutral in flavor and most often used in baking and dessert making. *Superfine sugar* is finely ground granulated sugar that dissolves quickly and is most often used in beverages and custards. *Confectioners'* or *10X sugar* is blended with cornstarch to prevent lumping and is often sieved or sifted before measuring and using. Confectioners' sugar should only be used in place of granulated sugar in recipes that specifically call for it. *Brown sugar* comes light and dark and has a higher moisture content than granulated sugar, because of the addition of cane molasses. Brown sugar must be stored tightly sealed to prevent hardening. Hardened brown sugar can be melted to a liquid or warmed in a microwave oven for a few seconds to soften. *Granulated brown sugar* pours like white sugar and can also be substituted, cup for cup, in recipes calling for regular light-brown sugar. *Maple sugar* is a slow-dissolving sweetener most often used in candy and syrup making.

Other staples that fare well on cupboard shelves and serve to keep your pantry well stocked for everyday and emergency use include:

■ **Canned meats and fish** (corned beef, chicken, clams, tuna, salmon, sardines, anchovies)
■ **Canned tomatoes and tomato products** (puree, paste, sauce)
■ **Canned soups and stocks, bouillon cubes**
■ **Canned and bottled fruit and vegetable juices**
■ **Evaporated and condensed milk; dry milk powder; shelf-stable milk in aseptic (sterilized) cartons**
■ **Unopened peanut butter, preserves, jams and jellies**
■ **Gelatin** (flavored and unflavored)
■ **Herbs, spices and flavorings** (vanilla, almond, rum extracts)
■ **Unopened condiments and sauces** (Worcestershire, soy sauce, relishes)

AISLE BY AISLE: A SUPERMARKET GUIDE TO GOOD EATING

What's in a Name? Product labeling laws are continually being revised to keep up with a flood of nutritionally modified products and to prevent words such as "low," "light" and "reduced" from being applied to foods that don't live up to health claims implied by the label. The best way to know what you're buying is to read the list of ingredients and to compare nutrition information from brand to brand. Remember that ingredients are listed in descending order by weight, so the first ingredient listed on a label is the one you're getting the most of in a processed food.

Nutrition labeling is voluntary for most foods but usually mandatory for products that make nutrition claims such as "high in Vitamin C" or "low-salt." These days, most American-made food products sold in supermarkets carry nutrition information on the package, so there may be reason to suspect those that don't.

BUYING THE BEST

FRUITS AND VEGETABLES

■ For the best flavor and optimal nutrition benefit, choose fresh produce over frozen, and frozen over canned. Canned and frozen fruits and vegetables fill a necessary void when fresh produce is out of season or unobtainable and when preparation time is limited. (*See Vegetables and Fruit chapter, pages 393 to 486, for specific produce-buying tips.*)
■ Buy unwrapped fresh fruits and vegetables; plastic-wrapped produce deteriorates more quickly and often you're seeing only the "good side" of the food.

CRACKERS AND CHIPS

■ Look for snacks that are baked instead of fried.
■ Check the nutrition information on the package for fat and compare nutritional profiles of similar products made by different manufacturers.

■ Choose whole-grain chips with seeds for added fiber.

COOKIES AND CAKES

■ Think plain: Instead of cream fillings, butter icings or sandwich-style cookies, buy unadorned baked goods and combine them with fresh fruit, fruit ices, lower-fat frozen yogurts, sherbets and ice milks, fruit syrups and toppings.

BREADS

■ Choose whole-grain and seeded loaves over refined for more fiber and flavor.

■ Compare brands and choose those with less fat per slice.

EGGS AND DAIRY

■ Buy clean, uncracked, Grade AA or A eggs that are stored in refrigerated food cases. *Grade* refers to the physical quality of the egg at packing time. There is no difference in nutritional value among the grades, only slight differences in the yolk firmness and thickness of the white.

■ Egg size is based on a minimum weight in ounces of a dozen eggs. A dozen jumbo eggs weighs 30 ounces, while a dozen small eggs weighs 18 ounces. Most recipes are tested with large eggs, so for the best results in home cooking, stick to large eggs, particularly in baking.

■ Small and medium-size eggs are convenient for cholesterol-restricted diets and for use in dishes such as omelets or scrambled eggs, where size is not paramount.

■ Nutritionally, brown eggs are the same as white eggs, although they are often more expensive. The color of the shell is determined by the breed of the hen.

■ The expiration or "sell-by" date on a carton of eggs can, by law, be up to 30 days after the pack date, so the closer the expiration date is to the date of purchase, the greater the chance your eggs are already a month old.

■ Look for reduced-fat snack cheeses, sour cream, cottage cheese and ricotta.

■ Choose strongly flavored hard and semi-soft cheeses for cooking—a little goes a long way. (*See Cheese Choices, page 171, for descriptions of individual cheeses.*)

■ Compare the nutritional profile of different brands and styles of yogurt. Choose plain lowfat yogurt and add your own fruit for flavor without added sugar.

■ There's no significant difference between the fat content of whole milk and 2% milk. Work your way down to 1% or skim milk: Buy a quart each of 2% and 1%; combine them in a pitcher at home. Let your taste buds adjust to reduced fat in milk, then move down a percent.

MEAT, POULTRY, FISH

■ Always check for freshness: one sure sign that meat or fish has been sitting around is a pool of liquid at the bottom of the package.

■ Choose fish fillets and steaks with a firm, fresh-cut appearance. The flesh begins to separate in older cuts of fish.

■ Compare cold-cut brands for total grams of fat per slice or serving and be sure the slices you're comparing are the same size by weight.

■ Have your butcher grind meat from leaner whole cuts. Combine lean ground turkey or chicken with ground meats used to make hamburgers and meatloaves.

DRESSINGS AND CONDIMENTS

■ All vegetable oils contain about the same amount of calories and fat. *None* contain cholesterol. (*See Oil You Need to Know, page 181.*)

■ Cholesterol-free doesn't mean fat-free. Check the nutrition information on mayonnaise and salad dressings for total grams of fat per serving.

■ Pickled foods are generally high in sodium. To reduce the salt in pickled cucumbers and peppers, rinse with cold water before eating.

CANNED GOODS

■ Choose reduced-sodium broths and tomato products used in cooking to better control the amount of salt in the finished dish. You can often add a small amount of salt yourself and still not reach the level of the original product. Or better yet, flavor your food with a splash of lemon juice, vinegar or wine and be generous with herbs and spices.

■ Look for canned fruit packed in un-

sweetened juice or light syrup made with less sugar.
- Lightly rinse and drain canned beans to remove excess salt before using.
- Look for reduced-sodium tuna packed in water or a mixture of oil and water.

BEFORE YOU BUY

To make short work of shopping, plan your menus in advance. Gather the recipes you'll be using and make a shopping list of the items you need according to how they are arranged in your supermarket. Working up and down the aisles in your mind, group together those items that are shelved next to each other so that when you shop, you can pick up everything you need from one aisle before moving on to the next. You'll save time by avoiding running back and forth for missed items.

HERBS AND SPICES

The word "herb" comes from the Latin "herba," meaning grass, and is generally used to describe the leaves of aromatic, non-woody plants and shrubs, such as parsley, basil and thyme. Spices are aromatic seasonings that come from woodier plants and trees, such as cinnamon bark and the clove buds of tropical evergreens. Whether you pick them from your garden or a supermarket shelf, herbs and spices add wonderful fragrance and exciting flavor to even the simplest of foods.

FRESH HERBS

If you grow your own herbs, pick them just before the flowers open to get the best flavor. When buying fresh herbs in the supermarket, look for fresh, moist, sprightly leaves with no signs of decay or wilting. To store fresh herbs, wash gently and shake off excess water. Wrap in paper toweling and refrigerate for up to 1 week. The exceptions are basil and mint, which turn black when damp. Store these herbs unwashed and upright with their stems in a vase of water in the refrigerator, covered loosely with a plastic bag. Clean and chop fresh herbs just before using and add to hot dishes toward end of cooking time. To dry fresh herbs, tie them in small bunches and hang them in a cool, airy place. When the bunches are brittle and dry, store them in tightly covered containers. You can freeze herbs and use them without defrosting in the same amounts as fresh.

Basil has a pungent flavor and clove-like fragrance that can perfume a room. Though its uses are limitless in soups, stews, sauces, salads and cheese dishes, basil is at its best with fresh ripe tomatoes.

Chives add delicate onion flavor when sliced or snipped with scissors and used to garnish soups, salads, pasta dishes, steamed vegetables and seafood or to flavor butter and cheese spreads. Clip garden chives at the base level to promote growth.

Cilantro (Chinese parsley, coriander) has an exotic, pungent flavor that many consider an acquired taste. Lovers of this unusual herb crave it in Mexican and South-east Asian dishes. Cilantro loses some of its strength in cooking.

Dill adds a light, lemony-fresh flavor to fish, potatoes, cream sauces for vegetables and yogurt-based dips and dressings.

Mint leaves can be infused to make teas, syrups, sauces, herb vinegars and jellies, or added to fruit salads and juices for a cool, refreshing flavor. Spearmint and peppermint are most common among the many varieties of mint.

Oregano is closely related to marjoram, and both are members of the mint family. The flavor of oregano varies from mild to strong, depending on where it grows, and some species are quite peppery. Add fresh oregano to lamb stew, bean dishes, roasted potatoes, tomato sauces and mixed vegetable salads.

Parsley is available with curly leaves or flat leaves. Flat-leaf parsley has a stronger, more distinctive flavor, but frilly sprigs of curly parsley are more decorative when used as a garnish. Chop parsley and add to potato or macaroni salad, egg dishes, tomato sauce, steamed vegetables and vegetable soups.

Rosemary has a powerful pine-like flavor and penetrating aroma. It has a particular affinity for lamb, but can be used to season roasted potatoes, lentils, tomato sauce or wine-based marinades. Older, stronger stems of rosemary are sometimes used as fragrant "skewers" for grilling cubes of meat and vegetables.

Sage has a strong, pleasant, somewhat musty flavor that enhances the flavor of pork, duck, veal and cheese dishes, and is especially delicious with lima beans.

Tarragon with its distinctive yet delicate licorice-like flavor is a pleasant accent for all types of poultry dishes. Use fresh tarragon leaves in creamy seafood sauces, chicken salad and omelets.

Thyme comes in many varieties, each with its own pungent flavor and fragrant aroma. Add sprigs of fresh thyme to seafood chowder, tomato or vegetable juice and beef stew. Strip the leaves from their stems and add to poultry stuffing and rice dishes or sprinkle on broiled fish.

DRIED HERBS AND SPICES

To test for freshness, pinch or crush a bit of dried herb or spice and sniff it. If it smells grassy or lacks the distinctive aroma of the seasoning, discard. The flavor of dried herbs and spices generally begins to fade about six months after the jar is opened. To prolong shelf life, store jars or tins in the refrigerator. If your refrigerator is too crowded, keep spices in a cool, dark cupboard, away from the heat of a stove or dishwasher. When substituting dried herbs for fresh, use 1 teaspoon of dried herbs for each tablespoon of fresh called for in the recipe. Crush the leaves in the palm of your hand just before using to help release flavor.

Allspice is sold as whole berries and ground powder. The flavor of this aromatic spice suggests a blend of cloves, cinnamon and nutmeg. Allspice is often used in savory Middle Eastern and Caribbean dishes as well as in fruit desserts and dressings.

Anise seeds add strong, sweet, licorice-like flavor to sweet breads, cookies, spice cakes, seafood and Spanish-style soups and stews. Crush seeds lightly before using to release more flavor.

Basil in its dried state is best used to flavor sauces, soups, stews and marinades, where its "green" flavor is released by the warmth of the cooking liquid.

Bay leaf is a highly aromatic herb, used especially in Mediterranean cooking to add pungent flavor to soups, stews, marinades, poaching liquids and pâtés. Add whole leaves during cooking, but be sure to remove them before serving.

allspice   anise seeds   basil   bay leaf

cardamom   caraway seeds   chili powder   celery seeds   cinnamon   fennel seeds

Caraway seeds flavor German, Scandinavian and Eastern European pork, poultry, cheese and cabbage dishes, as well as biscuits and breads. Crush seeds lightly before using to release flavor.

Cardamom is sold in the pod, whole seeds with pods removed, and ground. Used in both sweet and savory dishes, cardamom adds sweet, perfume-like flavor and aroma to Indian curries, Middle Eastern fruit dishes and Scandinavian baked goods.

Celery seed adds intense celery flavor to cheese spreads, tomato juice cocktails, coleslaw and salad dressings. Crush seeds lightly before using to release more flavor.

Chili powder is a blend of seasonings, including ground chili pepper, cumin, oregano, salt and garlic and sometimes allspice and cloves. Most popular in Mexican and American Southwestern cooking, chili powder adds punch to meat, bean and corn dishes and can be used to season sauces, dips and dressings.

Cinnamon is a dried bark sold in rolled stick or ground form. A warm, sweet spice most commonly used in baked desserts and with fruit, cinnamon is also used in savory Greek stews and casseroles, Middle Eastern meat dishes and in combination with coffee and chocolate around the world.

Cloves are available both as whole buds, from a tropical evergreen tree, and in ground form. Intensely spicy and highly aromatic, cloves season sweet and savory foods from cakes and fruit desserts to baked ham, onions and winter squash.

Coriander is sold as seeds or in ground form. Crush seeds and add to pickling brines, curries or slow-simmering Mediterranean stews. Ground coriander adds orange-like flavor to coffee cakes and creamy fruit salad dressings.

Cumin seeds can be crushed and added to chilies, curries, Tex-Mex meat stews and bean dishes. Lightly toast seeds in a dry skillet for enhanced flavor. Ground cumin is an aromatic addition to avocado dip, Mexican rice dishes, black bean soup or salad dressing.

Curry powder is a blend of many spices, including but not limited to ginger, cloves, cumin, coriander, ginger, turmeric and red peppercorns. Most often used in Indian curries and rice dishes, curry powder "sweetly" seasons fruit dressings, winter squash, deviled eggs and tomato or white sauce.

cloves   ginger   curry powder   coriander   mint   cumin

mace   dill   oregano   mustard   nutmeg   paprika

Dill as weed or seed adds a distinctively sour herb flavor to fish dishes, breads, flavored butters, cheese spreads and noodles. Dillweed, or dried dill leaf, is often used in yogurt or sour cream-based sauces and dressings and many Scandinavian dishes. Dill seed flavors pickling brines, breads and cooked cabbage dishes.

Fennel seed adds pleasant licorice-like flavor to fish dishes, sausage and pickled foods and is sometimes used to sweeten Italian tomato sauce. Crush seeds lightly before using to release flavor.

Ginger in its powdered form is ground from dried fresh ginger. Its peppery-hot, spicy flavor sweetens carrot, sweet potato, fruit and Oriental stir-fry dishes, as well as gingerbread and other baked desserts.

Mace begins as the lacy covering of a nutmeg seed and is ground for use in puddings, custards and baked goods, wherever a delicate, cinnamon-nutmeg flavor is desired. Like nutmeg, mace is also used in savory meat pâtés, cheese spreads and creamy beverages.

Mint in dried form has such intense flavor that a pinch is often enough to flavor creamy fruit salad dressings, steamed carrots or peas, candies and desserts. A sprinkling of dried mint wakes up the flavor of cheesy Italian dishes.

Mustard seeds come in a variety of colors, from white to black with a wide range of yellows in between. The seeds also vary in strength, from mild to hot. Most common in our markets are the mild yellow-white seeds used in pickling brines and crushed to make grainy mustard spreads and sauces. Ground yellow mustard powder is mildly hot and often added to cheese sauces, salad dressings, fruit chutney or curry blends.

Nutmeg comes whole as brown or limed-white kernels that can be grated as needed to add sweet, nutty spiciness to baked goods, cream sauces for pasta and vegetables, egg dishes, puddings and punches. Whole nutmeg kernels last indefinitely, while ground nutmeg more quickly loses its flavor and must be replaced.

Oregano is prized by Mediterranean cooks for its robust, somewhat bitter flavor. Essential for pizza and classic tomato sauce, dried oregano is also favored in lamb, fish, bean and summer vegetable dishes.

ground hot red pepper   peppercorns   rosemary   poppy seeds   sage   sesame seeds

summer savory   saffron   thyme   tarragon   turmeric

Paprika, hot or sweet, adds brick-red color as well as mild peppery flavor to seafood, potato and cheese dishes and is an essential ingredient in Hungarian and Spanish-style meat stews.

Pepper, ground hot red (cayenne). This is the powdered form of dried red chili peppers. It is used in a variety of dishes but most notably in Oriental stir-fries, seafood sauces, chilies and hot tomato sauces. How much you use depends on your tolerance for foods that "burn."

Peppercorns are dried pepper berries that grow in clusters, like grapes. Black pepper is picked while green to dry and darken in the sun. White pepper is soaked in water before drying to remove its outer red skin. One reason to choose white pepper is its milder flavor, but its use is often an aesthetic choice, to season light-colored soups and sauces. Freshly ground whole peppercorns are favored over packaged ground pepper for livelier flavor.

Poppy seeds add nutty crunch to cakes, breads, fruit salads, cheese sauces and noodle dishes. Store seeds in the freezer to extend their shelf life.

Rosemary has a strong, resinous flavor that is well retained when the needle-like leaf is dried. Use dried rosemary to season lamb, lentil and bean dishes and marinades for meat.

Sage is sold finely ground and in a less refined, fluffy, rubbed form. Its slightly bitter, pine-like flavor marries well with bean, cheese and pork dishes.

Saffron is the dried stigma of a non-poisonous crocus plant. Since more than 200,000 stigmas must be collected to make 1 pound of saffron, this is the world's costliest spice. It is used in minute quantities to add yellow-orange color and subtle flavor to soups, sauces, sweet breads and rice dishes.

Sesame seeds add sweet, nutty flavor to breads and biscuits, Oriental dishes, steamed vegetables and fruit salad. For more flavor, toast sesame seeds in a dry skillet over low heat, just until golden.

Summer savory is a mild, slightly peppery herb used to season green beans, sauerkraut, legumes, omelets and seafood dishes. Crush leaves slightly before using to release flavor.

Tarragon leaf adds mild anise or licorice-like flavor to seafood and poultry dishes, flavored vinegars and butters. Dried tarragon quickly loses flavor and must be replenished frequently.

Thyme in dried leaf form retains much of the powerful, pungent flavor of the fresh herb. Used widely in Mediterranean cooking, and often in concert with bay leaf, thyme flavors American favorites such as clam chowder, wild rice and Creole-style gumbos and shrimp dishes.

Turmeric adds more color than flavor to mustards, curries, cream sauces, relishes and marinades. It is often used in place of more costly saffron.

IN THE REFRIGERATOR

Refrigerator staples mostly mean eggs and dairy products, but also extend to open containers of foods from the pantry such as condiments, pickles, relishes, peanut butter, jams, jellies, nuts and coffee, as well as whole-wheat and other flours with higher fat contents that soon go rancid at room temperature.

Butter is usually sold as Grade AA, meaning superior quality, or Grade A, which means good quality. Whipped butter has air beaten into it for lighter texture and easier spreading and should not be substituted for bar butter in recipes. Sweet (*un*salted) butter, favored for its pure flavor and superior blending qualities, is often used for baking and dessert making. Tightly wrap butter to prevent absorption of refrigerator odors.

Eggs are considered to be nutrient-dense because their protein, vitamin and mineral content is high in proportion to their calorie count—a mere 80 calories per large egg. The best way to store eggs is to transfer them to a clean, covered container. Turn eggs large-end up to keep yolks centered. Eggs stored loose in the egg shelf of a refrigerator door are subject to repeated temperature fluctuations, breakage and absorption of odors from other foods. Handled properly, eggs keep well and last weeks beyond the expiration date. However, as an egg ages, the white thins out, the yolk falls flatter and eventually an "off" odor develops, signaling that the egg has passed its prime. Store leftover egg whites in a tightly closed container in the refrigerator for up to 4 days. Store unbroken egg yolks in water to cover in a tightly closed container in the refrigerator for up to 2 days.

Margarine is a vegetable fat that can usually be substituted for butter in cooking and baking. *Margarine spreads* and *diet margarines* often have a higher water content and are unsuitable baking substitutes.

Milk and cream products should be refrigerated as soon as you get them home from the market and will last up to a week beyond the sell-by date on the container, depending on storage conditions both in the market and in your refrigerator. Lower-fat milks have a slightly longer life than whole milk. *Homogenized whole milk* contains at least 3.25% milkfat and has been treated so that the fat (cream) will not separate out from the rest of the liquid. *Lowfat milk* has had some of its cream removed and contains 1% or 2% milkfat by weight. *Skim milk* has been skimmed of cream and contains less than .05% milkfat by weight. *Cultured buttermilk* is skim milk with a bacterial culture added to produce tangy taste and aroma. It often contains added salt to enhance flavor.

Half-and-half is a mixture of milk and cream that contains between 10.5% and 18% milkfat. *Light cream* contains between 18% and 30% milkfat. *Light whipping cream* has 30% to 36% milkfat. *Heavy cream* contains at least 36% milkfat and holds its whipped texture longer than whipping cream. *Sour cream* is pasteurized, acidified cream that contains at least 18% milkfat. Sour cream will curdle at high heat, so it should be stirred in at the end of any cooking time. *Crème fraîche* is a slightly thick, somewhat tart, fresh cream made originally in France and now produced in the United States. It is used as a dessert topping, in baking and as a final enrichment in sauces. To duplicate this cream at home, shake together 1 cup heavy cream and 2 teaspoons sour cream in a covered jar. Let stand at room temperature overnight or until thickened, then refrigerate for up to three weeks.

Yogurt usually contains as much milkfat as the fermented milk from which it is made. Nonfat yogurt contains less than 0.5% milkfat. Yogurt can be used as a lower-fat substitute for sour cream in cooking and baking; like sour cream, however, it will curdle at high heat and so should be stirred in at the end of cooking time.

AN EFFICIENT REFRIGERATOR

How you load your refrigerator depends on the style. Side-by-side refrigerators differ somewhat from wider refrigerators with top or bottom freezers, but the principles are the same: Foods that require maximum chilling go on the top shelf and all items should be arranged to allow maximum air flow. Place most reached-for foods in front, less used items in the back.

Top shelf: Store chilled gelatin and fruit desserts, juices in pitchers, well-wrapped raw or cooked meats, fish or poultry if meat-keeping drawer is too small or nonexistent. Also good for yogurt, cottage cheese, open cream cartons, milk cartons. (Milk can also be stored in top or middle door shelf if deep enough.)

Middle shelf: Place salads, cooked vegetables, leftovers, flours and condiments that don't fit into door shelves here. (Open catsup, mustard, horseradish, soy sauce, ethnic flavoring sauces, olives, pickles, peanut butter, jams, jellies, coffee and nuts should all be refrigerated.)

Bottom shelf: Good for eggs, covered pies and cakes, soups and stocks requiring slow chilling, loosely wrapped frozen foods in the process of thawing.

Meat keeper: Store well-wrapped luncheon meats, cheeses, bacon, raw and cooked meat, fish and poultry. If you have only one refrigerator storage drawer, keep cheeses and luncheon meats separate from uncooked meat, fish and poultry by placing them in sealable containers.

Crisper: Ideal for fruits and vegetables, lettuce and greens.

Door shelves—_Top_: Keep small cartons of juice, yogurt, condiments, dried spices and herbs, bottled salad dressings, butter (in butter keeper) here. _Middle_: A good space-saver for milk cartons and jugs, soft drinks, beer. _Bottom_: Any overflow from other shelves can go here.

FREEZER STORAGE

In most cases, freezing fresh food helps retain more of its natural flavor, color and nutritional qualities than other preservation methods.

■ For peak efficiency, a freezer should be 75% to 85% full at all times and kept at 0° temperature. At +10° and above, the bacteria and enzymes responsible for food spoilage are reactivated. If a freezer consistently registers over +10°, all foods should be used as soon as possible.

■ Cool hot food before freezing it; if possible, refrigerate for a few hours before freezing.

■ To protect flavor and prevent dehydration or "freezer burn," wrap food in airtight, vapor- and moisture-resistant packaging, squeezing out as much air as possible. Use freezer containers with tight-fitting lids, freezer bags, freezer wrap, heavy-duty aluminum foil or plastic wrap labeled "suitable for freezer."

■ Label all foods with the name of the food and the date of freezing. A useful rule: "first in, first out." For example, beans frozen in August should be used before beans frozen in September. Place foods with short freeze times in front and rotate packages so that foods frozen earlier will be used first.

■ Fast freezing best preserves the quality of food; arrange food packages in a single layer directly on freezer shelf and close to freezer walls. Cold air must circulate to bring food's temperature down quickly, so don't stack packages until after they are individually frozen.

■ Use foods within their recommended storage time. Foods stored longer than recommended may still be safe to eat, but will be less flavorful and nutritious.

FREEZING TECHNIQUES AND STORAGE TIMES

Freezing times are approximate, and based on freezers with temperatures at 0° F or below.

VEGETABLES
■ Blanch vegetables to destroy enzymes that affect flavor and texture.
■ Freeze fresh herbs: pack sprigs in sealed freezer bags.
■ Don't freeze cabbage, lettuce or other raw leafy greens, cucumbers, celery or radishes—they'll be mushy when thawed.

Maximum Freezing Time
Freeze up to 6 months.

FRUITS
■ Peel, pit and slice juicy fruits, such as peaches and pears, sprinkle with ascorbic acid to prevent darkening (follow package directions for mixing), then toss pieces with sugar (¼ cup to 1 pint fruit). Pack in clean freezer jars or freezer bags, seal and freeze.
■ Set fresh berries ¼ inch apart on a baking sheet; freeze; pour into freezer bags, seal and store in freezer.

Maximum Freezing Time
Freeze up to 12 months.

BAKED GOODS, BREAD
■ Baked quick and yeast breads freeze better than raw dough. Use yeast dough recipes designed for freezing.
■ Freeze fruit pies and cakes, Danish pastries, doughnuts, baked cookies and cookie dough.
■ Freeze cake layers, individually wrapped, without icing or filling.
■ Butter frosting can be frozen; cooked frostings do not freeze well.
■ Don't freeze cream, custard or meringue fillings.

Maximum Freezing Time
Freeze quick breads up to 2 months; yeast breads, 6 months; yeast dough, 2 weeks; cookies, 6 months; cookie dough, 4 months; pies, 1 month; unbaked pastry, 2 months; cakes, 6 months.

DAIRY
■ Milk and cream can be frozen but will separate when thawed. Heavy whipping cream will not whip when thawed.
■ Freeze stick butter, hard cheeses, processed cheese, raw egg whites; seal in plastic freezer bags.
■ Freezing adversely affects the texture of cottage cheese, sour cream, cooked eggs, yogurt and mayonnaise.

Maximum Freezing Time
Freeze milk up to 1 month; cream, 2 months; butter, 5 months; hard cheese, 6 months; processed cheese, 4 months; raw egg whites, 12 months.

MEAT, POULTRY, FISH
■ Before freezing whole poultry, remove giblets.
■ All raw meats can be frozen; cured meats such as ham, bacon and sausages can be frozen but have a shorter storage time than fresh. (Canned hams become watery and soft.)
■ If freezing any meat or fish for more than 2 weeks, remove from store package and rewrap snugly in heavy-duty freezer wrap.
■ Fatty fish such as salmon and catfish have a shorter freezer shelf life than lean fish such as bass, cod or perch.

Maximum Freezing Time
Freeze raw roasts, steaks and poultry up to 6 months; ground meat, 3 months; lamb or pork chops, 3 months; cured meats, 2 months; fatty fish, 2 months; lean fish, 6 months; raw shrimp, 9 months.

Caution: Never refrigerate or freeze home-stuffed whole poultry (still on carcass); it may become contaminated due to slow freezing or thawing. (See Turkey Talk, page 265.)

KITCHEN EQUIPMENT: THE BASICS

A well-equipped kitchen isn't just a luxury; it's essential to speedy meal preparation. Here's a list of must-haves to help you slice, peel, measure, cook and bake efficiently.

CUTTING EDGES

Newer stainless steel knives can hold a sharp edge, which they were unable to do in the past. Carbon steel knives hold a keen edge, but must be washed and dried immediately after use or they will stain and/or rust. Never put knives in the dishwasher; they tumble and become dull at once. Knives are best stored in the slots of a wooden block or on a magnetized wall panel.

What You Need:

Paring knife: 3½-inch blade for peeling, paring and fine chopping.

Utility knife: 5- to 7-inch blade for trimming meat, heavy-duty paring and peeling.

Chef's knife: 8-, 9- or 10-inch long, straight blade for chopping and dicing.

Slicer: a long, narrow-bladed knife for slicing cold meat, poultry, cheese.

Carving knife: 9-inch, thin-bladed knife for carving hot meats.

Serrated knife: for slicing bread and soft, juicy vegetables such as tomatoes.

Boning knife: narrow, thin knife used to remove raw meat, poultry or fish from the bone.

Grater: four-sided box grater for small jobs such as grating a little cheese or a single vegetable.

Knife sharpener: whetting stone or rod, or an electric sharpener.

Kitchen shears: for cutting through poultry bones and other uses.

Vegetable parer (swivel-bladed): indispensable and inexpensive; replace when dull.

POTS AND PANS

Flimsy, inexpensive pots and pans can tip over easily and often allow food to burn. Good pots come in a variety of materials suitable for specific uses.
- Cast iron is excellent for cooking foods that need a crust, like fried chicken.
- Food slides easily from the surface of a nonstick skillet, so little fat is needed for cooking.
- Copper is an excellent heat conductor and new interior surfaces make copper cooking equipment more durable than in the past.
- Heavy aluminum works well, but will discolor food cooked with eggs, wine or acid; treated or anodized aluminum will not discolor food.
- Stainless steel alone is a poor heat conductor, but with a layer of copper on the bottom, or a copper insert, it's ideal. The copper must be at least ⅛ inch thick.
- Top-of-the-stove guaranteed glass is heavy to handle, but can withstand extreme temperatures; you can cook food in it, freeze the pot and food when cool, then thaw and reheat.
- Heavy enamelware, an enamel coating over a steel base, is best for slow top-of-the-stove cooking (stews, for example) and can be presentable when brought to the table.

What You Need:

Saucepans: 1 quart, 2 quart, 3½ quart, with covers (5½ quart for quantity cooking).

Dutch oven: 5½ to 6 quart.

Frying pans or skillets: 8 inch (medium-size), 10 inch (large), 12 inch (extra-large) are standard.

Kettle: 8 to 10 quarts, with cover.

Roasting pan: shallow, at least 17 inches long, with roasting rack to fit the pan.

Casseroles: glass, porcelain and earthenware, in a variety of sizes, plus a 3-quart heavy round or oval casserole that's safe for stove top.

Double boiler: if not purchased, can be improvised from other pans by placing one inside the other with at least a 2-inch gap of space at the bottom.

Steamer: to fit inside a medium-size to large covered saucepan.

BAKING NECESSITIES

What You Need:

Rolling pin (with or without pastry cloth).

Cake pans: round 8 and 9 inch (one pair each), 8- or 9-inch square pan.

Loaf pans: for breads, cakes, quick breads; 9 x 5 x 3 inch, 8½ x 3⅝ x 2⅝ inch.

Baking or cookie sheets: at least two; as large as will fit in your oven.

Muffin pans: standard 6 cup and 12 cup.

Tart pan: 9 or 10 inch with removable bottom.

Pie plates: standard 9 or 10 inch; 9-inch deep-dish.

Springform pan: 9 inch.

Sifter: with squeeze handle.

Mixer: standard hand mixer for light beating; stand mixer for heavy duty or long-term beating.

Pastry blender: with wire cutter for blending flour and fat.

Jelly-roll pan: 15½ x 10½ x 1 inch is standard.

Cake racks: wire; assorted sizes for cooling baked goods.

Miscellaneous baking equipment: soufflé dishes, custard cups, pastry bag, dough scraper, biscuit cutters, cookie press, pastry wheel.

OTHER KITCHEN MUSTS

Chopping boards: at least two, one for meats and one for vegetables; thick, non-porous acrylic, plastic or hard rubber is preferable to wood in terms of food safety and cleaning.

Blender or food processor: for puréeing, crumbing, liquefying; a food processor is indispensable for chopping, slicing and shredding large quantities of food. (*See No Time to Cook, page 621.*)

Colander: large, for draining.

Sieve or strainer: ideally, one fine mesh stainless steel sieve and one with larger openings; can also be used as sifter—just tap the side.

Openers: heavy-duty hand can opener; church-key opener for bottles.

Measuring equipment: one set of metal measuring cups (¼-, ⅓-, ½- and 1-cup sizes) for measuring dry ingredients; 1-, 2- and 4-cup glass or plastic measuring cups with spouts, for measuring liquid ingredients; at least one set of measuring spoons, gathered on a ring (¼ teaspoon, ½ teaspoon, 1 teaspoon, 1 tablespoon); a small scale for weighing ounces and parts of ounces; heavy-duty scale for pounds of meat and vegetables.

Thermometers: instant-read thermometer, to insert at intervals into meats to measure internal temperature; candy/fry thermometer; oven thermometer to measure accuracy of oven thermostat; freezer and refrigerator thermometers.

Timer: essential to prevent burning and overcooking.

Miscellaneous: depending on how you cook and what you cook, you'll probably find a use for some of the following: food mill, juicer, garlic press, mixing bowls in a variety of sizes, slotted spoon, narrow metal spatula, wide metal turner (spatula), bulb baster, metal tongs, corkscrew, funnel, small and large whisks, skewers, wooden spoons, rubber spatulas, basting brushes, pastry brushes, rotary egg beater, potato masher, salad spinner.

Special-purpose but not-essential equipment: grapefruit knives, melon baller, apple corer, citrus zester, cherry pitter, egg slicer, potato ricer, nut grinder, lobster picks, trussing needle, meat pounder, fish poacher, pudding and gelatin molds.

CUTTING AND CHOPPING

In this era of the food processor, it is still worthwhile to know how to chop and dice with a knife. Although a food processor is efficient for some tasks, such as very fine chopping, it can never reproduce the appealing uniformity of hand chopping. And the more evenly an ingredient is chopped, diced or cubed, the more evenly it will cook.

Dicing is a more precise form of **chopping,** creating uniform, almost square pieces, about ¼ to ½ inch. **Cubing** results in pieces larger than ½ inch.

HOW TO JULIENNE

To cut a vegetable into julienne or long thin sticks, cut the vegetable lengthwise into slices. When cutting, curl under the fingertips of the hand holding the vegetable, and use the knuckles as a guide against the side of the knife to direct its movement. Stack the slices and cut lengthwise into thin sticks.

HOW TO DICE

To dice or cut a vegetable into small uni-

form square pieces, slice the vegetable lengthwise with several parallel, evenly spaced horizontal and vertical cuts, holding the vegetable together in its original shape. The spacing between the cuts will depend on how large or how small you want the pieces. Cut the vegetable crosswise, using your knuckles as a guide for the knife blade, and the slices will fall into diced pieces.

CHOP AN ONION FASTER

1. Cut peeled onion in half from top to bottom through root end. Lay onion half, cut side down, on cutting board. Steady onion with curled fingertips of one hand, hold knife blade horizontal to cutting board, and cut three or four parallel horizontal slices up to, but not through, root end.

2. Cut parallel vertical slices right up to, but not through, root end. Slice onion across at right angles to cuts from stem end to root end. Discard the tough root end. For smaller pieces, continue chopping.

CITRUS ZEST

The zest of a lemon, lime, orange or other citrus fruit is the perfumy, outermost colored part of the rind, with none of the bitter white pith attached. The zest, with its powerfully flavored citrus oil, can be used sparingly to add intense citrus flavor to all kinds of dishes, cooked and uncooked, from main courses to desserts.

A **zester** is a tool that removes citrus zest in thin strips. Use the strips whole to garnish everything from soup to dessert.

A **swivel-bladed vegetable peeler** removes long, wide strips of zest. Simmer whole strips in stocks or soups or other cooking broths for gently infused flavor. Or cut into thin strips or finely chop to use as a garnish.

FOOD SAFETY

Shop smart Healthful food is clean and safe, as well as nutritious. Start in the supermarket by buying the freshest food possible. Shop in stores that are clean and well maintained—where refrigerated foods are kept refrigerated, frozen food cases are ice-cold and frost-free and there are no signs of insect or rodent infestation.

The home front Back home, follow these simple rules for handling food in the kitchen:
■ Wash your hands before preparing food and again between handling raw meat, poultry or fish and raw vegetables or fruit to prevent transfer of bacteria.
■ Prepare foods on a clean work surface using clean utensils. Wash cutting boards, knives and utensils when switching from meat or poultry preparation to vegetable preparation. If possible, use separate cutting boards for animal foods and vegetable foods.
■ Keep all raw, fresh foods refrigerated until ready to use. Store cupboard foods in well-sealed containers. Store unrefrigerated foods away from heat sources such as the stove.
■ Thaw meat, poultry and fish overnight in the refrigerator, not at room temperature. Prepare thawed foods right away.
■ Be sure food is thoroughly cooked. This is particularly important when cooking meat, poultry, fish and eggs to destroy the bacteria responsible for food poisoning.
■ Rule of thumb: keep cold foods cold, hot foods hot. Most bacteria thrive when food is held at warm or lukewarm temperatures.
■ Sharp knives are safer to use than dull blades, which can easily slip from food and require more pressure to cut.
■ Disassemble blender or food processor before cleaning; carefully scrub blades free of food residue.

Safe food to go Whether you're carrying food in a picnic basket or a lunch box, meals that move have special safety requirements:

■ When preparing food for packing and traveling, pay special attention to the safe preparation techniques outlined above.

■ To keep food cold, pack the night before, in the carrying bag if possible, and refrigerate right up until ready to go.

■ Use clean, unbreakable, well-sealed storage containers, food storage bags, thermoses and carriers. Carry picnic foods in insulated coolers. For long storage (more than an hour or two), pack cooler with bags of ice or portable freezer packs.

■ Never leave perishable foods in a hot car or out in direct sunlight. Carry coolers on the passenger seat or floor of the car, rather than in the trunk where the temperature is higher. Refrigerate foods again when you get to where you're going or plan to eat them as soon as possible.

■ Take only what you need out of the cooler. Keep leftovers on ice if you plan to carry them home and serve them again.

MENU PLANNING

This is really where the fun begins—the cooking and tasting! In this chapter we've outlined the basics for healthful eating and meal preparation. In the following pages we offer hundreds of recipes you can organize into menus for every day, for weekend leisure time and for holidays, as well as other special events. To get you started, we've already incorporated many of the recipes into menus, which you'll find scattered throughout the book—some very simple and straightforward, others more sumptuous.

Whether planning a time-saving weekend dinner for three or four or a Saturday night buffet for twelve, keep the following basic principles in mind:

■ Select the "main course" first, but don't be trapped by traditional notions that you need a quarter of a chicken, a slab of beef or a pork chop. A lunch or dinner entrée could be Chicken Fajitas; Baked Ham and Brie Sandwich with Honey Mustard; Rice, Black-Eyed Peas and Chorizo Salad; or Tomato and Sweet Red Pepper Soup. Whatever your choice, balance it nutritionally with "side dishes," which may be nothing more than a salad or a slice of crusty bread.

■ Rethink the dinner plate trio: a protein, a starch and a vegetable. For instance, all three can be combined in a one-dish meal, such as Beef and Tostada Pie, or grains can be paired with legumes (Pasta with White Bean Sauce) to create a meatless meal that delivers complete protein.

■ Play different textures against each other—melt-in-your-mouth versus chewy, smooth against crisp. Mashed potatoes is a good choice with crunchy-coated chicken legs, or Grated Carrot Salad with Cilantro teams well with a silky puréed Asparagus Summer Soup.

■ Blend flavors, making sure they harmonize rather than compete. If a strongly flavored beef curry is the centerpiece, complement it with a softer and sweeter taste, such as a rice or couscous dish with apricots and raisins, and steamed carrots with a touch of nutmeg.

■ Consider how foods look on the plate, remembering that people first begin dining with their eyes. Combine interesting, contrasting colors (Baked Perch with Pecans and Orange Sauce, Snow Pea Sauté, and Watercress and Endive with Ginger Dressing) and mix a variety of food shapes and sizes—a large fish fillet, such as Baked Cod with Herbed Crumb Topping, with medium-size chunks of vegetables like Honeyed Carrots.

■ Make the plates work for you. If you're watching your weight, a smaller plate makes a moderate-sized meal look large; however, a large plate is a must for large meals, since small plates can cramp food. To take it one step further, if you have two sets of dinnerware, choose the set with the livelier border for foods that are a solid color, such as Pork Chops with Curried Pear Sauce. Plainer plates provide a good backdrop for multicolored foods such as Veal and Pepper Stew with Mushrooms, or Baked Ziti with Vegetables.

■ Finally, take advantage of the wonderful seasonal produce available in markets. Choose recipes that feature ingredients that are at their peak, for better flavor and lower prices. And enjoy!

CHAPTER 2

Walnut Bread (page 42).

BREADS, MUFFINS AND SUCH

CRACKED PEPPER AND HERB BREAD

Serve warm with butter or cheese or use as a sandwich bread.

Bake at 375° for 30 to 35 minutes.
Makes 2 loaves (24 slices each).
Nutrient Value Per Slice: 106 calories,
3 g protein, 2 g fat, 19 g carbohydrate,
103 mg sodium, 11 mg cholesterol.

5¼ to 6 cups all-purpose flour
3 tablespoons sugar
1 envelope active dry yeast
1¼ teaspoons salt
1¼ teaspoons cracked black pepper
1 teaspoon leaf thyme, crumbled
2 cups water
4 tablespoons (½ stick) *un*salted butter

Egg Wash:
1 egg beaten with 1 teaspoon water

1. Stir together 2 cups flour, sugar, yeast, salt, 1 teaspoon cracked pepper and the thyme in large bowl.
2. Heat the 2 cups water and butter in small saucepan until bubbles appear around edge of pan and butter melts (120° to 125°). Gradually beat water mixture into flour mixture until blended. Beat in 1 cup flour to make a thick batter. Stir in 2¼ cups flour to make a soft dough.
3. Turn dough out onto floured surface. Knead until smooth and elastic, about 10 minutes, adding more flour as needed to prevent sticking. Shape dough into ball. Place dough in greased bowl; turn to coat. Cover with clean towel. Let rise in warm place, away from drafts, until doubled in bulk, about 1 hour.
4. Punch dough down. Roll dough into 6-inch-long rope. Divide rope into 6 equal pieces. Roll each piece into 14-inch rope. Place 3 ropes side by side on large greased baking sheet; braid the 3 ropes together, pinching ends to seal.

Repeat with remaining 3 ropes. Cover and let rise in warm place until doubled in bulk, about 45 minutes.
5. Brush Egg Wash over breads. Sprinkle evenly with the remaining ¼ teaspoon cracked pepper.
6. Preheat oven to moderate (375°).
7. Bake bread in preheated moderate oven (375°) for 30 to 35 minutes or until golden brown and hollow sounding when lightly tapped. If browning too quickly, cover loosely with aluminum foil for last 5 to 10 minutes. Transfer to wire racks to cool.

STORING, FREEZING AND REHEATING YEAST BREADS

■ To keep home-baked breads for more than a few days, wrap tightly in plastic wrap or aluminum foil and store in the refrigerator. The moister the loaf, the less quickly it will dry out. Loaves stored in the refrigerator are less likely to get moldy and can be used for toast or crumbs when they start to dry out.

■ Homemade yeast breads freeze well, and when thawed and reheated, taste almost as good as when freshly baked. Frozen loaves of bread or leftover slices can be stored for up to 6 months. Wrap cooled loaves tightly in plastic wrap and overwrap with aluminum foil. Thaw, in wrapping, at room temperature for a few hours or overnight.

■ Rewrap thawed loaves of bread in aluminum foil and heat in a preheated 250° to 300° oven for 20 to 30 minutes, depending on the size of the loaf. Individual slices of frozen bread can be toasted straight from the freezer.

WINTER SOUP PARTY

Beet Soup with Vinegar (125)

White Bean and Kale Soup (123)

Sweet Potato Soup (135)

Spicy Red-Onion Flatbread (101)

Cracked Pepper and Herb Bread (this page)

Green Salad with Citrus Dressing (179)

Praline Ice Cream Cake (536) with Chocolate Sauce (537)

ALL ABOUT ACTIVE DRY YEAST

Yeast used in baking is a harmless sugar fungus that produces carbon dioxide gas bubbles, which force dough to expand and rise. Warm water reconstitutes and activates dry yeast granules and measured amounts of sugar help to feed the activity. The temperature of the water used to dissolve yeast is crucial: too low a temperature slows down the process and too high a temperature will kill the yeast. Active dry yeast is best dissolved at a temperature of 105° to 115°.

■ Store active dry yeast at cool room temperature or in the refrigerator and use before the expiration date printed on the package. Yeast can be frozen to extend its life for several months beyond the expiration date. Defrost at room temperature before using.

■ Expired dry yeast may no longer be active. If in doubt, "proof" the yeast to check that it is still alive: Dissolve yeast in warm water with a small amount of sugar as directed in your recipe. Stir and let stand for 5 to 10 minutes. If the liquid swells and foams, the yeast is active.

■ If you know your active dry yeast is fresh, you can omit the initial proofing and combine the yeast directly with the sugar, flour and other dry ingredients, thus putting the yeast directly in contact with its food source, the flour. Then add the liquid, heated to 120° to 125°, to the dry ingredients. The higher temperature is required since some of the heat needed to activate the yeast will be dissipated by the volume of the dry ingredients.

■ If your dry yeast is fresh, it makes no difference whether you first proof the yeast or add it directly to the dry ingredients. The finished product will be the same. Our recipes use both methods. Just be sure the liquid is at the proper temperature.

POTATO ONION BREAD

LOW-FAT

The breads can be baked in two 1½-quart casseroles to make round loaves.

Bake at 375° for 35 to 40 minutes.
Makes 2 loaves (10 slices each).
Nutrient Value Per Slice: 172 calories, 5 g protein, 3 g fat, 32 g carbohydrate, 193 mg sodium, 17 mg cholesterol.

1 pound potatoes, pared and cut into chunks
1 cup milk
¼ cup potato cooking water
6 green onions, finely chopped OR: 2 small bunches chives, snipped
3 tablespoons *un*salted butter
4 to 5½ cups all-purpose flour
2 tablespoons sugar
1 envelope active dry yeast
1½ teaspoons salt
¼ teaspoon ground black pepper
1 egg

1. Cook potatoes in boiling water to cover in medium-size saucepan for 15 to 20 minutes or until fork tender. Drain, reserving ¼ cup cooking liquid; return potatoes to saucepan. Mash potatoes.
2. Add milk, reserved ¼ cup cooking water, green onion and 2 tablespoons butter to potatoes. Heat over low heat until temperature reaches 120° to 125°.
3. Stir together 1½ cups flour, sugar, yeast, salt and pepper in large bowl. Beat in potato mixture with electric mixer until blended. Beat in egg. Beat in 1½ cups flour to make thick batter.
4. Stir in 1 cup flour with wooden spoon to make soft dough.
5. Turn dough out onto floured surface. Knead until smooth and elastic, about 10 minutes, adding more flour as needed to prevent sticking. Shape dough into ball. Place in large greased bowl; turn to coat. Cover with clean

(continued)

POTATO ONION BREAD SERVING IDEAS
Rich and satisfying, this bread is equally good with stews or as a sandwich maker.

POTATO ONION BREAD (*continued*)

towel. Let rise in warm place, away from drafts, until doubled in bulk, about 1 hour.

6. Punch dough down. Divide dough in half. Roll out one half of dough on floured surface with floured rolling pin into 11 × 7-inch rectangle. Starting at narrow end, roll dough up tightly; pinch seam to seal; press ends with sides of hands to seal. Fold ends under. Place, seam side down, in greased 8 × 4-inch loaf pan. Repeat with remaining half of dough. Cover with towel. Let rise in warm place, away from drafts, until doubled in bulk, about 1 hour.

7. Preheat oven to moderate (375°).

8. Melt remaining 1 tablespoon butter. Brush over loaves.

9. Bake loaves in preheated moderate oven (375°) for 35 to 40 minutes or until golden brown and hollow sounding when lightly tapped with fingers. Remove from pans to wire racks to cool.

OLIVE-HERB BREAD

LOW-FAT · LOW-CHOLESTEROL

An earthy bread, "ripe" with olives and enlivened with lemon rind.

Bake at 400° for 30 minutes.
Makes 2 loaves (12 slices each).
Nutrient Value Per Slice: 118 calories, 3 g protein, 2 g fat, 22 g carbohydrate, 203 mg sodium, 0 mg cholesterol.

1 teaspoon sugar
2 cups warm water (105° to 115°)
1 envelope active dry yeast
5 to 6 cups all-purpose flour
1 to 2 teaspoons salt, depending on saltiness of olives
⅓ cup finely chopped, pitted oil-cured olives

1 teaspoon grated lemon rind
2 teaspoons chopped fresh oregano
OR: marjoram
1 teaspoon chopped fresh thyme
1 tablespoon olive oil

1. Combine sugar and warm water in large bowl. Sprinkle yeast over top; stir to dissolve yeast. Let stand until foamy, about 10 minutes.

2. Stir in 2½ cups flour and salt. Beat with a wooden spoon about 3 minutes. Gradually beat in more flour, ½ cup at a time, to make a stiff dough.

3. Turn dough out onto floured work surface. Knead until smooth and elastic, about 5 to 10 minutes, adding more flour as needed to prevent sticking.

4. Place dough in lightly oiled bowl; turn to coat. Cover with clean towel. Let rise in warm place, away from drafts, until doubled in bulk, 1 to 1½ hours.

5. Meanwhile, combine olives, lemon rind, oregano, thyme and olive oil in small bowl. Let stand at room temperature while dough rises.

6. Punch dough down. Turn out onto work surface. Divide in half. Flatten each half. Spread olive mixture over each, dividing evenly. Working with one half at a time, press olive mixture into dough; fold over and knead a few times to distribute evenly. Form into round or oval loaves. Place on greased baking sheets. Cover with clean towel. Let rise in warm place, away from drafts, until doubled in bulk, 45 to 60 minutes.

7. Preheat oven to hot (400°).

8. Bake in preheated hot oven (400°) for 30 minutes or until golden brown and loaves sound hollow when lightly tapped with fingers. Cool on wire rack. Serve warm or at room temperature.

GRUYÈRE CHEESE BREAD

LOW-FAT

A *delicious bread that slices beautifully and makes wonderful toast—no need for butter here! Try it with your favorite sandwich filling—how about a ham and cheese melt? We achieve the sculpted top for this loaf by shaping the dough into 3 equal balls and placing them side by side in the loaf pan. (Pictured below.)*

Bake large loaf at 375° for 40 to 45 minutes; small loaves at 375° for 30 to 35 minutes.

Makes 1 large or 2 smaller loaves (18 slices).

Nutrient Value Per Slice: 207 calories, 7 g protein, 7 g fat, 27 g carbohydrate, 261 mg sodium, 55 mg cholesterol.

2 tablespoons sugar
¼ cup warm water (105° to 115°)
1 envelope active dry yeast
1 cup milk
1½ teaspoons salt
¼ teaspoon dry mustard
⅛ teaspoon ground hot red pepper
6 tablespoons *un*salted butter
2 eggs, slightly beaten
4½ to 5 cups all-purpose flour
1 cup shredded Gruyère, fontina or Swiss
    cheese (4 ounces)
½ cup diced (¼ inch) Gruyère, fontina or
    Swiss cheese (2 ounces)

Egg Wash:
1 egg beaten with 1 tablespoon water

1. Combine 1 teaspoon sugar and warm water in 1-cup measure. Sprinkle yeast over top; stir to dissolve yeast. Let stand until foamy, about 10 minutes.
2. Combine remaining sugar, milk, salt, mustard, hot red pepper and butter in small saucepan. Heat until butter melts. Pour into large bowl. Cool to lukewarm. Add eggs, yeast mixture and 2 cups flour. Beat with wooden spoon until smooth and slightly "stringy," about 2 minutes. Stir in shredded cheese. Gradually add remaining flour until dough is stiff and leaves side of bowl clean.
3. Turn dough out onto floured work surface. Knead until smooth and elastic, 5 to 10 minutes, adding more flour as needed to prevent sticking. Place dough in large greased bowl; turn to coat. Cover with clean towel. Let rise in warm place, away from drafts, until doubled in bulk, about 1 hour.
4. Punch dough down. Turn out onto work surface. Knead in diced cheese until evenly distributed. For large loaf, divide dough into thirds; shape each third into smooth round ball. Place balls in a row in greased 9 × 5 × 3-inch
(continued)

Top, Gruyère Cheese Bread (this page); bottom, Scandinavian Rye Bread with Fennel and Orange (page 44).

GRUYÈRE CHEESE BREAD (*continued*)

loaf pan. For smaller loaves, divide dough into sixths; shape each sixth into smooth round ball. Place 3 balls in a row in each of 2 greased 8½ × 4½ × 2⅝-inch loaf pans. Cover with clean towel. Let rise in warm place, away from drafts, until doubled in bulk, about 45 minutes.

5. Brush with Egg Wash for glossy crust. Place pan(s) on baking sheets to catch any drips.

6. Preheat oven to moderate (375°).

7. Bake in preheated moderate oven (375°) for 40 to 45 minutes for large loaf, 30 to 35 minutes for smaller loaves. If crust browns too quickly, tent with aluminum foil. Remove loaves from pan to wire racks to cool.

WALNUT BREAD

Great as a snacking bread or as the beginning for sandwiches. (Pictured on page 37.)

Bake at 400° for 15 minutes; then at 350° for 15 to 20 minutes.

Makes 1 round loaf (16 slices).
Nutrient Value Per Slice: 204 calories, 6 g protein, 8 g fat, 28 g carbohydrate, 311 mg sodium, 8 mg cholesterol.

1 teaspoon sugar
¼ cup warm water (105° to 115°)
1 envelope active dry yeast
1¼ cups milk
3 tablespoons *un*salted butter
2 teaspoons salt
4 to 4½ cups all-purpose flour
⅓ cup ground walnuts
½ cup coarsely chopped walnuts
1 egg white, slightly beaten
Toppings: poppy seeds, sesame seeds, caraway seeds, grated Parmesan cheese, coarse salt

BREAD GLAZES

Glazes improve the texture and appearance of the crust. Brush milk, evaporated milk, or egg yolk mixed with water onto dough before baking for a dark, shiny crust. A whole egg beaten with water gives a shiny finish. Egg white mixed with water also produces a shiny surface, but one that does not brown as much as if using a whole egg or yolk. For a softer crust, brush bread with oil or melted butter as soon as it comes out of the oven.

1. Combine ¼ teaspoon sugar and water in small bowl. Sprinkle yeast over top; stir to dissolve. Let stand until foamy, about 10 minutes.

2. Heat remaining sugar, milk, butter and salt in medium-size saucepan to melt butter. Pour into large bowl; cool to lukewarm (105° to 115°). Add yeast mixture. Stir in 2½ cups flour and ground nuts. Beat until smooth. Stir in enough flour to make soft, sticky dough.

3. Turn dough out onto floured surface. Knead until smooth and elastic, about 10 minutes, adding more flour as needed to prevent sticking. Place in large greased bowl; turn to coat. Cover with clean towel. Let rise in warm place, away from drafts, until doubled in volume, 1 to 1½ hours.

4. Punch dough down. Pinch off one-third. Pat remainder into 8-inch circle. Sprinkle with chopped walnuts; press in gently. Fold edges over to meet in center. Shape into ball. Flatten ball slightly. Push fingertips into center, gently pulling loaf apart to form 2-inch hole. Place on greased baking sheet.

5. Divide reserved dough into 5 equal pieces. Roll each into thin 12-inch rope; fold each in half; twist together to form braid. Arrange on top of loaf, from center to outside edge, spoke-fashion, and spacing evenly around the loaf; tuck ends under loaf. Cover with clean towel. Let rise in warm place, away from drafts, covered, until doubled in volume, about 1 hour.

6. Brush loaf with egg white. Sprinkle each section marked off with braids with a different topping.

7. Preheat oven to hot (400°).

8. Bake loaf in preheated hot oven (400°) for 15 minutes. Lower oven temperature to moderate (350°). Bake 15 to 20 minutes or until golden brown and hollow sounding when tapped with fingertips.

WILD RICE CASSEROLE BREAD

LOW-FAT · LOW-CHOLESTEROL

An easy yeast batter bread that requires no kneading and only one rising. The wild rice gives this hearty bread a slightly sweet, nutty flavor.

Bake at 375° for 50 to 60 minutes.
Makes 1 large loaf (24 slices).
Nutrient Value Per Slice: 121 calories, 4 g protein, 1 g fat, 24 g carbohydrate, 156 mg sodium, 3 mg cholesterol.

1 teaspoon sugar
2 cups warm water (105° to 115°)
2 envelopes active dry yeast
3 tablespoons honey
2 tablespoons *un*salted butter, melted
1½ teaspoons salt
1 cup whole-wheat flour
⅓ cup oat bran
½ cup nonfat dry milk powder
3½ cups all-purpose flour
1½ cups cooked wild rice (about ½ cup uncooked)
Oat bran, for topping and sprinkling baking dish

1. Combine sugar and warm water in large bowl. Sprinkle yeast over top; stir to dissolve yeast. Let stand until foamy, about 10 minutes. Stir in honey, butter and salt.
2. Combine whole-wheat flour, oat bran, milk powder and 1½ cups all-purpose flour in large bowl; add to yeast mixture. Beat at medium speed for 2 minutes. Stir in wild rice. Gradually beat in remaining all-purpose flour with wooden spoon. Beat, stretching dough, about 25 times. Cover with clean towel. Let rise in warm place, away from drafts, until doubled in bulk, about 1 to 1½ hours. (Don't punch down.)
3. Grease 2½- to 3-quart casserole or soufflé dish. Sprinkle with oat bran.
4. Beat dough with wooden spoon about 25 times. Turn dough into pre-

pared casserole or baking dish. Sprinkle top with oat bran.
5. Preheat oven to moderate (375°).
6. Bake in preheated moderate oven (375°) for 50 to 60 minutes or until nicely browned and bread sounds hollow when tapped with fingers. Cool bread in casserole for 10 minutes. Turn bread out onto wire rack. Serve slightly warm.

WINTER MORNING WARMER

Hot Oatmeal

Ham and Sweet Red Pepper Omelet

Wild Rice Casserole Bread
(this page)

Coffee, Tea or Hot Chocolate

WILD RICE BREAD SERVING IDEAS
Serve this hearty bread on its own with butter, cream cheese or chutney, or with strongly flavored stews and casseroles, roasted marinated meats and main-dish salads. A great base for hearty meat sandwiches.

SCANDINAVIAN RYE BREAD WITH FENNEL AND ORANGE

LOW-FAT · LOW-CHOLESTEROL

The flavors of rye, orange and fennel blend together perfectly. Use for ham or roast beef sandwiches, or even egg salad. (Pictured on page 41.)

Bake at 375° for 30 to 35 minutes.
Makes 2 loaves (12 slices each).
Nutrient Value Per Slice: 165 calories,
4 g protein, 3 g fat, 31 g carbohydrate,
258 mg sodium, 7 mg cholesterol.

Pinch sugar
¾ cup warm water (105° to 115°)
2 envelopes active dry yeast
1½ cups milk
¼ cup (½ stick) *un*salted butter
⅓ cup molasses
2½ teaspoons salt
2 tablespoons grated orange rind
2 tablespoons fennel seeds OR: anise
    seeds
3½ cups rye flour
3½ to 4 cups all-purpose flour

Egg Wash:
1 egg beaten with 2 tablespoons water

1. Combine sugar and warm water in 2-cup measure. Sprinkle yeast over top; stir to dissolve. Let stand until foamy, about 10 minutes.
2. Heat milk in small saucepan until small bubbles appear around edge of pan. Stir in butter, molasses and salt until butter is melted. Pour into large bowl. Cool to lukewarm. Stir in yeast mixture, orange rind, fennel seeds (reserving 1 teaspoon seeds for the topping), the rye flour and 1 cup all-purpose flour. Beat until smooth. Gradually beat in more all-purpose flour, ½ cup at a time, about 2½ cups total, to make a stiff dough.
3. Turn dough out onto floured surface.

Knead in enough of remaining all-purpose flour to make a very stiff dough.
4. Place dough in greased bowl; turn to coat. Cover with clean towel. Let rise in warm place, away from drafts, until doubled in bulk, 1 to 1½ hours.
5. Punch dough down. Turn dough out onto work surface. Divide in half. Knead each half a few times. Shape each half into a round or oval loaf. Place on opposite ends of large greased baking sheet. Let rise in warm place, away from drafts, covered, until doubled in bulk, about 40 minutes.
6. Brush loaves with Egg Wash. Make several ¼-inch-deep slices with single-edge razor blade in top of each loaf. Sprinkle loaves with the reserved fennel seeds.
7. Preheat oven to moderate (375°).
8. Bake loaves in preheated moderate oven (375°) for 30 to 35 minutes or until golden brown. Remove breads to wire rack to cool completely.

PARTY SANDWICHES
Cut the rye bread into small squares and use as the basis for appetizer sandwiches. The flavor of this bread will improve as it sits for a day or two.

LIGHTHOUSE DINNER

New England Clam Chowder (128)

Scandinavian Rye Bread with Fennel and Orange
(this page)

Winter Fruit Compote (529)

TOMATO, SPINACH AND CHEESE SWIRL BREAD

LOW-FAT

A dramatic tricolor bread, perfect for a buffet or impressive sandwiches. The olive oil gives the bread a rich taste. To make one large loaf, see sidebar on this page. (Pictured on page 46.)

Bake at 375° for 30 to 35 minutes.
Makes 2 small loaves (14 slices each).
Nutrient Value Per Slice: 127 calories, 4 g protein, 3 g fat, 21 g carbohydrate, 123 mg sodium, 9 mg cholesterol.

Sponge:
1 tablespoon sugar
1 cup warm water (105° to 115°)
1 envelope active dry yeast
1 teaspoon salt
¼ cup olive oil
1 cup all-purpose flour

Cheese Dough:
1 egg
½ cup warm milk (105° to 115°)
⅓ cup grated Parmesan cheese
2 to 2½ cups all-purpose flour

Tomato Dough:
¼ cup tomato paste
4 sun-dried tomatoes, packed in oil, finely chopped
¼ cup warm water (105° to 115°)
1½ to 2 cups all-purpose flour

Spinach Dough:
½ cup thawed, frozen chopped spinach
1 teaspoon leaf basil, crumbled
1¼ to 1¾ cups all-purpose flour

1. Prepare Sponge: Combine sugar and warm water in 2-cup measure. Sprinkle yeast over top; stir to dissolve yeast. Let stand until foamy, about 10 minutes.
2. Transfer to medium-size bowl. Add salt, olive oil and flour; beat until smooth. Divide sponge into thirds, about ½ cup each.
3. Prepare Cheese Dough: Beat together one-third sponge, egg, milk, Parmesan cheese and 1 cup flour in large bowl until smooth; beat for 1 minute. Stir in enough remaining flour to make soft dough. Transfer to floured work surface. Knead until smooth and elastic, 5 to 10 minutes, adding more flour as needed to prevent sticking. Place dough in greased bowl; turn to coat. Cover with oiled plastic wrap. Let rise in warm place, away from drafts, until doubled in bulk, about 1½ hours.
4. Prepare Tomato Dough: Beat together one-third sponge, tomato paste, sun-dried tomatoes, warm water and ½ cup flour in large bowl until smooth; beat for 1 minute. Stir in enough remaining flour to form soft dough. Transfer to floured work surface. Knead until smooth and elastic, 5 to 10 minutes, adding more flour as needed to prevent sticking. Place in greased bowl; turn to coat. Cover with oiled plastic wrap. Let rise in warm place, away from drafts, until doubled in bulk, about 1½ hours.
5. Prepare Spinach Dough: Place remaining one-third sponge and spinach in food processor. Whirl until spinach is pureed, about 1 minute. (Or finely chop spinach with knife, and then beat together with one-third of the Sponge in large bowl.) Beat together spinach mixture, basil and ½ cup flour in large bowl until smooth; beat for 1 minute. Stir in enough remaining flour to form soft dough. Transfer dough to floured work surface. Knead until smooth and elastic, 5 to 10 minutes, adding more flour as needed to prevent sticking. Place in greased bowl; turn to coat. Cover with oiled plastic wrap. Let rise in warm place, away from drafts, until doubled in bulk, about 1½ hours.
6. Grease 2 baking sheets.
7. Punch doughs down. Divide each in half. Roll half the cheese dough out on lightly floured surface with lightly floured rolling pin into 14×6-inch rectangle. Roll out half the tomato dough into 13½×5½-inch rectangle. Place on top of cheese dough. Repeat with half

(continued)

ONE LARGE LOAF
To make 1 large loaf, roll cheese dough out into 16×8-inch rectangle. Roll out other 2 doughs into 15½×7½-inch rectangles. Assemble as in Step 7. Bake loaves at 375° for 40 to 45 minutes.

Tomato, Spinach and Cheese Swirl Bread (page 45).

TOMATO, SPINACH AND CHEESE SWIRL BREAD
(*continued*)

the spinach dough, rolling into 13½ × 5½-inch rectangle, and placing on top of tomato dough. Roll up doughs together from long side. Pinch seam and ends to seal. Tuck ends under. Place, seam side down, on baking sheet. Cover with oiled plastic wrap. Repeat with remaining doughs and place on second baking sheet, to make second loaf. Let rise in warm place, away from drafts, until doubled in bulk, about 45 minutes.

8. Preheat oven to moderate (375°).

Cut several ¼-inch-deep slashes with single-edge razor blade or sharp knife on top of loaves.

9. Bake loaves in preheated moderate oven (375°) for 30 to 35 minutes or until golden brown and loaves sound hollow when tapped. Transfer to wire rack to cool.

HOW TO MAKE BREAD IN A PAN

(See Cinnamon-Swirl Bread with Currants and Almonds, page 49.)

PROOFING YEAST

1. Combine sugar and warm water in glass measuring cup. Sprinkle yeast over top; stir to dissolve yeast. Let stand until foamy, about 10 minutes.

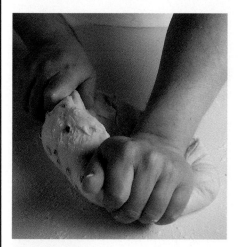

KNEADING DOUGH

2. Stretch or push ball of dough away from you with heel of hand.

3. Pull the dough back toward you, and at the same time give the dough a quarter turn. Continue the sequence, until dough is smooth and elastic, about 5 to 10 minutes, adding more flour as needed to prevent sticking.

FIRST RISING

4. Place the kneaded dough in a greased bowl; turn to coat. Cover with a clean towel. Let rise in a warm place, away from drafts, until doubled in bulk. To test, press two fingers into dough, ½ inch deep. If dents remain, the dough is properly risen. If dents fill in quickly, let rise another 15 minutes and test again. *(continued)*

SHAPING

5. Punch dough down. Roll dough out into 20 × 8-inch rectangle. Brush with melted butter. Sprinkle evenly with cinnamon-sugar.

6. Starting from short end, roll dough up, jelly-roll style.

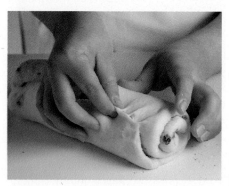

7. Pinch long seam together to seal. To smooth ends, press dough on each end with side of hand. Tuck thin strips formed under the loaf.

SECOND RISING

8. Place shaped loaf, seam side down, in greased 9 × 5 × 3-inch loaf pan. Cover with clean towel. Let rise in warm place, away from drafts, until doubled in bulk.

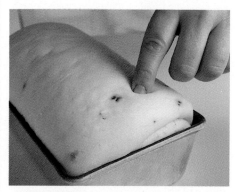

9. Test with fingers as in Step 4.

TESTING FOR DONENESS

10. Thump bottom (or top) of baked bread with fingers. If done, loaf will sound hollow.

CINNAMON-SWIRL BREAD WITH CURRANTS AND ALMONDS

A *warm and homey way to start the day—plain or toasted with butter. Or use for a ham sandwich or even egg salad. (See How-To, page 47.)*

Bake at 375° for 30 to 35 minutes.
Makes 1 loaf (12 slices).
Nutrient Value Per Slice: 266 calories, 7 g protein, 9 g fat, 40 g carbohydrate, 248 mg sodium, 33 mg cholesterol.

2 tablespoons sugar
¼ cup warm water (105° to 115°)
1 envelope active dry yeast
¾ cup milk
1 teaspoon salt
2 tablespoons *un*salted butter
1 egg, slightly beaten
½ cup finely chopped blanched almonds
⅓ cup currants
3½ to 4 cups all-purpose flour
2 tablespoons brown sugar
1 tablespoon ground cinnamon
3 tablespoons *un*salted butter, melted

1. Combine 1 teaspoon sugar and warm water in 1-cup measure. Sprinkle yeast over top; stir to dissolve yeast. Let stand until foamy, about 10 minutes.
2. Combine remaining sugar and the milk, salt and butter in small saucepan. Heat until butter melts. Pour into large bowl. Cool to lukewarm. Add yeast mixture, egg, almonds, currants and 2 cups flour. Beat with wooden spoon until smooth and slightly stringy, about 2 minutes. Gradually add enough of the remaining flour, about 1½ cups, to make a stiff dough.
3. Turn dough out onto floured work surface. Knead until smooth and elastic, 5 to 10 minutes, adding more flour as needed to prevent sticking. Place dough in large greased bowl; turn to coat.

Cover with clean towel. Let rise in warm place, away from drafts, until doubled in bulk, about 1 hour.
4. Mix together brown sugar and cinnamon in small bowl.
5. Punch dough down. Turn out onto lightly floured work surface. Roll out with lightly floured rolling pin into 20 × 8-inch rectangle. Brush with half the melted butter. Sprinkle evenly with cinnamon-sugar. Starting from short end, roll up dough jelly-roll fashion. Pinch long seam to seal. To smooth ends, press dough on each end with side of hand. Tuck the thin strips formed, under the loaf. Place, seam side down, in greased 9 × 5 × 3-inch loaf pan. Brush lightly with melted butter. Cover with clean towel. Let rise in warm place, away from drafts, until doubled in bulk and top is rounded over edge of pan, about 45 to 60 minutes. Brush with butter again.
6. Preheat oven to moderate (375°).
7. Bake in preheated moderate oven (375°) for 30 to 35 minutes or until golden brown and loaf sounds hollow when gently tapped with fingers. Remove loaf from pan to wire rack to cool. Serve slightly warm.

LUNCH BREAK

Curried Egg Salad and Ham Club Sandwich (110) with Cinnamon-Swirl Bread with Currants and Almonds (this page)

Apple and Pear Salad with Cider Dressing (175)

POPPY-SEED ONION ROLLS

Best fresh from the oven as a delicious dinner roll, or use for small roast beef or ham sandwiches.

Bake at 375° for 12 minutes.
Makes 12 rolls.
Nutrient Value Per Roll: 170 calories, 4 g protein, 7 g fat, 23 g carbohydrate, 350 mg sodium, 34 mg cholesterol.

Dough:
1 tablespoon sugar
¼ cup warm water (105° to 115°)
1 envelope active dry yeast
½ cup buttermilk
3 tablespoons *un*salted butter, at room
    temperature

1 egg
1½ teaspoons salt
2½ to 3 cups all-purpose flour

Filling:
3 tablespoons *un*salted butter
2 medium-size onions, finely chopped
1 tablespoon poppy seeds

1. Prepare Dough: Combine sugar and warm water in 1-cup measure. Sprinkle yeast over top; stir to dissolve yeast. Let stand until foamy, about 10 minutes.
2. Beat together yeast mixture, buttermilk, butter, egg, salt and 1 cup flour in large bowl until smooth. Stir in enough remaining flour, about 1½ cups, to form soft dough.
3. Turn dough out onto floured surface. Knead until smooth and elastic, 5 to 10 minutes, adding more flour as needed to prevent sticking. Place in greased bowl; turn to coat. Cover with oiled plastic wrap and towel. Let rise in warm place, away from drafts, until doubled in bulk, about 1 hour.
4. Prepare Filling: Heat butter in medium-size skillet over medium-low heat. Add onion; sauté until soft, about 5 minutes. Increase heat to medium; sauté, stirring constantly, until golden brown, about 2 minutes. Stir in poppy seeds. Let cool.
5. Punch dough down. Roll out on floured surface with lightly floured rolling pin into 16×10-inch rectangle. Spread with onion filling, leaving ½-inch border along one long edge. Starting with long side where filling is even with edge, roll dough up jelly-roll style. Pinch seam to seal. Cut crosswise into 12 equal slices. Lay rolls, cut-side down, 2 inches apart on large greased baking sheet. Press each roll to flatten slightly. Cover with oiled plastic wrap. Let rise in warm place, away from drafts, until doubled in bulk, about 45 minutes.
6. Preheat oven to moderate (375°).
7. Bake rolls in preheated moderate oven (375°) until golden brown, about 12 minutes. Serve warm.

COTTAGE CHEESE HERB ROLLS

LOW-FAT · LOW-CHOLESTEROL

Vary the herbs according to your own taste and their availability in the market. (Pictured at right.) Delicious with your favorite roast chicken recipe or ours (see recipe, page 232).

Bake at 375° for 12 minutes.
Makes 16 rolls.
Nutrient Value Per Roll: 105 calories, 3 g protein, 2 g fat, 18 g carbohydrate, 160 mg sodium, 14 mg cholesterol.

½ cup warm water (105° to 115°)
2 tablespoons honey
1 envelope active dry yeast
2 tablespoons vegetable oil
1 egg
⅓ cup lowfat cottage cheese
1 tablespoon dried dillweed
1 teaspoon salt
½ teaspoon leaf basil, crumbled
½ teaspoon leaf marjoram, crumbled
2½ to 3 cups all-purpose flour

1. Combine warm water and honey in 1-cup measure. Sprinkle yeast over top; stir to dissolve yeast. Let stand until foamy, about 10 minutes.
2. Beat together yeast mixture, oil, egg, cottage cheese, dillweed, salt, basil, marjoram and 1 cup flour in large bowl until smooth. Beat 1 minute. Stir in enough remaining flour, about 1½ cups, to make soft dough.
3. Turn dough out onto floured surface. Knead until smooth and elastic, about 5 to 10 minutes, adding more flour as needed to prevent sticking. Place dough in greased bowl; turn to coat. Cover with oiled plastic wrap. Let rise in
(continued)

Top, Golden Eggknots (page 52); bottom, Cottage Cheese Herb Rolls (this page).

COTTAGE CHEESE HERB ROLLS (*continued*)

warm place, away from drafts, until doubled in bulk, about 1 hour.

4. Grease sixteen 2½-inch muffin cups. Punch dough down. Roll into 16-inch long rope. Divide into 16 equal pieces.* Shape each piece into smooth ball. Place balls, smooth side up, in muffin cups. Cover with oiled plastic wrap. Let rise in warm place, away from drafts, until doubled in bulk, about 1 hour.

5. Preheat oven to moderate (375°).

6. Bake in preheated moderate oven (375°) for 12 minutes or until golden brown. Best served warm.

*Note: To create cloverleaf rolls, divide each of the 16 pieces into 3 equal pieces and roll into balls. Place 3 balls in each of the muffin-pan cups.

GOLDEN EGGKNOTS

LOW-FAT

It's the rich flavor of potatoes that makes these rolls so good. (Pictured on page 51.)

Bake at 375° for 12 minutes.

Makes 2 dozen rolls.

Nutrient Value Per Roll: 105 calories, 3 g protein, 3 g fat, 16 g carbohydrate, 123 mg sodium, 41 mg cholesterol.

1 medium-size potato (6 ounces), pared and cut into cubes
2 tablespoons sugar
1 envelope active dry yeast
¼ cup (½ stick) *un*salted butter, at room temperature
4 eggs
1 teaspoon salt
3½ to 4 cups all-purpose flour
Sesame seeds or poppy seeds, for topping

1. Boil potato in water to cover in small saucepan until tender. Drain, reserving ½ cup cooking water. Mash potato while still hot; you should have about ¾ cup mashed potato. Cool both potato and liquid just until warm (105° to 115°).

2. Combine 1 tablespoon sugar and reserved ½ cup cooking liquid in 1-cup glass measure. Sprinkle yeast over top; stir to dissolve yeast. Let stand until foamy, about 10 minutes.

3. Beat together yeast mixture, potato, butter, 3 eggs, remaining tablespoon sugar, salt and 1 cup flour in large bowl until smooth; beat 1 minute. Stir in enough remaining flour, about 2½ cups, to make soft dough.

4. Turn dough out onto floured surface. Knead until smooth and elastic, about 5 to 10 minutes, adding more flour as needed to prevent sticking. Place in greased bowl; turn to coat. Cover with oiled plastic wrap. Let rise in warm place, away from drafts, until doubled in bulk, about 1½ hours.

5. Punch dough down. Knead briefly on floured surface. Divide in half. Roll out each half into 12-inch rope. Cut each rope into 12 equal pieces. Roll each piece with palms into 9-inch ropes. Tie each rope to form loose knot. Place rolls, 2 inches apart, on 2 large greased baking sheets. Cover with oiled plastic wrap. Let rise in warm place, away from drafts, until doubled in bulk, for about 1 hour.

6. Beat remaining egg in small bowl. Brush rolls gently with egg. Sprinkle with either sesame or poppy seeds.

7. Preheat oven to moderate (375°).

8. Bake in preheated moderate oven (375°) for 12 minutes or until golden brown. Serve warm.

SAVE SOME EGGKNOTS

The Golden Eggknots recipe makes 24 rolls—freeze half to serve another time, if you wish.

SOUR CREAM APPLE-CRANBERRY COFFEE CAKE

A *sweet-tart breakfast or snack cake.*

Bake at 350° for 30 minutes.
Makes 12 servings.
Nutrient Value Per Serving: 233 calories,
4 g protein, 9 g fat, 34 g carbohydrate,
175 mg sodium, 40 mg cholesterol.

Dough:
¼ cup granulated sugar
¼ cup warm water (105° to 115°)
1 envelope active dry yeast
½ cup milk
¼ cup (½ stick) *un*salted butter
⅓ cup dairy sour cream
1 egg, slightly beaten
1 teaspoon vanilla
½ teaspoon salt
2 cups all-purpose flour

Fruit Filling:
2 Granny Smith apples (1 pound)
1 tablespoon *un*salted butter
1 cup fresh or frozen cranberries

Streusel:
⅓ cup all-purpose flour
¼ cup firmly packed light brown sugar
½ teaspoon ground cinnamon
2 tablespoons *un*salted butter, cold

1. Prepare Dough: Combine 1 tablespoon sugar and warm water in 1-cup measure. Sprinkle yeast over top; stir to dissolve yeast. Let stand until foamy, about 10 minutes.
2. Heat milk and butter in small saucepan over medium heat until warm; butter should not melt completely. Cool to lukewarm.
3. Beat together yeast mixture, remaining sugar, milk mixture, sour cream, egg, vanilla, salt and flour in large bowl until smooth; beat 1 minute. Scrape down side of bowl. Cover bowl with oiled plastic wrap. Let rise in warm place, away from drafts, until doubled in bulk, about 1 hour.
4. Grease 13 × 9 × 2-inch baking pan.

Stir down batter; spread evenly in pan. Cover with greased plastic wrap. Let rise in warm place, away from drafts, until almost doubled in bulk, about 45 minutes.
5. Prepare Fruit Filling: Pare, halve and core apples. Cut into ¾-inch cubes. Heat butter in large skillet over medium heat. Add apples; sauté 4 minutes or until partially cooked and very lightly browned. Cool slightly. Stir in cranberries.
6. Prepare Streusel: Combine flour, sugar and cinnamon in small bowl. Cut in butter with pastry blender until mixture is crumbly.
7. Spoon Filling and then Streusel evenly over batter.
8. Preheat oven to moderate (350°).
9. Bake in preheated moderate oven (350°) until bubbly and top is slightly crusty, about 30 minutes. Serve warm.

CHOCOLATE-ORANGE COFFEE CAKE BRAID

Chocolate and orange, a classic pairing, combine to make this large, not-too-sweet loaf that's sure to become a favorite for snacking, or even breakfast. (Pictured on page 55.)

Bake at 375° for 25 minutes.
Makes 24 slices.
Nutrient Value Per Slice: 161 calories,
4 g protein, 6 g fat, 23 g carbohydrate,
102 mg sodium, 41 mg cholesterol.

Dough:
¼ cup granulated sugar
¼ cup warm water (105° to 115°)
1 envelope active dry yeast
½ cup milk
¼ cup (½ stick) *un*salted butter, at room temperature
3 eggs, slightly beaten
1 tablespoon grated orange rind
¾ teaspoon salt
3¾ to 4 cups all-purpose flour

Filling:
3 squares (1 ounce each) semisweet chocolate, coarsely chopped
⅓ cup blanched almonds, toasted and cooled
1 egg, slightly beaten

Glaze:
½ cup 10X (confectioners') sugar
1 tablespoon honey
2 teaspoons milk
¼ cup sliced blanched almonds, toasted

1. Prepare Dough: Combine 1 tablespoon sugar and warm water in 1-cup glass measure. Sprinkle yeast over top; stir to dissolve yeast. Let stand until foamy, about 10 minutes.
2. Heat together milk and butter in small saucepan over medium heat until warm; butter does not need to melt completely. Cool to lukewarm.
3. Beat together yeast mixture, remaining sugar, milk mixture, eggs, orange rind, salt and 2 cups flour in large bowl until smooth; beat for 1 minute. Stir in enough remaining flour, about 1¾ cups, to make soft dough.
4. Transfer dough to floured work surface. Knead until smooth and elastic, 5 to 10 minutes, adding more flour as needed to prevent sticking. Place in greased bowl; turn to coat. Cover with oiled plastic wrap. Let rise in warm place, away from drafts, until doubled in bulk, about 1 hour.
5. Prepare Filling: Place chocolate in food processor or blender. Whirl until finely chopped. Add almonds. Whirl until finely chopped.
6. Punch dough down. Roll out on floured surface with lightly floured rolling pin into 16 × 14-inch rectangle. Cut lengthwise into 3 equal strips. Beat egg in small bowl. Brush 3 strips generously with all the egg. Sprinkle each strip with chocolate mixture, leaving ½-inch border along one long side on each strip. Starting with long side where filling is even with edge, roll up each strip jelly-roll style. Pinch seam and ends to seal.
7. Gently place strips, seam side down, on large greased baking sheet. Braid strips together. Pinch ends together; turn under. Cover with oiled plastic wrap. Let rise in warm place, away from drafts, until doubled in bulk, about 1 hour.
8. Preheat oven to moderate (375°).
9. Bake in preheated moderate oven (375°) for 25 minutes or until loaf sounds hollow when lightly tapped with fingers. If browning too quickly, tent with aluminum foil toward end of baking. Transfer to wire rack to cool.
10. Prepare Glaze: Stir together 10X sugar, honey and milk in small bowl until smooth. When bread is cool, drizzle with Glaze. Sprinkle with sliced almonds.

Top, Chocolate-Orange Coffee Cake Braid (page 54); bottom, Apricot Nut Twist (page 56).

APRICOT NUT TWIST

LOW-FAT

Bake at 350° for 20 to 25 minutes.
Makes 2 loaves (12 slices each).
Nutrient Value Per Slice: 188 calories,
4 g protein, 5 g fat, 31 g carbohydrate,
110 mg sodium, 35 mg cholesterol.

**NUT TWIST
SERVING IDEAS**
Serve for brunch or a
special holiday event
or just to jazz up an
everyday breakfast.
Filling variations are
included at the end of
this recipe. (Pictured
on page 55.)

Dough:

4 to 4½ cups all-purpose flour
½ cup granulated sugar
2 envelopes active dry yeast
¾ teaspoon salt
½ teaspoon ground cinnamon
¼ teaspoon ground nutmeg
1 cup milk
⅓ cup *un*salted butter
2 eggs

Filling:

½ pound dried apricots
1 cup water
¼ cup firmly packed light brown sugar
½ teaspoon ground cinnamon
½ cup finely chopped walnuts

Egg Wash:

1 egg beaten with 1 teaspoon water

1. Prepare Dough: Stir together 1 cup flour, granulated sugar, yeast, salt, cinnamon and nutmeg in large bowl.
2. Heat together milk and butter in small saucepan until bubbles appear around edge and butter melts (120° to 125°). Gradually beat milk mixture into flour mixture until blended. Beat in 2 eggs and 1 cup flour. With wooden spoon, stir in 2 cups flour to form dough.
3. Turn dough out onto floured surface. Knead until smooth and elastic, about 5 to 10 minutes, adding more flour as needed to prevent sticking. Shape dough into ball. Place in greased bowl; turn to coat. Cover with clean towel. Let rise in warm place, away from drafts, until doubled in bulk, about 1 hour.

4. Meanwhile, prepare Filling: Combine apricots and water in medium-size saucepan. Bring to boiling. Lower heat; cover and simmer until apricots are soft, about 20 minutes. Place mixture in food processor or, working in batches, in a blender. Add brown sugar and cinnamon. Whirl until pureed. Stir in walnuts. Let cool.
5. Punch dough down. Divide dough in half. Roll one-half of dough out on lightly floured surface with lightly floured rolling pin into 15 × 11-inch rectangle. Spread one-half of Filling over surface of dough, leaving ½-inch border all around edge. Starting at long side, roll up dough, jelly-roll fashion. Cut roll lengthwise in half.
6. Place halves, cut side up, next to each other on large greased baking sheet. Gently twist together to form rope, pinching ends to seal.
7. Repeat with remaining half of dough and Filling.
8. Cover with clean towels. Let rise in warm place, away from drafts, until doubled in bulk, about 30 minutes.
9. Preheat oven to moderate (350°).
10. Brush Egg Wash over twists.
11. Bake in preheated moderate oven (350°) for 20 to 25 minutes or until lightly browned. Cool on wire racks.

Filling Variations

Poppy Seed: Stir together 1 can (12½ ounces) poppy seed filling, ⅓ cup raisins, 2 teaspoons grated orange rind and 1 tablespoon orange juice in small bowl until blended. Use as directed in Step 5.
Prune: Bring 1 pound pitted prunes and ½ cup water to boiling in medium-size saucepan; cover and simmer until prunes are soft, about 30 minutes. Place mixture in food processor. Add ⅓ cup granulated sugar, 2 teaspoons grated lemon rind and ¼ cup lemon juice. Whirl until smooth. Use as directed in Step 5.

SPICED PEAR AND NUT TEA RING

For a special brunch or holiday time, or a quiet moment during a hectic afternoon.

Bake at 375° for 30 minutes.
Makes 1 ring (16 servings).
Nutrient Value Per Serving: 203 calories, 4 g protein, 6 g fat, 34 g carbohydrate, 112 mg sodium, 36 mg cholesterol.

Dough:
2¼ to 2½ cups all-purpose flour
1 envelope active dry yeast
¼ cup granulated sugar
½ teaspoon salt
½ cup milk
¼ cup (½ stick) *un*salted butter
1 egg, slightly beaten

Filling:
6 ounces dried pears
1 can (5.5 ounces) pear nectar
2 teaspoons chopped crystallized ginger
¼ teaspoon ground nutmeg
½ cup pecans, chopped

Egg Wash:
1 egg beaten with 1 teaspoon water

Glaze:
⅔ cup 10X (confectioners') sugar
1 tablespoon milk
¼ teaspoon vanilla

1. Prepare Dough: Stir together ½ cup flour, yeast, sugar and salt in large bowl.
2. Heat together milk and butter in small saucepan until bubbles appear around edge and butter melts (120° to 125°). Gradually beat milk mixture into flour mixture. Beat in 1 egg and ½ cup flour. Stir in 1¼ cups flour with wooden spoon to form soft dough.
3. Turn dough out onto floured surface. Knead until smooth and elastic, about 5 to 10 minutes, adding more flour as needed to prevent sticking. Shape dough into ball. Place in greased bowl; turn to coat. Cover with clean towel. Let rise in warm place, away from drafts, until doubled in bulk, about 1 hour.
4. Meanwhile, prepare Filling: Place pears, nectar and ginger in small saucepan. Bring to boiling over medium heat. Lower heat; cover and simmer 30 minutes or until pears are soft. Place in food processor or, working in batches, in a blender. Add nutmeg. Whirl until smooth. Transfer to bowl. Stir in pecans. Let cool.
5. Punch dough down. Roll dough out on lightly floured surface with lightly floured rolling pin into 17 × 13-inch rectangle. Spread dough with pear filling, leaving ½-inch border all around edge. Starting with long side, roll dough up, jelly-roll fashion. Shape into circle, pinching ends together to seal. Place on ungreased baking sheet. With scissors, cut slices, 1 inch apart, into outside edge without cutting all the way through to inside edge. Twist each piece so it lies flat, overlapping pieces slightly. Cover with clean towel. Let rise in warm place, away from drafts, until doubled, about 45 minutes.
6. Brush Egg Wash over bread.
7. Preheat oven to moderate (375°).
8. Bake in preheated moderate oven (375°) for 30 minutes or until golden brown. Cool on wire rack.
9. Prepare Glaze: Stir together 10X (confectioners') sugar, milk and vanilla in small bowl until smooth. Drizzle over the bread.

CALM TIME

Spiced Pear and Nut Tea Ring (this page)

Herbal Tea

¾ cup golden raisins
½ cup chopped blanched almonds
2 teaspoons grated lemon rind
¼ cup ground almonds

1. Sprinkle yeast over warm water in 2-cup glass measure; stir to dissolve yeast. Let stand until foamy, about 10 minutes.

2. Meanwhile, heat milk in small saucepan until bubbles appear around edge of pan. Cool to lukewarm. Stir milk into yeast mixture.

3. Beat together butter and sugar in large bowl until light and fluffy. Beat in eggs, one at a time, until blended. Beat in yeast mixture. Beat in salt and flour, 1 cup at a time, until smooth. Stir in raisins, chopped almonds and lemon rind. Cover bowl with clean towel. Let rise in warm place, away from drafts, until doubled in bulk, about 2 hours.

4. Butter 9-inch Kugelhopf or tube pan; sprinkle with ground almonds, turning pan to cover sides and bottom of pan.

5. Punch dough down. Spoon dough into pan. Cover and let rise in warm place until dough comes to about ¼ inch from top of pan, about 1 hour.

6. Preheat oven to moderate (350°).

7. Bake in preheated moderate oven (350°) for 40 to 45 minutes or until lightly browned. Cool in pan on wire rack 10 minutes. Invert onto wire rack; cool completely.

KUGELHOPF

Serve plain or toasted with jam. Our version is filled with raisins and almonds.

Bake at 350° for 40 to 45 minutes.
Makes 16 servings.
Nutrient Value Per Serving: 230 calories, 5 g protein, 10 g fat, 31 g carbohydrate, 215 mg sodium, 57 mg cholesterol.

1 envelope active dry yeast
¼ cup warm water (105° to 115°)
⅔ cup milk
½ cup (1 stick) *un*salted butter, at room temperature
½ cup sugar
3 eggs
1 teaspoon salt
3 cups all-purpose flour

HOLIDAY TEA

Cardamom Wreath (65)

Kugelhopf (this page)

Sour Cream
Apple-Cranberry Coffee
Cake (53)

Assorted Coffees, Teas and
Cordials

STICKY BUNS

Rich and gooey and loaded with pecans. Walnuts can be substituted for the pecans.

Bake at 375° for 25 minutes.
Makes 9 buns.
Nutrient Value Per Bun: 500 calories, 7 g protein, 28 g fat, 58 g carbohydrate, 279 mg sodium, 60 mg cholesterol.

Dough:
¼ cup granulated sugar
¼ cup warm water (105° to 115°)
1 envelope active dry yeast
½ cup milk
¼ cup (½ stick) *un*salted butter
1 egg, slightly beaten
½ teaspoon salt
2½ to 3 cups all-purpose flour

Topping:
½ cup firmly packed dark brown sugar
¼ cup (½ stick) *un*salted butter
2 tablespoons dark corn syrup
1¼ cups pecan halves

Filling:
2 tablespoons *un*salted butter, at room
    temperature
¼ cup granulated sugar
½ teaspoon ground cinnamon
½ cup pecans, chopped

1. Prepare Dough: Combine 1 tablespoon granulated sugar and warm water in 1-cup glass measure. Sprinkle yeast over top; stir to dissolve yeast. Let stand until foamy, about 10 minutes.
2. Heat together milk and butter in small saucepan until warm; butter should not melt completely. Cool to lukewarm.
3. Beat together yeast mixture, remaining sugar, milk mixture, egg, salt and 1 cup flour in large bowl until smooth; beat for 1 minute. Stir in enough remaining flour to form soft dough.
4. Transfer dough to lightly floured surface. Knead until smooth and elastic, about 5 to 10 minutes, adding more flour as needed to prevent sticking.

Place in greased bowl; turn to coat. Cover with oiled plastic wrap. Let rise in warm place, away from drafts, until doubled in bulk, about 1 to 1½ hours.
5. Prepare Topping: Combine brown sugar, butter and corn syrup in medium-size saucepan. Bring to a simmer, stirring, over medium heat; simmer 1 minute. Pour into greased 9 × 9 × 2-inch-square baking pan; spread evenly. Sprinkle with pecan halves.
6. Punch dough down. Roll out on lightly floured surface with lightly floured rolling pin into 12 × 12-inch square.
7. Prepare Filling: Spread butter over dough, leaving ½-inch border all

(continued)

STICKY BUNS (*continued*)

around. Combine sugar and cinnamon in small bowl. Sprinkle over butter. Sprinkle with chopped pecans. Roll dough up, jelly-roll style. Pinch seam to seal. Cut crosswise into 9 equal slices. Lay slices, cut side up, over topping in pan in 3 rows of 3 slices each. Cover with oiled plastic wrap. Let rise in warm place, away from drafts, until doubled in bulk, about 1 hour.

8. Preheat oven to moderate (375°).

9. Bake buns in preheated moderate oven (375°) until golden brown, about 25 minutes. Cover pan with serving dish and carefully invert. Let stand 5 minutes before removing pan. Spread any remaining topping over rolls. Serve warm.

POPPY-SEED COFFEE CAKE

Toasting *poppy seeds brings out their nutty flavor. This yeast-raised cake is ideal for breakfast or with afternoon coffee.*

Toast poppy seeds and almonds at 375° for 7 minutes; bake coffee cake at 375° for 50 minutes.

Makes 12 servings.

Nutrient Value Per Serving: 411 calories, 8 g protein, 22 g fat, 47 g carbohydrate, 179 mg sodium, 95 mg cholesterol.

⅓ cup poppy seeds
½ cup blanched slivered almonds
3½ cups all-purpose flour
¾ teaspoon salt
⅛ teaspoon ground nutmeg
⅛ teaspoon ground cloves
¾ cup firmly packed light brown sugar
¼ cup warm water (105° to 115°)
1 envelope active dry yeast
1 cup (2 sticks) *unsalted* butter, at room temperature

3 eggs
¾ cup buttermilk
1 tablespoon grated lemon rind
3 tablespoons lemon juice
½ teaspoon almond extract
¼ cup 10X (confectioners') sugar

1. Preheat oven to moderate (375°).

2. Toast poppy seeds and almonds on baking sheet, stirring occasionally, in preheated moderate oven (375°) until fragrant, about 7 minutes. Turn oven off.

3. Sift together flour, salt, nutmeg and cloves onto sheet of waxed paper.

4. Combine 1 tablespoon brown sugar and warm water in small bowl. Sprinkle yeast over top; stir to dissolve yeast. Let stand until foamy, about 10 minutes.

5. Beat together butter and remaining brown sugar in large bowl until light and fluffy. Beat in eggs, one at a time. Beat in yeast mixture, buttermilk, lemon rind, lemon juice and almond extract. Add flour mixture; beat 5 minutes or until very satiny and elastic. Beat in poppy seeds and almonds. Transfer dough to large greased bowl; turn to coat. Cover with oiled plastic wrap. Let rise in warm place, away from drafts, until doubled in bulk, about 1½ hours.

6. Generously grease and flour 12-cup Bundt pan.

7. Punch dough down. Transfer to prepared pan, smoothing top so it's even all around. Cover with oiled plastic wrap. Let rise in warm place, away from drafts, until almost doubled in bulk, about 1 hour.

8. Preheat oven to moderate (375°).

9. Bake in preheated moderate oven (375°) for 50 minutes or until golden brown. If top is overbrowning, tent with greased aluminum foil during last 15 minutes of baking. Cool coffee cake in pan on wire rack for 20 minutes. Run metal spatula around sides and center. Carefully invert onto cake plate. When cool, dust with 10X (confectioners') sugar.

FOCACCIA

An Italian flat bread that makes a delicious appetizer, or even a light lunch dish with a green salad. Experiment with your own toppings.

Bake at 400° for 25 to 30 minutes.
Makes 6 servings (12 pieces).
Nutrient Value Per Serving: 358 calories, 9 g protein, 13 g fat, 52 g carbohydrate, 206 mg sodium, 16 mg cholesterol.

2¾ to 3 cups all-purpose flour
1 envelope active dry yeast
½ teaspoon salt
1 cup milk
2 tablespoons *un*salted butter
3 tablespoons olive oil
1 large Spanish onion, halved and thinly
    sliced crosswise
1 large clove garlic, crushed
¼ cup packed fresh basil leaves, thinly
    sliced
1 tablespoon chopped fresh oregano OR:
    1 teaspoon dried
¼ teaspoon coarse black pepper

1. Stir together 1 cup flour, yeast and salt in large bowl.
2. Heat milk and butter in small saucepan until bubbles appear around edge of pan and butter has melted. Cool to lukewarm. Gradually beat milk mixture into flour mixture until blended. Beat in ¾ cup flour to make thick batter. Stir in 1 more cup flour with wooden spoon to make soft dough.
3. Transfer dough to floured work surface. Knead until smooth and elastic, 5 to 10 minutes, adding more flour as needed to prevent sticking. Shape into ball. Place in greased bowl; turn to coat. Cover bowl with towel. Let rise in warm place, away from drafts, until doubled in bulk, about 1 hour.
4. Punch dough down. Roll dough out on floured surface with floured rolling pin into 13 × 9-inch rectangle. Place in greased 13 × 9 × 3-inch baking dish; push dough up into corners of pan

slightly. Cover dish with towel. Let rise in warm place, away from drafts, until doubled in bulk, about 1½ hours.
5. Meanwhile, heat 2 tablespoons oil in large skillet over medium heat. Add onion and garlic; sauté until soft and lightly browned, 5 to 7 minutes.
6. Preheat oven to hot (400°).
7. With finger, make indentations over
(*continued*)

FOCACCIA (*continued*)

surface of dough, pressing almost to bottom of baking dish. Scatter onion mixture evenly over dough. Sprinkle with basil, oregano and pepper. Drizzle with remaining 1 tablespoon oil.

8. Bake in preheated hot oven (400°) for 25 to 30 minutes or until lightly browned. Cut crosswise into 12 strips. Serve while still warm.

SATURDAY NIGHT SNACK

Focaccia (61)

Cold Marinated Vegetables

Spiced Oatmeal Date Cookies (512)

PIZZA WITH RICOTTA, SPINACH AND PINE NUTS

LOW-FAT • LOW-CHOLESTEROL

Raisins add a slightly sweet touch to this rich pizza. For quicker preparation, use a packaged pizza dough, following package directions.

Bake at 500° for 13 to 15 minutes.
Makes 8 servings.
Nutrient Value Per Serving: 368 calories, 16 g protein, 12 g fat, 51 g carbohydrate, 480 mg sodium, 20 mg cholesterol.

1 envelope active dry yeast
¾ cup plus 2 tablespoons warm water (105° to 115°)
2¾ cups all-purpose flour
½ teaspoon salt
2 tablespoons yellow cornmeal
1 tablespoon olive oil

1 container (15 ounces) part-skim ricotta
1 package (10 ounces) frozen chopped spinach, thawed and well drained
½ cup grated Parmesan cheese
½ cup sun-dried tomatoes, packed in oil, blotted dry and coarsely chopped
½ cup golden raisins
¼ cup oil-cured black olives, pitted and finely chopped
¼ cup pine nuts
⅛ teaspoon black pepper

1. Sprinkle yeast over 6 tablespoons warm water in medium-size bowl; stir to dissolve yeast. Let stand until foamy, about 10 minutes.
2. Stir in ½ cup of the flour. Cover with plastic wrap. Let rise in warm place, away from drafts, until doubled in bulk, about 30 minutes. Stir in remaining ½ cup water, 2¼ cups flour and salt to form dough.
3. Transfer dough to floured work surface. Knead until smooth and elastic, 5 to 10 minutes, adding more flour as needed to prevent sticking. Place dough in oiled bowl; turn to coat. Cover with plastic wrap. Let rise in warm place, away from drafts, until doubled in bulk, about 1 hour.
4. Place oven rack in lowest position. Preheat oven to extremely hot (500°).
5. Punch dough down. Sprinkle cornmeal on large baking sheet. Roll dough out with floured rolling pin on sheet into 17×11-inch rectangle. Sprinkle oil on top.
6. Bake on lowest shelf in preheated extremely hot oven (500°) for 5 minutes.
7. Stir together ricotta, spinach, Parmesan, sun-dried tomato, raisins, olives, nuts and pepper in medium-size bowl. Spread on partially baked pizza dough.
8. Bake in preheated extremely hot oven (500°) for 8 to 10 minutes longer or until bottom is crisp and topping is hot.

PIZZA MAKE-AHEAD TIP: Prepare the pizza dough well in advance, let it rise once, punch it down, wrap, label, date and freeze. The dough will keep up to 2 weeks in the freezer. Thaw in refrigerator.

MEXICAN PIZZA

LOW-CHOLESTEROL

Bake at 450° for 17 to 20 minutes.
Makes 6 servings.
Nutrient Value Per Serving: 507 calories,
21 g protein, 22 g fat, 54 g carbohydrate,
697 mg sodium, 50 mg cholesterol.

1 envelope active dry yeast
1¼ cups warm water (105° to 115°)
½ cup yellow cornmeal, plus additional as
    needed
2½ cups all-purpose flour
¾ teaspoon salt
1 large red onion (8 ounces), halved and
    thinly sliced crosswise
1 teaspoon sugar
½ teaspoon ground coriander
½ teaspoon ground cumin
2 tablespoons olive oil
2 to 3 cups shredded Monterey Jack
    cheese (8 to 12 ounces)
1 can (4 ounces) chopped green chilies,
    drained
1 cup thinly sliced chorizo sausage
    (optional)
1 firm, ripe avocado, peeled, pitted and
    thinly sliced *(optional)*

1. Sprinkle yeast over ½ cup warm water in small bowl; stir to dissolve yeast. Let stand until foamy, about 10 minutes.
2. Stir in cornmeal. Cover with plastic wrap. Let stand 30 minutes. Transfer mixture to large bowl. Beat in remaining ¾ cup water, flour and salt.
3. Turn dough out onto lightly floured board. Knead until smooth and elastic, about 5 to 10 minutes, adding more flour as needed to prevent sticking. Form dough into ball. Place in lightly oiled bowl; turn to coat. Cover with plastic wrap. Let rise in warm place, away from drafts, until doubled in bulk, about 45 to 50 minutes.
4. Sprinkle large baking sheet or jelly-roll pan generously with cornmeal.
5. Punch dough down. Roll dough with floured rolling pin onto prepared baking sheet into 15 × 11-inch rectangle. Cover lightly with oiled plastic wrap. Let dough rise in warm place, away from drafts, until almost doubled in bulk, about 30 minutes.
6. Place oven rack in lowest position. Preheat oven to very hot (450°).
7. Combine onion, sugar, coriander, cumin and 1 tablespoon olive oil in a medium-size bowl. Drizzle dough with remaining tablespoon olive oil; press finger into dough to make indentations. Spread onion mixture over top of dough.
8. Bake pizza on lowest rack in preheated very hot oven (450°) for 7 minutes. Sprinkle cheese, green chilies and chorizo, if using, over top. Bake 10 to 13 minutes longer or until cheese is bubbly and crust is crisp. Remove from oven. Arrange avocado slices on top, if using. Serve.

STOLLEN

Bake at 375° for 30 to 35 minutes.
Makes 12 slices.
Nutrient Value Per Slice: 371 calories,
7 g protein, 14 g fat, 56 g carbohydrate,
203 mg sodium, 79 mg cholesterol.

HOLIDAY TREAT
Try toasting the Stollen and spreading with a little butter for Christmas morning breakfast. Perfect to bring to a holiday open house.

Dough:

½ cup dried apricot halves, coarsely
    chopped
½ cup dried pitted prunes, coarsely
    chopped
½ cup raisins
¼ cup dry sherry
½ cup firmly packed light brown sugar
1 cup warm milk (105° to 115°)
1 envelope active dry yeast
½ cup (1 stick) *un*salted butter, at room
    temperature
1 teaspoon salt
¼ teaspoon ground cinnamon
⅛ teaspoon ground nutmeg
1 tablespoon grated lemon rind
2 egg yolks, slightly beaten
3½ cups all-purpose flour
¾ cup sliced blanched almonds

Cinnamon Sugar:

2 tablespoons granulated sugar
¼ teaspoon ground cinnamon

Glaze:

3 tablespoons 10X (confectioners') sugar
1½ tablespoons heavy cream
1 egg yolk
½ teaspoon vanilla

1. Prepare Dough: Combine apricots, prunes, raisins and sherry in small bowl.
2. Combine 1 tablespoon brown sugar and ¼ cup warm milk in 1-cup glass measure. Sprinkle yeast over top; stir to dissolve yeast. Let stand until foamy, about 10 minutes.
3. Beat together butter and remaining brown sugar in large bowl until light and fluffy. Beat in yeast mixture, remaining milk, the salt, cinnamon, nutmeg, lemon rind and egg yolks. Beat in 3 cups flour until well combined and smooth. Stir in ½ cup flour, apricot mixture and almonds. Transfer to greased bowl; turn to coat. Cover with plastic wrap. Let rise in warm place, away from drafts, until doubled in bulk, about 1½ to 2 hours.
4. Punch dough down. Transfer to lightly floured work surface. Roll dough out with floured rolling pin into 13 × 8-inch rectangle.
5. Prepare Cinnamon Sugar: Combine sugar and cinnamon in small bowl. Sprinkle evenly over the dough. Fold dough in half lengthwise; pinch edges to seal. Transfer to greased baking sheet. Cover with oiled plastic wrap. Let rise in warm place, away from drafts, until almost doubled in bulk, about 40 minutes.
6. Prepare Glaze: Stir together 10X sugar, cream, egg yolk and vanilla in small bowl. Brush over stollen.
7. Preheat oven to moderate (375°).
8. Bake in preheated moderate oven (375°) for 15 minutes. Brush again with Glaze. Bake 10 minutes longer. Tent with aluminum foil. Bake 5 to 10 minutes longer or until golden. Cool on wire rack.

HOLIDAY GIFT BASKET

Stollen (this page)

Assorted Preserves

Candied Ginger

**Assorted Herbal Teas and
Flavored Coffees**

Mulled Cider Mix

HONEY BREAD

Try *this bread toasted, with cream cheese.*

Toast almonds at 350° for 10 minutes. Bake bread at 350° for 1 hour and 25 minutes.
Makes 1 loaf (12 slices).
Nutrient Value Per Slice: 267 calories, 6 g protein, 5 g fat, 51 g carbohydrate, 287 mg sodium, 19 mg cholesterol.

¾ cup unblanched almonds
2 cups all-purpose flour
1 cup whole-wheat flour
1½ teaspoons baking powder
1 teaspoon salt
¼ teaspoon baking soda
¼ teaspoon ground allspice
⅛ teaspoon ground cloves
⅛ teaspoon pepper
¾ cup firmly packed dark brown sugar
½ cup honey
1 egg
1 cup buttermilk
½ cup brewed coffee

1. Preheat oven to moderate (350°).
2. Toast almonds on baking sheet, stirring occasionally, in preheated moderate oven (350°) for 10 minutes or until fragrant. Cool. Coarsely chop. Leave oven on.
3. Grease 9 × 5 × 3-inch loaf pan.
4. Sift together all-purpose flour, whole-wheat flour, baking powder, salt, baking soda, allspice, cloves and pepper onto sheet of waxed paper. Stir together sugar, honey, egg, buttermilk and coffee in large bowl until well combined. Fold in flour mixture and nuts. Pour into prepared pan.
5. Bake in preheated moderate oven (350°) for 65 minutes. Tent with aluminum foil. Bake 20 minutes longer or until wooden pick inserted in center comes out clean. Cool bread in pan on wire rack for 20 minutes. Run a metal spatula around edges of pan. Invert bread onto platter. Invert again so that bread is right side up. Cool before slicing.

CARDAMOM WREATH

Bake at 350° for 20 minutes.
Makes 16 slices.
Nutrient Value Per Slice: 145 calories, 3 g protein, 5 g fat, 23 g carbohydrate, 118 mg sodium, 25 mg cholesterol.

Dough:
¼ cup granulated sugar
½ cup warm water (105° to 115°)
1 envelope active dry yeast
¼ cup nonfat dry milk powder
⅓ cup *uns*alted butter, at room temperature
1 egg
½ teaspoon salt
1 teaspoon grated lemon rind
1½ teaspoons grated orange rind
1 teaspoon ground cardamom
¼ teaspoon ground nutmeg
¼ teaspoon ground mace
2½ to 3 cups all-purpose flour

Glaze:
½ cup 10X (confectioners') sugar
5 teaspoons heavy cream

1. Prepare Dough: Combine 1 tablespoon sugar and warm water in 1-cup glass measure. Sprinkle yeast over top; stir to dissolve yeast. Let stand until foamy, about 10 minutes.
2. Beat together yeast mixture, remaining sugar, milk powder, butter, egg, salt, lemon rind, orange rind, cardamom, nutmeg, mace and 1 cup flour in large bowl until smooth; beat 1 minute. Stir in enough remaining flour, about 1½ cups, to make soft dough.
3. Turn dough out onto floured surface. Knead until smooth and elastic, 5 to 10 minutes, adding more flour as needed to prevent sticking. Place dough in oiled bowl; turn to coat. Cover with clean towel. Let rise in warm place, away from drafts, until doubled in bulk, about 2 hours.
4. Punch down dough. Divide into
(continued)

VERSATILE CARDAMOM WREATH
Nice for a quick Christmas break or gift giving at an open house. Make several and freeze for busy holiday times.

CARDAMOM WREATH (*continued*)

thirds. Roll each piece out on lightly floured surface to 30-inch rope. Braid ropes together; pinch ends together to form wreath. Place on greased baking sheet. Cover with oiled plastic wrap. Let rise in warm place, away from drafts, until doubled in bulk, about 1 hour.

5. Preheat oven to moderate (350°).

6. Bake in preheated moderate oven (350°) for 20 minutes or until browned. Cool on wire rack.

7. Prepare Glaze: Stir together 10X sugar and cream in small bowl until smooth. Drizzle over cooled wreath.

DOVE BREADS

These breads are a tradition at Easter. (Pictured on page 67.)

Bake at 400° for 10 minutes; then bake at 350° for 10 to 15 minutes.

Makes 12 small dove loaves (2 servings each).

Nutrient Value Per Serving: 183 calories, 4 g protein, 7 g fat, 25 g carbohydrate, 17 mg sodium, 69 mg cholesterol.

²/₃ cup sugar
½ cup warm water (105° to 115°)
2 envelopes active dry yeast
¾ cup (1½ sticks) *un*salted butter, at room temperature
4 eggs
2 egg yolks
1 tablespoon honey
1 teaspoon vanilla
½ cup finely chopped candied orange peel
2 tablespoons chopped orange rind
4 to 4¾ cups all-purpose flour, plus additional as needed

Glaze:
2 egg whites
2 tablespoons water
1 tablespoon sesame seeds

1. Combine 1 tablespoon sugar and warm water in small bowl. Sprinkle yeast over water; stir to dissolve. Let stand until foamy, about 10 minutes.

2. Beat together butter and remaining sugar in large bowl until light and fluffy. Beat in eggs, egg yolks, honey, vanilla, yeast mixture, candied peel and rind. On medium speed, beat in 2 cups flour. Stir in remaining 2 cups flour by hand with wooden spoon. Dough will be very thick and sticky. Cover bowl with clean towel.* Let rise in warm place, away from drafts, until doubled in volume, 2½ to 3 hours.

3. Lightly grease 2 large baking sheets. Punch dough down. Turn dough out onto well-floured surface. With well-floured hands, shape into 18-inch log. Cut into twelve 1½-inch pieces. Cut each piece in half; roll each half into 5-inch rope, tapering ends slightly; add more flour as needed to prevent sticking. Form dove shape by placing one rope on baking sheet. Make small indentation about one-third from one end. Place second rope across first at indentation, to make dove (*see picture, page 67*). Repeat with remaining ropes. Cover with towel. Let rise until doubled in volume, 45 to 60 minutes.

4. Prepare Glaze: Combine egg whites and water in small bowl. Brush over loaves. Sprinkle with sesame seeds.

5. Adjust oven racks to fit 2 baking sheets in oven. Preheat oven to hot (400°).

6. Bake breads in preheated hot oven (400°) for 10 minutes. Tent breads with aluminum foil. Reduce oven temperature to moderate (350°). Bake 10 to 15 minutes or until loaves are golden brown and firm. Remove to rack to cool.

***Note:** Dough can be made up to 3 days ahead and refrigerated before the first rising. To use, remove the dough from the refrigerator and let come to room temperature, 5 to 6 hours. Then proceed with Step 3.

HOT CROSS BUNS

LOW-FAT

Bake at 400° for 10 minutes; then at 350° for 10 minutes.
Makes 24 buns.
Nutrient Value Per Bun: 182 calories, 4 g protein, 5 g fat, 31 g carbohydrate, 127 mg sodium, 30 mg cholesterol.

2 envelopes active dry yeast
1 cup warm milk (105° to 115°)
4 to 4½ cups all-purpose flour
½ cup sugar
1¼ teaspoons salt
1 teaspoon grated orange rind
½ teaspoon ground cinnamon
¼ teaspoon ground allspice
¼ teaspoon ground cardamom
⅛ teaspoon ground cloves
⅛ teaspoon ground nutmeg
½ cup (1 stick) *un*salted butter, at room temperature
2 eggs, sightly beaten
½ teaspoon vanilla
1 cup dried currants

Sugar Glaze:
1 cup 10X (confectioners') sugar
4 teaspoons milk

1. Sprinkle yeast over ¼ cup of the warm milk in small bowl; stir to dissolve yeast. Let stand until foamy, about 10 minutes.
2. Whisk together 4 cups flour, sugar, salt, orange rind, cinnamon, allspice, cardamom, cloves and nutmeg in large bowl. Beat together yeast mixture, butter, eggs, vanilla and remaining ¾ cup milk in another bowl. Stir liquid ingredients into dry to form a ball.
3. Turn dough out onto floured work surface. Knead until smooth and elastic, 5 to 10 minutes, adding more flour as needed to prevent sticking. Knead in currants until well incorporated. Transfer to large, greased bowl; turn to coat. Cover bowl with clean towel. Let rise in warm place, away from drafts, until almost doubled, about 1½ hours.
4. Punch dough down. Divide dough in half. Roll each half into 12-inch-long log. Cut each log into twelve 1-inch pieces. With hand cupped, roll each piece into ball on unfloured work surface. Transfer each ball to greased baking sheet, spacing them 2 inches apart. Cover with damp cloth. Let rise in warm place, away from drafts, until almost doubled in bulk, about 1 hour.
5. Preheat oven to hot (400°).
6. Bake buns in preheated hot oven (400°) for 10 minutes. Lower oven temperature to moderate (350°). Bake 10 minutes or until golden. Tent with aluminum foil halfway through baking if browning too quickly. Transfer to wire rack to cool.
7. Prepare Sugar Glaze: Stir together 10X (confectioners') sugar and milk in small bowl until good drizzling consistency.
8. When buns are cool, drizzle cross on the top of each with glaze.

NOT JUST FOR EASTER
You'll find yourself wanting to make these classic sweet and pungent buns year-round. (Pictured below.)

Right, Dove Breads (page 66); left, Hot Cross Buns (this page).

HARVEST TREAT
The addition of
pumpkin brings color
and moistness to a
traditional cornbread
recipe. Delicious with
grilled or roasted
meats, stews and chil-
ies, and practically
anything cooked on
an outdoor grill. For
snacking, spread with
a little butter or
cream cheese.

PUMPKIN CORNBREAD

Bake at 400° for 25 to 30 minutes.
Makes 9 servings.
Nutrient Value Per Serving: 188 calories,
5 g protein, 7 g fat, 27 g carbohydrate,
460 mg sodium, 62 mg cholesterol.

¼ cup (½ stick) *un*salted butter
1 medium-size onion, finely chopped
1 cup yellow cornmeal
⅔ cup all-purpose flour
1 tablespoon baking powder
½ teaspoon baking soda
¾ teaspoon salt
¼ teaspoon pepper
2 tablespoons honey
1 cup pumpkin puree (not pie filling)
2 eggs, slightly beaten
¾ cup buttermilk

1. Preheat oven to hot (400°).
2. Heat 1 tablespoon butter in small
nonstick skillet over medium heat. Add
onion; sauté for 5 minutes or until softened and golden brown.
3. Combine cornmeal, flour, baking
powder, baking soda, salt and pepper in
large bowl.
4. Combine honey, pumpkin puree,
eggs, buttermilk and onion in medium-
size bowl.
5. Place remaining 3 tablespoons butter
in 9 × 9 × 2-inch-square baking pan.
Place in oven until butter is melted.
Swirl pan to coat with butter. Pour butter into pumpkin mixture; stir to combine. Add pumpkin mixture to dry
ingredients. Stir just until evenly moistened. Pour into pan; smooth top.
6. Bake in preheated hot oven (400°)
for 25 to 30 minutes or until wooden
pick inserted in center comes out clean.
Serve warm, cut into squares.

Top, Chocolate Loaf (page 70); bottom, Plum-Oatmeal Bread (page 70).

PLUM-OATMEAL BREAD

Good for breakfast, or just plain snacking. (Pictured on page 69.)

Bake at 350° for 45 minutes.
Makes 1 loaf (12 slices).
Nutrient Value Per Slice: 203 calories, 5 g protein, 7 g fat, 30 g carbohydrate, 203 mg sodium, 26 mg cholesterol.

2 teaspoons distilled white vinegar
Milk
2 cups all-purpose flour
⅓ cup firmly packed light brown sugar
2½ teaspoons baking powder
¾ teaspoon baking soda
¼ teaspoon salt
1 cup quick-cooking oats (not instant)
1 cup chopped, pitted firm-ripe plums
½ cup walnuts, chopped
1 egg
2 tablespoons vegetable oil

1. Preheat oven to moderate (350°). Grease and flour 8½ × 3⅝ × 2⅝-inch loaf pan.
2. Pour vinegar into 1-cup glass measure. Add milk to measure 1 cup total. Let stand 10 minutes to sour.
3. Combine flour, brown sugar, baking powder, baking soda and salt in medium-size bowl. Stir in oats, plums and walnuts.
4. Beat egg in bowl. Add soured milk and oil. Pour all at once into dry ingredients. Stir just until evenly moistened. Turn into pan.
5. Bake in preheated moderate oven (350°) for 45 minutes or until wooden pick inserted in center comes out clean. Remove bread from pan to wire rack to cool. Store overnight for easier slicing.

STORING AND FREEZING QUICK BREADS

■ Most quick breads, including coffee cakes, will store well, carefully wrapped, at room temperature for up to 2 or 3 days.
■ To freeze, carefully wrap in plastic wrap and then overwrap in aluminum foil. Freeze at 0° for up to 2 months. Thaw in wrapping at room temperature.

CHOCOLATE LOAF

LOW-FAT

Not too sweet—somewhere between a brownie and a bread. An afternoon break becomes something special with a slice of this bread and a freshly brewed cup of coffee or hot tea. Make this bread the day before you plan to serve it, since the flavor and texture improve on the second day. Wrap well and refrigerate. (Pictured on page 69.)

Bake at 350° for 45 to 50 minutes.
Makes 1 loaf (12 slices).
Nutrient Value Per Slice: 240 calories, 4 g protein, 8 g fat, 39 g carbohydrate, 227 mg sodium, 29 mg cholesterol.

1¾ cups all-purpose flour
½ cup unsweetened cocoa powder
1 teaspoon baking soda
½ teaspoon salt
1 tablespoon instant espresso powder
1 egg, slightly beaten
¼ cup (½ stick) *un*salted butter, melted
1 cup buttermilk
1 cup sugar
2 teaspoons vanilla
½ cup pecans, toasted and chopped
½ cup golden raisins

1. Preheat oven to moderate (350°). Grease 9 × 5 × 3-inch loaf pan.
2. Combine flour, cocoa, baking soda and salt in medium-size bowl.
3. Beat together espresso powder, egg, butter, buttermilk, sugar and vanilla in large bowl. Add dry ingredients; stir just until evenly moistened. Fold in pecans and raisins. Spoon into prepared pan; smooth top.
4. Bake in preheated moderate oven (350°) for 45 to 50 minutes or until wooden pick inserted in center comes out clean. Cool in pan on rack for 10 minutes. Remove from pan to rack. Cool completely before serving.

TOMATO AND CHEESE BREAD

Try *it toasted, spread with a little butter, or as a sandwich bread.*

Bake at 350° for 35 to 40 minutes.
Makes 1 loaf (12 slices).
Nutrient Value Per Slice: 203 calories, 6 g protein, 10 g fat, 23 g carbohydrate, 359 mg sodium, 70 mg cholesterol.

2½ cups all-purpose flour
1½ tablespoons sugar
2 teaspoons baking powder
¾ teaspoon salt
¼ teaspoon baking soda
⅛ teaspoon pepper
¾ cup plus 2 tablespoons shredded sharp
    Cheddar cheese
1½ teaspoons chopped fresh basil
1 cup finely chopped peeled, seeded
    tomatoes (about 1 pound)
1 tablespoon tomato paste
2 eggs, slightly beaten
6 tablespoons *un*salted butter, melted

1. Preheat oven to moderate (350°). Grease 9 × 5 × 3-inch loaf pan.
2. Stir together flour, sugar, baking powder, salt, baking soda and pepper in large mixing bowl. Stir in the ¾ cup Cheddar cheese and basil.
3. Combine tomatoes, tomato paste, eggs and butter in medium-size bowl; stir together to combine. Make well in center of dry ingredients; pour tomato mixture into well. Stir just until dry ingredients are evenly moistened. Do not overmix. Scrape mixture into prepared pan. Smooth top.
4. Bake in preheated moderate oven (350°) for 35 to 40 minutes or until wooden pick inserted in center comes out clean. After 30 minutes of baking time, sprinkle top with the 2 tablespoons Cheddar. Cool in pan on rack for 10 minutes. Remove from pan to rack. Serve warm or at room temperature.

RHUBARB AND ORANGE COFFEE CAKE

Bake at 350° for 30 minutes.
Makes 8 servings.
Nutrient Value Per Serving: 233 calories, 3 g protein, 7 g fat, 41 g carbohydrate, 165 mg sodium, 50 mg cholesterol.

1⅓ cups all-purpose flour
1½ teaspoons baking powder
Pinch salt
1 tablespoon grated orange rind
¼ cup (½ stick) *un*salted butter, at room
    temperature
¾ cup sugar
½ cup orange juice
1 egg, slightly beaten
1⅓ cups 1-inch chunks fresh rhubarb OR:
    frozen (12 ounces), thawed
    according to package directions
    and well drained

Topping:
2 tablespoons sugar
½ teaspoon ground cinnamon

1. Preheat oven to moderate (350°). Grease 9-inch tart pan with removable bottom or 9 × 9 × 2-inch-square baking pan.
2. Combine flour, baking powder, salt and orange rind in medium-size bowl.
3. Beat together butter and sugar in medium-size bowl until light and creamy, about 5 minutes. Stir in orange juice and egg until well mixed (mixture may look curdled).
4. Stir dry ingredients into liquid ingredients just until evenly moistened. Fold in rhubarb. Pour into baking pan.
5. Prepare Topping: Combine sugar and cinnamon in small bowl. Sprinkle over batter.
6. Bake in preheated moderate oven (350°) for 30 minutes or until wooden pick inserted in center comes out clean. If using tart pan, remove sides. Serve warm.

COFFEE CAKE CHANGE OF PACE
Cut-up strawberries can be substituted for the rhubarb.

BLUEBERRY-LEMON MUFFINS

LOW-FAT

Bake at 400° for 18 to 20 minutes.
Makes 18 muffins.
Nutrient Value Per Muffin: 142 calories, 4 g protein, 4 g fat, 23 g carbohydrate, 190 mg sodium, 22 mg cholesterol.

1 cup all-purpose flour
1 cup whole-wheat flour
½ cup wheat germ
2 tablespoons grated lemon rind
2 teaspoons baking powder
½ teaspoon baking soda
½ teaspoon salt
1¼ cups buttermilk
½ cup firmly packed light brown sugar
¼ cup granulated sugar
⅓ cup *un*salted butter, melted
1 egg, slightly beaten
1½ cups fresh or thawed frozen
   blueberries

1. Preheat oven to hot (400°). Line 18 muffin-pan cups (½-cup capacity) with paper liners.
2. Combine all-purpose flour, whole-wheat flour, wheat germ, lemon rind, baking powder, baking soda and salt in large bowl. Make well in center.
3. Beat together buttermilk, brown sugar, granulated sugar, butter and egg in medium-size bowl. Add all at once to well in dry ingredients; stir just until dry ingredients are completely moistened. Fold in blueberries. Do not overmix; batter will be lumpy.
4. Fill each cup with rounded ¼ cup batter.
5. Bake in preheated hot oven (400°) for 18 to 20 minutes or until lightly golden and wooden pick inserted in center comes out clean.
6. Cool muffins in pan on wire rack 5 minutes. Gently remove from muffin pans to wire rack to cool completely, unless serving warm.

HOW TO MAKE MUFFINS
The secret to perfect muffins: Don't over-beat the batter.
1. Stir together dry ingredients in a bowl. Make a well in the center of the dry ingredients. Combine the liquid ingredients and pour all at once into the well.

2. Stir the liquid ingredients into the dry ingredients just until the dry ingredients are moistened; do not overmix. The batter should be lumpy.

3. Spoon the batter into the muffin-pan cups, scraping the batter off the spoon with another spoon or spatula.

MAPLE-PECAN OATMEAL MUFFINS

A *hint of maple syrup combined with toasted pecans makes these delicious oatmeal muffins a family favorite. (Pictured at right.)*

Bake at 400° for 20 to 25 minutes.
Makes 12 muffins.
Nutrient Value Per Muffin: 232 calories, 4 g protein, 13 g fat, 26 g carbohydrate, 145 mg sodium, 32 mg cholesterol.

1 cup buttermilk
1 cup old-fashioned rolled oats (not quick-cooking)
⅓ cup *un*salted butter
¼ cup maple syrup
¼ cup firmly packed light brown sugar
1 egg
1 cup all-purpose flour
1 teaspoon baking powder
½ teaspoon baking soda
¼ teaspoon salt
1 cup coarsely chopped toasted pecans
2 tablespoons maple syrup
2 tablespoons finely ground pecans

1. Preheat oven to moderate (400°). Lightly grease or line with paper liners 12 muffin-pan cups (½-cup capacity).
2. Heat buttermilk in small saucepan over medium-low heat just until tiny bubbles form around edge of saucepan. Stir in oats until completely moistened. Add butter. Cover and let stand until cool and butter is melted. Beat in ¼ cup maple syrup, brown sugar and egg.
3. Meanwhile, combine flour, baking powder, baking soda, salt and toasted pecans in medium-size bowl. Make well in center of dry ingredients. Add oat mixture all at once to well; stir just until dry ingredients are completely moistened. Do not overmix; batter will be lumpy.
4. Fill each cup with ⅓ cup batter.
5. Bake in preheated moderate oven (400°) for 20 to 25 minutes or until lightly golden and wooden pick inserted in center comes out clean.
6. Cool muffins in pan on wire rack 5 minutes. Using thin metal spatula or knife, gently remove muffins from pan to wire rack. Brush top of each muffin with about ½ teaspoonful maple syrup. Sprinkle each with about ½ teaspoonful ground pecans. Serve immediately, or cool completely to serve later.

From top to bottom:
Cranberry-Raspberry Jam Muffins (page 74); Blueberry-Lemon Muffins (page 72); and Maple-Pecan Oatmeal Muffins (this page).

CRANBERRY-RASPBERRY JAM MUFFINS

LOW-FAT

Pictured on page 73, top.

Bake at 375° for 20 to 25 minutes.
Makes 12 muffins.
Nutrient Value Per Muffin: 227 calories,
4 g protein, 6 g fat, 40 g carbohydrate,
134 mg sodium, 32 mg cholesterol.

2 cups all-purpose flour
½ cup oat bran
1 teaspoon ground mace
1 teaspoon baking soda
¼ teaspoon salt
¾ cup plain yogurt
½ cup firmly packed light brown sugar
¼ cup granulated sugar
⅓ cup *un*salted butter, melted
1 egg, slightly beaten
2 teaspoons vanilla
1 cup fresh or frozen, thawed, cranberries
5 tablespoons raspberry jam

1. Preheat oven to moderate (375°).
Line 12 muffin-pan cups (½-cup capacity) with paper liners.
2. Combine flour, oat bran, mace, baking soda and salt in large bowl. Make well in center.
3. Beat together yogurt, brown sugar, granulated sugar, butter, egg and vanilla in medium-size bowl. Add all at once to well in dry ingredients, along with cranberries; stir just until dry ingredients are completely moistened. Do not overmix; batter will be lumpy.
4. Fill each cup with 2 level tablespoonfuls batter. With tip of wooden spoon handle, make slight indentation in batter. Spoon in 1 level teaspoonful raspberry jam; top with 2 to 3 level tablespoonfuls batter. With same wooden spoon, make another slight indentation in the batter. Fill with ¼ level teaspoonful raspberry jam.
5. Bake in preheated moderate oven (375°) for 20 to 25 minutes until lightly golden and wooden pick inserted in center without touching jam comes out clean.
6. Cool muffins in pan on wire rack 5 minutes. Gently remove from muffin pans to wire rack to cool completely, unless serving warm.

CORN MUFFINS

Bake at 400° for 20 to 25 minutes.
Makes 12 muffins. •
Nutrient Value Per Muffin: 166 calories,
6 g protein, 6 g fat, 23 g carbohydrate,
261 mg sodium, 33 mg cholesterol.

1 cup yellow cornmeal
1 cup all-purpose flour
1 teaspoon baking powder
1 teaspoon baking soda
1 tablespoon sugar
1 can (8½ ounces) creamed corn
¾ cup buttermilk
2 tablespoons *un*salted butter, melted
1 egg, slightly beaten
1 cup shredded sharp Cheddar cheese
    (4 ounces)

1. Preheat oven to hot (400°). Grease 12 muffin-pan cups (½-cup capacity).
2. Combine cornmeal, flour, baking powder, baking soda and sugar in large bowl. Make well in center.
3. Combine creamed corn, buttermilk, butter, egg and cheese in medium-size bowl. Add wet mixture all at once to well in dry ingredients; stir just until dry ingredients are moistened. Do not overmix; batter will be lumpy.
4. Spoon into muffin cups, dividing evenly.
5. Bake in preheated hot oven (400°) for 20 to 25 minutes or until lightly golden.
6. Cool muffins in pan on wire rack for 5 minutes. Run knife or thin metal spatula around edge of muffins; remove muffins from muffin cups. Serve warm.

CORN MUFFINS MADE BETTER
Creamed corn and Cheddar cheese add extra moistness and flavor to this muffin. Great for breakfast, with barbecued foods, and chicken and pork dishes. Excellent with Mexican food. (Pictured on page 75, bottom right.)

APPLE MUFFINS

Bake at 400° for 20 to 25 minutes.
Makes 12 muffins.
Nutrient Value Per Muffin: 196 calories,
4 g protein, 8 g fat, 28 g carbohydrate,
266 mg sodium, 29 mg cholesterol.

2 cups all-purpose flour
2 teaspoons baking powder
½ teaspoon baking soda
½ teaspoon salt
½ cup firmly packed light brown sugar
¾ teaspoon ground cinnamon
1 medium-size Granny Smith apple, pared,
     cored and cut into ¼-inch cubes
     (about 1 cup)
½ cup chopped walnuts
1 cup buttermilk
1 egg, slightly beaten
¼ cup (½ stick) *un*salted butter, melted

1. Preheat oven to hot (400°). Grease
12 muffin-pan cups (½-cup capacity).
2. Combine flour, baking powder, baking soda, salt, sugar, cinnamon, apple
and half the walnuts in large bowl.
Make well in center.
3. Combine buttermilk, egg and melted
butter in medium-size bowl. Add wet
mixture all at once to well in dry ingredients; stir just until dry ingredients are
moistened. Do not overmix; batter will
be lumpy.
4. Spoon batter into muffin cups, dividing evenly. Sprinkle with remaining
walnuts. Cups will be quite full.
5. Bake in preheated hot oven (400°)
for 20 to 25 minutes, or until lightly
golden and wooden pick inserted in
center comes out clean. Tent with aluminum foil if muffins brown too
quickly.
6. Cool muffins in pan on wire rack for
5 minutes. Run knife or thin metal
spatula around edges of muffins; remove
muffins from pan. Serve warm.

**Front left, Apple Muffins (this page);
right, Corn Muffins (page 74).**

BUTTERMILK BISCUITS WITH PARSLEY

You can substitute your favorite fresh herbs for the parsley—or omit the herbs altogether and you'll still have a fine biscuit.

Bake at 450° for 12 minutes.
Makes 10 biscuits.
Nutrient Value Per Biscuit: 166 calories, 3 g protein, 8 g fat, 21 g carbohydrate, 333 mg sodium, 10 mg cholesterol.

2 cups all-purpose flour
1 tablespoon baking powder
½ teaspoon baking soda
½ teaspoon salt
1 teaspoon sugar
3 tablespoons *un*salted butter, cut into
     small pieces
3 tablespoons solid vegetable shortening
2 tablespoons chopped parsley
¾ cup buttermilk

1. Preheat oven to very hot (450°). Grease baking sheet.
2. Combine flour, baking powder, baking soda, salt and sugar in medium-size bowl. Cut butter and shortening into flour mixture with pastry blender until mixture is crumbly. Add parsley and buttermilk; stir with fork until evenly moistened and mixture forms a ball. Do not overmix.
3. Turn dough out onto floured surface.

AFTER THE SNOWSTORM

Tomato and Sweet Red Pepper Soup (134)

Buttermilk Biscuits with Parsley (this page)

Chocolate Cake

Knead 4 times. Pat out to ¾-inch thickness. Cut into rounds with floured 2½-inch cutter. Place biscuits on prepared baking sheet. Pat out scraps once. Cut out more rounds.
4. Bake in preheated very hot oven (450°) for 12 minutes or until golden brown. Serve biscuits warm.

CREAM BISCUITS

A classic that's easy to prepare—and rich!

Bake at 450° for 12 minutes.
Makes 10 biscuits.
Nutrient Value Per Biscuit: 206 calories, 3 g protein, 12 g fat, 21 g carbohydrate, 316 mg sodium, 44 mg cholesterol.

2 cups all-purpose flour
1 tablespoon baking powder
1 teaspoon sugar
¾ teaspoon salt
1¼ cups heavy cream
1 tablespoon *un*salted butter, melted

1. Preheat oven to very hot (450°). Grease baking sheet.
2. Combine flour, baking powder, sugar and salt in medium-size bowl. Stir in heavy cream until mixture forms a ball. Do not overmix.
3. Turn dough out onto floured surface. Knead 4 times. Pat out to ¾-inch thickness. Cut into rounds with floured 2½-inch cutter. Place biscuits on baking sheet. Pat out scraps once. Cut out more rounds. Brush tops with melted butter.
4. Bake in preheated very hot oven (450°) for 12 minutes or until golden brown. Serve warm.

Top, Buttermilk Scones with Currants (page 78); bottom, Savory Cheese and Green Onion Scones (page 78).

SAVORY CHEESE AND GREEN ONION SCONES

BUTTERMILK SCONES WITH CURRANTS

SAVORY SCONES SERVING IDEAS
Offer these with a salad for lunch or with hearty soup for dinner, or on their own as a light snack. Butter is a welcome addition, or even cream cheese. (Pictured on page 77, bottom.)

BUTTERMILK MAKES IT BETTER
Buttermilk makes these scones very tender, and a hint of orange rind brightens their flavor. (Pictured on page 77, top.)

Bake at 400° for 15 to 18 minutes.
Makes 8 scones.
Nutrient Value Per Scone: 209 calories, 7 g protein, 10 g fat, 21 g carbohydrate, 307 mg sodium, 56 mg cholesterol.

1½ cups all-purpose flour
2½ teaspoons baking powder
1 tablespoon sugar
½ teaspoon leaf marjoram, crumbled
½ teaspoon dry mustard
¼ teaspoon salt
3 tablespoons *un*salted butter
1 cup shredded medium-sharp Cheddar
    cheese (4 ounces)
⅓ cup finely sliced green onion
½ to ⅔ cup milk
1 egg, slightly beaten

1. Preheat oven to hot (400°). Grease and flour large baking sheet.
2. Stir together flour, baking powder, sugar, marjoram, mustard and salt in large bowl. Cut in butter with pastry blender until mixture resembles coarse meal. Stir in cheese and green onion.
3. Whisk together ½ cup milk and the egg in small bowl. Make well in center of dry ingredients. Add milk mixture to well; stir just until combined; do not overmix. If mixture is too dry to come together, add remaining milk.
4. Transfer dough to lightly floured work surface. Pat into block 16 inches long, 3 inches wide and ¾ inch thick. Cut dough crosswise into four 4-inch pieces; cut each piece diagonally in half to make a total of 8 triangles; or cut block into eight 2-inch pieces. Place scones 1 inch apart on prepared baking sheet.
5. Bake in preheated hot oven (400°) for 15 to 18 minutes or until golden. Serve warm, or let cool.

Bake at 400° for 15 to 18 minutes.
Makes 8 scones.
Nutrient Value Per Scone: 172 calories, 4 g protein, 5 g fat, 27 g carbohydrate, 226 mg sodium, 39 mg cholesterol.

1½ cups all-purpose flour
2 tablespoons light brown sugar
2 teaspoons baking powder
1 teaspoon grated orange rind
¼ teaspoon baking soda
¼ teaspoon salt
3 tablespoons *un*salted butter
¼ cup dried currants
½ cup buttermilk
1 egg, slightly beaten
1 tablespoon granulated sugar
¼ teaspoon ground cinnamon, or to taste

1. Preheat oven to hot (400°). Grease and flour large baking sheet.
2. Stir together flour, light brown sugar, baking powder, orange rind, baking soda and salt in large bowl. Cut in butter with pastry blender until mixture resembles coarse meal. Stir in currants.
3. Whisk together buttermilk and egg in small bowl. Make well in center of dry ingredients. Add buttermilk mixture to well; stir just until combined; do not overmix.
4. Transfer dough to lightly floured surface. Shape dough into 8-inch circle. Transfer to prepared baking sheet. Score circle into eighths as if cutting a pie, cutting all the way through to baking sheet, but not separating wedges. (For easier cutting, dip knife in flour on board.)
5. Stir together granulated sugar and cinnamon in small bowl.
6. Bake in preheated hot oven (400°) for 12 minutes. Sprinkle cinnamon-sugar over top. Bake 3 to 6 minutes or until golden. Separate scones. Serve warm, or let cool.

FOUR-GRAIN PANCAKES

The secret to these thick but airy pancakes? Separating the eggs and beating the whites.

Toast oats at 400° for 7 minutes.
Makes 4 servings.
Nutrient Value Per Serving: 313 calories, 11 g protein, 12 g fat, 41 g carbohydrate, 635 mg sodium, 124 mg cholesterol.

½ cup old-fashioned rolled oats (not quick-cooking)
½ cup whole-wheat flour
½ cup all-purpose flour
2 tablespoons yellow cornmeal
4 teaspoons light brown sugar
1½ teaspoons baking powder
½ teaspoon baking soda
½ teaspoon salt
1 cup buttermilk
2 eggs, separated
2 tablespoons *un*salted butter, melted OR: 2 tablespoons vegetable oil
2 teaspoons vegetable oil

1. Preheat oven to hot (400°).
2. Toast oats on baking sheet in preheated hot oven (400°), shaking pan occasionally, until oats are fragrant and toasted, about 7 minutes. Transfer oats to food processor. Whirl until coarsely chopped. Transfer to large bowl.
3. Add whole-wheat flour, all-purpose flour, cornmeal, sugar, baking powder, baking soda and salt to oats. Whisk together buttermilk, egg yolks and melted butter in small bowl.
4. Beat egg whites in clean small bowl until stiff, but not dry, peaks form.
5. Make well in center of dry ingredients. Add buttermilk mixture to well; stir until combined. Fold in egg whites.
6. Heat large skillet or griddle over moderately high heat. Add the 2 teaspoons oil. Ladle in ¼ cup batter for each pancake. Cook until set and bubbly on top, about 2 minutes. Turn pancakes over; cook about 1 minute or until cooked through. Keep warm in preheated slow oven (250°).

Make-Ahead Tip: Prepare large batches of the dry mixture for these pancakes and store airtight at cool room temperature for up to several weeks. Add the liquid ingredients just before cooking.

APPLE PANCAKE

LOW-FAT

Bake at 375° for 25 to 30 minutes.
Makes 4 servings.
Nutrient Value Per Serving: 393 calories,
9 g protein, 13 g fat, 62 g carbohydrate,
617 mg sodium, 83 mg cholesterol.

3½ tablespoons *un*salted butter
1 pound Golden Delicious apples, pared,
    cored and sliced ½ inch thick
1 tablespoon lemon juice
2 teaspoons granulated sugar
1½ cups all-purpose flour
2 tablespoons firmly packed light brown
    sugar
1 teaspoon baking powder
½ teaspoon salt
¼ teaspoon baking soda
1 cup buttermilk
1 egg, slightly beaten

1. Preheat oven to moderate (375°).
2. Heat 2 tablespoons butter in large
ovenproof skillet* over moderate heat.
Add apple, lemon juice and granulated
sugar; cook, stirring, until crisp-tender,
5 minutes.
3. Stir together flour, light brown
sugar, baking powder, salt and baking
soda in large bowl. Stir together buttermilk and egg in small bowl. Make well
in center of dry ingredients. Add buttermilk mixture; stir to mix.
4. Add remaining butter to apples in
skillet. Melt over moderate heat. When
bubbly, spoon pancake mixture on top,
spreading it to sides of skillet.
5. Bake in preheated moderate oven
(375°) oven for 25 to 30 minutes or
until set and golden on top and wooden
pick inserted in center comes out clean.
Let stand 5 minutes. Loosen sides with
metal spatula. Invert onto serving plate.

*Note: If skillet is not ovenproof, wrap
handle with aluminum foil.

**APPLE PANCAKE
MAKE-AHEAD TIP:**
The apples can be
sautéed up to 2 hours
ahead and arranged
in a decorative pat-
tern in the skillet, and
then the pancake bat-
ter can be poured
over and the skillet
refrigerated. Bake just
before serving.

MOTHER'S DAY BREAKFAST
IN BED

Spiced Tea (560)

Apple Pancake (this page)

Honey-Raspberry Peaches
(477)

HUSH PUPPIES

*These cornmeal fritters are a delicious
complement to fried fish and chicken.*

Makes 6 servings (2 dozen).
Nutrient Value Per Serving: 238 calories,
6 g protein, 9 g fat, 34 g carbohydrate,
743 mg sodium, 37 mg cholesterol.

1¾ cups white cornmeal
1½ teaspoons salt
1 teaspoon baking powder
½ teaspoon baking soda
1 cup buttermilk
1 egg, slightly beaten
3 green onions, chopped
    Vegetable oil, for frying

1. Combine cornmeal, salt, baking
powder and baking soda in medium-size
bowl.
2. Beat together buttermilk and egg in
small bowl. Add to dry ingredients
along with onion; stir just to blend
ingredients.
3. Pour oil into heavy medium-size
saucepan to depth of 3 or 4 inches.
Heat oil over medium heat until deep-
fat frying thermometer registers 350°.
4. Scoop out 1 tablespoon of dough;
push off with rubber spatula into hot
oil. Fry a few at a time without crowding the saucepan. Fry, turning once,
until hush puppies turn a golden brown
and float to the top, 3 to 5 minutes.
Remove with slotted spoon to paper
toweling to drain. Keep warm in preheated slow oven (300°).

CHAPTER 3

APPETIZERS, SNACKS AND SANDWICHES

JALAPEÑO CHEESE SPREAD

For a special presentation, mound the spread (or shape it into a log) in the center of a serving platter and surround with our Salsa Fresca (see recipe, page 85) and an assortment of bagel chips, flatbread or melba rounds.

MICROWAVE DIRECTIONS FOR TOASTING SPICES FOR JALAPEÑO CHEESE SPREAD (HIGH POWER OVEN): Scatter nuts, chili powder and cumin over bottom of microwave-safe 9-inch pie plate. Microwave, uncovered, at 100% power 2½ to 3 minutes until nuts begin to darken and spices are fragrant.

Roast nuts and spices at 350° for 6 minutes.
Makes 1¼ cups. Recipe can be doubled.
Nutrient Value Per Tablespoon: 46 calories, 2 g protein, 4 g fat, 1 g carbohydrate, 64 mg sodium, 10 mg cholesterol.

¼ cup pine nuts OR: walnuts
1 teaspoon chili powder
½ teaspoon ground cumin
1 green onion, cut into 1-inch lengths
1 small clove garlic *(optional)*
½ pickled jalapeño pepper, seeded and chopped OR: 3 to 4 dashes liquid red-pepper seasoning
4 ounces light cream cheese OR: regular cream cheese
4 ounces plain goat cheese
1 tablespoon lemon juice

1. Preheat oven to moderate (350°). Fold 6-inch piece of foil over double; fold up edges to make tray. Place nuts, chili powder and cumin in center and place on baking sheet.
2. Bake nut mixture in preheated moderate oven (350°) for 6 minutes or until spices are fragrant and begin to darken. Cool completely.
3. Place green onion and garlic, if using, in food processor. Whirl until chopped. Add jalapeño and nuts and spices. Whirl until nuts are chopped. Add cream cheese, goat cheese and lemon juice. Whirl until blended.
4. Scrape spread into serving bowl. Cover tightly with plastic wrap and refrigerate at least 24 hours.

Make-Ahead Tip: The spread can be made up to 5 days ahead and refrigerated, tightly covered.

Preceding page, from top: Salmon Twists (page 88); Marinated Goat Cheese on Garlic Toast (page 92); and Gorgonzola and Pear Packets (page 91).

ARTICHOKE AND BLACK OLIVE SPREAD

LOW-CHOLESTEROL

Wonderful with sweet red pepper wedges or endive spears. Try this spread in sandwiches too, especially with smoked meats such as turkey and ham. (Pictured on page 83.)

Makes 1¼ cups. Recipe can be doubled.
Nutrient Value Per Tablespoon: 26 calories, 0 g protein, 2 g fat, 1 g carbohydrate, 72 mg sodium, 1 mg cholesterol.

1 jar (6 ounces) marinated artichoke hearts, drained and finely chopped
1 stalk celery, finely chopped
1 roasted sweet yellow pepper, chopped *(see How-To, page 433)*
¼ cup chopped pitted canned black olives
2 tablespoons chopped fresh basil OR: 2 to 3 teaspoons dried
3 tablespoons mayonnaise

Stir together artichoke, celery, yellow pepper, olives, basil and mayonnaise in medium-size bowl until combined. Scrape into serving bowl. Cover tightly with plastic wrap and refrigerate for at least 2 hours.

Make-Ahead Tip: The spread can be made up to 2 days in advance and refrigerated, covered.

SOUTHWEST TREAT

Jalapeño Cheese Spread
(this page) with Pita Chips

Stuffed Anaheim Peppers (437)

Coleslaw

Mexican Beer

Strawberry Ice

MUSHROOM AND CREAM CHEESE SPREAD

LOW-CHOLESTEROL · LOW-SODIUM

Serve *with melba toasts, wheat thins, pita chips or assorted raw vegetables. For a delicious pasta sauce, heat the spread, thinning with a little of the pasta cooking water or half-and-half, and toss with hot, cooked pasta. (Pictured below.)*

Makes 2 cups. Recipe can be doubled, tripled or quadrupled.

Nutrient Value Per Tablespoon: 22 calories, 1 g protein, 2 g fat, 2 g carbohydrate, 46 mg sodium, 2 mg cholesterol.

1 ounce dried mushrooms, domestic or
    imported
Boiling water
1 large onion, quartered
¾ pound fresh button mushrooms,
    trimmed
2 tablespoons olive oil
½ teaspoon leaf tarragon, crumbled
½ teaspoon salt
¼ teaspoon pepper
1 tablespoon brandy
1 tablespoon lemon juice
3 ounces light cream cheese OR: regular
    cream cheese

1. Soak mushrooms with enough boiling water to cover in small bowl for 15 minutes or until mushrooms are softened. Drain; rinse mushrooms well to remove sand. Squeeze dry. Trim off tough stems.
2. Place reconstituted mushrooms and onion in food processor. Pulse with on/off motion until finely chopped. Transfer to waxed paper.
3. Add half of fresh mushrooms to food processor. Whirl until finely chopped. Add remaining mushrooms. Whirl until finely chopped, scraping down the bowl as needed.
4. Heat oil in medium-size skillet over medium-high heat. Add dried mushroom-onion mixture; cook 3 minutes. Add chopped fresh mushrooms, tarragon, salt and pepper; cook 8 to 10 minutes or until all liquid from mushrooms is evaporated. Stir in brandy; cook 1 minute. Remove skillet from heat. Stir in lemon juice and cheese until smooth.
5. Scrape mixture into serving bowl, spreading level. Cover and refrigerate overnight for best flavor. Garnish with chives or parsley sprigs, if you wish.

Make-Ahead Tip: The spread can be prepared up to 5 days ahead and refrigerated, covered tightly with plastic wrap.

From bottom, clockwise: Mushroom and Cream Cheese Spread (this page); Artichoke and Black Olive Spread (page 82); Tuna and White Bean Spread (page 84); and Red Pepper and Chutney Cheese Spread (page 84).

BETTER SPREADS

- Instead of butter, margarine or mayo, spread your bread with healthful alternatives, like cranberry relish on a turkey sandwich, tomato salsa with chicken, applesauce with ham, hummus with vegetables or chutney with cheese. Be creative!
- Puree drained, canned beans in processor or blender, thinning with broth. Or, puree beans with equal parts nonfat yogurt or lowfat cottage cheese. Season with herbs, hot pepper sauce, anchovy paste or tomato paste.
- Use a food mill to puree leftover cooked vegetables or press through a wire mesh sieve with the back of a spoon. Thin out with leftover vegetable cooking liquid, broth, yogurt or olive oil. Flavor with herbs and spices.
- Mash or puree soft fresh fruit (banana, strawberries) or drained, canned fruit (peaches, pears) or leftover cooked fruit (baked apples, poached pears, stewed prunes), alone or with lowfat cottage cheese or ricotta. Season with cinnamon, nutmeg, honey mustard or chopped crystallized ginger.

TUNA AND WHITE BEAN SPREAD

LOW-CALORIE • LOW-FAT

Surround the spread with radicchio leaves or scoop into a hollowed-out red cabbage and serve with toasted slices of peasant bread or Italian bread. For a vegetable appetizer, spoon the spread into zucchini or cucumber rounds or cherry tomatoes. Also tasty as a lunchtime sandwich filling! (Pictured on page 83.)

Makes 2 cups. Recipe can be doubled.
Nutrient Value Per Tablespoon: 25 calories, 2 g protein, 1 g fat, 2 g carbohydrate, 28 mg sodium, 3 mg cholesterol.

½ cup parsley leaves
¼ cup basil leaves OR: 2 teaspoons dried
¼ medium-size red onion, cut in half
1 can (6½ ounces) water-packed tuna, drained
1 cup canned white beans, rinsed and drained
2 tablespoons lemon juice
¼ teaspoon salt *(optional)*
1 teaspoon drained capers
2 tablespoons mayonnaise
2 tablespoons lower-calorie ricotta cheese

1. Combine parsley and basil in a food processor. Whirl until chopped. Add onion. Whirl with short on/off pulses until chopped.
2. Flake tuna; add to processor, along with beans, lemon juice, salt if using, capers, mayonnaise and ricotta. Whirl with on/off pulses until medium-coarse texture; do not overprocess.
3. Scrape spread into serving dish. Cover tightly with plastic wrap and refrigerate for at least 2 hours for flavors to blend.

Make-Ahead Tip: The spread can be made up to 1 day ahead and refrigerated, covered.

RED PEPPER AND CHUTNEY CHEESE SPREAD

LOW-CALORIE

Accompany with crackers or raw vegetables or use as a sandwich spread—especially delicious with egg salad. (Pictured on page 83.)

Makes 2 cups. Recipe can be doubled.
Nutrient Value Per Tablespoon: 24 calories, 1 g protein, 1 g fat, 3 g carbohydrate, 45 mg sodium, 2 mg cholesterol.

1 tablespoon olive or vegetable oil
1 large (6 ounces) sweet red pepper, cored, seeded and chopped
1 medium-size red onion, chopped
¾ teaspoon curry powder
⅓ cup mango chutney, large pieces cut
2 tablespoons dry sherry
¼ teaspoon salt
4 to 6 drops liquid red-pepper seasoning
1 cup farmer's cheese OR: light cream cheese

1. Heat oil in skillet over medium heat. Add sweet pepper, onion and curry powder; cook 10 to 12 minutes, stirring occasionally, until softened. Stir in chutney and sherry; cook 1 minute. Remove skillet from heat.
2. Stir in salt and red-pepper seasoning. Stir in cheese until blended. Scrape into serving dish and bring to room temperature. Cover tightly with plastic wrap and refrigerate at least 4 hours.

Make-Ahead Tip: Spread can be made up to 2 days ahead and refrigerated.
Microwave Directions for Cooking Vegetable Mixture (High Power Oven): Combine oil, red pepper, onion and curry powder in microwave-safe 9-inch pie plate. Microwave, uncovered, at 100% power 8 minutes, stirring twice. Stir in chutney and sherry. Microwave, uncovered, at 100% power 2 minutes. Continue with Step 2.

SALSA FRESCA

**LOW-CALORIE · LOW-FAT
LOW-CHOLESTEROL**

Choose the ripest tomatoes for the freshest-tasting salsa. Serve with taco chips, flat-bread or pita chips or use to make our Seven-Layer Mexican Dip (see recipe, page 87). Spoon onto burgers, grilled meats or cooked vegetables as a lively accompaniment. (Pictured at right.)

Makes 2 cups. Recipe can be doubled.
Nutrient Value Per Tablespoon: 3 calories, 0 g protein, 0 g fat, 1 g carbohydrate, 19 mg sodium, 0 mg cholesterol.

1 pound plum tomatoes (about 10 medium-size)
½ small red onion, finely chopped
1 clove garlic, chopped
2 tablespoons fresh lime juice
1 to 2 tablespoons chopped cilantro OR: parsley
1 teaspoon chopped pickled jalapeño pepper OR: 3 to 4 dashes liquid red-pepper seasoning
¼ teaspoon salt

Core tomatoes and chop. Place tomatoes in colander set over bowl to drain out excess liquid. Reserve liquid for other uses such as adding to soup or sauces. Place tomato in medium-size bowl. Stir in red onion, garlic, lime juice, cilantro, jalapeño pepper and salt. Let stand at room temperature for 2 hours to blend flavors.

Make-Ahead Tip: The salsa can be made a day ahead and refrigerated, covered.

From left, clockwise: Spinach-Feta Cheese Dip (page 86); Salsa Fresca (this page); and Roasted Red-Pepper Dip (page 86).

Tablespoon for tablespoon, compare the fat and cholesterol contents in our chart of plain yogurt, mayonnaise and combinations from different varieties of the two.

MAYONNAISE VS. YOGURT: TABLESPOON TEE-OFF

	Calories	Fat	Cholesterol
Regular Mayonnaise	100	11g	5mg
Reduced-Calorie Mayonnaise	50	5g	5mg
Cholesterol-Free Mayonnaise	50	5g	0mg
Lowfat Plain Yogurt	9	.25g	1mg
Nonfat Plain Yogurt	7	0g	.30mg
½ mayonnaise & ½ lowfat yogurt	55	7g	3mg
½ reduced-calorie mayonnaise & ½ lowfat yogurt	30	3g	3mg

"SKINNY" DIPS

Reducing calories from fat doesn't mean doing without dips—it means "lightening up" on the ingredients used to make them.

- Instead of *all* sour cream, mix 2 parts lowfat plain yogurt with 1 part dairy sour cream.
- For a sour cream substitute that's practically fat-free, combine 3 parts lowfat cottage cheese and 1 part nonfat yogurt in a small food processor or blender and whirl until smooth. Season with lemon juice to taste.
- To cut back on calories from fat when a recipe calls for mayonnaise, use a half-and-half combination of regular mayonnaise and a reduced-calorie version, or mayonnaise and plain yogurt.
- Season a tomato salsa dip with flavored vinegar or lime juice, onion, garlic and fiery spices.
- A quick-fix dip: Puree rinsed and drained canned beans such as chick-peas or black beans, or leftover cooked vegetables like sweet peppers or eggplant, to a smooth dipping consistency. Flavor with lemon juice and herbs. For a "creamier" dip, stir in plain yogurt or pureed cottage cheese.

SPINACH-FETA CHEESE DIP

There are three delicious ways to serve this versatile dip: with raw vegetables, as a spread with toasted pita triangles, or atop a baked potato. For a thinner consistency, use undrained yogurt. (Pictured on page 85.)

Makes 2 cups.
Recipe can be halved or doubled.
Nutrient Value Per Tablespoon: 20 calories, 2 g protein, 1 g fat, 1 g carbohydrate, 61 mg sodium, 4 mg cholesterol.

2 cups lowfat plain yogurt
1 package (9 or 10 ounces) frozen leaf spinach, thawed according to package directions
1 small clove garlic
2 tablespoons chopped fresh dill OR: 2 teaspoons dried
4 ounces feta cheese, cut into cubes
1 teaspoon grated lemon rind
¼ teaspoon pepper
⅛ teaspoon salt

1. Set coffee filter or double thickness of paper toweling in strainer over small bowl. Spoon yogurt into filter. Refrigerate yogurt and let drain about 2 hours. (You should have about 1⅓ cups of yogurt.)
2. Squeeze liquid from spinach, pressing spinach between your palms.
3. Place garlic and dill in food processor. Whirl until finely chopped. Add spinach, feta, lemon rind, pepper and salt. Whirl 1 minute or until cheese is finely grated, scraping down side of bowl as needed. Add drained yogurt. Pulse with on/off motion just until the mixture is combined.
4. Scrape the spread into a serving bowl and serve.

Make-Ahead Tip: The dip can be prepared a day ahead and refrigerated.

ROASTED RED-PEPPER DIP

LOW-CHOLESTEROL

Terrific as a chilled dip with chips or raw vegetables, this vivid red puree is equally good tossed with hot pasta or spooned on a baked potato, and even becomes a sensational soup when thinned with a little chicken broth. (Pictured on page 85.)

Roast vegetables at 500° for 20 minutes.
Makes 2¼ cups. Recipe can be doubled.
Nutrient Value Per Tablespoon: 14 calories, 0 g protein, 1 g fat, 2 g carbohydrate, 54 mg sodium, 0 mg cholesterol.

1 red onion, unpeeled, halved
2 pounds sweet red peppers (about 4 large)
3 large cloves garlic, unpeeled
¼ cup walnuts
3 tablespoons grated Parmesan cheese
2 teaspoons red wine vinegar
¾ teaspoon salt

1. Preheat oven to extremely hot (500°).
2. Line jelly-roll pan with aluminum foil. Place onion and peppers on pan.
3. Bake in preheated extremely hot oven (500°) for 20 minutes. Halfway through cooking, add garlic and turn peppers over.
4. Remove from oven. Wrap onion, peppers and garlic in foil, crimping to seal. Let stand 10 minutes for easy peeling of vegetables.
5. Peel peppers and seed; peel onion and garlic. Place in food processor or blender. Add walnuts, Parmesan, vinegar and salt. Whirl 1 minute or until the mixture is smooth.
6. Transfer to serving dish and chill.

Make-Ahead Tip: The dip can be made up to 3 days ahead and refrigerated, tightly covered.

SEVEN-LAYER MEXICAN DIP

QUICK

Tortilla chips are the perfect accompaniment to this Family Circle favorite. To really cut preparation time, substitute store-bought guacamole for the homemade.

Makes about 6 cups. Recipe can be halved.
Nutrient Value Per ¼ Cup: 71 calories,
2 g protein, 5 g fat, 5 g carbohydrate,
157 mg sodium, 5 mg cholesterol.

1 clove garlic
1 can (16 ounces) pink or kidney beans, rinsed and drained
¼ cup mild or medium-hot picante sauce OR: salsa
1 teaspoon chili powder
¾ teaspoon ground cumin
1 recipe Guacamole (*see recipe, page 88*)
⅔ cup reduced-fat sour cream
¾ cup sliced pitted canned black olives
½ recipe (1 cup drained) Salsa Fresca (*see recipe, page 85*) OR: ½ cup chopped tomatoes, drained
1 large green onion, sliced
½ cup (2 ounces) shredded Cheddar cheese

1. Place garlic in food processor. Whirl until chopped. Add drained beans, picante sauce, chili powder and cumin. Whirl until smooth, about 1 minute. Spread in large serving dish.
2. Spread Guacamole over bean mixture, leaving a border of bean mixture showing. Spoon sour cream in center and spread level almost to edges, leaving guacamole border.
3. Sprinkle olives evenly on top. Spoon on salsa or tomatoes, spreading level. Sprinkle on green onion and cheese.
4. Cover and refrigerate up to 4 hours before serving.

MEXICAN DIP MAKE-AHEAD TIP:
The bean mixture, guacamole and salsa can all be made up to 1 day in advance and refrigerated, covered. The cheese and vegetables can be prepared and wrapped individually as well. Assemble the whole dip up to 4 hours before serving and refrigerate, covered.

TRY TOFU!

■ Tofu, or soybean curd, was invented in China about 2,000 years ago. Today, tofu cakes are packed in water to prevent drying out and sold in plastic tubs in the refrigerated section of supermarkets and health food stores, or in vacuum-sealed packages in produce departments.

■ Sometimes called "meat without bones," tofu is an inexpensive, low-calorie source of protein. A 4-ounce serving provides 100 calories, 9 grams protein, 6 grams fat and no cholesterol. It is also a good source of iron, calcium and Vitamin A.

■ Tofu comes in four consistencies: soft, with a custard-like texture that blends into dips and spreads; medium, for steaming or adding to soups; firm and extra-firm, for stir-frying, marinating and broiling. Tofu can be sliced, diced, grated, crumbled or pureed. It has no real flavor of its own, so can be added to almost any dish, where it soaks up flavors.

■ Refrigerate tofu in a dish of fresh water, covered, for up to 1 week; change water daily to prevent souring.

GUACAMOLE

LOW-CHOLESTEROL · QUICK

Spoon this creamy, mildly spicy dip into a hollowed-out avocado shell, and garnish with green onion or cilantro leaves. Serve with blue and yellow corn chips. Our Tofu Variation cuts the fat content in half.

Makes 1⅔ cups. Recipe can be doubled.
Nutrient Value Per Tablespoon: 26 calories, 0 g protein, 2 g fat, 1 g carbohydrate, 48 mg sodium, 0 mg cholesterol.

2 green onions, cut in 1-inch lengths
1 tablespoon chopped cilantro OR: parsley
2 ripe avocados
2 tablespoons lime juice (1 lime)
1 tablespoon medium or medium-hot picante sauce OR: salsa
½ teaspoon salt
⅛ to ¼ teaspoon liquid red-pepper seasoning

1. Place green onion and cilantro in food processor. Whirl until chopped.
2. Halve avocados. Peel and pit. Cut avocados into 2-inch pieces. Add about half of avocado to green onion mixture in processor. Add lime juice, picante sauce, salt and red-pepper seasoning. Whirl using on/off pulses until finely chopped. Add remaining avocado. Whirl with on/off motion to desired consistency.
3. Scrape guacamole into serving dish.

Make-Ahead Tip: The guacamole can be made up to 4 hours ahead and refrigerated, tightly covered with plastic wrap. Place pit in guacamole; remove before serving.

TOFU VARIATION

Nutrient Value Per Tablespoon: 16 calories, 1 g protein, 1 g fat, 1 g carbohydrate, 48 mg sodium, 0 mg cholesterol.

Substitute 4 ounces of tofu for 1 avocado; reduce lime juice to 1½ teaspoons. Process tofu and half the avocado as directed in Step 2 until smooth. Then proceed as directed.

SALMON TWISTS

These variations on cheese twists are delicious warm or at room temperature. (Pictured on page 81.)

Bake at 400° for 10 to 12 minutes.
Makes 16 servings (3 twists per serving). Recipe can be halved or doubled.
Nutrient Value Per Serving: 83 calories, 3 g protein, 5 g fat, 6 g carbohydrate, 134 mg sodium, 5 mg cholesterol.

1 can (7½ ounces) red salmon, drained and finely flaked
1 green onion, finely chopped
⅛ teaspoon ground hot red pepper
1 egg white
Half of 17¼-ounce package frozen puff pastry sheets, thawed according to package directions

1. Preheat oven to hot (400°).
2. Stir together salmon, green onion, hot red pepper and egg white.
3. Unfold pastry on lightly floured surface. Roll pastry out with lightly floured rolling pin into 20 × 12-inch rectangle. Starting at 12-inch end, spread half the pastry with the salmon mixture. Fold remaining pastry over filling, making 12 × 10-inch rectangle. Gently press layers together to seal.
4. Cut pastry lengthwise in half to make two 12 × 5-inch rectangles. Cut each rectangle crosswise into twenty-four 5 × ½-inch strips. Place about 1 inch apart on ungreased baking sheets, gently twisting each strip. Press ends onto sheet to prevent shrinkage.
5. Bake in preheated hot oven (400°) for 10 to 12 minutes or until golden.

Make-Ahead Tip: The filling can be made a day or two ahead and refrigerated, tightly covered.

CHICKEN-HONEY MUSTARD SPREAD

A *hearty cracker topper as well as a sandwich filler for your favorite bread. For a special treat, serve with our Chili-Corn Madeleines (see recipe, page 90). If you have leftover turkey or ham, substitute that for the chicken. (Pictured at right.)*

Makes 2¼ cups. Recipe can be doubled.
Nutrient Value Per Tablespoon: 43 calories,
2 g protein, 3 g fat, 1 g carbohydrate,
31 mg sodium, 19 mg cholesterol.

½ cup toasted pecans*
2 hard-cooked eggs
2 cups cubed, cooked chicken (8 ounces)
⅓ cup mayonnaise OR: reduced-fat sour
    cream
3 tablespoons prepared honey-mustard
1 stalk celery, finely chopped
2 tablespoons sliced chives

1. Place pecans in food processor. Whirl with on/off motion just until chopped. Transfer to waxed paper. Separate yolk and white of 1 hard-cooked egg; sieve the white and yolk separately onto sheets of waxed paper. Set aside for topping.
2. Cut remaining egg into quarters and place in food processor. Add chicken cubes, mayonnaise and mustard. Whirl for 1 minute or until blended, scraping down side of bowl as needed.
3. Set aside 3 tablespoons of the pecans for topping. Add remaining pecans to processor, along with celery and 1 tablespoon of the chives. Whirl with on/off motion just until combined.
4. Spread chicken mixture evenly into shallow 8-inch serving dish. Garnish with rows of the reserved sieved egg, chopped pecans and chives.

*Note: To toast pecans, place on baking sheet in preheated moderate oven (350°) for 8 minutes or until toasted, stirring occasionally.

Make-Ahead Tip: The spread can be made a day ahead and refrigerated, *ungarnished* and covered. Wrap garnishes separately and garnish up to 3 hours before serving.
Microwave Directions for Toasting Pecans (High Power Oven): Spread pecans in microwave-safe 9-inch pie plate. Microwave, uncovered, at 100% power 2 to 2½ minutes or until golden brown.

From top: Chicken-Honey Mustard Spread (this page) and Chili-Corn Madeleines (page 90).

CHILI-CORN MADELEINES

QUICK

These jalapeño-flecked little "breads" are nicely paired with our Super Watermelon Slush (page 552) or Spiced Lemonade (page 548) as well as beer or margaritas. (Pictured on page 89.)

Bake at 400° for 8 to 10 minutes.
Makes about 27 madeleines.
Recipe can be doubled.
Nutrient Value Per Madeleine: 73 calories, 2 g protein, 3 g fat, 10 g carbohydrate, 152 mg sodium, 23 mg cholesterol.

1 cup all-purpose flour
1 cup yellow cornmeal
1½ teaspoons baking powder
½ teaspoon baking soda
1 cup buttermilk
2 eggs
2 green onions, chopped
2 teaspoons sugar
1 teaspoon salt
¼ to ½ teaspoon ground hot red pepper
½ cup frozen whole-kernel corn, thawed
¼ cup drained pimiento pieces
1 jalapeño pepper, quartered and seeded

1. Preheat oven to hot (400°). Generously grease 27 madeleine forms.
2. Stir together flour, cornmeal, baking powder and baking soda in large bowl.
3. Combine buttermilk, eggs, green onion, sugar, salt and red pepper in food processor. Whirl until green onion is chopped. Add corn, pimiento and jalapeño pepper. Whirl with on/off motion or until corn, pimiento pieces and jalapeño pepper are finely chopped.
4. Pour egg mixture over dry ingredients; stir with large spoon just until blended (do not overmix). Spoon rounded measuring tablespoon of batter into each prepared form.
5. Bake in preheated hot oven (400°) for 8 to 10 minutes or until golden and tops spring back when lightly pressed with fingertip. Cool in pans on wire rack for 3 minutes. Gently loosen from pans with knife.

LOUISIANA SHRIMP

LOW-FAT

Serve the peppery shrimp, simmered in beer, in a large bowl with the cooking liquid and plenty of bread for soaking up the broth. Garnish with lemon wedges. The shrimp are also delicious served chilled.

Makes 12 servings.
Recipe can be halved or doubled.
Nutrient Value Per Serving: 120 calories, 19 g protein, 4 g fat, 2 g carbohydrate, 248 mg sodium, 145 mg cholesterol.

3 pounds medium-size or large shrimp
2 tablespoons *un*salted butter
1 large clove garlic, finely chopped
1 can (12 ounces) beer
½ teaspoon salt
½ teaspoon leaf thyme, crumbled
¼ to ½ teaspoon ground hot red pepper
¼ to ½ teaspoon black pepper
¼ teaspoon leaf oregano, crumbled
⅛ to ¼ teaspoon crushed red pepper flakes

1. Cut through shell of each shrimp along back to tail; remove vein, leaving shell on; or remove shells for easier handling when serving. *(See How-To, page 340.)*
2. Melt butter in large saucepan over medium heat. Add garlic; cook 1 minute. Add beer, salt, thyme, ground red pepper, black pepper, oregano and red pepper flakes. Bring to boiling. Lower heat; cover and simmer 10 minutes. Add shrimp; cover and simmer 1 to 2 minutes or until shrimp are tender. Do not drain. Serve hot or chilled with broth.

Make-Ahead Tip: The shrimp can be prepared a day ahead and refrigerated, covered, and then served chilled.

VERSATILE MADELEINE
For a knock-out accompaniment to chili and bean soups, top the madeleines with shredded Monterey Jack cheese and bake them in a moderate oven until the cheese is melted, 5 to 10 minutes. Serve with salads, split and fill with sandwich fixings, or tuck into lunch boxes.

MADELEINES MAKE-AHEAD TIP:
The madeleines can also be baked several hours before serving and reheated. Or they can be baked and frozen. To reheat, place frozen madeleines on a baking sheet and bake in preheated moderate oven (350°) for 10 minutes or until warm throughout.

GORGONZOLA AND PEAR PACKETS

The sweetness of the pear blends nicely with the pungent flavor of the cheese. Bring out a basket of these at your next weekend get-together. (Pictured on page 81.)

Bake at 425° for 12 to 15 minutes.
Makes 40 packets.
Recipe can be halved or doubled.
Nutrient Value Per Packet: 181 calories, 5 g protein, 13 g fat, 12 g carbohydrate, 260 mg sodium, 49 mg cholesterol.

---

6 ounces Gorgonzola cheese OR: blue cheese
1 large pear, cored and finely chopped
2 tablespoons finely chopped walnuts
1 egg, lightly beaten
½ cup (1 stick) *un*salted butter or margarine, melted
⅛ teaspoon ground hot red pepper
8 sheets phyllo, thawed according to package directions if necessary

1. Crumble Gorgonzola into medium-size bowl. Stir in pear, walnuts and egg.
2. Stir together melted butter and red pepper in small bowl.
3. Cut phyllo sheets lengthwise into 5 strips, each about 2½ inches wide. Keep phyllo covered with plastic wrap or damp paper toweling to prevent drying out.
4. Place one strip of phyllo on work surface; brush lightly with melted butter mixture. Place rounded measuring teaspoonful of cheese mixture at end of strip. Fold one corner of strip diagonally over filling so short end meets long end of strip, forming a right angle. Continue folding at right angles, like a flag, until strip ends. Place packet, seam side down, on baking sheet. Brush with melted butter mixture. Repeat with remaining strips and cheese mixture.
5. Preheat oven to hot (425°).
6. Bake packets in preheated hot oven

(425°) for 12 to 15 minutes or until golden brown. Serve hot.

Make-Ahead Tip: Pastries can be prepared several hours ahead up through Step 4. Cover with aluminum foil and refrigerate until ready to bake.

HOW TO MAKE PHYLLO PACKETS

1. Cut phyllo sheets lengthwise into 5 equal strips, each about 2½ inches wide. Keep phyllo covered with plastic wrap or damp paper toweling to prevent drying out. Place one strip of phyllo on work surface. Brush lightly with melted butter mixture. Spoon filling onto one end of strip.

2. Fold one end corner of strip diagonally over filling so short end meets long side of strip, forming a right angle and enclosing filling. Continue folding at right angles, like a flag, until strip ends and you have a triangular packet.

Originating in the Orient, phyllo, or filo, dough is associated with Greek and Middle Eastern cuisines and is frequently used in pastries stuffed with cooked meat, vegetables or fruit. Contrary to popular belief, phyllo is not high in fat or calories (each sheet contains approximately 30 calories); it's what you put on the dough that counts. Because of its delicacy, phyllo requires some care:
■ If dough is frozen, slowly thaw overnight in the refrigerator. Warm the refrigerated dough at room temperature for 2 hours before the package is opened.
■ Keep unopened or tightly re-closed packages of phyllo dough frozen or refrigerated for up to 1 month.
■ Exposure to air dries out the dough, so remove only as much as you need and return remainder to package, well wrapped. Keep phyllo covered with plastic wrap or a slightly damp towel while you are working with it.
■ If using melted butter between layers, don't saturate the dough. Rather, sparingly brush over most of the dough.
■ As an alternative to butter, coat each sheet lightly with non-stick vegetable-oil cooking spray.

MARINATED GOAT CHEESE ON GARLIC TOAST

Serve as an appetizer or with a salad for a light lunch. (Pictured on page 81.)

Bake toasts at 350° for 15 minutes.
Makes 10 servings (2 toasts per serving).
Recipe can be halved or doubled.
Nutrient Value Per Serving: 253 calories,
8 g protein, 18 g fat, 15 g carbohydrate,
337 mg sodium, 33 mg cholesterol.

½ small bunch arugula OR: watercress
    OR: parsley
⅓ cup olive oil
2 teaspoons balsamic vinegar OR: red
    wine vinegar
1 small clove garlic, crushed
⅛ teaspoon black pepper
1 package (11 ounces) goat cheese, cut
    into ¼-inch-thick slices
1 baguette or long, thin loaf French-style
    bread (8 ounces)
1 tablespoon *un*salted butter, melted
1 clove garlic, halved
1 ounce sun-dried tomatoes, chopped
    (optional)

1. Remove stems from arugula. Chop enough arugula to measure 1 tablespoon. Stir together chopped arugula, oil, vinegar, crushed garlic and pepper in small bowl.
2. Place cheese in single layer in large shallow dish. Pour oil mixture over cheese. Cover and refrigerate 1 hour.
3. Preheat oven to moderate (350°).
4. Prepare toasts: Diagonally slice baguette into ¼-inch slices. Brush both sides with butter. Place on baking sheet.
5. Bake in preheated moderate oven (350°) for 15 minutes or until golden. Rub warm toasts with garlic halves.
6. To serve, thinly slice remaining arugula. Place an equal amount on each toast. Remove cheese from marinade, reserving marinade. Top toast with cheese. Drizzle with reserved marinade. Top with sun-dried tomatoes, if you wish.

PINEAPPLE AND BACON BITES

LOW-CALORIE · QUICK

Arrange the chutney-accented bites on a platter or wooden tray covered with banana leaves and garnish with leaves from the pineapple crown. Check with your florist about the availability of banana leaves. (Pictured on page 93.) For even more flavor, grill these bites.

Broil 5 to 7 minutes.
Makes 18 servings
(2 appetizers per serving).
Recipe can be halved or doubled.
Nutrient Value Per Serving: 48 calories,
1 g protein, 2 g fat, 6 g carbohydrate,
75 mg sodium, 4 mg cholesterol.

1 medium-size fresh pineapple (about 4
    pounds) OR: 1 can (20 ounces)
    pineapple slices in juice, drained and
    each slice cut into quarters
¼ cup chutney
¼ teaspoon ground cinnamon
⅛ teaspoon ground hot red pepper
About 12 slices bacon

1. Remove crown from pineapple. Slice pineapple lengthwise into 4 wedges. Remove core from each wedge. Cut fruit in one piece from rind. (*See How-To, page 482.*) Cut each wedge crosswise into 9 equal pieces.
2. Stir together chutney, cinnamon and hot red pepper in large bowl. Add pineapple; toss to coat well.
3. Cut bacon crosswise into thirds. Wrap each pineapple slice with bacon slice; secure with wooden picks.
4. When ready to serve, preheat broiler. Arrange bacon-wrapped pineapple on rack in broiler pan.
5. Broil 5 to 7 minutes to crisp bacon.

Make-Ahead Tip: The bites can be prepared several hours ahead through Step 3 and then refrigerated, covered.

A TOMATO IN THE SUN
Like raisins and other dried fruit, sun-dried tomatoes are chewy and dense with flavor.
■ *Oil-packed tomatoes* are ready to use from the jar.
■ Crisp, *dry-packed tomatoes* may give you more for your money, but must be reconstituted before using: Cover with just-boiled water and let stand 10 to 20 minutes. Drain and dry slightly on paper toweling before using. Or, steam tomatoes in a steamer basket over simmering water in a covered saucepan until tender.
■ Add sun-dried tomatoes to cheese spreads, pasta sauces, stuffed mushrooms, salads, vegetable or bean dips. They're also good sprinkled on pasta or over a marinated cheese appetizer.

SESAME CHICKEN BROCHETTES

LOW-CALORIE · LOW-FAT

For a special presentation, arrange the brochettes along with our Pineapple and Bacon Bites (see recipe, page 92) on banana leaves on a wooden tray. Check with your florist about the availability of the leaves. (Pictured at right.) For summer entertaining, grill these brochettes.

Broil 5 to 7 minutes.
Makes about 10 skewers.
Recipe can be halved or doubled.
Nutrient Value Per Skewer: 85 calories, 11 g protein, 2 g fat, 4 g carbohydrate, 211 mg sodium, 26 mg cholesterol.

3 tablespoons reduced-sodium soy sauce
2 tablespoons sesame seeds
2 tablespoons plum preserves
1 tablespoon dry sherry
2 teaspoons Oriental sesame oil
1 teaspoon grated pared fresh ginger
1 clove garlic, crushed
1 pound boneless, skinned chicken
    breasts
4 green onions

1. Stir together soy sauce, sesame seeds, preserves, sherry, oil, ginger and garlic in medium-size bowl.
2. Cut chicken into about 30 pieces, about ¾ inch square. Cut green onions into 1½-inch pieces. Add chicken and green onions to soy mixture. Cover; refrigerate 2 hours, stirring occasionally. Soak 10 bamboo skewers in water.
3. To cook, preheat broiler.
4. Alternately thread 3 chicken pieces and 3 green onion pieces on each bamboo skewer. Reserve marinade. Place skewers on rack in broiling pan. Cover exposed part of bamboo with foil.
5. Broil, brushing with marinade and turning occasionally, until chicken is tender, 5 to 7 minutes. Discard any remaining marinade.

Microwave Directions (High Power Oven):
Use 6-inch bamboo skewers. Prepare and assemble skewers as above. Place skewers in microwave-safe 9-inch-square dish, with points of half the skewers facing one side and the points of the other half facing opposite side. Cover with waxed paper. Microwave at 100% power 5 to 5½ minutes or until chicken is cooked through.

From top: Sesame Chicken Brochettes (this page) and Pineapple and Bacon Bites (page 92).

EASY MINI-PIZZAS

LOW-CHOLESTEROL

Frozen bread dough makes these pizzas simple to fix for a hearty party snack or a festive light lunch. For cheese lovers, we've included a "white" variation.

MAKE-AHEAD TIP:
The tomato sauce can be prepared up to 3 days ahead and refrigerated, covered, until ready to assemble the pizzas.

Bake at 425° for 15 to 20 minutes.
Makes 16 individual pizzas.
Recipe can be halved or doubled.
Nutrient Value Per Pizza: 109 calories, 3 g protein, 4 g fat, 16 g carbohydrate, 329 mg sodium, 3 mg cholesterol.

Easy Tomato Sauce:
1 tablespoon olive oil
2 cloves garlic, finely chopped
1 can (14½ ounces) stewed tomatoes, crushed
1 teaspoon sugar
¼ teaspoon leaf oregano, crumbled
¼ teaspoon salt
⅛ teaspoon black pepper

1 loaf (1 pound) frozen bread dough, thawed according to package directions
2 ounces part-skim mozzarella cheese, shredded
¼ cup Greek olives, pitted and chopped OR: pitted canned black olives, chopped

1. Prepare Easy Tomato Sauce: Heat oil in medium-size saucepan over medium-high heat. Add garlic; cook 1 minute. Add tomatoes, sugar, oregano, salt and pepper. Lower heat; simmer, uncovered, stirring occasionally, until mixture is reduced to 1¼ cups, about 20 minutes.
2. Preheat oven to hot (425°). Grease large baking sheets.
3. Cut bread dough crosswise into ½-inch-thick slices. Place about 3 inches apart on prepared baking sheets. Knead each piece with fingers into a 3-inch round.
4. Spread equal amount of sauce on each round. Top with cheese and olives.
5. Bake in preheated hot oven (425°) for 15 to 20 minutes or until crusts are browned and topping is bubbly.

WHITE CHEESE TOPPING VARIATION

Nutrient Value Per Pizza: 121 calories, 5 g protein, 4 g fat, 15 g carbohydrate, 197 mg sodium, 9 mg cholesterol.

Heat 1 tablespoon olive oil in large skillet. Add 2 small sweet red and/or sweet yellow peppers, cut into thin strips; cook, stirring, until soft. Stir together 1 cup part-skim ricotta cheese, ⅓ cup shredded part-skim mozzarella cheese and ¼ cup grated Parmesan cheese in large bowl. Spread mixture evenly on bread dough rounds. Top with cooked peppers. Sprinkle pizzas with a total of 3 tablespoons shredded part-skim mozzarella cheese. Bake as above.

CARAMELIZED ONION TARTLETS

These are wonderful warm or chilled, and the Sesame-Seed Pastry adds subtle flavor and texture. (Pictured at right.)

Bake at 400° for 20 minutes.
Makes 26 tartlets.
Recipe can be halved or doubled.
Nutrient Value Per Tartlet: 90 calories, 2 g protein, 6 g fat, 8 g carbohydrate, 82 mg sodium, 28 mg cholesterol.

Sesame-Seed Pastry:
1⅓ cups all-purpose flour
½ cup (1 stick) cold *un*salted butter, cut into small pieces
¼ cup sesame seeds
¼ teaspoon salt
3 to 4 tablespoons cold water

Caramelized Onion Filling:
1 tablespoon *un*salted butter
1 tablespoon vegetable oil
2 large Spanish or Vidalia onions, thinly sliced and slices halved
1 tablespoon sugar
2 eggs
¾ cup milk
⅛ teaspoon salt

1. Prepare Sesame-Seed Pastry: Place flour, butter, sesame seeds and salt in medium-size bowl. Blend mixture with pastry blender, 2 knives or fingertips until coarse-crumbed. Add cold water, 1 tablespoon at a time, mixing with fork just until moist enough to hold together. Shape into ball. Wrap in plastic wrap and refrigerate 1 hour.
2. Roll pastry out with floured rolling pin on floured surface to ⅛-inch thickness. Cut pastry into circles using 3-inch-round cookie cutter. Press pastry circles into 26 greased 2½- to 3-inch tartlet pans. Refrigerate until ready to fill.
3. Prepare Caramelized Onion Filling: Heat butter and oil in large skillet over medium heat. Add onion and sugar; cook, stirring frequently, for 15 minutes

or until onions are caramelized, dark to medium brown; do not let burn. Cool slightly.
4. When ready to bake, preheat oven to hot (400°).
5. Place pastry-lined tartlet pans on baking sheet. Divide onion mixture equally among tartlet shells. Lightly beat eggs in small bowl. Beat in milk and salt. Pour mixture over onions in shells, dividing equally.
6. Bake in preheated hot oven (400°) for 20 minutes or until set. Serve warm or chilled.

Make-Ahead Tip: The onion mixture can be prepared 2 days ahead and refrigerated. Return to room temperature before using. The baked filled tartlets themselves can be served chilled.

From top: Sour Cream and Prosciutto Tartlets (page 96) and Caramelized Onion Tartlets (this page).

TARTLET PASTRY MAKE-AHEAD TIP:
The unbaked pastry dough or tartlet shells can be made ahead, wrapped and refrigerated for up to 3 days. Keep dough at room temperature until soft enough to roll. The dough can also be frozen for up to 6 weeks.

SOUR CREAM AND PROSCIUTTO TARTLETS

Plan ahead: the Sesame-Seed Pastry needs to be made an hour beforehand. (Pictured on page 95.)

Bake at 425° for 10 to 12 minutes.
Makes 48 tartlets.
Recipe can be halved or doubled.
Nutrient Value Per Tartlet: 28 calories, 1 g protein, 2 g fat, 2 g carbohydrate, 42 mg sodium, 5 mg cholesterol.

½ **Sesame-Seed Pastry recipe** *(see Caramelized Onion Tartlets, page 95)*
1½ **teaspoons grated Parmesan cheese**

Sour Cream and Prosciutto Filling:
1 cup reduced-fat sour cream
3 tablespoons well-drained, finely chopped roasted red pepper, homemade *(see How-To, page 433)* OR: jarred
1 teaspoon anchovy paste *(optional)*
⅛ teaspoon leaf oregano, crumbled
1 small clove garlic, finely chopped
8 thin slices prosciutto
Fresh oregano sprigs OR: parsley, for garnish *(optional)*

1. Prepare the half recipe Sesame-Seed Pastry, adding the Parmesan to the flour mixture. Shape into ball; wrap in plastic wrap and refrigerate 1 hour.
2. To bake, preheat oven to hot (425°).
3. Roll pastry out on floured surface with floured rolling pin to ⅛-inch thickness. Cut pastry into circles using 2-inch-round cookie cutter. Press circles into forty-eight ½-inch tartlet pans or mini-muffin pans. (Work in batches if you don't have enough pans.)
4. Bake in preheated hot oven (425°) for 10 to 12 minutes or until lightly browned. Cool in pans. Remove tartlet shells from pans.
5. Prepare Filling: Stir together sour cream, red pepper, anchovy paste, if using, oregano and garlic in small bowl. Spoon mixture equally into shells.

6. Cut each prosciutto slice lengthwise into thirds, then crosswise in half. Starting at narrow end of each piece, loosely roll up strip, jelly-roll fashion. Top each tart with prosciutto roll. Garnish with oregano or parsley.

GARLIC PITA CHIPS

LOW-CALORIE · LOW-CHOLESTEROL
QUICK

These are also superb with soups and salads. Try experimenting with other toppings such as grated Parmesan cheese or grated lemon rind. (Pictured on page 97.)

Bake at 300° for 15 to 18 minutes.
Makes 64 chips.
Recipe can be halved or doubled.
Nutrient Value Per Chip: 19 calories, 0 g protein, 1 g fat, 2 g carbohydrate, 36 mg sodium, 0 mg cholesterol.

1 package (8 ounces) small whole-wheat pita breads
½ cup chopped fresh parsley
2 egg whites, lightly beaten
¼ cup olive oil
3 small cloves garlic, finely chopped
½ teaspoon coarse (kosher) salt

1. Preheat oven to slow (300°). Lightly coat 2 or 3 baking sheets with nonstick vegetable-oil cooking spray.
2. Cut each pita into 4 wedges, then gently cut or pull each wedge apart, to form a total of 64 triangles.
3. Combine parsley, egg white, olive oil, garlic and salt in small bowl. Spoon some of the parsley mixture over rough side of each triangle. Place triangles, parsley-side up, in single layer on baking sheets.
4. Bake in preheated slow oven (300°) for 15 to 18 minutes or until edges of triangles are toasted and parsley topping is set. Cool chips on baking sheets on wire racks.

PITA CHIPS MAKE-AHEAD TIP
The chips can be prepared up to 8 hours in advance. To recrisp them, place them in a very slow oven (250°) for 10 to 15 minutes.

CHILI NUTS

LOW-CHOLESTEROL

These piquant nibbles are excellent accompaniments to lemonade, cider and iced tea—as well as beer, margaritas or Bloody Marys. Walnuts, pecans or almonds can be substituted for the cashews. (Pictured at right.)

Bake at 300° for 25 minutes.
Makes 12 servings. Recipe can be doubled.
Nutrient Value Per Serving: 167 calories, 5 g protein, 14 g fat, 9 g carbohydrate, 255 mg sodium, 0 mg cholesterol.

1 egg white
¾ **pound unsalted cashews**
2 **teaspoons coarse (kosher) salt**
1 **teaspoon sugar**
1 **teaspoon crushed red pepper flakes**
½ **teaspoon ground cumin**
½ **teaspoon leaf oregano, crumbled**
¼ **teaspoon ground hot red pepper**

1. Preheat oven to slow (300°). Generously grease jelly-roll pan.
2. Lightly beat egg white in medium-size bowl. Add cashews; toss gently to coat.
3. Combine salt, sugar, red pepper flakes, cumin, oregano and ground red pepper in small bowl. Sprinkle over nuts; toss to coat evenly. Spread nuts on prepared pan.
4. Bake in preheated slow oven (300°), stirring 2 or 3 times to separate nuts, for 25 minutes or until golden and fragrant.
5. Cool nuts completely. Store in airtight container.

Make-Ahead Tip: Store at room temperature for up to 1 week, or frozen in an
(continued)

From top: Chili Nuts (this page); Zucchini-Stuffed Mushrooms (page 98); and Garlic Pita Chips (page 96).

CHILI NUTS *(continued)*

airtight container for up to 1 month. To enhance flavor, warm nuts in 250° oven 10 to 15 minutes before serving.

Microwave Directions (High Power Oven):
Prepare cashew mixture as in above recipe through Step 3. Spread cashews evenly on bottom of microwave-safe 12-inch quiche dish. Microwave, uncovered, at 100% power 7 minutes until nuts are golden and fragrant, stirring well after 4 minutes. Stir again after removing from microwave oven; nuts will continue to cook.

ZUCCHINI-STUFFED MUSHROOMS

PARTY PLATTER
Arrange the mushrooms on a tray with our Chili Nuts *(see recipe, page 97)* and Garlic Pita Chips *(see recipe, page 96)* for tasty hors d'oeuvres. The zucchini filling is also delicious as a stuffing for tomatoes or as a side dish with grilled meats. *(Pictured on page 97.)*

Bake at 375° for 15 minutes.

Makes 16 servings.
Recipe can halved or doubled.
Nutrient Value Per Serving: 129 calories, 5 g protein, 9 g fat, 9 g carbohydrate, 229 mg sodium, 25 mg cholesterol.

1 pound zucchini
¼ teaspoon salt
2 pounds large mushrooms
¼ cup (½ stick) *un*salted butter, melted
1 clove garlic, finely chopped
4 sun-dried tomatoes packed in oil, finely chopped (about 2 tablespoons) (optional)
¾ cup part-skim ricotta cheese
⅓ cup crushed cracker crumbs OR: potato chips
¼ teaspoon leaf oregano, crumbled
Pinch pepper
¼ cup grated Parmesan cheese

1. Shred zucchini; toss with salt in colander. Place over bowl and let stand 30 minutes. Squeeze dry.
2. Meanwhile, wipe mushrooms with paper toweling. Remove stems; reserve stems for soup or other uses.
3. Reserve 1 tablespoon melted butter. Brush mushrooms with remaining butter.
4. Sauté garlic in reserved tablespoon butter in skillet for 1 minute. Add zucchini; sauté 2 minutes. Let cool slightly. Stir in sundried tomatoes if using, ricotta, crumbs, oregano, pepper and Parmesan.
5. Preheat oven to moderate (375°).
6. Spoon zucchini mixture into mushrooms, dividing equally. Place on baking sheet.
7. Bake in preheated moderate oven (375°) for 15 minutes or until hot and bubbly.

Make-Ahead Tip: The filling can be made a day ahead and refrigerated, covered. The mushrooms can be assembled earlier in the day, placed on a tray, covered tightly with plastic wrap and refrigerated. Remove from refrigerator about 30 minutes before baking.

Microwave Directions (High Power Oven):
Reduce butter to 3 tablespoons. Follow Steps 1 and 2 of recipe. Place butter in microwave-safe 1½-quart casserole. Microwave, uncovered, at 100% power 60 to 75 seconds to melt. Remove 2 tablespoons of the butter and brush on mushrooms; reserve. Add garlic to casserole. Microwave, uncovered, at 100% power 1½ minutes. Add zucchini. Microwave, uncovered, at 100% power 3 minutes. Stir in tomatoes, ricotta, crumbs, oregano, pepper and Parmesan. Spoon filling into mushrooms. Place half the stuffed mushrooms around edge of microwave-safe 12-inch quiche dish. Cover with waxed paper. Microwave at 100% power 6 minutes, rotating dish after 3 minutes. Let stand, covered, 2 minutes. Repeat with remaining mushrooms.

SNACK ATTACK! CRACKERS, TOASTS AND CHIPS*

Start with crackers and chips that are low in calories, fat and sodium, top them with a healthful spread, and you can indulge without guilt!

How to Choose Healthful Chips?

Read labels! Check the nutrition information and ingredient list on the package, compare brands, and choose those that are lower in fat and sodium. And beware of the "no cholesterol" banner; it's the total fat that counts.

Best bets Rice cakes, matzohs (made without eggs), crisp breads, pretzels, graham crackers, melba toast, bread sticks, zwieback and bagel, pita or tortilla chips that are *baked*, not fried. *Any* low- or no-salt crackers or chips with 2 grams of fat or less per ½-ounce serving are your best health bets of all.

Ak-Mak Crackers Stone-ground wheat and sesame seeds provide lively flavor. (1 cracker = less than 1 g fat, 40 mg sodium)

Club Crackers Similar in consistency and flavor to Ritz crackers, with rich, buttery flavor. (4 crackers = 70 cal, 4 g fat, 120 mg sodium)

Corn Chips High in fat and sodium. Look for baked variety to reduce fat intake somewhat. (1 ounce = 150 to 160 cal, 9 to 11 g fat)

Graham Crackers Lightly sweetened, with distinctive wheat flavor and texture; great with mild cheeses and nut butters. (2 crackers = 60 cal, 1 g fat, 90 mg sodium)

Melba Toast Available plain and in many varieties such as wheat, rye, sesame, garlic and onion. (3 slices = 50 to 60 cal, 1 to 2 g fat, 130 to 140 mg sodium)

Potato Chips If you must eat potato chips, take out your portion before you start eating, then put the rest of the package away. Unsalted variety has a more pronounced potato flavor. (1 ounce = 140 to 170 cal, 6 to 13 g fat)

Pretzels Look for unsalted tops or rub off some of the salt from salted variety. (1 ounce = 100 cal, 0 g fat, 650 mg sodium; 110 cal, 0 g fat, 80 mg sodium for unsalted variety)

Ritz Crackers Perfect size for canapés, rich and crunchy. (4 crackers = 70 cal, 4 g fat, 120 mg sodium)

Ry Krisp One of a variety of Scandinavian-style wheat and rye crackers. Sturdy, with a good chew, large enough to make open-face sandwiches or accompaniments to soups. (2 triple crackers = 50 cal, 2 g fat, 160 mg sodium)

Saltines Simple squares that go well with soups. (5 crackers = 60 cal, 2 g fat, 180 mg sodium; 135 mg sodium for unsalted tops)

Stoned Wheat Thins The hearty, "wheaty" flavor makes these good bases for cheese. (4 crackers = 144 mg sodium)

Table Water Biscuits English, very crisp, mildly flavored crackers, traditionally served with cheese.

Triscuits Shredded Wheat Crackers (3 crackers = 60 cal, 2 g fat, 75 mg sodium; 35 mg sodium for low-salt variety)

Wheatmeal Biscuits Similar to graham crackers in flavor and texture but much higher in fat content. Can double as a cookie.

Wheat Thins Delicate, thin, crisp squares with hearty wheat flavor. (8 crackers = 70 cal, 3 g fat, 120 mg sodium; 60 mg sodium for low-salt variety)

Tortilla Chips Fried corn chips available plain or flavored with cheese spices, etc. Traditionally served with guacamole, salsa and other dips. (1 ounce = 140 cal, 7 g fat, 240 mg sodium for nacho cheese variety)

Zwieback Literally "twice baked," these toast slices can be used with soft cheeses and spreads, jams and fruit butters. (2 slices = 60 cal, 1 g fat, 20 mg sodium)

* Complete nutritional information unavailable for all entries.

CORNMEAL PARMESAN PRETZELS

LOW-CALORIE · LOW-FAT
LOW-CHOLESTEROL

JUST A PRETZEL?
A delicious cross between a breadstick and a pretzel, these are especially good dipped in mustard. We use a food processor to prepare the dough, but your hands will work just as well. (Pictured on page 101.)

**PRETZEL
MAKE-AHEAD TIP:**
Store the pretzels in airtight containers for up to 1 week.

**POPCORN
MAKE-AHEAD TIP:**
Store the popcorn in an airtight container at room temperature for up to 2 weeks.

Bake at 400° for 17 to 20 minutes.
Makes 10 pretzels. Recipe can be doubled.
Nutrient Value Per Pretzel: 77 calories, 2 g protein, 1 g fat, 15 g carbohydrate, 132 mg sodium, 1 mg cholesterol.

¾ teaspoon active dry yeast
¼ teaspoon sugar
½ cup warm (105° to 115°) water
1 cup all-purpose flour
½ cup cornmeal
2 tablespoons grated Parmesan cheese
½ teaspoon salt
¼ teaspoon liquid red-pepper seasoning

1. Sprinkle yeast and sugar over water in glass measure. Stir to dissolve yeast. Let stand until foamy, about 10 minutes.
2. Combine flour, cornmeal, 1 tablespoon Parmesan, salt and red-pepper seasoning in food processor. Pulse with on/off motion to combine. Stir yeast mixture; with machine running, pour yeast mixture in through opening. Whirl for 30 seconds to knead.
3. Scrape dough into greased bowl. Turn to coat. Cover with towel. Let rise in warm place, away from drafts, for 40 minutes or until doubled in bulk.
4. Lightly coat 2 baking sheets with nonstick vegetable-oil cooking spray.
5. Punch down dough. Roll out on floured surface to 20-inch log. Cut crosswise into ten 2-inch-long pieces. Roll each piece to 14-inch strip and shape into pretzel. Place on prepared sheets. Let rise 20 minutes.
6. When ready to bake, preheat oven to hot (400°).
7. Brush pretzels lightly with water. Sprinkle on remaining Parmesan.
8. Bake in preheated hot oven (400°) for 17 to 20 minutes or until golden. Transfer to racks to cool.

MAPLE-SESAME GLAZED POPCORN

LOW-CALORIE · LOW-FAT
LOW-CHOLESTEROL · LOW-SODIUM
QUICK

You won't believe how addictive this popcorn is—and how low-calorie! (Pictured on page 101.)

Warm in 250° oven.
Makes 8 cups.
Recipe can be halved or doubled.
Nutrient Value Per ½ Cup: 42 calories, 1 g protein, 1 g fat, 8 g carbohydrate, 5 mg sodium, 1 mg cholesterol.

8 cups hot-air popped popcorn
1½ tablespoons sesame seeds
¼ cup maple syrup
3 tablespoons light brown sugar
⅛ teaspoon ground cinnamon
1½ teaspoons *unsalted* butter

1. Preheat oven to very slow (250°). Lightly spray very large ovenproof bowl, preferably glass or ceramic, and baking sheet with nonstick cooking spray.
2. Add popcorn to bowl. Place in preheated very slow oven (250°) to warm while preparing the glaze. Place sesame seeds in small dish.
3. Stir together maple syrup, brown sugar and cinnamon in small, heavy-bottomed saucepan. Bring to boiling over medium heat; cook to hard ball stage (250° on candy thermometer). Stir in butter and cook to hard crack stage (300° on candy thermometer).
4. Remove popcorn from oven. Pour about half of glaze over popcorn, working quickly and tossing with metal spoon to coat popcorn. Sprinkle on sesame seeds; pour on remaining glaze and toss until evenly coated. (If mixture cools down too quickly, warm in oven until softened enough to mix.)
5. Spoon onto prepared baking sheet and spread into small clumps. Cool.

SPICY RED-ONION FLATBREAD

LOW-CALORIE · LOW-FAT
LOW-CHOLESTEROL

We use a food processor to make our dough, but you can certainly knead it by hand. (Pictured at right.)

Bake at 375° for 12 to 15 minutes.
Makes 40 squares.
Nutrient Value Per Square: 23 calories, 1 g protein, 0 g fat, 4 g carbohydrate, 37 mg sodium, 0 mg cholesterol.

1 teaspoon active dry yeast
½ teaspoon sugar
⅔ cup warm (105° to 115°) water
1¼ cups all-purpose flour
½ cup rye flour OR: whole-wheat flour
½ teaspoon salt
1 tablespoon olive oil
1 clove garlic, chopped
¼ teaspoon crushed red pepper flakes
1 teaspoon poppy seeds
1 small red onion, sliced thin
¼ teaspoon coarse (kosher) salt

1. Sprinkle yeast and sugar over warm water in glass measure. Stir to dissolve yeast. Let stand until foamy, about 10 minutes.
2. Combine all-purpose flour, rye flour and salt in food processor. Stir yeast mixture. With machine running, pour yeast mixture in through opening. Whirl 30 seconds to knead.
3. Scrape dough into greased bowl; turn to coat. Cover with cloth. Let rise in warm place, away from drafts, for 40 minutes or until doubled in bulk.
4. When ready to bake, preheat oven to moderate (375°). Lightly coat 2 baking sheets with nonstick vegetable-oil cooking spray.
5. Divide dough in half. Roll each half out on floured surface into thin, free-form rectangle, about 13 × 10 inches. Transfer to baking sheets.
6. Stir together oil, garlic and red pepper flakes in small dish. Brush over flatbread. Sprinkle on poppy seeds, red onion and coarse salt.
7. Bake in preheated moderate oven (375°) for 12 to 15 minutes or until golden. Slide bread onto cutting board; cut while still hot into 20 pieces. Repeat with remaining bread. Serve hot or warm.

Make-Ahead Tip: The bread can be made ahead without the topping and stored in an airtight container for up to a week. The bread can be recrisped in a slow oven (250°) for 10 to 15 minutes. The dough can be made ahead and frozen.

From top:
Maple-Sesame Glazed Popcorn (page 100);
Cornmeal Parmesan Pretzels (page 100);
and Spicy Red-Onion Flatbread (this page).

MORE THAN A SNACK
Delicious on its own or with soup or a selection of cheeses, this flatbread can also be served with dips such as Pesto (see recipe, page 202).

FRUIT AND CHEESE MINI-SNACKS

LOW-CALORIE · LOW-FAT
LOW-SODIUM · QUICK

The dried fruit in this snack will satisfy your sweet cravings without a lot of extra calories, while the reduced-calorie cheese helps keep the fat down. Try other chopped fresh herbs for the coating, such as oregano or marjoram. (Pictured below.)

Makes 16 snacks. Recipe can be doubled.
Nutrient Value Per Snack: 42 calories,
2 g protein, 1 g fat, 6 g carbohydrate,
45 mg sodium, 5 mg cholesterol.

2 ounces shredded reduced-calorie Ched-
    dar cheese, at room temperature
2 ounces light cream cheese
4 drops liquid red-pepper seasoning
½ cup (1½ ounces) dried apple, chopped
⅓ cup (2 ounces) dried apricots,
    chopped
¼ cup (1 ounce) dried pineapple,
    chopped
½ cup chopped parsley

1. Beat together Cheddar cheese, cream cheese and red-pepper seasoning in small bowl until blended, about 1 minute.
2. Stir in dried apple, apricot and pineapple with wooden spoon. Using 1 level measuring tablespoon, form mixture into balls, rolling between palms. Roll balls in chopped parsley.

Make-Ahead Tip: The snacks can be refrigerated for up to 2 weeks in an airtight container.

From top: Fruit and Cheese Mini-Snacks (this page) and Pineapple Fig Bars (page 103).

PINEAPPLE FIG BARS

LOW-FAT

Having a sweet snack craving? Reach for our homemade version of the familiar store-bought variety. For a dessert, serve with wedges of fresh pineapple. (Pictured on page 102.)

Bake at 350° for 20 minutes.
Makes 16 bars. Recipe can be doubled.
Nutrient Value Per Bar: 96 calories,
2 g protein, 2 g fat, 18 g carbohydrate,
48 mg sodium, 14 mg cholesterol.

Crust:
½ cup whole-wheat flour
½ cup all-purpose flour
1 tablespoon dark brown sugar
⅛ teaspoon salt
2 tablespoons margarine
½ cup lowfat ricotta cheese

Filling:
1 can (8 ounces) crushed pineapple,
    packed in juice
¾ cup dried figs, tips trimmed and halved
3 tablespoons dark brown sugar
1 teaspoon grated orange rind OR: lemon
    rind
1 egg
1 egg white, beaten
1 teaspoon granulated sugar

1. Prepare Crust: Combine flours, brown sugar, salt and margarine in food processor. Whirl until blended. Add ricotta. Whirl just until mixture is combined and begins to form a ball. (The ingredients can also be mixed together in a bowl: Cut margarine into dry ingredients, then stir in ricotta.) Divide in half. Flatten into rectangles. Wrap in plastic wrap and chill at least 1 hour.
2. Meanwhile, prepare Filling: Drain pineapple in sieve, pressing to remove excess liquid. Combine figs, sugar and orange rind in same processor bowl (no need to wash). Whirl until finely chopped. Add whole egg and drained pineapple. Pulse with on/off motion just until combined. (The ingredients can also be chopped with a knife and then combined.)
3. Preheat oven to moderate (350°). Coat large baking sheet with nonstick vegetable-oil cooking spray.
4. Roll each half of dough out into 12 × 5-inch rectangle. Spoon half of filling (½ cup) down center of dough in 2½-inch-wide strip, leaving ½-inch border on ends. Fold one side of dough over filling. Brush with egg white. Fold over other side of dough to cover. Press ends to seal. Transfer to baking sheet. Brush top with half the egg white. Poke small holes in top for steam vents. Sprinkle with half the granulated sugar. Repeat with remaining dough and filling.
5. Bake in preheated moderate oven (350°) for 20 minutes or until lightly golden. Remove from sheets to racks to cool. Cut each roll into 1½-inch lengths.

Make-Ahead Tip: The bars can be made up to a week ahead and refrigerated in airtight containers.

SOUTHERN JAMBOREE

Chili Nuts (97)

Pineapple and Bacon Bites
(92)

Louisiana Shrimp (90)

**Zucchini-Stuffed
Mushrooms** (98)

Crusty Herbed Cauliflower
(411)

Jalapeño Cheese Spread
(82) **with Crackers and
Vegetables**

Pineapple Fig Bars
(this page)

Peach and Passion Punch
(554)

OPEN-FACE CALIFORNIA CHICKEN SALAD SANDWICH

LOW-CALORIE · LOW-CHOLESTEROL
QUICK

Although this sandwich is served cold, it is also delicious warm: Before topping with the avocado and sprouts, place under a preheated broiler until the cheese is melted.

Makes 6 sandwiches.
Recipe can be halved or doubled.
Nutrient Value Per Sandwich: 238 calories, 17 g protein, 12 g fat, 18 g carbohydrate, 331 mg sodium, 46 mg cholesterol.

¼ cup reduced-calorie mayonnaise
3 tablespoons chopped fresh cilantro OR: parsley
1 tablespoon grated onion
¼ teaspoon chili powder
¼ teaspoon salt
⅛ teaspoon ground hot red pepper
2½ cups cooked cubed chicken (about 10 ounces)
6 slices rye bread, lightly toasted
Green leaf lettuce
1 large tomato, cut into 6 slices
2 ounces Monterey Jack cheese with jalapeño pepper, shredded *(optional)*
1 ripe avocado, peeled, pitted and sliced
½ cup alfalfa sprouts

1. Stir together mayonnaise, cilantro, onion, chili powder, salt and hot red pepper in medium-size bowl. Add chicken; toss to coat well. Refrigerate until ready to serve.
2. To assemble, line bread slices with lettuce. Top with chicken salad, tomato slices, cheese, avocado slices and sprouts, dividing equally.

Make-Ahead Tip: The chicken salad can be made ahead and refrigerated for up to 2 days, covered.

THE BEST OF BREAD

The perfect sandwich starts with the kind of bread you can really sink your teeth into. Introduce yourself to the wide variety of crusty, chewy and diversely shaped breads available in bakeries and supermarket bakeshops.

Bagel —Chewy, doughnut-shaped bread with smooth, shiny crust and doughy interior. Split mini-bagels in half; cut larger bagels horizontally into three slices for easier handling. Bagels are best toasted and eaten open-faced with thin layers of spreadable fillings such as light cream cheese or farmer's cheese, tuna or egg salad.

Baguette —Long, thin, crusty-on-the-outside, chewy-on-the-inside variation of French bread made with yeast. Slice into small rounds for quick snack sandwiches, or lengthwise—top with salad spreads, sliced meats, grilled vegetables, thinly sliced or melted cheese.

Black Bread —A dense, chewy, peasant-style bread. Color comes from coffee and/or molasses and its earthy flavor from rye or pumpernickel flour. Fat round or oval-shaped loaf; slices well and holds up to overstuffed meat, cheese and vegetable sandwiches.

Brioche —Butter, eggs and a small dose of sugar give this topknotted loaf a cake-like texture. Its rich and slightly sweet flavor combines well with sliced ham and melted cheese.

Challah —Traditionally shaped in a braid, this light-textured, glazed Jewish egg bread has a slightly sweet flavor. Use thick-sliced for French toast or thin-sliced for sandwiches.

Cornbread —Grainy texture and crunchy bite are found in both quick and yeast bread versions.

Top sliced cornbread or round, toaster-ready corncakes with chili bean, saucy chicken, barbecued pork or ground beef mixtures.

Crepe —Fill these thin French pancakes with soft spreads and fillings like egg salad, ham salad, even peanut butter and jelly.

Croissant —Delicate, crescent-shaped puffs of flaky, golden, butter-rich pastry. Best served warm with a thin layer of moist filling such as crab salad or thinly

sliced meats and tender, leafy salad greens.

Crumpet —The original "English muffin" is spongier than its American counterpart and traditionally served unsplit and open-faced at teatime with butter or jam. Top toasted crumpets with melted cheese or use to make mini-pizzas.

Focaccia —Flat squares or rounds of dense, chewy, dimpled bread. Serve as pizza-like bases for

From bottom, clockwise: Crepes, Pumpernickel, Brioche, Pita Bread, Bagels and Crumpets.

open-faced sandwiches. Best if heated before serving; brush lightly with olive oil and sprinkle with fresh herbs or top with grated or shredded cheese, sliced fresh or dried tomatoes, sautéed onions, roasted peppers, olives or thinly sliced shreds of ham or prosciutto.

Pita Bread —Round, flat, Middle Eastern bread, regular or whole wheat, that forms its own pocket. Fill with chunky meat, cheese or mixed salad combinations.

Potato Bread —Moist texture and crispy crust with neutral flavor that's perfect for roast beef or broiled steak sandwich

with a sharp, mustardy dressing.

Pumpernickel Bread —Moist and dark, it gets its color from unsweetened cocoa powder or molasses and a combination of rye and whole-wheat flours. Hearty flavor holds up to strong cheese and meat combinations or cured meats like corned beef and pastrami. Try pumpernickel-raisin with baked ham, creamy Brie and sliced apples or pears.

Semolina Bread —Amber durum wheat flour gives this French- or Italian-style loaf its golden color and smooth texture. Use as you would Italian- or French-style breads, for overstuffed heroes,

or thinly sliced and toasted with garlic, olive oil and herbs.

Sourdough Bread —Available in a wide variety of shapes, such as loaves, rolls or baguettes. Sourdough breads are started with a fermented flour-based culture that gives the bread a distinctive tangy flavor that goes well with roast meats and grilled chicken, meatloaf or grilled vegetables and cheese.

Tortilla —Corn or flour versions. Serve warm and filled with shredded cheese, chopped vegetables, ground or sliced meat, and other chopped fillings, such as chili mixed with sweet peppers.

From top: Semolina Bread, French Bread, Challah, Black Bread and Croissants.

From bottom, clockwise: Cornbread, Focaccia, Sourdough Bread, Potato Bread, Corn Tortilla and Flour Tortilla.

STIR-FRY PORK AND VEGETABLE BURRITOS

LOW-CALORIE · LOW-FAT
LOW-CHOLESTEROL · QUICK

An unusual sandwich that mixes two cuisines: An Oriental hot pork and vegetable mixture wrapped in a warm tortilla brushed with plum sauce.

Heat tortillas at 350° for 10 minutes.
Makes 8 burritos.
Recipe can be halved or doubled.
Nutrient Value Per Burrito: 237 calories, 10 g protein, 5 g fat, 37 g carbohydrate, 344 mg sodium, 18 mg cholesterol.

8 large flour tortillas
3 tablespoons dry sherry
1½ tablespoons reduced-sodium soy sauce
1½ tablespoons sugar
2 tablespoons vegetable oil
8 ounces pork tenderloin, thinly sliced crosswise and slices halved lengthwise
½ medium-size sweet red pepper, cored, seeded and slivered
¼ pound fresh snow peas OR: frozen, thawed
2 green onions, cut into 1½-inch lengths and slivered
4 cups shredded green cabbage
¼ cup bottled Oriental plum sauce

1. Preheat oven to moderate (350°).
2. Wrap tortillas in aluminum foil. Combine sherry, soy sauce and sugar in small cup.
3. Heat tortillas in preheated moderate oven (350°) for 10 minutes or until very warm.
4. Meanwhile, heat very large skillet or wok over medium-high heat. Add 1 tablespoon oil. When oil is hot, add pork. Stir-fry 3 minutes or until browned and just cooked through. Remove with slotted spoon to small bowl.
5. Add remaining oil to skillet. When oil is hot, add red pepper, snow peas and green onion; stir-fry 2 minutes. Add cabbage and reserved sherry mixture; stir-fry 1 minute. Return meat to skillet; cover and cook 2 minutes or until cabbage just starts to wilt.
6. Remove tortillas from oven. Brush each with plum sauce. Fill center of each tortilla with pork mixture. Fold up bottom of tortilla and fold sides over so burrito can be eaten in hand. If you like, let everyone brush and fill his or her own tortilla.

LOWER-CALORIE BURRITOS VARIATION
Omit the tortillas and wrap the filling in spinach, cabbage or lettuce leaves.

STEAK SANDWICH WITH YOGURT-MUSTARD SAUCE

LOW-CALORIE · LOW-FAT
LOW-CHOLESTEROL

STEAK SANDWICH MAKE-AHEAD TIP:
You can make the sauce up to 8 hours ahead and refrigerate; covered.

Guaranteed to satisfy the largest appetite. The sauce can double as a salad dressing.

Broil steak 10 to 12 minutes.
Makes 6 sandwiches.
Recipe can be halved or doubled.
Nutrient Value Per Sandwich: 299 calories, 19 g protein, 8 g fat, 36 g carbohydrate, 609 mg sodium, 38 mg cholesterol.

½ cup lowfat plain yogurt
2 teaspoons Dijon-style mustard
⅛ teaspoon salt
1 jar (6 ounces) marinated artichoke hearts

¾ pound top round steak, in one piece
1 sweet red pepper OR: 1 bottled roasted red pepper
1 loaf French- or Italian-style bread
1 small red onion, thinly sliced

1. Preheat broiler.
2. Combine yogurt, mustard and salt in small bowl.
3. Drain artichokes, reserving marinade in medium-size bowl. Coarsely chop artichokes. Score top and bottom of steak with sharp knife. Add to artichoke marinade, turning to coat.
4. Broil pepper 6 inches from heat until blackened on all sides. Place in paper bag and close. When cool enough to handle, remove blackened skin from pepper. Core, seed and thinly slice pepper. Leave broiler on.
5. Broil steak 6 inches from heat for 5 to 6 minutes on each side for medium-rare or until desired doneness; brush with marinade after turning. Let stand 10 minutes. Thinly slice.
6. Meanwhile, cut bread crosswise into thirds. Slice each third in half horizontally. Toast bread. Brush a little yogurt sauce on each slice.
7. Arrange steak slices, artichokes, roasted pepper and onion on the cut side of each of the 6 slices of bread. Drizzle each sandwich with a little yogurt sauce. Serve sandwiches warm and pass remaining sauce.

SATISFYIN' SANDWICH AND SALAD

Steak Sandwich with Yogurt-Mustard Sauce (this page)

Romaine and Curly Endive with Anchovy Vinaigrette

Vanilla Ice Cream with Pineapple Sauce (537)

BAKED HAM AND BRIE SANDWICH WITH HONEY MUSTARD

QUICK

If you like "melts," omit the top slice of pumpernickel and run the sandwich under the broiler to melt the cheese.

Makes 4 sandwiches.
Recipe can be halved or doubled.
Nutrient Value Per Sandwich: 445 calories, 25 g protein, 20 g fat, 45 g carbohydrate, 1,260 mg sodium, 74 mg cholesterol.

1 teaspoon sugar
¼ teaspoon ground cinnamon
1 small red apple, cored and thinly sliced
2 teaspoons lemon juice
8 slices pumpernickel-raisin bread
¼ cup honey mustard
Romaine lettuce leaves
¼ pound sliced honey-baked ham
½ pound Brie cheese, sliced

1. Stir together sugar and cinnamon in medium-size bowl. Add apple and lemon juice; gently toss.
2. For one sandwich, spread 2 slices of bread with some of the mustard. Top one slice, mustard-side up, with lettuce leaves, one-quarter of the ham, one-quarter of the Brie and one-quarter of the apple slices. Place second slice of bread, mustard-side down, over apples. Cut sandwich in half. Repeat to make 3 more sandwiches.

HAM AND BRIE VARIATIONS
This combination also makes a great club sandwich using cinnamon-raisin bread instead of the pumpernickel. To make the club version, layer the mustard, lettuce, ham, cheese and apples with 3 slices of the bread to make one sandwich. If honey mustard is not available, make your own: Stir together ¼ cup Dijon-style mustard with seeds and 1 tablespoon honey.

TOFU SANDWICH SPREAD
Puree crumbled, soft tofu in food processor or blender with honey, fruit, yogurt and spices for a sweet sandwich spread, or puree into bean or vegetable mixtures for a savory spread.

CURRIED EGG SALAD AND HAM CLUB SANDWICH

LOW-FAT · QUICK

A *spicy variation on the usual egg salad.*

EGG SALAD VARIATIONS
Double up on the whites and cut back on the yolks for a healthier egg salad sandwich. Add finely chopped vegetables for color, flavor and crunch. Add chopped olives or marinated artichokes for zest. Moisten with equal parts mayonnaise and nonfat yogurt; mix in mustard or soy sauce for extra bite.

Makes 4 sandwiches.
Recipe can be halved or doubled.
Nutrient Value Per Sandwich: 413 calories, 19 g protein, 14 g fat, 53 g carbohydrate, 1,026 mg sodium, 221 mg cholesterol.

⅓ cup lower-calorie mayonnaise
¼ cup finely chopped sweet red pepper
1 tablespoon finely chopped onion
1½ teaspoons curry powder
¼ teaspoon salt
⅛ teaspoon black pepper
4 hard-cooked eggs, peeled and chopped
½ bunch watercress, stems removed OR: shredded Romaine lettuce OR: other lettuce
12 slices cracked-wheat bread, lightly toasted
¼ cup chutney
4 slices turkey-ham (4 ounces)

1. Stir together mayonnaise, sweet red pepper, onion, curry powder, salt and black pepper in medium-size bowl. Gently stir in eggs with rubber scraper. Cover; refrigerate until ready to serve.
2. For 1 sandwich, place some watercress on one bread slice. Top with one-quarter of the egg salad. Spread another slice of bread with some of the chutney. Place bread, chutney side up, on egg salad. Top with 1 slice of turkey-ham. Spread a third slice of bread with some chutney. Place bread, chutney side down, on top of ham. Cut sandwich in half or quarters. Secure with wooden pick (be sure to remove before eating). Repeat to make 3 more sandwiches.

Make-Ahead Tip: Egg salad can be made ahead and refrigerated for up to 2 days, covered.

TUNA NIÇOISE PITA POCKETS

LOW-CALORIE · LOW-FAT
LOW-CHOLESTEROL

In these sandwiches, the traditional salad Niçoise ingredients are combined as a multicolored filling. You can also serve the salad on its own.

Makes 4 servings.
Recipe can be halved or doubled.
Nutrient Value Per Serving: 301 calories, 15 g protein, 8 g fat, 44 g carbohydrate, 486 mg sodium, 9 mg cholesterol.

½ **pound small red potatoes, scrubbed**
¼ **pound green beans, trimmed and cut into 1-inch lengths**
1 **can (6½ ounces) solid white tuna, packed in oil, drained**
½ **sweet red pepper, halved crosswise, cored, seeded and cut into ⅓-inch slivers**
1 **tablespoon finely chopped red onion**
6 **Niçoise OR: oil-cured black olives, pitted and finely chopped** (optional)
2 **tablespoons olive oil**
2 **tablespoons red wine vinegar**
½ **teaspoon anchovy paste** (optional)
¼ **teaspoon leaf oregano, crumbled**
Salt and pepper, to taste
4 **regular-size whole-wheat pita pocket breads**
Romaine lettuce leaves

1. Cook potatoes in large saucepan of boiling salted water for 15 minutes or until tender. Remove with slotted spoon from water; drain.
2. Cook green beans in same saucepan of boiling water for 2 minutes or until crisp-tender. Immediately plunge beans into bowl of ice water to stop cooking.
3. Peel potatoes, if desired. Thinly slice into large bowl. Drain beans very well; add to potatoes. Flake tuna with fork into the bowl. Add red pepper, onion and olives if using.

4. Whisk together oil, vinegar, anchovy paste if using and oregano in small bowl. Let stand 5 minutes for flavors to blend. Pour dressing over potato and tuna mixture; toss gently to blend. Season with salt and pepper.
5. Carefully split open tops of pita pockets, but do not cut in half. Tuck lettuce leaves into pitas. Fill with tuna mixture.

Microwave Directions for Cooking Potatoes and Green Beans (High Power Oven): Place potatoes and 2 tablespoons water in microwave-safe 1-quart casserole. Cover with lid. Microwave at 100% power 5 minutes until tender. Drain. Place green beans and 1 tablespoon water in same casserole. Cover with lid. Microwave at 100% power 3 to 3½ minutes until tender-crisp. Drain and plunge into ice water as above.

PITA POCKET
MAKE-AHEAD TIP:
The tuna filling can be made up to a day ahead, covered and refrigerated.

MUFFULETTA

LOW-FAT · LOW-CHOLESTEROL

In New Orleans, a muffuletta is made with salami and provolone cheese. To cut back on saturated fat, we've used lean baked ham and turkey in this make-ahead sandwich. For smaller servings, cut into 6 equal wedges.

Makes 4 servings.
Nutrient Value Per Serving: 452 calories, 20 g protein, 11 g fat, 68 g carbohydrate, 1,351 mg sodium, 20 mg cholesterol.

1 jar (16 ounces) marinated mixed vegetables, drained and coarsely chopped
¼ cup green olives with pimiento, finely chopped
1 tablespoon olive oil
1 clove garlic, finely chopped
¼ teaspoon leaf oregano, crumbled
1 round loaf (8 inches) bread, unsliced
3 ounces thinly sliced lean baked ham
3 ounces thinly sliced deli turkey breast

1. Combine mixed vegetables and olives in small bowl.
2. Heat oil in small saucepan over medium-low heat. Add garlic and oregano; cook 2 minutes, do not brown. Halve bread horizontally. Pull out some of bread from each half. Brush inside of bottom half with oil mixture. Top with half of vegetables. Add ham and turkey. Top with remaining vegetables. Cover with top half of bread.
3. Wrap sandwich in plastic wrap. Refrigerate at least 2 hours or overnight. Cut into 4 wedges to serve.

Make-Ahead Tip: The sandwich can be made a day ahead, tightly wrapped and refrigerated.

BROCCOLI-WALNUT SANDWICH ROLL

LOW-CHOLESTEROL

An impressive sandwich roll made easy with frozen bread dough. (Pictured at top right.)

Bake at 400° for 30 minutes.
Makes 12 servings (1 roll).
Nutrient Value Per Serving:
192 calories, 8 g protein, 8 g fat,
22 g carbohydrate, 292 mg sodium,
10 mg cholesterol.

2 teaspoons olive oil
1 small onion, slivered
2 cloves garlic, finely chopped
2 packages (10 ounces each) frozen
    chopped broccoli, thawed and well
    drained
¼ cup water
1 cup shredded reduced-fat Cheddar
    cheese (4 ounces)
½ cup toasted walnuts, finely chopped
¼ cup grated Parmesan cheese
1 loaf frozen bread dough (1 pound),
    thawed according to package
    directions to room temperature

1. Heat olive oil in large skillet. Add onion; cook 2 minutes or until tender. Add garlic; cook 30 seconds. Add broccoli and water; cook, covered, 5 minutes or until broccoli is just tender. Uncover; cook 1 minute or until liquid evaporates. Remove from heat. Stir Cheddar cheese, walnuts and Parmesan cheese into broccoli. Cool before filling sandwich.
2. Preheat oven to hot (400°). Coat baking sheet with nonstick vegetable-oil cooking spray.

(continued)

**From top: Broccoli-Walnut
Sandwich Roll (this page) and
Chicken and Basil Party
Sandwich (page 114).**

Try small changes and new additions to your favorite every-day sandwiches.

- Mix sweet and savory sandwich combinations such as baked ham and Camembert cheese on raisin bread; roast pork and pear or banana slices on walnut bread; melted Cheddar or Gorgonzola and tart apple slices on date-nut bread.

- Fill a hero with less meat, more flavorful vegetables, like roasted peppers, mixed lettuce greens, fresh or sun-dried tomatoes, sprouts, cucumbers or any leftover cooked vegetable. Sprinkle with chopped fresh or dried herbs and drizzle with olive oil.

- Combine finely diced ham, chicken or turkey breast with chopped toasted walnuts. Add just enough applesauce, apple butter or cranberry relish to make a spreadable salad.

- Instead of frying cheese sandwiches, bake them open-faced in a moderate oven or toaster oven. Place chopped olives, toasted nuts, leftover vegetables or fresh fruit between bread and cheese before baking.

BROCCOLI-WALNUT SANDWICH ROLL

(continued)

3. Roll thawed dough out on lightly floured surface to 12×12-inch square. (If dough is too springy, let rest for a moment between rolls.) Spread cooled filling down center of dough in strip about 3½ inches wide, to within 1 inch of each end. Fold ends over filling. Fold sides over and pinch to seal. (Be careful not to stretch dough or it may break during baking.) Roll onto baking sheet so loaf is seam-side-down.

4. Bake in preheated hot oven (400°) for 30 minutes or until lightly browned and hollow-sounding when tapped on top. Remove bread from baking sheet to wire rack. Let stand 15 minutes before slicing. Serve warm.

GRADUATION DAY BUFFET

Rite of Spring Punch (554)

Pineapple and Bacon Bites (92)

Mexican Pizza (63)

Broccoli-Walnut Sandwich Roll (113)

Rotelle with Mozzarella and Roasted Peppers (201)

Kitchen Sink Cookies (512) and Toffee Crunch Bars (520)

CHICKEN AND BASIL PARTY SANDWICH

LOW-CALORIE · LOW-FAT

LOW-CHOLESTEROL · QUICK

Serve either warm or chilled—the sandwich is equally good either way. (Pictured on page 113, bottom.)

Broil chicken for 10 to 12 minutes.

Makes 8 servings.

Nutrient Value Per Serving: 231 calories, 19 g protein, 6 g fat, 24 g carbohydrate, 452 mg sodium, 44 mg cholesterol.

---

2 whole boneless, skinned chicken breasts (about 1¾ pounds)
¼ cup light olive oil vinaigrette
1 bunch fresh basil
½ cup lower-calorie mayonnaise
1 tablespoon tomato paste
¼ teaspoon pepper
1 clove garlic, crushed
1 loaf (10 ounces) Italian bread with seeds
2 ounces part-skim mozzarella cheese, sliced
1 plum tomato, sliced

1. Preheat broiler.

2. Toss chicken breasts with vinaigrette in large bowl. Remove chicken from vinaigrette, reserving vinaigrette. Place chicken on rack in broiler pan.

3. Broil 3 inches from heat source, turning and brushing with reserved vinaigrette occasionally, for 10 to 12 minutes or until cooked through.

4. Meanwhile, chop enough basil to measure ¼ cup. Stir together chopped basil, mayonnaise, tomato paste, pepper and garlic in small bowl.

5. Cut chicken lengthwise into thin slices. If not using chicken right away, cover and refrigerate until ready to use.

6. To serve, slice bread horizontally in half. Spread mayonnaise mixture over cut sides of each bread half. Line bottom half of bread with some basil leaves. Top with chicken and cheese. Alternately arrange tomato slices and some basil leaves on top of cheese. Top with remaining bread half, mayonnaise side down. Cut crosswise into 1-inch slices. Garnish with any remaining basil.

Make-Ahead Tip: If serving the chicken cold, broil ahead and refrigerate, covered, for up to 2 days.

Chicken, Okra and Sausage Gumbo (page 122).

CHAPTER 4

SOUPS AND STEWS

VEGETABLE STOCK

LOW-CALORIE · LOW-SODIUM · LOW-FAT
LOW-CHOLESTEROL

U*se this broth as a base for vegetarian soups and stews, or substitute it for chicken broth in your favorite recipes. Since this broth is subtly flavored, it does not take well to freezing.*

Makes about 8 cups.
Nutrient Value Per Cup: 59 calories,
2 g protein, 0 g fat, 14 g carbohydrate,
20 mg sodium, 0 mg cholesterol.

4 large tomatoes, cored and quartered
3 large carrots, pared and cut into thick
    slices
2 large (about 1 to 1¼ pounds)
    all-purpose potatoes, quartered
2 large onions, unpeeled and quartered
2 celery stalks, cut into thick slices
1 large apple, cored and quartered
½ bunch parsley
5 cloves garlic, unpeeled
10 peppercorns
1 bay leaf
8 cups water

1. Combine tomato, carrot, potato, onion, celery, apple, parsley, garlic, peppercorns, bay leaf and water in a 5-quart Dutch oven or large saucepot. Bring to boiling over high heat. Reduce heat to low; cover and simmer 1 hour.
2. Remove from heat and let stand 30 minutes. Strain, reserving cooked vegetables for other uses. Cool broth. Refrigerate.

Make-Ahead Tip: The broth can be refrigerated, covered, for up to several days.

CHICKEN STOCK

LOW-CALORIE · LOW-SODIUM · LOW-FAT
LOW-CHOLESTEROL

Makes about 12 cups.
Nutrient Value Per Cup: 44 calories,
1 mg protein, 2 g fat, 6 g carbohydrate,
32 mg sodium, 0 mg cholesterol.

1 chicken (3 pounds), quartered
2 pounds chicken wings OR: chicken
    necks and gizzards
2 large carrots, scraped and halved
2 large stalks celery with tops, halved
1 small bunch parsley
1 bay leaf
1 large leek, well cleaned, with 3 inches
    of greens OR: 1 large onion, peeled
    and studded with 1 whole clove
⅛ teaspoon salt
6 to 8 peppercorns
12 to 14 cups water, or as needed

1. Combine chicken, wings, carrot, celery, parsley, bay leaf, leek, salt and peppercorns in large Dutch oven or stockpot. Add 12 to 14 cups of cold water or enough to cover the ingredients by 2 inches. Slowly bring to boiling, skimming any scum that rises to surface.
2. Partially cover pot and simmer 2 hours. Strain through colander lined with double-thickness dampened cheesecloth. Discard solids, reserving chicken for other uses, if you wish. Cool stock in separate smaller bowls (*see Storing Stock, page 118*). Then refrigerate, covered, until next day.
3. Skim fat from surface of stock. Transfer stock to large saucepan. Bring to boiling. Pour into three 1-quart refrigerator or freezer containers, or ice cube trays. Let cool. Refrigerate or freeze.

Make-Ahead Tip: This stock can be refrigerated, covered, for up to 3 days, or frozen for up to 2 months. Bring to boiling before using.

VERSATILE VEGETABLE STOCK
The stock is delicious on its own as a first course, garnished with tortellini, spätzle or thinly sliced cooked carrots. As a bonus, puree the drained, cooked vegetables and use a little as a thick base for creamy soups and stews. Remove the peppercorns, onion and garlic skins, parsley and bay leaf before pureeing.

SKIMMING THE FAT
To defat meat stock, make it a day ahead; refrigerate so fat rises to top and solidifies. Then just scrape off fat.

POULTRY STOCK
■ Don't throw away a cooked carcass! Although raw meat yields a more flavorful stock or broth, the carcass of cooked poultry still has a lot of flavor locked within it, especially with a little meat attached.
■ Take stock in parts: legs, wings, backs and necks make a rich broth.

TURKEY STOCK

LOW-CALORIE • LOW-SODIUM
LOW-FAT • LOW-CHOLESTEROL

Here's a good way to use the turkey carcass left over after a holiday meal, or the bones left over from roasting a whole turkey breast (see turkey breast recipes, pages 269 to 272).

Makes about 8 cups.
Nutrient Value Per Cup: 46 calories,
1 g protein, 2 g fat, 7 g carbohydrate,
8 mg sodium, 0 mg cholesterol.

1 turkey carcass, with some meat left on
8 cups water
2 carrots, sliced
2 celery stalks, sliced
1 medium-size onion, sliced
1 large clove garlic, sliced
1 large sprig parsley
1 bay leaf
2 teaspoons leaf basil, crumbled
1 teaspoon leaf thyme, crumbled

1. Cut carcass into pieces with cleaver or large knife. Place in large kettle or stock pot. Add water, carrot, celery, onion, garlic, parsley, bay leaf, basil and thyme. Bring to boiling. Lower heat; simmer, partially covered, 3 to 4 hours, skimming and discarding any foam from surface.
2. Carefully strain through colander lined with double-thickness dampened cheesecloth. Discard solids. Cool stock in separate smaller bowls (see Storing Stock, page 118). Then refrigerate, covered, overnight.
3. Skim fat and discard. Transfer stock to large saucepan. Bring to boiling. Pour in refrigerator or freezer containers, or ice cube trays. Let cool. Refrigerate or freeze stock.

Make-Ahead Tip: The stock can be refrigerated, covered, for up to 3 days, or frozen for up to 2 months. Bring to boiling before using.

DUCK STOCK

If you are cooking duck legs or breasts from a whole duck (see Duck Stew with Vegetables, page 289, and Sautéed Duck Breasts with Orange Sauce, page 290), save the carcasses, either in the refrigerator for a day or two or in the freezer for up to 2 months, and make this flavorful broth—it's great for soup and sauces.

Makes about 11 cups.
Nutrient Value: Unavailable.*

2 duck carcasses (from 2 ducks, 4½
    pounds each), cut up
13 cups cold water
2 large onions, thinly sliced
2 stalks celery, thinly sliced
2 large carrots, thinly sliced
3 cloves garlic, peeled
Sprig rosemary
6 sprigs parsley
2 bay leaves

1. Combine carcasses, water, onion, celery, carrot, garlic, rosemary, parsley and bay leaves in large pot. Bring to boiling over moderate heat. Skim off any scum. Lower heat; gently simmer, partially covered, 3 hours.
2. Strain stock through colander lined with double-thickness dampened cheesecloth. Discard solids. Cool stock in separate smaller bowls (see Storing Stock, page 118). Then refrigerate, covered, overnight.
3. Skim fat from surface of stock and discard. Transfer stock to large saucepan. Bring to boiling. Pour in refrigerator or freezer containers, or ice cube trays. Let cool. Refrigerate or freeze stock.

***Note:** Nutrition information for duck carcass unavailable.
Make-Ahead Tip: Refrigerate stock for up to 3 days, covered, or freeze for up to 2 months. Bring to boiling before using.

ALTERNATIVES TO HOMEMADE STOCKS

■ Even dedicated cooks rely on canned chicken and beef broths, especially as the springboard for more complex soups, sauces and risottos (see page 214). Although they take up more storage space than their powdered or cubed cousins, their flavor is usually more true to the real thing. Look for the lower-sodium versions.
■ Some excellent frozen stock concentrates are now available, many of them with no artificial ingredients or salt. Use almost full strength in sauces or dilute to use in soups.
■ If you are unable to make fish stock from scratch, substitute bottled clam broth as a good alternative. But remember, it is salty.
■ Powdered and cubed bouillon dissolve quickly, so it can be added dry to liquids that are a bit lackluster. Both keep well, sealed in a moisture-proof package, in a small amount of cupboard space. Look for the lower- or no-salt varieties of chicken or beef bouillon.

BEEF STOCK

Roasting bones adds a rich flavor and color. You can, however, skip this step and begin with Step 3.

Bake bones at 400° for 30 minutes.
Makes about 8 cups.
Nutrient Value: Unavailable.*

4 **pounds beef and/or veal bones**
12 **cups water**
1 **medium-size onion, coarsely chopped**
3 **large carrots, chopped**
6 **sprigs fresh parsley**
1 **teaspoon whole peppercorns, or to taste**
4 **cloves garlic, halved**
1 **bay leaf**
2 **whole cloves**
1 **teaspoon leaf thyme, crumbled**
½ **teaspoon celery seeds**

1. Preheat oven to hot (400°).
2. Roast bones in roasting pans for 30 minutes, turning once. Discard fat.
3. Combine bones, water, onion, carrot, parsley, peppercorns, garlic, bay leaf, cloves, thyme and celery seeds in large pot. Bring to boiling over medium-high heat. Lower heat; simmer, partially covered, at least 4 hours. Frequently skim foam; do not stir or boil.
4. Strain stock through colander lined with double-thickness dampened cheesecloth. Discard solids. Cool stock in separate smaller bowls (see Storing Stock, at left). Then refrigerate, covered, overnight.
5. Skim fat and discard. Transfer stock to large saucepan. Bring to boiling. Pour in refrigerator or freezer containers, or ice cube trays. Let cool. Refrigerate or freeze stock.

*Note: Nutrition information unavailable for bones.
Make-Ahead Tip: The stock can be refrigerated, covered, for up to 3 days, or frozen for up to 2 months. Bring to boiling before using.

STORING STOCK
■ Cool the stock to 40°, uncovered, as quickly as possible. Pour into smaller bowls and stir often to aerate. Then refrigerate, covered, overnight and remove the solidified fat from the surface.
■ If the stock has been refrigerated for 2 or 3 days, bring it to boiling before using to be sure there is no souring.
■ If you plan to freeze stock, omit the salt and season to taste for a particular recipe.
■ If you're short on freezer space, simmer the de-fatted broth in a saucepan until it has an almost a syrupy consistency. This highly concentrated mixture freezes well and is easily added to water in a saucepan to make a flavorful broth.
■ For single serving or for using in sauces, freeze the stock in ice cube trays, then transfer the cubes to a freezer-proof bag or container.
■ Be sure to label and date the frozen stock and use within 2 months.

QUICK BEEF STOCK

LOW-CALORIE • LOW-FAT
LOW-CHOLESTEROL

Here's a fast version of beef stock which will add more flavor to all your homemade soups and casseroles.

Makes about 4 cups.
Nutrient Value Per Cup: 30 calories, 1 g protein, 1 g fat, 5 g carbohydrate, 148 mg sodium, 0 mg cholesterol.

1 **pound lean ground beef**
4 **cups cold water**
1 **carrot, chopped**
1 **large onion, chopped**
1 **stalk celery, chopped**
½ **teaspoon salt**
¼ **teaspoon pepper, or to taste**

1. Brown beef in large saucepan. Add water. Bring to boiling slowly.
2. Add carrot, onion, celery, salt and pepper. Simmer, partially covered, for 1 hour. Skim fat from surface.
3. Strain through colander lined with double-thickness dampened cheesecloth. Discard solids. Cool stock in separate smaller bowls (see Storing Stock, at left). Then refrigerate stock, covered, overnight.
4. Skim fat from surface of stock and discard. Transfer stock to large saucepan. Bring to boiling. Pour in refrigerator or freezer containers, or ice cube trays. Let cool. Refrigerate or freeze stock.

Make-Ahead Tip: The stock can be refrigerated, covered, for 2 or 3 days, or frozen for up to 2 months. Bring to boiling before using.

FISH STOCK

P*repared from the bones or frames, heads and tails of non-oily fish, fish stock or broth is ready in about 30 minutes.*

Makes about 8 cups.
Nutrient Value: Unavailable.*

2 tablespoons *un*salted butter
2 medium-size onions, halved and sliced crosswise
2 stalks celery, sliced
1 carrot, sliced
¼ cup parsley stems
3 to 3½ pounds fish bones, heads and tails from flounder, halibut, cod or other non-oily fish, rinsed
¼ teaspoon leaf thyme, crumbled
1 bay leaf
1 bottle (750 ml) dry white wine

1. Heat butter in large nonaluminum pot over medium heat. Add onion; cook, covered, stirring often, until softened, 5 to 10 minutes. Add celery and carrot; cook, covered, 3 to 4 minutes. Add parsley, fish bones, heads and tails; cook, uncovered, 2 to 3 minutes.
2. Add thyme, bay leaf and wine, and water if necessary to cover all the ingredients. Cover and bring to boiling. Skim any foam from surface and discard. Lower heat; simmer, partially covered, about 30 minutes.
3. Strain broth through large sieve or colander lined with double-thickness dampened cheesecloth. Gently press down on solids to extract liquid. Discard solids. Cool stock in separate smaller bowls (*see Storing Stock, page 118*). Then refrigerate or freeze stock.

*Note: Nutrition information unavailable for fish bones.
Make-Ahead Tip: The stock can be refrigerated, covered, for up to 2 days, or frozen for up to 2 months. Bring to boiling before using.

HOW TO MAKE A PUREED SOUP

1. Place small pieces of cooked broccoli* in blender or food processor. Add ½ cup chicken broth or other liquid.
*Note: Other good choices are carrots, green beans, beets, cauliflower, potatoes and even mixtures of leftover cooked vegetables.

2. Whirl until a thick, smooth puree. With motor running, pour more liquid through small opening in top cover until soup is as thick or thin as desired.

3. Pour soup into saucepan and heat to serving temperature. Season as you wish with herbs, salt and pepper.

STOCKS AND BROTHS: THEIR MANY USES

■ If a soup recipe calls for water, substitute broth for extra flavor and richness.
■ Cook vegetables in broth instead of water.
■ Use broth as some or all of the liquid in stews, combined with wine and/or vegetable juice.
■ Make a delicious skillet sauce by adding a little broth after the sautéed food and excess fat have been removed from the skillet. Bring the mixture to simmer, stirring to release the cooked-on pieces from the pan. Continue to cook until the sauce is reduced to desired thickness, adding a touch of cream or pureed vegetables for added richness and thickness.
■ Braised foods such as pot roasts are first browned all over, then simmered slowly in liquid. Broths, alone or in combination with wine, impart flavor to the meat and become the basis for a rich sauce once the meat is cooked.
■ A good broth transforms rice into something special, whether it's a simple pilaf or a more painstakingly prepared risotto (*see page 214*).

CHEDDAR CHEESE AND ASPARAGUS SOUP

QUICK

After adding cheese, cook over medium-low heat to prevent cheese separating. (Pictured on page 121.)

**Makes 4 servings (5 cups).
Recipe can be halved or doubled.**
Nutrient Value Per Serving: 605 calories, 31 g protein, 45 g fat, 19 g carbohydrate, 1,084 mg sodium, 147 mg cholesterol.

3 tablespoons *un*salted butter
½ pound asparagus, trimmed and cut into
    ½-inch pieces
1 clove garlic, crushed
3 tablespoons all-purpose flour
4 cups milk
3 cups shredded sharp Cheddar cheese
    (12 ounces)
2 teaspoons Dijon-style mustard
½ teaspoon salt
⅛ teaspoon white pepper
Pinch grated nutmeg

1. Melt butter in heavy, medium-size saucepan over medium heat. Add asparagus and garlic; sauté, stirring occasionally, about 5 minutes. Gradually blend in flour; cook, stirring constantly, 3 to 5 minutes. Reduce heat to medium-low. Gradually stir in 1 cup milk and the shredded cheese; cook, stirring occasionally, about 5 minutes or until cheese is melted and smooth.
2. Stir in remaining milk, mustard, salt, pepper and nutmeg. Gently heat, stirring occasionally, until soup is hot. Remove garlic before serving. Garnish with shredded cheese, if you wish.

Other Than Asparagus: You can substitute other cooked vegetables for the asparagus, such as tiny broccoli flowerets, cut green beans, green peas or pearl onions. For extra color, add ¼ to ½ cup sautéed diced sweet red pepper.

SPICY CORN CHOWDER

LOW-FAT · LOW-CHOLESTEROL

For a less spicy version of this soup, eliminate the jalapeño pepper. Serve with tortilla chips or bread sticks. (Pictured on page 121.)

**Makes 8 servings (8 cups).
Recipe can be halved or doubled.**
Nutrient Value Per Serving: 148 calories, 6 g protein, 5 g fat, 23 g carbohydrate, 595 mg sodium, 9 mg cholesterol.

1 tablespoon vegetable oil
1 large onion, diced (1 cup)
2 cans (13¾ ounces each) chicken broth
    OR: homemade (*see recipe, page
    116*)
1 package (16 ounces) frozen corn
    kernels
2 cups milk
1 large sweet red pepper, cored, seeded
    and diced (1¼ cups)
1 jalapeño pepper, seeded and finely
    chopped
½ pound all-purpose potatoes, cut into
    ½-inch pieces
½ teaspoon salt

1. Heat oil in large saucepan over medium heat. Add onion; cook, stirring occasionally, 10 minutes. Add 1½ cups chicken broth and corn. Bring to boiling over high heat. Lower heat; simmer 5 minutes.
2. Remove 1½ cups corn mixture with slotted spoon and place in blender or food processor. Whirl until pureed.
3. Return puree to saucepan. Add remaining chicken broth, milk, red pepper, jalapeño pepper, potato and salt. Bring to boiling over high heat. Lower heat; cover and simmer 10 minutes or until vegetables are tender.

Make-Ahead Tip: The soup can be made a day ahead and refrigerated, covered. Gently reheat.

BLACK BEAN SOUP

LOW-FAT · LOW-CHOLESTEROL

Dress up this classic favorite with a dollop of yogurt or sour cream, sieved hard-cooked egg, chopped onion and/or chopped cilantro. (Pictured at right.)

Makes 8 servings (9 cups).
Recipe can be halved or doubled.
Nutrient Value Per Serving: 241 calories, 11 g protein, 6 g fat, 37 g carbohydrate, 663 mg sodium, 5 mg cholesterol.

2 cups dried black beans, picked over
    and rinsed
Water for soaking
8 cups water
½ pound bacon, left in slices
2 large onions, chopped (2 cups)
2 cloves garlic, finely chopped
1 bay leaf
2¼ teaspoons salt
½ teaspoon leaf oregano, crumbled
¼ teaspoon leaf thyme, crumbled
⅛ teaspoon ground hot red pepper
3 medium-size carrots, pared and finely
    chopped
⅓ cup chopped cilantro OR: parsley
3 tablespoons red wine vinegar
1 tablespoon dry sherry (optional)

1. Cover beans with water in large Dutch oven or saucepan. Let stand 4 hours or overnight. Or to quick-soak beans, bring beans to boiling in water over high heat; cook 2 minutes. Remove from heat and let stand 1 hour.
2. Drain beans. Return to pan. Add 8 cups fresh water. Add bacon, half the onion, the garlic, bay leaf, salt, oregano, thyme and red pepper. Bring to boiling over high heat. Lower heat; cover and simmer 1½ hours. Add remaining onion and the carrot. Cover and simmer 1½ hours, adding additional water if necessary.
3. Remove bacon and discard. Place 1 cup of solid mixture in food processor or blender. Whirl until smooth puree.

From top: Cheddar Cheese and Asparagus Soup (page 120); Black Bean Soup (this page) and Spicy Corn Chowder (page 120).

Return to saucepan. Stir in cilantro, vinegar, and sherry if using. Heat through. Remove bay leaf before serving. Garnish with sprigs of cilantro and a touch of sour cream, if you wish.

Make-Ahead Tip: This soup can be made up to 2 days ahead. Omit the cilantro, vinegar and sherry in Step 3. Refrigerate, covered, or freeze for up to 2 months. Defrost overnight in the refrigerator and reheat. After reheating, stir in cilantro, vinegar and sherry. For left-over frozen soup, stir in a little extra vinegar and/or sherry to pick up flavor after reheating.

BASIC BLACK BEANS

Black turtle beans are a staple in Caribbean, Mexican and South American cooking and a famous food for soup making. (See Legumes Primer, page 227.)

■ How is black bean soup seasoned? Mexican black bean soup carries the flavors of sherry, oregano and lemon. In Brazil, chopped bacon or sausage and hard-cooked eggs inevitably come with a bowl of black beans. Island chefs may add spicy cloves or a hot pepper.

■ Other ways to dress up a basic black bean soup: sliced green or red onion; tomato salsa; lemon, lime or orange wheels; shredded cheese; cilantro or watercress sprigs; grated carrot; chopped olives.

ONE WAY OR ANOTHER: GUMBO THICKENERS

There are two ways to thicken a gumbo. Use either one, but not both, or you'll never get the stew off the spoon.

■ Gumbos made with cut-up okra thicken as they cook from the sticky substance released by the vegetable into the stew.

■ Filé powder, a thickener made from dried, ground sassafras leaves, becomes stringy when boiled. To prevent this, stir the filé into finished gumbo, off the heat, or even pass it at the table so diners can thicken their own stews to taste.

FREEZING SOUPS

■ Most soups freeze well, except those containing cheese, cream or other dairy products since they may separate and curdle when thawed and reheated. Freeze the soup without these particular ingredients, then add when gently reheating.

■ Freeze soups in individual microwave-proof containers, for a quick microwavable lunch or snack.

■ Some vegetable pieces and pasta become soft when frozen and reheated. For a better texture, add these ingredients to the soup as it is reheated.

CHICKEN, OKRA AND SAUSAGE GUMBO

LOW-CALORIE · LOW-FAT

For a slightly different flavor twist, substitute Italian-style pork sausages or breakfast sausage links for the turkey sausage. Leftover turkey can be substituted for the chicken. To reduce fat, remove the skin from the chicken before cooking. (Pictured on page 115.)

Makes 8 servings (about 11 cups). Recipe can be halved or doubled.

Nutrient Value Per Serving: 227 calories, 26 g protein, 7 g fat, 15 g carbohydrate, 1,307 mg sodium, 74 mg cholesterol.

---

1 broiler-fryer chicken (about 3 pounds), cut up
4 cups chicken broth, canned OR: homemade (*see recipe, page 116*)
2 cloves garlic, finely chopped
1 bay leaf
1½ teaspoons salt
1 teaspoon leaf thyme, crumbled
½ teaspoon pepper
½ pound turkey sausage links
2 cans (16 ounces each) tomatoes, broken up
1 large onion, chopped
1 pound okra, fresh or frozen, cut into ½-inch pieces
1 cup frozen whole-kernel corn
¼ teaspoon liquid red-pepper seasoning

1. Combine chicken, broth, garlic, bay leaf, salt, thyme and pepper in large Dutch oven or saucepan. Bring to boiling over high heat. Lower heat; cover and simmer 25 minutes or until chicken is tender. Remove chicken with slotted spoon from broth. Skim fat from broth. When cool enough to handle, remove bones and skin from meat; discard. Cut meat into bite-size pieces. Leave broth in pan.
2. Meanwhile, cook sausages in small skillet over medium-high heat until

brown all over. Drain on paper toweling. When cool enough to handle, cut into ½-inch-thick slices.
3. Add tomato, onion and sausage to broth in pan. Cover and simmer 10 minutes. Add okra, corn, liquid red-pepper seasoning and reserved chicken. Cover and simmer 10 minutes or until okra is tender. Remove bay leaf.

Make-Ahead Tip: The recipe can be prepared through Step 2 up to 2 days ahead and refrigerated. The finished soup can be frozen for up to 1 month, then defrosted overnight in the refrigerator and reheated.

Microwave Directions for Cooking Sausage (High Power Oven): Prick sausage links in several places with fork. Place in microwave-safe 9-inch pie plate. Cover with double-thickness paper toweling. Microwave at 100% power 4 minutes, turning sausage over after 2 minutes. Let stand, covered, 2 minutes.

KENTUCKY DERBY DAY

Ginger Juleps (553) with Gorgonzola and Pear Packets (91)

Chicken, Okra and Sausage Gumbo (this page)

Baked Ham

Cream Biscuits (76)

Cheese and Chili Baked Grits (222)

Sautéed Spinach with Golden Raisins (447)

Citrus Layer Cake (507)

WHITE BEAN AND KALE SOUP

LOW-FAT · LOW-CHOLESTEROL

If frozen kale is not available, substitute frozen spinach in this thick, hearty soup, ideal for the coldest of days.

Makes 8 servings (8 cups).
Recipe can be halved or doubled.
Nutrient Value Per Serving: 203 calories, 12 g protein, 6 g fat, 27 g carbohydrate, 899 mg sodium, 4 mg cholesterol.

½ pound dried navy beans, picked over and rinsed
Water
2 tablespoons olive oil
3 stalks celery, diced
2 medium-size carrots, pared and sliced
1 medium-size onion, diced
1 clove garlic, finely chopped
2 ounces prosciutto, diced
1 can (46 ounces) chicken broth OR: homemade (*see recipe, page 116*)
½ teaspoon pepper
1 package (10 ounces) frozen chopped kale OR: frozen chopped spinach
½ cup small shell pasta
Grated Parmesan cheese *(optional)*

1. Place beans in large saucepan. Add enough water to cover beans by 2 inches. Bring to boiling over high heat; boil 5 minutes. Remove from heat; cover and let stand 1 hour. Drain.
2. Heat oil in large saucepan or Dutch oven over medium-high heat. Add celery, carrot, onion, garlic and prosciutto; cook, stirring frequently, 5 minutes. Add beans, chicken broth and pepper. Bring to boiling over high heat. Lower heat; cover and simmer 1 hour or until beans are tender.
3. With slotted spoon, remove 1 cup beans to bowl. Mash beans with potato masher or fork. Return mashed beans to saucepan. Add kale. Bring to boiling over high heat. Lower heat; simmer 10 minutes or until kale is heated through.
4. Meanwhile, prepare pasta according to package directions; drain. Stir pasta into soup. If you like, serve with freshly grated Parmesan cheese.

BEAN SOUP MAKE-AHEAD TIP:
You can soak the beans overnight, drain and rinse, and then proceed with Step 2. The soup can be made up to 2 days ahead and refrigerated, covered. Gently reheat.

SEAFOOD SOUP WITH FENNEL

LOW-CALORIE · LOW-FAT

*A*ny firm-fleshed white fish such as cod, grouper or tile fish may be substituted for the scrod. Serve with lots of crusty bread.

Makes 6 servings (8 cups).
Recipe can be halved or doubled.
Nutrient Value Per Serving: 178 calories, 20 g protein, 6 g fat, 8 g carbohydrate, 412 mg sodium, 77 mg cholesterol.

2 tablespoons olive oil
2 small heads fennel (about 12 ounces), trimmed, cored and sliced (2½ cups)
1 medium-size onion, sliced
1 medium-size carrot, pared and sliced
2 large cloves garlic, finely chopped
2 cups seeded and diced tomatoes
1 teaspoon leaf thyme, crumbled
½ teaspoon salt
¼ teaspoon pepper
Pinch powdered saffron *(optional)*
2 cups water
1 bottle (8 ounces) clam juice
½ cup dry white wine
1 dozen littleneck or cherrystone clams, scrubbed
½ pound scrod fillet, cut into chunks
½ pound medium-size shrimp, peeled, deveined and cut lengthwise in half *(See How-To, page 340)*

1. Heat oil in large saucepan or Dutch oven over medium-high heat. Add fennel, onion, carrot and garlic; cook 5 minutes. Add tomato, thyme, salt, pepper, and saffron if using; cook, stirring frequently, 5 minutes.
2. Add water, clam juice and white wine. Bring to boiling over high heat. Add clams. Lower heat; cover and simmer 5 minutes or until clams begin to open. Discard any unopened clams. Add scrod and shrimp. Cook, covered, 3 to 4 minutes or until fish flakes when tested with fork and shrimp turn opaque.

BEET SOUP WITH VINEGAR

LOW-CALORIE · LOW-FAT
LOW-CHOLESTEROL

A *splash of balsamic vinegar makes our meaty borscht a little different.*

Makes 6 servings (7 cups).
Recipe can be halved or doubled.
Nutrient Value Per Serving: 167 calories, 17 g protein, 6 g fat, 11 g carbohydrate, 758 mg sodium, 49 mg cholesterol.

1 pound lean stew beef, such as chuck, bottom round or shank, cut into 1-inch cubes
1¾ cups water
1 can (13¾ ounces) beef broth OR: homemade (*see recipe, page 118*)
1 bay leaf
1 teaspoon salt
1 pound beets, tops removed to within 1 inch of beet and washed OR: 1 can (16 ounces) whole beets, drained*
½ cup cold water
2 medium-size onions, thinly sliced
1 large turnip, pared and cut into ½-inch cubes (1 cup)
¼ cup tomato puree
¼ cup balsamic vinegar OR: red wine vinegar
¼ teaspoon pepper
1 cup thinly sliced red or green cabbage

1. Combine beef, the 1¾ cups water, beef broth, bay leaf and ½ teaspoon salt in large Dutch oven or saucepan. Bring to boiling over high heat. Lower heat; cover and simmer about 1 hour or until beef is almost tender.
2. Meanwhile, combine beets, except for one, and enough water to cover in large nonaluminum saucepan. Bring to boiling. Lower heat; cover and simmer 30 to 40 minutes or until tender.
3. Peel, shred and mix remaining beet with the ½ cup cold water in small bowl. Set aside.

4. Drain whole beets when tender. When cool enough to handle, peel and cut into ½-inch cubes.
5. Add cubed beets, onion, turnip, tomato puree, vinegar, remaining ½ teaspoon salt and the pepper to beef in pan. Cover and simmer 30 minutes.
6. Drain reserved shredded beet; add to beef mixture along with cabbage. Cover and simmer 15 minutes or until the beef and vegetables are tender. Remove bay leaf before serving.

*Note: If using canned beets, shred 1 beet as in Step 3, but don't soak. Cut remaining beets in ½-inch cubes and add in Step 5.
Make-Ahead Tip: Soup can be frozen for up to 1 month; defrost overnight in refrigerator and reheat.
Microwave Directions for Cooking Beets (High Power Oven): Use four 4-ounce beets. Place 3 of the beets and 2 tablespoons water in microwave-safe 1½-quart casserole. Cover with lid. Microwave at 100% power 9 to 11 minutes until tender.

RED AS A BEET
Served hot as a meaty main-dish soup, or cold and clear as a first course, a true *borscht* gets its crimson glow from ruby-red beets.
■ The original borscht came from the Ukrainians, who used pork, ham or other meats to flavor the hot vegetable broth and add substance to the soup. Sugar and vinegar often add a sweet-and-sour tang.
■ Cold borscht is a meatless, warm-weather soup made simply from beets and cooking broth or water, seasoned with sugar and lemon juice or vinegar.

THE MANY FLAVORS OF MINESTRONE

Literally translated, *minestrone* means "big soup" and that means something different in every region of Italy. While it's always a hearty vegetable soup, key ingredients vary around the country. Minestrone from southern Italy is heavy with tomato and garlic. Fresh herbs dominate the soups of the northwest. Tuscan minestrone contains beans and pasta or bread, while Milanese minestrone is thick with rice. Florentine chefs never add grated cheese, yet in many areas it's a must. But all Italians agree on one thing—minestrone is best made ahead of time and reheated, allowing the flavors to mellow and meld.

BEGIN WITH SOUP

■ Keep first-course soup portions small, to avoid spoiling appetites for the remaining courses. Serve in small bowls, cups or ramekins.
■ Carefully balance the first-course soup with the rest of the meal. If the entree contains cream, avoid a creamy soup. Serve a lighter soup for meals with heartier entrees, more substantial soups for a lighter meal.

MINESTRONE

LOW-FAT · LOW-CHOLESTEROL

Even better the second or third day.

**Makes 8 servings (about 10 cups).
Recipe can be halved or doubled.**
Nutrient Value Per Serving: 180 calories, 8 g protein, 5 g fat, 28 g carbohydrate, 704 mg sodium, 0 mg cholesterol.

½ cup dried white pea beans, picked over and rinsed
Water
2 tablespoons olive oil
1 large onion, chopped
3 stalks celery, chopped
2 cloves garlic, finely chopped
4 cups chicken broth, canned OR: homemade (*see recipe, page 116*)
2 teaspoons leaf basil, crumbled
2 cans (16 ounces each) tomatoes, broken up
2 medium-size carrots, pared and chopped
½ cup orzo (rice-shaped) pasta
2 medium-size zucchini, chopped (2 cups)
¼ teaspoon pepper
Freshly grated Parmesan or Romano cheese

1. Cover beans with water in large Dutch oven or saucepan. Refrigerate overnight. Or to quick-soak beans, bring beans to boiling in water over high heat; cook 2 minutes. Remove from heat and let stand 1 hour.
2. Drain beans. Place in small bowl.
3. In same saucepan, heat oil over medium heat. Add onion and celery; sauté, stirring occasionally, 8 to 10 minutes or until tender. Add garlic; sauté, stirring occasionally, for 2 minutes.
4. Add chicken broth, beans and basil. Bring to boiling over high heat. Lower heat; cover and simmer 1 hour. Add tomato, carrot, orzo and zucchini. Return to boiling. Lower heat; cover and simmer 15 minutes or until vegetables and orzo are tender. Serve with grated cheese.

Make-Ahead Tip: This soup can be made ahead and refrigerated, covered, for up to 3 days. Gently reheat.

MUSHROOM AND GREEN ONION SOUP

If dried Chilean mushrooms are not available, you can substitute dried shiitake, porcini or Polish mushrooms. To lower the fat, substitute milk for the heavy cream.

Makes 6 servings (about 7 cups).
Recipe can be halved or doubled.

Nutrient Value Per Serving: 275 calories, 4 g protein, 23 g fat, 15 g carbohydrate, 927 mg sodium, 75 mg cholesterol.

2 ounces dried Chilean mushrooms
2 cups warm water
4 cups beef broth, canned OR: homemade
    (*see recipe, page 118*)
¼ cup (½ stick) *un*salted butter
3 bunches green onions, trimmed of 2
    inches of greens, thinly sliced (3 cups)
2 cloves garlic, crushed
⅛ teaspoon pepper
3 tablespoons all-purpose flour
1 cup heavy cream OR: milk
3 to 4 tablespoons finely chopped parsley
6 fresh white button mushrooms,
    stemmed and thinly sliced

1. Combine dried mushrooms and warm water in medium-size bowl. Let soak 30 minutes or until mushrooms are softened. Lift mushrooms out of water and reserve. Strain water through fine-meshed sieve lined with paper toweling or cheesecloth into small bowl. Reserve. Run mushrooms under cold water to remove any remaining grit.
2. Combine reserved mushrooms, strained soaking liquid and beef broth in medium-size saucepan. Bring to boiling over medium heat. Lower heat; simmer, covered, for 30 minutes or until mushrooms are tender. Drain mushrooms, reserving cooking liquid. Finely chop mushrooms. Strain liquid through fine-meshed sieve lined with paper toweling or cheesecloth to make certain no grit remains. Reserve liquid and mushrooms separately.

3. Melt butter in heavy-bottomed Dutch oven or saucepan over low heat. Add green onion, garlic, 2 to 3 tablespoons reserved liquid and pepper. Cover casserole and cook until green onion is soft, about 3 minutes.
4. Whisk in flour until well blended. Stir in remaining reserved liquid. Bring to boiling. Lower heat. Add reserved mushrooms. Cover; simmer 20 minutes.
5. Stir in cream; cook just until heated through; do not boil. Serve at once, garnished with parsley and sliced raw button mushrooms.

MUSHROOM SOUP MAKE-AHEAD TIP:
The soup can be prepared a day ahead through Step 4 and refrigerated, covered, for 2 or 3 days, or frozen for up to 1 month. Defrost overnight in the refrigerator and reheat. Finish as in Step 5.

NEW ENGLAND CLAM CHOWDER

For many more seafood recipes, see our Fish and Shellfish chapter, page 295. To reduce fat, substitute milk for the light cream.

Makes 8 servings (about 12 cups).
Recipe can be halved or doubled.
Nutrient Value Per Serving: 292 calories, 17 g protein, 16 g fat, 21 g carbohydrate, 143 mg sodium, 83 mg cholesterol.

24 chowder clams (about 13 pounds)
¼ cup (½ stick) *un*salted butter
1½ cups chopped onion
3 tablespoons all-purpose flour
2 cups water
3 large all-purpose potatoes (1½ pounds), cut in small cubes
½ teaspoon white pepper
1½ cups light cream OR: milk

Chopped parsley
Oyster crackers *(optional)*

1. Pick over clams, discarding any with broken shells. Scrub to remove sand. Rinse. Open clams over bowl to catch clam liquor. Strain liquor into bowl through sieve lined with cheesecloth. (You should have 2 cups of liquor.) Remove clam meat from shells. Coarsely chop. Refrigerate. (You should have about 2 cups of chopped clams.)
2. Heat butter in large saucepan over medium-low heat. Add onion; cook 8 minutes or until tender. Stir in flour until blended; cook, stirring, 1 minute.
3. Add reserved clam liquor, water, potatoes and pepper. Bring to boiling. Lower heat; simmer 10 minutes or until potatoes are tender.
4. Add clam meat; cook 3 minutes. Add cream; cook just until heated through. Ladle into bowls and garnish with parsley. Serve with oyster crackers, if you wish.

ONION SOUP WITH CHEESE CROUTONS

Toast bread at 325° for 15 minutes; melt cheese at 375°.
Makes 4 servings.
Recipe can be halved or doubled.
Nutrient Value Per Serving: 420 calories, 16 g protein, 24 g fat, 36 g carbohydrate, 1,050 mg sodium, 48 mg cholesterol.

2 to 3 Spanish onions (about 2 pounds)
2 tablespoons vegetable oil
2 tablespoons *un*salted butter
1 clove garlic, finely chopped
2 tablespoons all-purpose flour
2 cans (13¾ ounces each) beef broth OR: homemade (*see recipe, page 118*)
1 bay leaf
¼ to ½ teaspoon leaf thyme, crumbled
¼ to ½ teaspoon salt *(optional)*
4 slices French bread, diagonally sliced (¾ inch thick)
1 clove garlic, crushed
4 thin slices Gruyère cheese, or as needed
2 teaspoons grated Parmesan cheese
2 teaspoons lemon juice
Pepper, to taste

1. Peel onions and trim ends. Cut onions in half lengthwise; cut crosswise into thin slices.
2. Heat together oil and butter in large, heavy-bottomed saucepan or Dutch oven. Add onions; stir to coat well. Reduce heat to medium-low; cover and cook, stirring occasionally, until onions are very limp and just beginning to color, about 20 minutes.
3. Stir in chopped garlic. Increase heat to medium. Cook, uncovered, stirring frequently until onions are amber or caramel colored, about 30 minutes. Stir more frequently toward end of cooking time to prevent sticking.
4. Sprinkle onions with flour; stir to combine. Cook over medium heat 2 to 3 minutes, stirring frequently.
5. Stir in 1 cup broth, scraping up any

browned bits from bottom. Bring to gentle boiling; cook 1 minute. Stir in bay leaf, thyme, remaining broth and salt if using. Simmer, partially covered, 20 to 30 minutes.
6. Preheat oven to 325°.
7. Place bread slices on cookie sheet. Trim if necessary so slices fit into soup bowls. Place in preheated slow oven (325°) until golden brown and crispy, about 15 minutes. Increase oven temperature to moderate (375°).
8. Remove croutons from oven. Rub each crouton on both sides with crushed garlic clove. Place Gruyère cheese on each crouton so top is covered. Sprinkle each with ½ teaspoon Parmesan. Return to moderate oven (375°) until cheese is melted and golden brown, about 2 minutes.
9. Flavor soup with lemon juice and pepper to taste. Discard bay leaf. Ladle soup into 4 soup crocks or bowls. With spatula, transfer one crouton to each crock of soup. Serve immediately.

SLOWER IS BETTER
The secret to this classic onion soup recipe is patience—slowly cook the onions to develop a deep, rich flavor. To reduce the fat, omit the cheese-topped croutons.

ONION SOUP MAKE-AHEAD TIP:
The soup can be prepared a day ahead through Step 5, and refrigerated, covered. Gently reheat and proceed with Step 6.

HOT AND SOUR SOUP WITH TOFU

LOW-CALORIE · LOW-CHOLESTEROL
QUICK

Makes 8 servings (about 8 cups).
Recipe can be halved or doubled.
Nutrient Value Per Serving: 198 calories, 12 g protein, 11 g fat, 16 g carbohydrate, 589 mg sodium, 0 mg cholesterol.

3 tablespoons vegetable oil
2 large sweet red peppers, cored, seeded and cut into ¾ × ¼-inch strips (about ¾ cup)
1 small bunch green onions, cut diagonally into ¾-inch pieces (about 1½ cups)
2 cups chicken broth, canned OR: homemade (see recipe, page 116)
2 cups Vegetable Stock (see recipe, page 124) OR: water
2 tablespoons soy sauce
2 teaspoons red wine vinegar
½ teaspoon crushed red pepper flakes
¼ teaspoon salt
⅛ teaspoon pepper
2 tablespoons cornstarch
3 tablespoons water
1 teaspoon Oriental sesame oil
½ pound snow peas, fresh or frozen
1 pound firm tofu, drained and cut into ½-inch cubes
1 can (8 ounces) sliced water chestnuts, drained

1. Heat oil in large saucepan over medium-high heat. Add peppers and onion; stir-fry about 5 minutes.
2. Add chicken broth, Vegetable Stock and soy sauce. Bring to boiling. Lower heat; simmer for about 5 minutes.
3. Stir together vinegar, red pepper flakes, salt, pepper, cornstarch, water and sesame oil in small bowl until smooth. Add to soup with fresh snow peas; cook for about 5 minutes or until thickened and bubbly.
4. Add tofu, frozen snow peas if using, and water chestnuts. Gently heat through.

Microwave Directions (High Power Oven):
Reduce oil to 2 tablespoons. Combine oil, red peppers and green onion in microwave-safe 4½-quart casserole with lid. Microwave, covered, at 100% power 6 minutes, stirring once. Stir in broths and soy sauce. Microwave, covered, at 100% power 9 to 10 minutes or until boiling. Stir together vinegar, pepper flakes, salt, pepper, cornstarch, water and sesame oil until smooth. Stir into casserole with snow peas. Microwave, covered, at 100% power for 3 minutes until mixture thickens and boils. Stir again. Add tofu and water chestnuts. Microwave, covered, at 100% power for 3 minutes.

CURRIED PUMPKIN-CAULIFLOWER SOUP

LOW-FAT · LOW-CHOLESTEROL

For more special occasions, dollop with plain yogurt, top with spicy-sweet chutney and sprinkle with golden raisins. Other vegetables, such as pearl onions, can be substituted for the cauliflower. Garnish with a little shredded coconut or chopped parsley. (Pictured at bottom right.)

Makes 6 servings (6 cups).
Recipe can be halved or doubled.
Nutrient Value Per Serving: 119 calories,
3 g protein, 4 g fat, 19 g carbohydrate,
429 mg sodium, 10 mg cholesterol.

2 tablespoons *un*salted butter
2 cups coarsely chopped cauliflower
1 large onion, chopped
2 to 3 teaspoons curry powder
4 cups Vegetable Stock *(see recipe, page 116)* OR: chicken broth, canned OR: homemade *(see recipe, page 116)*
1 can (16 ounces) solid-pack pumpkin puree
1 teaspoon salt
⅓ cup coarsely chopped cashew nuts *(optional)*

1. Melt butter in large, heavy saucepan over medium heat. Add cauliflower; sauté about 5 minutes or until almost tender. Remove cauliflower with slotted spoon to medium-size bowl. Reserve.
2. Add onion and curry powder to saucepan; sauté about 5 minutes or until almost tender. Add 2 cups Vegetable Broth. Bring to boiling. Lower heat; cover and simmer for 15 minutes.
3. Cool mixture slightly. Working in batches, place mixture in blender.
(continued)

From top: Vegetable Soup (page 132) and Curried Pumpkin-Cauliflower Soup (this page).

SOUPS: THE THICK AND THE THIN OF IT

■ Puree leftovers to start a soup. Starchy fruits and vegetables such as bananas, potatoes, turnips and winter squash make thicker purees, while watery fruits and vegetables like melon, juicy pears, cucumbers and tomatoes make thinner purees.

■ To thicken stocks and broths for a heartier soup, stir in pureed cooked vegetables, beans, potatoes, rice or pasta (1 cup of starchy puree will thicken approximately 8 cups of soup).

■ To make soup from a vegetable puree, simply thin with stock or bouillon and season to taste.

SERVING SOUP

■ For a casual presentation, serve soups in mugs, accompanied by crackers or breadsticks.

■ Serve squash and pumpkin soups in their shells. Acorn squash makes a rustic single-serving container.

■ Smaller portions of rich soups look appealing in dessert dishes, ramekins or cups set in saucers.

■ To display them at their hearty best, ladle chunky soups with lots of ingredients into wide, shallow bowls.

CURRIED PUMPKIN-CAULIFLOWER SOUP

(*continued*)

Whirl until smooth puree, about 1 minute. Return broth mixture to saucepan.

4. Add remaining 2 cups broth, pumpkin, salt and reserved cauliflower to saucepan. Bring to boiling over medium-high heat. Lower heat; cover and simmer 10 minutes or until cauliflower is tender. Stir in the cashews, if using.

Make-Ahead Tip: This soup can be made ahead and refrigerated, covered, for up to 3 days. Gently reheat. If using the cashews, do not add until serving time.

VEGETABLE SOUP

LOW-FAT · LOW-CHOLESTEROL

Experiment with your own favorite vegetables. Use our Vegetable Stock to make this soup truly vegetarian. (Pictured on page 131, top.)

Makes 8 servings (about 8 cups).
Recipe can be halved or doubled.
Nutrient Value Per Serving: 147 calories, 4 g protein, 7 g fat, 20 g carbohydrate, 601 mg sodium, 8 mg cholesterol.

2 tablespoons olive oil
2 tablespoons *un*salted butter
2 medium-size leeks, trimmed, thoroughly washed and finely chopped
2 medium-size sweet green peppers, cored, seeded and chopped
2 medium-size sweet red peppers, cored, seeded and chopped
2 cloves garlic, crushed
2 teaspoons leaf basil, crumbled
½ pound small mushrooms, quartered
2 tablespoons all-purpose flour
6 cups Vegetable Stock (*see recipe, page 116*) OR: chicken broth, canned OR: homemade (*see recipe, page 116*)

2 medium-size yellow squash, cut lengthwise in quarters and crosswise in ¼-inch-thick slices
2 medium-size zucchini squash, cut lengthwise in quarters and crosswise in ¼-inch-thick slices
2 teaspoons salt
¼ teaspoon pepper
Freshly grated Parmesan cheese (*optional*)

1. Heat olive oil and butter in large Dutch oven or saucepan over medium heat. Add leeks, green and red peppers, garlic and basil; sauté 5 minutes. Add mushrooms; sauté about 5 minutes or until lightly browned.

2. Push vegetables to one side of pan. Gradually stir in flour. Cook, stirring constantly, 3 to 5 minutes or until thickened and bubbly. Gradually add broth, stirring constantly, until well blended and smooth.

3. Add yellow squash, zucchini, salt and pepper. Bring to boiling. Cover; lower heat and simmer 10 minutes or until vegetables are tender. Serve with grated Parmesan, if you wish.

Make-Ahead Tip: The soup can be made ahead and refrigerated, covered, for up to 3 days. Gently reheat.

MEATLESS FEAST

Vegetable Soup (this page)

Brown Rice, Nut and Kale Loaf (213)

Cucumber and Radish with Yogurt

Melon and Blueberries with Yogurt Topping (542)

ASPARAGUS SUMMER SOUP

When asparagus is not in season, substitute fresh green beans, trimmed and cut into 1-inch pieces. For a lighter soup, omit the heavy cream.

Makes 8 servings (about 9 cups).
Recipe can be halved or doubled.

Nutrient Value Per Serving: 225 calories, 6 g protein, 17 g fat, 15 g carbohydrate, 736 mg sodium, 50 mg cholesterol.

---

1 pound fresh asparagus, trimmed and peeled
5 tablespoons *un*salted butter
2 leeks, white part only and 2 inches of the green, thinly sliced and well washed (3 cups)
5 cups chicken broth, canned OR: homemade (*see recipe, page 116*)
1 pound fresh spinach, stemmed, washed and dried
1 teaspoon sugar
2½ tablespoons all-purpose flour
¼ teaspoon salt
⅛ teaspoon white pepper
1 cup fresh peas (from about 1 pound pods) OR: 1 cup frozen peas
½ to 1 cup heavy cream OR: milk
1 cup heart of Boston or Bibb lettuce, leaves separated, washed and dried
Finely snipped fresh chives and/or watercress leaves, for garnish

1. Cut asparagus stalks into 1-inch pieces; reserve tips separately.
2. Heat 2 tablespoons butter in heavy saucepan or Dutch oven. Add leeks and ⅓ cup broth; cover and cook over medium heat until the stalks of the leeks are tender, about 5 minutes. Add asparagus stalks. Cover and cook 3 minutes. Add remaining broth. Bring to boiling. Lower heat; simmer until asparagus is very tender, 10 to 12 minutes.
3. Add 2 packed cups of spinach (reserve remaining spinach for Step 5)

and the sugar to saucepan. Cook until spinach is tender, about 5 minutes. Working in batches, place liquid and solids in food processor. Whirl until very smooth. Set aside.
4. Heat remaining butter in saucepan. Whisk in flour until well blended. Cook, stirring, 1 minute; do not let brown. Whisk in pureed soup until

(continued)

From top: Asparagus Summer Soup (this page) and Tomato and Sweet Red Pepper Soup (page 134).

SOUP GARNISHES

Garnishes balance texture, flavor and color of soups.

- Top a creamy soup with a crunchy garnish such as croutons, toasted sliced almonds, pumpkin seeds, thinly sliced carrot or tiny broccoli flowerets.
- Enhance pale soups with colorful garnishes such as chopped fresh herbs, finely chopped green onion, chopped sweet red or green pepper, and drained, diced tomatoes.
- Add a cool garnish to a spicy soup, such as a dollop of plain yogurt blended with shredded cucumber.
- Consider the Japanese notion of garnishes for clear or broth soups, and treat each bowl as a work of art. Slices of fresh wild mushrooms, a decoratively cut carrot slice or a sprig or two of parsley create a dramatic effect.
- Swirl or drizzle a light-colored puree into a darker-colored soup or vice versa. Corn chowder is uplifted by a swirl of red pepper puree; tomato soup gets pizazz from a small dollop of pesto-flavored whipped cream or yogurt.
- Leftover vegetables, pasta and rice make great garnishes.

ASPARAGUS SUMMER SOUP (*continued*)

smooth and blended. Bring to boiling. Season soup with salt and pepper. Lower heat. Add peas; simmer until barely tender, about 5 minutes, or less time if peas are frozen. Add asparagus tips; simmer until the asparagus is tender, about 5 minutes.

5. Add heavy cream and heat through; do not boil. Stir in remaining spinach and lettuce. Gently heat; do not boil; the lettuce should remain somewhat crisp. Garnish with chives and/or watercress.

Make-Ahead Tip: The soup can be made ahead through Step 4 and refrigerated for a day or two, or frozen for up to 1 month. Defrost overnight in the refrigerator, gently reheat, and proceed with Step 5.

TOMATO AND SWEET RED PEPPER SOUP

This tasty soup works best with the ripest tomatoes you can find. But good-quality drained canned tomatoes are a fine substitute. For a lighter soup with less fat, omit the sour cream.

Makes 8 servings (8 cups).
Recipe can be halved or doubled.
Nutrient Value Per Serving: 173 calories, 4 g protein, 14 g fat, 10 g carbohydrate, 760 mg sodium, 29 mg cholesterol.

5 tablespoons *un*salted butter
1 teaspoon olive oil
1 large onion, quartered and thinly sliced
4 tomatoes (6 ounces each), peeled, seeded and chopped (3 cups)
2 sweet red peppers, cored, seeded and diced (2½ cups)
1 tablespoon fresh thyme leaves OR: 1½ teaspoons dried
2 teaspoons sweet paprika

⅛ teaspoon sugar
6 cups chicken broth, canned OR: homemade (*see recipe, page 116*)
Salt and pepper, to taste
1½ tablespoons all-purpose flour
¾ cup dairy sour cream OR: heavy cream
1 cup finely diced ripe tomatoes
1 cup finely diced sweet green and red pepper
2 to 3 tablespoons snipped fresh chives

1. Heat together 3 tablespoons butter and the olive oil in large saucepan or pot over medium heat. Add onion; cook until soft but not browned, about 5 minutes. Stir in tomato, red pepper, thyme, paprika and sugar. Cook over medium-low heat until all the tomato juices have evaporated, about 25 minutes.

2. Stir in chicken broth and salt and pepper to taste. Bring to boiling. Lower heat; simmer, partially covered, for 25 minutes.

3. Strain soup, reserving broth and solids separately. Working in batches if necessary, place solids in food processor or blender. Whirl until a smooth puree. Whisk puree into reserved liquid in a bowl.

4. Melt remaining butter in saucepan over medium heat. Stir in flour; cook, stirring, for 1 minute; do not let brown. Slowly whisk in soup. Bring to boiling. Lower heat; simmer, partially covered, for 10 minutes.

5. Whisk sour cream or heavy cream into soup. Gently heat through; do not let boil. Adjust seasoning. Garnish with peppers and chives.

Make-Ahead Tip: The soup may be prepared ahead through Step 4 and refrigerated, covered, for up to 3 days, or frozen for up to 1 month. Defrost overnight in the refrigerator, gently reheat and then proceed with Step 5.

SWEET POTATO SOUP

If your taste runs to the less spicy, omit the jalapeño pepper. For a lighter soup, omit the heavy cream and substitute nonfat plain yogurt for the sour cream.

Makes 8 servings (about 8 cups).
Recipe can be halved or doubled.
Nutrient Value Per Serving: 238 calories, 5 g protein, 14 g fat, 24 g carbohydrate, 834 mg sodium, 38 mg cholesterol.

---

3 tablespoons *un*salted butter
1 cup finely chopped onion
3 sweet potatoes (1½ pounds), peeled and chopped
6 cups chicken broth, canned OR: homemade (*see recipe, page 116*)
1 jalapeño pepper, seeded and thinly sliced
1½ cups corn kernels, fresh or frozen
½ cup heavy cream
¼ teaspoon salt
⅛ teaspoon pepper
½ cup dairy sour cream OR: nonfat plain yogurt
1½ teaspoons fresh lime juice
½ teaspoon grated lemon rind
2 to 3 tablespoons tiny fresh cilantro leaves OR: parsley leaves

1. Melt butter in large saucepan or Dutch oven over medium heat. Add onion; sauté until onion begins to brown, about 5 minutes. Reduce heat to medium-low; cover and cook until onion is soft and nicely browned, about 10 minutes. Stir in sweet potato and chicken broth. Bring to boiling. Lower the heat; simmer, partially covered, for about 25 minutes or until the potatoes are tender.
2. Strain soup through colander, reserving solids and liquid separately, transferring liquid to saucepan. Working in batches if necessary, place solids in food processor. Whirl until smooth puree. Whisk puree into reserved liquid in saucepan. Stir in jalapeño pepper and corn; simmer 5 minutes or until jalapeño pepper is crisp-tender. Whisk cream, salt and pepper into soup.
3. Whisk together sour cream, lime juice and lemon rind in small bowl. Serve soup in individual soup bowls. Garnish with a dollop of sour cream mixture and a sprinkle of cilantro leaves or parsley.

CREAM OF BROCCOLI AND STILTON SOUP

For a lighter soup, omit the half-and-half. Reserve 1 cup of the broth after straining in Step 4 and puree the Stilton with it rather than the half-and-half.

Makes 12 servings (about 12 cups).
Recipe can be halved or doubled.
Nutrient Value Per Serving: 190 calories, 7 g protein, 16 g fat, 5 g carbohydrate, 858 mg sodium, 42 mg cholesterol.

---

8 ounces Stilton cheese
7 tablespoons *un*salted butter
1 bunch broccoli (about 12 ounces), trimmed, peeled and cut into 1-inch pieces (about 4 cups)
⅓ cup diced celery
1 cup finely chopped onion
¼ teaspoon white pepper
7 cups chicken broth, canned OR: homemade (*see recipe, page 116*)
2½ tablespoons all-purpose flour
1¼ cups half-and-half OR: heavy cream OR: milk

1. Trim Stilton of outer yellow-brown crust and use only the center. You should have about 6 ounces. Crumble cheese and set aside.
2. Melt 4 tablespoons butter in large, heavy saucepan or Dutch oven. Add broccoli, celery, onion and white pepper. Partially cover and simmer just until tender, about 5 minutes.

(continued)

SWEET POTATO SOUP MAKE-AHEAD TIP:
The soup can be made ahead through Step 2, without adding the cream, and refrigerated, covered, for up to 3 days, or frozen for up to 1 month. Defrost in the refrigerator overnight. To serve the soup, gently heat. Whisk in cream. Heat through; do not let boil. Proceed with Step 3.

THE WAY TO PUREE

■ Use a *food mill* to make a puree from fibrous foods such as asparagus, green beans and fresh peas or from foods that have been cooked with their skin on, such as eggplant or tomatoes.

■ Press well cooked, skinned, mashed foods such as potatoes, rutabaga and turnips through a *coarse-mesh sieve* to strain out lumps or stray bits of skin.

■ A *blender* is fine for pureeing small batches of liquidy soups, while a *food processor* is better for pureeing larger or thicker mixtures.

■ For the smoothest puree, whirl soup mixture in a blender or processor first, then press through a fine-mesh strainer. For How to Make a Pureed Soup, see page 119.

CREAM OF BROCCOLI AND STILTON SOUP
(*continued*)

BROCCOLI AND STILTON SOUP SERVING IDEAS
Serve as a first course to your favorite chicken dish or for lunch with crusty whole-wheat or rye bread.

WHAT COLOR IS YOUR GAZPACHO?
Gazpacho is a cool, light, refreshing soup made from finely diced fresh vegetables. Gazpacho may be predominantly red or green, depending on the vegetables used. For a creamy pink gazpacho, stir in sour cream or yogurt just before serving. Gazpacho is sometimes thickened with fresh bread crumbs soaked in water.

A GAZPACHO OCCASION
Serve as a first course or as a light luncheon with a grilled chicken sandwich such as our Chicken and Basil Party Sandwich *(see recipe, page 114)*. Also try gazpacho as a light and satisfying snack.

3. Stir in broth. Bring to boiling. Lower heat; simmer, covered, 30 to 35 minutes or until vegetables are very tender.

4. Strain soup, reserving solids and liquid separately. Place solids, working in batches if necessary, with ½ cup reserved liquid in food processor. Whirl until very smooth puree. Whisk puree into remaining liquid in medium-size bowl. Set aside.

5. Melt remaining butter in saucepan over moderate heat. Whisk in flour until well combined; cook, whisking constantly, until mixture is hazelnut brown, about 2 minutes; be careful not to scorch flour. Whisk in soup until blended. Bring to boiling. Lower heat; simmer, whisking occasionally, for 15 minutes.

6. Combine half-and-half and Stilton cheese in food processor. Whirl until mixture is smooth. Whisk cheese mixture into soup until well blended. Gently heat through; do not boil.

Make-Ahead Tip: The soup may be prepared up to 2 days ahead through Step 5 and then refrigerated, covered, or frozen for up to 1 month. Defrost overnight in the refrigerator. Gently reheat. Then proceed with Step 6.

GAZPACHO

LOW-CALORIE • LOW-FAT
LOW-CHOLESTEROL

A *food processor and canned vegetable juice make short work of this warm-weather favorite. For a milder version, replace the spicy juice with regular vegetable juice.*

Makes 8 servings (about 8 cups).
Recipe can be halved or doubled.
Nutrient Value Per Serving: 101 calories, 3 g protein, 4 g fat, 15 g carbohydrate, 774 mg sodium, 0 mg cholesterol.

1 can (64 ounces) spicy vegetable juice
1 cup diced celery
1 cup diced sweet green pepper
1 cup diced, pared, seeded cucumber
¾ cup chopped green onion
¼ cup lime juice (2 limes)
1½ cups diced avocado (1 medium-size)
Garnishes *(optional):* dairy sour cream,
    fresh coriander, diced celery, diced
    sweet green pepper, diced cucumber
    or chopped green onion

1. Place 3 cups spicy vegetable juice, ½ cup diced celery, ½ cup diced green pepper, ½ cup diced cucumber, ½ cup chopped green onion and lime juice in large food processor, or working in batches, in regular processor. Whirl until smooth. Pour mixture into bowl.

2. Stir in remaining 5 cups spicy vegetable juice, ½ cup diced celery, ½ cup diced green pepper, ½ cup diced cucumber, ¼ cup chopped green onion and the avocado. Chill before serving. Garnish, if you wish.

Make-Ahead Tip: The soup can be prepared a day ahead and refrigerated, covered.

COLD CHERRY-BUTTERMILK SOUP

LOW-CALORIE · LOW-FAT
LOW-CHOLESTEROL · LOW-SODIUM

Serve as a first course, or as a dessert with assorted cookies, or even as a sauce over ice cream or cake. Garnish with a dollop of sour cream or yogurt or a tiny scoop of vanilla ice cream.

Makes 10 servings (about 6 cups).
Recipe can be halved or doubled.
Nutrient Value Per Serving: 130 calories, 3 g protein, 1 g fat, 31 g carbohydrate, 58 mg sodium, 2 mg cholesterol.

3 cans (17 ounces each) sweet pitted
　　cherries, drained
2 tablespoons finely chopped crystallized
　　ginger
2 cups buttermilk
¼ cup port wine

Place cherries and crystallized ginger in food processor. Whirl until smooth puree. Pour cherry mixture into large bowl. Stir in buttermilk and wine. Refrigerate until chilled.

CHILLED MINTED PEACH SOUP

LOW-CALORIE · LOW-FAT
LOW-CHOLESTEROL · LOW-SODIUM

This soup is best made with fresh peaches, but canned is an easy substitute.

Makes 10 servings (about 5 cups).
Recipe can be halved or doubled.
Nutrient Value Per Serving: 90 calories, 2 g protein, 1 g fat, 18 g carbohydrate, 22 mg sodium, 5 mg cholesterol.

3 pounds ripe peaches, peeled, pitted and
　　cut into quarters*
2 tablespoons brown sugar, or more to
　　taste
1 container (8 ounces) lowfat vanilla
　　yogurt
½ cup half-and-half
1 tablespoon finely chopped fresh mint

Place peaches and brown sugar in food processor. Whirl until smooth puree. Pour peach mixture into large bowl. Whisk in yogurt, half-and-half and mint. Chill before serving.

*Note: For canned peach version of this soup, use 2 cans (29 ounces each) large peach halves, drained. Omit the brown sugar and use 2 tablespoons finely chopped fresh mint.

From top: Cold Cherry-Buttermilk Soup and Chilled Minted Peach Soup (both this page).

COLD SOUPS MAKE-AHEAD TIP:
These soups can be made a day ahead and refrigerated, covered.

DESSERT SAUCE
Serve Chilled Minted Peach Soup over ice cream sundaes and plain cakes, and no one will guess that your sauce is a soup.

VEAL AND PEPPER STEW MAKE-AHEAD TIP:

This stew can be made up to 2 days ahead and refrigerated, covered, and the flavor will improve. Gently reheat.

VEAL AND PEPPER STEW WITH MUSHROOMS

LOW-CALORIE

Refrigerate overnight, then remove any excess fat from the surface. Serve the stew with rice, noodles or spätzle.

Makes 6 servings. Recipe can be doubled.
Nutrient Value Per Serving: 305 calories, 33 g protein, 13 g fat, 13 g carbohydrate, 739 mg sodium, 125 mg cholesterol.

¼ cup all-purpose flour
1 teaspoon salt
½ teaspoon pepper
2 pounds boneless veal shoulder, cut into 1½-inch pieces
4 tablespoons olive oil
2 cups onion wedges (about 2 medium-size onions)
2 large cloves garlic, finely chopped
¾ cup dry red wine
1 can (13¾ ounces) beef broth OR: homemade (see recipe, page 118)
1 bay leaf
3 cups mushroom halves (about ½ pound)

1 large sweet red pepper, cored, seeded and cut into 1½-inch pieces
1 large sweet yellow pepper, cored, seeded and cut into 1½-inch pieces
Chopped parsley and/or thinly sliced raw mushrooms, for garnish (optional)

1. Combine flour, salt and pepper on waxed paper. Dredge veal in flour.
2. Working in batches to avoid overcrowding, brown veal in 3 tablespoons oil in large saucepan or Dutch oven over medium-high heat. Remove veal as it browns to a bowl.
3. Add remaining tablespoon oil to drippings in saucepan. Place over medium heat. Add onion and garlic; sauté 5 minutes. Add wine; increase heat to high, stirring up any browned bits from bottom of saucepan. Return veal to saucepan. Add beef broth and bay leaf. Bring to boiling. Lower heat; cover and simmer 45 minutes.
4. Stir in mushrooms and peppers. Bring to boiling. Lower heat; cover and simmer 30 minutes or until meat and vegetables are tender. Skim any fat from the surface and discard. Remove bay leaf before serving. Garnish with chopped parsley and/or very thin slices of raw mushrooms, if you wish.

LAMB STEW WITH POTATO TOPPING

The mounds of potatoes slowly melt into the hot stew.

Bake potatoes at 350° for 1 hour.
Makes 6 servings.
Recipe can be halved or doubled.
Nutrient Value Per Serving: 444 calories, 35 g protein, 15 g fat, 42 g carbohydrate, 473 mg sodium, 109 mg cholesterol.

2 pounds boneless lamb shoulder, cut into 1-inch cubes
1 tablespoon vegetable oil
2 cloves garlic, sliced
1 bay leaf
1 teaspoon leaf thyme, crumbled
2 cups beef broth, canned OR: homemade (*see recipe, page 118*)
½ cup dry white wine OR: beef broth
1 package (12 ounces) frozen baby carrots
1¼ pounds baking potatoes
1¼ pounds sweet potatoes
2 tablespoons *un*salted butter
¼ cup milk
Salt and pepper, to taste
2 cups frozen pearl onions

1. Preheat oven to moderate (350°).
2. Working in batches, brown lamb in oil in large saucepan over medium-high heat. As lamb browns, remove to bowl. Remove all but about ½ tablespoon fat from drippings.
3. Add garlic, bay leaf and thyme to drippings in pan; cook over medium heat, stirring occasionally, 1 minute. Add beef broth and wine, stirring up any browned bits from bottom of saucepan. Add lamb and carrots to saucepan. Bring to boiling. Lower heat; cover and simmer 1 hour and 15 minutes.
4. Meanwhile, bake white and sweet potatoes in preheated moderate oven (350°) for 1 hour or until soft. When cool, remove skins from potatoes.

5. Beat together white potatoes, 1 tablespoon butter, milk and salt and pepper to taste in medium-size bowl with electric mixer until smooth. Repeat with sweet potatoes and remaining tablespoon butter.
6. Stir pearl onions into stew. Bring to boiling over high heat. Lower heat; cover and simmer 10 to 15 minutes or until lamb and vegetables are tender.
7. Spoon mashed potatoes on top of stew. Increase heat to medium; cover and cook 10 minutes or until heated through. Remove bay leaf.

Make-Ahead Tip: The stew can be made up to 2 days ahead through Step 3 and refrigerated, covered. After the stew has been refrigerated, remove the fat from the surface. Gently reheat; proceed with Step 4.

SLASHING THE FAT
■ When making stock, allow enough time to cool and refrigerate the stock so you'll be able to remove the solidified fat from the surface.
■ For fast de-fatting, pour the broth into a shallow metal baking pan and place in the freezer until the fat floats to the top.
■ Refrigerate canned broth before opening it. The fat will be floating on the top.

HOW TO MAKE CROUTONS

Croutons add crunch and are a good way to use leftover bread. Prepare a few days ahead to save time, and then re-crisp in warm oven.

■ For best results, cut bread into uniform pieces: cubes, diamonds, triangles or circles.

■ Make with Italian or French bread, or from any other bread, including firm pieces of cornbread.

■ For seasoned croutons, sprinkle with sesame seeds, poppy seeds, caraway seeds or curry powder before baking or sautéing.

■ For lightly sautéed croutons, use a non-stick skillet. Heat olive oil or butter in the skillet over medium heat. For extra flavor, add a clove or two of garlic, crushed but left whole, while the butter or oil heats. Remove garlic before adding bread. Add bread, a little at a time, and sauté until golden brown. Place on paper toweling to drain.

■ To oven-bake croutons, place bread pieces on baking sheet lightly coated with nonstick vegetable-oil cooking spray and bake in 350° oven for 10 to 15 minutes or until golden brown.

TEX-MEX BEEF STEW WITH CORN

A *hearty stew, chunky with pieces of corn on the cob.*

Makes 6 servings.
Recipe can be halved or doubled.
Nutrient Value Per Serving: 375 calories, 36 g protein, 15 g fat, 23 g carbohydrate, 691 mg sodium, 91 mg cholesterol.

3 tablespoons all-purpose flour
¼ teaspoon salt
¼ teaspoon pepper
2 pounds beef stew meat, cut into 1½-inch cubes
3½ tablespoons vegetable oil
2 medium-size onions, cut into wedges (about 2 cups)
1 can (4 ounces) chopped green chilies
1 teaspoon ground coriander
1 teaspoon ground cumin
½ teaspoon leaf oregano, crumbled
1 can (16 ounces) whole tomatoes, in thick puree
1 cup beef broth, canned OR: homemade (*see recipe, page 118*)
¼ cup catsup
2 zucchini (about 6 ounces each), cut into 1-inch pieces
2 ears fresh or frozen corn on the cob, each cut into 6 pieces
Dairy sour cream and/or thin strips sweet red pepper, for garnish *(optional)*

1. Combine flour, salt and pepper on waxed paper. Dredge beef cubes in flour mixture to coat.
2. Working in batches, brown beef in 2½ tablespoons oil in large saucepan or Dutch oven over medium-high heat. Remove beef as it browns to a bowl.
3. Add remaining 1 tablespoon vegetable oil to saucepan and heat. Add onion, chilies, coriander, cumin and oregano; cook 5 minutes, stirring frequently. Add tomatoes, broth and catsup, stirring up any browned bits from bottom of saucepan. Return beef to saucepan. Bring to boiling. Lower heat; cover and simmer 1 hour.
4. Add zucchini and corn. Bring to boiling. Lower heat; cover and simmer 30 minutes or until beef and vegetables are tender. Garnish with dollop of dairy sour cream and/or sweet red pepper.

Make-Ahead Tip: The stew can be made up to 2 days ahead and refrigerated, covered. Gently reheat.

PORK STEW WITH MANGO AND PLANTAINS

If you are not able to locate a mango for this stew, substitute sweet potatoes.

Makes 8 servings.
Recipe can be halved or doubled.
Nutrient Value Per Serving: 379 calories, 24 g protein, 16 g fat, 36 g carbohydrate, 401 mg sodium, 77 mg cholesterol.

¼ cup all-purpose flour
½ teaspoon salt
½ teaspoon pepper
2 pounds pork stew meat, cut into ¾-inch cubes
3 tablespoons vegetable oil
1 large onion, cut into ¾-inch pieces
2 medium-size sweet red peppers, cored, seeded and cut into ¾-inch pieces
2 cloves garlic, finely chopped
1 can (13¾ ounces) beef broth OR: homemade (*see recipe, page 118*)
1 cup water
Cinnamon stick (½ inch)
4 whole cloves
⅛ teaspoon leaf oregano, crumbled
2 large plantains OR: green bananas, cut into ¾-inch-thick slices
2 medium-size tomatoes, cut in wedges
1 large mango (about 1¼ pounds), pared, pitted and cut into ¾-inch cubes (about 3 cups)

1. Combine flour, ¼ teaspoon salt and ¼ teaspoon pepper in plastic bag. Add pork; shake vigorously to coat.
2. Heat 1 tablespoon oil in large Dutch oven or saucepan over medium-high heat. Working in batches, sauté pork in oil 5 to 8 minutes or until browned on all sides. Remove pieces as they brown to platter lined with paper toweling to drain. Add 1 tablespoon more oil as needed.
3. Reduce heat to moderate. Add remaining oil to saucepan. Add onion,
(*continued*)

PLANTAINS: NOT JUST ANOTHER BANANA

Though they look like jumbo bananas and are, in fact, related, plantains are tougher, thicker-skinned, starchier and must be cooked before eating. More often than not they are served as a side dish or in a savory soup or stew.

■ Green, unripe plantains have a bland flavor and are usually used in stews and soups, as a fried snack, or boiled and mashed like potatoes.

■ Ripe, brown plantains have a flavor similar to sweet potato or winter squash and can be baked or sautéed.

■ Overripe plantains have a black skin and a banana-like flavor and are often cooked in a spicy sugar syrup and served as a dessert or as a sweet side dish with meat, rice and beans.

■ To peel a plantain, cut off each end with a sharp knife. Cut the fruit crosswise in half. Make lengthwise cuts down the ridges of each half. Peel skin off to the side.

PORK STEW WITH MANGO AND PLANTAINS
(*continued*)

red pepper and garlic; sauté 5 to 8 minutes or until golden.

4. Add pork, beef broth, water, cinnamon, cloves, oregano and remaining ¼ teaspoon salt and pepper. Bring to boiling. Lower heat; cover and simmer 30 minutes or until pork is almost tender.

5. Add plantains; cover and simmer 3 to 5 minutes or just until tender. Add tomatoes and mango; heat through.

Make-Ahead Tip: The stew can be prepared through Step 4 and refrigerated, covered, for up to 3 days or frozen for up to 1 month. Defrost overnight in the refrigerator, gently reheat and then proceed with Step 5.

CAROLINA CHICKEN STEW WITH LIMA BEANS AND CORN

LOW-CALORIE · LOW-FAT
LOW-CHOLESTEROL

This chicken stew takes its inspiration from a version originally made with rabbit or squirrel. For a lower-fat version, remove the skin before cooking.

Makes 12 servings.
Recipe can be halved or doubled.
Nutrient Value Per Serving: 198 calories, 19 g protein, 4 g fat, 22 g carbohydrate, 552 mg sodium, 42 mg cholesterol.

1 broiler-fryer chicken (about 3½ pounds), cut up
4 cups chicken broth, canned OR: homemade (*see recipe, page 116*)
2 stalks celery, sliced
1 teaspoon leaf thyme, crumbled
¾ teaspoon leaf marjoram, crumbled
½ teaspoon salt

½ teaspoon pepper
1 pound (2 large) all-purpose potatoes, pared and cut into ½-inch cubes
2 medium-size onions, coarsely chopped
1 can (16 ounces) crushed tomatoes
4 medium-size carrots, pared and cut into ¾-inch cubes
1 package (10 ounces) frozen baby lima beans
1 package (10 ounces) frozen whole-kernel corn

1. Combine chicken, chicken broth, celery, thyme, marjoram, salt and pepper in large saucepan or Dutch oven. Bring to boiling. Lower heat; cover and simmer for about 30 minutes or until chicken is tender and no longer pink near bone. Remove chicken from broth. Skim fat from broth. When chicken is cool enough to handle, remove meat from bones and remove skin. Cut meat into bite-size pieces. Reserve.

2. Add potato, onion, tomato and carrot to saucepan. Cover and return to boiling over medium heat; lower heat and simmer 20 minutes. Add lima beans and corn; simmer, covered, 10 minutes. Stir in reserved chicken. Gently heat through.

Make-Ahead Tip: The stew can be made up to 3 days ahead and refrigerated, covered, or frozen for up to 1 month. Defrost in the refrigerator overnight and gently reheat.

STEW FOR A CROWD

Zucchini-Stuffed Mushrooms (98)

Carolina Chicken Stew with Lima Beans and Corn (this page)

Buttermilk Biscuits with Parsley (76)

Citrus Layer Cake (507)

Warm Spinach and Pear Salad with Bacon Dressing (page 177).

CHAPTER 5

SALADS AND DRESSINGS

SUPER SALADS

Take advantage of the new abundance of salad greens at supermarkets and farmstands, or grow your own for fresh-picked flavor. Create multi-flavored, multi-textured salads from mixed greens (and whites and reds) by choosing three or four varieties from the following categories:

CRUNCHY

Bean sprouts: Crisp and white; use as is, or blanch for 30 seconds to remove rawness; refresh in ice water and drain well before adding to salad.

Iceberg lettuce: Tight, heavy head of crisp, pale green leaves; neutral flavor. Remove core before chopping or tearing for salad.

Napa

Savoy

Green cabbage (Napa, Savoy, Chinese): Smooth or deeply crinkled, pale green to white leaves; remove tough core when using in salad.

PEPPERY

Watercress: Small, dark green, slightly curly leaves; discard larger, tougher stems.

Arugula: Also known as rocket. Choose smaller, bright green leaves; discard wilted leaves.
Nasturtium: Edible green leaves of the flowering plant.

TENDER

Green leaf lettuce: Also known as salad bowl; tender, crinkly leaf with a crisp stem.

Boston lettuce: Large, loose-leaf head of fragile medium-green leaves.

Bibb lettuce: Small head of loose, buttery-textured pale green leaves.

Mâche: Also known as lamb's lettuce or field salad. Tiny, blue-green, spoon-shaped leaves with a chewy texture.

BOLD FLAVORED

Spinach: Very dark green, crinkly or flat leaves.

Romaine: Loose head of sturdy, long-stemmed, dark green leaves with pale yellow-white inner leaves.

COLORFUL

Radicchio: A bright, purplish-red bitter chicory with white stem; long, loose-leaved head, or small, compact head; bitter flavor.

Red leaf lettuce: Relative of green leaf with tender, crinkly, bronze-tipped leaves on a crisp stem.

Red cabbage: Crunchy texture, deep purple color with contrasting white; best shredded and added to green salads in small amounts.

BITTER

green chicory

Chicory: Comes in several varieties such as a **green chicory** with broad, dandelion-like leaves; **Belgian endive** with small, tight, white head with yellow-tipped leaves, shaped like corn in the husk;

Belgian endive

curly endive

escarole

and **red chicory** or **radicchio. Curly endive,** a loose head of frilly green and yellow leaves, and *escarole*, a loose head of broad, medium-green leaves, might also be labeled chicory.

beet greens

dandelion

mustard greens

Greens: Young, tender beet, collard, dandelion, mustard and turnip greens all add a pleasant bitter flavor when added to mixed green salads in small amounts.

CLEAN GREENS

■ Look for freshness in *all* salad greens; avoid signs of wilting or decay.
■ Remove broken or bruised leaves before cleaning or storing greens.
■ Store unwashed greens in open or perforated plastic bags in the crisper section of the refrigerator.
■ Beet, collard, dandelion, mustard and turnip greens should be used within 1 day.
■ Tender-leaf lettuce, spinach and arugula can be stored for up to 2 days.

■ Bean sprouts, watercress and loose-leaf lettuces can be held for up to 4 days.
■ Romaine, radicchio and iceberg lettuce will keep for up to 1 week.
■ Green or red cabbage can be refrigerated for up to 2 weeks.
■ Wash greens in sink or large bowl filled with warm water. Drain well and dry in salad spinner or blot gently with paper toweling. Be sure to rinse especially sandy greens such as arugula and spinach in several changes of clean water.
■ To keep *clean* greens crisp and fresh until mealtime, wrap in paper toweling and store in a closed plastic bag in the refrigerator. With delicate-leaf greens like mâche or arugula, wrap toweling around roots only. Place watercress stems in glass of water and cover the leaves with plastic bag.

Drying Salad Greens
For the driest greens (and to avoid excess water clinging to leaves, which will dilute a salad dressing), whirl the greens in a salad spinner. If not using the greens right away, store in a paper-lined plastic bag in the crisper section of the refrigerator.

ARUGULA AND RED LEAF LETTUCE WITH RASPBERRY DRESSING

LOW-CHOLESTEROL · QUICK

The peppery arugula pairs well with the sweet raspberry dressing. Wash the arugula well since it can be very sandy. Use extra dressing for other salads or marinating chicken or pork chops.

Makes 4 servings.
Recipe can be halved or doubled.
Nutrient Value Per Serving: 190 calories, 5 g protein, 14 g fat, 13 g carbohydrate, 186 mg sodium, 0 mg cholesterol.

Raspberry Dressing:
¼ cup raspberry vinegar
¼ cup vegetable oil
¼ teaspoon salt
⅛ teaspoon pepper

Salad:
2 bunches arugula, trimmed, washed, dried and torn into bite-size pieces (about 5 cups)
1 small head red leaf lettuce, trimmed, washed, dried and torn into bite-size pieces
1 head Bibb lettuce, trimmed, washed, dried and torn into bite-size pieces
1 medium-size sweet red pepper, cored, seeded and cut into slivers
1 cup frozen lima beans, cooked according to package directions

1. Prepare Raspberry Dressing: Combine vinegar, oil, salt and pepper in screw-top jar. Shake to blend.
2. Prepare Salad: Place greens in large salad bowl. Drizzle with ¼ cup dressing; toss to coat. Arrange red pepper slivers and lima beans over top. Pass extra dressing with salad.

Make-Ahead Tip: The dressing can be prepared several days ahead and refrigerated. The greens can be prepared a day ahead and refrigerated in plastic bags.

SLENDERIZING SALADS

Salads are healthful foods but can actually *contribute* to an unhealthy amount of fat in your diet. Greens and vegetables tossed with vinaigrettes, or other oil-based dressings, will always be high in fat relative to the calories they provide. *(See Dressing Slim, page 179.)* That's because most of the calories come from the salad oil in the dressing, while very few are contributed by vegetables and flavorings. To stick closer to the 30% solution for keeping fat down in your diet *(see page 15),* drizzle a *measured* tablespoon of dressing over individual salads. The nutrition information for many of our salads is based on 1 tablespoon of dressing, which should be enough to pleasantly enhance the flavor of the greens and vegetables in one serving of salad.

MAKE IT A MAIN-DISH SALAD

To easily transform Arugula and Red Leaf Lettuce with Raspberry Dressing into a main dish, add 12 to 16 ounces of thinly sliced cooked pork (broiled thin loin pork chops work well) that has been marinated in the salad dressing for about 30 minutes.

MÂCHE AND BIBB LETTUCE WITH BALSAMIC VINEGAR DRESSING

LOW-CHOLESTEROL · QUICK

*M*âche and Bibb lettuces are very delicately flavored, so drizzle the salad with a small amount of the dressing.

Makes 4 servings.
Recipe can be halved or doubled.
Nutrient Value Per Serving: 258 calories, 3 g protein, 24 g fat, 11 g carbohydrate, 1,106 mg sodium, 0 mg cholesterol.

Balsamic Vinegar Dressing:
1½ tablespoons olive oil
1½ tablespoons vegetable oil
1 tablespoon balsamic vinegar OR: red wine vinegar
¼ teaspoon salt
⅛ teaspoon pepper

Salad:
4 cups loosely packed mâche (about ¼ pound), trimmed, washed and dried
3 heads Bibb lettuce, trimmed, washed and dried (about 8 cups)
4 sun-dried tomatoes, packed in oil, cut into thin slices
1 green onion, white part only, cut lengthwise into thin strips

1. Prepare Balsamic Vinegar Dressing: Combine olive and vegetable oils, vinegar, salt and pepper in small screw-top jar. Shake to blend.
2. Prepare Salad: Arrange mâche and Bibb lettuce on 4 individual salad plates. Scatter sun-dried tomato and green onion over greens, dividing evenly. Drizzle each salad with very small amount of dressing.

Make-Ahead Tip: The dressing can be made several days ahead and refrigerated, covered.

CAESAR SALAD WITH HARD-COOKED EGG

QUICK

*O*ur Caesar salad uses finely chopped hard-cooked eggs rather than raw egg. If you're not a lover of anchovies, feel free to omit them. The salad, which should be served as soon as it is dressed, makes a substantial first course or a light supper with a selection of home-baked breads.

Makes 6 servings.
Recipe can be halved or doubled.
Nutrient Value Per Serving: 228 calories, 9 g protein, 16 g fat, 13 g carbohydrate, 466 mg sodium, 77 mg cholesterol.

Dressing:
⅓ cup olive oil
3 tablespoons lemon juice
1 clove garlic, mashed to a paste
1 teaspoon Worcestershire sauce
¼ teaspoon salt
⅛ teaspoon pepper

Salad:
3 cups 1-inch bread cubes, preferably day-old, toasted
1 large head Romaine lettuce, separated into leaves and broken into bite-size pieces
2 hard-cooked eggs, finely chopped
⅓ cup freshly grated Parmesan cheese
6 anchovy fillets, or to taste

1. Prepare Dressing: Combine olive oil, lemon juice, garlic, Worcestershire sauce, salt and pepper in screw-top jar. Shake to blend.
2. Prepare Salad: Combine toast cubes and lettuce in large salad bowl. Add eggs, Parmesan and dressing; toss to combine. Garnish with anchovy fillets. Serve immediately.

Make-Ahead Tip: The dressing can be made up to 3 days ahead and refrigerated, covered.

MÂCHE MAKES A MEAL
To create a main-dish salad from Mâche and Bibb Lettuce with Balsamic Vinegar Dressing, add 8 ounces of goat cheese, cut into thin slices. Since mâche is very expensive, serve this salad for special occasions.

HOW TO HARD-COOK EGGS
■ Place eggs in single layer in saucepan.
■ Add cool tap water to cover by 1 inch.
■ Gently heat to *almost* boiling. Simmer, without boiling, 10 minutes.
■ Remove eggs with slotted spoon to bowl of cold water and let stand 5 minutes.
■ To store, do not crack shell. Place hard-cooked eggs in clean container, covered, and refrigerate for up to 1 week. If using immediately, crack shell and use egg according to the recipe.

RADICCHIO AND ESCAROLE WITH TAMARI DRESSING

LOW-CHOLESTEROL · QUICK

Need a main dish salad? Add 12 ounces of thinly sliced or shredded cooked chicken meat that has been marinated in the salad dressing for about 15 minutes.

Makes 4 servings.
Recipe can be halved or doubled.
Nutrient Value Per Serving: 123 calories, 2 g protein, 11 g fat, 5 g carbohydrate, 100 mg sodium, 0 mg cholesterol.

Tamari Dressing:
½ cup vegetable oil
¼ cup olive oil
¼ cup rice vinegar
2 teaspoons tamari soy sauce
2 teaspoons lemon juice
½ teaspoon pepper
½ teaspoon Oriental sesame oil
¼ teaspoon salt

Salad:
¼ pound snow peas
1 small head Boston lettuce, trimmed, washed, dried and torn into bite-size pieces
¼ head escarole, trimmed, washed, dried and torn into bite-size pieces
1 head radicchio, trimmed, washed, dried and torn into bite-size pieces

1. Prepare Tamari Dressing: Combine vegetable oil, olive oil, vinegar, soy sauce, lemon juice, pepper, sesame oil and salt in small screw-top jar. Shake to blend.
2. Prepare Salad: String snow peas. Steam just until snow peas have lost their raw taste, about 2 minutes. Rinse in colander under cold running water to stop cooking. Blot snow peas dry with paper toweling.
3. Toss Boston lettuce and escarole

pieces and snow peas separately with 1 tablespoon dressing.
4. Arrange radicchio, Boston lettuce, escarole and snow peas on salad plates. Pass remaining dressing.

Make-Ahead Tip: The dressing can be made several days ahead and refrigerated, covered. The greens can be prepared a day ahead and refrigerated in plastic bags.

WATERCRESS AND ENDIVE WITH GINGER DRESSING

LOW-CHOLESTEROL · QUICK

Make this a main-dish salad by adding 12 to 16 ounces of cold, cooked, shelled and deveined medium-size to large shrimp.

Makes 4 servings.
Recipe can be halved or doubled.
Nutrient Value Per Serving: 106 calories, 2 g protein, 8 g fat, 8 g carbohydrate, 125 mg sodium, 0 mg cholesterol.

Ginger Dressing:
5 tablespoons vegetable oil
2 tablespoons olive oil
2 tablespoons rice vinegar
2 tablespoons lemon juice
2 teaspoons Dijon-style mustard
1 teaspoon ground ginger
¼ teaspoon salt
¼ teaspoon pepper

Salad:
1 large bunch watercress, trimmed, washed and dried (about 6 cups)
½ cucumber (halved crosswise), halved lengthwise, seeded and cut crosswise into thin slices
1 navel orange, peeled, thinly sliced and slices halved
4 to 5 slices red onion, separated into rings
1 head Belgian endive, trimmed and cut diagonally into thin slices OR: 2 bunches arugula, trimmed, washed and dried

1. Prepare Ginger Dressing: Combine vegetable and olive oils, vinegar, lemon juice, mustard, ginger, salt and pepper in screw-top jar. Shake to blend.
2. Prepare Salad: Arrange watercress, cucumber, orange, onion and endive on salad plates. Drizzle 1 tablespoon dressing over each salad.

WATERCRESS AND ENDIVE MAKE-AHEAD TIP: The dressing can be prepared several days ahead and refrigerated, covered. The greens can be prepared a day ahead and refrigerated in plastic bags.

BELGIAN ENDIVE AND BOSTON LETTUCE WITH CUMIN DRESSING

LOW-CHOLESTEROL · QUICK

For a main-dish seafood salad, add 12 to 16 ounces cooked scallops that have been marinated in the dressing for 30 minutes. If using large sea scallops, slice each scallop in half horizontally.

Makes 4 servings.
Recipe can be halved or doubled.
Nutrient Value Per Serving: 180 calories, 3 g protein, 16 g fat, 10 g carbohydrate, 95 mg sodium, 0 mg cholesterol.

Cumin Dressing:
½ cup olive oil
¼ cup vegetable oil
6 tablespoons lime juice
1 teaspoon ground cumin
½ teaspoon grated lime rind
½ teaspoon salt
¼ teaspoon white pepper

Salad:
1 small avocado
1 tablespoon lime juice
2 heads Belgian endive, trimmed and
    separated into leaves OR: 1 large
    bunch watercress, trimmed, washed
    and dried
1 head Boston lettuce, trimmed, washed
    and dried (about 8 cups)
4 radishes, thinly sliced

1. Prepare Cumin Dressing: Combine olive and vegetable oils, lime juice, cumin, lime rind, salt and pepper in screw-top jar. Shake to blend.
2. Prepare Salad: Halve avocado and remove pit. Cut each half lengthwise into quarters. Remove skin. Cut each piece diagonally into slivers. Toss with the 1 tablespoon lime juice in small bowl.
3. Arrange endive spears on 4 salad plates. Arrange Boston lettuce over top. Scatter radish and avocado over top. Drizzle each with 1 tablespoon dressing. Pass remainder.

Make-Ahead Tip: The dressing can be made several days ahead and refrigerated, covered.

GRATED CARROT SALAD WITH CILANTRO

LOW-CALORIE · LOW-CHOLESTEROL
QUICK

Serve this light, refreshing salad with roasted or grilled meats (excellent with hamburgers) and poultry, or as a relish with stews and curries.

Makes 6 servings (4 cups).
Recipe can be halved or doubled.
Nutrient Value Per Serving: 95 calories, 1 g protein, 5 g fat, 13 g carbohydrate, 225 mg sodium, 0 mg cholesterol.

Lemon Dressing:
3 tablespoons lemon juice
2 tablespoons olive oil
½ teaspoon sugar
½ teaspoon salt
¼ teaspoon pepper

Salad:
1½ pounds carrots, pared and grated
½ cup finely chopped green onion
2 tablespoons finely chopped cilantro
1 teaspoon grated lemon rind
1 teaspoon toasted cumin seeds*

1. Prepare Lemon Dressing: Whisk together lemon juice, olive oil, sugar, salt and pepper in large bowl.
2. Prepare Salad: Add carrot, green onion, cilantro, lemon rind and cumin seed to dressing; toss to mix. Serve immediately.

*Note: Toast cumin seeds in dry skillet over medium heat, tossing until aromatic and lightly browned.
Make-Ahead Tip: The salad can be made up to 2 hours ahead and refrigerated, covered.

APPLE COLESLAW WITH SWEET & SOUR DRESSING

LOW-CHOLESTEROL

Apple makes this slaw particularly refreshing. Make several hours ahead or even the day before so the flavors have a chance to mellow. Garnish with chopped fresh dill, chives or parsley.

Makes 8 servings (10 cups).
Recipe can be halved or doubled.
Nutrient Value Per Serving: 194 calories, 2 g protein, 14 g fat, 17 g carbohydrate, 408 mg sodium, 0 mg cholesterol.

Sweet & Sour Dressing:
½ cup vegetable oil
½ cup cider vinegar
2 tablespoons Dijon-style mustard
1 tablespoon sugar
1 teaspoon celery seeds
1 teaspoon salt
¼ teaspoon pepper, or to taste

Coleslaw:
1 head (about 2 pounds) red cabbage, cored and shredded
2 Granny Smith apples, pared, cored and thinly sliced
3 carrots, pared and grated
1 sweet red pepper, cored, seeded and cut into thin strips
1 yellow onion, finely chopped

1. Prepare Sweet & Sour Dressing: Combine oil, vinegar, mustard, sugar, celery seeds, salt and pepper in screw-top jar. Shake to blend.
2. Prepare Coleslaw: Add cabbage, apple, carrot, red pepper and onion to dressing; toss to mix. Let salad stand at room temperature, covered, for 2 hours.

Make-Ahead Tip: The salad can be made a day ahead and refrigerated, covered.

SWEET POTATO AND APPLE SALAD

LOW-CHOLESTEROL

The mix of sweet potato and apple (you might try pear) in this salad is delicious. If you have leftovers during the holidays, add cooked whole cranberries and diced cooked turkey (or chicken) to create a main dish.

Makes 6 servings. Recipe can be doubled.
Nutrient Value Per Serving: 426 calories,
5 g protein, 25 g fat, 48 g carbohydrate,
217 mg sodium, 0 mg cholesterol.

Orange Dressing:
⅓ cup vegetable oil
3 tablespoons red wine vinegar
3 tablespoons orange juice
2 teaspoons grated orange rind
½ teaspoon salt

Salad:
3 cups cooked, cubed sweet potatoes
    (about 1½ pounds raw)
1 Granny Smith apple, pared, cored and
    cut into cubes
¼ cup finely chopped shallots OR: green
    onion
1 bunch watercress, stems removed
1 small Belgian endive, cored and
    separated into leaves
½ cup toasted pecans, coarsely chopped
Julienned orange rind, for garnish
    (optional)

1. Prepare Orange Dressing: Combine vegetable oil, vinegar, orange juice, orange rind and salt in screw-top jar. Shake to blend.
2. Prepare Salad: Combine sweet potatoes, apple and shallots in a bowl. Add half the dressing; stir to coat. Add remaining dressing to watercress in separate bowl.
3. Place watercress on serving plate or individual salad plates. Arrange sweet potato mixture and endive leaves over watercress. Garnish with pecans, and orange rind, if you wish.

Make-Ahead Tip: The sweet potato and apple mixture can be made up to 2 hours ahead. Cover with plastic wrap and let stand at room temperature. Toss the watercress with the remaining dressing just before serving. The dressing can be made up to 3 days ahead and refrigerated, covered.

THREE-BEAN SALAD WITH RED ONION

LOW-CHOLESTEROL

This salad is a wonderful accompaniment to roast meats and poultry. Make the salad at least several hours ahead so the flavors can mellow.

THREE-BEAN SALAD MAKE-AHEAD TIP:
The salad can be made up to 2 days ahead and refrigerated, covered.

Makes 6 servings.
Recipe can be halved or doubled.
Nutrient Value Per Serving: 254 calories, 7 g protein, 13 g fat, 31 g carbohydrate, 292 mg sodium, 0 mg cholesterol.

Cider Vinegar Dressing:
¼ cup cider vinegar
3 tablespoons sugar
½ teaspoon salt
¼ teaspoon pepper
⅓ cup vegetable oil

Salad:
1 pound cooked wax beans OR: canned, drained and rinsed
1 pound cooked green beans OR: canned, drained and rinsed
1 can (16 ounces) kidney beans, drained and rinsed
1 cup finely chopped red onion
1 cup finely chopped sweet red pepper
½ cup finely chopped celery
¼ cup finely chopped parsley

1. Prepare Cider Vinegar Dressing: Whisk together vinegar, sugar, salt and pepper in large bowl. Add oil in thin stream, whisking until thoroughly combined.
2. Prepare Salad: Add wax beans, green beans, kidney beans, onion, red pepper, celery and parsley to dressing; toss to mix. Let salad stand, covered, at room temperature for 2 hours or refrigerate overnight.

WINTER ROOT SALAD WITH HONEY-MUSTARD DRESSING

LOW-CHOLESTEROL

This shredded, slightly crunchy salad serves well as a sharply flavored first course or appetizer, or as an accompaniment to roast meats, such as pork or chicken.

Makes 8 servings (4 cups).
Recipe can be halved or doubled.
Nutrient Value Per Serving: 111 calories, 1 g protein, 7 g fat, 12 g carbohydrate, 259 mg sodium, 0 mg cholesterol.

Salad:
3 carrots
3 parsnips
1 large leek
2 tablespoons olive oil
1 sweet red pepper, cored, seeded and
    cut into thin strips

Honey-Mustard Dressing:
2 tablespoons red wine vinegar
2 tablespoons olive oil
2 teaspoons Dijon-style mustard
1 teaspoon honey
¾ teaspoon salt

Lettuce leaves

1. Prepare Salad: Fit food processor with shredding disk. Cut carrots and parsnips into lengths to fit horizontally into food processor feed tube. Process with shredding blade. Or chop by hand. Cut off all but 1 inch of green top of leek. Trim off end; cut lengthwise into 2-inch slivers. Rinse well in colander to remove all sand.
2. Heat 2 tablespoons oil in large skillet or Dutch oven over medium heat. Add leeks; sauté 4 minutes. Add carrot, parsnip and red pepper; cook, covered, for 5 to 8 minutes or until tender-crisp. Spoon into medium-size bowl.
3. Prepare Dressing: Whisk together red wine vinegar, oil, mustard, honey and salt in small bowl. Stir Dressing into vegetables. Refrigerate, covered, for at least 3 hours.
4. To serve, line plate or shallow bowl or individual salad plates with lettuce leaves. Spoon salad in center. Serve chilled or at room temperature.

Make-Ahead Tip: The salad can be prepared up to 3 days ahead and refrigerated, covered.

THE MUSTARD MARKET

The many flavors of mustard available on supermarket shelves lend themselves to a wide range of uses:
■ **Beer mustard** has a robust flavor that stands up to strong cheeses, smoked meats and sausages; also perfect as a pretzel dip.
■ **Dijon** and **Dijon-style mustards** are flavored with white wine and often with herbs; use on sandwiches and in sauces and savory crumb toppings for fish and vegetables.
■ **Honey mustard** is mild and sweet; use as a ham glaze, on cold cuts, in a fruit salad dressing, on hot dogs, or mixed with yogurt for a chip dip.
■ **Horseradish mustard** complements the flavor of corned beef, pastrami or pot roast.
■ **Hickory smoke mustard** lends barbecued flavor to roast poultry, beef or pork.
■ **Raspberry** and other **fruit-flavored mustards** add a sweet and tangy touch to turkey or chicken sandwiches and roast duck or roast pork.

CAULIFLOWER SALAD WITH BASIL DRESSING

LOW-CHOLESTEROL · QUICK

*P*repare salad at least 30 minutes before serving to allow vegetables to marinate.

Makes 4 servings (6 cups).
Recipe can be doubled.
Nutrient Value Per Serving: 150 calories, 3 g protein, 12 g fat, 10 g carbohydrate, 307 mg sodium, 0 mg cholesterol.

Basil Dressing:
3 tablespoons olive oil
2 tablespoons lemon juice
2 flat anchovies *(optional)*
¼ teaspoon salt
⅛ teaspoon sugar
¼ cup parsley leaves
¼ cup basil leaves
1 green onion, cut into 1-inch pieces

Salad:
1 small head cauliflower (1 pound), cut
    into small flowerets
1 box (9 ounces) frozen Italian beans
12 cherry tomatoes, halved
8 dry-cured black olives, pitted and cut
    into slivers OR: canned ripe black
    olives, cut into slivers

1. Prepare Basil Dressing: Combine oil, lemon juice, anchovies if using, salt, sugar, parsley, basil and green onion in blender or food processor. Whirl until smooth.
2. Prepare Salad: Steam cauliflower on steamer rack in covered pan for 12 minutes or until tender. Place in medium-size bowl. Steam Italian beans for 4 minutes. Place in small bowl.
3. Pour dressing over cauliflower, tossing to coat. Thirty minutes before serving, toss in tomatoes and olives. Toss in Italian beans. Serve chilled or at room temperature.

Make-Ahead Tip: The vegetables can be cooked a day ahead, and the cauliflower mixed with the dressing, and both refrigerated separately, covered. Then proceed with Step 3.
Microwave Directions for Cooking Cauliflower and Beans (High Power Oven): Place cauliflowerets and 2 tablespoons water in microwave-safe 1½-quart casserole with lid. Microwave, covered, at 100% power 4 minutes until tender. Drain and rinse with cold water. Cook frozen Italian beans in same casserole following package directions. Drain and rinse.

SZECHUAN EGGPLANT AND SNOW PEA SALAD

LOW-CALORIE · LOW-CHOLESTEROL
QUICK

The possibilities for this salad are endless: a piquant accompaniment to roast meats, especially pork or ribs; spooned over pasta or couscous; stuffed in a pita-bread pocket; or for breakfast in an omelet or a frittata.

Makes 10 servings (5 cups).
Recipe can be halved or doubled.
Nutrient Value Per Serving: 79 calories, 1 g protein, 6 g fat, 7 g carbohydrate, 286 mg sodium, 0 mg cholesterol.

3 tablespoons olive oil or vegetable oil
1 large eggplant (about 1½ pounds), peeled and cut into 1-inch cubes
1 large onion, coarsely chopped
2 cloves garlic, chopped
½ cup tomato sauce
2 tablespoons soy sauce
2 tablespoons red wine vinegar
1 tablespoon Oriental sesame oil
¼ teaspoon liquid red-pepper seasoning
⅓ cup chopped cilantro OR: parsley
¼ pound snow peas, halved crosswise

1. Heat oil in large 12-inch skillet or Dutch oven over medium heat. Add eggplant and onion; cook, covered, for 10 to 12 minutes or until almost tender.
2. Stir in garlic, tomato sauce, soy sauce, vinegar, sesame oil and red-pepper seasoning; simmer about 6 minutes or until eggplant is just tender. Stir in cilantro and snow peas. Remove from heat and keep covered 2 minutes. Turn into serving bowl. Serve warm, at room temperature or chilled.

CELERY ROOT SALAD WITH HORSERADISH DRESSING

LOW-CALORIE · LOW-CHOLESTEROL

A lemony, crunchy make-ahead salad that stands up well to grilled or barbecued meats such as flank steak.

Makes 6 servings (3 cups).
Recipe can be halved or doubled.
Nutrient Value Per Serving: 96 calories, 1 g protein, 7 g fat, 9 g carbohydrate, 359 mg sodium, 0 mg cholesterol.

Salad:
1 lemon
1 celery root (about 1¼ pounds), peeled
2 green onions

Horseradish Dressing:
¼ cup chopped parsley
3 tablespoons olive oil
2 teaspoons prepared horseradish
¾ teaspoon salt
¼ teaspoon pepper

1. Prepare Salad: Set steamer rack in covered pan with 1 inch water; bring to simmer.
2. Juice lemon and reserve juice. Place lemon halves in medium-size bowl and fill with water.
3. Cut celery root into feed-tube-size pieces for food processor. Process with shredding disc. Or cut into matchstick-size pieces with knife. Place in lemon water to prevent discoloring. Cut green onions into 2-inch lengths; slice into thin slivers.
4. Drain celery root. Place in steamer; cover and cook 5 minutes or until tender-crisp. Toss with reserved lemon juice in bowl. Add green onion.
5. Prepare Horseradish Dressing: Combine parsley, oil, horseradish, salt and pepper in small bowl. Add to celery root. Refrigerate for at least 2 hours. Serve cold or at room temperature.

CELERY ROOT SALAD SERVING IDEAS
Use Celery Root Salad with Horseradish Dressing as a topping for meat sandwiches or as a substitute for coleslaw—it's great picnic food. For a first course, serve on a bed of greens, garnished with cherry tomatoes and chopped parsley. For a variation, try half celery root and half turnip.

CELERY ROOT SALAD MAKE-AHEAD TIP:
The salad can be made up to 2 days ahead and refrigerated, covered.

EGGPLANT AND SNOW PEA SALAD MAKE-AHEAD TIP:
The salad can be prepared up to 3 days ahead, but don't mix in the snow peas. Instead, cook the snow peas separately in boiling water for 30 seconds; drain and rinse under cold water. Refrigerate the eggplant mixture and the snow peas separately, covered. Stir the snow peas into the salad just before serving.

⅓ cup red wine vinegar
¾ teaspoon leaf oregano, crumbled
¼ teaspoon salt
2 sweet red and/or yellow peppers, cored, seeded and cut into ¾-inch-thick slices
1 large Spanish onion, thinly sliced
1 eggplant (about 1 pound), thinly sliced and each slice cut into thirds OR: 1 pound small eggplants, cut into spears
1 medium-size zucchini, thinly sliced
1 bunch arugula

1. Preheat the oven to moderate (350°).
2. Toast bread on baking sheet in preheated moderate oven (350°) for 15 minutes or until golden. Increase oven temperature to broil.
3. Rub warm toasts with garlic halves; set toasts aside. Finely chop garlic.
4. Stir together oil, vinegar, oregano, salt and chopped garlic in small bowl. Arrange peppers in single layer on broiler-pan rack. Brush with some of the oil mixture.
5. Broil peppers, turning and brushing peppers with some of the oil mixture occasionally, until browned and tender, 10 to 15 minutes. Remove peppers to large bowl.
6. Place onion on broiler rack. Brush with some of the oil mixture. Broil, turning and brushing with some of the oil mixture once, until browned and tender, about 10 minutes. Remove onion to bowl with peppers.
7. Repeat with eggplant and zucchini, broiling each until browned and tender, 3 to 5 minutes, turning and brushing with some of the oil mixture. Add to bowl with vegetables; gently toss.
8. To serve: Arrange arugula and bread toasts on platter. Drizzle with some of the remaining oil mixture. Top with roasted vegetables. Drizzle with any remaining oil mixture.

Make-Ahead Tip: The vegetables, without the bread, can be prepared several hours ahead and refrigerated, covered. Toast and add the bread, rubbed with garlic, just before serving.

ROASTED VEGETABLE SALAD

LOW-CHOLESTEROL

The toasted garlic bread is a wonderful foil to the flavors of this salad, which can be served warm or chilled. If chilled, prepare bread just before serving so it stays crisp.

Toast bread at 350° for 15 minutes; broil vegetables about 30 minutes.
Makes 6 servings.
Recipe can be halved or doubled.
Nutrient Value Per Serving: 314 calories, 6 g protein, 19 g fat, 31 g carbohydrate, 326 mg sodium, 1 mg cholesterol.

Half loaf French or Italian bread, diagonally sliced into ¼-inch-thick slices
1 clove garlic, halved
½ cup olive oil

TRY IT GRILLED!
This Roasted Vegetable Salad is especially flavorful when the vegetables are grilled over charcoal. Add thin slices of mozzarella cheese or grilled chicken breasts to create a main-dish salad.

ASPARAGUS, ENDIVE AND TOMATO SALAD

LOW-CALORIE · LOW-CHOLESTEROL
QUICK

Creamy Tarragon Dressing is the ideal complement to the first of the spring asparagus.

Makes 6 servings.
Recipe can be halved or doubled.
Nutrient Value Per Serving: 91 calories, 4 g protein, 6 g fat, 8 g carbohydrate, 66 mg sodium, 6 mg cholesterol.

Creamy Tarragon Dressing:
⅓ cup reduced-calorie sour cream
¼ cup reduced-calorie mayonnaise
¼ cup milk
1 tablespoon tarragon vinegar
¼ teaspoon leaf tarragon, crumbled
¼ teaspoon coarse black pepper

Salad:
1 pound thin asparagus, trimmed
1 head Romaine lettuce, cored and separated into leaves
4 plum tomatoes, cut into wedges
1 head Belgian endive, separated into leaves

1. Prepare Creamy Tarragon Dressing: Stir together sour cream, mayonnaise, milk, vinegar, tarragon and pepper in small bowl. Reserve.
2. Prepare Salad: Cook asparagus in ½ inch boiling water in large skillet, covered, 3 to 4 minutes or until crisp-tender. Drain; rinse with cold water; drain again.
3. To serve, arrange lettuce on serving platter. Top with asparagus, tomatoes and endive. Just before serving, spoon dressing over salad.

Make-Ahead Tip: The salad and dressing can be made several hours ahead and refrigerated separately, covered. Top salad with dressing just before serving.

MICROWAVE DIRECTIONS FOR COOKING ASPARAGUS (HIGH POWER OVEN):
Place asparagus and 2 tablespoons water in microwave-safe 8- or 9-inch square dish. Cover with microwave-safe plastic wrap, slightly vented at one corner. Microwave at 100% power 4 minutes or until tender-crisp. Carefully uncover. Drain and rinse with cold water as above.

TOASTING SESAME SEEDS
To toast sesame seeds, toss in dry, heavy skillet over medium heat until light brown, 2 to 3 minutes.

VEGETABLE SALAD MAKE-AHEAD TIP:
Vegetables can be prepared a day ahead and refrigerated separately, covered.

ORIENTAL VEGETABLE SALAD

LOW-CHOLESTEROL · QUICK

Serve with roast pork or chicken or broiled fish. For a main dish, just add leftover cooked meat.

Makes 6 servings.
Recipe can be halved or doubled.
Nutrient Value Per Serving: 133 calories, 4 g protein, 10 g fat, 9 g carbohydrate, 349 mg sodium, 0 mg cholesterol.

½ pound green beans
¼ pound snow peas

Dressing:
3 tablespoons vegetable oil
2 tablespoons tamari soy sauce
1 tablespoon rice vinegar
1 teaspoon Oriental sesame oil
1 green onion, finely chopped
1 small clove garlic, finely chopped

1 small head Chinese cabbage, coarsely shredded
1 package (3½ ounces) enoki mushrooms *(see page 425)*
1 tablespoon sesame seeds, toasted

1. Cook green beans in 2 inches boiling water in medium-size saucepan until crisp-tender, 5 to 8 minutes. Remove beans with slotted spoon to colander. Rinse with cold water to stop cooking.
2. Return water in saucepan to boiling. Add snow peas; cook until crisp-tender, 2 to 3 minutes. Drain in colander; rinse with cold water to stop cooking.
3. Prepare Dressing: Stir together vegetable oil, tamari, vinegar, sesame oil, green onion and garlic in small bowl.
4. To serve: Pat beans and snow peas dry with paper toweling. Arrange cabbage, beans, snow peas and mushrooms on platter. Sprinkle with sesame seeds. Just before serving, drizzle with dressing.

CHINESE NEW YEAR CELEBRATION

Bok Choy Strudel with Mushrooms and Onions (401)

Oriental Vegetable Salad (this page)

Baked Boneless Turkey Breast with Honey-Hoisin Sauce (271)

Sautéed Peas with Water Chestnuts (431)

Steamed Rice

Pineapple-Strawberry Ice (535) with Double-Ginger Molasses Crisps (513)

CHICKEN COUSCOUS SALAD WITH PINEAPPLE DRESSING

LOW-FAT · LOW-CHOLESTEROL

Couscous, or semolina grain, is an excellent foil for the lively flavors of the dried fruits and spicy dressing.

Makes 6 servings.
Recipe can be halved or doubled.
Nutrient Value Per Serving: 419 calories, 30 g protein, 9 g fat, 56 g carbohydrate, 566 mg sodium, 55 mg cholesterol.

Salad:
1¼ pounds boneless, skinned chicken breasts
1 can (13¾ ounces) chicken broth
3 carrots, pared, halved lengthwise and sliced crosswise
1 onion, chopped
1 large clove garlic, crushed
1 cup frozen whole-kernel corn
4 ounces mixed dried fruit, chopped (1 cup)
1 cup couscous

Pineapple Dressing:
¾ cup pineapple juice
2 tablespoons olive oil OR: vegetable oil
2 tablespoons cider vinegar
2 tablespoons chutney OR: orange marmalade
½ teaspoon salt
6 drops liquid red-pepper seasoning

Garnish:
¼ cup chopped pistachios OR: walnuts
Leaf lettuce, for garnish

1. Prepare Salad: Slice chicken breasts into strips. Bring broth to simmering in medium-size saucepan. Add chicken pieces; simmer 4 to 5 minutes or until cooked through. Remove with slotted spoon to serving bowl; cover with plastic wrap.
2. Add carrot, onion and garlic to broth. Cook 6 minutes or until crisp-tender. Add corn; cook 2 minutes. Strain, reserving liquid; add vegetables to chicken. Discard garlic.
3. Measure enough cooking liquid into saucepan to prepare couscous according to package directions. Add dried fruit; bring to boiling. Stir in couscous; remove from heat and let stand, covered, 3 minutes. Fluff and spoon into serving dish.
4. Prepare Pineapple Dressing: Combine pineapple juice, olive oil, vinegar, chutney, salt and red-pepper seasoning in blender or food processor. Whirl until smooth. Pour over salad; toss to coat. Refrigerate to chill. Garnish with pistachios and leaf lettuce. Serve chilled or at room temperature.

(continued)

CHICKEN COUSCOUS SALAD MAKE-AHEAD TIP:
The salad can be made up to 2 days ahead without the garnishes and refrigerated, covered.

CHICKEN COUSCOUS SALAD WITH PINEAPPLE DRESSING (continued)

CHICKEN COUSCOUS SALAD VARIATIONS
Try substituting wild rice, kasha or white rice for the couscous, and cooked pork tenderloin or turkey breast for the chicken. For an elegant version, add a little saffron to the cooking liquid for the couscous.

Chicken Couscous Microwave Directions (High Power Oven): Combine chicken strips and ¼ cup of the broth in microwave-safe 2-quart casserole with lid. Microwave, covered, at 100% power 6 minutes, stirring twice. Remove chicken with slotted spoon. Add carrot, onion and garlic to casserole. Microwave, covered, at 100% power 5 minutes. Stir in corn. Microwave, covered, at 100% power 1 minute. Strain, reserving liquid. Add chicken to vegetables. Add enough chicken broth to cooking liquid to prepare 1 cup couscous according to package directions; pour into casserole. Add dried fruit. Microwave, covered, at 100% power 6 to 7 minutes to boiling. Stir in couscous; let stand, covered, 3 minutes. Stir in chicken and vegetables. Prepare Dressing as in Step 4; toss with couscous mixture.

SUMMER SOUP 'N' SALAD BAR

Gazpacho (136)

Asparagus Summer Soup (133)

Arugula and Red Leaf Lettuce with Raspberry Dressing (147)

Savory Cheese and Green Onion Scones (78)

Melon and Shrimp with Cilantro-Lime Dressing (170)

Chicken Couscous Salad with Pineapple Dressing (161)

CHICKEN, GREEN BEAN AND POTATO SALAD WITH HERB-YOGURT DRESSING

LOW-CALORIE • LOW-FAT • QUICK

This salad takes advantage of leftover chicken, or you can purchase already roasted chicken from the deli counter.

Makes 4 servings.
Recipe can be halved or doubled.
Nutrient Value Per Serving: 328 calories, 35 g protein, 9 g fat, 27 g carbohydrate, 128 mg sodium, 82 mg cholesterol.

1 container (8 ounces) lowfat plain yogurt
2 tablespoons Basil Vinaigrette *(recipe follows)*
1 pound new potatoes, scrubbed
½ pound green beans, trimmed
4 cooked chicken breast halves (about 1½ pounds), skinned, boned and sliced (about 13 ounces)

1. Combine yogurt and Basil Vinaigrette in small bowl.
2. Simmer potatoes in large pot water until tender, about 15 minutes. Add green beans for last 5 minutes. Drain; halve or quarter potatoes if large.
3. Arrange chicken, potatoes and green beans on bed of lettuce, if you wish. Drizzle with dressing.

Basil Vinaigrette: Place 1 clove garlic, ¼ cup firmly packed basil leaves and 2 teaspoons fresh thyme, or ½ teaspoon dried, in food processor or blender. Whirl until chopped. Blend in ⅔ cup olive oil, ⅓ cup balsamic vinegar or red wine vinegar, ⅛ teaspoon salt and ⅛ teaspoon pepper.
Make-Ahead Tip: The salad can be arranged up to 2 hours ahead and refrigerated, covered. Drizzle with yogurt-vinaigrette mixture just before serving.

ORIENTAL ORANGE AND CHICKEN SALAD

LOW-CALORIE · LOW-FAT

You can substitute cubed cooked turkey or pork tenderloin for the chicken.

Makes 4 servings.
Recipe can be halved or doubled.

Nutrient Value Per Serving: 349 calories, 38 g protein, 10 g fat, 27 g carbohydrate, 476 mg sodium, 82 mg cholesterol.

1 cup orange juice
1 tablespoon soy sauce
1 tablespoon honey
1¼ pounds boneless, skinned chicken breasts
¼ pound snow peas, trimmed
¼ cup fresh cilantro leaves OR: parsley, chopped
2 tablespoons rice wine vinegar OR: cider vinegar
4 cups sliced Napa cabbage OR: iceberg lettuce
1 cup sliced radishes
2 green onions, sliced
½ cup salted cashews
1 navel orange, peeled, halved and sliced or cut into pieces

(continued)

SOY SAUCE SELECTS

Natural soy sauce is made from fermented soybeans, wheat and salt. *Japanese* and *Chinese* soy sauces are produced from natural fermentation. *Domestic* soy sauce is synthetically produced and rapidly fermented, so does not have the same intense flavor as naturally brewed, imported soy sauces. Flavor, saltiness and color vary among brands and types of soy sauce.

- **Light soy sauce,** available in supermarkets, is thin and salty; most often used in salads, marinades, clear soups and stir frys.
- **Dark soy sauce** is thicker, sweeter, blacker and less salty than light soy because it is aged longer and flavored with molasses. Dark soy is used as a dipping sauce and to season heavy stews and meat dishes.
- **Tamari soy sauce** is traditionally brewed from soybeans, water and salt, but some brands do contain wheat. Tamari's richer flavor, darker color and thicker consistency are the result of longer fermentation.
- **Reduced-sodium or "lite" soy sauces** have been developed for those who wish to cut back on salt. They contain an average of half the salt of regular soy sauce.

ORIENTAL ORANGE AND CHICKEN SALAD MAKE-AHEAD TIP:

Salad components can be prepared a day ahead and refrigerated separately; don't add dressed chicken to salad until serving.

REACH FOR CHORIZO

Spicy pork chorizo has been unofficially dubbed the national sausage of Spain and Mexico and is also used in Caribbean and Latin American cooking. Since several combinations of seasonings, including garlic, red chilies, cumin, oregano, cloves and paprika, may be used to flavor chorizo, the taste and texture of the links vary from source to source. *Spanish chorizo* is a firm, easily sliced sausage made with roughly chopped smoked pork while *Mexican chorizo* is usually a dry, crumbly sausage made from fresh pork. Grill or broil whole chorizos to serve on their own, or remove the sausage from its casing, crumble or thinly slice, and sauté gently before adding to soups and stews, or rice, egg and bean dishes.

CHORIZO SALAD MAKE-AHEAD TIP:

The rice mixture can be prepared a day ahead and refrigerated, covered.

ORIENTAL ORANGE AND CHICKEN SALAD

(*continued*)

1. Heat juice, soy sauce and honey in medium-size skillet over medium heat. Add chicken; simmer, covered, 10 minutes or until cooked through, turning halfway through. Remove chicken with slotted spoon to cutting board. Cut into ¾-inch cubes.

2. Add snow peas to simmering cooking liquid; cook 30 seconds. Remove with slotted spoon to small bowl.

3. Continue cooking juice mixture until reduced to ½ cup. Pour into medium-size bowl. Stir in chicken, cilantro and vinegar. Refrigerate about 2 hours.

4. Meanwhile, arrange cabbage on serving platter or individual salad plates. Add radishes, green onion and snow peas. Cover with plastic wrap and refrigerate until ready to serve.

5. To serve: Remove chicken with slotted spoon from dressing and mound in center of platter. Spoon on dressing. Garnish with cashews and orange.

RICE, BLACK-EYED PEAS AND CHORIZO SALAD

LOW-CHOLESTEROL

A *spicy main-dish salad. Substitute black beans or lima beans for the black-eyed peas, and ham or kielbasa for the chorizo.*

Makes 6 servings.
Recipe can be halved or doubled.
Nutrient Value Per Serving: 551 calories, 23 g protein, 26 g fat, 57 g carbohydrate, 480 mg sodium, 20 mg cholesterol.

Salad:
1 large onion, chopped
2 teaspoons olive oil
⅔ cup uncooked converted white rice

1⅓ cups water
¾ teaspoon grated lemon rind
¼ teaspoon salt
2 chorizo (3 ounces each), diagonally sliced ½ inch thick
2½ cups cooked black-eyed peas, dried, canned or frozen

Dressing:
1 large (9 ounces) ripe tomato, peeled, seeded and cut into chunks
2 tablespoons olive oil
1 tablespoon red wine vinegar
¼ teaspoon salt
¼ teaspoon leaf oregano, crumbled

3 cups washed and dried salad greens, such as red leaf, green leaf or arugula
1 large ripe tomato (9 ounces), diced

1. Prepare Salad: Cook onion in oil in medium-size saucepan, covered, over moderate heat, stirring occasionally, until softened, about 6 minutes. Stir in rice to coat; cook 1 minute. Add water, lemon rind and salt. Bring to boiling. Lower heat; simmer, covered, 15 minutes. Stir in chorizo; cook 5 minutes or until heated through. Transfer to large bowl. Stir in black-eyed peas. Reserve.

2. Prepare Dressing: Combine tomato, olive oil, vinegar, salt and oregano in food processor or blender. Whirl until smooth, about 40 seconds. Pour over rice mixture; toss gently to coat. Cool to room temperature.

3. Place greens on serving platter or plates. Spoon rice mixture on top. Sprinkle with diced tomato.

SUNDAY AFTERNOON SALAD

Rice, Black-Eyed Peas and Chorizo Salad (this page)
Corn Muffins (74)

ORIENTAL STEAK SALAD

LOW-FAT · LOW-CHOLESTEROL

Although the combination of flank steak and pasta in a salad may seem odd, its inspiration is a dish commonly found in Oriental cuisines. Our version uses ingredients readily available in the supermarket. If you prefer, substitute 3 cups cooked rice for the pasta.

Broil flank steak 12 minutes.
Makes 4 servings.
Recipe can be halved or doubled.
Nutrient Value Per Serving: 473 calories, 32 g protein, 15 g fat, 52 g carbohydrate, 314 mg sodium, 57 mg cholesterol.

Oriental Dressing:
3 tablespoons reduced-sodium soy sauce
3 tablespoons rice wine vinegar OR: cider vinegar
2½ tablespoons vegetable oil
1 tablespoon brown sugar
1 teaspoon Oriental sesame oil

Salad:
1 flank steak (1 pound), about ½ inch thick
3 pieces orange rind, each 3 × ½ inch (optional)
1 clove garlic, crushed
8 ounces uncooked capellini, spaghettini or other thin pasta
2 large sweet red peppers, cored, seeded and thinly sliced
1 cucumber, pared, halved lengthwise, seeded and cut crosswise into thin half-slices
2 carrots, pared and shredded

1. Prepare Oriental Dressing: Combine soy sauce, vinegar, vegetable oil, sugar and sesame oil in jar with tight-fitting lid; shake well to combine.
2. Prepare Salad: Place steak in self-sealing plastic bag. Add orange rind, garlic and 3 tablespoons dressing. Seal bag and shake. Refrigerate for 2 hours or overnight. Turn bag occasionally.

3. Cook pasta in large pot of boiling water according to package directions. One minute before pasta is done, drop peppers and cucumbers into water. Drain; rinse under cold running water; drain again. Transfer pasta, peppers and cucumber to large mixing bowl. Add carrot and remaining dressing; toss well.
4. Preheat broiler. Remove flank steak from bag; discard marinade.
5. Broil steak on broiler-pan rack 6 inches from heat for about 6 minutes per side or until medium-rare (timing will vary, depending upon thickness of meat). Let meat stand 10 minutes. Thinly slice across grain. Cut each slice in half lengthwise. Add to pasta mixture. Toss again and serve.

ORIENTAL STEAK SALAD MAKE-AHEAD TIP:
The dressing can be prepared several hours or a few days in advance and refrigerated, covered. Marinate the flank steak in the refrigerator for at least 2 hours or up to 8 hours before cooking.

½ pound fresh mushrooms, sliced
1 tablespoon chopped fresh rosemary OR:
    1 teaspoon dried
¼ teaspoon leaf thyme, crumbled
⅔ cup uncooked wild rice
⅓ cup uncooked basmati rice OR:
    Texmati rice OR: white rice
2 small summer squash (8 ounces),
    halved lengthwise and sliced
    crosswise
3 tablespoons white wine vinegar
½ teaspoon salt
¼ teaspoon pepper
1 pound chunk smoked turkey, cut into
    2 × ½ × ½-inch sticks
3 medium-size plum tomatoes, sliced

1. Soak dried mushrooms in boiling water to cover for 20 minutes. Drain, reserving and straining soaking liquid for another use, if you wish. Rinse mushrooms well. Pat dry with paper toweling. Cut off any tough stems and discard. Chop mushrooms. Slice leek; rinse in colander under running water to remove all sand. Pat slices dry with paper toweling.

2. Heat 2 tablespoons oil in skillet over medium heat. Add leek; sauté 4 minutes. Stir in soaked dried and fresh mushrooms, rosemary and thyme. Sauté 6 minutes or until liquid has evaporated. Scrape into large mixing bowl.

3. Bring large pot of water to boiling. Add wild rice; boil 25 minutes. Stir in basmati rice; boil 12 minutes. Stir in summer squash; boil 3 minutes more or until rices are tender. Drain in colander; add rice mixture to mushroom mixture in bowl.

4. Combine remaining 2 tablespoons oil, vinegar, salt and pepper in small bowl. Add along with smoked turkey to rice mixture; toss to coat. Cover and refrigerate at least 2 hours or overnight. Taste and add additional vinegar if needed. Serve chilled or at room temperature, garnished with tomato slices.

Make-Ahead Tip: The salad can be made up to 2 days ahead without the tomato garnish and refrigerated, covered.

WILD RICE, MUSHROOM AND SMOKED TURKEY SALAD

LOW-CHOLESTEROL

DON'T SKIMP ON WATER
Cooking rice, uncovered, in a large quantity of water keeps the grains separate, which is an admirable quality for rice salad.

*P*lain *roast turkey, cooked pork, or cubes of ham or ham and cheese can be substituted for the turkey. The salad also makes a wonderful filling for hollowed-out tomatoes or blanched zucchini boats.*

Makes 4 servings. Recipe can be doubled.
Nutrient Value Per Serving: 453 calories, 29 g protein, 19 g fat, 44 g carbohydrate, 1,398 mg sodium, 50 mg cholesterol.

1 package (½ ounce) dried mushrooms
1 leek, trimmed
4 tablespoons olive oil OR: vegetable oil

Thai Shrimp Salad with Coconut and Ginger

LOW-CALORIE

This recipe is a good introduction to some of the flavor combinations found in Thai cuisine: coconut, ginger, lime and hot pepper. Sea scallops or slivered chicken meat can be substituted for the shrimp.

Makes 4 servings.
Recipe can be halved or doubled.
Nutrient Value Per Serving: 247 calories, 20 g protein, 14 g fat, 11 g carbohydrate, 305 mg sodium, 140 mg cholesterol.

1 tablespoon olive or vegetable oil
1 pound medium-size raw shrimp (30 to 35), peeled and deveined
1 clove garlic, chopped
2 teaspoons grated, pared fresh ginger
1 jalapeño pepper, seeded and chopped
¾ cup coconut milk* OR: canned coconut milk
1 teaspoon grated lime rind
¼ teaspoon salt
1 red apple, cored and cubed
Red lettuce leaves
1 sweet red pepper, cored, seeded and cut into squares
3 green onions, sliced
3 stalks celery, diagonally sliced
1 teaspoon lime juice
½ cup roasted peanuts *(optional)*

1. Heat oil in skillet over medium heat. Add shrimp; cook, covered, 4 to 5 minutes or until opaque, turning halfway through cooking. Remove shrimp with slotted spoon to bowl.
2. Add garlic, ginger and jalapeño to skillet; cook 1 minute, stirring. Stir in coconut milk, lime rind and salt. Pour over shrimp. Stir in apple. Cover and refrigerate at least 3 hours.

(continued)

THAI SHRIMP SALAD WITH COCONUT AND GINGER (*continued*)

3. Arrange lettuce leaves on serving platter. Arrange red pepper, green onion and celery on top.

4. To serve: Spoon shrimp and apples with slotted spoon onto platter. Stir lime juice into coconut milk mixture and pass separately. Garnish salad with peanuts, if you wish.

*Note: To prepare an easy version of coconut milk, bring 1 cup milk to simmering in medium-size saucepan. Add 2 cups shredded sweetened coconut; cook 1 minute. Remove from heat and let stand 30 minutes. Drain in sieve, pressing out excess liquid. Discard coconut. Makes ¾ cup milk.

Make-Ahead Tip: The shrimp and the apple with the coconut mixture can be prepared a day ahead and refrigerated, separately. The salad can be prepared up to 3 hours ahead through Step 3 and refrigerated, covered.

Microwave Directions (High Power Oven):
To prepare coconut milk, pour milk into microwave-safe 4-cup measure. Microwave, uncovered, at 100% power 2½ to 3 minutes to simmering. Stir in coconut. Microwave, uncovered, at 100% power 30 seconds. Proceed as above. To prepare shrimp mixture, stir together oil, garlic, ginger and jalapeño pepper in microwave-safe 2-quart casserole with lid. Microwave, uncovered, at 100% power 2 minutes. Stir in shrimp. Microwave, covered, at 100% power 3 to 3½ minutes until cooked, stirring once. Stir in coconut milk, lime rind, salt and apple. Cover and refrigerate at least 3 hours. Finish recipe as above.

PARTY AT THE BAR
Plan a salad bar with 4 or 5 salads—mixed greens, pasta, rice, vegetable, meat or seafood, fruit—and set out go-withs: crumbled bacon, croutons, nuts and seeds. Include lowfat dressings such as our Buttermilk Dressing with Dill, page 177. Fill baskets with assorted breads *(see The Best of Bread, page 105)* and have a variety of cheeses nearby. After the party, consult the cheese storage guide on page 172.

BROWN RICE, PEANUT AND BROCCOLI SALAD WITH TAMARI DRESSING

This lunchtime salad uses leftover chicken, either from your own kitchen or already cooked from the deli. Increase portion sizes to serve 4 for dinner.

Makes 6 servings.
Recipe can be halved or doubled.
Nutrient Value Per Serving: 387 calories, 17 g protein, 23 g fat, 31 g carbohydrate, 409 mg sodium, 21 mg cholesterol.

1 cup long- or short-grain brown rice
2 cups broccoli flowerets and tender stems, cut into 1-inch pieces (about 6 ounces)
¼ cup olive oil OR: vegetable oil
½ teaspoon grated lemon rind
2 tablespoons fresh lemon juice
1 tablespoon tamari soy sauce
1 teaspoon grated, pared fresh ginger
1 clove garlic, crushed
1 cup shredded cooked chicken
1 cup coarsely chopped dry-roasted peanuts
¼ cup thinly sliced green onion (both white and green parts)

1. Cook brown rice without salt following package directions. Cool.

2. Cook broccoli in vegetable steamer over simmering water in covered saucepan until tender-crisp, about 5 minutes. Drain; rinse with cold water to stop cooking; drain well.

3. Whisk together oil, lemon rind, lemon juice, tamari sauce, ginger and garlic in large bowl. Add rice, broccoli, chicken and peanuts; toss gently to blend. Sprinkle with green onion. Serve at room temperature.

Make-Ahead Tip: The rice and broccoli can be prepared a day ahead and refrigerated separately, covered.

SAFFRON SEAFOOD SALAD

LOW-FAT

This is a spectacular salad for a small intimate party. If good fresh mussels are hard to find, use all shrimp or increase the amounts of scallops and shrimp.

Makes 4 servings. Recipe can be doubled.
Nutrient Value Per Serving: 440 calories, 29 g protein, 13 g fat, 50 g carbohydrate, 713 mg sodium, 99 mg cholesterol.

Dressing:
½ cup parsley leaves
3 tablespoons olive oil
3 tablespoons sherry wine vinegar OR: red wine vinegar
¼ teaspoon salt
¼ teaspoon pepper

Salad:
1¼ cups chicken broth
2 cloves garlic, chopped
1 pound mussels, scrubbed and debearded
½ pound raw shrimp, peeled and deveined
½ pound raw bay scallops
2 pinches (a loose ⅛ teaspoon) saffron threads
1 cup converted long-grain white rice
1 yellow squash (8 ounces), quartered lengthwise and sliced crosswise
1 large sweet green pepper, cored, seeded and cubed
2 cups diced plum tomatoes (14 ounces)

1. Prepare Dressing: Combine parsley, olive oil, vinegar, salt and pepper in blender or food processor. Whirl until smooth. Reserve.
2. Prepare Salad: Bring ¼ cup chicken broth and garlic to boiling in medium-size saucepan, covered. Add mussels; cook, covered, 4 to 6 minutes or until shells open. Discard any unopened shells. Transfer mussels with slotted spoon to bowl. Reserve.
3. Add shrimp and scallops to simmering broth in saucepan; cook, covered, 5 minutes or until opaque. Transfer with slotted spoon to small bowl; cover.
4. Add remaining 1 cup chicken broth and saffron to saucepan. Bring to boiling. Stir in rice. Lower heat; simmer, covered, for 10 minutes. Stir in squash and green pepper; cook 10 minutes or until rice is tender and liquid is absorbed. Transfer to clean bowl.
5. Add 2 tablespoons dressing to shrimp and scallops. Add remaining dressing to rice mixture.
6. To serve: Arrange rice, shrimp mixture, tomatoes and mussels on platter or plates. Serve warm or chilled.

SEAFOOD SALAD MAKE-AHEAD TIP:
The various components of this salad, except for the mussels, can be made a day ahead and refrigerated, covered. Cook the mussels the same day you plan to serve the salad.

MELON AND SHRIMP WITH CILANTRO-LIME DRESSING

A *cooling salad with lots of fiery taste.*

Broil for 5 minutes.
Makes 4 servings.
Nutrient Value Per Serving: 274 calories, 22 g protein, 13 g fat, 19 g carbohydrate, 374 mg sodium, 140 mg cholesterol.

Marinade:
1 tablespoon finely chopped, seeded jalapeño pepper
1 tablespoon olive oil OR: vegetable oil
1 large clove garlic, crushed
¼ teaspoon crushed red pepper flakes
¼ teaspoon salt

1 pound large raw shrimp (about 20), peeled and deveined
2 green onions
1 cup diced plum tomatoes (about 2)
2 teaspoons finely chopped mint *(optional)*
8 cups torn pieces curly leaf lettuce
1 tablespoon finely chopped fresh coriander OR: parsley
1 ripe cantaloupe
12 thin slices cucumber
Cilantro-Lime Dressing *(recipe follows)*

1. Prepare Marinade: Whisk together jalapeño pepper, olive oil, garlic, red pepper flakes and salt in small bowl.
2. Combine marinade and shrimp in small bowl. Cover and refrigerate about 1 hour.
3. Preheat broiler.
4. Broil shrimp on rack 2 inches from heat for 5 minutes or until cooked through, turning once. Cool shrimp slightly. Discard marinade.
5. Chop white part of 1 green onion; place in small bowl. Stir in tomatoes and mint, if using.
6. Diagonally slice remaining green onion; combine with lettuce and coriander in large bowl.
7. Cut melon into 12 wedges; seed and pare. Arrange melon, lettuce mixture, cucumber slices and shrimp on salad plates, dividing equally. Sprinkle tomato mixture over each. Drizzle each salad with 1 tablespoon dressing. Serve remaining dressing on side, if you wish.

Cilantro-Lime Dressing: Whisk together ⅓ cup olive oil, 2 tablespoons lime juice, 2 tablespoons finely chopped fresh cilantro, 1 small clove garlic, crushed, and ½ teaspoon salt in small bowl. Remove garlic clove before serving.

CHEESE CHOICES

Natural cheeses are classified by texture from soft to very hard. Within each category there are wide varieties of styles and flavors. Which cheese you choose depends on how you use it.

SOFT CHEESES

Brie, Camembert: mild to slightly tangy; creamy, soft-ripened cheeses with firm, edible rind; soft center becomes runny at room temperature; veined variety has mellow blue cheese flavor. Serve as dessert or snacking cheese with fruit and nuts, as an hors d'oeuvre with crackers, or sliced and spread on sandwiches.

Cottage cheese: mildly tangy, spreadable, curd cheese; available in creamy, dry-curd and low fat styles including pressed farmer's cheese, pickled liptauer, large-curd pot cheese and rich, creamy ricotta. Use for eating and baking.

Chèvre: a soft, white, tart French goat cheese, also produced in this country; sometimes coated in an edible gray ash or rolled in herbs. Slice into rounds and marinate; serve with crackers and fruit; melt into sauces and add to casseroles.

Cream cheese: smooth, somewhat tangy cheese made from cream and milk; fresh, French-style cream cheese is sold as Chantilly in flavors ranging from fruit to herb to chocolate; Neufchâtel or Neufchâtel variety differs from cream cheese only in its lower fat content. Classic ingredient in cheesecake; use for sandwiches, dips and spreads, sauces, pastry filling.

Explorateur, St. André: very rich, smooth, triple-cream (75% butterfat) dessert cheeses. Serve as a final dinner course with fruit, nuts, sweet wine.

Mascarpone: Italian double-cream (rich) cheese with buttery flavor and a slight tang; sometimes flavored with sweet liqueurs or fruit or savory seasonings such as smoked ham or mustard. Use

From left: Stilton, Edam, Fontina, white Cheddar, Feta and Bel Paese.

plain or sweetened versions as a dessert cheese, savory versions for appetizers and sauces.

SEMISOFT TO FIRM CHEESES

Bel Paese: mellow to slightly tart. A good snack cheese with crackers and/or fruit; shred for an omelet; cube for a salad; substitute in recipes calling for mozzarella.

Blue: crumbly; sharp and tangy; blue- or green-veined; varieties include Italian Gorgonzola, French Roquefort, English Stilton. Sprinkle over salad or fruit; melt over hot vegetables; puree with yogurt, sour cream or cream cheese for dip or spread.

Cheddar: white, yellow or orange with flavor ranging from mild to sharp, depending on age and curing process. All-purpose cheese for eating or cooking.

Edam: mild, nutty flavor; Dutch yellow cheese sold with red wax coating; similar to but firmer and less rich than Gouda. Use both for cooking and eating.

Feta: crumbly, salty brine cheese made from sheep or goat's milk. Use in salads, pita pocket sandwiches, and cooking.

Fontina: nutty, mild-flavored cheese from Italy or Scandinavia; good melting cheese. Use for

SOFT CHEESES

Front row, from left: cream cheese, Explorateur, chèvre and Brie. Back row, from left: ricotta, Mascarpone, cottage cheese, St. André and pot cheese.

SEMISOFT TO FIRM CHEESES

Front row, from left: Port Salut, Muenster, mozzarella and provolone. Second row, from left: Gjetost, Samsoe, Jarlsberg and Monterey Jack.

sauces, fondues; substitute for mozzarella.

Gjetost: strong, sweet, caramel-brown Norwegian cheese made with goat's milk whey; lacks a true cheese flavor. Serve with sliced apples or in a sandwich made with dark, crusty bread.

Jack (Monterey): mild white cheese, originally from California. Good for cooking, eating, shredding over hot foods; often used in Southwestern cooking.

Mozzarella: mild flavor; available smoked or fresh. Marinate to use as an hors d'oeuvre; slice for sandwiches; shred and use in cooking and casseroles.

Muenster: creamy white with edible orange rind; available in bricks and slices. Shred for soups and casseroles; slice for sandwiches.

Port Salut: smooth, elastic texture; strong flavor and aroma reminiscent of Limburger. Eat out of hand or in sandwich made with dark, hearty bread.

Provolone: salty, smoky, mellow to sharp. Slice for sandwiches and antipasto plates; grate for pasta dishes.

Samsoe: nutty, mildly sweet Danish cheese with small holes. Use in sandwiches or salads; melt into sauces, casseroles, fondues.

Swiss: nutty flavor; elastic texture; Swiss-style cheeses include Emmenthaler, Jarlsberg and Gruyère. Better melting qualities when aged; use for sandwiches, salads, cooking.

HARD (GRATING) CHEESES

Aged asiago: rich, salty Italian cheese. Grate into soups, sauces, casseroles.

Parmesan: grainy, off-white cheese. Used primarily for grating over pasta or salads and in cooking.

Pecorino: dry, pungent cheese made from sheep's milk. Grate and use as for Parmesan.

Romano: grating cheese similar to but sharper than Parmesan.

Sapsago: dry, pale green cheese; flavored and colored with clover. Grate and add to cream sauces or soups.

PROCESSED AND LOW-CALORIE CHEESE BLENDS

Processed cheeses and spreads, including reduced-calorie and reduced-fat cheese products, contain less milk fat and more water than natural cheeses. As a result, they differ from their counterparts in flavor, texture and melting quality and cannot always be substituted in cooking or baking.

WELL-KEPT CHEESE

■ Store *soft* cheeses in coldest section of the refrigerator in original containers, or wrap tightly with plastic wrap or foil, 1 to 2 weeks.

■ Refrigerate *hard* and *semisoft* or *semi-firm* cheese tightly wrapped in plastic or waxed paper; overwrap with foil. Wrap strong-flavored cheeses and store in tightly covered containers. Keep hard, semisoft and semi-firm cheese 3 weeks to 2 months, depending on variety.

■ Freeze *hard, semisoft* and *semi-firm* natural (unprocessed) cheeses in freezer wrap in small pieces (up to 1 pound) for up to several months. Thaw in refrigerator; use as soon as possible.

■ Do not freeze *processed cheese* or *cheese spreads, cream* or *cottage cheese.*

HARD (GRATING) CHEESES

From left: Pecorino, Romano, Parmesan, aged Asiago and sapsago.

BREAD AND VEGETABLE SALAD WITH MOZZARELLA

This main-dish salad is inspired by panzanella, originally a poor man's dinner in Tuscany. Serve as a first course or salad course, or with a glass of white wine or mineral water for lunch. To speed up preparation, substitute jarred roasted red peppers for the whole fresh peppers which you roast yourself.

Toast bread at 400° for 8 minutes; broil peppers 17 minutes; broil zucchini 10 minutes.
Makes 4 servings.
Recipe can be halved or doubled.
Nutrient Value Per Serving: 452 calories, 16 g protein, 30 g fat, 31 g carbohydrate, 386 mg sodium, 45 mg cholesterol.

Dressing:
⅓ cup firmly packed fresh basil leaves
5 tablespoons olive oil
4 anchovy fillets, rinsed and dried (optional)
2½ tablespoons balsamic vinegar
2 cloves garlic

Salad:
4 ounces (½ loaf) Italian bread, cut into 1-inch cubes (3 cups)
4 large sweet red peppers (8 ounces each)
2 zucchini, diagonally sliced into 16 long rounds
8 ounces whole-milk or part-skim mozzarella cheese, cut into 16 slices

1. Preheat oven to hot (400°).
2. Prepare Dressing: Combine basil, olive oil, anchovies if using, vinegar and garlic in food processor or blender. Whirl until basil and anchovies are pureed. Cover and set aside.
3. Prepare Salad: Toast bread cubes on baking sheet in preheated hot oven (400°), stirring occasionally, until crisp and golden, about 8 minutes. Transfer to large mixing bowl. Increase oven temperature to broil.
4. Broil peppers on broiler pan 6 inches from heat, turning, until blackened all over, about 15 minutes. Transfer peppers to paper bag and seal. When cool enough to handle, core and peel peppers and discard seeds. (See How-To, page 433.) Cut peppers into thick lengthwise slices, about 6 per pepper. Add to bread cubes in bowl.
5. Sprinkle zucchini with a little water. Broil on broiler pan 4 inches from heat for 5 minutes per side or until browned. Add to bread and peppers in bowl. Add mozzarella.
6. Pour dressing over salad; toss well to combine. Let stand 30 minutes at room temperature for bread to soften slightly. Serve.

Make-Ahead Tip: The vegetables can be roasted up to 2 days ahead and refrigerated, covered, while the croutons and dressing can be prepared several days ahead. The salad with dressing should not be assembled until 30 minutes before serving.

TROPICAL FRUIT SALAD WITH GINGER-YOGURT DRESSING

LOW-FAT · LOW-SODIUM
LOW-CHOLESTEROL · QUICK

This sweet and tangy salad is wonderful on its own or as an accompaniment to roast meats or poultry. Use all mango if you wish, or substitute grapes for some of the fruit. Garnish with fresh mint sprigs, crystallized ginger and/or sliced star fruit.

SALAD DAYS

Try the Ginger-Yogurt Dressing in your favorite chicken salad recipe. Need a main-dish salad? Add roasted pork or chicken.

Makes 6 servings. Recipe can be doubled.
Nutrient Value Per Serving: 144 calories, 2 g protein, 3 g fat, 31 g carbohydrate, 33 mg sodium, 2 mg cholesterol.

Ginger-Yogurt Dressing:
1 piece fresh ginger (4 inches)
⅓ cup lowfat plain yogurt
1 tablespoon mayonnaise
1 tablespoon honey

Salad:
1 medium-size honeydew melon OR: cantaloupe
1 ripe mango (about 1½ pounds)
1 ripe papaya (about 1¼ pounds)

1. Prepare Ginger-Yogurt Dressing: Peel ginger; grate over bowl or plate. Squeeze grated ginger to extract as much juice as possible; you should have about 4 teaspoons. Transfer juice to small mixing bowl; discard solids.
2. Whisk together ginger juice, yogurt, mayonnaise and honey. Cover and refrigerate until serving time.
3. Prepare Salad: Halve melon and remove seeds. Using large melon baller, scoop out melon balls; you should have about 3 cups. Peel mango; cut into spears. Peel papaya; halve and remove seeds. Cut flesh into spears. Arrange melon, mango and papaya on 6 cold serving plates or serve in scooped-out mango, papaya or melon halves. Pour dressing over each or spoon dressing into hollowed-out melon half. Or toss all the fruits together in large serving bowl and drizzle with dressing.

Make-Ahead Tip: The dressing can be made several days ahead and refrigerated. The fruit can be prepared earlier in the day and refrigerated, but the salad shouldn't be dressed until just before serving.

APPLE AND PEAR SALAD WITH CIDER DRESSING

QUICK

In the fall, take advantage of the crisp apples and ripe pears in the market. We've used blue cheese, but feel free to experiment with others. To make a main course, increase the amount of cheese.

Toast nuts at 350° for 7 minutes.
Makes 6 servings.
Recipe can be halved or doubled.
Nutrient Value Per Serving: 310 calories, 8 g protein, 23 g fat, 22 g carbohydrate, 408 mg sodium, 21 mg cholesterol.

Cider Dressing:
2 tablespoons vegetable oil
1 tablespoon apple cider
1 tablespoon apple cider vinegar
1 tablespoon honey

Salad:
⅔ cup pecan halves (3 ounces) OR: walnuts
1 bunch watercress, trimmed, washed and dried
2 crisp red apples, such as McIntosh, Empire or Ida Red, halved, cored and thinly sliced
2 firm ripe pears, halved, cored and thinly sliced
6 ounces blue cheese, crumbled OR: goat cheese

1. Preheat oven to moderate (350°).
2. Prepare Cider Dressing: Combine oil, cider, cider vinegar and honey in small jar with tight-fitting lid; shake well to combine.
3. Prepare Salad: Toast pecans on baking sheet in preheated moderate oven (350°) for 7 minutes or until crisp and fragrant; set aside.
4. Arrange watercress on 6 chilled serving plates. Arrange apple and pear slices on top. Sprinkle with blue cheese and pecans. Shake dressing once more and drizzle over each. Or arrange salad on large serving platter.

Make-Ahead Tip: The dressing can be made several days ahead and refrigerated, covered.

Microwave Directions for Toasting Pecans (High Power Oven): Spread pecans in microwave-safe 9-inch pie plate. Microwave, uncovered, at 100% power 3 to 3½ minutes or until toasted.

PEACH AND PLUM SALAD WITH RED CURRANT DRESSING

LOW-SODIUM · LOW-CHOLESTEROL

QUICK

*S*erve this as a side dish or as a dessert. *A good accompaniment with roast pork, chicken or duck, or even venison.*

Toast nuts at 350° for about 5 minutes.
Makes 4 servings.
Recipe can be halved or doubled.
Nutrient Value Per Serving: 226 calories, 7 g protein, 9 g fat, 34 g carbohydrate, 33 mg sodium, 4 mg cholesterol.

Red Currant Dressing:
2 tablespoons red currant jelly
1 tablespoon water
⅔ cup lowfat plain yogurt
1 tablespoon whole-milk or part-skim
     ricotta cheese
1 teaspoon fresh lime juice

Salad:
½ cup slivered almonds (2 ounces)
2 large ripe peaches (9 ounces each)
4 ripe red plums (3 ounces each), pitted
     and cut into ¼-inch-thick wedges

1. Preheat oven to moderate (350°).
2. Prepare Red Currant Dressing: Melt jelly with water in small saucepan over low heat. Whisk together yogurt, jelly, ricotta and lime juice in small bowl. Cover and refrigerate until serving time.
3. Prepare Salad: Toast almonds on baking sheet in preheated moderate oven (350°) for about 5 minutes or until lightly golden.
4. Blanch peaches in small pot of boiling water for 1 minute. Remove with slotted spoon. When cool enough to handle, peel with paring knife or swivel-bladed vegetable peeler. Pit and cut into ¼-inch-thick wedges.
5. Arrange peaches and plums on 4 chilled serving plates. Drizzle dressing over each and sprinkle with nuts.

Make-Ahead Tip: The dressing can be prepared several days ahead and refrigerated, covered.

MICROWAVE DIRECTIONS FOR MELTING JELLY (HIGH POWER OVEN):
Combine jelly and water in microwave-safe 1-cup measure. Microwave, uncovered, at 100% power 30 seconds.

MICROWAVE DIRECTIONS FOR TOASTING ALMONDS (HIGH POWER OVEN):
Spread almonds on microwave-safe dinner plate. Microwave, uncovered, at 100% power 3 minutes, stirring once.

WARM SPINACH AND PEAR SALAD WITH BACON DRESSING

LOW-CHOLESTEROL • QUICK

Serve as a first course, or a light luncheon dish with whole-grain bread. Vary the flavor and texture by substituting apples, peaches, papayas or melon for the pear. (Pictured on page 143.)

Makes 6 servings.
Recipe can be doubled.
Nutrient Value Per Serving: 123 calories, 3 g protein, 10 g fat, 7 g carbohydrate, 236 mg sodium, 8 mg cholesterol.

1 bag (10 ounces) fresh spinach, rinsed, dried and torn into bite-size pieces
4 slices bacon
1 tablespoon vegetable oil
1 small onion, diced
2 tablespoons cider vinegar
1 teaspoon spicy brown mustard
½ teaspoon sugar
¼ teaspoon salt
⅛ teaspoon pepper
1 pear, cored and thinly sliced

1. Place spinach in large bowl.
2. Cook bacon in large skillet over medium-high heat until crisp. Remove to paper toweling to drain. Discard all but 3 tablespoons drippings from skillet.
3. Add oil to drippings in skillet and heat. Add onion; cook until tender, about 3 minutes. Stir in vinegar, mustard, sugar, salt and pepper. Bring to boiling. Remove from heat.
4. Add pear to spinach. Pour hot dressing over spinach and pear; toss well to coat. Crumble bacon and sprinkle over salad. Serve immediately.

Microwave Directions for Making Dressing (High Power Oven): Halve bacon slices. Place in single layer on microwave-safe bacon rack in microwave-safe shallow dish, about 12 × 8 inches. Microwave, uncovered, at 100% power 3 to 3½ minutes until crisp. Remove to paper toweling to drain. Remove rack from dish. Combine 3 tablespoons bacon drippings, oil and onion in same dish. Microwave, uncovered, at 100% power 3 minutes. Transfer mixture to microwave-safe 2-cup measure; stir in vinegar, mustard, sugar, salt and pepper. Microwave, uncovered, at 100% power 1 minute to boiling.

BUTTERMILK DRESSING WITH DILL

LOW-CALORIE • LOW-FAT
LOW-CHOLESTEROL • LOW-SODIUM
QUICK

Assertively flavored with fresh dill, this dressing matches well with a variety of partners: leafy greens, cooked vegetables such as sliced red potatoes, or even a pasta salad. You can substitute finely chopped chives, or any other fresh green herb, for the dill. Using buttermilk keeps both the calories and fat low.

Makes 1⅓ cups.
Recipe can be halved or doubled.
Nutrient Value Per Tablespoon:
7 calories, 0 g protein, 0 g fat, 1 g carbohydrate, 38 mg sodium, 0 mg cholesterol.

1 cup buttermilk
⅓ cup cider vinegar
1 shallot, thinly sliced OR: green onion, thinly sliced
2 tablespoons finely chopped fresh dill OR: 2 teaspoons dried dillweed
1 teaspoon sugar
¼ teaspoon salt
⅛ teaspoon ground hot red pepper

Combine buttermilk, vinegar, shallot, dill, sugar, salt and pepper in blender. Whirl until well combined, about 15 seconds.

PREPARED MUSTARD, PERSONALIZED
Sweeten store-bought mustards with maple syrup, honey or fruit spread, or add a savory touch with grated horseradish or citrus peel, crushed peppercorns and dried herbs. Refrigerate for at least a few days for flavors to develop before using. Makes a wonderful holiday gift.

BUTTERMILK
Contrary to its name, buttermilk does not contain butter. Although originally a by-product of butter-making, buttermilk today is made from pasteurized lowfat or skim milk that is fermented in a manner similar to yogurt or sour cream. During an incubation period, lactose (milk sugar) is converted to lactic acid, which gives buttermilk its characteristic acidic flavor and thick consistency. Buttermilk adds tang to cold soups, fruit shakes and salad dressings and imparts a tender crumb to pancakes, waffles and baked goods.

BUTTERMILK DRESSING MAKE-AHEAD TIP:
Dressing can be prepared up to 3 days ahead and refrigerated, covered.

CURRIED YOGURT DRESSING

LOW-CALORIE · LOW-SODIUM
LOW-CHOLESTEROL · QUICK

This versatile dressing, accented with fresh cilantro, is delicious with assertive leafy greens, cooked vegetables or even as a dipping sauce for raw vegetables. Use the low-calorie yogurt base to experiment with a variety of herbs and spices. If cilantro is unavailable, substitute finely chopped fresh chives or parsley.

Makes 1½ cups.
Recipe can be halved or doubled.
Nutrient Value Per Tablespoon:
17 calories, 1 g protein, 1 g fat,
1 g carbohydrate, 38 mg sodium,
3 mg cholesterol.

1 cup plain yogurt
½ cup dairy sour cream OR:
    reduced-calorie sour cream OR:
    no-fat sour cream
2 tablespoons lemon juice
1 tablespoon finely chopped cilantro
1 clove garlic, finely chopped *(optional)*
1 teaspoon curry powder, or to taste
1 teaspoon Dijon-style mustard
¼ teaspoon salt
⅛ teaspoon ground hot red pepper

Whisk together yogurt, sour cream, lemon juice, cilantro, garlic if using, curry powder, mustard, salt and hot pepper in small bowl until smooth.

Make-Ahead Tip: Dressing can be made up to 3 days ahead and refrigerated.

CURRIED YOGURT DRESSING OTHER WAYS
Toss Curried Yogurt Dressing with hot cooked pasta for a quick sauce, or drizzle over your favorite chicken, turkey, fruit or fish salad.

RUSSIAN DRESSING

LOW-CALORIE · LOW-CHOLESTEROL
QUICK

This is our reduced-calorie, lower-fat version of a classic Russian dressing. Serve on leafy greens, as a dip with cooked or raw vegetables, or as a spread on meat, poultry and cheese sandwiches.

Makes 2 cups.
Recipe can be halved or doubled.
Nutrient Value Per Tablespoon:
23 calories, 0 g protein, 2 g fat,
2 g carbohydrate, 85 mg sodium,
0 mg cholesterol.

⅔ cup reduced-calorie mayonnaise
⅔ cup lowfat plain yogurt
⅓ cup chili sauce
2 tablespoons finely chopped sweet green pepper
2 tablespoons finely chopped pimiento
2 tablespoons finely chopped celery
2 tablespoons finely chopped onion
1 tablespoon lemon juice
¼ teaspoon salt
¼ teaspoon pepper

Whisk together mayonnaise, yogurt, chili sauce, green pepper, pimiento, celery, onion, lemon juice, salt and pepper in bowl.

Make-Ahead Tip: Dressing can be made up to 3 days ahead and refrigerated.

LUNCH ON THE DECK

Open-Face California
Chicken Salad Sandwich
(104)

Green Salad with Russian
Dressing (this page)

Pineapple Fig Bars (103)

CITRUS DRESSING

LOW-SODIUM · LOW-CHOLESTEROL
QUICK

Drizzle over fruit and poultry or fruit and meat salads, or avocado and crisp vegetable salads. Try as a marinade for poultry or seafood, or as a sauce for grilled poultry and leafy green combinations.

Makes 1 cup. Recipe can be doubled.
Nutrient Value Per Tablespoon:
44 calories, 0 g protein, 5 g fat,
1 g carbohydrate, 35 mg sodium,
0 mg cholesterol.

⅓ cup orange juice
¼ cup lemon juice
2 tablespoons raspberry vinegar OR:
    balsamic vinegar OR: red wine
    vinegar
2 tablespoons finely chopped shallot OR:
    green onion
1 teaspoon grated lemon rind
1 teaspoon grated orange rind
¼ teaspoon salt
⅓ cup vegetable oil
1 tablespoon finely chopped mint

Combine orange juice, lemon juice, vinegar, shallot, lemon rind, orange rind and salt in blender. Whirl until well combined, about 15 seconds. With machine running, add oil in thin stream, then the mint, and blend until smooth and thoroughly incorporated, about 20 seconds.

Make-Ahead Tip: Dressing can be made up to 3 days ahead and refrigerated.

GINGER-SESAME DRESSING

LOW-CHOLESTEROL · QUICK

Robustly flavored with Oriental sesame oil and fresh ginger, this dressing goes well with seafood, poultry, pasta and vegetable salads.

Makes 1 cup. Recipe can be doubled.
Nutrient Value Per Tablespoon:
93 calories, 0 g protein, 10 g fat,
0 g carbohydrate, 62 mg sodium,
0 mg cholesterol.

2 tablespoons rice vinegar OR: white wine
    vinegar
2 tablespoons lemon juice
1 tablespoon finely chopped, pared fresh
    ginger
1 tablespoon Dijon-style mustard
1 clove garlic, finely chopped
¼ teaspoon salt
⅛ teaspoon pepper
½ cup vegetable oil
¼ cup Oriental sesame oil
1 tablespoon finely chopped cilantro OR:
    parsley

Combine vinegar, lemon juice, ginger, mustard, garlic, salt and pepper in blender. Whirl until combined, about 15 seconds. With machine running, add oils in thin stream and blend until smooth and thoroughly incorporated, about 20 seconds. Add the cilantro.

Make-Ahead Tip: Dressing can be made up to 3 days ahead and refrigerated, covered.

DRESSING SLIM
■ Use buttermilk, yogurt or pureed lowfat cottage cheese as a base for creamy, low-calorie salad dressings. Season with dry or prepared mustard; herbs and spices; crushed poppy, fennel or celery seeds; honey; hot sauce; grated onion; or citrus peel. To vary the dressing consistency, thin out with fruit or vegetable juice.
■ Use fat-free prepared salsa as a salad dressing or make your own from juicy, finely chopped, flavorful vegetables—ripe tomatoes, roasted peppers, green olives, red onions, cucumbers. Stir in fresh lemon, lime or grapefruit juice or an herb-flavored vinegar.

VINEGAR

Vinegar is made by a controlled fermentation process that turns alcohol into acetic acid. In fact, the word vinegar comes from the French *vin* (wine) and *aigre* (sour).

Vinegar adds a tang to salad dressings and sauces, helps tenderize lean cuts of meat when used in a marinade, and acts as a preservative in pickled foods. Today, vinegar is used more and more to flavor foods that have been modified to reduce fat or sodium.

Supermarkets now carry a wide assortment of vinegars, each of which plays a distinctive role in the kitchen.

■ **Wine vinegar** is most often used for salad dressing, marinades and sauces. Use *red wine vinegar* for robust salads made with strongly flavored greens such as escarole or spinach and in marinades and sauces for red meats. Use *white wine vinegar* or Champagne vinegar with more delicate greens such as Boston or Bibb lettuce and in fish or poultry dishes.

■ **Balsamic vinegar** is a dark red Italian vinegar made from unfermented grapes and aged in wooden casks to achieve a mellow finish. Mild and sweet, balsamic vinegar is often used without oil to dress a salad. Try a sprinkle on fresh fruit and berries.

■ **Sherry vinegar** is a sweet, full-flavored Spanish wine vinegar. Use to dress salads made with fruits and cheese or sprinkle on green vegetables.

■ **Rice vinegar** is a sweet vinegar with low acidity. Traditionally used in Chinese and Japanese cooking, rice vinegar extends beyond its native cuisines, adding a mild spark of flavor to any seafood, poultry or vegetable combination.

■ **Berry vinegar,** infused with the fruity flavor of blueberries, raspberries or other berries, adds a fresh, gentle piquancy to salad dressings and poultry dishes. Add to sautéed sweet vegetables such as carrots or onions.

■ **Herb vinegar** is usually made from white wine vinegar infused with fresh herbs such as tarragon or dill. Excellent for flavoring poultry or vegetable dishes or dressing light green salads.

■ **Distilled white vinegar,** made from grain alcohol, is highly acidic and best used for pickling.

■ **Cider vinegar,** made from fermented apple juice, is mildly acidic, almost sweet, and most often used for pickling, potato salad, and as a substitute in Chinese cooking when rice vinegar is unavailable.

■ **Malt vinegar** has a strong, lemon-like flavor that serves as a tangy foil to the blandness of fried fish and potato dishes.

Dark vinegars, from left: malt, raspberry, red wine, sherry and balsamic.

Light vinegars, from left: Champagne, rice, tarragon, white wine, distilled white and cider.

OIL YOU NEED TO KNOW

Which oil to use when? Knowing the different characteristics of cooking and salad oils will help you use each type to its best advantage. While many oils can be used interchangeably, some are more suited to cooking and others are best used for flavoring. For example, it would be impractical to deep-fry a fritter in an expensive, extra-virgin olive oil, and the oil's low burning point would prevent proper cooking. Likewise, a devoted Italian cook would shudder at using a bland vegetable oil in a basil pesto, where a richly flavored olive oil is imperative to the success of the sauce.

Olive oil is available in different grades and varies in color, flavor and aroma, depending on the variety of olive and extraction or

olive oil

corn oil

soybean oil

safflower oil

canola oil

peanut oil

Oriental sesame oil

walnut oil

refining method used to produce the oil. Unrefined *extra virgin olive oil* has the lowest acidity and richest flavor of all olive oils. Its color varies from deep golden to dark green. Extra-virgin olive oil is the most expensive grade and is best used in small amounts for flavoring salads and sauces. *Virgin olive oil*, also unrefined, varies in flavor but is slightly more acidic and less fruity than extra-virgin. Virgin olive oil is usually combined with refined olive oil to improve the flavor and produce the product which is simply labeled *olive oil* or *pure olive oil.* Use olive oil in vinaigrette dressings or for light sautéing. Virgin olive oil is also blended with a lower grade oil that has been extracted through the use of solvents from pomace, or olive residue, to produce inexpensive *olive pomace oil.* The best use for olive pomace oil is all-purpose sautéing and shallow frying.

Corn, cottonseed, soybean, safflower, canola and peanut oils are neutral-flavored cooking oils that won't mask the true taste of foods. Varying combinations of these oils are often sold as all-purpose vegetable oils. Use for all types of frying and for mixing with herbs and flavorful vinegars in vinaigrette dressings.

Clear **sesame oil,** used mostly for cooking, adds a mild nutlike flavor to foods, but is not to be confused with **Oriental sesame oil,** a heavy, deep-brown oil used to flavor foods with the taste of toasted sesame seeds. Oriental sesame oil is never used as a cooking oil and if used in a cooked dish, is usually added at the end to prevent burning.

Unrefined and uniquely flavorful **walnut, almond, hazelnut and avocado oils** are usually used in small amounts in salads made with assertive greens such as arugula, escarole and spinach.

Tropical oils from *palm* and *coconut* are more frequently found in prepared foods than on supermarket shelves as cooking oils.

Flavored oils, usually made from olive or grapeseed oil, are infused with flavor from fresh herbs, garlic, peppercorns and other seasonings. Use in salad dressings and marinades or brush on grilled foods.

CARE AND KEEPING
The less refined, more flavorful olive, nut and seed oils are also more perishable. Store all oils in airtight containers in a cool, dark place for up to 6 months (olive oil will keep for up to 2 years). Refrigerate unrefined oils during hot weather; the oil will congeal and although some cloudiness may develop, the quality of the oil is unaffected. Before using refrigerated oil, bring to room temperature or run container under warm water to remove cloudiness and liquefy oil. Rancid oil is easily recognized by a distinct "off" flavor that signals time for replacement.

HORSERADISH DRESSING

QUICK

If you are lucky enough to find fresh horseradish, by all means use it, but sparingly since it is much more pungent than the bottled variety. This is the perfect partner for meat or vegetable salads, and it even makes a lively dip for vegetables.

Makes ⅔ cup. Recipe can be doubled.
Nutrient Value Per Tablespoon:
92 calories, 1 g protein, 9 g fat,
3 g carbohydrate, 190 mg sodium,
10 mg cholesterol.

1 cup dairy sour cream OR:
    reduced-calorie sour cream
½ cup reduced-calorie mayonnaise
3 tablespoons cider vinegar
3 tablespoons drained bottled horseradish
2 tablespoons finely chopped onion
½ teaspoon salt
⅛ teaspoon ground hot red pepper

Combine sour cream, mayonnaise, vinegar, horseradish, onion, salt and red pepper in blender. Whirl until well combined, about 15 seconds.

CREAMY BLACK PEPPER DRESSING

LOW-SODIUM · LOW-CHOLESTEROL
QUICK

Goes well over greens, steamed vegetables, chilled sliced beef or fruit salads.

Makes 1 cup dressing.
Recipe can be doubled.
Nutrient Value Per Tablespoon:
32 calories, 1 g protein, 3 g fat,
1 g carbohydrate, 32 mg sodium,
3 mg cholesterol.

½ cup reduced-calorie sour cream
⅓ cup reduced-calorie mayonnaise
¼ cup milk
1 tablespoon lemon juice
1 teaspoon Worcestershire sauce
½ teaspoon cracked black pepper
½ teaspoon grated lemon rind

Stir together sour cream, mayonnaise, milk, lemon juice, Worcestershire sauce, pepper and lemon rind in small bowl until well blended.

GREEN GODDESS DRESSING

LOW-CHOLESTEROL · QUICK

Here's our version of this classic. Serve over greens, steamed vegetables, chilled cooked fish or chicken. Excellent as a dip with lightly cooked or raw vegetables, or drizzled over an open-faced avocado and sprout sandwich (see page 104).

Makes 1¼ cups. Recipe can be doubled.
Nutrient Value Per Tablespoon:
44 calories, 0 g protein, 4 g fat,
1 g carbohydrate, 81 mg sodium,
1 mg cholesterol.

1 cup reduced-calorie mayonnaise
¼ cup finely chopped parsley
¼ cup milk
2 tablespoons tarragon vinegar
½ teaspoon leaf tarragon, crumbled
⅛ teaspoon pepper
2 anchovy fillets, finely chopped
1 green onion, finely chopped
1 clove garlic, crushed

Stir together mayonnaise, parsley, milk, vinegar, tarragon, pepper, anchovy, green onion and garlic in small bowl until well blended. Remove garlic before serving.

MAKE-AHEAD TIP:
The three dressings on this page can be made up to 3 days ahead and refrigerated, covered.

GETTING DRESSED
Salad dressing should complement, not overpower, the flavor and texture of salad greens.
■ Sturdy leaf lettuces like romaine, radicchio, iceberg and endive hold up better under heavy or creamy dressings than more tender greens, which fare best beneath a light oil and vinegar dressing.
■ Vinaigrettes made with fruity extra-virgin olive oils and full-bodied vinegars such as balsamic or sherry wine are best tossed with boldly flavored greens like spinach, chicory and romaine, greens that can stand up to intense flavors.
■ Lightly seasoned dressings made with vegetable oils or pure olive oil and mild wine or herb vinegars allow the more delicately flavored greens to maintain their individual character.
■ To keep your salad from wilting on the plate, salt the dressing, not the greens, and toss the greens with the dressing just before serving.

MAKE-AHEAD TIP:
The three dressings on this page can be made up to 3 days ahead and refrigerated, covered.

HONEY-POPPY SEED DRESSING

LOW-CALORIE · LOW-FAT
LOW-CHOLESTEROL · QUICK

Making fruit salad? Then here's your dressing. Stir in ¼ teaspoon vanilla extract for fuller flavor.

Makes 1 cup. Recipe can be doubled.
Nutrient Value Per Tablespoon:
16 calories, 1 g protein, 0 g fat,
2 g carbohydrate, 10 mg sodium,
1 mg cholesterol.

1 container (8 ounces) plain yogurt
1 tablespoon poppy seeds
1 tablespoon honey
1 teaspoon orange juice
½ teaspoon cider vinegar
¼ teaspoon grated orange peel

Stir together yogurt, poppy seeds, honey, orange juice, vinegar and orange peel in small bowl.

THOUSAND ISLAND DRESSING

QUICK

One of our favorites. Serve over greens, steamed vegetables, chilled cooked sliced beef or meat salads.

Makes 1⅓ cups. Recipe can be doubled.
Nutrient Value Per Tablespoon:
46 calories, 0 g protein, 4 g fat,
2 g carbohydrate, 92 mg sodium,
10 mg cholesterol.

1 cup reduced-calorie mayonnaise
2 tablespoons chili sauce
2 tablespoons milk
1 tablespoon sweet pickle relish
1 tablespoon finely chopped parsley
½ teaspoon paprika
⅛ teaspoon pepper
1 hard-cooked egg, peeled and chopped

Stir together mayonnaise, chili sauce, milk, relish, parsley, paprika and pepper in small bowl until well blended. Gently stir in egg.

TOMATO BASIL DRESSING

LOW-SODIUM · LOW-CHOLESTEROL
QUICK

Serve over greens, steamed vegetables, chilled cooked chicken or fish or warm pasta. To sweeten the garlic, blanch peeled clove in boiling water for 1 to 2 minutes before using.

Makes 1 cup.
Recipe can be doubled.
Nutrient Value Per Tablespoon:
45 calories, 0 g protein, 4 g fat,
1 g carbohydrate, 43 mg sodium,
0 mg cholesterol.

1 large tomato, peeled, seeded and
    chopped OR: 1 can (8¼ ounces)
    tomatoes, drained
½ small sweet red pepper, finely chopped
½ cup packed fresh basil leaves
1 clove garlic
2 tablespoons white wine vinegar
1 tablespoon tomato paste
½ teaspoon sugar
¼ teaspoon salt
⅛ teaspoon black pepper
⅓ cup olive oil

Combine tomato, red pepper, basil, garlic, vinegar, tomato paste, sugar, salt and pepper in food processor or blender. Whirl until pureed. With machine running, slowly add oil in thin stream until well blended.

Fusilli with Meatballs (page 190).

CHAPTER 6

PASTA, GRAINS AND BEANS

PASTA AND NOODLE TYPES

Fresh pasta: This pasta is made one of two ways: by mixing wheat flour either with eggs or with water. Fresh pasta cooks very quickly: begin testing for doneness about 1 minute after adding to boiling water.

Italian-style dried: Imported from Italy and domestically produced, this long-keeping pasta is based on a wheat dough that is extruded through dies or formed in molds to create literally hundreds of shapes. Whatever the size, shape or brand, the best-quality pasta is made from hard durum wheat, ground into semolina or durum flour, which gives the pasta a firm texture.

Flavored pastas: Many "flavored" dried pastas are little more than regular pasta colored with a little vegetable juice; other types, such as whole-wheat or spinach, are much more flavorful. Also, look for carrot, beet, wild mushroom and herb varieties, and the slightly more exotic spice pastas such as saffron and chili powder. Flavored fresh pastas generally have a more pronounced flavor and can include everything from tomato and basil to blue corn

and cilantro. For flavored dried pastas, select lighter sauces; for flavored fresh pastas, stronger sauces pair well.

Domestic dried egg noodles: Available in thin or thick ribbons, delicate strands or squares, these noodles are richer, softer and more complexly flavored than dried pasta made from semolina and water. These characteristics make the noodles better suited to mild cheese and meat sauces, which don't overpower the flavor of the noodle, rather than more full-flavored preparations.

Asian egg noodles: These versatile noodles are available dried or fresh. The dried often come in nests, and whether dried or fresh, the noodles are softer than Italian-style pasta and overcooking should be avoided. Toss cooked noodles with a spicy sesame sauce and chopped green onion; stir-fry with meat, fish and/or vegetables; or pan-fry into pancake-like bases for other stir-fried combinations.

Cellophane noodles: Made from rice, wheat, seaweed and/or mung beans, these Asian noodles

are so named because they become translucent during cooking. Chewy with a gelatinous texture and bland flavor, they are the perfect backdrop for flavorful Asian preparations. First soaked for about 20 minutes, the noodles take only a few minutes to cook.

Soba noodles: Japanese noodles made from the flour of a buckwheat-like grain, which lends its taupe color and unique flavor. Soba noodles can be served hot in soup, or more typically chilled with an array of condiments such as grated fresh ginger, chopped green onion and prepared green horseradish.

Somen and udon: Japanese wheat-based noodles, which differ in width: somen are very narrow; udon, wider. In Japan, somen are served in bowls of ice water with a soy dipping sauce and other condiments. Udon are often prepared in hot, substantial soups laden with vegetables, fish and/or eggs. Somen are available in dried form, while udon come fresh and dried, although the fresh are very perishable and should be eaten as soon after purchasing as possible.

FLAVORED PASTAS
chili pepper — beet — saffron — dill — spinach

tomato — squid ink — whole wheat — ginger carrot

PASTA: GETTING IN SHAPE

For pictures of some of the following pastas, see below and on page 188.

Agnolotti ("Priests' Caps"): crescent-shaped pockets filled with meat or cheese

Alphabet letters

Anellini: tiny pasta rings

Bucatini: short, straight macaroni

Cannelloni: large cylindrical tubes for stuffing, saucing or baking

Capellini ("Angel's Hair"): very fine pasta strands

Cavatelli: small shells with ruffled edges

Conchiglie ("Conch Shells")

Ditali ("Thimbles"): stubby macaroni

Egg noodles: wide and thin noodles, and squares

Farfalle/farfallone ("Butterflies"): bow ties, small and big

Fedelini ("Little Faithful Ones"): very fine spaghetti

Fettuccine/fettucce ("Ribbons"): narrow and wide pasta ribbons

Fusilli ("Little Springs"): pasta twists

Lasagna: straight- and rippled-edged; wider than fettuccine

Manicotti ("Muffs"): giant tubes to be stuffed, sauced and baked

Margherita ("Daisies"): narrow noodles with one rippled edge

Maruzze ("Seashells")

Mezzani: short, curved macaroni

Mostaccioli ("Little Moustaches")

Orecchiette ("Little Ears"): pasta curls

Orzo: rice-shaped pasta

Pappardelle: broad noodles classically topped with game sauces

Pastina ("Tiny Dough"): Tiny pasta shapes for soups and side dishes, including Acini di Pepe ("Peppercorns"), Stelline ("Little Stars"), and Semi de Mela/Melone ("Apple/Melon Seeds")

Penne ("Quills"): thin tubes with diagonally cut ends

Perciatelli: long, thin macaroni resembling thick spaghetti

Pizzoccheri: thick buckwheat noodles

Radiatore: rippled, thick, short pasta ideally suited for chunky sauces

Ravioli: pasta pillows with filling

Rigatoni: large, grooved macaroni

Rotelle/ruote ("Wheels"): small/spiked wheels

Spaghetti: long thin rods ranging from capellini (very thin), and spaghettini (thin) to spaghetti (medium) and spaghettoni (thick)

Tagliatelle: egg noodles resembling fettuccine

Tortellini/Tortelloni: stuffed pasta bundles

Trenette: similar to tagliatelle, but narrower and thicker

Tubetti ("Small Tubes"): small, hollow tubes

Vermicelli: very fine spaghetti or egg noodles

Ziti ("Bridegrooms"): large tubes with a slight curve

From left, vermicelli, linguine, capellini, spaghetti, lasagna, spaghettini, fettuccine, fusilli.

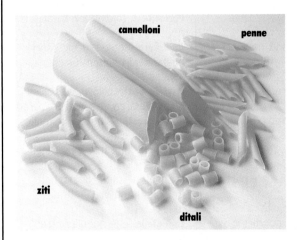

cannelloni

penne

ziti

ditali

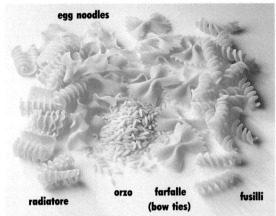

egg noodles

radiatore

orzo

farfalle
(bow ties)

fusilli

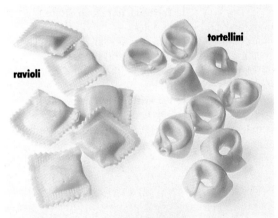

ravioli

tortellini

capellini
(angel's hair)

tagliatelle

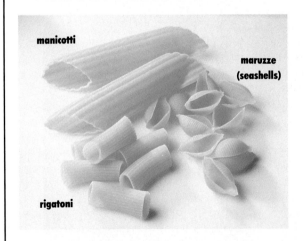

manicotti

maruzze
(seashells)

rigatoni

rotelle

orecchiette #48

pastina

orecchiette #91

TURKEY TETRAZZINI

The perfect dish for leftover turkey, or even chicken or ham, for that matter.

Bake at 375° for 20 to 25 minutes.
Makes 8 servings.
Recipe can be halved or doubled.
Nutrient Value Per Serving: 581 calories, 38 g protein, 26 g fat, 48 g carbohydrate, 539 mg sodium, 132 mg cholesterol.

1 pound vermicelli
5 tablespoons butter
3 tablespoons all-purpose flour
2 cups chicken broth
1 cup heavy cream OR: half-and-half OR: milk
2 tablespoons dry sherry
¾ cup grated Parmesan cheese
¼ teaspoon black pepper
2 cups thinly sliced mushrooms (12 ounces)
1 small sweet red pepper, cored, seeded and diced
3 green onions, sliced (⅓ cup)
4 cups cubed (¾ inch) cooked turkey (1½ pounds)

1. Preheat oven to moderate (375°). Grease 13 × 9 × 2-inch baking dish.
2. Cook pasta according to package directions until *al dente*, firm but tender. Drain.
3. Melt 3 tablespoons butter in medium-size saucepan over medium heat. Whisk in flour; cook, whisking, 1 minute. Whisk in broth. Bring to boiling. Lower heat; simmer 1 minute. Add cream, sherry, ¼ cup Parmesan cheese and black pepper; simmer 2 minutes. Set aside.
4. Melt remaining butter in large skillet over medium-high heat. Add mushrooms, sweet red pepper and green onion; sauté for 2 minutes or until slightly softened.
5. Combine pasta, sauce, mushroom mixture and turkey in large bowl. Pour into prepared baking dish. Sprinkle with remaining ½ cup Parmesan.

6. Bake in preheated moderate oven (375°) until bubbly and brown, 20 to 25 minutes.

Microwave Directions (High Power Oven):
Ingredient Changes: Reduce butter to 4 tablespoons; use 1 can (about 14 ounces) chicken broth; add ½ teaspoon of paprika.
Directions: Combine 1 tablespoon butter, mushrooms, red pepper and green onions in microwave-safe 8-cup measure. Microwave, uncovered, at 100% power 3 minutes, stirring once. Transfer mixture to microwave-safe 4½-quart casserole. Place remaining 3 tablespoons butter in same measure. Microwave, uncovered, at 100% power 1½ to 2 minutes to melt. Whisk in flour. Gradually stir in chicken broth and sherry until smooth. Microwave, uncovered, at 100% power 5 minutes to full boil, whisking twice. Whisk in cream, all the Parmesan and black pepper. Add to casserole with cooked vermicelli and turkey. Mix well. Microwave, uncovered, at 100% power 10 minutes, stirring once. Stir again after removing from microwave. Sprinkle with paprika. Microwave, uncovered, at 100% power 3 minutes.

PASTA PROFILE

■ Cooking pasta *al dente,* or firm to the bite, preserves some of the vitamins and minerals that are lost into the cooking water with longer cooking times.
■ Regular pasta contains virtually no fat or sodium. Even egg noodles contribute less than 1 gram of fat from a ¾-cup serving.
■ Whole-wheat pasta provides 4 times the dietary fiber as regular pasta for approximately the same number of calories.
■ Pasta is a significant source of iron and B-vitamins, because of the enrichment of durum wheat or semolina flour milled for pasta making.

FUSILLI WITH MEATBALLS

*O*ur sauce is flecked with olives and raisins, and our spicier-than-usual meatballs are "extended" with wheat germ rather than bread crumbs. For a leaner version, make the meatballs with ground turkey. (Pictured on page 185.)

Bake meatballs at 400° for 8 minutes.
Makes 6 servings.
Recipe can be halved or doubled.
Nutrient Value Per Serving: 752 calories, 29 g protein, 34 g fat, 83 g carbohydrate, 645 mg sodium, 113 mg cholesterol.

Sauce:
2 tablespoons olive oil
1 large onion, thinly sliced
2 jars (7 ounces each) roasted red peppers, drained
⅓ cup red wine OR: chicken broth OR: water
1 can (28 ounces) tomatoes, in puree
1 tablespoon tomato paste
¾ cup sliced, pitted, ripe black olives
⅓ cup golden raisins
⅛ teaspoon ground hot red pepper
2 tablespoons butter

Meatballs and Pasta:
1 pound ground beef
1 small clove garlic, finely chopped
3 tablespoons grated Parmesan cheese
3 tablespoons milk
⅓ cup wheat germ
1 egg
1 teaspoon ground sage
½ teaspoon leaf thyme, crumbled
½ teaspoon ground cumin
¼ teaspoon salt
⅛ teaspoon pepper
1 pound fusilli
2 tablespoons chopped parsley

1. Prepare Sauce: Heat oil in large skillet over medium heat. Stir in onion; sauté until browned, about 12 minutes.
2. Meanwhile, empty one of the drained jars of peppers into blender or food processor. With motor running, gradually add wine and whirl until smooth puree. Dice remaining jar of peppers.
3. Add pureed and diced peppers, tomatoes, tomato paste, olives, raisins and ground red pepper to onion; stir with wooden spoon to combine and break up tomatoes. Cover and simmer 30 minutes. Stir in butter. Keep warm.
4. Preheat oven to 400°. Cover 15½ × 10½ × 1-inch jelly-roll pan with aluminum foil. Spray with nonstick vegetable-oil cooking spray.
5. Prepare Meatballs and Pasta: Combine beef, garlic, Parmesan cheese, milk, wheat germ, egg, sage, thyme, cumin, salt and pepper in medium-size bowl. Form beef mixture into about forty-eight 1-inch balls. Place in single layer on prepared pan.
6. Bake in preheated hot oven (400°) for 8 minutes or until cooked through.
7. Meanwhile, cook pasta according to package directions. Drain.
8. Toss together sauce, meatballs and pasta in large serving bowl. Sprinkle with parsley.

Make-Ahead Tip: Both the sauce and the meatballs can be made a few days ahead and refrigerated, covered.
Microwave Directions (High Power Oven):
Ingredient Changes: Eliminate wine in the sauce.
Directions: Prepare meatballs as above. Shape into 12 balls. Place around edge of microwave-safe 10-inch pie plate. Cover with waxed paper. Microwave at 100% power 5 minutes, turning dish once. Let stand, covered. Puree and chop roasted red peppers as above, but without the wine. Combine onion and oil in microwave-safe 4-quart casserole with lid. Microwave, uncovered, at 100% power 4 minutes, stirring once. Stir in pureed and chopped peppers, tomatoes, tomato paste, olives, raisins and hot pepper. Microwave, covered, at 100% power 10 minutes. Microwave, covered, at 70% power 10 minutes. Stir in butter, cooked pasta, meatballs and parsley. Microwave, covered, at 100% power 3 minutes.

HOW TO COOK PERFECT PASTA
Perfectly cooked pasta is moist, tender and just slightly resistant to the bite—what the Italians call *al dente,* or "to the tooth." Fresh pasta needs much less cooking than dried pasta, literally just a minute or two. Because pasta's main contribution to a dish is its texture, proper cooking is important. For each *pound* of pasta, observe these simple steps:
■ For best results, pasta must be added to *boiling* water. Bring 4 to 6 quarts of water to a rolling boil in a large pot. Add salt, if you wish.
■ Add pasta gradually so the water returns to boiling quickly and the pasta does not clump. If boiling subsides, cover the pot briefly until the water returns to boiling. Use a long-handle fork to push down pieces and stir briefly to separate.

BAKED ZITI WITH VEGETABLES

LOW-FAT · LOW-CHOLESTEROL

*B*ake this as one large casserole or as individual servings.

Bake at 375° for 25 minutes for large casserole, or 20 minutes for small casseroles.
Makes 4 servings.
Nutrient Value Per Serving: 487 calories, 21 g protein, 15 g fat, 71 g carbohydrate, 1,007 mg sodium, 22 mg cholesterol.

2 tablespoons olive oil
1 medium-size sweet green pepper, cored, seeded and diced
1 medium-size sweet red pepper, cored, seeded and diced
2 large onions, coarsely chopped
2 large cloves garlic, finely chopped
¼ pound mushrooms, chopped
1 can (16 ounces) whole tomatoes, undrained
1 can (8 ounces) tomato sauce
¼ cup dry red wine
1 teaspoon leaf basil, crumbled
½ teaspoon salt
½ teaspoon pepper
¼ teaspoon leaf oregano, crumbled
½ pound fresh spinach, cleaned and stemmed
½ cup frozen corn kernels
8 ounces ziti, cooked according to package directions
1 container (8 ounces) part-skim ricotta cheese
¼ cup grated Parmesan cheese

1. Heat 1 tablespoon oil in large skillet over medium heat. Add green and red pepper; sauté until barely tender, about 5 minutes. Remove with slotted spoon and set aside.
2. Heat remaining tablespoon oil in skillet. Add onion; sauté until softened, 4 to 5 minutes. Add garlic and mushrooms; sauté 2 minutes.
3. Break up tomatoes with fork and add

with liquid to skillet along with tomato sauce, wine, basil, salt, pepper and oregano. Bring to boiling. Lower heat; simmer, uncovered, until slightly thickened, about 20 minutes. Add spinach and corn; cook, stirring, until the spinach wilts.
4. Preheat oven to moderate (375°). Coat inside of one 2½-quart casserole dish or insides of four 2½-cup casserole dishes with nonstick vegetable-oil cooking spray.
5. Combine ziti, tomato mixture, ricotta and two-thirds of peppers in large bowl. Spoon ziti mixture into prepared casserole(s). Sprinkle with Parmesan.

(continued)

PERFECT PAIRINGS: PASTAS & SAUCES

Although, in a pinch, most pastas can be served with most sauces, classic pasta preparations combine "like with like."

- Thick, creamy sauces need a shape or thick noodle to cling to, such as fettuccine.
- Thinner, more delicate pastas such as capellini and thin spaghetti are the right match for light sauces, including garlic and oil and broths.
- Egg noodles are satisfying accompaniments to stews.
- Special pastas such as large manicotti and lasagna are made for filling, saucing and baking casserole-style.
- Tiny stars, orzo and alphabet letters can be tossed with butter or a simple sauce and served as a side dish, used to stuff vegetables, poultry or fish, or simmered in soups at the end of the cooking.
- Flavor and color are important, too. Whole-wheat pasta needs an assertive sauce that can stand up to its nutty character. Milder-flavored additions, such as carrot, and those with bold taste should be matched with complementary sauces. Sauces for vividly hued pastas should be selected with color in mind.

BAKED ZITI WITH VEGETABLES (continued)

6. Bake in preheated moderate oven (375°) for 25 minutes for large casserole or 20 minutes for small casseroles. Garnish with remaining peppers.

Make-Ahead Tip: The casserole(s) can be assembled 2 or 3 hours ahead and refrigerated, covered. Bring to room temperature. Proceed with Step 6.

Microwave Directions (High Power Oven):
Ingredient Changes: Drain off ½ cup liquid from canned tomatoes; eliminate wine.
Directions: Combine peppers and 1 tablespoon oil in microwave-safe 2½-quart casserole. Microwave, uncovered, at 100% power 3 minutes, stirring once. Remove peppers and reserve. Combine remaining oil, onion, garlic and mushrooms in same casserole. Microwave, uncovered, at 100% power 6 minutes, stirring once. Stir in tomatoes, tomato sauce, basil, salt, pepper and oregano. Cover with lid. Microwave at 100% power 8 minutes. Stir in spinach and corn. Microwave, uncovered, at 100% power 2 minutes. Add cooked ziti, ricotta, Parmesan and two-thirds of the peppers to casserole. Stir well. Sprinkle remaining peppers over top. Microwave, uncovered, at 70% power 10 minutes. Cover and let stand 10 minutes.

CROWD-PLEASING PASTA

Baked Ziti with Vegetables (191)

Garden Salad with Green Goddess Dressing (183)

Summer or Winter Fruit Compote (528 or 529)

FETTUCCINE WITH ONION SAUCE

QUICK

The secret ingredient in this sauce is a generous splash of bourbon. The alcohol cooks away, leaving a sweet, slightly spicy taste.

Makes 4 servings.
Recipe can be halved or doubled.
Nutrient Value Per Serving: 555 calories, 19 g protein, 18 g fat, 80 g carbohydrate, 862 mg sodium, 118 mg cholesterol.

4 tablespoons (½ stick) *un*salted butter
5 large yellow onions, finely chopped (about 5 cups)
2 carrots, pared and finely chopped
½ teaspoon salt
⅓ cup bourbon
1⅔ cups chicken broth
⅛ to ¼ teaspoon black pepper
¾ pound fettuccine OR: egg noodles
6 tablespoons grated Parmesan cheese

1. Melt 3 tablespoons butter in large, heavy skillet over low heat. Add onion and carrot; sprinkle with salt; toss to coat. Cover and cook, stirring frequently, until onion is very soft and transparent, about 6 minutes.
2. Add bourbon. Increase heat to medium-high; cook 4 minutes. Add chicken broth; cook until almost all liquid has evaporated, about 5 minutes. Add pepper. Reserve.
3. Meanwhile, cook pasta according to package directions until *al dente*, firm but tender. Drain well, reserving 3 tablespoons pasta cooking liquid.
4. Over low heat, swirl remaining 1 tablespoon butter and 3 tablespoons pasta cooking liquid into onion mixture in skillet. Season with more salt and pepper, if you wish. Gently toss pasta and sauce together in large serving bowl. Sprinkle each serving with Parmesan.

LINGUINE WITH ZUCCHINI SAUCE

LOW-FAT · LOW-CHOLESTEROL · QUICK

Makes 4 servings.
Recipe can be halved or doubled.
Nutrient Value Per Serving: 494 calories, 20 g protein, 16 g fat, 12 g carbohydrate, 289 mg sodium, 23 mg cholesterol.

12 ounces linguine
2 tablespoons olive oil
2 cloves garlic, thinly sliced
1½ pounds zucchini, coarsely shredded
¼ cup plain yogurt
¾ cup coarsely shredded Cheddar
     cheese (3 ounces)
¼ teaspoon salt
¼ teaspoon pepper

1. Cook linguine according to package directions until *al dente*, firm but tender.

2. Meanwhile, heat oil in large, heavy skillet over medium-high heat. Add garlic; cook, stirring, until lightly browned, about 30 seconds. Add one-fourth of zucchini. Increase heat to high; cook, stirring, until zucchini is well coated with oil. Add remaining zucchini; cook, tossing occasionally, until tender, about 3 minutes. Turn into large serving bowl.

3. Drain linguine. Add to zucchini along with the yogurt; toss to mix. Add the cheese, salt and pepper. Serve immediately.

Microwave Directions (High Power Oven):
Cook linguine as above. Combine oil and garlic in microwave-safe 3-quart casserole. Microwave, uncovered, at 100% power 2 minutes. Stir in zucchini. Cover with lid. Microwave at 100% power 6 minutes, stirring once. Add linguine, yogurt, cheese, salt and pepper to casserole; toss to mix. Serve immediately.

QUICK AS BOILING WATER

You can prepare Linguine with Zucchini Sauce in the amount of time it takes to cook the pasta. Garnish with a cherry tomato half and a sprig of dill, if you wish.

COOKING DRIED PASTA

■ Dried pasta may take from 4 to 15 minutes to cook, depending on the shape and thickness.
■ Begin testing when the water returns to boiling. Estimate about 4 minutes for thin pasta, 8 minutes or more for thick. Or follow the package directions and begin testing after the shorter time suggested.
■ To test, lift out a piece, run it under cold water, and bite it. The pasta should be flexible, firm but cooked through.

LASAGNA TORTE

LOW-CHOLESTEROL

This free-standing vegetarian lasagna takes on a new shape. Top with candles and you have a centerpiece for a birthday party.

Bake at 350° for 50 to 60 minutes.
Makes 8 servings.
Nutrient Value Per Serving: 457 calories, 25 g protein, 21 g fat, 44 g carbohydrate, 740 mg sodium, 68 mg cholesterol.

1 tablespoon olive oil
1 large onion, finely chopped
1 can (28 ounces) tomatoes in puree
2 cloves garlic, finely chopped
2 medium-size carrots, pared and
    shredded
¼ cup chopped fresh basil OR: 1
    tablespoon dried
½ teaspoon salt
2 pounds fresh spinach OR: 2 packages
    (10 ounces each) frozen leaf spinach,
    thawed and squeezed dry
12 lasagna noodles
2 cups whole-milk ricotta cheese
½ cup grated Parmesan cheese
¼ teaspoon pepper
2 cups shredded fontina cheese (8
    ounces)

1. Heat oil in large skillet over low heat. Add onion; sauté until soft, about 8 minutes. Place in medium-size bowl.
2. Add tomatoes to skillet, breaking up with spoon. Add garlic and carrots. Bring to boiling. Lower heat; simmer, covered, 10 minutes. Uncover and simmer 10 minutes. Stir in basil and salt. Set sauce aside.
3. Stem and wash fresh spinach. Place in large pot over high heat; cook until wilted, about 3 minutes. Drain and squeeze dry.
4. Cook lasagna noodles according to package directions. Drain.
5. Preheat oven to moderate (350°). Line 9-inch springform pan with aluminum foil; grease foil.
6. Add ricotta, Parmesan and pepper to reserved onion; stir to combine.
7. Trim lasagna noodles to fit pan. Fit 4 noodles into pan, overlapping slightly. Cover with one-third ricotta mixture, spreading evenly. Top with one-third spinach, one-quarter sauce and one-quarter fontina. Repeat two more times using noodle trimmings as one layer. Top with the last layer of noodles, the remaining quarter of sauce and fontina.
8. Bake in preheated moderate oven (350°) until hot, 50 to 60 minutes. Let stand 5 minutes before serving. Remove sides of pan. Cut into wedges to serve.

MACARONI WITH FOUR CHEESES

We use Cheddar, Gruyère, blue and Parmesan cheeses to dress up Mom's classic. Experiment with different shapes of short pastas, and for an attractive presentation, sprinkle the bread crumb mixture in diagonal bands across the top.

Bake at 375° for 25 to 30 minutes.
Makes 8 servings.
Nutrient Value Per Serving: 571 calories, 26 g protein, 27 g fat, 54 g carbohydrate, 725 mg sodium, 80 mg cholesterol.

1 pound elbow macaroni
5 tablespoons butter or margarine
1 onion, finely chopped
1 clove garlic, finely chopped
3 tablespoons all-purpose flour
3 cups hot lowfat (1%) milk
2 cups shredded sharp Cheddar cheese, (½ pound)
½ cup grated Parmesan cheese
1 cup shredded Gruyère cheese OR: Swiss cheese (4 ounces)
½ cup crumbled blue cheese
6 drops liquid red-pepper seasoning
½ teaspoon dry mustard
½ teaspoon salt
⅛ teaspoon pepper
4 plum tomatoes, peeled, seeded and diced
1 cup fresh bread crumbs
1 tablespoon chopped parsley

1. Cook macaroni following package directions until *al dente*, firm but tender. Drain; rinse with cold water; drain again.
2. Preheat oven to moderate (375°). Grease 13 × 9 × 2-inch baking dish.
3. Melt 3 tablespoons butter in medium-saucepan over medium heat. Add onion and garlic; sauté 4 minutes. Stir in flour; cook 1 minute. Gradually whisk in hot milk. Bring to boiling, stirring frequently; cook 1 minute. Remove from heat.

4. Reserve ¼ cup each Cheddar and Parmesan cheese. Stir remaining Cheddar, Parmesan, Gruyère, blue cheese, red-pepper seasoning, dry mustard, salt and pepper into sauce until cheeses just melt. Combine macaroni, sauce and tomatoes in large bowl. Pour into prepared baking dish.
5. Bake in preheated moderate oven (375°) for 15 minutes. Combine reserved Cheddar, Parmesan, bread crumbs and parsley in small bowl. Melt remaining 2 tablespoons butter in small saucepan. Add to crumb mixture; stir to combine. Sprinkle over top of macaroni. Bake 10 to 15 minutes longer or until bubbly and top is browned.

(continued)

MACARONI MAKE-AHEAD TIP:
The whole dish can be assembled several hours ahead and refrigerated. Increase the baking time appropriately if taking from refrigerator.

MACARONI WITH FOUR CHEESES (*continued*)

Microwave Directions (High Power Oven):
Ingredient Changes: Decrease butter to 3 tablespoons; eliminate bread crumbs and parsley.
Directions: Combine onion, garlic and butter in microwave-safe 8-cup measure. Microwave, uncovered, at 100% power 3 minutes, stirring once. Stir flour into onion mixture until smooth. Gradually mix in milk. Microwave, uncovered, 7 to 9 minutes to a full boil, whisking after 3 and 6 minutes. Stir in all of the cheeses and seasonings until smooth. Place cooked macaroni in microwave-safe 4-quart casserole. Pour in cheese sauce and tomatoes. Mix well to blend ingredients. Microwave, uncovered, at 70% power 12 minutes. Let stand, covered, 5 minutes.

CHEESE! AND MACARONI

Macaroni with Four Cheeses (195)

Sautéed Swiss Chard with Lemon and Garlic

Thin Breadsticks

Melon Chunks with Honey and Lime

LEMON LINGUINE WITH WHITE CLAM SAUCE

LOW-FAT • LOW-CHOLESTEROL • QUICK

This *quick recipe can be easily made from ingredients you probably have on hand.*

Makes 6 servings.
Recipe can be halved or doubled.
Nutrient Value Per Serving: 437 calories, 27 g protein, 8 g fat, 12 g carbohydrate, 295 mg sodium, 43 mg cholesterol.

---

1 pound linguine
Grated rind and juice of 1 small lemon
1 tablespoon olive oil
1 medium-size onion, finely chopped
2 cloves garlic, finely chopped
½ teaspoon leaf oregano, crumbled
⅛ teaspoon crushed red pepper flakes
1 cup dry white wine
3 cans (6½ ounces each) chopped clams in broth
1 bottle (8 ounces) clam juice
1 tablespoon *un*salted butter
1 tablespoon all-purpose flour
¾ cup chopped parsley
½ cup grated Parmesan cheese

1. Cook linguine according to package directions until *al dente*, firm but tender. Drain; toss in large bowl with lemon rind and juice.
2. Meanwhile, prepare sauce: Heat oil in medium-size saucepan over medium heat. Add onion; sauté 3 minutes or until onion begins to soften. Add garlic, oregano, red pepper flakes and wine. Bring to boiling; cook 5 minutes or until reduced by half.
3. Strain clams over the saucepan; reserve clams. Add bottled clam juice to onion mixture in saucepan. Return to boiling over high heat; cook until liquid is reduced by half, 5 to 8 minutes. (You should have about 2 cups.) Transfer to bowl.
4. Melt butter in saucepan. Stir in flour and cook, stirring, 1 minute. Add reserved broth mixture along with chopped clams. Simmer 3 minutes. Remove saucepan from heat. Stir in ½ cup parsley and the Parmesan.
5. Toss pasta with clam sauce in bowl. Garnish with remaining parsley.

FETTUCCINE WITH SCALLOPS

LOW-FAT · QUICK

Makes 4 servings.
Recipe can be halved or doubled.
Nutrient Value Per Serving: 626 calories, 38 g protein, 15 g fat, 81 g carbohydrate, 527 mg sodium, 135 mg cholesterol.

1 package (9 ounces) frozen artichoke hearts
2 teaspoons olive oil
1 ounce sun-dried tomatoes (dry-packed), cut into slivers
2 tablespoons finely chopped shallots OR: white part of green onion
1 clove garlic, finely chopped
12 ounces bay scallops OR: sea scallops, cut into 1-inch pieces
¼ cup dry vermouth
1 cup lowfat (1%) milk
½ cup half-and-half
⅓ cup (2 ounces) grated Parmesan cheese
¼ teaspoon pepper
2 tablespoons chopped fresh basil OR: 2 teaspoons dried
12 ounces fettuccine

1. Bring small saucepan of water to boiling. Add artichoke hearts; cook 5 minutes. Drain. When cool enough to handle, cut each piece in half.
2. Heat oil in large nonstick skillet over medium heat. Add sun-dried tomatoes, shallot and garlic; cook 2 minutes. Add scallops and vermouth; cook 2 to 4 minutes or until scallops begin to turn opaque (they will not be cooked through at this point). Remove scallops with slotted spoon and set aside.
3. Add milk, half-and-half, Parmesan and pepper to skillet. Lower heat; simmer, stirring occasionally, 2 to 3 minutes or until sauce is smooth and slightly thickened. Add reserved artichoke hearts, basil and scallops. Cook, stirring, until artichoke hearts are heated through and scallops are opaque in center, about 2 minutes.
4. Meanwhile, cook fettuccine according to package directions. Drain. Arrange on serving platter. Spoon sauce over. Toss and serve.

Microwave Directions (High Power Oven):
Ingredient Changes: Thaw artichokes; increase oil to 1 tablespoon; eliminate milk; increase half-and-half to ¾ cup.
Directions: Place artichokes and ¼ cup water in microwave-safe 3-quart casserole with lid. Microwave, covered, at 100% power 3 minutes. Drain and reserve. Combine oil, tomatoes, shallots and garlic in same casserole. Microwave, covered, at 100% power 2 minutes. Add scallops and vermouth. Microwave, covered, at 100% power 4 minutes. Add half-and-half, cheese, pepper and artichokes. Microwave, covered, at 100% power 3 minutes. Add cooked fettuccine and basil to casserole; toss to combine ingredients.

SUN-DRIED FLAVOR
Sun-dried tomatoes enliven Fettuccine with Scallops—try adding these tomatoes to some of your favorite pasta sauces.

ORIENTAL NOODLE SALAD

LOW-CHOLESTEROL

Colorful and crunchy, this salad is ideal for a party crowd. To make a main-dish salad, add cooked shrimp or chicken.

Makes 12 servings.
Recipe can be halved or doubled.
Nutrient Value Per Serving: 201 calories, 5 g protein, 10 g fat, 22 g carbohydrate, 306 mg sodium, 5 mg cholesterol.

Salad:
½ pound capellini or other thin pasta
2 medium-size carrots, pared and cut into matchsticks
6 ounces snow peas, cut into matchsticks
1 medium-size sweet red pepper, cored, seeded and diced
2 green onions, sliced (½ cup)
1 can (8 ounces) bamboo shoots, drained
1 can (8 ounces) sliced water chestnuts, drained
1 can (15 ounces) baby corn, drained and cut into ½-inch slices

Dressing:
¼ cup reduced-sodium soy sauce
¼ cup rice wine vinegar
1 tablespoon Oriental sesame oil
2 tablespoons chopped cilantro OR: parsley
1 tablespoon finely chopped, pared fresh ginger
½ teaspoon pepper
½ cup chicken broth
½ cup mayonnaise
¼ cup chopped peanuts

1. Prepare Salad: Cook pasta according to package directions. Add carrots and snow peas during last 30 seconds of cooking time. Drain; rinse with cold water; drain well. Combine pasta, sweet red pepper, green onion, bamboo shoots, water chestnuts and baby corn in large bowl.
2. Prepare Dressing: Stir together soy sauce, vinegar, sesame oil, cilantro and ginger in small bowl. Add Dressing to pasta; toss well to combine. Refrigerate, covered, until serving. Whisk together chicken broth and mayonnaise in small bowl until smooth. Refrigerate, covered, until serving.
3. To serve: Toss salad with mayonnaise mixture. Garnish with peanuts.

Make-Ahead Tip: The salad and mayonnaise mixture can be prepared separately up to 2 days ahead and refrigerated, covered. Toss with the mayonnaise mixture just before serving.

Orzo with Carrot and Fennel (page 200).

ORZO WITH CARROT AND FENNEL

LOW-CHOLESTEROL · QUICK

Transform this salad into a dinner entree by adding cooked chicken or a pickup from the deli, such as smoked turkey.

Makes 6 servings.
Recipe can be halved or doubled.
Nutrient Value Per Serving: 265 calories, 7 g protein, 10 g fat, 37 g carbohydrate, 317 mg sodium, 0 mg cholesterol.

Salad:
1¼ cups orzo pasta
2 cups broccoli flowerets (1 small head)
2 carrots, pared and diced (1 cup)
½ fennel bulb, diced (1¼ cups)
¼ cup diced red onion

Dressing:
¼ cup olive oil
¼ cup basil leaves, cut into thin strips
3 tablespoons balsamic vinegar OR: red wine vinegar
¾ teaspoon salt
1 small clove garlic, finely chopped

1. Prepare Salad: Cook orzo according to package directions. Drain; rinse under cold water; drain well. Transfer to large bowl.
2. Meanwhile, cook broccoli in 1 inch boiling water in large saucepan, covered, for 2 minutes or until crisp-tender. Drain; rinse under cold water; drain well. Transfer to bowl with orzo. Add carrot, fennel and red onion to the same bowl.
3. Prepare Dressing: Whisk together olive oil, basil, vinegar, salt and garlic in small bowl. Pour dressing over orzo and vegetables; toss to coat. Serve immediately or cover and refrigerate to serve cold later.

ORZO WITH CARROT AND FENNEL MAKE-AHEAD TIP:
The salad and dressing can be prepared separately a day ahead and refrigerated, covered. Toss together just before serving.

TORTELLINI SALAD MAKE-AHEAD TIP:
The salad can be made a day or 2 ahead and refrigerated, covered. After being refrigerated, the pasta may absorb some liquid from sauce. You may wish to toss in 1 to 2 tablespoons milk to retain creamy consistency.

MEAT AND CHEESE TORTELLINI SALAD

LOW-CALORIE · LOW-FAT
LOW-CHOLESTEROL · QUICK

This dish is at home in many places: a buffet table, Sunday night supper, a picnic and probably a lot of other places we haven't even thought of. Serve warm or chilled.

Makes 8 servings.
Recipe can be halved or doubled.
Nutrient Value Per Serving: 295 calories, 17 g protein, 9 g fat, 37 g carbohydrate, 679 mg sodium, 50 mg cholesterol.

½ pound meat tortellini
½ pound cheese tortellini
1 package (10 ounces) frozen peas
1 sweet red pepper, cored, seeded and cubed
1 tablespoon olive oil OR: vegetable oil
1 large onion, chopped
3 cloves garlic, sliced
½ teaspoon paprika
1 cup ricotta cheese
2 tablespoons tomato paste
¼ cup grated Parmesan cheese
1 teaspoon salt
6 to 8 drops liquid red-pepper seasoning
½ cup basil leaves, slivered

1. Cook tortellini according to package directions. Stir in peas and red pepper during last 2 minutes of cooking. Drain and place in large bowl.
2. Meanwhile, heat oil in skillet over medium-low heat. Add onion; cook, covered, 8 minutes. Stir in garlic and paprika; cook 4 minutes or until onion is softened. Scrape into blender.
3. Add ricotta, tomato paste, Parmesan, salt and red-pepper seasoning to blender. Whirl until smooth. Scrape onto pasta. Add slivered basil; toss until combined. Serve warm or chilled.

ROTELLE WITH MOZZARELLA AND ROASTED PEPPERS

Roast vegetables at 450° for 20 to 25 minutes.

Makes 6 servings.

Recipe can be halved or doubled.

Nutrient Value Per Serving: 310 calories, 14 g protein, 14 g fat, 32 g carbohydrate, 364 mg sodium, 22 mg cholesterol.

Salad:

1 sweet red pepper, cored, seeded and cut into 1-inch pieces

1 sweet yellow pepper, cored, seeded and cut into 1-inch pieces

1 sweet green pepper, cored, seeded and cut into 1-inch pieces

½ pint cherry tomatoes, each cut in half

8 ounces rotelle pasta

1 package (8 ounces) part-skim mozzarella cheese, cut into ½-inch cubes

Dressing:

3 tablespoons olive oil

1½ tablespoons lemon juice

2 teaspoons finely chopped fresh thyme OR: ½ teaspoon dried

½ teaspoon salt

½ teaspoon coarse black pepper

1. Preheat oven to very hot (450°).

2. Prepare Salad: Place peppers and cherry tomatoes in single layer in jelly-roll pan.

3. Roast vegetables in preheated very hot oven (450°) for 20 to 25 minutes or until peppers are tender and browned.

4. Meanwhile, cook pasta according to package directions. Drain; rinse under cold water; drain well. Transfer to large bowl. Add mozzarella.

5. Prepare Dressing: Whisk together olive oil, lemon juice, thyme, salt and pepper in small bowl.

6. Pour dressing over pasta mixture. Add roasted vegetables to pasta mixture; toss to coat. Serve warm or cover and refrigerate to serve cold later.

A VERSATILE DISH

Serve the rotelle warm or cold and for a change of pace, use tricolor rotelle. For a main-dish salad, add a full-flavored deli meat such as salami, pepperoni or ham. For a vegetarian main-dish salad, toss in chick-peas.

ROTELLE MAKE-AHEAD TIP:

The vegetables, pasta and dressing can be prepared separately a day ahead and refrigerated, covered. Combine just before serving.

PASTA WITH CREAM CHEESE PESTO

QUICK

Makes 4 servings.
Recipe can be halved or doubled.
Nutrient Value Per Serving: 639 calories, 17 g protein, 34 g fat, 70 g carbohydrate, 336 mg sodium, 99 mg cholesterol.

12 ounces bow ties OR: fettuccine

Pesto:
2 cloves garlic, peeled
1½ cups firmly packed fresh basil leaves
¾ cup firmly packed flat-leaf Italian parsley leaves
⅓ cup olive oil
⅓ cup pecans OR: walnuts
¼ cup chicken broth
¼ teaspoon salt
3 tablespoons grated Parmesan cheese
2 ounces cream cheese

1. Cook pasta according to package directions until *al dente*, firm but tender.
2. Meanwhile, prepare Pesto: For sweeter-tasting garlic, blanch garlic in small pot boiling water 2 minutes. Drain. Transfer to food processor along with basil, parsley, oil, pecans, broth and salt. Whirl until creamy. Stir in Parmesan.
3. Drain pasta; reserve ½ cup liquid.
4. Combine cream cheese and reserved pasta water in very large skillet over moderate heat. Add pesto, stirring to combine. Add hot pasta; toss to coat. Serve immediately, passing additional Parmesan cheese, if you wish.

PASTA WITH QUICK TOMATO SAUCE

LOW-CHOLESTEROL · QUICK

This sauce can be served over any type of pasta. Garnish with basil, if you wish.

Makes 4 servings.
Recipe can be halved or doubled.
Nutrient Value Per Serving: 378 calories, 9 g protein, 15 g fat, 53 g carbohydrate, 328 mg sodium, 0 mg cholesterol.

8 ounces pasta

Tomato Sauce:
3 cloves garlic, crushed
¼ cup olive oil
1 can (28 ounces) crushed tomatoes
2 pieces (3 × ½ inch each) orange rind
1 cinnamon stick, split lengthwise
2 teaspoons sugar *(optional)*
2 tablespoons chopped fresh basil OR: ½ teaspoon dried

1. Cook pasta according to package directions.
2. Prepare Sauce: Meanwhile, sauté garlic in oil in large nonaluminum skillet over low heat until lightly golden, 3 to 4 minutes. Add tomato, orange rind and cinnamon; cook, uncovered, stirring occasionally, for 12 to 15 minutes or until lightly thickened. Stir in sugar if tomatoes are particularly acidic. Remove and discard orange rind and cinnamon. Stir in basil.
3. Drain pasta. Add to skillet and toss with sauce. Serve.

A RICHER PESTO
Our version of pesto includes cream cheese, which creates a smoother, richer sauce. To reduce calories and fat, omit the cream cheese and simply toss the room-temperature pesto with hot cooked pasta. You can also dab a little pesto on hot cooked vegetables or a baked potato for a change of pace.

PESTO MAKE-AHEAD TIP:
The pesto, without the additions of the cream cheese, Parmesan and the pasta cooking water, can be refrigerated and covered with a thin film of olive oil for several days, or frozen for up to 2 months. Add cream cheese, Parmesan and pasta cooking water just before serving.

TOMATO SAUCE MAKE-AHEAD TIP:
Sauce can be made several days ahead, without the basil. Refrigerate covered. Reheat gently. Stir in basil, proceed.

20-MINUTE PASTA AL PESTO

Roasted Red Peppers, Marinated Artichoke Hearts and Olives

Pasta with Cream Cheese Pesto (this page)

Breadsticks

Neapolitan Ice Cream

PASTA WITH MUSHROOMS AND ZUCCHINI

QUICK

Dried porcini or shiitake mushrooms give this dish a rich "earthy" flavor.

Makes 4 servings.
Recipe can be halved or doubled.
Nutrient Value Per Serving: 410 calories, 12 g protein, 19 g fat, 47 g carbohydrate, 594 mg sodium, 30 mg cholesterol.

¼ ounce dried porcini OR: dried shiitake
    mushrooms
1 cup boiling water
8 ounces linguine, spaghetti, fettuccine or
    egg noodles
3 ounces pancetta OR: bacon, finely
    chopped (scant ½ cup)
1 small zucchini (4 ounces), quartered
    lengthwise and sliced crosswise, OR:
    yellow squash
8 ounces fresh mushrooms, cleaned,
    trimmed and thinly sliced (3 cups)
¼ teaspoon salt
⅛ teaspoon pepper
1 cup chicken broth
2 tablespoons *un*salted butter
2 tablespoons chopped parsley

1. Place porcini in small bowl; pour boiling water over. Let stand at room temperature 10 minutes to soften.
2. Cook pasta according to the package directions.
3. Heat large skillet over moderately low heat. Add pancetta; cook 2 minutes.* Add zucchini; cook 3 minutes, stirring frequently.
4. Remove porcini from soaking liquid; strain liquid through sieve lined with double-thickness dampened cheesecloth to remove any grit; reserve liquid. Rinse and chop porcini; remove tough stems.
5. Add porcini to skillet along with fresh mushrooms, salt and pepper.

Cover and cook 5 minutes, stirring occasionally. Add chicken broth and reserved porcini liquid; cook, uncovered, over high heat for 5 to 7 minutes or until lightly thickened. Lower heat to low; swirl in butter until creamy. Swirl in parsley.
6. Drain pasta. Toss with sauce. Stir in parsley. Serve.

*Note: If using bacon, cook until crisp.

PASTA WITH CAPONATA

QUICK

Canned caponata, an eggplant-based salad, is one of those supermarket ingredients that are frequently overlooked. Get in the habit of using quality canned products in a variety of homemade dishes. Here, the caponata makes the pasta sauce quick and easy.

Makes 4 servings.
Recipe can be halved or doubled.
Nutrient Value Per Serving: Unavailable.*

8 ounces shells, fusilli or penne

Caponata Sauce:
1 tablespoon olive oil
1 medium-size sweet green pepper, cored,
    seeded and chopped
2 cloves garlic, thinly sliced
2 cans (7¾ ounces each) caponata
    (eggplant appetizer)
⅓ cup water
2 tablespoons chopped fresh basil OR:
    parsley

1. Cook pasta according to package directions.
2. Meanwhile, prepare sauce: Heat oil in large skillet over low heat. Add green pepper; cover and cook, stirring occasionally, for 7 minutes or until
(continued)

PASTA WITH CAPONATA MICROWAVE DIRECTIONS (HIGH POWER OVEN):
Ingredient Changes: Eliminate water.
Directions: Combine oil and green pepper in microwave-safe 2½-quart casserole with lid. Microwave, uncovered, at 100% power 3 minutes. Stir in garlic. Microwave, covered, at 100% power 1 minute. Stir in caponata. Microwave, covered, at 100% power 5 minutes. Add cooked pasta and basil. Toss and serve.

PASTA WITH CAPONATA (*continued*)

tender. Add garlic; cover and cook for 2 minutes.

3. Add caponata and water; cook, uncovered, over low heat until heated through, about 5 minutes. Stir in basil.

4. Drain pasta. Add to skillet and toss with sauce. Serve.

Make-Ahead Tip: The sauce can be prepared a few days ahead, omitting the final addition of the basil, and refrigerated, covered. To serve, heat gently over low heat, stir in the basil and proceed with recipe.

*Note: Nutrient information for canned caponata is unavailable.

PASTA PRONTO

Pasta with Caponata (203)

Belgian Endive and Boston Lettuce with Cumin Dressing (151)

Sorbet

PASTA WITH HAM, PEAS AND CREAM MICROWAVE DIRECTIONS (HIGH POWER OVEN):

Ingredient Changes:
Eliminate water; reduce cream to ¾ cup.

Directions:
Combine butter, onion and garlic in microwave-safe 2-quart casserole. Cover with lid. Microwave at 100% power 5 minutes, stirring once. Add ham and cream. Microwave, uncovered, at 100% power 3 minutes. Add peas, marjoram, nutmeg and pepper. Microwave, uncovered, at 100% power 1 minute. Add cooked pasta and Parmesan cheese. Toss to mix ingredients. Cover and let stand 5 minutes.

PASTA WITH HAM, PEAS AND CREAM

QUICK

You can substitute cooked or smoked chicken or turkey for the ham.

Makes 4 servings.
Recipe can be halved or doubled.
Nutrient Value Per Serving: 551 calories, 20 g protein, 30 g fat, 51 g carbohydrate, 616 mg sodium, 109 mg cholesterol.

8 ounces rotelle, penne, bow ties or shells

Ham, Peas and Cream:
2 teaspoons *un*salted butter
1 medium-size onion, finely chopped
⅓ cup water
2 cloves garlic, finely chopped
1 cup chopped cooked ham (6 ounces)
1 cup heavy cream OR: half-and-half
1 cup frozen peas, thawed
¼ teaspoon leaf marjoram, crumbled
⅛ teaspoon grated nutmeg
⅛ teaspoon pepper
⅓ cup grated Parmesan cheese

1. Cook pasta according to package directions.

2. Meanwhile, prepare sauce: Melt butter in large skillet over moderately low heat. Add onion and water; cover and cook, stirring occasionally, until softened, about 7 minutes. Add garlic; cook, uncovered, 2 minutes or until very fragrant.

3. Add ham and cream. Bring to boiling over moderately high heat; cook 5 to 7 minutes or until thick enough to coat back of spoon. Stir in peas, marjoram, nutmeg and pepper; cook until heated through.

4. Drain pasta. Add to skillet and toss with hot sauce. Add cheese and toss again. Serve, passing a pepper mill and extra Parmesan cheese, if you wish.

TOSS-TOGETHER PASTA

Pasta with Ham, Peas and Cream (this page)

Green Salad with Tomato Basil Dressing (184)

Spumoni Ice Cream

20-Minute Pastas

Clockwise from upper left: Pasta with Cream Cheese Pesto (page 202); Pasta with Sweet Red Pepper Sauce (page 206); Pasta with Caponata (page 203); Pasta with Ham, Peas and Cream (page 204); Pasta with White Bean Sauce (page 208); Pasta with Garlic and Bread Crumbs (page 206); Pasta with Mexican Sauce (page 207); Pasta with Mushrooms and Zucchini (203); Pasta with Sausage and Broccoli (page 207); Pasta with Quick Tomato Sauce (page 202).

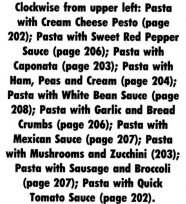

PASTA WITH SWEET RED PEPPER SAUCE MAKE-AHEAD TIP:
The sauce can be made several days ahead and refrigerated, covered.

MICROWAVE DIRECTIONS FOR SAUCE (HIGH POWER OVEN):
Stir together oil and almonds in microwave-safe 9-inch pie plate. Microwave, uncovered, at 100% power 2½ minutes. Stir in garlic. Microwave, uncovered, at 100% power 1 minute. Continue with recipe at right.

PASTA WITH GARLIC AND BREAD CRUMBS MICROWAVE DIRECTIONS (HIGH POWER OVEN):
Place oil and garlic in microwave-safe 9-inch pie plate. Microwave, uncovered, 2 minutes. Discard garlic. Stir in bread crumbs. Microwave, uncovered, at 100% power 1½ minutes. Add lemon juice, water, parsley and salt; swirl to combine. Toss with cooked pasta.

PASTA WITH SWEET RED PEPPER SAUCE

LOW-CHOLESTEROL · QUICK

To make this sauce even more special, roast your own peppers (see How-To, page 433). Garnish with slivered almonds, if you wish.

Makes 4 servings.
Recipe can be halved or doubled.
Nutrient Value Per Serving: 516 calories, 15 g protein, 18 g fat, 75 g carbohydrate, 526 mg sodium, 0 mg cholesterol.

12 ounces penne, fusilli, shells or bow-tie pasta

Sweet Red Pepper Sauce:
3 tablespoons olive oil
3 cloves garlic, smashed and peeled
⅓ cup slivered almonds
2 jars (7 ounces each) roasted red peppers, drained, rinsed and patted dry (2 cups)
½ cup chicken broth
3 tablespoons tomato paste
1 tablespoon balsamic vinegar OR: red wine vinegar
½ teaspoon salt
½ teaspoon sugar *(optional)*

1. Cook pasta according to package directions.
2. Meanwhile, prepare sauce: Heat oil in medium-size skillet over moderate heat. Add garlic; cook until lightly golden, about 2 minutes. Add almonds; cook 2 minutes or until lightly golden. Transfer to food processor along with peppers, chicken broth, tomato paste, vinegar, salt and sugar if peppers are particularly acidic. Whirl until pureed and smooth. Transfer to a large serving bowl.
3. Drain cooked pasta. Toss with sauce. Serve hot, warm or at room temperature.

PASTA WITH GARLIC AND BREAD CRUMBS

LOW-CHOLESTEROL · QUICK

This simple sauce goes well with any thin spaghetti shape. For extra zip, add 3 or 4 flat anchovy fillets, chopped, and a pinch of hot red pepper flakes as you brown the crumbs.

Makes 4 servings.
Recipe can be halved or doubled.
Nutrient Value Per Serving: 572 calories, 11 g protein, 29 g fat, 67 g carbohydrate, 301 mg sodium, 0 mg cholesterol.

12 ounces spaghettini or capellini

Garlic and Bread Crumbs:
½ cup olive oil
4 cloves garlic, peeled and left whole
⅓ cup fresh bread crumbs
2 tablespoons lemon juice
2 tablespoons water
¼ cup chopped parsley
½ teaspoon salt

1. Cook pasta according to package directions.
2. Meanwhile, prepare Garlic and Bread Crumbs: Heat oil and garlic in large skillet over low heat; cook until garlic is golden, about 7 minutes. Remove garlic and discard.
3. Add crumbs to oil; cook 3 to 4 minutes or until crisp and golden. Add lemon juice, water, parsley and salt; swirl to combine.
4. Drain pasta. Transfer to serving bowl. Pour sauce over hot pasta; toss and serve.

PASTA WITH MEXICAN SAUCE

QUICK

Makes 4 servings.
Recipe can be halved or doubled.
Nutrient Value Per Serving: 601 calories,
25 g protein, 27 g fat, 65 g carbohydrate,
565 mg sodium, 80 mg cholesterol.

8 ounces bow ties, shells, penne or rigatoni
Mexican Sauce:
3 tablespoons *un*salted butter
1 small sweet green pepper, cored,
    seeded and finely chopped
3½ tablespoons all-purpose flour
½ teaspoon chili powder
2¼ cups whole or lowfat milk
1 can (4 ounces) chopped green chilies
1½ cups shredded Monterey Jack cheese
    (6 ounces)
1 cup frozen whole-kernel corn, thawed
    and drained

1. Cook pasta according to package
directions.
2. Meanwhile, prepare Sauce: Heat
butter in large saucepan or Dutch oven
over low heat. Add green pepper; cook,
stirring frequently, for 3 minutes. Stir
in flour and chili powder until well
mixed; cook 3 minutes or until bubbly.
Stir in milk and green chilies until
smooth. Bring to boiling over moderate
heat, stirring constantly. Lower heat.
Stir in cheese and corn; cook until the
cheese has melted and the corn is
heated through.
3. Drain pasta. Add to saucepan and
toss with sauce.

Microwave Directions (High Power Oven):
Ingredient Changes: Reduce flour to 3
tablespoons; reduce milk to 2 cups.
Directions: Combine butter and green
pepper in microwave-safe 2½-quart casserole. Microwave, uncovered, at 100%
power 4 minutes, stirring once. Stir in
flour and chili powder. Gradually whisk

in milk until smooth. Add to casserole
with green chilies. Microwave, uncovered, at 100% power 7 minutes to a full
boil, stirring twice. Stir in cheese and
corn until cheese is melted. Mix in
cooked pasta. Cover and let stand 5
minutes.

PASTA WITH SAUSAGE AND BROCCOLI

LOW-CHOLESTEROL · QUICK

Makes 4 servings.
Recipe can be halved or doubled.
Nutrient Value Per Serving: 539 calories,
20 g protein, 26 g fat, 57 g carbohydrate,
780 mg sodium, 54 mg cholesterol.

8 ounces large pasta shells, penne or bow
    ties
Sausage and Broccoli:
2 teaspoons olive oil
4 sweet Italian sausages (10 ounces), skin
    removed and meat crumbled
1 medium-size onion, finely chopped
1 cup chicken broth
½ cup chopped tomatoes
⅓ cup raisins
⅛ to ¼ teaspoon ground hot red pepper
2½ cups (5 ounces) small broccoli
    flowerets (about 1 head)

1. Cook pasta according to package
directions.
2. Meanwhile, prepare Sausage and
Broccoli: Heat oil in large skillet over
moderate heat. Add sausage; cook, stirring occasionally, until browned, about
5 minutes. Add onion; cover and cook
5 minutes, stirring occasionally. Add
broth, tomatoes, raisins and ground red
pepper. Bring to boiling over moderate
heat. Add broccoli; cover and cook
until broccoli is tender, 5 to 7 minutes.
(continued)

THE CASSEROLE CONNECTION
You can transform
Pasta with Mexican
Sauce into spicy mac-
aroni and cheese by
pouring the pasta and
sauce into a lightly
buttered 11 × 7-inch
baking pan, topping
with bread crumbs,
and baking for 20
minutes in a 350°
oven.

QUICKER-COOKING SAUSAGE
For Pasta with Sau-
sage and Broccoli, we
speed prep time by
taking the sausage
out of its casing. To
remove the casing
easily, use a knife or
scissors to slit the sau-
sage open, then
remove the meat.
Garnish this dish with
toasted pignoli (pine
nuts), if you wish.

PASTA WITH SAUSAGE AND BROCCOLI
(*continued*)

3. Drain pasta. Add to skillet and toss with sauce. Serve.

Microwave Directions (High Power Oven):
Ingredient Changes: Eliminate oil; reduce ground hot red pepper to a pinch.
Directions: Crumble sausage into microwave-safe 2-quart casserole. Cover with paper toweling. Microwave at 100% power 3 minutes. Drain off fat. Stir in onion. Cover with lid. Microwave at 100% power 3 minutes. Add broth, tomatoes, raisins and hot pepper. Re-cover. Microwave at 100% power 3 minutes to boiling. Stir in broccoli. Re-cover. Microwave at 100% power 3 minutes. Mix in cooked pasta. Cover and let stand 5 minutes, stirring once.

PASTA WITH WHITE BEAN SAUCE

LOW-FAT · LOW-CHOLESTEROL · QUICK

Mashing *some of the beans makes this sauce extra creamy. Garnish with a fresh sage leaf, if you wish.*

Makes 4 servings.
Recipe can be halved or doubled.
Nutrient Value Per Serving: 430 calories, 19 g protein, 12 g fat, 62 g carbohydrate, 729 mg sodium, 8 mg cholesterol.

8 ounces rigatoni, penne, bow ties or
    shells

White Bean Sauce:
2 tablespoons olive oil
1 medium-size onion, finely chopped
2 cloves garlic, thinly sliced
2 carrots, halved lengthwise and thinly
    sliced crosswise
1 can (16 ounces) white beans, drained
    and rinsed
1 cup chicken broth

¾ teaspoon leaf sage, crumbled
¼ teaspoon salt
2 tablespoons lemon juice
½ cup grated Parmesan cheese
3 tablespoons chopped parsley

1. Cook pasta according to package directions.
2. Meanwhile, prepare Sauce: Heat oil in large skillet over moderate heat. Add onion; cook, stirring frequently, for 5 minutes or until onion is softened. Add garlic; cook 1 minute. Add carrot; cook 5 minutes, stirring occasionally. Add beans, broth, sage and salt; cook 5 minutes, mashing about one-quarter of the beans with wooden spoon against side of skillet. Add lemon juice; cook 2 minutes. Add Parmesan and parsley.
3. Drain pasta. Add to skillet and toss with sauce.

Microwave Directions (High Power Oven):
Ingredient Changes: Reduce chicken broth to ¾ cup; reduce the sage to ½ teaspoon.
Directions: Combine oil, onion, garlic and carrot in microwave-safe 2½-quart casserole with lid. Microwave, uncovered, at 100% power 5 minutes, stirring once. Mash about one-quarter of the beans. Add whole and mashed beans, chicken broth, sage, salt and lemon juice to casserole. Microwave, covered, at 100% power 5 minutes. Stir in cheese, parsley and cooked pasta.

SIMPLE PASTA SUPPER

Pasta with White Bean Sauce (this page)

Mixed Greens with Oil and Vinegar

Italian Bread

Berries

SHAPES MADE FOR SAUCING
Hearty sauces with chunky ingredients call for pasta shapes with nooks and crannies to hold the sauce. Penne, macaroni and fusilli capture the beans in a White Bean Sauce or the vegetables in a fresh vegetable mixture.

RICE PRIMER

long-grain   medium-grain   short-grain

Although more than 40,000 varieties of rice exist worldwide, only a few are generally consumed in North America.

Rices are commercially classified by size, and different-size rices when cooked will differ in texture—long-grain rice cooks fluffier than short-grain. One type of rice is not necessarily "better" than another; fluffy rice is preferred in some dishes, sticky rice in others.

Most rice sold commercially has been enriched with iron, niacin and thiamin. However, all rice must be milled—that is, the hull, or outer coating, removed—for the grain to be edible.

Long-grain rice: Available in both white and brown varieties, the grains are four to five times as long as they are wide and when cooked are fluffy and separate. Used in such dishes as meat or chicken with rice and gravy, or as plain boiled rice flavored with butter and herbs, or for Middle Eastern pilafs and the fragrant rice dishes of India.

Medium-grain white rice: This rice is shorter and plumper than long-grain, and clings together, making it excellent for croquettes, molded dishes and rice pudding. Somewhat fluffy just after it is cooked, the rice clumps as it cools. Used in Spanish paella and in Caribbean dishes, such as Cuban black beans and rice.

Short-grain white rice: Shorter than medium-grain and softer and stickier when cooked, this rice, sometimes called "round rice," is the grain of choice in Japan and China since its cohesiveness makes it easier to eat with chopsticks.

Arborio rice: An Italian rice, grown in the Po valley for centuries, is technically a medium-grain rice, although it's usually identified as short-grain. It is preferred for risotto, the creamy Italian dish in which each grain is very tender, yet distinct.

Sweet or glutinous rice: Also known as waxy rice, this short-grained variety is sweet and very sticky and used extensively in Oriental dishes.

Aromatic rice: A family distinguished by a nutty, fresh aroma sometimes described as "popcorn," frequently found in specialty shops. The best known is *basmati,* a long-grain white rice from Northern India and Pakistan that needs washing and, often, preliminary soaking before cooking. Brand-name aromatic rices are grown in this country, and they include: *Texmati,* a basmati-type rice sold both as white and brown rices; a wild pecan version from Louisiana; and a gourmet rice from Arkansas. You may also find aromatic-style rice in your supermarket.

Wild rice: Not a true rice, but actually a purplish-black North American grass. Dried, parched and husked, it has a nutty flavor and chewy texture, a perfect match for meat and game dishes. Although more expensive (and longer-cooking than regular

aromatic   Texmati   basmati

rice), a little goes a long way: wild rice can be extended with white rice, a combination with a special flavor and an attractive speckled appearance.

PROCESSING

White or polished rice: This rice is stripped of its husk, bran, polish and germ, so choose an enriched variety that replaces some of the nutrients lost in the processing.

Brown rice: A tan-colored rice of any shape from which only the inedible hull has been removed by milling, leaving the bran layers intact and thus retaining more nutrient value than other, polished types. Brown rice requires longer cooking than white rice, and its chewy texture and nutty flavor are appreciated in many vegetarian combinations such as rice and vegetable casseroles. The oil in the bran layers can become rancid, so it is best to use this rice quickly and to keep it refrigerated.

Parboiled or converted white rice: The unhulled rice grain is soaked, pressure-steamed, dried and then milled—a process which forces some of the nutrients from the bran and the germ into the center of the rice kernel and which allows the rice grains to remain separate and fluffy when cooked. This rice requires a slightly longer cooking time in more water than does regular-milled rice.

Instant or precooked white rice: Partially or fully cooked before being dehydrated, this convenient rice cooks quickly, but with less texture and nutrient value than others.

wild rice   brown rice   converted rice

CURRIED RICE PILAF

LOW-FAT · LOW-CHOLESTEROL

Serve with roast pork, lamb or chicken, or grilled lamb chops. If you can't find either imported or domestic basmati rice, use long-grain white rice. To create a main dish, add cooked chicken, pork or ham.

Makes 8 servings.
Recipe can be halved or doubled.
Nutrient Value Per Serving: 225 calories, 5 g protein, 6 g fat, 38 g carbohydrate, 384 mg sodium, 0 mg cholesterol.

2 tablespoons vegetable oil
1 large onion, thinly sliced
1½ teaspoons curry powder
1½ cups basmati OR: Texmati rice OR: long-grain white rice
¼ cup currants
1 cinnamon stick
3 cups chicken broth
1 medium-size sweet red pepper, cored, seeded and thinly sliced
1 small carrot, pared and shredded
½ cup frozen peas
¼ cup sliced almonds, toasted

1. Heat oil in large skillet over medium heat. Add onion; sauté until browned, about 7 minutes. Stir in curry powder and rice. Add currants, cinnamon stick and broth. Bring to boiling. Lower heat; cover and simmer 10 minutes.
2. Stir in sweet red pepper and carrot; cover and simmer 5 minutes. Sprinkle with peas. Remove from heat and let stand, covered, 10 minutes. Sprinkle with almonds and serve.

Microwave Directions (High Power Oven):
Scatter almonds over bottom of 2½-quart microwave-safe casserole with lid. Microwave, uncovered, at 100% power 3 minutes. Remove and reserve. Combine oil and onion in same casserole. Microwave, uncovered, at 100% power 5 minutes, stirring once. Stir in curry powder and rice. Add currants, cinna-mon stick and broth. Microwave, covered, at 100% power 10 minutes to boiling. Stir in red pepper and carrot. Microwave, covered, at 50% power 10 minutes. Stir in peas. Let stand, covered, 5 minutes. Sprinkle with almonds and serve.

■ Do not stir rice while it is cooking or it will become mushy (except for risotto; *see recipes, pages 214–216).*

■ When the rice is finally cooked in the pot, gently fluff with a fork to let the steam escape and keep the grains separate.

■ Rice reheats with excellent results. Add 2 tablespoons of liquid for each cup of cooked rice. Cover the saucepan and cook on top of the stove over low heat for about 5 minutes or until heated through. In a microwave oven (High Power Oven), heat 1 cup cooked rice at 100% power for 1 minute. Or cook 1 cup frozen rice at 100% power for 2 minutes. Fluff with a fork. Additional microwaving time is needed if reheating 2 or 3 cups cooked or frozen cooked rice.

■ Milled white rices keep almost indefinitely on the shelf. Store opened rice in a tightly covered container. It's best to store brown rice and wild rice in the refrigerator since the oils can turn rancid.

■ Leftover cooked rice can be refrigerated, tightly covered, for up to 4 days, or frozen for up to 3 months.

WHITE AND WILD RICE WITH APRICOTS AND PECANS

LOW-CHOLESTEROL

Serve with poultry, or roasted and grilled meats, or use as a stuffing for poultry, onions and other vegetables. Prunes, raisins or dried cherries may be substituted for the apricots. Add some leftover cooked chicken to the rice mixture, and you've created a main dish.

Makes 8 servings.
Recipe can be halved or doubled.
Nutrient Value Per Serving: 184 calories, 4 g protein, 8 g fat, 25 g carbohydrate, 315 mg sodium, 8 mg cholesterol.

2 tablespoons *un*salted butter
1 large onion, diced
2 carrots, pared and diced
½ cup wild rice, rinsed and drained
2¼ cups chicken broth
½ cup converted white rice
½ cup coarsely chopped toasted pecans
⅓ cup dried apricots, quartered

1. Heat butter in 4-quart saucepan over medium-high heat. Add onion and carrots; cook, stirring occasionally, until softened, about 5 minutes. Stir in wild rice and chicken broth. Bring to boiling. Lower heat; cover and simmer 45 minutes or until rice is almost cooked through.
2. Stir in white rice. Bring to boiling. Lower heat; cover and simmer 20 minutes or until rice is tender and liquid is absorbed. Stir in pecans and apricots; heat through.

BROWN RICE, NUT AND KALE LOAF

This loaf is delicious with roasted meats or egg dishes or will serve four as a vegetarian main dish. Serve either cold or at room temperature—great picnic food!

Bake at 350° for 55 minutes.
Makes 6 servings.
Nutrient Value Per Serving: 353 calories, 12 g protein, 19 g fat, 37 g carbohydrate, 745 mg sodium, 81 mg cholesterol.

1¾ cups water
1¾ teaspoons salt
1 cup brown rice
2 tablespoons *un*salted butter
1 large onion, finely chopped
2 medium-size carrots, pared and
    shredded
2 cloves garlic, finely chopped
½ teaspoon leaf marjoram, crumbled
½ teaspoon leaf thyme, crumbled
2 eggs
2 egg whites
2 packages (10 ounces each) frozen
    chopped kale, thawed, drained and
    squeezed of excess liquid
1 cup walnuts, finely chopped
½ teaspoon pepper

1. Bring water and ½ teaspoon salt to boiling in small saucepan. Add rice. Return to boil. Lower heat; cover and simmer for 35 minutes. Remove from heat. Let stand, covered, 20 minutes.
2. Preheat oven to moderate (350°). Lightly butter 9 × 5 × 3-inch glass or aluminum loaf pan.
3. Meanwhile, heat butter in 10-inch skillet over medium-low heat. Add onion, carrot, garlic, marjoram and thyme; sauté, stirring occasionally, for 5 to 7 minutes or until onion and carrot are tender. Set aside.
4. Beat together slightly eggs and egg whites in large bowl. Add kale, stirring well to separate strands. Add rice,

onion mixture, walnuts, pepper and remaining 1¼ teaspoons salt; mix until thoroughly moistened. Spoon mixture evenly into prepared pan, lightly pressing mixture down. Cover with aluminum foil.
5. Bake in preheated moderate oven (350°) for 45 minutes. Remove foil. Bake an additional 10 minutes. Remove to wire rack and let stand 15 minutes. Gently run a small, thin sharp knife around edges of pan to loosen. Place serving dish on top; invert loaf onto dish. Serve immediately or refrigerate to serve chilled. To serve, slice crosswise with serrated knife, using gentle back-and-forth sawing motion.

Make-Ahead Tip: The loaf can be prepared a day ahead and refrigerated, covered.

Microwave Directions (High Power Oven): Cook rice as above. Coat inside of microwave-safe 2-quart casserole with lid with nonstick spray. Combine butter, onion, carrot, garlic, marjoram and thyme in casserole. Microwave, uncovered, at 100% power 7 minutes, stirring once. Combine ingredients in large bowl as directed in Step 4. Spoon into same casserole. Cover with lid. Microwave at 100% power 5 minutes. Uncover and microwave at 70% power 5 minutes. Cover and let stand 5 minutes. Unmold onto serving plate as directed above.

FAR EAST SAMPLER

Hot and Sour Soup with
Tofu (130)

Brown Rice, Nut and Kale
Loaf (this page)

Shredded Chinese Green
Cabbage Salad with Bean
Sprouts

Plums and Fortune Cookies

RICE REPORT
■ **Brown rice** contains twice as much fiber as white rice, but because of enrichment, white rice contains almost three times the amount of iron.
■ **Wild rice** is richer in protein and vitamins, significantly higher in fiber and somewhat lower in calories than either white or brown rice.
■ **All rice** is sodium-free unless you add salt during cooking.

TEX-MEX RICE CASSEROLE

A *flavorful side dish to team with hamburgers or grilled steaks.*

Combine rice, corn, garlic, green onion, milk, chili powder, liquid red-pepper seasoning, salt and pepper in microwave-safe 2-quart casserole with lid. Microwave, covered, at 100% power 10 minutes, stirring once. Stir again. Overlap tomato slices around edge of casserole; sprinkle with cheese. Microwave, uncovered, at 100% power 3 minutes. Cover and let stand 5 minutes.

Bake at 350° for 35 to 40 minutes.
Makes 8 servings.
Nutrient Value Per Serving: 280 calories, 12 g protein, 11 g fat, 33 g carbohydrate, 349 mg sodium, 36 mg cholesterol.

3 cups cooked basmati rice OR: other aromatic rice *(see page 209)* OR: white rice
1 package (10 ounces) frozen whole-kernel corn, thawed and patted dry
1 clove garlic, finely chopped
⅓ cup sliced green onion
1½ cups milk
1 teaspoon chili powder
½ teaspoon liquid red-pepper seasoning
½ teaspoon salt
¼ teaspoon pepper
2 cups shredded sharp Cheddar cheese (8 ounces)
1 large tomato, thinly sliced

1. Preheat oven to moderate (350°). Grease a 2-quart casserole.
2. Mix together rice, corn, garlic, green onion, milk, chili powder, red-pepper seasoning, salt, pepper and 1½ cups Cheddar cheese. Pour into casserole. Arrange tomato slices on top, overlapping slightly.
3. Bake in preheated moderate oven (350°) until heated through, 35 to 40 minutes. Sprinkle with remaining ½ cup cheese for last 5 minutes of cooking. Let casserole stand for 10 minutes before serving.

RISOTTO

Here's *our basic recipe for this classic, slow-cooking rice dish, followed by variations on pages 215 and 216. Feel free to improvise on your own by adding leftovers.*

Makes 4 servings.
Nutrient Value Per Serving: 386 calories, 8 g protein, 15 g fat, 53 g carbohydrate, 495 mg sodium, 21 mg cholesterol.

2 tablespoons olive oil
2 tablespoons *un*salted butter
1 medium-size onion, finely chopped
1¼ cups (9 ounces) arborio rice
4½ cups simmering homemade Chicken Stock *(see recipe, page 116)* OR: 3 cups water combined with 1½ cups canned chicken broth, simmering
⅓ cup grated Parmesan cheese

1. Heat oil and 1 tablespoon butter in medium-size heavy-bottomed saucepan over low heat. Add onion; cook, stirring occasionally, until softened and golden, about 7 minutes. Add rice; stir to coat and cook 1 minute.
2. Add ½ cup chicken broth, or water and broth mixture; stir until liquid has been absorbed. Continue adding broth, ½ cup at a time, stirring constantly until each addition is absorbed before adding the next ½ cup, and until there is only 1 cup broth remaining.
3. Add the remaining broth, ⅓ cup at a time, stirring and cooking as above, until rice is just cooked through; rice will have a slight "bite," but there should be no starchy center. The whole cooking time will be about 30 minutes.
4. Stir in Parmesan cheese and remaining tablespoon butter. Serve immediately.

RISOTTO WITH CHICKEN

LOW-FAT · LOW-CHOLESTEROL

Makes 4 servings.

Nutrient Value Per Serving: 424 calories, 22 g protein, 12 g fat, 55 g carbohydrate, 586 mg sodium, 82 mg cholesterol.

1½ tablespoons *un*salted butter
1 tablespoon olive oil
1 medium-size onion, finely chopped
2 cloves garlic, finely chopped
1 carrot, pared and finely chopped (½ cup)
1¼ cups arborio rice (9 ounces)
3½ cups simmering homemade Chicken Stock (*see recipe, page 116*) OR: 2 cups water combined with 1½ cups canned chicken broth, simmering
12 ounces boneless, skinned chicken thighs or breasts, cut into ½-inch chunks
¼ teaspoon salt

1. Heat butter and oil in medium-size heavy-bottomed saucepan over low heat. Add onion; cook, stirring occasionally, until softened and golden, about 7 minutes. Add garlic; cook 1 minute. Add carrot; cook 4 minutes longer, stirring occasionally. Add rice; stir to coat and cook 1 minute.
2. Add ½ cup chicken broth, or water and broth mixture; stir until liquid has been absorbed. Continue adding broth ½ cup at a time, stirring continually until liquid is absorbed before adding another ½ cup, and until there is only 1 cup broth remaining.
3. Stir in chicken and salt. Add remaining broth, ⅓ cup at a time, stirring and cooking as above, until chicken is cooked through and rice is just cooked through; rice will have slight "bite," but there should be no starchy center. Total cooking time will be about 30 minutes. Serve immediately.

HOW TO MAKE RISOTTO WITH CHICKEN
1. Add arborio rice to cooked onion, garlic and carrot mixture. Stir to coat rice.

2. Add ½ cup simmering broth and stir until liquid is absorbed. Continue adding broth ½ cup at a time, stirring until liquid is absorbed before adding another ½ cup, and until there is only 1 cup remaining. Stir in other main ingredients. Add remaining 1 cup broth, ⅓ cup at a time.

3. Finished rice should be bathed in a "creamy" sauce; rice should have a slight "bite," but there should be no starchy center.

RISOTTO WITH SHRIMP

LOW-FAT

Makes 4 servings.
Nutrient Value Per Serving: 454 calories,
19 g protein, 14 g fat, 54 g carbohydrate,
403 mg sodium, 120 mg cholesterol.

2 tablespoons olive oil
1 medium-size onion, finely chopped
1 small sweet red pepper, cored, seeded
    and finely chopped
1¼ cups arborio rice (9 ounces)
12 ounces large shrimp, shelled and
    deveined
1 tablespoon tomato paste
⅔ cup dry white wine
2 cups water
1 bottle (8 ounces) clam broth
¼ teaspoon salt
2 tablespoons *un*salted butter

1. Heat oil in medium-size heavy-bottomed saucepan over low heat. Add onion and pepper; cook, stirring occasionally, until softened, about 7 minutes. Stir in rice; stir for 1 minute.
2. Place 3 ounces shrimp in food processor or blender. Whirl until pureed. Stir into rice. Stir in tomato paste and wine. Cook, stirring, until all wine is absorbed.
3. Combine water and clam broth; bring to simmering. Add ½ cup of water and clam broth mixture to rice, stirring continually until all liquid is absorbed. Continue adding liquid, ½ cup at a time, stirring constantly until liquid is absorbed before adding another ½ cup, and until there is only 1 cup of liquid remaining.
4. Add remaining shrimp and salt. Add the remaining liquid, ⅓ cup at a time, stirring and cooking as above, until shrimp is cooked through and rice is just cooked through; rice will have a slight "bite," but there should be no starchy center. The total cooking time will be about 30 minutes. Stir in butter. Serve immediately.

KASHA WITH KALE AND MUSHROOMS

LOW-FAT

Makes 6 servings (6 cups).
Recipe can be doubled.
Nutrient Value Per Serving: 177 calories,
7 g protein, 6 g fat, 26 g carbohydrate,
393 mg sodium, 46 mg cholesterol.

2 tablespoons *un*salted butter
1 large onion, chopped
2 cloves garlic, finely chopped
¼ pound small mushrooms, sliced
½ pound fresh kale, stems removed,
    washed, well drained and thinly cut
    crosswise OR: 1 package (10 ounces)
    frozen kale, thawed and well drained
    OR: spinach OR: collard greens
1 egg
1 cup whole kasha
2 cups chicken broth
1 teaspoon lemon juice
¼ teaspoon pepper

1. Melt butter in large skillet over medium heat. Add onion; sauté 5 minutes or until slightly softened. Add garlic; sauté 1 minute. Add mushrooms; sauté 8 to 10 minutes or until softened. During last 2 to 3 minutes, add kale; cook, stirring occasionally, just until kale is wilted or until thawed frozen kale is heated through. Remove vegetables with slotted spoon to medium-size bowl. Increase heat to medium-high.
2. Beat egg slightly in small bowl; stir in kasha to coat. Add kasha mixture to skillet; cook, stirring constantly, until kasha and egg separate, about 3 minutes. Add chicken broth. Bring to boiling. Lower heat; cover and simmer about 10 minutes or until liquid is absorbed. Add reserved vegetables. Heat through.

BIG SHRIMP FLAVOR
Pureeing a portion of the shrimp and adding it toward the beginning of the cooking gives Risotto with Shrimp a really rich shrimp flavor. Serve as a main dish for a special luncheon, or in smaller portions as a first course.

KASHA WITH KALE SERVING IDEAS
Kasha, or roasted buckwheat, can be served as a side dish in place of rice or grains. This vegetable-kale side dish would complement most lamb or pork dishes.

GRAINS PRIMER

Grains or edible seeds come from a group of plants called cereals. Grains provide some protein and a good amount of carbohydrates.

Amaranth (AM-ah-ranth): A tiny, poppy seed-sized grain loaded with protein and calcium. Serve as you would rice. Use the toasted grain in pancake, muffin and cake batters.

whole hulled barley

pearl barley

Barley: A stubby grain resembling an overstuffed oat flake. Pearl barley, the grain stripped of husks and embryo, is white and relatively fast-cooking, and comes in three sizes: coarse, medium and fine. Pearl barley is often made into a soup along with mushrooms and lamb. It's also a delicious stuffing for poultry, fish and vegetables, and a tasty alternative to rice as a side dish. Whole hulled barley, available in health food stores, derives its gritty texture, brown color and high fiber content from the outer coating that's left on.

Buckwheat: Like wild rice, buckwheat is technically a grass, not a grain. The most commonly available form is buckwheat groats or kasha—roasted, hulled buckwheat kernels. With a deep, nutty flavor and tan color, kasha is often paired with pasta bow ties to make a dish called kasha varnishkas. The whole and coarse-ground forms cook a bit more slowly than the medium or fine, but retain their pleasant chewiness. Buckwheat is also available untoasted; this cooks to a more delicate flavor and texture. Prepare untoasted buckwheat as you would rice. Buckwheat flour, with its distinctive lavender tinge, is used to make blini, the flavorful yeast-raised pancakes served with caviar or smoked fish, sour cream or melted butter.

Corn: A native American grain widely enjoyed in foods as diverse as corn chips, succotash and grits.
Corn on the cob, summer's prize vegetable, should be eaten as soon after picking as possible to maximize its sweetness.
Canned corn is available in whole-kernel and cream-style forms. Both have the same number of calories, although whole-kernel corn is a bit higher in vitamins and minerals.
To make *cornmeal,* the whole kernel of corn is conventionally ground or stone ground. In modern conventional grinding (also known as enriched-degerminated), the corn kernels are dried first, then pulverized between heavy steel rollers, which removes the hull fiber and the germ. Stone-ground cornmeal is ground between millstones, which crush the whole kernels along with their germ and hull, both retaining nutrients and enhancing flavor. Since there is more fat in the germ, the stone-ground variety needs to be refrigerated, and may be kept for up to 4 months. Both varieties are enriched to comply with USDA standards. Cornmeal is either yellow, white or blue, depending on the type of corn used. Yellow has slightly more vitamins than white and more beta carotene. Blue cornmeal from the Southwest, with a pronounced "corny" flavor, is higher in protein, magnesium, iron, zinc and fat than the yellow or white hues; however it's lower in calcium and phosphorus. With those slight variations in mind, all three

CORN

yellow cornmeal   blue cornmeal   grits   white cornmeal   popcorn

OATS

steel-cut oats   old-fashioned oats   quick-cooking oats   oat bran   oat flour

varieties are interchangeable in cooking. To add a pleasant crunch to biscuits, cakes, cookies, pancake batters and pie crusts, replace about ¼ of the flour with cornmeal. Or dust poultry or fish with cornmeal instead of bread crumbs before sautéing.

Popcorn is made from hard-starch corn, which enhances popping. A hot-air popper eliminates the need for any oil in cooking. High in fiber and low in sodium, this all-American snack food clocks in at just 23 calories per cup, if you hold the melted butter.

Grits is coarsely ground, hulled kernels of mature, dried corn, and like cornmeal, is available commercially ground and stone-ground. Seek out the stone-ground variety for flavor, appearance and nutritive content; the commercially ground sort is still high in fiber and rich in protein, and to some tastes, appealingly fluffier when cooked. An instant kind is also available.

Millet: These diminutive beige kernels resemble rice when cooked. Use as a side dish or stuffing, or substitute for rice in classic preparations such as jambalaya and croquettes. Millet is also ground into meal and flour for baking. Puffed millet is eaten as a cereal.

Oats: There's more to oats than just oatmeal, and even in that category, there's a variety of choices. Oats are high in vitamin B-1 and contain good amounts of B-2 and E.

Oat groats are the whole kernels, stripped of the hull after being cleaned and toasted. They retain almost all of the grain's original nutrient value. Oat groats can be used in the same manner as rice, as a side dish, cereal, stuffing or salad base. Oat groats can also be grown into high-protein sprouts.

Steel-cut oats, also known as Scotch or Irish oats, are groats broken into 2 or 3 parts. They are usually cooked and eaten as a breakfast cereal, retaining more "chew" than rolled oats.

Old-fashioned rolled oats are made from groats that are steam-cooked, then flattened.

Quick-cooking rolled oats are made by steam-cooking and flattening cut groats.

Instant oatmeal, made from cut groats that have been pre-cooked, dried and then rolled, is prepared by pouring boiling water over the dry cereal right in the bowl for eating. Compared to old-fashioned or quick-cooking rolled oats, however, it usually contains sugar and salt.

Oat flour is made from ground groats; you can also make your own version by grinding rolled oats in a blender or food processor. Use in breads, muffins and scones. For yeast breads, oat flour must be mixed with all-purpose flour, since it doesn't have the gluten necessary for rising.

Oat bran, the outer casing of the oat, is high in soluble fiber. Sprinkle onto cold cereals or prepare hot as you would rolled oats, or add to some of your favorite recipes such as meatloaf.

Quinoa (KEEN-wah): A pale, amber seed from the Andes, where it's been a staple for centuries. Rich in calcium (one cup of cooked quinoa has the same calcium as a quart of milk!), quinoa is considered a complete protein since it contains all eight essential amino acids. Quinoa has a grasslike scent, which diminishes with cooking. The grain is now being grown domestically, although the South American variety is still preferred by aficionados. Altiplano, grown in Bolivia and Peru, is the best of the three available varieties (the second-best is valley, and the lowest-quality is sea-level) because it is sweet, succulent and delicately colored. Dry-toasting before cooking enhances flavor. Use as you would rice, in soups, side dishes and salads. It's available as a grain and ground into a flour and used in such products as pasta. Look for it in some specialty food shops and health food stores.

kasha   millet   amaranth   quinoa   triticale

Semolina: The hard heart of durum wheat is ground into a flour used for making pasta, or it is processed into granules for making couscous. On its native turf, such as Morocco, couscous is hand-prepared from semolina at home. In this country, couscous is available ready-made. The traditional Middle Eastern variety of couscous requires a steaming and fork-fluffing process that takes at least an hour.

couscous   semolina

Although purists quiver, instant couscous, prepared in less than 10 minutes, makes a fine, if admittedly less fluffy, substitute for the real thing. Try couscous as a nice switch from rice and use as a base for stews, or for a delicious salad with Middle Eastern undertones.

Triticale: A relative newcomer to the grain world, triticale is a man-made hybrid of wheat and rye, with a higher protein content and a more desirable amino acid breakdown than either grain. It's available in whole berries, flakes and flour. The berries, similar to wheat berries in appearance, have a more pronounced flavor. Triticale flakes can be used just about anywhere you'd use oat flakes, such as a cereal, as a meatloaf binder, or even in cookies. Triticale flour needs to be blended with a high-gluten flour, such as bread flour, to produce baked goods with the right texture.

Wheat: *Bran* is the fiber-rich outer layer of the wheat berry, and is available in unprocessed and processed forms. *Unprocessed bran,* sometimes referred to as miller's bran, can be used in muffin or pancake batters, and substituted for part or all of the bread crumbs in recipes such as meatloaf or breaded fish or chicken. Pulverize the bran in a blender to use in more delicate baking.
Processed bran resembles prepared cereal in that it contains sugar and salt; its high-fiber profile salvages its reputation.

Bulgur cooks quickly since the wheat berries have been steamed, then dried and cracked into coarse, medium or fine pieces. Coarse bulgur, similar to rice, is ideally suited to pilafs and stuffings; medium grind is perfect for salads such as tabbouleh, the Middle Eastern grain dish heavily flavored with mint, parsley and lemon juice; fine grind is often used in bread baking.
Cracked wheat is wheat berries first dried, then cracked, to sharply reduce cooking time.
Wheat berries are the whole kernel of the wheat, with only the inedible hull removed.
Wheat flakes are cooked, rolled wheat berries, similar to rolled oats, and they can be prepared in the same manner.
Wheat germ is the heart of the wheat and is available raw and toasted. Sprinkle on cereals, and add to cake, muffin and pancake batters. Use to coat foods for sautéing or oven-frying.

WHEAT

wheat berries   bulgur   bran   cracked wheat   wheat flakes   wheat germ

BULGUR BAKED WITH GARLIC AND VEGETABLES

LOW-FAT

A *delicious complement to roasted meats, this hearty casserole could also occupy a spot on a vegetarian buffet table.*

Bake garlic at 350° for 45 minutes; bake casserole at 325° for 50 minutes.
Makes 6 servings.
Nutrient Value Per Serving: 274 calories, 12 g protein, 9 g fat, 42 g carbohydrate, 623 mg sodium, 77 mg cholesterol.

1 whole bulb garlic
1½ cups bulgur
1½ cups boiling water
2 tablespoons lemon juice
1½ teaspoons salt
¼ teaspoon pepper
2 tablespoons olive oil
3 medium-size onions, coarsely chopped
1 large sweet red pepper, cored, seeded and coarsely chopped (2 cups)
1 bunch broccoli, trimmed, divided into flowerets, stems removed and saved for another use (4 to 5 cups flowerets)
⅓ cup water
2 eggs
1 cup milk

1. Preheat oven to moderate (350°). Wrap garlic bulb in aluminum foil.
2. Roast garlic in preheated moderate oven (350°) for 45 minutes or until tender when pierced with fork. Set the garlic aside.
3. Lower oven temperature to slow (325°). Lightly grease 2½-quart (11¾ × 7½ × 1¾-inch) shallow baking dish.
4. Place bulgur in medium-size bowl. Pour boiling water over. Let stand 15 to 20 minutes.
5. Meanwhile, squeeze garlic pulp into bulgur, along with 1 tablespoon lemon juice, 1 teaspoon salt and the pepper; stir to mix.
6. Heat olive oil in large skillet over medium heat. Add onion and red pepper; sauté 3 to 5 minutes or until slightly softened. Remove to small bowl. Add broccoli to skillet; sauté, stirring occasionally, for 2 minutes. Add water; cover and simmer 2 to 3 minutes or until just tender. Drain any excess liquid. Return red pepper-onion mixture to skillet. Stir in remaining 1 tablespoon lemon juice and ½ teaspoon salt. Remove from heat.
7. Beat eggs slightly in small bowl; stir in milk. Stir mixture into bulgur. Place three-quarters of bulgur mixture in bottom of prepared dish. Cover with vegetable mixture; top with remaining bulgur.
8. Bake in preheated slow oven (325°) for 50 minutes or until heated through.

Microwave Directions (High Power Oven):
Ingredient Changes: Increase oil to 3 tablespoons; add 1 tablespoon water. Reduce milk to ¾ cup; eliminate the ⅓ cup water.
Directions: Place garlic, 1 tablespoon oil and 1 tablespoon water in microwave-safe 2-cup measure. Cover with microwave-safe plastic wrap, vented at one edge. Microwave at 100% power 2½ to 3 minutes until tender when pierced with a fork. Squeeze garlic pulp from skin into small bowl. Stir in 2 tablespoons lemon juice. Prepare bulgur as above; stir in pureed garlic, salt and pepper. Combine remaining 2 tablespoons oil, onion and red pepper in microwave-safe 2½-quart casserole with lid. Microwave, covered, at 100% power 4 minutes, stirring once. Add broccoli. Microwave, covered, at 100% power 5 minutes, stirring once. Beat eggs slightly in small bowl; stir in milk. Stir into bulgur. Add bulgur mixture to casserole; stir to mix well. Microwave, covered, at 100% power 3 minutes. Microwave, uncovered, at 50% power 10 minutes. Cover and let stand 5 minutes.

GRAINS NUTRIENT PROFILE

The closer you come to the whole form of any grain, the more nutritious it is. For example, whole wheat loses its fiber-rich bran layer and nutrient-dense germ portion when processed into white flour. To increase the protein and fiber content of your diet, substitute barley, bulgur (cracked wheat) or kasha (buckwheat groats) for rice as a side dish.

BARLEY-VERMICELLI PILAF

LOW-CHOLESTEROL

Try this pilaf as a replacement for potatoes—it's very good with roasted meats. Add a little leftover cooked chicken or beef, and you have a main dish.

Makes 6 servings.
Recipe can be halved or doubled.
Nutrient Value Per Serving: 266 calories, 8 g protein, 9 g fat, 40 g carbohydrate, 456 mg sodium, 10 mg cholesterol.

2 tablespoons *un*salted butter
3 ounces vermicelli, broken into 1- to 2-inch pieces
1 small onion, chopped
½ small sweet red pepper, cored, seeded and diced
1½ cups thinly sliced mushrooms
2½ cups chicken broth
1 cup pearl barley
⅛ teaspoon pepper
⅓ cup chopped toasted walnuts
1 tablespoon chopped parsley

1. Melt butter in medium-size saucepan over medium heat. Add vermicelli; sauté, stirring constantly, about 3 minutes or until lightly browned. Remove with slotted spoon and reserve.
2. Add onion, sweet red pepper and mushrooms to saucepan; sauté 2 minutes or until slightly softened. Add 2 cups broth, barley and pepper. Bring to boiling. Lower heat; cover and simmer 20 minutes.
3. Add remaining broth and the vermicelli; cover and simmer, stirring frequently, for 10 minutes. Remove from heat; let stand, covered, for 5 minutes. Stir in nuts and parsley.

Barley-Vermicelli Pilaf (this page)

Almond-Raisin Conscous (page 222).

ALMOND-RAISIN COUSCOUS

LOW-FAT · QUICK

Serve this flavorful grain dish with roasted meats such as pork or chicken, or as an accompaniment to eggs for a brunch. (Pictured on page 221.)

Makes 4 servings.
Recipe can be halved or doubled.
Nutrient Value Per Serving: 358 calories, 10 g protein, 12 g fat, 54 g carbohydrate, 374 mg sodium, 16 mg cholesterol.

⅓ cup blanched, slivered almonds
1 large orange
1¼ cups chicken broth
1 cinnamon stick, broken
2 tablespoons *un*salted butter
1 cup couscous
¼ cup pitted prunes, quartered
¼ cup golden raisins

1. Toast almonds in dry 2-quart saucepan over medium heat, stirring occasionally, 3 to 4 minutes. Remove almonds; reserve.
2. Meanwhile, grate enough rind from orange to measure 1 teaspoon. Squeeze enough juice to measure ¼ cup.
3. In same saucepan, combine chicken broth, cinnamon stick, butter, orange rind and orange juice. Bring to boiling. Stir in couscous, prunes and raisins. Remove saucepan from heat; cover and let stand 5 minutes.
4. To serve: Remove cinnamon stick. Stir in toasted almonds.

CHEESE AND CHILI BAKED GRITS

Bake at 375° for 45 minutes.
Makes 6 servings.
Nutrient Value Per Serving: 250 calories, 10 g protein, 13 g fat, 23 g carbohydrate, 514 mg sodium, 101 mg cholesterol.

2 tablespoons *un*salted butter
1 medium-size onion, chopped
1 small jalapeño pepper, seeded and finely chopped OR: 2 to 4 dashes liquid red-pepper seasoning
2 cloves garlic, finely chopped
1¾ teaspoons chili powder
2 cups chicken broth
1 cup old-fashioned grits (not quick-cooking)
2 eggs
4 ounces Cheddar cheese, shredded (1 cup)

1. Preheat oven to moderate (375°). Lightly butter 1-quart baking casserole.
2. Melt butter in medium-size saucepan over medium-low heat until hot. Add onion; sauté for about 5 minutes or until almost tender. Add jalapeño and garlic; sauté for about 2 minutes. Stir in chili powder.
3. Increase heat to medium. Add chicken broth. Bring to boiling. Reduce heat to low; gradually whisk in grits. Cook, stirring constantly, for 1 to 2 minutes or until grits thickens. Remove from heat.
4. Beat eggs slightly in small bowl. Quickly beat small amount of hot grits into eggs. Return to saucepan with remaining grits, stirring constantly. Stir in cheese; pour into prepared casserole.
5. Bake, uncovered, in preheated moderate oven (375°) for 45 minutes or until golden.

POLENTA TORTE

Bake at 400° for 30 minutes.
Makes 8 servings.
Nutrient Value Per Serving: 260 calories,
13 g protein, 12 g fat, 24 g carbohydrate,
578 mg sodium, 35 mg cholesterol.

1 package (10 ounces) frozen chopped
    spinach, thawed
1 package (10 ounces) frozen chopped
    kale, thawed
2 tablespoons olive oil
1 small onion, finely chopped
2 cloves garlic, finely chopped
¼ pound smoked ham, cut into small
    cubes
¼ teaspoon pepper
5 cups water
1½ cups yellow cornmeal
½ teaspoon salt
⅓ cup grated Romano cheese OR:
    Parmesan
1½ cups shredded fontina cheese OR:
    mozzarella

1. Squeeze spinach and kale dry.
2. Heat oil in large skillet over medium
heat. Add onion and garlic; sauté 3
minutes. Add spinach, kale, ham and
pepper; sauté 4 minutes.
3. Preheat oven to hot (400°). Butter
2½-quart soufflé dish, or line 8-inch
springform pan with heavy-duty aluminum foil; butter sides and bottom.
4. Bring 4 cups water to boiling in large
saucepan. Stir together remaining 1 cup
water, the cornmeal and salt in a bowl.
Gradually stir cornmeal mixture into
boiling water. Simmer over medium
heat for 10 minutes, stirring constantly.
5. Spread one-third of polenta in prepared dish. Cover with half the greens,
half the Romano and one-third of the
fontina. Repeat layering one more time.
Spread with remaining polenta; sprinkle
with remaining fontina.
6. Bake in preheated hot oven (400°)
for 30 minutes. Let stand for 10 minutes before serving. If using springform
pan, remove sides.

Microwave Directions (High Power Oven):
Combine oil, onion and garlic in
microwave-safe 2-quart casserole.
Microwave, uncovered, at 100% power
3 minutes. Add spinach, kale, ham and
pepper. Microwave, uncovered, at
100% power 5 minutes. Transfer vegetable mixture to small bowl. Combine
water, cornmeal and salt in microwave-
safe 2-quart measure. Cover with paper
toweling. Microwave at 100% power 7
minutes. Whisk well. Microwave,
uncovered, at 100% power 4 minutes.
Whisk again. Assemble torte in same
2-quart casserole in same way as
directed in Step 5. Microwave, uncovered, at 50% power 5 minutes. Let
stand, covered, 5 minutes.

BEFORE-THEATER DINNER

Polenta Torte (this page)

**Braised Artichoke with
Sweet Red Pepper** (394)

Plum Port-Wine Ice (539)

MORE ABOUT TORTE
Polenta Torte is one
of our favorites. To
serve, spoon directly
from the soufflé dish,
or for a spectacular
presentation, bake in
an eight-inch spring-
form pan and
unmold. Experiment
with a variety of dif-
ferent greens. If fro-
zen kale is
unavailable, use all
frozen spinach. Serve
with grilled or roasted
meats, or with a
whole-grain bread
for lunch. A glass of
Italian red wine
would be a nice
addition.

QUICK RED BEANS AND RICE WITH SAUSAGE

QUICK

DRIED BEAN TIPS
- Purchase dried beans that are bright in color, which is an indication of freshness, and uniform in size and shape so they'll cook evenly.
- Store dried beans, tightly covered, in a cool, dry place.
- Cooked beans can be refrigerated for up to 4 days, or frozen for up to 4 months.

In New Orleans, red beans and rice is traditionally served on a Monday to use Sunday's leftover ham bone. We've replaced ham bone with kielbasa. Since beans and rice form a complete protein, they combine with a small amount of meat in this recipe to form a main dish.

Makes 4 servings.
Recipe can be halved or doubled.
Nutrient Value Per Serving: 605 calories, 26 g protein, 21 g fat, 77 g carbohydrate, 970 mg sodium, 38 mg cholesterol.

1 tablespoon olive oil
½ pound smoked kielbasa, cut into
    ½-inch pieces
6 green onions, sliced (½ cup)
1 large onion, chopped (1 cup)
1 small sweet red pepper, cored, seeded
    and chopped
3 stalks celery, chopped

2 cloves garlic, finely chopped
2 cans (19 ounces each) kidney beans,
    drained and rinsed
2 cups water
½ teaspoon leaf thyme, crumbled
½ teaspoon leaf oregano, crumbled
¼ teaspoon crushed red pepper flakes
¼ teaspoon black pepper
1 bay leaf
1 box (7 ounces) pecan rice, cooked
    according to package directions OR:
    regular white rice

1. Heat oil in large skillet over medium heat. Add sausage; sauté until browned, about 5 minutes. Remove with slotted spoon to paper toweling to drain.
2. Reserve 2 tablespoons green onion for garnish. Add remaining green onion, chopped onion, sweet red pepper, celery and garlic to skillet; sauté 4 minutes or until vegetables are softened. Add beans, water, thyme, oregano, pepper flakes, black pepper and bay leaf to vegetables. Bring to boiling. Lower heat; simmer 10 minutes.
3. Mash about one-quarter of beans with potato masher. Add sausage; simmer 5 minutes, stirring frequently. Remove bay leaf. Garnish with reserved green onion. Serve with rice.

Microwave Directions (High Power Oven):
Ingredient Changes: Eliminate oil; reduce water to 1½ cups.
Directions: Place kielbasa in microwave-safe 2-quart casserole with lid. Microwave, uncovered, at 100% power 2 minutes. Remove to paper toweling to drain. Reserve 2 tablespoons green onion for garnish. Combine remaining green onion, onion, red pepper, celery and garlic in same casserole. Microwave, covered, at 100% power 6 minutes, stirring once. Add beans, water, thyme, oregano, pepper flakes, pepper and bay leaf. Microwave, covered, at 100% power 7 minutes to boiling. Mash about one-quarter of the beans. Add kielbasa. Microwave, uncovered, at 70% power 5 minutes. Sprinkle with reserved green onion.

VEGETARIAN FOUR-BEAN CHILI

LOW-CALORIE · LOW-FAT
LOW-CHOLESTEROL

Our version, *without chicken broth, is so full of vegetables and beans that even meat-lovers won't miss the meat. The secret ingredient? Beer. Serve with rice and grated cheese.*

Makes 8 servings.
Recipe can be halved or doubled.
Nutrient Value Per Serving: 286 calories, 14 g protein, 4 g fat, 51 g carbohydrate, 866 mg sodium, 0 mg cholesterol.

1 tablespoon vegetable oil
2 large onions, chopped
1 medium-size sweet green pepper, cored, seeded and chopped
3 cloves garlic, finely chopped
2 medium-size carrots, pared and cut in ½-inch dice
1 small zucchini, halved lengthwise and thickly sliced crosswise
1 small summer squash, halved lengthwise and thickly sliced crosswise
2 tablespoons chili powder
½ teaspoon leaf oregano, crumbled
1 teaspoon ground cumin
2 cans (28 ounces each) tomatoes, in puree
1 can (12 ounces) beer
1 teaspoon salt
1 can (1 pound) black beans, drained and rinsed
1 can (1 pound) black-eyed peas, drained and rinsed
1 can (1 pound) kidney beans, drained and rinsed
1 can (1 pound) chick-peas, drained and rinsed

1. Heat oil in large pot over medium heat. Add onion, green pepper and garlic; sauté 4 minutes or until onion is softened. Add carrot; cover and cook 2 minutes. Add zucchini, summer squash, chili powder, oregano and cumin; sauté 1 minute. Add tomatoes, breaking up with wooden spoon, the beer and salt. Bring to boiling. Lower heat; simmer, partially covered, 15 minutes.
2. Stir in all the beans. Simmer, stirring, until heated through.

CHILI
MAKE-AHEAD TIP:
The chili can be made several days ahead and refrigerated, covered.

CHILLY OUTSIDE?
CHILI INSIDE!

Red Onion and Orange Salad

Vegetarian Four-Bean Chili
(this page)

Pita Bread

Blueberry Cheesecake

1½ teaspoons lemon juice
½ teaspoon salt
⅛ teaspoon pepper

1. Combine water and lentils in medium-size saucepan. Bring to boiling over medium heat. Lower heat; simmer, covered, 40 minutes or until lentils are tender and liquid is absorbed.
2. Preheat oven to slow (325°). Lightly grease 13 × 9 × 2-inch baking dish.
3. Wrap tortillas securely in aluminum foil. Heat in preheated slow oven (325°) for 10 minutes.
4. Meanwhile, heat oil in large skillet over medium heat. Add onion, celery, garlic and ginger; sauté 5 minutes or until onion is softened. Stir in pear, coconut, lemon juice, salt and pepper; cook, stirring occasionally, 10 minutes or until heated through. Add lentils; mix together.
5. Remove tortillas from oven. Increase oven temperature to moderate (375°).
6. Removing one tortilla at a time from foil, fill center of each tortilla with about ⅓ cup lentil mixture, spreading across diameter of tortilla. Fold sides over top of filling. Place burritos, seam side down, in prepared dish. Cover with aluminum foil.
7. Bake in preheated moderate oven (375°) for 10 minutes or until heated through.

Make-Ahead Tip: The filling can be made a day ahead and refrigerated, covered.

SPICY LENTIL BURRITOS

LOW-FAT • LOW-CHOLESTEROL

BURRITOS GO FAST
Looking for something different in a vegetarian recipe? Try our spicy mix of fresh pear, shredded coconut and lentils wrapped in tortillas and baked. Serve as a main dish or side dish, with a dollop of sour cream or yogurt, or chutney. A perfect dish to add spark to a buffet table. Garnish with celery leaves.

Heat tortillas at 325° for 10 minutes; bake burritos at 375° for 10 minutes.
Makes 8 burritos.
Recipe can be halved or doubled.
Nutrient Value Per Burrito: 239 calories, 10 g protein, 4 g fat, 42 g carbohydrate, 350 mg sodium, 0 mg cholesterol.

2 cups water
1 cup dried lentils, picked over and rinsed
1 package (10 ounces) flour tortillas
1 tablespoon olive oil
1 medium-size onion, chopped
¼ cup chopped celery
1 clove garlic, finely chopped
1 teaspoon grated, pared fresh ginger
1 pear, pared, cored and chopped
¼ cup shredded coconut

TORTILLAS NEUVAS

Spicy Lentil Burritos
(this page)

Cold Green Bean Salad

Spiced Tangerines and Oranges (472)

LEGUMES PRIMER

Almost every culture's cuisine features beans, and their cousins, peas and lentils. Beans, as they are collectively known, are the seeds of leguminous plants (plants with nodules on the roots that contain nitrogen-fixing bacteria) that have been dried and then shelled. They will keep for years, and when rehydrated— that is, cooked in liquid—they swell to double or triple their size. Like pasta, beans tend to be bland, but that is one of their virtues. As they cool in liquid, they can absorb any number of delicious and complex flavors.

Black beans (turtle beans) are shiny black South American beans, often combined with rice throughout the Southern Hemisphere. They have a full flavor, and are commonly used to make black bean soup and stews.

Black-eyed peas are creamy colored with a black eye or dot. They have an earthy flavor and mealy texture and do not need presoaking. Black-eyed peas are

featured in hoppin' John, the Southern rice, pea and salt pork dish that, when eaten on New Year's Day, is said to bring good fortune.

Chick-peas (garbanzo beans, ceci) look like small, wrinkled beige nuts. Their nutty taste and firm texture make them a salad bar favorite. Chick-peas are often used in fritters, such as falafel, and ground with sesame paste for the dip *hummus bi tahini.*

cranberry beans   pinto

Cranberry beans (rosecoco, Roman, borlotti) look and taste like pinto beans, but the color is reversed (dark pink markings on beige background). Use like pinto beans in Southwestern and Italian dishes.

Fava beans (broad beans) are usually found dried or canned but they also can be eaten raw when they're just picked in the spring. The dried beans are creamy, and wrinkled and can be tough when cooked, but are

good as a puree, especially if passed through a food mill to remove the skins.

Kidney beans are commonly deep red, medium-size and shaped like a kidney but are also colored white, brown and black. They have a meaty flavor and mealy texture. This is the bean for chili, Louisiana red beans and rice, and one of the beans in a four-bean salad.

Lentils need no soaking. They cook quickly, but must be watched as they will lose texture if overcooked. Types include: *brown lentils,* flavorful, served in France in butter, in the Middle

East with olive oil, and used in soup; *green lentils,* also known as Egyptian lentils, are olive green, have a light fresh flavor and firm texture, and are served cold in salad; *red lentils* are bland, are often sold as split lentils, and have a beautiful orange-pink color that turns yellowish in cooking. All lentils are good for purees.

nor yellow split peas require any soaking.

Pinto beans look like cranberry beans, but are reversed in color, with beige markings on pink background. Their shape and taste are similar to that of cranberry beans.

Soybeans are round in shape and very hard. The soybean is enormously valuable as a food, but almost all preparation is commercial, such as bean curd, soy sauce, emulsifiers in candy and extenders for imitation cheeses and other similar mock foods.

Lima beans (butter beans) are flattish beans, creamy white to pale green, and large or small in size. They have bland flavor and soft texture. Dried limas, cooked and pushed through a food mill to remove skins, make a smooth, delicious puree to serve with lamb stew.

cannellini beans   **white beans**

White beans are a family of beans including great Northern, navy, small white, white kidney and pea beans. Mostly ivory-white and small to medium in size, white beans have a mild flavor. You'll find them in French cassoulet, Boston baked beans, Senate bean soup and Italian bean dishes.

Cannellini beans are white, medium-size beans favored in Italian cooking. Try them in salads with a garlicky dressing, or in *pasta e fagioli* (beans and pasta).

Mung beans come in different colors but green is most common. A staple starch used to make noodles, bean curd and sauces in Asian cooking, mung beans in America are most often seen sprouted in salads.

Peas, either the split garden or field type, are used for hearty winter soup, often made with ham bone or hock. Neither green

BEAN SOAKING

Almost all dried legumes must be soaked in water before they can be cooked. This process returns moisture to the beans, and begins to break down the complex sugars that cause flatulence. *Exceptions:* Black-eyed peas, split peas and lentils do not need soaking, only rinsing before cooking. Chick-peas, fava beans, soy beans and old beans must be soaked for 24 hours.

Slow soak Pick the beans over, discarding shriveled ones and bits of dirt. Rinse well. Cover with unsalted cold water by 2 inches. After 2 minutes, remove any "floaters," grit or shriveled beans. Soak 8 hours or overnight. (If your kitchen is very warm, refrigerate the beans to avoid souring.) This method helps beans retain their shape when cooked. Discard soaking water; rinse beans well.

Quick soak Wash and pick over as for the Slow Soak. Place in large pan, cover with unsalted water by 2 inches. Bring to boiling; boil 2 minutes. Remove pan from heat. Soak, covered, 1 hour. Drain; rinse well.

COOKING PERFECT BEANS

- Place drained, soaked beans in large pot and add 3 cups liquid for each cup of beans; liquid should cover beans by 1 inch. Add any seasonings, except salt, which can toughen beans; add salt after beans are tender.

- Bring beans slowly to boiling; remove scum that rises to top. Simmer, covered, for the time indicated on the package directions. Beans should be tender to the bite, but still firm enough to retain shape.

- Most dried beans more than double in cooking, except for chick-peas and soybeans, which triple in size.

CHICK-PEAS WITH VEGETABLES AND FETA CHEESE

LOW-CHOLESTEROL

A vegetarian main dish with lots of taste and texture that is particularly good served over white or brown rice.

Bake at 375° for 45 minutes.
Makes 4 main-dish servings.
Nutrient Value Per Serving: 402 calories, 18 g protein, 16 g fat, 50 g carbohydrate, 816 mg sodium, 23 mg cholesterol.

8 ounces dried chick-peas, picked over and rinsed (1 cup)*
Water
¾ cup finely crumbled feta cheese
2 to 3 teaspoons Dijon-style mustard
4 medium-size tomatoes
¾ teaspoon salt
¼ teaspoon pepper
2 tablespoons olive oil
1 large onion, coarsely chopped
1 large sweet red or yellow pepper, cored, seeded and coarsely chopped
1¼ teaspoons leaf marjoram, crumbled
2 cloves garlic, finely chopped
1 large yellow squash, coarsely chopped OR: cut into chunks
1 large zucchini, coarsely chopped OR: cut into chunks

1. Combine chick-peas and enough water to cover in large saucepan. Refrigerate and soak 24 hours. Or for quick soaking, bring beans and water to boiling over medium heat. Cover and boil 2 minutes. Remove from heat. Let stand for 1 hour.
2. Drain beans. Return to saucepan. Add enough water to cover beans by 1 inch. Bring to boiling over high heat. Lower heat; cover and simmer for 1 to 1½ hours or until beans are tender; add more liquid if necessary.
3. Drain beans. Transfer to lightly greased shallow 2-quart baking dish, 8×8×2 inches. Stir in feta and mustard. Chop 2 of the tomatoes; stir into beans with salt and pepper.
4. Preheat oven to moderate (375°).
5. Heat 1 tablespoon oil in large skillet over medium heat. Add onion, sweet pepper and marjoram; sauté 5 minutes or until onion is softened. Add garlic; sauté 2 minutes. Stir into bean mixture.
6. Heat remaining tablespoon oil in same skillet. Add yellow squash and zucchini; sauté 5 minutes.
7. Meanwhile, seed and chop remaining 2 tomatoes; stir into squash mixture. Spoon over bean mixture. Cover dish with aluminum foil.
8. Bake in preheated moderate oven (375°) for 45 minutes.

*Note: You can substitute 3 cups drained and rinsed, canned chick-peas (two 16-ounce cans) for the dried chick-peas. Reduce the salt in the above recipe to ⅛ teaspoon. Begin with Step 3.

CHICK-PEA MAKE-AHEAD TIP:
The beans can be cooked a day or two ahead and refrigerated. The onions and squash can be chopped the day before, tightly sealed in plastic bags and refrigerated. The casserole can also be assembled through Step 7 several hours ahead, and refrigerated, covered. Increase baking time.

THREE-BEAN PIZZA

LOW-FAT · LOW-CHOLESTEROL · QUICK

This is a real knife-and-fork pizza with a "meaty" taste. Feel free to substitute your favorite beans.

Bake at 425° for 10 to 15 minutes.
Makes 4 servings.
Nutrient Value Per Serving: 494 calories, 22 g protein, 16 g fat, 64 g carbohydrate, 1,338 mg sodium, 25 mg cholesterol.

1 tablespoon olive oil
1 large onion, coarsely chopped
3 cloves garlic, finely chopped

1 can (15 ounces) black beans, drained and rinsed
1 can (8 ounces) chick-peas, drained and rinsed
1 can (8 ounces) red kidney beans, drained and rinsed
1 jar (12 ounces) chunky salsa
¼ cup chopped cilantro OR: parsley
1 tube (10 ounces) refrigerated pizza dough
4 ounces shredded Monterey Jack cheese (1 cup)

1. Preheat oven to hot (425°).
2. Heat oil in large skillet over medium heat. Add onion; sauté 3 minutes or until softened. Add garlic; sauté 2 minutes. Add black beans, chick-peas, red kidney beans, salsa and cilantro to skillet; cook, stirring occasionally, until heated through, about 5 minutes.
3. Meanwhile, prepare the pizza dough for a 12-inch pie according to the package directions.
4. Sprinkle dough with half the cheese. Spoon bean mixture on top of cheese; spread to cover entire surface. Sprinkle with remaining cheese.
5. Bake in preheated hot oven (425°) for 10 to 15 minutes or until hot and bubbly and cheese is melted.

MEATLESS ITALIAN BUFFET

Eggplant Sandwiches with Goat Cheese (419)

Three-Bean Pizza (this page)

Pasta with Sweet Red Pepper Sauce (206)

Bulgur Baked with Garlic and Vegetables (220)

Radicchio and Escarole with Tamari Dressing (149)

Assorted Frozen Fruit Yogurts

**Roasted Turkey Breast with
Cornbread-Pecan Stuffing (page 271)**

CHAPTER 7

POULTRY

WHOLE ROASTED CHICKEN WITH LEMON HERB BUTTER

UNDER THE SKIN
Whole Roasted Chicken is a fine centerpiece for a special dinner—and it's easy to prepare. The flavor secret is an herb-butter mixture spread under the skin of the bird. (See How-To, page 250.)

CHICKEN CHAT
From single-serving drumsticks and breast halves to roasters that will feed a crowd, there's a chicken part for every occasion and every budget.

Roast at 350° for about 2 hours.
Makes 8 servings.
Nutrient Value Per Serving: 357 calories, 35 g protein, 22 g fat, 1 g carbohydrate, 343 mg sodium, 119 mg cholesterol.

1 roasting chicken (about 5 pounds)
1 medium-size onion
1 tablespoon lemon juice
1 teaspoon grated lemon rind
¾ teaspoon leaf thyme, crumbled
¾ teaspoon leaf basil, crumbled
¾ teaspoon salt
¼ teaspoon paprika
¼ teaspoon pepper
2 tablespoons *un*salted butter, melted

1. Preheat oven to moderate (350°).
2. Prepare chicken: Remove neck and giblets and reserve for another use. Rinse bird well with cold water inside and out. Pat dry with paper toweling. Starting from edge of neck cavity, gently loosen and lift skin covering breast and legs, being careful not to tear skin.
3. Finely chop enough onion to measure 1 tablespoon; cut remaining onion into quarters. Place onion quarters into cavity of chicken.
4. Stir together chopped onion, lemon juice and rind, thyme, basil, salt, paprika and pepper in small bowl. Rub all but 1 tablespoon herb mixture under skin of chicken; stretch skin back in place. Stir melted butter into remaining herb mixture. Place chicken, breast-side up, on rack in large roasting pan. Brush with some of the butter mixture.
5. Roast in preheated moderate oven (350°) for about 2 hours or until instant-read meat thermometer inserted into thigh meat without touching bone registers 180°. Brush chicken occasionally with remaining butter mixture and pan drippings. Let stand 15 minutes before carving.

CHICKEN COOKING TIMES

Chicken Type/Part	Baking or Roasting 350° to 400°	Broiling 6"–8" from heat	Poaching or Braising	Sautéing or Frying 350° to 375°
Breast quarter	40–60	15–20 per side		25
Leg/thigh combo	40–45	8–10 per side		15–20
Bone-in half-breast	35–45	8–10 per side	20–25	20–25
Skinless, boned breast half	25–30	5 per side	15–20	10–12
Flattened skinless breast half	15	2–3 per side		2–4
Fillet	15–20	2–3 per side		4–6
Drumstick	40–45	8–10 per side	25–30	15–20
Thigh	45–50	10–12 per side	30–35	20–25
Wing	25–35	5–8 per side	15–20	10–15
Whole chicken (fryer)	1½–2¼ hours			
Roaster	2–3 hours			
Cornish hen, 1 pound	60–70			

Chart times are approximate and given in minutes, unless otherwise indicated.

CHICKEN PHYLLO PIE

LOW-CHOLESTEROL

Bake eggplant at 425° for 20 minutes.
Bake phyllo pie at 350° for 60 minutes.
Makes 12 servings.
Nutrient Value Per Serving: 431 calories,
24 g protein, 22 g fat, 35 g carbohydrate,
298 mg sodium, 68 mg cholesterol.

1 chicken (about 4 pounds), quartered*
½ cup plus 1 tablespoon olive oil
2 medium-size onions, chopped
1 sweet red pepper, cored, seeded and
    chopped
1 cup whole blanched almonds, toasted
    and ground**
¾ teaspoon salt
¼ teaspoon white pepper
1 egg, beaten
1 eggplant (1½ pounds)
1 teaspoon curry powder
½ teaspoon ground turmeric
1 cup couscous
½ chopped fresh parsley
10 phyllo sheets (17 × 12 inches), thawed
    according to package directions
Chutney-Yogurt Sauce *(recipe follows)*

1. Combine chicken with enough water
to cover in medium-size saucepan. Bring
to boiling. Lower heat; simmer 35 minutes or until meat is no longer pink
near bone. Remove chicken; let cool.
Skim fat from surface of cooking liquid.
Boil liquid, reducing to 2 cups; reserve
liquid. When chicken is cool enough to
handle, remove and discard skin. Shred
chicken into bowl (you should have
about 4 cups cooked chicken).
2. Preheat oven to hot (425°).
3. Heat the 1 tablespoon oil in skillet
over medium heat. Add onion and red
pepper; sauté 10 minutes or until onion
is softened. Add to chicken, along with
3 tablespoons ground almonds, ½ teaspoon salt, the white pepper and half
the egg; stir to combine.
4. Slice eggplant lengthwise into ½-
inch-thick slices. Brush both sides with

a total of 3 tablespoons olive oil. Place
on baking sheet.
5. Bake eggplant in preheated hot oven
(425°) for 20 minutes; turn slices once.
6. Meanwhile, combine 2 cups reserved
broth, curry, turmeric and remaining ¼
teaspoon salt in saucepan. Bring to boiling. Stir in couscous; cook 1 minute.
Cover; remove from heat and let stand
5 minutes. Stir in parsley and remaining
half of egg.
7. Lower oven temperature to moderate
(350°). Lay phyllo sheets flat on dry
surface. Cover with damp toweling to
prevent drying. Lightly grease 10-inch
skillet with oil. Brush sheet of phyllo
(continued)

A PARTY DISH
Special-for-company
dish Chicken Phyllo
Pie is a delicious com-
bination of chicken,
eggplant, almonds
and flaky phyllo
pastry. Perfect for a
buffet, this pie takes a
little work, but the
results are well worth
it. See the Note on
page 234 for a short-
cut using leftover
cooked chicken.

CHICKEN PHYLLO PIE
(*continued*)

lightly with oil. Place in skillet; sprinkle on scant tablespoon of almonds. Repeat with 4 more sheets, placing each sheet at 45° angle to last. Press sheets against side of skillet.

8. Spoon chicken mixture into skillet, pressing level. Arrange eggplant slices on top. Spread with couscous mixture. Brush each of the remaining sheets of phyllo with oil; sprinkle each lightly with almonds (reserve 2 tablespoons). Place phyllo sheets one at a time on top of mixture in skillet, arranging in same manner as bottom sheets. Tuck excess into sides of pan.

9. Bake in preheated moderate oven (350°) for 45 minutes or until metal skewer inserted in center comes out hot. Carefully invert skillet onto cookie sheet. Remove skillet. Sprinkle pie with remaining 2 tablespoon almonds. Return to oven. Bake 15 minutes more or until phyllo is golden and crisp. Slice into wedges. Serve with Chutney-Yogurt Sauce.

Notes: *Four cups of leftover cooked chicken pieces or deli chicken and 2 cups of chicken broth can be substituted for the whole chicken.
**To toast almonds, bake on baking sheet in preheated 375° oven for 8 minutes or until golden, stirring occasionally.

Chutney-Yogurt Sauce: Combine 2 tablespoons chutney and 2 tablespoons dairy sour cream in blender. Whirl until smooth. Scrape into bowl. Stir in ½ cup yogurt.

JAMAICAN JERKED CHICKEN

This highly seasoned dish uses a fair amount of allspice, a favorite Jamaican spice. We've included a range on the "hot" seasonings, so make this as hot or as mild as you wish.

CHICKEN PHYLLO PIE MAKE-AHEAD TIP:
Step 1 can be prepared a day ahead as can the Chutney-Yogurt Sauce and refrigerated, covered.

WHOLE CHICKENS
Available in different sizes, to suit the cooking method and the family. The *broiler,* also known as the fryer or broiler-fryer, 2½ to 4 pounds, is usually the least expensive chicken per pound. (A 3-pound chicken yields about 4 servings.) The *roaster,* 3 to 6 pounds, is ample for a small crowd since it has a higher meat-to-bone ratio. Stuff in the same way as a turkey for a festive meal. (It yields about 4 to 6 servings). The *stewing hen,* about 4½ to 7 pounds, is an older bird, so while it's not particularly tender, it does have lots of flavor to impart to soups and stews.

QUARTERED CHICKENS
Ideal for those with big appetites, with a mix of white and dark meat portions (1 quarter per serving).

Bake at 400° for 35 minutes; broil 4 to 5 minutes.
Makes 6 servings.
Recipe can be halved or doubled.
Nutrient Value Per Serving: 416 calories, 32 g protein, 28 g fat, 8 g carbohydrate, 282 mg sodium, 103 mg cholesterol.

4 teaspoons allspice berries, crushed in mortar and pestle OR: 2 teaspoons ground allspice
6 cloves garlic, crushed
2 tablespoons chopped, pared fresh ginger
2 tablespoons dark brown sugar
1 teaspoon ground cinnamon
½ to 1 teaspoon chopped seeded jalapeño pepper
¼ to ½ teaspoon ground hot red pepper
¼ to ½ teaspoon black pepper
½ teaspoon salt
⅓ cup olive oil
⅓ cup sliced green onion
¼ cup red wine vinegar
2 tablespoons lime juice
1 broiler-fryer (about 3½ pounds), cut into 12 pieces (2 drumsticks, 2 thighs, breast cut in 4 pieces, wing tips removed, wings halved)

1. Combine allspice, garlic, ginger, sugar, cinnamon, jalapeño, red pepper, black pepper, salt, oil, onion, vinegar and lime juice in food processor or blender. Whirl until smooth.

2. Place chicken pieces in large nonaluminum pan; rub with marinade. Gently lift skin up and rub marinade under skin; stretch skin back in place. Cover with plastic wrap. Refrigerate 2 hours.

3. Preheat oven to hot (400°). Transfer chicken to broiler-proof baking pan that will hold pieces in one layer.

4. Bake in preheated hot oven (400°) for 35 minutes or until no longer pink near bone. Raise oven temperature to broil.

5. Broil chicken 4 inches from heat for 4 to 5 minutes or until lightly crisped.

CHICKEN WITH FENNEL AND OLIVES

Richly *flavored with Mediterranean accents—fennel and black olives—this chicken dish is special enough for a weekend party. Serve with orzo.*

Makes 6 servings.
Recipe can be halved or doubled.
Nutrient Value Per Serving: 426 calories, 33 g protein, 30 g fat, 6 g carbohydrate, 573 mg sodium, 125 mg cholesterol.

1 fresh fennel bulb (about ¾ pound)
1 tablespoon vegetable oil
1 broiler-fryer (3 to 3½ pounds), cut into eighths
1 small onion, chopped
1 clove garlic, finely chopped
1 can (16 ounces) tomatoes in juice, chopped
¼ cup water
¼ teaspoon salt
⅛ teaspoon pepper
¼ cup Greek olives, pitted and chopped

1. Cut root end from fennel. Remove enough fennel sprigs to measure ¼ cup; set aside. Cut bulb into thin slices.
2. Heat oil in large skillet over medium heat. Add chicken; brown on all sides, removing pieces to plate as they brown. Drain and discard all but 1 tablespoon drippings from skillet.
3. To drippings in skillet, add fennel, onion and garlic; cook, stirring, until lightly browned. Add tomatoes, water, salt, pepper and reserved fennel sprigs. Bring to boiling.
4. Return chicken to skillet. Lower heat; cover and simmer until chicken is tender and no longer pink near bone, about 30 minutes. Add olives; heat through.

Make-Ahead Tip: This whole dish can be made a day ahead, refrigerated, covered, and then gently reheated to serve.

HOW TO COOK CHICKEN

- **Oven-baking:** Dip chicken parts in egg, egg white, milk, buttermilk or honey-mustard, then fresh bread crumbs to coat. Or bake uncoated, basting occasionally with pan drippings, melted butter, or fruit or vegetable juice.
- **Broiling:** Rub with oil or butter and herbs and/or garlic, if you wish.
- **Poaching:** Simmer in water or water and chicken broth (to cover), seasoned with bay leaf, celery stalk, carrot and thyme.
- **Braising:** Brown in fat, then cook, covered, in a small amount of liquid such as water or wine, in a pot or Dutch oven; add vegetables such as mushrooms, onions, sweet peppers and carrots, and/or herbs such as tarragon or marjoram.
- **Sautéing** or **stir-frying:** Slide chicken pieces, usually in a uniform size, into a hot pan, cooking them quickly in a small amount of oil. The smaller the pieces, the faster the cooking.

POACHED CHICKEN BREASTS WITH MINT-SPINACH SAUCE

LOW-CALORIE · LOW-FAT · QUICK

This light and easy chicken entree is ready in almost the time it takes to make the sauce in a food processor. Speaking of the sauce, try it on fish—it's delicious. Garnish with baby carrots and pattypan squash for an elegant touch.

Makes 4 servings.
Recipe can be halved or doubled.
Nutrient Value Per Serving: 186 calories, 35 g protein, 2 g fat, 4 g carbohydrate, 273 mg sodium, 83 mg cholesterol.

Chicken broth OR: water
4 boneless, skinned chicken breast halves
   (about 5 ounces each)

1 small onion, chopped
½ teaspoon reduced-calorie margarine
   OR: *un*salted butter
2 cups fresh spinach, rinsed well, drained
   and stemmed (about 8 ounces)
2 tablespoons fresh mint leaves
½ cup nonfat plain yogurt
1 teaspoon lemon juice
⅛ teaspoon salt

1. Pour enough broth into medium-size skillet to just cover chicken breasts. Bring liquid to boiling. Lower heat. Add chicken. Cover and simmer until cooked through, about 15 minutes.
2. Meanwhile, sauté onion in margarine in nonstick skillet until softened, 3 to 4 minutes. Add spinach; cook until wilted. Transfer to strainer; squeeze out excess water.
3. Combine mint and spinach in food processor or blender. Whirl until chopped. Add yogurt, lemon juice and salt. Whirl until pureed.
4. When chicken is cooked, slice across grain into ¼-inch-thick slices. Spoon pool of sauce on each of 4 plates. Arrange sliced breasts on top of sauce.

Make-Ahead Tip: The sauce can be made ahead and refrigerated, covered. Let come to room temperature.
Microwave Directions (High Power Oven):
Combine onion and margarine in microwave-safe 10-inch pie plate. Cover with another pie plate, inverted. Microwave at 100% power 2 minutes. Add spinach. Microwave, covered, at 100% power 3 minutes. Transfer spinach mixture to strainer; squeeze out moisture with wooden spoon. Place spinach and mint in food processor or blender. Whirl until chopped. Add yogurt, lemon juice and salt. Whirl until combined. Transfer to small bowl; cover. Place chicken in same pie plate, spoke-fashion, with thickest portions towards edge. Add 1 tablespoon chicken broth or water. Microwave, covered, at 100% power 5½ minutes until cooked through. Let stand, covered, 1 minute. Serve as above.

CHICKEN BREASTS IN ORANGE SAUCE

LOW-CALORIE · LOW-FAT
LOW-CHOLESTEROL

Skinless chicken breasts are nicely complemented with an orange sauce sharpened with a little vinegar. Garnish with an orange slice and sprigs of fresh parsley and serve at room temperature, if you wish.

Makes 4 servings.
Recipe can be halved or doubled.
Nutrient Value Per Serving: 260 calories, 29 g protein, 8 g fat, 16 g carbohydrate, 215 mg sodium, 68 mg cholesterol.

2 whole chicken breasts (about 12 ounces each), halved and skin removed
¼ teaspoon salt
⅓ cup all-purpose flour
2 tablespoons olive oil
⅓ cup finely chopped shallots (about 6 shallots) OR: white part of green onion
¼ cup dry white wine
¾ cup fresh orange juice
3 tablespoons balsamic vinegar OR: red wine vinegar
2 tablespoons finely chopped parsley

1. Sprinkle chicken with salt. Dredge in flour, shaking off excess. Heat oil in very large nonaluminum skillet over moderate heat. Add chicken; cook until well browned on both sides, about 5 minutes per side. Remove to bowl.
2. Reduce heat to low. Add shallot to skillet; cook, stirring frequently, until shallots are softened, about 7 minutes. Add wine; cook, scraping up any browned bits from bottom of skillet with wooden spoon, for 2 minutes.
3. Add orange juice and vinegar. Bring to boiling. Add chicken. Lower heat; cover and simmer 25 minutes or until no longer pink near bone; turn over pieces halfway through. Stir in parsley. Serve hot or at room temperature.

Make-Ahead Tip: The whole dish can be prepared a day ahead and refrigerated. Gently reheat in a skillet, covered.
Microwave Directions (High Power Oven):
Ingredient Changes: Reduce wine to 1 tablespoon; orange juice to ½ cup; balsamic vinegar to 2 tablespoons; add 2 teaspoons cornstarch.
Directions: Combine shallots and oil in microwave-safe 4-cup measure. Microwave, uncovered, at 100% power 4 minutes, stirring once. Whisk together wine, orange juice, vinegar and corn-
(continued)

CHICKEN BREASTS

Available in several forms: the more processed the cut, the faster the cooking time. *Whole* or *halved* chicken breasts are the least expensive (½ breast per serving). *Boned* chicken breasts are more expensive, although there's less waste ounce for ounce (½ breast per serving). *Boneless, skinned* chicken breasts are extra-lean, extra-quick to prepare (½ boneless, skinned breast, about 4 ounces, per serving).

CHICKEN BREASTS IN ORANGE SAUCE
(*continued*)

starch in small bowl until smooth. Stir into measure. Microwave, uncovered, at 100% power 3 minutes, whisking once. Whisk again when cooked. Pour into microwave-safe 10-inch pie plate. Place chicken in sauce, spoke-fashion, with thicker parts towards outside of plate. Cover with microwave-safe plastic wrap. Microwave at 100% power 8 to 8½ minutes until done, turning plate once. Sprinkle with salt and parsley. Let stand, covered, for 2 minutes.

CHICKEN BREASTS WITH RASPBERRY SAUCE

LOW-CALORIE · QUICK

An *elegant dish for company, or for brightening up the dinner table mid-week, and it takes practically no time to prepare. Garnish with whole raspberries and sprigs of thyme.*

Makes 4 servings.
Recipe can be halved or doubled.
Nutrient Value Per Serving: 329 calories, 35 g protein, 14 g fat, 18 g carbohydrate, 406 mg sodium, 98 mg cholesterol.

4 boneless, skinned chicken breast halves
  (about 1¼ pounds)
2 tablespoons all-purpose flour
1½ tablespoons vegetable oil
1 package (12 ounces) dry-pack frozen
  raspberries, thawed
¾ cup chicken broth
¼ teaspoon leaf thyme, crumbled
2 teaspoons cornstarch
2 tablespoons butter, cut up
2 tablespoons red wine vinegar
2 teaspoons lemon juice
1 teaspoon sugar
⅛ teaspoon salt

1. Shake chicken with flour in bag to coat. Sauté chicken in oil in large, heavy skillet over medium-high heat until browned, 3 to 4 minutes. Lower heat to medium; sauté other side 3 to 4 minutes or until cooked through. Transfer to warm platter. Discard fat from pan; wipe pan.
2. Reserve ¼ cup raspberries for garnish. Add remaining raspberries, ½ cup chicken broth and the thyme to skillet. Bring to boiling. Lower heat; simmer 2 to 3 minutes or until raspberries are reduced to saucy consistency.
3. Force raspberry mixture through strainer with back of spoon; discard seeds. Return puree to skillet.
4. Stir together cornstarch and remaining chicken broth in small bowl until smooth. Stir into puree. Bring to boiling, stirring. Lower heat; simmer to thicken, about 2 minutes. Remove from heat. Stir in butter, red wine vinegar, lemon juice, sugar, salt and the reserved raspberries.
5. Ladle sauce onto 4 warm plates. Slice breasts lengthwise. Arrange slices over sauce.

CHICKEN BREASTS WITH GREEN MOLE SAUCE

LOW-CALORIE · QUICK

The mole (mo-LAY) sauce, made with chilies, cilantro and sunflower seeds, is also delicious with broiled pork chops and grilled hamburgers and even steamed vegetables, especially squashes.

Broil chicken for 6 minutes.
Makes 4 servings.
Recipe can be halved or doubled.
Nutrient Value Per Serving: 255 calories, 36 g protein, 10 g fat, 4 g carbohydrate, 365 mg sodium, 82 mg cholesterol.

Green Mole Sauce:
1 tablespoon vegetable oil
1 medium-size onion, coarsely chopped
1 clove garlic, crushed
⅛ teaspoon ground cumin
1 canned green chili
⅓ cup fresh cilantro leaves
¼ cup parsley leaves
¼ cup shelled sunflower seeds
1 cup chicken broth
½ cup water
2 teaspoons lime juice

4 boneless, skinned chicken breast halves (about 5 ounces each)
Sliced or whole green onion, tomato wedges, lime wedges and lettuce, for garnish

1. Preheat broiler. Lightly grease broiler-pan rack.
2. Prepare Green Mole Sauce: Heat oil in medium-size skillet over medium heat. Add onion, garlic and cumin; cook until onion is tender, 3 minutes. Place in food processor or blender along with chili, cilantro, parsley, sunflower seeds, broth and water. Whirl until pureed (mixture will be slightly grainy). Return mixture to skillet; simmer, stir-
(continued)

CHICKEN BREASTS WITH GREEN MOLE SAUCE
(*continued*)

ring occasionally, 20 minutes or until thickened. Stir in lime juice.

3. Broil chicken 6 inches from heat for 3 minutes on each side or just until cooked through. Serve with sauce.

Make-Ahead Tip: The sauce can be prepared a day ahead and refrigerated, covered. Gently reheat to serve.

Microwave Directions (High Power Oven):
Ingredient Changes: Decrease chicken broth to ⅔ cup; eliminate water.
Directions: Combine oil, onion and garlic in microwave-safe 4-cup measure. Cover with microwave-safe plastic wrap, vented at one edge. Microwave at 100% power 3 minutes. Place in food processor along with other ingredients listed in Step 2. Whirl until pureed. Return to measure. Microwave, covered, at 100% power 4½ minutes. Pour about two-thirds of sauce into microwave-safe 10-inch pie plate. Arrange chicken, spoke-fashion, over sauce. Cover with microwave-safe plastic wrap, vented at one edge. Microwave at 100% power 5 to 5½ minutes, turning plate after 3 minutes. Serve with remaining sauce.

DOWN-HOME DINNER

Southern-Fried Chicken Strips (this page)

Okra Succotash (426)

Savory Sweet Potato Pudding (442)

Ice Cream with Maple Praline Sauce (538)

FRESH CHICKEN?

Follow these tips for buying *fresh* chicken:
■ The chicken should smell fresh—this can mean no smell at all or a pleasant "chicken aroma." So when you get the chicken home, unwrap and sniff. If it smells "off," return it to the store.
■ Avoid packages with accumulated juice or blood in the bottom; this indicates the chicken was frozen or near-frozen, then thawed and held too long.
■ The whole bird, in particular the breast, should be plump and firm to the touch, with a layer of fat under the skin.
■ The skin itself should be moist, supple and smooth with no dry spots and with no tears or signs of bruising. Skin color is arbitrary since some consumers prefer white skin, others yellow, so producers vary the chickens' diet accordingly. But there should be no discoloration to the skin, and the flesh should be pink, not gray.

SOUTHERN-FRIED CHICKEN STRIPS

LOW-CALORIE • LOW-CHOLESTEROL
QUICK

Succulent little chicken morsels assertively seasoned with black and red pepper. Serve with shoe-string potatoes, if you wish.

Makes 4 servings.
Recipe can be halved or doubled.
Nutrient Value Per Serving: 273 calories, 28 g protein, 12 g fat, 11 g carbohydrate, 213 mg sodium, 68 mg cholesterol.

¼ cup milk
½ cup lowfat plain yogurt
1 pound boneless, skinned chicken
    breasts, cut into strips about
    3 × ½ × ½ inches
¾ cup all-purpose flour
¾ teaspoon leaf thyme, crumbled
½ teaspoon salt
½ teaspoon black pepper
¼ teaspoon ground hot red pepper
Vegetable oil, for frying

1. Combine milk and yogurt in medium-size bowl. Add chicken strips; toss to mix well.
2. Combine flour, thyme, salt, black pepper and red pepper on piece of waxed paper.
3. Pour about ¼-inch oil into cast-iron skillet. Heat over medium-high heat.
4. Lift chicken pieces out of yogurt mixture; they should be evenly but thinly coated. Toss chicken, a few pieces at a time, with flour mixture.
5. When oil is hot (about 325°), add coated strips, being careful not to crowd skillet; work in batches if necessary. Fry until chicken is browned on bottom. Turn to brown other side. Remove from oil with slotted spoon to paper toweling to drain.
6. Serve chicken immediately.

Stir-Fried Chicken with Cashews and Green Onion

LOW-CHOLESTEROL · QUICK

Makes 4 servings.
Recipe can be halved or doubled.
Nutrient Value Per Serving: 342 calories, 30 g protein, 20 g fat, 11 g carbohydrate, 453 mg sodium, 66 mg cholesterol.

1 egg white
1 tablespoon plus 1 teaspoon cornstarch
2 tablespoons reduced-sodium soy sauce
1 pound boneless, skinned chicken
    breasts, cubed
1 teaspoon sugar
¼ cup chicken broth
1 tablespoon dry sherry OR: chicken broth
½ cup unsalted cashews
3 tablespoons peanut oil OR: sesame oil
⅓ cup sliced green onion
¼ teaspoon crushed red pepper flakes

1. Mix together egg white, the 1 tablespoon cornstarch and 1 tablespoon soy sauce in small bowl. Add chicken; stir to coat all pieces. Let stand 15 minutes.
2. Stir together sugar, chicken broth, sherry, the remaining 1 teaspoon cornstarch and remaining 1 tablespoon soy sauce in small bowl until smooth.
3. Sauté cashews in 1 tablespoon oil in large skillet or wok over medium heat until lightly browned on all sides. Remove and reserve.
4. Drain chicken mixture in strainer. Heat remaining 2 tablespoons oil in skillet. Add chicken; stir-fry over

(continued)

BONELESS IS BETTER
Using boneless chicken breasts in our stir-fried chicken takes all the effort out of this dish. Serve over rice or noodles, if you wish. Garnish with green onions.

CHICKEN NUTRIENT SCORE CARD
■ A three-ounce serving of roast chicken provides an average of 180 calories and supplies approximately half the recommended daily allowance of protein.
■ *Dark meat* chicken is only slightly higher in calories than light meat. However, a higher percentage of the calories in dark meat comes from fat, while a higher percentage of calories in light meat comes from protein.
■ Meat from the leg or thigh contains twice the amount of fat as an equal serving of breast meat.
■ Removing the skin before cooking or eating reduces the amount of fat in a serving of both dark and light meat by up to one-half.
■ Cholesterol, which is concentrated more in the meat than in the skin, is similar for all cuts of chicken and ranges from 70 to 80 mg per serving.

STIR-FRIED CHICKEN WITH CASHEWS AND GREEN ONION (*continued*)

medium-high heat until browned on all sides, stirring constantly. Add green onion and pepper flakes; stir-fry 30 seconds longer.

5. Stir chicken broth mixture again; add to skillet along with cashews. Cook until mixture is bubbly and thickened.

STIR-FRY WITH STYLE

Stir-Fried Chicken with Cashews and Green Onion (241)

Rice

Coffee Ice Cream with Chocolate Syrup

NO FRESH TOMATOES?
If ripe tomatoes are unavailable, substitute canned tomatoes in Baked Tomato-Cilantro Chicken.

BAKED TOMATO-CILANTRO CHICKEN

Bake at 400° for 20 to 25 minutes.
Makes 4 servings.
Recipe can be halved or doubled.
Nutrient Value Per Serving: 357 calories, 35 g protein, 20 g fat, 9 g carbohydrate, 511 mg sodium, 91 mg cholesterol.

1 tablespoon lime juice
½ teaspoon salt
⅛ teaspoon ground hot red pepper
4 boneless, skinned chicken breast halves (about 1 pound), slightly flattened
3 tablespoons olive oil
1 medium-size onion, chopped
1 small sweet green pepper, cored, seeded and chopped
1 clove garlic, finely chopped
¼ cup chopped fresh cilantro OR: 2 teaspoons dried cilantro and 3 tablespoons chopped fresh parsley
1¼ pounds ripe tomatoes, sliced (about 4 medium-size)
4 ounces shredded Monterey Jack cheese (1 cup)
Parsley sprigs OR: cilantro sprigs, for garnish *(optional)*
Lime slices, for garnish *(optional)*

1. Preheat oven to hot (400°).
2. Combine lime juice, ¼ teaspoon salt and the ground pepper in medium-size bowl. Add chicken; turn to coat. Let stand 10 minutes.
3. Heat 2 tablespoons oil in large skillet over medium heat. Add chicken; sauté until lightly browned on both sides. Remove to paper toweling to drain. Heat remaining 1 tablespoon oil in skillet. Add onion, green pepper and garlic; sauté until tender but not browned, about 4 minutes. Remove from heat. Stir in cilantro.
4. Place about two-thirds of tomato slices in bottom of 9-inch-square baking dish, or divide among 4 individual 2-cup baking dishes. Sprinkle with two-thirds of the onion mixture and remaining ¼ teaspoon salt. Sprinkle with about two-thirds cheese. Arrange chicken in layer over cheese. Top with remaining tomato and onion mixture.
5. Bake in preheated hot oven (400°) for 15 to 20 minutes, or 10 to 15 minutes for individual dishes, or until chicken is tender. Sprinkle with remaining cheese. Bake 5 minutes longer or until cheese is melted. Garnish with parsley or cilantro and lime slices, if you wish.

CHICKEN WITH ONIONS AND BALSAMIC VINEGAR

LOW-CALORIE · LOW-FAT · QUICK

Sweet with the taste of cooked onion and sharp with the taste of vinegar, this dish may be served hot or at room temperature, making it an excellent choice to bring along on a picnic or to serve as part of a buffet.

Makes 4 servings.
Recipe can be halved or doubled.
Nutrient Value Per Serving: 290 calories, 35 g protein, 9 g fat, 15 g carbohydrate, 298 mg sodium, 82 mg cholesterol.

2 tablespoons olive oil
4 boneless, skinned chicken breast halves (about 5 ounces each)
¼ cup all-purpose flour
2 large onions, halved and thinly sliced
1 carrot, pared and cut into 3 × ⅛-inch strips
⅓ cup balsamic vinegar OR: red wine vinegar
1 tablespoon tomato paste
⅔ cup chicken broth
½ teaspoon chopped fresh rosemary OR: ¼ teaspoon dried

1. Heat 1 tablespoon oil in large skillet over moderately high heat. Dredge chicken in flour, shaking off excess. Add chicken to skillet; cook until golden brown, about 3 minutes per side. Remove chicken; wipe out pan.
2. Reduce heat to low. Add remaining tablespoon oil and onion to skillet. Cook, uncovered, stirring occasionally, for 5 minutes. Add carrot; cook 4 minutes longer.
3. Stir in vinegar and tomato paste; cook 3 minutes. Add chicken broth and rosemary. Bring to boiling over moderate heat. Return chicken to pan. Lower heat; cover and simmer 8 to 10 minutes or until chicken is cooked through.

CHICKEN ROLL-UPS WITH MANDARIN SAUCE

LOW-CALORIE · LOW-FAT
LOW-CHOLESTEROL · QUICK

This is a showy dish for a special dinner that looks more difficult to prepare than it really is. Serve with rice, if you wish.

Bake at 450° for 15 minutes.
Makes 4 servings.
Recipe can be halved or doubled.
Nutrient Value Per Serving: 221 calories, 22 g protein, 3 g fat, 28 g carbohydrate, 356 mg sodium, 49 mg cholesterol.

4 small boneless, skinned chicken breast halves (about 3 ounces each), pounded very thin
1½ teaspoons Oriental sesame oil
¾ teaspoon leaf rosemary, crumbled
½ teaspoon salt
⅛ teaspoon pepper
1 package (9 ounces) frozen whole green beans, thawed and drained
¼ cup fresh whole-wheat bread crumbs (½ to ¾ slice bread)

Mandarin Sauce:
1 cup orange juice
1 tablespoon cornstarch
1 can (11 ounces) mandarin oranges, drained
¼ teaspoon lemon juice

1. Place oven rack in upper third of oven. Preheat oven to very hot (450°). Lightly coat 12 × 8 × 2-inch (2-quart) baking dish with nonstick vegetable-oil cooking spray.
2. Brush one side of each breast with ½ teaspoon of the sesame oil. Sprinkle same side equally with ½ teaspoon of the rosemary, the salt and pepper.
3. Place one-fourth of the beans on each chicken breast. Roll each up, using fingers to hold beans inside. Place roll-ups, seam-side down, in prepared
(continued)

CUTTING CLEAN

To prevent any bacteria present in raw chicken from being transferred to other foods, scrub hands, utensils and work surfaces with soap and hot water after handling chicken and before handling other foods. Scour cutting boards, then rinse and dry them, before and after using the board for carrying, carving and slicing cooked poultry. Use *another* cutting board for vegetables, fruits or other foods that will be eaten raw. Thick, nonporous acrylic, plastic or hard rubber is preferable to wood in terms of food safety and cleaning.

CHICKEN ROLL-UPS WITH MANDARIN SAUCE
(*continued*)

dish. Lightly brush roll-ups with remaining oil. Sprinkle with crumbs and remaining rosemary.

4. Bake in preheated very hot oven (450°) for 15 minutes. Remove from oven. Let the roll-ups stand 5 minutes before slicing.

5. Meanwhile, prepare Mandarin Sauce: Stir together orange juice and cornstarch in small saucepan until smooth and well blended. Bring to boiling over medium heat; cook, stirring, until thickened, 2 to 3 minutes. Stir in oranges. Heat through. Stir in lemon juice. Keep warm.

6. Slice roll-ups ½-inch thick. Arrange on dinner plates. Spoon sauce over.

Microwave Directions (High Power Oven):

Assemble roll-ups as in above recipe. Place, seam-side down, in microwave-safe 10-inch pie plate. Brush with sesame oil and sprinkle with bread crumbs and rosemary as directed in Step 3 of the recipe. Cover plate with microwave-safe plastic wrap, slightly vented at one edge. Microwave at 100% power 8 minutes, rotating plate one-quarter turn after 4 minutes. Let stand, covered, 2 minutes. Prepare Mandarin Sauce: Combine orange juice and cornstarch in microwave-safe 4-cup measure; whisk until well blended. Microwave, uncovered, at 100% for 4 minutes to a full boil, whisking well after 2 minutes and after 4 minutes. Stir in drained mandarin oranges. Microwave, uncovered, at 100% power 1 minute until hot. Stir in lemon juice.

CHICKEN FAJITAS

QUICK

If you have some fresh cilantro on hand, add to the salsa or sprinkle it in the fajitas. The salsa is also delicious with grilled meats, hamburgers and egg dishes.

Broil chicken for 8 minutes; warm tortillas at 350° for 8 minutes.
Makes 4 servings.
Recipe can be halved or doubled.
Nutrient Value Per Serving: 471 calories, 34 g protein, 23 g fat, 36 g carbohydrate, 733 mg sodium, 78 mg cholesterol.

1 pound boneless, skinned chicken breast halves
1 tablespoon vegetable oil
1¼ teaspoons ground cumin

Salsa:
1 can (16 ounces) whole tomatoes, in juice
1 can (4 ounces) chopped green chilies
2 green onions, finely chopped

8 flour tortillas (7-inch diameter)
1 avocado, peeled, pitted and sliced
½ cup dairy sour cream OR: plain yogurt
1 lime, cut into wedges, for garnish

1. Preheat broiler. Place chicken on broiler-pan rack. Rub chicken with oil; sprinkle with cumin.
2. Broil chicken 6 inches from heat, turning once, for 8 minutes or until no longer pink in center. Remove and cover with aluminum foil to keep warm. Reduce oven temperature to moderate (350°).
3. Meanwhile, prepare Salsa: Drain tomatoes, reserving ⅓ cup liquid. Coarsely chop tomatoes. Place tomatoes and reserved liquid in medium-size bowl. Stir in green chilies and green onion.
4. Stack tortillas and wrap in aluminum foil. Place in preheated moderate oven (350°) until warmed, about 8 minutes.
5. Cut chicken across grain into thin

slices. To serve, divide chicken equally among tortillas. Top with avocado and sour cream. Serve with lime wedges and Salsa.

Make-Ahead Tip: The Salsa can be prepared a day ahead and refrigerated.

SOUTHWEST CHICKEN DINNER

Chicken Fajitas (this page)

Mexican Corn with Red Pepper and Green Onion

Vanilla Ice Cream with Toasted Chopped Pecans

WHAT'S A FAJITA?
The original Texas *fajita* is simply a marinated skirt steak that has been broiled or grilled and then sliced. But now the word is often used to mean a Southwestern sandwich made with strips of highly seasoned, grilled beef, chicken or pork wrapped in a flour tortilla. Fajitas are usually accompanied by an assortment of sautéed vegetables, salsa and guacamole, which are added to the sandwich or eaten on the side.

CHICKEN LEGS WITH HONEY-MUSTARD CRUMB COATING

LOW-CALORIE

This dish is equally delicious at room temperature, and it's great for picnics. The coating works well on other chicken parts and Cornish hens.

Bake at 400° for 25 minutes.
Makes 4 servings.
Recipe can be halved or doubled.
Nutrient Value Per Serving: 261 calories, 24 g protein, 11 g fat, 17 g carbohydrate, 605 mg sodium, 91 mg cholesterol.

¼ cup Dijon-style mustard
2 tablespoons honey
3½ teaspoons lemon juice
½ teaspoon leaf oregano, crumbled
⅛ teaspoon ground cloves
4 whole chicken legs with thighs (about 2½ pounds), skinned and cut halfway through thigh-leg joint
1 cup fresh bread crumbs
4 teaspoons vegetable oil

1. Whisk together mustard, honey, lemon juice, oregano and cloves in shallow pie plate. Dip chicken in mustard mixture to coat. Dip in bread crumbs. Place on wire rack that has been sprayed with nonstick vegetable-oil cooking spray. Refrigerate 1 hour.
2. Preheat oven to hot (400°). Line baking sheet with aluminum foil. Spray with nonstick vegetable-oil cooking spray. Lay chicken pieces on baking sheet. Drizzle chicken with oil.
3. Bake in preheated hot oven (400°) for 25 minutes or until crisp and cooked through. Serve with additional sauce, if you like.

Make-Ahead Tip: The honey-mustard mixture can be made several hours or a day ahead and refrigerated, covered.

HONEY MUSTARD DIP
If you like, double the amount of honey-mustard mixture and set aside half, before coating the chicken, to use as a dipping sauce.

LEG PRESENTATION
Cutting the chicken leg at the joint, but not all the way through, makes for a neat presentation.

VCR PARTY

Seven-Layer Mexican Dip (87) with Tortilla Chips

Chicken Legs with Honey-Mustard Crumb Coating (this page)

Szechuan Eggplant and Snow Pea Salad (157)

Pear-Cranberry Upside-Down Cake (500)

Spicy Chicken Legs with Chick-Peas (page 248)

SPICY CHICKEN LEGS WITH CHICK-PEAS

LOW-CALORIE · LOW-CHOLESTEROL

Chicken legs and thighs remain moist in this rich and flavorful stew. Serve with couscous, if you like. Other chicken parts and split Cornish hens would also work well in this recipe; just adjust the cooking time accordingly. (Pictured on page 247.)

Makes 4 servings.
Recipe can be halved or doubled.
Nutrient Value Per Serving: 243 calories, 20 g protein, 11 g fat, 16 g carbohydrate, 758 mg sodium, 70 mg cholesterol.

1 tablespoon vegetable oil
2 teaspoons *unsalted* butter
1 teaspoon ground cumin
¼ teaspoon salt
⅛ teaspoon ground hot red pepper
4 whole chicken legs and thighs (about 2½ pounds), skinned and cut halfway through leg-thigh joint
1 large onion, halved and cut into 1-inch chunks
1 can (14½ ounces) no-salt-added stewed tomatoes
¾ cup chicken broth
⅓ cup pitted green olives, halved
¾ cup drained and rinsed canned chick-peas
1 tablespoon lemon juice
2 tablespoons chopped parsley

1. Heat oil and butter in large skillet over moderate heat. Rub cumin, salt and ground red pepper over chicken. Add chicken to skillet; cook until browned, about 4 minutes per side. Remove chicken.
2. Add onion to skillet; cook, stirring frequently, 4 minutes. Return chicken to skillet along with stewed tomatoes, broth and olives. Bring to boiling. Lower heat; cover and simmer 25 minutes or until chicken is cooked through.
3. Stir in chick-peas and lemon juice;

cook 2 minutes or until chick-peas are heated through. Stir in parsley. Serve.

Make-Ahead Tip: Legs can be prepared a day ahead through Step 2 and refrigerated. Gently reheat, covered, in a preheated moderate oven (350°) or in a skillet over low heat. Complete Step 3.

CHICKEN LEGS WITH GINGER-FENNEL COATING

LOW-CALORIE

Packed with lots of flavor, these chicken legs take just minutes to prepare for the oven. Serve with couscous, or basmati or Texmati rice. And the leftovers are delicious cold.

Bake at 400° for 45 minutes.
Makes 4 servings.
Recipe can be halved or doubled.
Nutrient Value Per Serving: 335 calories, 37 g protein, 19 g fat, 2 g carbohydrate, 674 mg sodium, 128 mg cholesterol.

1½ tablespoons fennel seeds, crushed
1½ teaspoons ground ginger
1 teaspoon salt
¾ teaspoon ground cloves
¼ to ½ teaspoon ground hot red pepper
4 whole chicken legs (about 2½ pounds)

1. Preheat oven to hot (400°).
2. Combine fennel seeds, ginger, salt, cloves and red pepper in plastic bag. Add chicken legs to bag; shake to coat. Arrange legs in roasting pan lined with aluminum foil.
3. Bake in preheated hot oven (400°) for 45 minutes or until meat is no longer pink near bone.

Make-Ahead Tip: The chicken legs can be coated and refrigerated, covered, several hours ahead.

REHEATING CHICKEN
Cooked poultry that is not eaten immediately should be kept hot (not lukewarm, which encourages spoilage) and eaten within a reasonable amount of time, or else refrigerated. To be on the safe side, thoroughly reheat chicken dishes refrigerated for 2 or 3 days; this means bringing them to a high temperature again before serving.

CHICKEN LEGS WITH 40 CLOVES OF GARLIC

Bake at 425° for 35 to 40 minutes; toast bread at 425° for 5 minutes.

Makes 8 servings.

Recipe can be halved or doubled.

Nutrient Value Per Serving: 489 calories, 30 g protein, 19 g fat, 47 g carbohydrate, 712 mg sodium, 104 mg cholesterol.

---

6 whole chicken legs (about 3 pounds)
40 unpeeled cloves garlic
1 pound small red potatoes, quartered
1 teaspoon salt
1 teaspoon leaf rosemary, crumbled
½ teaspoon cracked black pepper
2 tablespoons vegetable oil
1 loaf Italian or French bread, cut in half lengthwise

1. Preheat oven to hot (425°). Spray large roasting pan with nonstick vegetable-oil cooking spray.

2. Cut each chicken leg at joint to separate leg from thigh. Combine chicken, garlic, potatoes, salt, rosemary and pepper in roasting pan. Add vegetable oil; toss to coat.

3. Bake, stirring occasionally, in preheated hot oven (425°) for 35 to 40 minutes or until chicken, garlic and potatoes are tender. Remove from oven, but do not turn oven off.

4. Place bread, cut-side up, on baking sheet. Bake 5 minutes or until lightly toasted. Pinch cooked garlic out of skins and spread on toasted bread. Serve with chicken and potatoes.

AN ENTERTAINING DISH

A variation on the famous French classic, Chicken Legs with 40 Cloves of Garlic is perfect for entertaining. It needs little attention while cooking and can be served hot, chilled or at room temperature. And don't worry, all that garlic sweetens as it cooks.

CHICKEN LEGS MAKE-AHEAD TIP:

The dish can be prepared a day ahead through Step 3 and refrigerated, covered. Gently reheat in preheated moderate oven (350°) or serve at room temperature or chilled.

CAJUN SPICED CHICKEN LEGS

The surprise in this dish is the okra stuffing spread under the skin. For a little less spice, reduce the amount of liquid red-pepper seasoning. Serve with basmati rice. If okra is unavailable, substitute lima beans.

Bake in 400° oven for 40 to 45 minutes.
Makes 4 servings.
Recipe can be halved or doubled.
Nutrient Value Per Serving: 358 calories, 38 g protein, 19 g fat, 7 g carbohydrate, 339 mg sodium, 129 mg cholesterol.

2 green onions, finely chopped
1 sweet red pepper, cored, seeded and finely chopped
¼ pound fresh or thawed frozen okra, finely chopped OR: thawed frozen lima beans, finely chopped
1 slice white bread, torn into small pieces
1½ teaspoons liquid red-pepper seasoning
¼ teaspoon salt
¼ teaspoon ground black pepper
4 whole chicken legs (about 2½ pounds)

1. Preheat oven to hot (400°).
2. Stir together green onion, red pepper, okra, white bread, ½ teaspoon red-pepper seasoning, salt and black pepper in small bowl.
3. Carefully push fingers between skin and meat of each chicken leg to form pocket. Place some stuffing into each pocket. Secure with wooden picks.
4. Line a small roasting pan with aluminum foil. Spray the foil with non-stick vegetable-oil cooking spray. Place chicken, skin side up, on the foil. Brush chicken with remaining 1 teaspoon red-pepper seasoning.
5. Bake in preheated hot oven (400°) for 40 to 45 minutes or until chicken is no longer pink near bone; baste occasionally with pan drippings. Remove wooden picks before serving.

STUFFING BUTTER UNDER SKIN
Loosen edge of skin with fingers. Gently push fingers between skin and meat, without tearing skin, to form a pocket. Spoon butter or other seasoning into the pocket. Fold back skin, returning it to its original position.

BOILED CHICKEN DINNER

LOW-FAT

Makes 4 servings.
Recipe can be halved or doubled.
Nutrient Value Per Serving: 359 calories,
39 g protein, 8 g fat, 32 g carbohydrate,
1,182 mg sodium, 130 mg cholesterol.

4 cups chicken broth, canned OR:
    homemade (*see recipe, page 116*)
4 whole chicken legs (about 2½ pounds),
    skinned
3 carrots, cut diagonally into 2-inch
    pieces
3 celery stalks, cut diagonally into 2-inch
    pieces
1 large onion, cut into wedges
1 piece fresh ginger (2 inches), pared and
    sliced
1 large clove garlic, sliced
½ teaspoon whole black peppercorns
4 medium-size red potatoes (about 1
    pound), scrubbed and each cut in
    half

1. Bring chicken broth to boiling in
5-quart saucepot or Dutch oven. Add
chicken legs, carrot, celery, onion, ginger, garlic and peppercorns. Return to
boiling. Lower heat; cover and simmer
20 minutes. Add potatoes; return to
boiling. Lower heat; cover and simmer
15 to 20 minutes or until vegetables are
tender and chicken is no longer pink
near bone.
2. Strain chicken and vegetables,
reserving broth. Skim fat from broth.
Arrange boiled chicken and vegetables
on platter. Serve broth as first course or
spoon over chicken and vegetables.

CHICKEN LEGS
Drumsticks with thighs
attached are for
dark-meat lovers.
Cook as you would
drumsticks. Chicken
leg quarters with part
of breast attached
are also available (1
leg per serving).

ONE-POT MEAL
Boiled Chicken Dinner
is an entire meal from
one pot—what could
be easier? Serve the
savory broth as a first
course, or spoon over
the chicken and vege-
tables. The fresh gin-
ger adds a nice touch
to the broth.

**BOILED CHICKEN
DINNER MAKE-AHEAD
TIP:**
The dish can be made
a day ahead and
refrigerated, covered.
If refrigerated,
remove the fat from
the top. Gently reheat
the dish on top of the
stove.

DEVILED DRUMSTICKS

LOW-CALORIE · QUICK

The chicken can be prepared with or without the skin. Serve over rice, noodles or orzo.

Makes 4 servings.
Recipe can be halved or doubled.
Nutrient Value Per Serving: 217 calories, 26 g protein, 8 g fat, 8 g carbohydrate, 278 mg sodium, 94 mg cholesterol.

1 tablespoon vegetable oil
8 chicken drumsticks (about 2 pounds), skinned
1 small onion, chopped
1 carrot, chopped
1 celery stalk, chopped
⅔ cup water
3 tablespoons spicy brown mustard
1 tablespoon Worcestershire sauce
1 tablespoon light brown sugar
¼ teaspoon black pepper

1. Heat oil in large nonstick skillet. Add chicken; brown on all sides, removing drumsticks to plate as they brown.
2. Add onion, carrot and celery to drippings in skillet; cook, stirring, until softened, about 2 minutes. Add water, mustard, Worcestershire sauce, brown sugar and pepper. Bring to boiling. Return chicken to skillet. Lower heat; cover and simmer 20 minutes or until chicken is no longer pink near bone.

TRICK-OR-TREAT SUPPER

Spicy Corn Chowder (120)

Deviled Drumsticks (this page)

Butternut Squash with Pear and Ginger (452)

Double Chocolate-Chunk Cookies (511)

DEVILED DRUMSTICKS MAKE-AHEAD TIP:
The dish can be prepared a day ahead and refrigerated, covered. Gently reheat, covered, in preheated moderate oven (350°) or in skillet over very low heat.

CHICKEN DRUMSTICKS
Drumsticks are fun food, a meal that even little hands can handle. Bake or sauté and use for quick dinners or chill for lunch boxes or picnics (2 drumsticks per serving).

CITRUS-BROILED CHICKEN DRUMSTICKS

LOW-CALORIE

Here's a chicken dish that can be broiled or grilled, with or without the skin.

Broil for 30 minutes.
Makes 4 servings.
Recipe can be halved or doubled.
Nutrient Value Per Serving: 298 calories, 30 g protein, 13 g fat, 13 g carbohydrate, 608 mg sodium, 98 mg cholesterol.

1 cup bottled barbecue sauce
2 tablespoons orange juice
1 tablespoon grated orange rind
1 tablespoon dark brown sugar
½ teaspoon grated lemon rind
8 chicken drumsticks (about 2 pounds)

1. Stir together barbecue sauce, orange juice and rind, brown sugar and lemon rind in small saucepan. Bring to boiling. Lower heat; simmer, uncovered, 10 minutes or until thickened slightly.
2. Preheat broiler. Arrange chicken on rack in broiler pan.
3. Broil 6 inches from heat for 10 minutes. Brush with some of the sauce; broil 3 minutes longer. Turn chicken; broil 10 minutes. Brush with remaining sauce; broil 5 minutes or until chicken is no longer pink near bone.

DRUMMING UP DINNER

Citrus-Broiled Chicken Drumsticks (this page)

Rice

Stir-Fried Celery with Garlic and Ginger (412)

Ice Milk

CHICKEN WITH SWEET RED PEPPER AND SNOW PEAS

LOW-CALORIE · LOW-CHOLESTEROL
QUICK

Boneless thighs make this stir-fry a snap to prepare. Serve with rice, and fortune cookies for dessert.

Makes 4 servings.
Recipe can be halved or doubled.
Nutrient Value Per Serving: 241 calories, 21 g protein, 11 g fat, 17 g carbohydrate, 380 mg sodium, 71 mg cholesterol.

2 tablespoons reduced-sodium soy sauce
1 tablespoon honey
4 teaspoons white wine vinegar
½ teaspoon ground ginger
2 tablespoons vegetable oil
12 ounces boneless, skinned chicken thighs, cut into 1-inch chunks
1 large onion, halved and cut into eighths
1 large sweet red pepper, cored, seeded and cut into 1-inch chunks
2 cloves garlic, slivered
1 package (6 ounces) frozen snow pea pods, thawed and drained
8 ounces fresh bean sprouts

1. Combine soy sauce, honey, vinegar and ginger in small bowl.
2. Heat 1 tablespoon oil in very large skillet over high heat. Add chicken; stir-fry until cooked through, about 4 minutes. Remove chicken with slotted spoon to bowl.
3. Reduce the heat to medium-low. Add the remaining 1 tablespoon oil to the skillet, along with onion and red pepper; stir-fry until crisp-tender, 4 minutes. Add the garlic; stir-fry 1 minute longer. Add the soy mixture. Bring to boiling. Add the snow peas, bean sprouts and chicken; stir-fry just until heated through, about 2 minutes.

CHICKEN THIGHS
Economical and with lots of flavor, dark meat can be broiled, braised or sautéed, with or without the skin (2 to 3 thighs per serving).

STORING CHICKEN
■ Uncooked chicken will keep in the refrigerator for up to 2 days in its original packaging, depending on label date.
■ To freeze, over-wrap original packaging with more plastic wrap or aluminum foil for double protection. Use within 2 months to maintain best quality.

CITRUS-BROILED CHICKEN DRUMSTICKS MAKE-AHEAD TIP:
The sauce can be prepared a day or two ahead and refrigerated, covered.

CHICKEN THIGHS WITH PRUNES AND PORT

LOW-CALORIE

The prunes and port make this chicken dish richly satisfying for a cold weather dinner, and a hint of vanilla and cloves adds a little mystery. Serve with noodles, rice or pan-broiled potatoes.

Makes 4 servings.
Recipe can be halved or doubled.
Nutrient Value Per Serving: 286 calories, 24 g protein, 11 g fat, 23 g carbohydrate, 465 mg sodium, 100 mg cholesterol.

½ cup dry red wine
½ cup medium-size pitted prunes
½ teaspoon salt
⅛ teaspoon ground cloves
1¼ pounds skinned chicken thighs
¼ cup all-purpose flour
1 tablespoon vegetable oil
1 medium-size onion, finely chopped
⅓ cup ruby port wine
¼ cup chicken broth
⅛ teaspoon pepper
1 tablespoon *un*salted butter
¼ teaspoon vanilla

1. Combine red wine and prunes in small saucepan. Bring to boiling. Remove from heat; let the mixture stand at room temperature.
2. Rub ¼ teaspoon salt and the cloves into chicken. Dredge with flour. Heat oil in large skillet over moderate heat. Add chicken; cook until browned on both sides, 4 to 5 minutes per side. Remove to bowl.
3. Reduce heat to low. Add onion to skillet; cook, stirring frequently, until very soft, about 10 minutes. Raise heat to moderate. Add port; cook 2 minutes. Add prune mixture, chicken broth, remaining ¼ teaspoon salt and the chicken. Bring to boiling. Lower heat; cover and simmer 15 minutes or until chicken is cooked through.
4. Remove chicken to platter. Add pepper, butter and vanilla to skillet; swirl over low heat until butter has melted. Pour sauce over chicken.

Make-Ahead Tip: The recipe can be prepared through Step 3 a day ahead and then refrigerated, covered. Gently reheat and complete Step 4.

CURRY CONDIMENTS
See page 466–484
for a variety of fruit
relishes and compotes
that would go well
with curries.

CURRIED CHICKEN

LOW-CALORIE · QUICK

Makes 4 servings.
Recipe can be halved or doubled.
Nutrient Value Per Serving: 190 calories,
23 g protein, 8 g fat, 5 g carbohydrate,
237 mg sodium, 94 mg cholesterol.

1 pound boneless, skinned chicken thighs,
    cut into 2-inch chunks
1 tablespoon vegetable oil
1 large onion, finely chopped
3 cloves garlic, finely chopped
1 teaspoon ground turmeric
½ teaspoon ground cumin
½ teaspoon ground coriander
¼ teaspoon ground ginger
¼ teaspoon salt
⅛ teaspoon ground cloves
⅛ teaspoon ground nutmeg
½ cup chopped tomato
⅓ cup water

1. Sauté chicken in oil in large skillet
over moderate-high heat until browned
all over, about 5 minutes. Remove to
bowl.
2. Reduce heat to low. Add onion and
garlic to skillet; cook, stirring frequently, until lightly browned and soft,
5 to 7 minutes. Stir in turmeric, cumin,
coriander, ginger, salt, cloves and nutmeg; cook 1 minute. Stir in tomato and
(continued)

**HOMEMADE CURRY
POWDER**
Our Curried Chicken
uses a combination of
spices rather than
store-bought curry
powder to give this
dish a rich, deep fla-
vor. Serve with a
variety of condiments
such as shredded
coconut, raisins,
chopped nuts,
chopped sweet red
pepper, yogurt and
parsley leaves.

CURRIED CHICKEN (*continued*)

water; cook 1 minute. Add chicken. Bring to boiling. Lower heat; cover and simmer 15 to 20 minutes or until chicken is cooked through and sauce is richly flavored.

CURRY IN A HURRY

Curried Chicken (255)

Almond-Raisin Couscous (222)

Sautéed String Beans and Garlic

Lemon Sherbet with Raspberry Vanilla Sauce (538)

CHICKEN THIGHS TERIYAKI

LOW-CALORIE · LOW-FAT

Broil for 12 to 14 minutes.
Makes 4 servings.
Recipe can be halved or doubled.
Nutrient Value Per Serving: 175 calories, 23 g protein, 4 g fat, 10 g carbohydrate, 698 mg sodium, 92 mg cholesterol.

Marinade:
½ cup sake* OR: dry white wine
¼ cup reduced-sodium soy sauce
2 tablespoons chopped, pared fresh ginger
2 tablespoons sugar
1 large clove garlic, chopped

1½ pounds skinless chicken thighs
1½ teaspoons cornstarch
1 teaspoon vinegar
Orange slices, for garnish (*optional*)

1. Prepare Marinade: Combine sake, soy sauce, ginger, sugar and garlic in blender. Whirl until blended. Strain through fine-mesh sieve into plastic food storage bag; discard solids.
2. Score smooth side of each chicken thigh with sharp knife into ½-inch diamond pattern (score marks should be about ¼ inch deep). Add chicken to marinade in plastic bag; seal. Refrigerate 4 to 24 hours; turning occasionally.
3. Preheat broiler. Line broiler pan with aluminum foil. Spray rack with nonstick vegetable-oil cooking spray.
4. Remove chicken from marinade and place, scored-side down, on broiler-pan rack. Reserve marinade.
5. Broil chicken 5 inches from heat for 7 minutes. Turn chicken over and broil another 5 to 7 minutes or until meat is no longer pink near bone.
6. Meanwhile, measure remaining marinade. If necessary, add water to make ¾ cup. Place marinade in small heavy saucepan; boil for 2 to 3 minutes. Stir in cornstarch to dissolve. Cook over medium heat, stirring, until boiling and thick. Remove from heat. Stir in vinegar.
7. Transfer cooked chicken to dinner plates. Pour juices from broiling into sauce. Spoon over chicken. Garnish with orange slices, if you wish.

*Note: Sake is a Japanese wine traditionally served warm in small porcelain cups. Made from fermented rice, the alcoholic drink is also used in sauces and marinades.

TEMPTING TERIYAKI

Chicken Thighs Teriyaki
(this page)

Brown Rice

Steamed Broccoli

Almond Cookies

CURRIED CHICKEN MAKE-AHEAD TIP:
This dish can be prepared a day ahead and then refrigerated, covered. Reheat, covered in a preheated moderate oven (350°) or in a skillet over very low heat.

TERIYAKI MARINADE
The marinade is also good with strongly flavored fish, such as bluefish or swordfish, or with pork or beef.

CHICKEN THIGHS TERIYAKI MAKE-AHEAD TIP:
The chicken can be marinated a day ahead and refrigerated, covered.

NUTTY CHICKEN WINGS

Whole-wheat crackers and smoked almonds combine to make a crunchy coating for these wings.

Bake at 400° for 35 minutes.
**Makes 4 main-dish servings or
8 appetizer or hors d'oeuvre servings.
Recipe can be halved or doubled.**
Nutrient Value Per Wing: 194 calories,
13 g protein, 14 g fat, 6 g carbohydrate,
116 mg sodium, 62 mg cholesterol.

1 cup smoked almonds
22 whole-wheat crackers
2 eggs
16 chicken wings (about 3½ pounds)

1. Preheat oven to hot (400°). Spray 2 jelly-roll pans with nonstick vegetable-oil cooking spray.
2. Combine almonds and crackers in food processor or blender. Whirl until finely ground. Place crumbs in pie plate. Beat eggs slightly in small bowl. Dip chicken wings in egg, then in crumbs to coat. Arrange chicken wings in jelly-roll pans.
3. Bake in preheated hot oven (400°) for 35 minutes or until no longer pink near bone. Serve the wings hot or at room temperature.

Make-Ahead Tip: The recipe can be prepared through Step 2 several hours ahead and refrigerated, covered.

SOUTHWESTERN CHICKEN POT PIE

The black beans are an unexpected touch in our version of this favorite.

Bake at 350° for 35 to 40 minutes.
Makes 6 servings.
Nutrient Value Per Serving: 583 calories,
29 g protein, 29 g fat, 55 g carbohydrate,
1,068 mg sodium, 116 mg cholesterol.

Cornmeal Pastry:
1 cup all-purpose flour
½ cup yellow cornmeal
½ teaspoon salt
½ cup (1 stick) *un*salted butter
¼ cup cold water

Filling:
4 green onions, cut diagonally into ½-inch
    pieces
2 carrots, pared, halved lengthwise and
    sliced crosswise
2 teaspoons chili powder
3 tablespoons *un*salted butter
3 tablespoons all-purpose flour
1½ cups milk
1 cup chicken broth
3 cups cooked chicken meat, cubed
    (about 12 ounces)
1 can (15 to 16 ounces) black beans,
    drained and rinsed
1 can (10 ounces) corn kernels with red
    and green peppers, drained
1 can (4 ounces) chopped green chilies,
    drained *(optional)*
¼ teaspoon salt

1. Prepare Cornmeal Pastry: Combine flour, cornmeal and salt in medium-size bowl. With pastry blender or 2 knives, cut in butter until mixture resembles coarse crumbs. Sprinkle cold water, 1 tablespoon at a time, over mixture, tossing lightly with fork after each addition until pastry is moist enough to hold together. Shape pastry into ball. Cover with plastic wrap and refrigerate until needed.

(continued)

CHICKEN WINGS

Serve wings as an informal entrée. Wing tips removed, they make great finger food such as our Nutty Chicken Wings *(this page)* with a crunchy almond coating. (Save the wing tips for making stock.) Some companies distribute "drummettes," cut from the lower portion of the wing (4 wings per serving).

CHICKEN NUGGETS

Precooked, bite-size pieces of chicken, breaded or batter-dipped, and ready for reheating and serving with a sauce for a casual dinner or before-meal munching (4 servings per pound).

SOUTHWESTERN CHICKEN POT PIE
(*continued*)

2. To bake, preheat the oven to moderate (350°).

3. Prepare Filling: Cook green onion, carrot and chili powder in butter in 10-inch skillet over medium-high heat, stirring occasionally, until slightly soft-ened, about 5 minutes. Add flour; cook, stirring constantly, 1 minute or until smooth and bubbly. Stir in milk and chicken broth; cook, stirring constantly, until mixture thickens, 1 to 2 minutes. Stir in cooked chicken, black beans, corn kernels, green chilies and salt. Spoon chicken mixture into $13 \times 9 \times 2$-inch baking dish.

4. Roll pastry out on lightly floured surface with floured rolling pin into rectangle 1 inch larger than baking dish. Center pastry over filling. Fold overhang over pastry; press to form dec-orative edge. Using sharp knife, cut decorative vents in pastry.

5. Bake in preheated moderate oven (350°) for 35 to 40 minutes or until pastry is golden and chicken mixture is heated through.

SUNDAY NIGHT SUPPER

Southwestern Chicken
Pot Pie (257)

Peach and Plum Salad with
Red Currant Dressing (176)

Chocolate-Amaretto
Pudding (530)

CHICKEN TURNOVERS

Prepare the dough the night before you plan on using it, or to speed up preparation, use a store-bought refrigerator crescent dough and form it into turnovers. For appetizer portions, make smaller turnovers. Also delicious using leftover cooked turkey, beef, veal or pork.

Bake at 400° for 25 minutes.
Makes 4 main-dish turnovers.
Recipe can be halved or doubled.
Nutrient Value Per Turnover: /79 calories, 33 g protein, 41 g fat, 70 g carbohydrate, 660 mg sodium, 137 mg cholesterol.

Dough:
2 cups all-purpose flour
¼ cup cornmeal
2½ teaspoons sugar
½ teaspoon salt
½ cup (1 stick) plus 1 tablespoon *un*salted butter
4 teaspoons solid vegetable shortening
¾ cup lowfat plain yogurt

Filling:
¼ cup finely chopped shallots OR: green onion
1 tablespoon olive oil
8 ounces mushrooms, trimmed and finely chopped (2 cups)
½ medium-size sweet red pepper, cored, seeded and chopped
2 tablespoons all-purpose flour
1½ teaspoons sweet paprika
½ teaspoon salt
⅛ teaspoon pepper
⅓ cup lowfat plain yogurt
10 ounces cooked chicken, chopped (about 2 cups)

1. Prepare Dough: Stir together flour, cornmeal, sugar and salt in large bowl. With pastry blender or 2 knives, cut in butter and vegetable shortening until mixture resembles coarse meal. Stir in yogurt, mixing just until mixture comes together. Divide dough in half, wrap in plastic wrap and refrigerate several hours or overnight.

2. Prepare Filling: Sauté shallots in oil in large skillet over low heat, stirring frequently, for 5 minutes. Add mushrooms and sweet red pepper; cover and cook 5 to 7 minutes over low heat or until mushrooms have given off their liquid and peppers are soft. Stir in flour, paprika, salt and pepper; cook 2 minutes. Stir in yogurt and chicken. Cool to room temperature.

3. Preheat oven to hot (400°). Grease 1 large or 2 small baking sheets.

4. Working with half the dough at a time, roll out one 12 × 12-inch square. Cut in half diagonally into 2 triangles, then in half again to form 4 triangles. Place triangles on prepared baking sheet. Top each triangle with one-fourth of the filling, leaving a ½-inch border all around. Brush border with water. Roll out remaining dough to 12 × 12-inch square. Cut into 4 triangles as with first piece. Place one

(continued)

CHICKEN TURNOVERS (*continued*)

triangle on top of each triangle on baking sheet. Seal edges with fingers. Prick tops of turnovers several times with fork.

5. Bake in preheated hot oven (400°) for 25 minutes or until crisp and golden brown.

**TURNOVERS
MAKE-AHEAD TIP:**
The dough can be prepared several days ahead, wrapped and refrigerated. The unbaked turnovers can be frozen, and then baked in a pre-heated 375° oven for 5 to 10 minutes longer than in Step 5 at right.

```
┌─────────────────────────────┐
│      FINGER FOOD FEAST      │
│                             │
│   Chicken Turnovers (259)   │
│                             │
│   Stuffed Pepper Wedges     │
│           (435)             │
│                             │
│    Cherry Tomatoes with     │
│   Green Goddess Dressing    │
│    (183) for Dipping        │
│                             │
│       Fruit Skewers         │
└─────────────────────────────┘
```

CHICKEN PATTIES

LOW-CALORIE

A *classic way to use up leftover chicken and mashed potatoes, or any cooked meat, including crabmeat and shrimp.*

**CHICKEN PATTIES
MAKE-AHEAD TIP:**
The patties can be prepared up to 3 hours ahead through Step 3 and refrigerated, covered.

**Makes 4 servings (8 patties).
Recipe can be halved or doubled.**
Nutrient Value Per Serving: 328 calories, 25 g protein, 20 g fat, 12 g carbohydrate, 471 mg sodium, 114 mg cholesterol.

¾ cup water
¼ teaspoon salt
8 ounces all-purpose potatoes, pared and cut in chunks*
2 cloves garlic, peeled
½ cup plus 2 tablespoons grated Parmesan cheese
1½ cups finely diced cooked chicken (about 8 ounces)
1 egg, separated
2 tablespoons chopped parsley

2 teaspoons lemon juice
3 tablespoons fine dry bread crumbs
3 tablespoons olive oil OR: vegetable oil
Lemon wedges *(optional)*

1. Bring water and ⅛ teaspoon salt to boiling in small saucepan. Add potato and garlic; boil gently, uncovered, for 15 to 20 minutes or until potato is tender. Mash potato and garlic with water until creamy. Stir in ½ cup Parmesan. Transfer to large bowl. Let stand until potatoes come to room temperature.

2. Stir in chicken, egg yolk, parsley and lemon juice. Beat egg white in small bowl until stiff but not dry peaks form. Fold into chicken mixture. Form into 8 elongated patties.

3. Combine bread crumbs and remaining 2 tablespoons Parmesan cheese in shallow pie plate or on sheet of waxed paper. Dredge patties in crumb mixture; place on plate. Refrigerate patties, covered, for at least 1 hour or for up to 3 hours before sautéing.

4. Heat oil in large skillet over moderate heat. When oil is very hot, add patties; cook until golden brown and crisp, about 3 minutes per side. Serve with lemon wedges, if you wish.

*Note: One cup of leftover mashed potatoes can be substituted for the cooked all-purpose potatoes in Step 1. Add just enough hot water, about ¼ cup, to loosen potatoes and make them creamy. Continue with Step 1 in recipe.

```
┌─────────────────────────────┐
│       LEFTOVER MADNESS      │
│                             │
│  Chicken Patties (this page)│
│                             │
│  Marinated Vegetable Salad  │
│         on Greens           │
│    (leftover vegetables in  │
│       Italian Dressing)     │
│                             │
│        Fruit Salad          │
└─────────────────────────────┘
```

JUNIPER MARINADE

Makes enough for 3-pound chicken or 3-pound piece of pork.
Recipe can be halved or doubled.
Nutrient Value Per Serving: Insignificant.

2 teaspoons juniper berries
2 teaspoons coarse (kosher) salt
¼ teaspoon sugar
⅛ teaspoon ground cloves
⅛ teaspoon pepper
1 bay leaf, crumbled

Crush juniper berries in mortar and pestle or mini chopper. Combine with salt, sugar, cloves, pepper and bay leaf. Use to marinate chicken. With your fingers, loosen skin from chicken. Rub marinade under and on top of skin. Or rub marinade over pork. Refrigerate, covered, 2 hours. Cook chicken or pork as desired.

Make-Ahead Tip: The marinade can be prepared several days ahead and stored, tightly covered, in a cool place.

YOGURT MARINADE

LOW-FAT · LOW-CHOLESTEROL

Makes enough for 1½ pounds of chicken.
Recipe can be halved or doubled.
Nutrient Value Per ¼ Cup: 37 calories, 3 g protein, 1 g fat, 4 g carbohydrate, 176 mg sodium, 3 mg cholesterol.

1 container (8 ounces) lowfat plain yogurt
⅓ cup firmly packed cilantro leaves OR: parsley
2 tablespoons chopped fresh mint
1 teaspoon grated, pared fresh ginger
½ teaspoon ground coriander
¼ teaspoon ground cumin
¼ teaspoon salt
⅛ teaspoon ground hot red pepper

Combine all ingredients in food processor or blender. Whirl until smooth. Use to marinate chicken, covered and refrigerated, for 3 hours. To cook, lift pieces out of marinade and cook as desired. Spoon on remaining marinade for the last half of the cooking.

Make-Ahead Tip: The marinade can be prepared a day ahead and refrigerated, covered.

ORIENTAL MARINADE

LOW-CHOLESTEROL

Makes enough for 1¼ pounds of chicken.
Recipe can be halved or doubled.
Nutrient Value Per 3 Tablespoons: 73 calories, 1 g protein, 3 g fat, 10 g carbohydrate, 603 mg sodium, 0 mg cholesterol.

¼ cup reduced-sodium soy sauce
2 tablespoons firmly packed dark brown sugar
3 strips (3 × ½ inch each) orange rind
2 tablespoons orange juice
2 teaspoons vegetable oil
1 teaspoon Oriental sesame oil
2 cloves garlic, crushed
1 cinnamon stick, split lengthwise
⅛ teaspoon ground cloves

Combine soy sauce, brown sugar, orange rind, orange juice, vegetable oil, sesame oil, garlic, cinnamon and cloves in small jar with tight-fitting lid. Shake well to combine. Use to marinate chicken. Place chicken in plastic bag; add marinade and close to seal. Refrigerate 3 hours or overnight, turning bag occasionally to redistribute marinade. Cook chicken as desired, brushing with marinade every 5 minutes.

Make-Ahead Tip: The marinade can be prepared several days ahead and refrigerated, covered.

JUNIPER MARINADE
While there is no real substitute for juniper berries, you can still make this dry marinade by using an equivalent amount of sage and marjoram for the juniper.

YOGURT MARINADE
This marinade works well with skinless chicken, and is also ideal for broiling or grilling since it keeps the chicken moist. Try with pork or veal chops. If fresh cilantro is unavailable, substitute fresh parsley.

ORIENTAL MARINADE
This marinade, which is enough for 1¼ pounds chicken, is delicious on whole chicken or chicken parts, as well as game hens, duck, flank steak and even on vegetables. Chicken prepared this way tastes even better at room temperature and is excellent for picnics. Remove the skin for a lower-fat version.

THANKSGIVING FEAST

Caramelized Onion Tartlets (95) with Maple Cider Toddy (553)

Cream of Broccoli and Stilton Soup (135)

Roast Turkey (263) with Cornbread and Dried Fruit Stuffing (291)

Apple-Cranberry Relish (466)

Yogurt Mashed Potatoes (439)

Old-Fashioned Corn Pudding (415)

Cranberry Beans and Kale (398)

Honeyed Carrots with Ginger and Orange (408)

Walnut Tart (496)

Apple Pie with Streusel Topping (493)

ROAST TURKEY WITH WILD AND PECAN RICE STUFFING

Roast at 400° for 15 minutes; then at 325° for 3¼ hours.
Makes 10 servings with leftovers.
Nutrient Value Per Serving (4 ounces cooked turkey with ½ cup stuffing and gravy):
481 calories, 45 g protein, 22 g fat,
25 g carbohydrate, 890 mg sodium,
170 mg cholesterol.

Wild and Pecan Rice Stuffing *(see recipe, page 294)*

Turkey:
1 turkey (about 12 pounds), thawed if frozen *(see page 265)*
¾ teaspoon salt
½ teaspoon pepper
2 cups water
2 carrots, pared and cut into 1-inch pieces
2 stalks celery, cut into 1-inch pieces
2 medium-size onions, peeled and quartered
4 parsley sprigs

Giblet Gravy:
Turkey giblets
1 can (13¾ ounces) chicken broth
1 bay leaf
2 cups defatted pan drippings
¼ cup all-purpose flour
Salt and pepper, to taste

1. Prepare stuffing. This can be made separately a day ahead and refrigerated, covered, and then brought to room temperature before stuffing the bird.
2. Prepare Turkey: Preheat oven to hot (400°). Remove neck and giblets from turkey; reserve for gravy. Rinse turkey with cold water, inside and out. Pat dry with paper toweling. Sprinkle neck and body cavities with ½ teaspoon salt and ¼ teaspoon pepper.
3. Spoon cooled stuffing loosely into both cavities. (Transfer any leftover rice mixture to baking pan and cover. Place in oven with turkey for last 30 minutes of roasting time, to heat through.) Tie legs to tail with string; skewer neck skin to back. Place turkey, breast-side up, on rack in roasting pan with tight-fitting cover. (If no cover is available, prepare loose tent of foil to be sealed tightly around rim of pan.) Add water, carrot, celery, onion and parsley to pan. Sprinkle turkey with remaining salt and pepper.
4. Roast turkey, uncovered, in preheated hot oven (400°) for 15 minutes. Reduce oven temperature to slow (325°). Cover pan with tight-fitting lid or aluminum foil. Roast 2½ hours. Uncover and roast 45 minutes longer or until meat thermometer registers 180° to 185° and center of stuffing registers 160° to 165°; drumstick should move up and down freely; juices should run clear when thigh is pierced. Remove from oven. Let stand 15 to 30 minutes before carving. *(See carving how-to, page 264.)* Reserve drippings in roasting pan.
5. Meanwhile, prepare gravy: Combine giblets (except liver), chicken broth and bay leaf in medium-size saucepan. Bring to boiling. Lower heat; cover and simmer 1 hour or until tender. Add liver; simmer 15 minutes. Drain mixture, reserving broth. Discard bay leaf. Remove meat from neck; finely chop with giblets; reserve.
6. When turkey is done, strain drippings from roasting pan into clear glass 4-cup measure. Discard solids. Skim off fat; reserve 2 tablespoons. You should have at least 2 cups of drippings. Add enough giblet broth to make a total of 3¾ cups. Heat 2 tablespoons reserved fat in small saucepan. Stir in flour; cook 2 minutes. Gradually whisk in broth mixture. Cook over medium heat, whisking, until thickened and bubbly. Skim foam. Lower heat; add giblets and simmer 5 minutes. Add salt and pepper. Pour into gravy boat.
7. To store leftovers, remove stuffing from turkey and refrigerate the bird and stuffing separately.

WILD AND PECAN RICE STUFFING
The rice stuffing is also delicious with our Prune-Stuffed Loin of Pork (see page 378). Feel free to substitute your own stuffing for this bird or try our others (pages 291 to 294).

HOW TO CARVE A TURKEY
(Carver is left-handed)

1. Line roasting pan across width with strip of folded heavy-duty foil. Center roasting rack over foil and place bird on rack. When turkey is done, lift bird and rack out of pan by lifting the two ends of the foil. Let stand 15 to 30 minutes.

2. Remove leg: Place turkey, breast-side up, on cutting board. Steady bird with carving fork. Slice through skin between breast and thigh. Pull back leg to locate joint. Cut through joint to remove whole leg.

3. Divide leg: To separate drumstick and thigh, slightly stretch them apart to find joint. With firm, downward movement of knife, cut through joint.

4. Carve drumstick: Position narrow end of leg between tines of carving fork to avoid piercing meat. Holding carving knife parallel to bone, cut slices from drumstick.

5. Carve thigh and wing: Working parallel to bone, cut slices from thigh. To remove wing (not pictured), cut through skin at corner of breast around wing. Move wing to locate joint. Cut through joint to remove wing with small part of breast.

6. Carve breast: Starting at outside of breast, cut down diagonally to produce thin slices. Repeat all carving steps with other side of bird when you need to refill platter.

TURKEY TALK

FRESH TURKEYS
Keep refrigerated at all times. Cook within 1 or 2 days of purchase.

FROZEN WHOLE TURKEYS
Store in the original wrapper for up to 12 months at 0°F or lower.

THAWING
Never thaw turkey at room temperature; instead, use one of the methods below. Once the turkey is thawed, cook or refrigerate it immediately.

Conventional (Long) Method
Thawing time: 3 to 4 days, or about 24 hours for each 5 pounds of a whole frozen turkey.
- Leave turkey in original wrapper until ready to cook.
- Place frozen turkey on a tray and defrost in the refrigerator.

Cold Water (Short) Method
- Thawing time: about 30 minutes per pound of whole frozen turkey.
- Leave turkey in original wrapper.
- Place turkey in sink or large pan.
- Cover turkey completely with cold water.
- Change the water every 30 minutes, but refill the sink or pan immediately with cold water so the turkey is constantly immersed.

STUFFING
When? Just before you roast your turkey is the time to stuff it. You run the risk of food poisoning if you stuff the bird earlier.
How much? Allow ¾ cup stuffing per pound of bird for turkeys weighing more than 10 pounds; ½ cup of stuffing per pound for smaller birds.
Note: Do not freeze stuffing inside the bird, whether it's uncooked or the cooked leftovers from dinner. Always remove *all* stuffing

and wrap and refrigerate separately.

TESTING FOR DONENESS
- Your turkey is done when a meat thermometer inserted in meatiest part of thigh (without touching the bone) reads 180° to 185°F; in the center of the stuffing it reads 160° to 165°F.
- Turkey juices run clear when thigh is pierced with knife point.
- Drumsticks move up and down easily.

RESTING PERIOD
Let turkey stand at room temperature 15 to 30 minutes to allow juices to settle and meat to firm up for easier carving.

GOT A QUESTION?
If you run into snags making your turkey for Thanksgiving dinner, help is as near as your telephone. The toll-free hotline below operates even on Thanksgiving day!
- U.S.D.A. Meat and Poultry Hotline: 1-800-535-4555. This service answers questions year-round about meat and poultry products, and it expands its hours for the holidays.

EVERYDAY TURKEY
Most famous for its role as the holiday classic, turkey is now available in a tempting array of smaller cuts and parts, making it practical for everyday meals.
- **Turkey wings** make a particularly rich stock, and they're also great eating in stews and fricassees (1½ servings per pound).
- **Turkey thighs** are also good soup and stew makers (2½ servings per pound).
- **Turkey drumsticks** can be roasted like the whole bird, or skinned and cut up into bite-size pieces and stir-fried (about 2 servings per pound).
- **Turkey breast,** on the bone or off, can be roasted and sliced as you would serve a big bird. Since it's all white meat, however, be extra careful not to overcook and dry out the meat. Baste with wine and/or broth for moist results (2½ servings per pound).
- **Turkey cutlets** are boned and skinned sliced portions of the breast. Use them interchangeably with veal and chicken cutlets (4 servings per pound).

CONVENTIONAL OVEN: TIMETABLE FOR ROASTING TURKEY (325°)

Weight (pounds)	Stuffed (hours)	Unstuffed (hours)
6 to 8	3 to 3½	2½ to 3½
8 to 12	3½ to 4¼	3 to 4
12 to 16	4 to 5	3½ to 4½
16 to 20	4½ to 5½	4 to 5
20 to 24	5 to 6½	4½ to 5½

TURKEY DRUMSTICKS, OSSO BUCO STYLE

Fresh ginger and orange juice give this dish a real pick-me-up. And the garnish, a mixture of basil, orange rind and garlic, adds a final zip. Serve with orzo or rice.

TURKEY DRUMSTICKS MAKE-AHEAD TIP:

The dish can be prepared a day ahead and refrigerated, covered. Reheat in a preheated moderate oven (350°) or on the stove top.

Bake at 350° for 40 to 45 minutes.

Makes 4 servings.

Recipe can be halved or doubled.

Nutrient Value Per Serving: 459 calories, 49 g protein, 18 g fat, 22 g carbohydrate, 325 mg sodium, 171 mg cholesterol.

Drumsticks:

2½ tablespoons olive oil

4 skinless turkey drumsticks (about 12 ounces each)

¼ teaspoon salt

½ cup all-purpose flour

1 large onion, finely chopped

4 cloves garlic, crushed

2 teaspoons finely chopped, pared fresh ginger

⅔ cup dry white wine

¾ cup chopped tomato

4 strips orange rind (3 × ½ inch each)

½ cup fresh orange juice

Garnish:

2 tablespoons finely chopped fresh basil OR: parsley

1 teaspoon finely chopped garlic

½ teaspoon finely chopped orange rind

1. Preheat oven to moderate (350°).

2. Heat oil in Dutch oven or large saucepan over moderate heat. Sprinkle turkey with salt. Dredge in flour, shaking off excess. Add to Dutch oven, working in batches if necessary; cook until turkey is browned all over, about 10 minutes. Remove to bowl.

3. Reduce heat to low. Add onion, garlic and ginger to Dutch oven; cook, uncovered, stirring frequently, until lightly browned and softened, about 10 minutes. Add wine. Increase heat to moderate; cook 2 minutes. Add tomato, orange rind, orange juice and turkey. Bring to boiling. Cover.

4. Bake in preheated moderate oven (350°) for 40 to 45 minutes or until tender.

5. Meanwhile, prepare Garnish: Combine basil, garlic and orange rind in small bowl.

6. Spoon turkey and liquid onto serving plates. Sprinkle a little of the Garnish over each serving.

BRAISED DRUMSTICK DINNER

Turkey Drumsticks, Osso Buco Style (this page)

Noodles

Banana Semifreddo (533)

SHALLOT AND HERB STUFFED TURKEY DRUMSTICKS

P*repare this under-the-skin stuffing as much as 3 days in advance, if you like. You may also use it for chicken or game hens. For really large appetites, serve one drumstick per serving.*

Bake at 375° for 45 minutes.
Makes 6 servings.
Nutrient Value Per Serving: 350 calories, 35 g protein, 21 g fat, 3 g carbohydrate, 189 mg sodium, 106 mg cholesterol.

⅓ cup finely chopped shallots
⅓ cup packed parsley leaves
1 tablespoon fresh tarragon leaves
1 tablespoon chopped green onion
3 pieces pared fresh ginger, each size of a quarter
¼ teaspoon salt
2½ tablespoons fresh lemon juice
¼ cup olive oil
4 turkey drumsticks (about 12 ounces each)

1. Preheat oven to moderate (375°). Lightly grease an 11 × 7-inch or 13 × 9-inch baking pan; set aside.
2. Combine shallots, parsley, tarragon, green onion, ginger and salt in workbowl of a food processor and whirl until blended. Add lemon juice and oil and whirl until pasty.
3. Push your fingers under the skin of the drumsticks, separating it from the flesh. Spoon about 2 tablespoons of the paste under the skin, spreading it over the turkey flesh and pulling skin back in place to cover. Repeat with remaining drumsticks. Place in prepared pan.
4. Bake in preheated moderate oven (375°) until tender, about 45 minutes, basting every 15 minutes. To serve, slice drumsticks.

ROASTED TURKEY DRUMSTICKS AND LENTIL CASSEROLE

A *soul-warming dish seasoned with rosemary and fennel and flecked with pieces of pepperoni. Serve with crusty Italian bread and rice.*

Bake at 325° for 2 hours.
Makes 6 servings.
Recipe can be halved or doubled.
Nutrient Value Per Serving: 456 calories, 47 g protein, 17 g fat, 27 g carbohydrate, 562 mg sodium, 110 mg cholesterol.

4 turkey drumsticks (about 12 ounces each)
½ cup parsley leaves
3 cloves garlic, sliced
Grated rind of 1 lemon
½ teaspoon fennel seeds
1 tablespoon olive oil
1 large onion, chopped
1 sweet green pepper, cored, seeded and cut into squares
1 stalk celery, chopped
¾ teaspoon leaf rosemary, crumbled
1 can (13¾ ounces) beef broth
1 can (16 ounces) tomatoes
¼ cup chopped pepperoni (1 ounce)
1 cup dried lentils, rinsed

1. Preheat oven to slow (325°). Pull back skin from drumsticks. Place in 13 × 9 × 2-inch baking dish.
2. Chop together parsley, garlic, lemon rind and fennel seeds until medium-fine, either with a knife or in small food processor. Rub a little on flesh of each drumstick. Re-cover with skin. Reserve remaining parsley mixture.
3. Bake in preheated slow oven (325°) for 45 minutes.
4. Meanwhile, heat oil in medium-size skillet over medium heat. Add onion, green pepper, celery and rosemary; cook 8 minutes or until softened. Add beef
(continued)

DRUMSTICKS AND LENTIL CASSEROLE MAKE-AHEAD TIP:
The dish can be prepared a day or two ahead and refrigerated, covered. Reheat, covered, in a preheated moderate oven (350°).

ROASTED TURKEY DRUMSTICKS AND LENTIL CASSEROLE (continued)

broth, tomatoes and pepperoni. Bring to boiling, breaking up tomatoes with spoon. Remove from heat.

5. Sprinkle lentils and remaining parsley mixture in baking dish around turkey legs. Add tomato mixture from skillet. Tent dish with aluminum foil. Return to oven.

6. Bake in preheated slow oven (325°) for 1 hour and 15 minutes or until lentils and drumsticks are tender. Remove dish to wire rack and let stand at least 15 minutes for lentils to absorb excess broth. To serve, slice drumsticks.

WINTER WARMER

Tomato Soup with Orange Zest and Chives

Roasted Turkey Drumsticks and Lentil Casserole (267)

Yogurt Mashed Potatoes (439)

Butterscotch Ice Cream

TURKEY BREAST STUFFED WITH CHILIES AND CHEESE

This is a terrific party dish that can be made ahead and served either warm or at room temperature. Try this at holiday time instead of the usual roast whole turkey or gigantic baked ham.

Bake at 325° for 1¾ to 2¼ hours.
Makes 12 servings.
Nutrient Value Per Serving: 387 calories, 56 g protein, 14 g fat, 7 g carbohydrate, 370 mg sodium, 206 mg cholesterol.

1 fresh or frozen bone-in turkey breast (6 to 6½ pounds) with skin, thawed if frozen

Stuffing:
3 green onions, chopped
1 sweet red pepper, cored, seeded and chopped
½ cup (1 stick) *un*salted butter
1 teaspoon ground cumin
½ teaspoon ground coriander
½ teaspoon ground chili powder
½ teaspoon salt
¼ teaspoon pepper
1 can (4 ounces) chopped green chilies, drained
3 cups dry day-old coarse bread crumbs
1½ cups shredded Monterey Jack cheese (about 5 ounces)
2 eggs, slightly beaten

Picante or chili sauce *(optional)*

1. To bone breast: Place breast, skin-side down, on cutting board. Cut between bone and flesh; pull bone away as you loosen it. At base of breastbone, be careful not to cut through skin. Do not remove skin.
2. Place boned breast, skin-side down, on work surface. Trim excess fat. Trim off tendon. Cut away oval fillet from each side of breast; set aside. Starting in

center of thickest part on one-half of breast, cut meat horizontally in half but not all the way through. Spread meat out like open book. Repeat with other side. Cover with plastic wrap. Pound with skillet to even thickness. Refrigerate until ready to stuff.
3. Prepare Stuffing: Sauté green onion and sweet red pepper in 2 tablespoons butter in medium-size skillet over medium heat until tender, about 5 minutes. Add cumin, coriander, chili powder, salt and pepper; sauté about 1 minute. Add chilies. Remove from heat. Stir in crumbs, cheese and eggs.
4. Preheat oven to slow (325°).
5. To stuff: Spread double-thickness
(continued)

TURKEY BREAST MAKE-AHEAD TIP:
The recipe can be prepared through Step 3 up to 2 hours ahead and refrigerated, covered.

TURKEY BREAST STUFFED WITH CHILIES AND CHEESE (continued)

cheesecloth, 35 × 16 inches, on board. Place turkey, skin-side down, on cloth. Spread stuffing evenly over breast, leaving ½-inch border all around. Place reserved fillets, end to end, lengthwise, down center. Roll up breast from long side; fasten with wooden picks. Bring skin up and over turkey from both ends; secure with wooden picks. Wrap turkey in cheesecloth. Tie with kitchen string every 2 inches. Place, seam-side down, in roasting pan.

6. Melt remaining butter in small saucepan. Pour over turkey to soak cheesecloth.

7. Roast in preheated slow oven (325°), basting often with pan drippings, for 1¾ to 2¼ hours or until instant-read thermometer registers 170° when inserted in thickest part. Remove to cutting board; let stand 20 minutes.

8. Remove and discard string, cheesecloth and wooden picks. Cut turkey into thick slices. Serve hot or at room temperature, with picante or chili sauce, warmed or at room temperature, if you wish.

SUMMER CONCERT IN THE PARK

Artichoke and Black Olive Spread (82) with Assorted Crackers

Cold Cherry-Buttermilk Soup (137)

Turkey Breast Stuffed with Chilies and Cheese (269)

Grated Carrot Salad with Cilantro (152)

Hazelnut Shortbread (517) with Summer Fruit Compote (528)

TURKEY WITH PEARS AND SWEET GINGER CREAM

LOW-CALORIE · LOW-FAT
LOW-CHOLESTEROL · LOW-SODIUM
QUICK

A *flavorful dish to serve chilled or at room temperature for lunch or a light supper along with warmed bread and a small green salad. Use leftover cooked turkey breast or deli turkey.*

Makes 4 servings.
Recipe can be halved or doubled.
Nutrient Value Per Serving: 243 calories, 20 g protein, 6 g fat, 29 g carbohydrate, 42 mg sodium, 49 mg cholesterol.

½ cup reduced-calorie sour cream
1½ teaspoons finely chopped crystallized ginger
½ teaspoon lemon juice
¼ teaspoon ground cumin
⅛ teaspoon dry mustard
Dash liquid red-pepper seasoning
4 Anjou pears, halved and cored
8 ounces sliced, cooked turkey breast

1. Combine sour cream, crystallized ginger, lemon juice, cumin, mustard and red-pepper seasoning in small bowl.

2. Place 2 pear halves on each of 4 salad plates. Arrange turkey on pears. Spoon 2 tablespoons cream mixture over each serving.

ROASTED TURKEY BREAST WITH CORNBREAD-PECAN STUFFING

LOW-FAT

Looking for an alternative to the holiday turkey? Try this delicious stuffed breast— there's no wrestling with legs or wings. (Pictured on page 231.)

Bake at 375° for 4 hours.
Makes 16 servings.
Nutrient Value Per Serving: 487 calories, 77 g protein, 12 g fat, 14 g carbohydrate, 522 mg sodium, 243 mg cholesterol.

1 whole turkey breast on bone (about 12 pounds)
¼ cup (½ stick) *un*salted butter
1 cup chopped celery
1 cup chopped onion
½ cup chopped parsley
1¼ teaspoons poultry seasoning
1 teaspoon salt
½ teaspoon black pepper
4 cups cubed day-old white bread (8 slices)
4 cups crumbled cornbread (8 slices)
¾ cup milk
¾ cup chicken broth
1 egg, beaten
1 cup toasted pecans, coarsely chopped

1. Rinse breast and pat dry. Place rack in roasting pan. Place aluminum foil on rack. Pierce foil in 6 places for excess liquid to drain. Place breast on foil.
2. Heat butter in large skillet over medium heat. Add celery, onion and parsley; cook 10 minutes until softened. Stir in seasonings.
3. Meanwhile, combine bread cubes, cornbread, milk, broth and egg in large bowl. Stir in onion mixture and pecans.
4. Preheat oven to moderate (375°). Spoon stuffing under breast. Cover pan with lid or tight-fitting aluminum foil.

5. Bake in preheated moderate oven (375°) for 3 hours. Uncover and bake an additional 1 hour or until instant-read thermometer inserted in meat and stuffing registers 170°. Let turkey stand at least 20 minutes before carving. Serve with stuffing.

BAKED BONELESS TURKEY BREAST WITH HONEY-HOISIN SAUCE

LOW-CALORIE

Slices of this turkey breast can be served warm, at room temperature, or chilled.

Bake at 350° for 1½ hours.
Makes 12 servings.
Nutrient Value Per Serving: 343 calories, 45 g protein, 14 g fat, 5 g carbohydrate, 454 mg sodium, 133 mg cholesterol.

1 whole turkey breast (about 6 pounds)
2 tablespoons hoisin sauce
2 tablespoons soy sauce
1 tablespoon dry sherry
2 tablespoons honey
1 tablespoon catsup
1 tablespoon grated, pared fresh ginger
1 tablespoon chopped shallot OR: white part green onion
¼ teaspoon ground pepper
2 teaspoons cornstarch
1 tablespoon cold water
¾ cup chicken broth

1. Slide fingers between meat and skin on one side of breast close to ribs. Pull skin off meat and discard; repeat with other side. Trim off any remaining skin or fat with sharp knife.
2. Remove flesh from bones by scraping knife against rib bones and working up to the breastbone and cartilage. Repeat with other side. Cut whole breast off

(continued)

FOR A SMALLER ROASTED TURKEY BREAST

If a 12-pound whole turkey breast is too big for your small crowd, select a 6- to 8-pound whole breast on the bone, and begin to check the internal temperature after 2 hours.

TURKEY BREAST WITH HONEY-HOISIN SAUCE MAKE-AHEAD TIP:

The turkey can be cooked up to 3 days ahead and refriger-ated, covered. Serve at room temperature or chilled. Or reheat slices with sauce, cov-ered, in preheated moderate oven (350°).

BAKED BONELESS TURKEY BREAST WITH HONEY-HOISIN SAUCE (continued)

breast cage, being careful not to cut breast in half. Remove tendons by cutting on either side; grasp the tendons with toweling to prevent slipping and scrape away flesh.

3. Roll up breast from a long side. Tie crosswise with kitchen string in several

places. Tie lengthwise in 2 or 3 places.

4. Preheat oven to moderate (350°).

5. Place turkey on rack in roasting pan. Add ¼ cup water to pan. Combine hoisin sauce, soy sauce, sherry, 1 tablespoon honey, catsup, ginger, shallot and pepper in small bowl. Brush basting sauce over roast. Cover tightly with aluminum foil.

6. Bake in preheated moderate oven (375°) for 60 minutes, covered, basting halfway through cooking. Uncover. Cook, basting occasionally, 30 minutes more or until an instant-read thermometer registers 170° when inserted into thickest part. Let stand at least 20 minutes. Remove strings. Slice.

7. Meanwhile, stir together cornstarch and water in small cup. Measure out ½ cup pan drippings into small saucepan. Add chicken broth, 1 tablespoon honey and any remaining basting sauce. Bring to boiling. Stir in cornstarch mixture; cook 1 minute or until thickened and bubbly. Strain into gravy boat. Serve with sliced turkey.

Microwave Directions (High Power Oven):

Bone and roll turkey breast as in Steps 1 to 3. Place in microwave-safe 13 × 9 × 2-inch baking dish. Do not add water. Combine hoisin sauce, soy sauce, sherry, 1 tablespoon honey, catsup, ginger, shallot and pepper in small bowl; brush over roast. Cover turkey with another baking dish, inverted. Microwave at 100% power 10 minutes, turning dish once. Microwave at 50% power 40 to 43 minutes until internal temperature reaches 170°, turning roast over after 25 minutes. Let stand, covered, 10 minutes. Prepare sauce: Whisk together cornstarch, water, chicken broth and remaining 1 tablespoon honey in microwave-safe 2-cup measure until smooth. Microwave, uncovered, at 100% power 3 minutes to a full boil, whisking after 1½ minutes.

WALNUT-CRUSTED TURKEY CUTLETS WITH FONTINA CHEESE SAUCE

QUICK

The crusty coating of the turkey slices contrasts nicely with the rich cheese sauce. Serve with new potatoes and sautéed mushrooms. Try this recipe with chicken cutlets.

Bake at 375° for 10-to 15 minutes.
Makes 4 servings.
Recipe can be halved or doubled.
Nutrient Value Per Serving: 508 calories, 39 g protein, 34 g fat, 12 g carbohydrate, 405 mg sodium, 168 mg cholesterol.

2 slices whole-wheat bread, quartered
¼ cup toasted walnuts
¼ teaspoon black pepper
1 egg
3 tablespoons olive oil
1 pound turkey cutlets

Fontina Sauce:
1 tablespoon oil
½ cup finely chopped onion
    (1 medium-size)
1 tablespoon all-purpose flour
½ teaspoon ground sage
½ cup half-and-half
1 cup shredded fontina cheese
    (4 ounces)
Chopped parsley, for garnish

1. Combine bread, walnuts and pepper in food processor or blender. Whirl until medium-coarse crumbs, about 1 minute. Scrape into shallow dish. Beat egg in second shallow dish.
2. Heat oil in skillet over medium heat. Dip cutlets in egg, then in crumb mixture to coat. Add half of cutlets to skillet; cook 5 to 6 minutes or until both sides are golden, turning once. Place in ovenproof serving dish or 13 × 9 × 2-inch baking dish. Repeat with remaining cutlets.

(continued)

EASY & ELEGANT TURKEY

Endive and Orange Salad with Ginger-Sesame Dressing (179)

Walnut-Crusted Turkey Cutlets with Fontina Cheese Sauce (this page)

Roasted Sweet Potato Wedges with Garlic

Brownie Sundae with Chocolate Sauce (537)

**WALNUT-CRUSTED TURKEY CUTLETS
WITH FONTINA CHEESE SAUCE** (*continued*)

3. Preheat oven to moderate (375°).
4. Prepare Sauce: Wipe out skillet with paper toweling. Heat oil in skillet over medium heat. Add onion to skillet; sauté 4 minutes or until softened. Stir in flour and sage; cook, stirring, 2 minutes. Whisk in half-and-half. Bring to simmering until smooth and thickened. Remove from heat. Stir in fontina until blended and smooth. Spoon over cutlets.
5. Bake cutlets in preheated moderate oven (375°) for 10 to 15 minutes or until heated through. Garnish with chopped parsley.

Make-Ahead Tip: The cutlets can be prepared through Step 2 and refrigerated, covered, up to 2 hours ahead.

PIQUANT TURKEY CUTLETS

LOW-CALORIE · QUICK

These are quick and easy to prepare with a full rich flavor—sun-dried tomatoes provide an extra zip. Serve with pasta as a side dish. This recipe also works well with chicken, veal and pork cutlets.

Makes 4 servings.
Recipe can be halved or doubled.
Nutrient Value Per Serving: 346 calories, 32 g protein, 18 g fat, 9 g carbohydrate, 702 mg sodium, 87 mg cholesterol.

⅓ cup sun-dried tomatoes, dry pack
2 tablespoons olive oil
4 turkey cutlets (4 to 5 ounces each)
¼ cup all-purpose flour
½ cup dry white wine
¾ cup reduced-sodium chicken broth
1 tablespoon capers
½ teaspoon leaf marjoram, crumbled
1 tablespoon *un*salted butter

1. Bring medium-size saucepan of unsalted water to boiling. Add sun-dried tomatoes; blanch 30 seconds. Drain, rinse and drain again. Thinly slice.
2. Heat oil in large skillet over moderately high heat. Dredge turkey in flour. Add to skillet; sauté 2 to 3 minutes per side or until browned all over. Remove cutlets to plate. Drain fat from skillet.
3. Add wine to skillet. Increase heat to high; cook 2 minutes. Add chicken broth, capers, marjoram and sun-dried tomatoes. Lower heat to moderate; cook 4 minutes or until slightly reduced. Return cutlets to skillet. Reduce heat to low; cook 2 minutes longer. Add butter, swirling skillet just until butter has melted. Serve immediately.

TURKEY AND EGGPLANT PARMESAN

Baking rather than frying the eggplant eliminates extra fat.

Bake eggplant at 400° for 25 minutes;
bake casserole for 15 minutes.
Makes 4 servings.
Nutrient Value Per Serving: 456 calories,
43 g protein, 22 g fat, 23 g carbohydrate,
1,047 mg sodium, 148 mg cholesterol.

---

1 eggplant (about 1¼ pounds)
1¼ cups fresh bread crumbs
½ cup chopped parsley
½ cup grated Parmesan cheese
1 egg
½ teaspoon salt
¼ teaspoon black pepper
3 tablespoons vegetable oil
1 pound turkey cutlets
1½ cups prepared or homemade tomato
    sauce
1 cup shredded part-skim mozzarella
    cheese (4 ounces)

1. Preheat oven to hot (400°). Spray
13 × 9 × 2-inch baking dish with nonstick vegetable-oil cooking spray. Peel
eggplant; slice lengthwise into ¾-inch-
thick slices. Use 4 center-cut slices;
reserve remaining eggplant for another
use.
2. Combine bread crumbs, parsley and
Parmesan in shallow dish. Beat together
egg, salt and pepper in another dish.
3. Dip eggplant slices in egg mixture,
then in crumbs to coat. Place in baking
dish in single layer. Drizzle with 1
tablespoon oil.
4. Bake in preheated hot oven (400°)
for 25 minutes or just until eggplant is
tender.
5. Meanwhile, heat remaining oil in
nonstick skillet. Dip half the cutlets in
egg, then in crumb mixture to coat.
Add cutlets to skillet; sauté for 5 minutes, turning halfway during cooking

after first side is golden. Repeat with
remaining cutlets.
6. Place cutlets on top of cooked eggplant slices. Spoon sauce evenly over
cutlets. Sprinkle on mozzarella. Return
to oven.
7. Bake in preheated hot oven (400°)
for 15 minutes or until heated through
and cheese is bubbly.

Make-Ahead Tip: The eggplant and turkey can be prepared separately up to 4
hours ahead and refrigerated, covered.

TURKEY PAPRIKASH

LOW-CALORIE · QUICK

A TASTE OF PAPRIKA
A quick, flavorful dish, Turkey Paprikash takes just minutes to prepare. For best flavor, use a good-quality Hungarian paprika. Serve over rice, noodles or toast points and garnish with chopped parsley, if you wish.

PAPRIKA
■ *Sweet paprika* powder is made from certain dried, sweet red peppers which have had their hot inner membranes removed before grinding. It is often used to add mild flavor and a sprinkle of color to both warm and cold foods.
■ *Hot paprika* is also made from sweet red peppers, but with hot membranes intact. This pepper adds a more pungent flavor to soups, stews and casseroles.
■ While an assortment of chilies flavors the foods of Mexico, Asia, India and America, ground red paprika is the pepper of choice in European, Middle Eastern, Spanish and North African dishes, and is known as the national spice of Hungary.

Makes 4 servings.
Recipe can be halved or doubled.
Nutrient Value Per Serving: 253 calories, 31 g protein, 9 g fat, 12 g carbohydrate, 642 mg sodium, 78 mg cholesterol.

1 pound turkey cutlets
⅓ cup reduced-calorie sour cream
¼ cup lowfat plain yogurt
1 teaspoon lemon juice
1 tablespoon olive oil or vegetable oil
2 cups sliced red onions (8 ounces)
2 cloves garlic, sliced
⅛ teaspoon leaf thyme, crumbled
1 cup chicken broth
1 tablespoon tomato paste
1 tablespoon all-purpose flour
½ teaspoon salt
2½ tablespoons sweet paprika

1. Cut turkey into 1-inch-wide strips. Stir together sour cream, yogurt and lemon juice in small bowl.
2. Heat oil in medium-size skillet over medium-low heat. Add onion, garlic and thyme; cook, covered, about 12 minutes or until soft. Combine onion mixture, broth, tomato paste, flour and salt in food processor or blender. Whirl until pureed.
3. Scrape puree into skillet. Bring to boiling. Lower heat. Stir in turkey pieces; simmer, covered, for 8 minutes or until opaque. Stir in paprika; cook 2 minutes. Stir in sour cream mixture; bring just to simmering; do not boil. Remove from heat and serve.

SPICY TURKEY

Romaine and Curly Endive Salad

Turkey Paprikash (this page)
with Egg Noodles

Green Beans

Poundcake with Berries in Syrup

YUCATAN-STYLE TURKEY CUTLETS

LOW-CALORIE · QUICK

The cutlets are flavored with cumin and chili powder. Serve with parslied rice and garnish with green olives.

Makes 4 servings.
Recipe can be halved or doubled.
Nutrient Value Per Serving: 263 calories, 28 g protein, 13 g fat, 8 g carbohydrate, 404 mg sodium, 78 mg cholesterol.

1 pound turkey cutlets
3 tablespoons all-purpose flour
2 tablespoons vegetable oil
1 tablespoon *un*salted butter
½ teaspoon ground chili powder
¼ teaspoon ground cumin
⅔ cup reduced-sodium chicken broth
⅓ cup orange juice
1 tablespoon tomato paste
2 teaspoons liquid from green olives
2 green onions, sliced
3 tablespoons chopped green olives
2 tablespoons chopped pumpkin seeds
    OR: sunflower seeds *(optional garnish)*

1. Dredge cutlets in flour in pie plate. Pat off excess flour; place cutlets on waxed paper. Measure out 2 tablespoons flour and reserve for sauce.
2. Heat oil in skillet over medium heat. Add cutlets; sauté 8 to 10 minutes or until golden on both sides. Transfer to serving plate. Pour off oil from skillet.
3. Heat butter in skillet. Stir in chili powder, cumin and reserved flour; cook, stirring, 2 minutes. Remove from heat. Whisk in the chicken broth, orange juice, tomato paste, olive liquid and green onion until the mixture is well blended and smooth.
4. Return to heat. Bring to boiling; cook, stirring, 2 minutes, until thickened and bubbly. Add cutlets; cook until heated through, about 4 minutes.

Spoon onto serving plate. Sprinkle with olives, and pumpkin seeds if you wish.

Make-Ahead Tip: The cutlets and the sauce can be prepared separately earlier in the day and refrigerated. To serve, gently reheat together in a skillet.

12 no-salt saltine crackers (½ cup crumbs)
3 tablespoons sesame seeds
½ teaspoon leaf basil, crumbled
1 egg
1 pound turkey cutlets
3 tablespoons vegetable oil
¼ cup orange juice
1 teaspoon cornstarch
¼ cup chardonnay or other dry white wine OR: chicken broth
½ cup grapefruit juice
2 teaspoons honey
¼ cup chopped golden raisins
2 green onions, sliced
¼ teaspoon salt
2 tablespoons dairy sour cream

1. Preheat oven to very slow (250°). Crush crackers in bag with rolling pin until finely crumbed. Toss together cracker crumbs, sesame seeds and basil in pie plate. Beat egg in second pie plate.

2. Dip cutlets in egg, then in crumbs to coat; place on waxed paper.

3. Heat half the oil in medium-size skillet over medium heat. Add half the cutlets; sauté 8 to 10 minutes or until golden on both sides, turning over once. Place on ovenproof serving platter; cover loosely with aluminum foil. Keep warm in oven. Repeat with remaining oil and cutlets.

4. Stir together orange juice and cornstarch in small bowl until smooth.

5. Return skillet to heat. Add wine; bring to boiling, scraping up any browned bits from bottom of skillet. Stir in grapefruit juice, honey, raisins, green onion and salt. Bring to boiling. Stir in cornstarch mixture; cook, stirring, 2 minutes or until thickened and bubbly. Remove from heat. Stir in sour cream. Spoon sauce over cutlets and serve.

Make-Ahead Tip: The turkey cutlets can be coated up to 4 hours ahead and refrigerated, covered.

Sesame-Coated Turkey Cutlets with Citrus Sauce

QUICK

Quick enough for everyday meals—special enough for guests. Try with chicken cutlets. Serve with rice or orzo, and for a special touch, garnish with orange wedges, including blood orange.

Makes 4 servings.
Recipe can be halved or doubled.
Nutrient Value Per Serving: 400 calories, 31 g protein, 19 g fat, 24 g carbohydrate, 303 mg sodium, 127 mg cholesterol.

TURKEY TAMALE PIE

LOW-CALORIE · LOW-CHOLESTEROL

Makes 4 servings.
Nutrient Value Per Serving: 317 calories, 19 g protein, 14 g fat, 32 g carbohydrate, 887 mg sodium, 57 mg cholesterol.

½ cup yellow cornmeal
½ cup chicken broth
⅓ cup lowfat plain yogurt
½ teaspoon salt
1 medium-size onion, finely chopped
1 teaspoon vegetable oil
1 clove garlic, finely chopped
8 ounces ground turkey
1 tablespoon chili powder
½ teaspoon leaf oregano, crumbled
½ teaspoon ground cumin
⅛ teaspoon pepper
1 can (14½ ounces) whole tomatoes, undrained
1 cup frozen whole-kernel corn
½ cup sliced pitted canned black olives
½ cup shredded medium-sharp Cheddar cheese (2 ounces)

1. Combine cornmeal, broth, yogurt and ¼ teaspoon salt in small bowl.
2. Sauté onion in oil in 10-inch non-stick skillet over medium heat, 3 to 4 minutes. Add garlic; cook 30 seconds. Crumble turkey into skillet; sprinkle with chili powder, oregano, cumin, remaining ¼ teaspoon salt and the pepper. Cook, stirring, until no pink remains, 2 to 3 minutes.
3. Add tomatoes with their juice, crushing tomatoes with wooden spoon. Add corn. Bring to boiling. Lower heat to simmer. Pour two-thirds of yogurt mixture into simmering turkey mixture; stir and simmer 3 minutes. Do not let boil. Smooth top; scatter ¼ cup olive slices over top. Drizzle remaining yogurt mixture over top; sprinkle with cheese. Cover and simmer over very low heat, without stirring, for 15 to 20 minutes or until set. Sprinkle remaining olives over top.

4. Remove from heat. Let stand, covered, for 10 minutes. Serve hot, spooning onto plates, or let cool completely and cut into wedges to serve.

Make-Ahead Tip: The pie can be prepared a day ahead and refrigerated, covered, and then served cold.
Microwave Directions (High Power Oven):
Ingredient Changes: Reduce chili powder to 2 teaspoons; reduce oregano and cumin to ¼ teaspoon *each*.
Directions: Combine cornmeal, chicken broth, yogurt and ¼ teaspoon salt in small bowl; reserve. Combine onion, garlic and oil in microwave-safe 1½-quart casserole with lid. Microwave, covered, at 100% power 2 minutes. Crumble turkey into casserole; stir in chili powder, oregano and cumin.
(continued)

SAVORY PIE
Turkey Tamale Pie is prepared in a skillet on top of the stove. It will be soft and spoonable if served right away; but if made ahead, it will set and then it can be cut into wedges. Ground beef can be substituted for the turkey.

TURKEY TAMALE PIE (*continued*)

Microwave, uncovered, at 100% power 4 minutes, breaking up chunks with a fork after 2 minutes. Drain off ¼ cup liquid from canned tomatoes and save for another use. Break up tomatoes; add to casserole with corn, remaining ¼ teaspoon salt and the pepper. Microwave, covered, at 100% power 7 minutes until bubbling all over, stirring once. Stir two-thirds of cornmeal mixture into casserole. Microwave, uncovered, at 100% power 2 minutes. Stir and smooth top. Sprinkle with ¼ cup of the olives. Drizzle remaining cornmeal mixture over top. Microwave, uncovered, at 70% power 3 minutes. Sprinkle cheese over top; turn dish. Microwave, uncovered, at 100% power 4 minutes. Sprinkle remaining ¼ cup olives over top. Cover and let stand 3 minutes.

TURKEY TACOS

LOW-CALORIE · LOW CHOLESTEROL
QUICK

Made with ground turkey, these tacos are a lighter alternative to their beef cousin and take practically no time at all to prepare.

Makes 4 servings.
Recipe can be halved or doubled.
Nutrient Value Per Serving: 267 calories, 13 g protein, 12 g fat, 26 g carbohydrate, 436 mg sodium, 41 mg cholesterol.

½ pound ground turkey
1 small onion, chopped
1 tablespoon vegetable oil
1 can (10 ounces) pinto beans
⅔ cup hot or mild salsa
8 packaged taco shells

Garnish:
Chopped avocado, chopped or sliced tomato, shredded Monterey Jack cheese and shredded lettuce

1. Sauté turkey and onion in oil in large skillet until lightly browned, about 5 minutes, stirring to break up clumps. Drain beans and rinse. Push turkey to one side of skillet; add beans. Mash one-third of beans with fork. Stir in half the salsa. Heat until hot.
2. To serve, divide mixture into taco shells. Serve with remaining salsa, the avocado, tomato, cheese and lettuce.

Make-Ahead Tip: The filling can be prepared earlier in the day and refrigerated, covered. Gently reheat.
Microwave Directions (High Power Oven): Combine onion and oil in microwave-safe 1½-quart casserole. Cover with lid. Microwave at 100% power 2 minutes. Crumble turkey into casserole. Re-cover. Microwave at 100% power 2½ minutes, stirring once. Add beans and salsa as directed above. Microwave, uncovered, at 100% power 2 minutes, stirring once. Serve as above.

GROUND TURKEY BURGERS

LOW-CALORIE · LOW-CHOLESTEROL

Serve these flavorful burgers with a yogurt-chutney sauce on the side, if you like. Using water and just a small amount of oil to cook the onions makes a leaner burger, as does the ground turkey.

Broil for 8 to 10 minutes.
Makes 4 servings.
Recipe can be halved or doubled.
Nutrient Value Per Serving: 137 calories, 13 g protein, 7 g fat, 5 g carbohydrate, 216 mg sodium, 52 mg cholesterol.

2 medium-size onions, finely chopped
1 tablespoon olive oil
¾ cup water
2 cloves garlic, finely chopped
1¼ pounds ground turkey
3 tablespoons chopped fresh dill
    OR: 1 tablespoon dried
2 tablespoons lowfat plain yogurt
2 tablespoons chutney, chopped
½ teaspoon salt
⅛ teaspoon pepper

1. Cook onion in oil in large skillet, covered, over low heat, stirring occasionally, for 5 minutes. Add ¼ cup of the water; cook, uncovered, until evaporated, about 5 minutes. Repeat, adding remaining water ¼ cup at a time. Add garlic; cook 2 minutes longer. Transfer to large bowl.
2. When mixture has cooled, add turkey, dill, yogurt, chutney, salt and pepper. Form into 4 equal patties, ¾ inch thick.
3. Preheat broiler. Spray broiler-pan rack with nonstick vegetable-oil cooking spray.
4. Broil 6 inches from heat for 5 minutes. Turn burgers over; broil 3 to 5 minutes longer or until cooked through.

RAVIOLI WITH TURKEY AND MUSHROOM FILLING

Makes 4 servings.
Recipe can be halved or doubled.
Nutrient Value Per Serving: 619 calories, 33 g protein, 20 g fat, 73 g carbohydrate, 698 mg sodium, 78 mg cholesterol.

Ravioli:
½ cup finely chopped shallots (about 6)
    OR: green onion
2 tablespoons olive oil
2 cloves garlic, finely chopped
8 ounces domestic mushrooms, trimmed and very thinly sliced (2½ cups)
4 ounces shiitake mushrooms, trimmed and very thinly sliced (1½ cups)
½ teaspoon salt
⅛ teaspoon pepper
2 tablespoons bourbon OR: chicken broth
12 ounces ground turkey
2 tablespoons chopped parsley
1 teaspoon fresh sage leaves, finely chopped OR: ½ teaspoon dried
1 package 3-inch-square wonton wrappers (1 pound)

Sauce:
2 tablespoons finely chopped shallots
    OR: green onion
2 tablespoons *un*salted butter
1 tablespoon all-purpose flour
1 cup chicken broth
1 teaspoon lemon juice
2 tablespoons chopped parsley
Grated Parmesan cheese *(optional)*

1. Prepare Ravioli: Cook shallots in oil in large skillet over low heat, stirring frequently, until soft, about 7 minutes. Add garlic; cook 2 minutes. Add mushrooms, shiitake, ¼ teaspoon salt and the pepper; cover and cook, stirring occasionally, for 10 minutes or until soft. Uncover. Add bourbon; cook 2 minutes. Transfer to large bowl.
2. Add turkey, parsley, sage and remaining salt to bowl; mix well.

(continued)

RAPID RAVIOLI
Prepared wonton wrappers, available at greengrocers and supermarkets, make our ravioli a quick yet elegant dish. If shiitake mushrooms are not available, increase the amount of domestic mushrooms. Substitute ground chicken, beef, pork or veal for the turkey, if you wish. For a special garnish, add sautéed mushrooms and a stalk of broccoli rabe.

TURKEY BURGERS MAKE-AHEAD TIP:
Patties can be assembled an hour or two ahead and refrigerated, covered.

RAVIOLI WITH TURKEY AND MUSHROOM FILLING (*continued*)

3. Lay 24 wonton wrappers on work surface. Spoon generous tablespoon of filling into center of each. Brush edges of wrappers with water. Place second wrapper on top of each, pressing all around the edges with fingers to seal ravioli.

4. Cook ravioli in large pot of boiling salted water until cooked through, about 5 minutes. Drain.

5. Meanwhile, prepare Sauce: Cook shallots in 1 tablespoon butter in large skillet over moderate heat, stirring fre-

quently, for 3 minutes. Stir in flour; cook 2 minutes. Stir in broth. Increase heat to high; cook, stirring occasionally, 4 minutes or until lightly thickened. Stir in lemon juice and parsley. Remove from heat. Swirl in remaining butter. Pour over hot drained ravioli. Pass Parmesan cheese, if you wish.

Make-Ahead Tip: If the wrappers have not been frozen previously, you can freeze the filled ravioli in a single layer on a baking sheet. Transfer to a freezer bag and freeze for up to 3 months. Also, the filling can be made a day ahead and refrigerated.

TURKEY EMPANADAS

You can substitute ground pork or beef for the turkey, and a packaged pastry product for our homemade dough. Try smaller versions for an appetizer.

Bake at 375° for 25 minutes.
Makes 6 servings.
Recipe can be halved or doubled.
Nutrient Value Per Serving: 554 calories, 24 g protein, 30 g fat, 46 g carbohydrate, 491 mg sodium, 123 mg cholesterol.

Dough:
1½ cups all-purpose flour
¾ cup cornmeal
1 tablespoon sugar
1 teaspoon chili powder
¾ teaspoon salt
¼ teaspoon ground cumin
10 tablespoons (1¼ sticks) chilled
    *un*salted butter, cut in pats
1 container (8 ounces) lowfat plain yogurt

Filling:
1¼ pounds ground turkey
1 tablespoon olive oil
3 cloves garlic, chopped
4 green onions, sliced
½ teaspoon leaf oregano, crumbled
¼ teaspoon ground cumin
¼ teaspoon ground allspice
2 tablespoons tomato paste
¼ cup chopped, pitted dry-cured black
    olives OR: canned black olives
1 tablespoon lime juice
1 teaspoon sugar

Egg Glaze:
1 egg
1 teaspoon water

1. Prepare Dough: Combine flour, cornmeal, sugar, chili powder, salt, cumin and butter in food processor. Whirl until texture resembles coarse meal. Add yogurt. Pulse with on-and-off motion just until mixture masses together. Or, mix dry ingredients together in a bowl. Cut in butter until mixture is crumbly. Stir in yogurt.

2. Turn dough out onto lightly floured surface. Divide into 6 equal portions; shape each into a disk. Cover and refrigerate.

3. Meanwhile, prepare Filling: Heat medium-size skillet over medium-high heat. Add turkey; cook, breaking up meat with wooden spoon, until no longer pink, about 6 minutes. Drain turkey in colander. Wipe out skillet with paper toweling.

4. Heat oil in skillet over medium heat. Add garlic, green onion, oregano, cumin and allspice; cook, stirring, 3 minutes. Remove from heat. Stir in tomato paste. Stir in drained turkey, olives, lime juice and sugar.

5. Preheat oven to moderate (375°).

(continued)

(continued)

SAUCE FOR EMPANADAS
Serve these cumin- and allspice-seasoned pastry turnovers with salsa and nonfat sour cream on the side.

TURKEY EMPANADAS (*continued*)

Lightly spray baking sheet with nonstick vegetable-oil cooking spray.

6. Roll each round of dough out on lightly floured surface into an 8-inch circle. Spoon about ½ cup of filling on one-half of each round, leaving 1-inch border. Stir together egg and water in small bowl to make Egg Glaze. Brush border with Egg Glaze. Fold dough over filling, pressing out all air. Crimp edges with fork or fingers to seal. Place on baking sheet. Brush Egg Glaze lightly over empanadas.

7. Bake in preheated moderate oven (375°) for 25 minutes or until golden. Serve hot or warm, with plain yogurt.

EMPANADA MAKE-AHEAD TIP:

The dough can be prepared up to 2 days ahead and refrigerated, wrapped, while the filling can be prepared the day before. The cooked, filled empanadas can be frozen in a single layer on a baking sheet, and then stored in a freezer bag. Reheat in a preheated moderate oven (375°).

PAINTING PARTY

Cornmeal Parmesan Pretzels (100)

Guacamole (88) with Vegetable Dippers

Turkey Empanadas (283)

Fudgy Brownies (521)

TURKEY SAUSAGE BREAKFAST PATTIES

LOW-CALORIE · QUICK

*S*tart the day with this leaner version of a breakfast favorite, with sautéed apples and maple syrup, or serve for brunch, lunch or a light dinner. Use also as a filling for stuffed vegetables.

Makes 12 patties (2 patties per serving). Recipe can be halved or doubled.
Nutrient Value Per Pattie: 121 calories, 11 g protein, 5 g fat, 7 g carbohydrate, 343 mg sodium, 41 mg cholesterol.

TURKEY SAUSAGE BREAKFAST PATTIES MAKE-AHEAD TIP:

The patties can be prepared a day ahead and refrigerated, covered. Or, freeze uncooked patties on waxed-paper-lined baking sheets until solid. Double wrap in plastic bags and freeze for up to 3 months. Thaw in refrigerator in single layer and cook as in Step 4.

½ cup old-fashioned oats
2 egg whites
2 tablespoons maple syrup
½ teaspoon liquid red-pepper seasoning
1½ teaspoons salt
¾ teaspoon rubbed sage
¼ teaspoon ground nutmeg
¼ teaspoon ground ginger
1½ pounds ground turkey
½ Granny Smith apple, cored and shredded
½ cup finely chopped onion (1 medium-size)
3 tablespoons all-purpose flour
Vegetable oil, for frying

1. Place oats in food processor or blender. Whirl until texture of coarse meal.

2. Stir together egg whites, maple syrup, red-pepper seasoning, salt, sage, nutmeg and ginger in large bowl. Add turkey, apple, onion and oats.

3. Divide mixture into 12 equal portions (3 ounces each) and shape into patties. Dredge lightly in flour and place on waxed paper.

4. Heat 1 teaspoon oil in large nonstick skillet. Add patties; fry over medium-high heat for 6 minutes or until browned on both sides, turning over once. Add more oil, as needed.

MORNING WAKE-UP CALL

Potato and Red Onion Frittata (445)

Turkey Sausage Breakfast Patties (this page)

Berry Peachy Fizz (549)

GROUND TURKEY AND HAM MINI-LOAVES

LOW-CALORIE

Ground turkey and turkey-ham are used to good advantage in these single-serving loaves. Serve with baked potato and green beans. Not only are these a tasty entree, but they are equally delicious packed whole for picnics, or sliced as an appetizer or for sandwiches.

Bake at 350° for 35 minutes.
Makes 6 mini-loaves.
Recipe can be halved or doubled.
Nutrient Value Per Loaf: 315 calories, 27 g protein, 14 g fat, 20 g carbohydrate, 980 mg sodium, 118 mg cholesterol.

Mini-Loaves:
2 teaspoons dry mustard
2 teaspoons water
¾ cup old-fashioned oats
1 tablespoon olive oil OR: vegetable oil
1 sweet red pepper, cored, seeded and chopped
3 green onions, sliced
2 cloves garlic, chopped
1 teaspoon leaf tarragon, crumbled
¼ teaspoon leaf thyme, crumbled
1 teaspoon salt
1½ pounds ground turkey
¼ pound turkey-ham, finely chopped
1 egg
2 tablespoons catsup

Glaze:
½ cup catsup
2 tablespoons dark brown sugar
1 teaspoon spicy brown mustard

1. Stir together mustard and water in large bowl. Let stand at least 15 minutes. Meanwhile, place oats in food processor or blender. Whirl until texture resembles coarse meal.
2. Heat oil in medium-size skillet over medium heat. Add red pepper; cook 6 minutes. Add green onion, garlic, tarragon, thyme and salt; cook, stirring, 3 minutes. Scrape into large bowl with mustard mixture. Add oats, turkey, turkey-ham, egg and catsup to bowl; mix together.
3. Preheat oven to moderate (350°). Lightly grease $13 \times 9 \times 2$-inch baking pan. Divide mixture into 6 equal portions (6 ounces each) and shape into mini-loaves, about $4 \times 2 \times 1\frac{1}{2}$ inches. Arrange evenly in prepared pan.
4. Bake in preheated moderate oven (350°) for 20 minutes.
5. Meanwhile, prepare Glaze: Stir together catsup, sugar and brown mustard in small bowl until smooth. Spoon evenly over loaves.
6. Bake another 15 minutes or until juices run clear when pierced with skewer. Spoon any leftover Glaze into sauceboat and serve on side with mini-loaves.

MINI-LOAVES MAKE-AHEAD TIP:
The loaves may be shaped a day ahead and refrigerated, covered. The uncooked loaves can be frozen, wrapped, for up to 2 months, then thawed in the refrigerator and baked as at left.

HERB-STUFFED CORNISH HENS WITH POTATOES

Bake at 400° for 1 hour.
Makes 4 servings.
Recipe can be halved or doubled.
Nutrient Value Per Serving: 587 calories, 39 g protein, 36 g fat, 27 g carbohydrate, 694 mg sodium, 145 mg cholesterol.

2 tablespoons olive oil
1½ pounds baking potatoes, pared and sliced ¼ inch thick
2 Cornish game hens (1¼ pounds each)
1 teaspoon salt
4 cloves garlic, peeled
1 teaspoon leaf rosemary, crumbled
2 small whole lemons OR: 1 large lemon, halved

1. Preheat oven to hot (400°). Spread 1 tablespoon oil in bottom of 11 × 7 × 2-inch baking pan.
2. Cook potatoes in large pot of boiling salted water for 10 minutes. Drain; rinse under cold running water. Drain; dry on paper toweling.
3. Sprinkle outside and inside of each hen with salt. Place 2 cloves garlic and ¼ teaspoon rosemary in each cavity. Prick lemon skins in several places with paring knife; place either 1 small or half a large lemon in the cavity of each hen. Truss hens.
4. Arrange potatoes in bottom of prepared pan, slightly overlapping (there will be about 3 layers). Sprinkle with remaining rosemary. Place hens on top; brush lightly with remaining oil.
5. Bake in preheated hot oven (400°) for 1 hour or until golden brown and no longer pink near bone. Serve half a hen per person.

WELCOME CHRISTMAS

Champagne with Salmon Twists (90)

Mushroom and Green Onion Soup (127)

Herb-Stuffed Cornish Hens with Potatoes (this page)

Brussels Sprouts with Roasted Chestnuts (405)

Roasted Beets (400), Steamed Baby Carrots with Lemon-Dill Butter (409), Baked Celery Root (413)

Apple and Pear Salad with Cider Dressing (175)

Lemon Pecan Torte (501)

Cranberry Fool (530)

"Welcome Christmas" Feast (see menu, page 286)

CORNISH HENS WITH GREEN GRAPES

Makes 4 servings.
Recipe can be halved or doubled.
Nutrient Value Per Serving: 455 calories, 36 g protein, 24 g fat, 21 g carbohydrate, 462 mg sodium, 110 mg cholesterol.

2 Cornish game hens (about 1¼ pounds each), split
⅛ teaspoon ground cloves
¼ cup all-purpose flour
2 tablespoons vegetable oil
3 tablespoons Cognac OR: brandy
½ cup white wine
1 small onion, finely chopped
1 cup (8 ounces) seedless green grapes, halved
2 cloves garlic, crushed
¼ teaspoon ground allspice
¼ teaspoon salt
8 peppercorns
1¼ cups reduced-sodium chicken broth
½ cup whole seedless green grapes (optional)

1. Rub hens with cloves. Dredge in flour, shaking off excess. Heat oil in Dutch oven over moderate heat. Add hens; cook until browned, about 4 minutes per side. Remove from pot.
2. Add Cognac and white wine; cook 2 minutes, stirring up any browned bits. Add onion, grape halves, garlic, allspice, salt, peppercorns and chicken broth. Bring to boiling. Add hens. Lower heat; cover and simmer 25 minutes or until hens are cooked through.
3. Remove hens to serving platter. Strain sauce through fine-meshed sieve; skim off fat. Pour sauce over hens. Garnish with whole grapes, if you wish.

BOOK COVER PHOTOGRAPH

Pictured on the cover is the recipe at right. It is served with cooked green beans and rice with sweet peppers. The sauce for the hens can be passed separately.

A WELL-BRED BIRD

Cornish game hens are 5-week-old hens weighing between 1 and 2 pounds, with a direct blood-line to the British poultry breed Cornish. Sold fresh whole or split, or frozen whole, these tiny birds have a fine, dense texture and delicate, sweet taste. One bird is 2 servings or 1 very generous portion.

DUCK STEW WITH WINTER VEGETABLES

LOW-CALORIE

See *"What to Do with Two Ducks?,"* page 290.

Makes 4 servings.
Recipe can be halved or doubled.
Nutrient Value Per Serving: 291 calories, 22 g protein, 14 g fat, 20 g carbohydrate, 353 mg sodium, 83 mg cholesterol.

2 tablespoons olive oil
4 duck legs (about 7 ounces each), skinned
⅓ cup all-purpose flour
8 ounces parsnips, pared and thickly sliced (1 cup)
4 ounces white turnips, pared and cut into 1-inch chunks (¾ cup)
2 carrots, pared and thickly sliced
2 teaspoons sugar
⅓ cup Duck Stock *(see recipe, page 117)* OR: chicken broth
⅓ cup canned crushed tomatoes
¼ teaspoon salt
¼ teaspoon ground allspice
⅛ teaspoon ground nutmeg

1. Heat oil in Dutch oven over moderately high heat. Dredge duck legs in flour. Add to Dutch oven; cook until browned on both sides, about 5 minutes per side. Remove to bowl.
2. Add parsnip, turnip, carrot and sugar to pan. Lower heat to medium; cook, stirring, until vegetables have caramelized, about 5 minutes. Add Duck Stock, tomatoes, salt, allspice, nutmeg and duck legs to pan. Bring to boiling. Lower heat; cover and simmer until tender, about 45 minutes. Skim fat.

Make-Ahead Tip: Prepare a day ahead, cover and refrigerate. Remove fat from top. Reheat.

SAUTÉED DUCK BREASTS WITH ORANGE SAUCE

Be sure to use a light-colored skillet so you can gauge the proper color of the Orange Sauce. Garnish with thin threads of orange rind and serve with rice. The sauce can also be served with a whole roasted duck, sautéed chicken breasts or calf's liver.

Makes 4 servings.
Recipe can be halved or doubled.
Nutrient Value Per Serving: 474 calories, 24 g protein, 36 g fat, 12 g carbohydrate, 199 mg sodium, 105 mg cholesterol.

4 boneless duck breast halves (6 to 7 ounces each)

Orange Sauce:
2 tablespoons sugar
1 tablespoon lemon juice
¾ cup fresh orange juice
½ cup Duck Stock *(see recipe, page 117)* OR: chicken broth
¼ teaspoon grated orange rind
1 teaspoon cornstarch
1 tablespoon cold water

1. Remove as much excess fat from duck breasts as possible without removing skin. Prick skin all over with thin-tined fork. Heat large skillet over moderately high heat. When skillet is hot, add duck breasts, skin-side down. Reduce heat to low; cook 15 minutes, carefully draining fat from skillet several times during cooking. Turn breasts skin-side up; cook 4 to 5 minutes longer or until cooked through. Remove to platter and keep warm.

2. Prepare Orange Sauce: Combine sugar and lemon juice in same skillet over moderately high heat; cook, stirring occasionally, until pale amber, about 4 minutes. Carefully pour in orange juice, stock and orange rind; cook 5 minutes longer or until reduced to ⅔ cup.

3. Stir together cornstarch and water in small cup until smooth. Whisk into sauce mixture. Bring to boiling; boil 1 minute.

4. To serve: Slice duck breasts diagonally across width. Serve 1 sliced breast per person. Pour Orange Sauce over.

CORNBREAD AND DRIED FRUIT STUFFING

LOW-FAT

Bake cornbread at 400° for 20 to 25 minutes.
Toast cubes at 350° for 12 minutes.
Use to stuff turkey or chicken, or bake at
350° for 35 to 40 minutes.
**Makes about 10 cups (enough for a
12-pound turkey).**
Nutrient Value Per Cup: 257 calories,
5 g protein, 8 g fat, 43 g carbohydrate,
359 mg sodium, 25 mg cholesterol.

Cornbread:
1 cup all-purpose flour
1 cup cornmeal
3 tablespoons sugar
1½ teaspoons baking powder
½ teaspoon baking soda
½ teaspoon salt
½ teaspoon sweet paprika
⅛ teaspoon ground hot red pepper
1 cup buttermilk
¼ cup vegetable oil
1 egg

Stuffing:
¾ cup pitted prunes, halved (5 ounces)
⅔ cup dried apricots, halved (4 ounces)
½ cup warm water
1 tablespoon *un*salted butter
1 large onion, finely chopped
2 cloves garlic, thinly sliced
1 cup chicken broth

1. Prepare Cornbread: Preheat oven to
hot (400°). Lightly grease 9 × 9 × 2-
inch-square baking pan.
2. Stir together flour, cornmeal, sugar,
baking powder, baking soda, salt,
paprika and ground red pepper in large
bowl. Whisk together buttermilk, oil
and egg in small bowl. Stir into flour
mixture just until no lumps remain.
Pour into prepared pan.
3. Bake in preheated hot oven (400°)
for 20 to 25 minutes or until golden
and wooden pick inserted in center
comes out clean. Cool in pan on wire

rack to room temperature. Invert.
When completely cool, cut cornbread
into 1-inch cubes. Place on baking
sheet. Bake in preheated moderate oven
(350°) for 12 minutes to dry out.
4. Prepare Stuffing: Combine prunes
and apricots in medium-size bowl. Add
the warm water; set aside. Heat butter
in large skillet over low heat. Add
onion and garlic; sauté for 10 to 12
minutes or until very soft. Transfer mixture to very large bowl. Add cornbread
cubes, chicken broth, prunes and apricots with soaking water; mix.
5. Stuff turkey or chicken and roast
according to your favorite recipe or ours
(*Roast Turkey with Wild and Pecan Rice
Stuffing, page 263*). Or, spoon into
greased 13 × 9 × 2-inch baking dish.
Bake, covered, in preheated moderate
oven (350°) for 35 to 40 minutes or
until heated through. Uncover for last
10 minutes for a crispy top.

STUFFING SHORTCUT
If you don't wish to
prepare your own
cornbread, use 8 cups
of packaged pre-
pared cornbread
stuffing and skip the
toasting in Step 3.

ORZO AND SPINACH STUFFING

LOW-CHOLESTEROL

Use to stuff turkey or chicken, or bake at 375° for 40 minutes.
Makes 6 cups (enough for an 8-to-10 pound turkey).
Nutrient Value Per Cup: 266 calories, 10 g protein, 7 g fat, 45 g carbohydrate, 338 mg sodium, 0 mg cholesterol.

½ cup chopped green onion (both white and green parts)
2 cloves garlic, finely chopped
1 tablespoon olive oil
1 package (10 ounces) frozen chopped spinach, thawed and drained
¼ teaspoon sugar
1 can (14½ ounces) chicken broth
1 cup water
1¼ cups uncooked orzo
¾ teaspoon grated lemon rind
½ teaspoon leaf marjoram, crumbled
2 teaspoons lemon juice
½ cup raisins
¼ cup pine nuts OR: almonds

1. Cook onion and garlic in oil in large skillet over moderate heat, stirring occasionally, for 2 minutes. Add spinach and sugar; cook 4 minutes or until spinach is heated through.
2. Bring chicken broth and water to boiling in large saucepan. Add orzo, lemon rind and marjoram. Lower heat; simmer, uncovered, until tender, about 10 minutes. Stir in lemon juice, raisins, pine nuts and spinach mixture.
3. Stuff turkey or chicken and roast according to your favorite recipe or ours (*Roast Turkey with Wild and Pecan Rice Stuffing, page 263*). Or spoon stuffing into lightly buttered 13×9×2-inch baking dish. Bake, covered, in pre-heated moderate oven (375°) for 40 minutes or until heated through. Uncover last 10 minutes for crusty top.

ENOUGH STUFFING

Amount of Stuffing	Size of Bird It Will Stuff	Number of Servings
2 cups	3 to 4 pounds	2 to 3
3 cups	5 to 6 pounds	4 to 5
4 cups	6 to 8 pounds	6
6 cups	8 to 10 pounds	8
8 cups	10 to 12 pounds	10
12 cups	12 to 15 pounds	12 to 14
16 cups	15 to 20 pounds	18 to 20

SAUSAGE AND FRUIT STUFFING

Serve with roast chicken, turkey or pork.

Use to stuff turkey or chicken, or bake at 325° for 40 minutes.
Makes about 10 cups (enough for a 12-pound turkey).
Nutrient Value Per Cup: 312 calories, 10 g protein, 20 g fat, 22 g carbohydrate, 599 mg sodium, 69 mg cholesterol.

1 pound sweet Italian sausage
¼ cup (½ stick) *un*salted butter
2 stalks celery, chopped
1 large onion, diced
1 red apple, cored and chopped
1 pear, cored and chopped
½ cup dried apricots, chopped
¼ teaspoon leaf thyme, crumbled
¼ teaspoon salt
¼ teaspoon pepper
10 cups white bread cubes (about 15 slices)
¼ cup chopped parsley
1 egg, slightly beaten

1. Remove and discard casings from sausages. Crumble sausage into large saucepan. Cook over medium heat until sausage is browned. With slotted spoon, remove sausage from saucepan.
2. To drippings in pan, add butter, celery, onion, apple, pear, apricots, thyme, salt and pepper; cook, stirring occasionally, until vegetables and fruit are soft, about 10 minutes. Remove from heat. Stir in bread cubes, parsley, egg and sausage until well mixed.
3. Stuff chicken or turkey and roast according to your favorite recipe or ours (*Roast Turkey with Wild and Pecan Rice Stuffing, page 263*). Or, spoon stuffing into greased, shallow 2-quart baking dish. Bake, covered, in preheated slow oven (325°) for 40 minutes or until heated through. Uncover for the last 10 minutes of baking time for a crusty top.

Sausage and Fruit Stuffing (this page).

Rye Bread and Cabbage Stuffing (page 294).

WILD AND PECAN RICE STUFFING

The wild rice is extended with pecan or white rice. Serve as a side dish with roast meats such as pork or use to stuff a turkey or chicken.

WILD AND PECAN RICE STUFFING MAKE-AHEAD TIP:

The rice mixture can be made a day ahead and refrigerated, covered. Bring to room temperature before stuffing the bird.

Makes about 7 cups (enough for a 10-pound turkey).
Nutrient Value Per ½ Cup: 204 calories, 4 g protein, 13 g fat, 19 g carbohydrate, 436 mg sodium, 21 mg cholesterol.

¾ cup wild rice
3 cups chicken broth
1 cup dry white wine
8 tablespoons (1 stick) *un*salted butter
1 cup pecans, chopped
½ cup finely chopped cooked ham
2 Granny Smith apples, cored and chopped
¼ teaspoon ground cinnamon
2 tablespoons orange-flavored liqueur (optional)
½ teaspoon salt
¼ teaspoon pepper
¾ cup pecan rice *(see page 209)* OR: white rice

1. Pick over wild rice. Rinse in bowl of cold water. Drain in fine-mesh sieve.
2. Combine wild rice, broth, wine and 2 tablespoons butter in large saucepan. Bring to boiling. Lower heat and simmer, covered, for 40 minutes.
3. While rice is cooking, melt remaining 6 tablespoons butter in large skillet over medium heat. Add pecans; sauté until lightly browned, 3 to 4 minutes. Add ham, apples and cinnamon; sauté until apples are almost cooked, about 5 minutes. Add liqueur if using, salt and pepper; cook 3 minutes. Set aside.
4. Add pecan rice to wild rice. Simmer, covered, another 20 minutes or until rice is done.
5. Drain remaining liquid from rice. Return rice to saucepan. Stir in ham mixture.

6. Or use to stuff turkey or chicken and roast according to your favorite recipe or ours (*Roast Turkey with Wild and Pecan Rice Stuffing, page 263*).

RYE BREAD AND CABBAGE STUFFING

Equally good with roast turkey, chicken or pork. (Pictured on page 293.)

Use to stuff turkey or chicken, or bake at 325° for 40 minutes.
Makes 9 cups (enough for a 10- to 12-pound turkey).
Nutrient Value Per Cup: 200 calories, 4 g protein, 11 g fat, 24 g carbohydrate, 552 mg sodium, 27 mg cholesterol.

½ cup (1 stick) *un*salted butter
1 small head green cabbage, thinly sliced (about 12 cups)
1 large onion, chopped
10 cups rye bread cubes (about 12 slices)
2 tablespoons chopped parsley
1 teaspoon salt
¼ teaspoon ground black pepper
1 cup water

1. Melt butter in large saucepan. Add cabbage and onion; cook, stirring occasionally, until cabbage is tender and lightly browned. Remove saucepan from heat. Add bread cubes, parsley, salt and pepper and mix well.
2. Add the water; toss to moisten.
3. Stuff the turkey or chicken and roast according to your favorite recipe or ours (*Roast Turkey with Wild and Pecan Rice Stuffing, page 263*). Or, spoon the stuffing into a greased, shallow 2-quart baking dish. Bake, covered, in a preheated moderate oven (325°) for 40 minutes or until heated through. Uncover for the last 10 minutes of baking for a crusty top.

Flounder Stuffed with Vegetables
(page 301)

CHAPTER 8

FISH AND SHELLFISH

FISH AND SHELLFISH PRIMER

FISH FARMING

What: Aquaculture, the raising of seafood in a controlled environment, is a relatively new industry in the United States and one that is rapidly growing with improved technology. The aim of fish farming is to ensure a steadier supply of fresh fish throughout the year, regardless of season, and to help keep the price of seafood down.

Where: In the United States, catfish, crayfish, rainbow trout and oysters are the primary farm-raised species. Much of the salmon and shrimp available in our fish markets has been imported from farms overseas, but it is expected that aquaculture in this country will expand to include these species and others as we improve our methods of farming.

Why: In addition to those fish mentioned above, aquaculture allows for the development of hybrid fish that are less bony, more meaty and more flavorful, and it also enables the introduction and increased availability of once-exotic fish, such as sweet, white-fleshed tilapia. As fish farming continues to develop, aquaculturists hope to duplicate natural environments more accurately to improve diet and disease resistance in species farmed, and to improve the quality, flavor and nutritional value of the fish.

HOW TO BUY AND STORE FISH

■ Whenever possible, buy fish openly displayed on ice in refrigerated cases in a fish market or good supermarket. Whole fish should have bright eyes that bulge a little, shiny scales and red gills. Fillets, steaks and other cuts should be unblemished, without tears, translucent and firm yet springy to the touch (even through any plastic wrap). Avoid fresh fish that smells "fishy" or like ammonia, or is discolored around the edges. Fresh ocean fish smells briny.

■ To store whole fish or parts, rinse with cold water, place in airtight plastic bag and refrigerate at about 32°F. until ready to cook. Store fresh fish no more than one day.

■ Frozen fish should be chosen using the same criteria as all frozen foods: The package should be intact and frozen solid in a tight wrapping with no ice crystals and no discoloration. Avoid packages that are above the frost line in a store's display freezer. Store frozen fish in a cold freezer (0°F) in original wrapping for up to six months. Place package on a plate and thaw overnight in the refrigerator. For a hurry-up defrost, thaw in original wrapper under cold running water. Or thaw in a microwave oven following manufacturer's directions.

■ Wash hands, cutting boards, knives and other utensils thoroughly with hot soapy water before and after handling raw seafood.

FATTY FISH FACTS

Seafood has earned its reputation as a lowfat, high-protein addition to our diet.

■ Very lean, white-fleshed fish, such as flounder, sole, red snapper and sea bass, contain only 1 gram of fat and provide fewer than 100 calories per 3-ounce serving.

■ Fattier, oily fish such as tuna, trout, catfish, bluefish and salmon are slightly higher in calories and contain 3 to 7 grams of fat per serving.

■ Both lean and fatty fish contain an average of 50 mg of cholesterol in a 3-ounce serving.

■ The fat in fish is rich in healthful omega-3 fatty acids. Omega-3 refers to the chemical structure of a particular type of polyunsaturated fat found in all seafood that helps improve blood flow to the heart.

■ Shellfish are low in calories and fat. Crustaceans (lobster, shrimp, crab and crayfish) are generally higher in cholesterol than most mollusks (clams, mussels and oysters) and fin fish.

■ Shrimp has more cholesterol than light or dark meat chicken, but less saturated and total fat.

HOW TO BUY AND STORE SHELLFISH

Shellfish is the overall name for a variety of edibles from the sea. *Crustaceans* include shrimp, crayfish, crabs and lobster. In the large *mollusk* family are clams, oysters, mussels and scallops, as well as octopus and squid.

■ Live shellfish should be active, or at least react by moving when prodded. Bivalves—mollusks with two shells, such as mussels, clams and oysters—must have tightly-closed, unbroken shells.

■ Place live shellfish on top of wet paper towels in open plastic or paper bags in the refrigerator; they need air and moisture. Clams, oysters and mussels can keep for one or two days. Cook lobsters and crabs on the day you buy them.

■ Picked, cooked crabmeat is graded: The choicest is lumpmeat or backfin; special grade includes lumpmeat and flakes from the whole body; regular or flake crabmeat consists of meat from the entire body except the lumpmeat. Refrigerate fresh crabmeat and use as soon as possible.

Broiled Bluefish with Fennel and Tomato

LOW-CALORIE

The flavor of tomatoes and fennel is a wonderful complement to bluefish. Serve with fresh corn on the cob and new potatoes.

Broil for 6 minutes; then bake at 400° for 6 to 8 minutes.
Makes 6 servings.
Recipe can be halved or doubled.
Nutrient Value Per Serving: 322 calories, 33 g protein, 16 g fat, 11 g carbohydrate, 713 mg sodium, 89 mg cholesterol.

4 tablespoons olive oil
1 medium-large fennel bulb (about 12 ounces), cut into ¼-inch-thick slices
1 large onion, finely chopped
2 cans (14½ ounces each) tomatoes in juice, drained and chopped
3 cloves garlic, finely chopped
½ teaspoon leaf thyme, crumbled
1 bay leaf
4 tablespoons finely chopped fresh basil
    OR: 1¼ teaspoons dried
½ teaspoon salt
¼ teaspoon pepper
1 cup Fish Stock (*see recipe, page 119*)
    OR: chicken broth
2 pounds bluefish fillets
¼ teaspoon fennel seeds, crushed

1. Heat 3 tablespoons oil in medium-size saucepan over medium heat until hot. Add fennel; sauté for 5 minutes or until golden. Transfer to plate; keep warm.
2. Add onion to saucepan; sauté 3 minutes. Add tomatoes, 2 cloves garlic, the thyme, bay leaf, 2 tablespoons basil, ¼ teaspoon salt, ⅛ teaspoon pepper and stock to saucepan. Bring to boiling. Lower heat; simmer, covered, stirring occasionally, for 20 minutes. Remove and discard bay leaf.
3. Preheat broiler.

4. Season bluefish with remaining olive oil, garlic, salt and pepper and the fennel seeds. Arrange on broiler-pan rack.
5. Broil fish 4 inches from heat for 6 minutes or until browned. Reduce oven temperature to 400°. Bake fish for 6 to 8 minutes more or until it flakes easily when tested with fork.
6. Arrange fish on platter. Spoon fennel and tomato sauce over and around fish. Sprinkle with remaining basil.

Make-Ahead Tip: The sauce can be prepared a day ahead and refrigerated.

BLUEFISH
Found along the Atlantic coast, bluefish has soft-textured, flaky, dark flesh that is very oily and full-flavored. Remove the darker strip of flesh that runs down the center of the fillet before cooking as it may have a strong "fishy" flavor. Bluefish is best when baked, broiled or grilled.

CATFISH AND BLACK BEAN STEW

LOW-CALORIE · LOW-CHOLESTEROL
QUICK

Makes 4 servings.
Recipe can be halved or doubled.
Nutrient Value Per Serving: 318 calories,
28 g protein, 12 g fat, 24 g carbohydrate,
595 mg sodium, 66 mg cholesterol.

2 tablespoons olive oil
1 large onion, finely chopped
1 large sweet green pepper, cored,
    seeded and cut into ½-inch dice
2 cloves garlic, finely chopped
1 can (15 ounces) black beans, rinsed
    and drained
½ cup chopped canned tomato
½ cup clam broth
¼ teaspoon leaf oregano, crumbled
1 pound catfish fillets
⅛ teaspoon ground allspice
⅛ teaspoon ground cloves
⅛ teaspoon ground hot red pepper

1. Heat 2 teaspoons oil in large skillet over low heat. Add onion; cover and cook, stirring occasionally, for 7 minutes or until tender. Add green pepper, garlic and 1 teaspoon oil; cover and cook, stirring occasionally, 5 minutes. Stir in beans, tomato, clam broth and oregano; cover and cook 5 minutes over moderate heat.

2. Meanwhile, rub catfish with allspice, cloves and ground red pepper. Heat remaining tablespoon oil in second large skillet over high heat. Add fish; sauté on one side until fish has colored, about 3 minutes. Turn fish over and place, colored-side up, on top of beans in first skillet. Cover and cook over moderate heat for 5 to 7 minutes or until fish is cooked through.

CATFISH STEW SERVING IDEAS
Serve with basmati or plain white rice, and an assortment of steamed vegetables. Mackerel, red snapper or sea bass can be substituted for the catfish.

CATFISH STEW MAKE-AHEAD TIP:
The black bean mixture can be prepared up to 2 days ahead and refrigerated, covered.

CATFISH
A firm, white-fleshed fish with a pleasant, almost sweet taste. Most catfish are farm-raised in freshwater ponds in the American South and sold as fillets. Both mild and spicy flavoring suit catfish, and almost any cooking method is appropriate.

PAN-FRIED CATFISH WITH CORNMEAL CRUST

LOW-CALORIE · LOW-CHOLESTEROL

*O*ften the best way to cook something is the simplest—here's a good example. Serve the catfish with homemade tartar or horse-radish sauce. If catfish is unavailable, substitute sole or flounder. Serve with Hush Puppies (see page 80).

Makes 4 servings.
Recipe can be halved or doubled.
Nutrient Value Per Serving: 299 calories, 26 g protein, 13 g fat, 19 g carbohydrate, 232 mg sodium, 75 mg cholesterol.

4 catfish fillets (4 to 5 ounces each)
1 cup buttermilk
¼ teaspoon salt
⅔ cup cornmeal
2 tablespoons oil

1. Place catfish fillets in buttermilk in shallow dish. Refrigerate 30 minutes. Remove catfish from milk; sprinkle with salt. Dip fish in cornmeal to coat both sides.
2. Heat oil in large skillet over moderately high heat. Add catfish. Reduce heat to moderate; cook until browned, about 3 minutes. Turn fish over carefully; cook 3 minutes or until browned and cooked through. With spatula, carefully transfer to serving plates. Serve.

FRIDAY FISH FRY

Pan-Fried Catfish with Cornmeal Crust (this page)

Coleslaw

Oranges in Caramel Sauce (525)

COD WITH ALMONDS

QUICK

What could be easier than this flash-in-the-pan fish preparation—extra tasty when made in an iron skillet over a campfire.

Makes 4 servings.
Recipe can be halved or doubled.
Nutrient Value Per Serving: 335 calories, 34 g protein, 19 g fat, 7 g carbohydrate, 703 mg sodium, 89 mg cholesterol.

---

2 tablespoons cornstarch
1 teaspoon salt
4 cod fillets (about 5 to 6 ounces each)
1 tablespoon olive oil
2 tablespoons *un*salted butter
½ cup slivered almonds
1 tablespoon chopped parsley
1 teaspoon lemon juice
Lemon wedges, for garnish

1. Combine cornstarch and salt on waxed paper. Dip each cod fillet in cornstarch mixture to coat; set aside.
2. Heat oil and 1 tablespoon butter in large skillet over medium-high heat. Add fillets, half at a time; cook 5 to 6 minutes, turning once. With slotted spatula, remove cod fillets to platter; keep warm.
3. Heat remaining 1 tablespoon butter in skillet. Add almonds; cook 3 minutes or until almonds are lightly browned. Stir in parsley and lemon juice. Spoon sauce over cod fillets. Garnish platter with lemon wedges.

BAKED COD WITH HERBED CRUMB TOPPING

LOW-CALORIE · LOW-FAT
LOW-CHOLESTEROL · QUICK

Mild cod fillets benefit from the flavorful rosemary and mustard seasoning in this dish. Try the same topping with other thick fish fillets, such as tilefish or grouper.

Bake at 400° for 17 minutes.
Makes 4 servings.
Recipe can be halved or doubled.
Nutrient Value Per Serving: 184 calories, 26 g protein, 5 g fat, 7 g carbohydrate, 246 mg sodium, 61 mg cholesterol.

1 tablespoon Dijon-style mustard
1 tablespoon lemon juice
4 cod fillets (about 5 to 6 ounces each)
1 cup fresh dry bread crumbs
2 tablespoons chopped parsley
1 tablespoon finely cut chives OR: green
    onion tops
1½ teaspoons chopped fresh rosemary
    OR: ½ teaspoon dried
1 tablespoon olive oil

1. Preheat oven to hot (400°). Lightly grease baking dish.
2. Stir together mustard and ¾ tea-spoon lemon juice in small bowl. Spread mustard mixture over tops of fish fillets. Mix together crumbs, parsley, chives, rosemary, oil and remaining lemon juice in small bowl. Press mixture firmly into mustard-covered tops of fillets. Transfer to prepared baking dish.
3. Bake in preheated hot oven (400°) for about 17 minutes or until top is lightly browned and fish is cooked through.

GONE FISHIN' DINNER

Baked Cod with Herbed Crumb Topping (this page)

Gingered Broccoli and Grapefruit (403)

Mixed Green Salad with Buttermilk Dressing with Dill (177)

Orange Sherbet with Raspberries

FLOUNDER STUFFED WITH VEGETABLES

LOW-CALORIE

This stuffing method would also work well with sole or any thin, delicate fish fillets. Garnish with lemon zest and fennel fronds or frilly lettuce. Try the fennel butter on other fish or on grilled or broiled chicken breasts. (Pictured on page 295.)

Bake at 400° for 16 minutes.
Makes 4 servings.
Recipe can be halved or doubled.
Nutrient Value Per Serving: 196 calories, 27 g protein, 8 g fat, 3 g carbohydrate, 347 mg sodium, 84 mg cholesterol.

1 carrot, pared
½ bulb fennel (5 ounces)
½ sweet red pepper, cored and seeded
2 tablespoons *un*salted butter
1 teaspoon grated lemon rind
¼ teaspoon salt
⅛ teaspoon pepper
4 flounder fillets (1¼ pounds)

1. Preheat oven to hot (400°). Coat 13 × 9 × 2-inch baking dish with non-stick vegetable-oil cooking spray.
2. Cut carrot into 3 × ⅜-inch strips; reserve. Chop 1 tablespoon feathery fennel tops; reserve. Cut fennel and red pepper into 3 × ⅜-inch strips.

(continued)

FLOUNDER
A mild-flavored, lean saltwater flatfish, flounder has a delicate texture. Many of the varieties of "sole" found in fish markets actually are types of flounder. Most are sold whole or as skinned, boneless fillets and there are only subtle differences among the species. Bake, steam or grill whole flounder; poach, sauté, steam or roll up and bake fillets.

FLOUNDER STUFFED WITH VEGETABLES
(*continued*)

3. Heat 1 tablespoon butter in large skillet over medium heat. Add carrot, fennel and red pepper. Reduce heat to low; sauté 8 minutes until crisp-tender.
4. Combine remaining butter, lemon rind, salt, pepper and reserved chopped fennel tops. Set aside.
5. Cut flounder fillets in half lengthwise. Place, skin-side up, on work surface. Divide vegetable mixture evenly among fillets, placing 1½ inches down from thick end. Starting at thick end, roll fillets up jelly-roll fashion. Place, seam-side down, in prepared baking dish. Cover pan with aluminum foil.
6. Bake in preheated hot oven (400°) for 15 minutes. Remove foil. Spread fennel butter over fish. Bake, uncovered, until fish is cooked through, about 1 minute.

Make-Ahead Tip: The fennel butter can be made a day ahead and refrigerated, covered.

Microwave Directions (High Power Oven):
Place 1 tablespoon butter in microwave-safe 13 × 9 × 2-inch baking dish. Microwave, uncovered, 45 to 60 seconds to melt. Stir in carrot, fennel and red pepper. Cover with microwave-safe plastic wrap. Microwave at 100% power 5 minutes. Pierce plastic wrap. Carefully uncover. Assemble flounder rolls as in Step 5. Place in same baking dish. Re-cover with microwave-safe plastic wrap. Microwave at 100% power 5½ minutes. Pierce wrap. Carefully uncover. Spread with fennel butter. Microwave, uncovered, at 100% power 30 seconds.

MAKE IT WITH MAYONNAISE

Horseradish mayonnaise is an easy treatment for any thin fish fillets, such as perch or sole. If using fish thicker than ½ inch, broil first briefly, then top with mayonnaise and continue with recipe.

FLOUNDER WITH HORSERADISH MAYONNAISE

LOW-CHOLESTEROL · QUICK

Broil 6 minutes.
Makes 4 servings.
Recipe can be halved or doubled.
Nutrient Value Per Serving: 236 calories, 22 g protein, 16 g fat, 1 g carbohydrate, 198 mg sodium, 65 mg cholesterol.

⅓ cup mayonnaise
1 clove garlic, finely chopped
1 tablespoon chopped parsley
2 teaspoons drained prepared horseradish
1 teaspoon grated lemon rind
⅛ teaspoon pepper
4 flounder fillets (1 pound)

1. Combine mayonnaise, garlic, parsley, horseradish, lemon rind and pepper in small bowl.
2. Preheat broiler. Grease broiler pan. Place fish on pan. Spread mayonnaise mixture on each fillet to ¼ inch from edge.
3. Broil 4 inches from heat for 6 minutes or until fish is cooked through and top is browned and bubbly.

FISH WITH A KICK

Flounder with Horseradish Mayonnaise (this page)

Rice with Red Pepper

Steamed Carrots

Sautéed Apples

PAN-FRIED FLOUNDER WITH ALMONDS AND SAGE

QUICK

This recipe can be used for any thin fish fillets that cook quickly. Experiment with other nuts and herbs.

Makes 4 servings.
Recipe can be halved or doubled.
Nutrient Value Per Serving: 320 calories, 29 g protein, 20 g fat, 6 g carbohydrate, 310 mg sodium, 84 mg cholesterol.

1 clove garlic
⅓ cup almonds
2 tablespoons all-purpose flour
1 tablespoon leaf sage, crumbled
1 tablespoon fresh parsley leaves
¼ teaspoon salt
⅛ teaspoon pepper
4 flounder fillets (1¼ pounds)
2 tablespoons *un*salted butter
2 tablespoons olive oil

1. Place garlic in small food processor or blender. Whirl until finely chopped. Add almonds, flour, sage, parsley, salt and pepper. Whirl until almonds are finely chopped. Remove mixture to sheet of waxed paper. Coat fillets on both sides, pressing nut mixture onto fillets.

2. Heat 1 tablespoon each butter and oil in large skillet over medium heat. Add 2 fillets; cook 3 to 4 minutes or until golden brown. Carefully turn fish over; cook another 3 to 4 minutes or until fish is cooked through, reducing heat if necessary. Transfer fish to platter and keep warm. Wipe skillet out with paper toweling. Repeat with remaining butter, oil and fish. Serve immediately.

DINNER ON CAPE COD

Pan-Fried Flounder with Almonds and Sage (this page)

Crab and Corn Cakes (335) with Tartar Sauce

Apple Coleslaw with Sweet and Sour Dressing (152)

Zucchini with Lemon (449)

Blueberry-Peach Cobbler (527)

Poached Halibut with Tomatoes and Black Olives (page 305)

POACHED HALIBUT WITH TOMATOES AND BLACK OLIVES

LOW-CALORIE · LOW-CHOLESTEROL

Any firm-fleshed white fish would work in this dish, and poaching keeps the fish moist. Serve with steamed new potatoes for soaking up the sauce and a green bean salad for crunch. (Pictured on page 304).

Bake at 350° for 20 minutes.
Makes 6 servings.
Recipe can be halved or doubled.
Nutrient Value Per Serving: 241 calories, 27 g protein, 9 g fat, 12 g carbohydrate, 594 mg sodium, 39 mg cholesterol.

2 tablespoons olive oil
2 medium-size yellow onions, sliced
3 cloves garlic, finely chopped
½ cup dry white wine
1 can (28 ounces) crushed tomatoes, in puree
1½ teaspoons chopped fresh basil OR: ½ teaspoon dried
1½ teaspoons chopped fresh thyme OR: ½ teaspoon dried
½ teaspoon salt
¼ teaspoon black pepper
4 tablespoons chopped fresh basil OR: parsley
6 halibut steaks (about 2 pounds)
1 teaspoon lemon juice, or to taste
24 pitted oil-cured black olives

1. Preheat oven to moderate (350°).
2. Heat oil in medium-size saucepan over medium heat. Add onion; sauté 3 minutes or until softened. Add garlic; sauté 1 minute. Add wine; cook until liquid is reduced to 1 tablespoon, stirring to prevent scorching. Add tomatoes, 1½ teaspoons basil, thyme, ¼ teaspoon salt and ⅛ teaspoon pepper. Bring to boiling. Lower heat; simmer, stirring occasionally, for 10 minutes. Stir in 3 tablespoons chopped fresh basil.

3. Meanwhile, sprinkle halibut with lemon juice and remaining salt and pepper.
4. Spoon half the sauce in bottom of flameproof 11 × 7 × 2-inch baking pan or other 2-quart pan. Arrange fish over sauce. Top with remaining sauce. Bring to simmering on top of stove.
5. Bake, covered with aluminum foil, in preheated moderate oven (350°) for 10 minutes. Add olives. Bake for 10 minutes or until fish flakes easily when tested with fork.
6. Arrange fish on platter and keep warm. Cook sauce in baking pan over medium heat on stove top until thick. Spoon over fish. Garnish with remaining tablespoon basil.

Make-Ahead Tip: The sauce can be prepared up to a day ahead and refrigerated, covered.
Microwave Directions (High Power Oven):
Ingredient Changes: Reduce wine to 2 tablespoons; reduce crushed tomatoes to 1½ cups; reduce fresh basil and thyme *each* to 1 teaspoon; reduce salt to ¼ teaspoon and pepper to ⅛ teaspoon.
Directions: Combine onion, garlic and oil in microwave-safe 4-cup measure. Microwave, uncovered, 4 minutes, stirring once. Add wine, tomatoes, 1½ teaspoons basil, thyme, salt and pepper. Cover with microwave-safe plastic wrap. Microwave at 100% power 4 minutes. Stir in 3 tablespoons chopped fresh basil. Spoon half the sauce into a microwave-safe 2-quart casserole. Sprinkle halibut with lemon juice; arrange over sauce. Top with remaining sauce. Cover with waxed paper. Microwave at 100% power 5 minutes. Sprinkle with olives. Re-cover. Microwave at 100% power 2 minutes or until fish flakes easily when tested with fork. Garnish with remaining 1 tablespoon chopped basil.

HALIBUT
A deep-water fish, technically a flounder, halibut is found in the Atlantic and Pacific oceans. Unlike most forms of flounder, halibut is large enough to be cut into steaks. Its firm, sweet flesh lends itself to poaching, steaming, baking, broiling, sautéing and grilling and can be cut into cubes and skewered for kabobs.

CURRIED MACKEREL

Mackerel combines well with the strong flavor of curry, and apple adds a gentle note of sweetness. Any robust-flavored fish, such as bluefish, can be substituted for the mackerel. Serve with rice pilaf or, for a special occasion, saffron rice.

Makes 6 servings.
Recipe can be halved or doubled.
Nutrient Value Per Serving: 476 calories, 31 g protein, 33 g fat, 13 g carbohydrate, 625 mg sodium, 117 mg cholesterol.

2 pounds mackerel fillets
1¼ teaspoons curry powder
½ teaspoon salt
¼ teaspoon pepper

MACKEREL

Soft-fleshed and somewhat fatty, mackerel must be eaten very fresh. Chub mackerel, from the Pacific Ocean, are similar to Atlantic varieties, but smaller. Both have pink-gray flesh that turns white when cooked. Spanish mackerel have paler flesh and milder flavor. All can be braised, stewed, baked, broiled or grilled.

All-purpose flour for dredging fish
2 tablespoons *un*salted butter
1 large onion, finely chopped
1 sweet red pepper, cored, seeded and diced
1 stalk celery, sliced
3 cloves garlic, finely chopped
1 Granny Smith apple, pared, cored and diced small
1 tablespoon all-purpose flour
1½ cups Fish Stock (*see recipe, page 119*) OR: chicken broth
½ cup plain yogurt OR: dairy sour cream
Fresh lemon juice, to taste
3 tablespoons vegetable oil
2 tablespoons finely chopped fresh cilantro OR: parsley

1. Season fish with ¼ teaspoon curry powder and ⅛ teaspoon each of salt and pepper. Dredge fillets in flour, shaking off the excess.
2. Heat butter in large, deep skillet over moderately low heat. Add onion, red pepper, celery and garlic; cook, covered, stirring occasionally, for 5 minutes. Add apple; cook, covered, for 3 minutes. Stir in remaining curry powder and the 1 tablespoon flour; cook, stirring, 1 minute. Add stock and remaining salt and pepper. Bring to boiling. Lower heat; simmer, stirring, for 10 minutes.
3. Meanwhile, heat oil in second large skillet over moderately high heat. Add fish fillets, skin-side up; cook 2 minutes. Turn fish over; cook 1 minute.
4. Stir yogurt and lemon juice to taste into curry mixture in skillet. Transfer fish with slotted spatula to curry mixture. Simmer, but do not boil, partially covered, 5 minutes or until fish flakes easily when tested with fork. Sprinkle fish with cilantro and serve.

SAUTÉED BREADED MONKFISH

LOW-CALORIE · LOW-CHOLESTEROL
QUICK

While you don't usually think of pounding fish, the firm texture of monkfish lends itself nicely to this treatment and makes cooking time truly fast.

Makes 4 servings.
Recipe can be halved or doubled.
Nutrient Value Per Serving: 231 calories, 19 g protein, 11 g fat, 12 g carbohydrate, 157 mg sodium, 29 mg cholesterol.

1 pound cleaned monkfish fillets
1 egg white
1 tablespoon water
⅔ cup plain dry bread crumbs
2 to 3 tablespoons vegetable oil
Lemon wedges

1. Slice monkfish ½ inch thick. Place fish on sheet of waxed paper or plastic wrap. Cover with another sheet of same. Pound fish with flat edge of meat pounder or skillet bottom to ¼-inch thickness. Whisk together the egg white and water in a shallow dish or pie plate.
2. Dip fish pieces into egg white mixture, then into bread crumbs. Place on sheet of waxed paper. Refrigerate 1 hour.
3. Heat 2 tablespoons oil in large skillet over high heat. Add fillets to skillet in single layer without crowding skillet; reserve any remaining fillets. Cook 3 minutes. Lower heat to medium. Turn fish over; cook 3 minutes or until golden brown and cooked through. Repeat with any remaining fillets, adding more oil to prevent sticking, if necessary. Divide into 4 servings. Serve with lemon wedges.

SAUTÉED BREADED MONKFISH MAKE-AHEAD TIP: Recipe can be prepared through Step 2 up to 4 hours ahead and refrigerated, covered.

MONKFISH
Also known as anglerfish or lotte, monkfish is a firm, white-fleshed fish from the New England coast with a taste similar to that of lobster and scallops. In fact, it is their voracious appetite for shellfish that gives monkfish their unique flavor, lending a certain credibility to the expression "You are what you eat." Generally, only the tail of monkfish is eaten (although tiny medallions of monkfish cheeks are sometimes available) and it is sold whole, filleted or sometimes cut into cubes. Monkfish can be cooked by any method, but because it rapidly loses moisture, it is most often braised or stewed.

OCEAN PERCH

A firm-fleshed, flavorful saltwater fish from northeastern Atlantic waters, ocean perch is a member of the rockfish family. Deep-sea redfish, from the same family, are often sold as ocean perch. Bake, grill or steam whole fish; poach, pan-fry or bake fillets.

SECRET FLAVORING

Grapefruit juice adds a little tartness to the sauce for the baked perch—try a sprinkle for seasoning other plainly prepared fish.

BAKED PERCH WITH PECANS AND ORANGE SAUCE

LOW-CALORIE · QUICK

Bake at 400° for 10 minutes.
Makes 4 servings.
Recipe can be halved or doubled.
Nutrient Value Per Serving: 308 calories, 35 g protein, 14 g fat, 12 g carbohydrate, 271 mg sodium, 161 mg cholesterol.

4 perch fillets (1½ pounds)
½ cup pecans, toasted and chopped
1 tablespoon *un*salted butter, softened
1 teaspoon all-purpose flour
1 large navel orange
⅓ cup orange juice
¼ cup grapefruit juice OR: lemon juice

1 tablespoon snipped chives OR: finely chopped green onion tops
¼ teaspoon salt

1. Preheat oven to hot (400°). Spray 15½ × 10½ × 1-inch jelly-roll pan with nonstick vegetable-oil cooking spray. Place fish on pan. Sprinkle with pecans.
2. Combine butter and flour in small bowl until well mixed. Grate 2 teaspoons rind from orange and reserve. Remove peel and white pith from orange. Section orange and coarsely chop.
3. Bake fish in preheated hot oven (400°) for 10 minutes or until fish flakes easily when tested with fork.
4. While fish is baking, prepare sauce: Place orange and grapefruit juices in small saucepan. Bring to simmering over medium heat. Whisk in flour mixture. Simmer 1 minute. Stir in grated orange rind, chives, salt and chopped orange flesh. Keep warm. Serve with fish.

Orange Roughy with Citrus Sauce

LOW-CHOLESTEROL · QUICK

If orange roughy is not available, substitute grouper, tilefish, snapper or catfish.

Makes 4 servings.
Recipe can be halved or doubled.
Nutrient Value Per Serving: 293 calories, 18 g protein, 19 g fat, 11 g carbohydrate, 212 mg sodium, 32 mg cholesterol.

1 pound orange roughy fillets, about ½ inch thick
½ cup milk
¼ teaspoon salt
⅓ cup all-purpose flour
2 tablespoons plus 1 teaspoon olive oil or vegetable oil
1 tablespoon finely chopped garlic
3 tablespoons fresh lime juice
2 tablespoons fresh lemon juice
1 tablespoon fresh orange juice
1 tablespoon finely chopped parsley
2 teaspoons snipped chives OR: finely chopped green onion tops
1 tablespoon *un*salted butter

1. Let fillets soak in milk in shallow dish for 10 minutes. Remove fish from milk; sprinkle with salt. Dredge fish in flour, shaking off excess.

ROUGH 'N' READY FISH

Orange Roughy with Citrus Sauce (this page)

Rice with Cilantro

Sliced Tomato Salad

Applesauce with Cookies

---

2. Heat the 2 tablespoons oil in a large skillet over moderately high heat. Add fish; cook until golden brown on one side, about 3 minutes. Carefully turn fish over; cook second side until golden brown and fish is cooked through, 3 to 4 minutes longer.

3. Remove fish to serving platter. Wipe skillet clean. Reduce temperature to low. Add remaining teaspoon oil to skillet. Add garlic; cook 30 seconds. Add lime, lemon and orange juices, parsley and chives. Add butter; swirl skillet until just creamy. Pour sauce over fish and serve immediately.

ORANGE ROUGHY
An exotic newcomer from the deep waters off New Zealand and in the South Pacific. So named for its bright red-orange skin, it has firm, pearly-white flesh and is rather bland in flavor. Usually sold as fillets, orange roughy can be cooked by any method and seasoned to taste.

POMPANO WITH TOMATO AND FETA CHEESE IN PACKETS

QUICK

Strongly flavored pompano stands up well to the tomatoes, peppers and feta cheese. Cooking fish in a sealed packet makes for moist fish and easy cleanup. Try with mackerel or bluefish.

POMPANO
A fish from the Florida coast which is small, firm-fleshed, slightly oily, sweet-flavored and somewhat flat-bodied. It is usually sold whole or butterflied and best when baked, broiled or grilled.

Bake at 450° for 15 minutes.
Makes 4 servings.
Recipe can be halved or doubled.
Nutrient Value Per Serving: 354 calories, 30 g protein, 20 g fat, 15 g carbohydrate, 724 mg sodium, 80 mg cholesterol.

1 tablespoon olive oil
1 large onion, cut into ½-inch dice
1 sweet yellow pepper, cored, seeded and cut into ¾-inch dice
2 large cloves garlic, finely chopped
1 can (14½ ounces) whole tomatoes, drained
1 can (8 ounces) tomato sauce
1 teaspoon leaf oregano, crumbled
1 teaspoon leaf basil, crumbled
⅛ teaspoon pepper
4 pompano fillets (1¼ pounds)
6 tablespoons crumbled feta cheese (1½ ounces)

1. Heat oil in large skillet over medium-low heat. Add onion; sauté for 8 minutes or until softened. Add yellow pepper and garlic; sauté for 3 minutes. Add tomatoes, tomato sauce, oregano, basil and pepper. Increase heat to medium-high, stirring to break up tomatoes; cook, stirring frequently, for 5 minutes.
2. Preheat oven to very hot (450°).
3. Place 4 pieces aluminum foil, each 18 × 12 inches, on work surface. Place one fillet in center of each piece of foil. Divide sauce evenly over fish. Sprinkle fish with feta cheese.
4. Fold long edges of foil together 3 times to seal. Fold short edges over 2 or 3 times to seal ends of packets. Place packets on large baking sheet.
5. Bake in preheated very hot oven (450°) for 15 minutes or until fish flakes easily when tested with a fork. (Carefully open one of the packets to test the fish.) Carefully unfold foil to serve, or let the diners do it themselves.

Microwave Directions (High Power Oven):
Ingredient Changes: Reduce oregano and basil *each* to ¾ teaspoon; use 4 sheets parchment paper, each 16 × 12 inches.
Directions: Stir together oil, onion, garlic and pepper in microwave-safe 4-cup measure. Microwave, uncovered, at 100% power 5 minutes. Stir in cut-up drained tomatoes, tomato sauce, oregano, basil and pepper. Cover with microwave-safe plastic wrap, vented at one edge. Microwave at 100% power 5 minutes. Assemble packets as above, using parchment paper. Place packets in microwave oven, no dish needed. Microwave at 100% power 8 minutes until fish flakes easily when tested with fork.

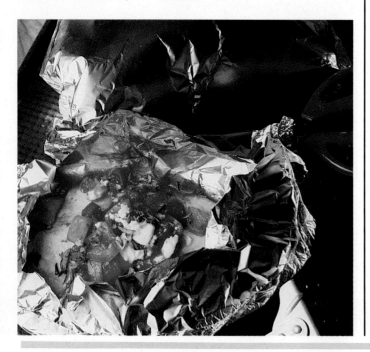

BAKED WHOLE STUFFED RED SNAPPER

This dish makes a wonderful presentation. Although it may appear somewhat daunting to prepare, it is really quite simple. As an alternative, use smaller whole fish or fillets. See our variations on page 312.

Bake at 400° for 40 to 50 minutes.
Makes 6 servings.
Nutrient Value Per Serving: 458 calories, 39 g protein, 23 g fat, 22 g carbohydrate, 697 mg sodium, 152 mg cholesterol.

Stuffing:
¼ cup (½ stick) *un*salted butter
1 medium-size onion, finely chopped
1 stalk celery, finely chopped
1 cup cooked chopped fresh spinach (1 pound) OR: 1 package (10 ounces) frozen, thawed
2 cloves garlic, finely chopped
1½ cups coarse dry bread crumbs
1½ teaspoons grated lemon rind
¼ cup finely chopped parsley
½ teaspoon leaf thyme, crumbled
½ teaspoon salt
¼ teaspoon black pepper
¼ cup heavy cream OR: milk
1 egg, lightly beaten

1 whole cleaned red snapper (3½ to 4 pounds)
½ teaspoon salt
¼ teaspoon black pepper
¼ cup (½ stick) *un*salted butter, melted

1. Preheat oven to hot (400°). Line shallow baking pan or broiler pan with aluminum foil and butter generously.
2. Prepare Stuffing: Heat butter in medium-size saucepan over medium heat. Add onion and celery to saucepan; cook, covered, over medium heat, stirring occasionally, for 5 minutes. Add spinach and garlic; cook, stirring occasionally, for 3 minutes.
3. Transfer spinach mixture to bowl. Add bread crumbs, lemon rind, parsley, thyme, salt, pepper, cream and egg; mix well.
4. Sprinkle inside of red snapper with half the salt and pepper. Loosely pack fish with some of the stuffing. (Wrap remaining stuffing in buttered foil to enclose it.) Close fish opening with wooden picks or skewers. Brush both sides of fish with some of melted butter. Sprinkle with remaining salt and pepper.
5. Arrange fish in prepared baking pan or broiler pan. Add stuffing package to pan.
6. Bake fish and stuffing in preheated hot oven (400°) for 40 to 50 minutes or *(continued)*

BAKED WHOLE STUFFED RED SNAPPER
(*continued*)

until fish flakes easily when tested with fork, basting fish occasionally with melted butter and pan juices.

7. To serve: Arrange fish on platter. Remove wooden picks. Surround fish with additional stuffing. Fillet top side of fish and scoop out the stuffing to accompany it. Remove bones from fish. Serve bottom half with additional stuffing.

Variations: For a 1¼-pound cleaned red snapper, halve recipe for stuffing, but include 1 egg. Bake for 15 to 17 minutes or until fish flakes when tested with fork. For two 8-ounce fillets, halve recipe for stuffing and bake separately in a buttered gratin dish for about 15 minutes. Brush fillets with 1 to 2 tablespoons melted butter and sprinkle with ⅛ teaspoon each of salt and pepper. Bake in a second buttered gratin dish for 8 to 10 minutes or until fish flakes when tested.

RED SNAPPER

This name is given to many, many fish, but the true red snapper, with pink skin, bright red eyes and lean, sweet, flaky flesh, is found in the Atlantic waters of the American South and in the Gulf of Mexico. Sometimes red-skinned West Coast rockfish or red perch is sold as snapper. Roasting is a preferred way of preparing snapper, but all cooking methods are suitable.

BAKED RED SNAPPER WITH TOMATOES AND OLIVES

LOW-CALORIE · LOW-FAT
LOW-CHOLESTEROL

A *robustly flavored dish accented with a pickled jalapeño pepper. Omit the pepper if you wish, or increase the amount for a spicier flavor.*

Bake at 350° for 20 minutes.
Makes 6 servings.
Recipe can be halved or doubled.
Nutrient Value Per Serving: 256 calories, 33 g protein, 8 g fat, 12 g carbohydrate, 873 mg sodium, 56 mg cholesterol.

2 pounds red snapper fillets
1 tablespoon lime juice
½ teaspoon salt
¼ teaspoon pepper
2 tablespoons olive oil
1 cup finely chopped onion
½ cup finely chopped sweet green pepper
3 cloves garlic, finely chopped
1 can (28 ounces) crushed tomatoes, in puree
½ cup chopped pimiento-stuffed olives (3-ounce jar)
2 tablespoons drained capers
1 pickled jalapeño pepper, seeded and finely chopped, or to taste *(optional)*
3 tablespoons finely chopped fresh cilantro OR: parsley
½ teaspoon leaf oregano, crumbled
½ teaspoon leaf basil, crumbled
½ teaspoon leaf thyme, crumbled
1 bay leaf

1. Preheat oven to moderate (350°). Pat fish fillets dry with paper toweling. Sprinkle with lime juice and ⅛ teaspoon each of salt and pepper.
2. Heat oil in medium-size saucepan over medium heat. Add onion, green pepper and garlic; cook, stirring occasionally, for 3 minutes. Add tomatoes, olives, capers, jalapeño pepper if using, 2 tablespoons cilantro, oregano, basil, thyme, bay leaf and remaining salt and pepper. Simmer, stirring occasionally, for 20 minutes or until thickened.
3. Arrange red snapper fillets in 2-quart flameproof baking dish. Cover fillets with sauce. Bring to boiling on top of the stove.
4. Bake fillets, covered with foil, in preheated moderate oven (350°) for 20 minutes or until fish flakes easily when tested with fork. Remove and discard bay leaf. Sprinkle with remaining cilantro.

Make-Ahead Tip: The sauce can be prepared a day ahead and refrigerated, covered.

Salmon with Lentils and Wasabi-Chive Sauce (page 314)

SALMON WITH LENTILS AND WASABI-CHIVE SAUCE

LOW-CALORIE

WASABI
The Japanese version of horseradish, wasabi can be found in the Oriental foods section of some supermarkets and in shops specializing in Oriental ingredients.

SALMON
A large, full-flavored and firm-textured fish, salmon is somewhat sweet and fatty. Most species of wild salmon are from the Pacific Northwest. Both Atlantic and Pacific salmon are raised in fish farms worldwide. The color of salmon varies from white to pink to bright orange-red, depending on the species. Bake, grill, broil or poach whole salmon, steaks and butterfly cuts; steam, poach, bake or grill fillets.

This recipe may seem unusual, borrowing elements from French provincial cooking and the Orient, but the results are delicious. Watch out, the sauce is hot. Try with other strong-flavored fishes or with chicken. Garnish with radicchio or other lettuce leaves.

Broil for 8 minutes.
Makes 4 servings.
Recipe can be halved or doubled.
Nutrient Value Per Serving: 343 calories, 37 g protein, 12 g fat, 19 g carbohydrate, 496 mg sodium, 83 mg cholesterol.

Lentils:
1 cup dried lentils (4 ounces), picked
    over and rinsed
2 cups water
½ onion, chopped
2 cloves garlic, crushed
½ teaspoon salt
1 tablespoon rice wine vinegar

Salmon:
4 salmon fillet pieces (about 1¼ pounds)
½ cup sake OR: dry white wine
2 tablespoons lemon juice
2 teaspoons grated fresh ginger
2 teaspoons tamari soy sauce OR: regular
    soy sauce

Wasabi-Chive Sauce:
1 teaspoon water
½ teaspoon wasabi powder OR: 1
    teaspoon prepared horseradish
¼ cup reduced-calorie sour cream
2 teaspoons snipped chives
⅛ teaspoon salt

½ cup sliced canned water chestnuts, cut
    into slivers *(optional)*

1. Prepare Lentils: Combine lentils, water, onion and garlic in small saucepan. Bring to boiling. Lower heat; simmer, covered, for 30 minutes or until lentils are tender. Remove garlic. Stir in salt and rice wine vinegar.
2. Meanwhile, prepare Salmon: Combine salmon, sake, lemon juice, ginger and tamari in plastic food storage bag. Push out all air and seal. Let stand 20 minutes at room temperature.
3. Preheat broiler. Spray broiler-pan rack with nonstick cooking spray.
4. Broil salmon 5 inches from heat for 8 minutes or until cooked through, turning over halfway through cooking.
5. Meanwhile, prepare Wasabi-Chive Sauce: Stir together water and wasabi in small bowl; let stand 5 minutes. Stir in sour cream, chives and salt.
6. To serve, stir water chestnuts, if using, into hot lentils. Divide lentils among 4 serving plates. Place salmon on lentils. Spoon sauce over salmon.

Make-Ahead Tip: The lentils can be prepared up to 2 days ahead and refrigerated, covered. Gently reheat, adding a little water if necessary.

SHOWER LUNCHEON

Celery Root Salad with
Horseradish Dressing (157)

Salmon with Lentils and
Wasabi-Chive Sauce (this
page)

Assorted French Cheeses

Walnut Bread (42)

Endive, Watercress and
Romaine Salad

Berry Tart (495)

PEPPER-COATED SALMON WITH LEEKS

LOW-CALORIE · QUICK

Bake at 375° for 12 minutes.
Makes 4 servings.
Recipe can be halved or doubled.
Nutrient Value Per Serving: 322 calories,
30 g protein, 16 g fat, 14 g carbohydrate,
359 mg sodium, 96 mg cholesterol.

1¼ pounds salmon fillets, cut into 4 equal
  pieces
½ teaspoon salt
½ teaspoon cracked pepper
2 tablespoons *un*salted butter
2 leeks (12 ounces), well washed and
  thinly sliced (3 cups)
1 shallot OR: white part green onion,
  chopped
2 teaspoons all-purpose flour
½ cup dry white wine
2 tablespoons half-and-half

1. Preheat oven to moderate (375°).
2. Place salmon on waxed paper. Sprinkle ¼ teaspoon salt and the pepper on both sides of fish, pressing to adhere.
3. Heat butter in heavy ovenproof skillet (cast iron)* over medium heat. Add leeks and shallot; cook, stirring, 6 minutes or until softened. Stir in remaining ¼ teaspoon salt, the flour and wine. Bring to simmering. Remove from heat. Place salmon fillets on leek mixture.
4. Bake in preheated moderate oven (375°) for 12 minutes or until the fish is cooked through, turning fish over halfway through cooking.
5. Place fish on dinner plates. Stir half-and-half into leek mixture until combined. Spoon over fish and serve, or serve leek mixture on the side.

*Note: If your skillet does not have a metal handle, cover with foil to ovenproof up to 375°.
Microwave Directions (High Power Oven):
Ingredient Changes: Decrease wine to 3

tablespoons; increase half-and-half to 3 tablespoons.
Directions: Sprinkle salmon with salt and pepper as in Step 1. Place butter in microwave-safe baking dish, about 9 × 9 × 2 inches. Microwave, uncovered, at 100% power 1 to 1½ minutes to melt. Stir in leeks and shallots. Microwave, uncovered, at 100% power 6 minutes. Stir in remaining salt, flour and wine. Fold under thinner parts of fillets to make even thickness if necessary. Place in baking dish. Cover with microwave-safe plastic wrap, vented at one edge. Microwave at 100% power 6 to 7 minutes or until cooked through. Carefully remove plastic wrap. Place salmon on dinner plates. Stir half-and-half into leek mixture. Microwave, uncovered, at 100% power 30 seconds. Spoon over salmon.

DRAMATIC PRESENTATION
Pepper-Coated Salmon with Leeks is sure to wow company. For a dramatic garnish, serve salmon on a cross-hatching of thinly sliced cooked leek greens.

BROILED SEA BASS WITH MUSTARD GLAZE AND TOMATO RELISH

MUSTARD GLAZE
Broiling with the mustard glaze lends itself to less delicate types of fish, which are not overpowered by the mustard and pungent relish. The tomato relish would work well with mackerel and bluefish, and even chicken.

BROILED SEA BASS MAKE-AHEAD TIP:
The relish can be made a day ahead and refrigerated, covered.

SEA BASS
A lean saltwater fish, sea bass is similar to freshwater bass in its mild flavor and firm texture. Varieties of sea bass include stripers, blackfish and grouper, which are sold whole or as steaks or fillets. Poach, steam or add to stew, or marinate and broil or grill.

LOW-CALORIE · LOW-CHOLESTEROL

Broil 8 minutes.
Makes 4 servings.
Recipe can be halved or doubled.
Nutrient Value Per Serving: 260 calories, 32 g protein, 12 g fat, 4 g carbohydrate, 638 mg sodium, 70 mg cholesterol.

Tomato Relish:
4 plum tomatoes, seeded and diced
8 Greek olives, pitted and chopped OR: canned black olives
1 green onion, chopped
2 tablespoons chopped fresh dill OR: 1½ teaspoons dried
¼ teaspoon salt
⅛ teaspoon pepper
2 tablespoons olive oil
1 teaspoon red wine vinegar

2 tablespoons Dijon-style mustard
4 sea bass fillets (about 1½ pounds)

1. Prepare Tomato Relish: Stir together tomatoes, olives, green onion, dill, salt, pepper, 1 tablespoon oil and the vinegar in medium-size bowl. Set aside.
2. Preheat broiler. Spray broiler-pan rack with nonstick cooking spray.
3. Stir together remaining oil and mustard in small bowl. Place fillets on broiler rack. Brush fillets with mustard mixture.
4. Broil fish 4 inches from heat for 8 minutes or until fish is cooked through and top is browned. Serve with relish.

SHARK WITH THAI COCONUT SAUCE

LOW-CHOLESTEROL • QUICK

Shark is now more readily available in supermarkets, but you can also substitute swordfish in this recipe. The lemon grass adds a special spiciness; check stores that carry Oriental ingredients if you can't find it in your supermarket. Garnish with lime wedges and julienned zucchini.

Broil 8 to 10 minutes.
Makes 4 servings.
Recipe can be halved or doubled.
Nutrient Value Per Serving: 307 calories, 32 g protein, 19 g fat, 4 g carbohydrate, 464 mg sodium, 73 mg cholesterol.

Coconut Sauce:
2 green onions
1 cup coconut milk*
2 stalks lemon grass, cut ½ inch thick
    OR: 2 strips lemon peel
1 clove garlic, finely chopped
1 small fresh jalapeño pepper, seeded and chopped
1 canned anchovy, chopped
1 teaspoon cornstarch
¼ teaspoon salt

1¼ pounds shark OR: swordfish fillets, about ¾ inch thick
2 teaspoons lime juice
2 teaspoons soy sauce
1 tablespoon chopped cilantro OR: parsley

1. Prepare Sauce: Slice 1 green onion top and reserve. Slice remaining white part and other green onion and place in small saucepan. Stir in coconut milk, lemon grass, garlic, jalapeño, anchovy, cornstarch and salt until well combined. Bring to boiling, whisking; simmer 5 minutes. Cover and let stand while cooking fish.
2. Preheat broiler.
3. Place fish on broiler-pan rack sprayed with nonstick cooking spray. Combine lime juice and soy sauce in small dish. Brush over fish.
4. Broil fish 5 inches from heat for 8 to 10 minutes or until cooked through, turning over halfway through cooking and brushing with soy mixture.
5. Strain sauce into sauceboat. Stir in cilantro and reserved sliced green onion top. Serve with broiled fish.

*Note: To make an easy coconut milk, simmer together 2 cups shredded, sweetened coconut and 1¼ cups milk in small saucepan for 1 minute. Let stand 10 minutes. Strain in sieve, pressing solids to extract as much liquid as possible. Discard solids.

SHARK
Meat sold commercially is usually from mako, thresher, black-tip and angel sharks. The flesh is firm and white to pink and the taste similar to that of swordfish, but not as sweet. Shark is sold as steak and fillets which can be cooked by any method.

STEAMED SOLE FILLETS WITH SPICY BEAN SAUCE

LOW-CALORIE · LOW-CHOLESTEROL
QUICK

Steaming is an easy way to cook fish and keep it moist. Use any thin, mild-tasting fish fillet. Bottled black bean sauce is available in the Oriental foods section of some supermarkets and in shops specializing in Oriental ingredients.

Makes 4 servings.
Recipe can be halved or doubled.
Nutrient Value Per Serving: 177 calories, 23 g protein, 7 g fat, 4 g carbohydrate, 490 mg sodium, 54 mg cholesterol.

Marinade:
1 tablespoon rice wine vinegar OR: cider vinegar
1 tablespoon rice wine OR: dry sherry
2 teaspoons bottled black bean sauce
1 teaspoon finely chopped pared fresh ginger
1 teaspoon Oriental sesame oil

1 pound sole fillets (4 fillets)

Spicy Bean Sauce:
1 cup chicken broth
2 tablespoons bottled black bean sauce
1 tablespoon rice wine OR: dry sherry
1 tablespoon reduced-sodium soy sauce
1 teaspoon Oriental sesame oil
2 teaspoons cornstarch

1 tablespoon corn oil
¼ cup finely chopped green onion
1 tablespoon finely chopped pared fresh ginger
2 teaspoons finely chopped garlic

1. Prepare Marinade: Combine vinegar, wine, black bean sauce, ginger and sesame oil in small bowl. Spread 1 teaspoon marinade on skinned side of each fillet. Fold fillets in half. Arrange in single layer on heatproof plate. Sprinkle fillets with the remaining marinade. Let stand for 10 minutes.

2. Arrange plate with fish on rack over simmering water in saucepan. Cover saucepan and steam fillets for 5 minutes or just until fish flakes when tested with fork.

3. Meanwhile, prepare Spicy Bean Sauce: Combine chicken broth, black bean sauce, rice wine, soy sauce, sesame oil and cornstarch in small bowl until smooth.

4. Heat corn oil in skillet over medium heat. Add green onion, ginger and garlic; stir-fry 1 minute. Add sauce; simmer 5 minutes.

5. Pour off juices from plate with sole. Spoon sauce over fish and serve.

FIT FOR THE STEAMER

Steamed Sole Fillets with Spicy Bean Sauce (this page)

Steamed Rice

Steamed Carrots

Belgian Endive and Boston Lettuce with Cumin Dressing (151)

Plum Port-Wine Ice (539)

SWORDFISH WITH TOMATOES AND RAISINS

LOW-CALORIE · LOW-CHOLESTEROL
QUICK

This dish is equally good with cod.

Makes 4 servings.
Recipe can be halved or doubled.
Nutrient Value Per Serving: 240 calories,
22 g protein, 14 g fat, 14 g carbohydrate,
283 mg sodium, 39 mg cholesterol.

¼ cup golden raisins
½ cup hot water
2 tablespoons olive oil
2 swordfish steaks (8 ounces each),
    halved
5 ounces fresh fennel bulb, cut in ½-inch
    dice (1 cup)
2 cloves garlic, finely chopped
1 can (13⅓ ounces) plum tomatoes,
    drained and chopped
6 dashes liquid red-pepper seasoning
¼ teaspoon salt
¼ cup pine nuts *(optional)*
1 tablespoon chopped fennel fronds

1. Place raisins in small bowl. Pour hot
water over; set aside.
2. Heat 1 tablespoon oil in large skillet
over moderate heat. Add swordfish;
cook until golden brown, about 4 minutes. Turn fish over; cook 2 minutes
longer. Remove to serving platter.
3. Add remaining tablespoon oil to
skillet. Add fennel; sauté over moderate
heat for 7 minutes or until soft and
lightly browned. Reduce heat to low.
Add garlic; cook 1 minute, stirring frequently. Add raisins, their soaking liquid, tomato, liquid red-pepper seasoning
and salt; cook 4 minutes. Add swordfish. Cover and cook 4 to 5 minutes or
until fish is cooked through.
4. Transfer fish to serving platter. Stir
pine nuts, if using, into sauce. Stir in
fennel fronds. Spoon sauce over fish.

SWORDFISH WITH ORANGE-GINGER MARINADE

LOW-CALORIE · LOW-CHOLESTEROL

Try the marinade with chicken or pork,
and you can substitute mackerel or cod for
the swordfish. This dish also works well on
the barbecue. Serve with broiled or grilled
orange wedges and baby corn.

Broil 8 minutes.
Makes 4 servings.
Recipe can be halved or doubled.
Nutrient Value Per Serving: 173 calories,
20 g protein, 6 g fat, 7 g carbohydrate,
92 mg sodium, 39 mg cholesterol.

Orange-Ginger Marinade:
1 cup fresh orange juice
2 teaspoons corn oil OR: peanut oil
1¼ teaspoons ginger juice*
½ teaspoon sugar
⅛ teaspoon ground cardamom
⅛ teaspoon ground hot red pepper

2 swordfish steaks (8 ounces each),
    halved

1. Prepare Marinade: Boil orange juice
in small saucepan over high heat until
reduced to ½ cup, about 5 minutes.
Remove from heat.
2. Stir oil, ginger juice, sugar, cardamom and ground red pepper into orange
juice in saucepan. Let cool slightly.
Transfer to shallow dish or self-sealing
bag. Place fish in marinade. Refrigerate
2 hours, turning fish occasionally.
3. Preheat broiler. Spray broiler-pan
rack with nonstick vegetable-oil cooking spray. Place fish on rack. Spoon
half the marinade over fish.
4. Broil fish 6 inches from heat for 4
minutes or until fish has darkened.
Turn fish over. Spoon remaining marinade over fish. Broil 4 minutes longer
(continued)

SWORDFISH
These fish are caught
in tropical and tem-
perate waters on
both coasts. The meat
is firm and somewhat
oily, with sweet, rich
flavor. Most swordfish
is sold as steaks that
can be broiled,
grilled, cubed for bro-
chettes or braised.

SWORDFISH WITH ORANGE-GINGER MARINADE
(*continued*)

or until fish easily flakes when tested
with a fork.

*Note: To make ginger juice, pare
3-inch piece of fresh ginger and grate

into bowl. Squeeze grated pulp, extracting as much juice as possible. Discard
pulp.

Make-Ahead Tip: The marinade can be
made several days ahead and refrigerated, covered. Marinate the fish in the
refrigerator, covered, up to 4 hours
ahead.

TROUT WITH MISO SAUCE AND MUSHROOMS

QUICK

This recipe may seem exotic, but it's simple and quick to prepare. The fillets are crunchy with cracker crumbs and sauced with a mushroom cream accented with miso and rice wine vinegar. Try with flounder or perch. Serve with steamed snow peas.

Makes 4 servings.
Recipe can be halved or doubled.
Nutrient Value Per Serving: 399 calories, 35 g protein, 23 g fat, 14 g carbohydrate, 458 mg sodium, 149 mg cholesterol.

1 egg
¼ cup cracker crumbs, such as saltines
3 tablespoons sesame seeds
¼ teaspoon pepper
4 trout fillets (about 1¼ pounds), skinned
1 tablespoon *un*salted butter
1 tablespoon olive oil OR: vegetable oil
1½ cups (4 ounces) sliced mushrooms
¼ cup reduced-sodium chicken broth
    OR: water
¼ cup half-and-half
3 tablespoons rice wine vinegar OR: cider vinegar
2 tablespoons miso OR: soy sauce
1 teaspoon sugar

1. Beat egg in shallow pie plate. Stir together crumbs, sesame seeds and pepper on piece of waxed paper.

(continued)

TROUT WITH MISO SAUCE AND MUSHROOMS
(*continued*)

2. Dip fish fillets in egg, then crumb mixture to coat evenly. Place on clean waxed paper.

3. Heat butter and oil in medium-size skillet over medium heat. Add fillets; cook 6 minutes or until fish flakes easily when tested with fork, turning halfway through cooking. Transfer to serving plate and cover with aluminum foil to keep warm.

4. Add mushrooms to skillet; sauté over medium-high heat for 4 minutes or until lightly colored. Reduce heat to low; stir in chicken broth, half-and-half, vinegar, miso and sugar. Bring to boiling; boil, stirring, 1 minute. Spoon sauce evenly over fish.

EXOTIC TROUT

Trout with Miso Sauce and Mushrooms (321)

Carrots Glazed with Orange Marmalade

Rice with Chopped Parsley

Pear Gratin

TROUT WITH ROASTED GARLIC CREAM

Baking the garlic softens the strong flavor and makes it sweet. Try the savory cream with flounder fillets, or with roasted or broiled chicken.

Bake garlic at 350° for 45 minutes; toast almonds for 8 to 10 minutes.
Makes 4 servings.
Recipe can be halved or doubled.
Nutrient Value Per Serving: 362 calories, 33 g protein, 20 g fat, 11 g carbohydrate, 212 mg sodium, 87 mg cholesterol.

TROUT
A slightly oily, somewhat sweet, medium-firm fish, trout can be found in fresh or salt water. Freshwater rainbow trout are a favorite of fishermen in western states but are commercially available from trout farms throughout the country. Wild brook trout are fished from Eastern lakes and streams, and brown trout are found in waters throughout the United States. Both species are farmed in limited quantities and can sometimes be found in fish markets. Bake, broil, grill, poach or pan-fry whole or filleted trout.

Roasted Garlic Cream:
4 cloves garlic, unpeeled
2 tablespoons sliced almonds
2 tablespoons parsley
¼ cup reduced-calorie sour cream
1 tablespoon lemon juice
¼ teaspoon salt
⅛ teaspoon ground white pepper

⅓ cup all-purpose flour
4 trout fillets (about 1¼ pounds)
2 tablespoons olive oil OR: vegetable oil

1. Preheat oven to moderate (350°).
2. Prepare Roasted Garlic Cream: Wrap garlic in aluminum foil. Place in small baking dish with ½ inch water.
3. Bake in preheated moderate oven (350°) for 45 minutes. Meanwhile, place almonds on small sheet of aluminum foil. Bake 8 to 10 minutes or until golden.
4. When cool enough to handle, squeeze garlic out of skins into small food processor or blender. Add 1 tablespoon of the almonds and the parsley. Whirl until smooth. Scrape into small bowl. Stir in sour cream, lemon juice, salt and pepper. Reserve.
5. Place flour in plastic food storage bag. Add fillets; shake to coat. Heat oil in medium-size skillet over medium heat. Add fillets; cook 6 minutes or until golden, turning halfway through cooking. Sprinkle with remaining tablespoon almonds, and serve with Roasted Garlic Cream.

Make-Ahead Tip: The garlic cream can be made up to 2 days ahead and refrigerated, covered.
Microwave Directions for Roasting Garlic and Toasting Almonds (High Power Oven): Place garlic in microwave-safe 4-cup measure. Cover tightly with microwave-safe plastic wrap. Microwave at 100% power for 6 to 8 minutes or until very tender. To toast almonds, microwave in single layer on microwave-safe paper toweling at 100% power for 4 to 6 minutes, stirring once.

BROILED LEMON-LIME TUNA STEAKS

LOW-CALORIE · LOW-CHOLESTEROL
LOW-SODIUM

Use all lemon or all lime juice if you wish, instead of blending the two. The marinade works well with other strong-flavored fish such as swordfish and bluefish. Garnish with dill sprigs and sprouts.

Broil about 10 minutes.
Makes 4 servings.
Recipe can be halved or doubled.
Nutrient Value Per Serving: 234 calories, 27 g protein, 12 g fat, 3 g carbohydrate, 114 mg sodium, 43 mg cholesterol.

¼ cup fresh lemon juice
¼ cup fresh lime juice
2 tablespoons olive oil
1 tablespoon finely chopped fresh dill
    OR: 1½ teaspoons dried
2 cloves garlic, finely chopped
⅛ teaspoon salt
⅛ teaspoon pepper
1 pound tuna steaks, ½ inch thick

1. Mix together lemon juice, lime juice, olive oil, dill, garlic, salt and pepper in nonmetallic dish. Add tuna steaks; turn to coat. Refrigerate, cov-ered, for 1 hour, turning once halfway through.

2. Preheat broiler. Spray broiler-pan rack with nonstick vegetable-oil cooking spray.

3. Remove tuna steaks to broiler rack. Broil 6 to 7 inches from heat for 5 minutes, brushing occasionally with marinade. Turn and repeat with other side for 5 minutes or until cooked through. Discard any remaining marinade.

Make-Ahead Tip: The marinade can be made a day ahead and refrigerated, covered. The fish, however, should only be put in the marinade 1 hour ahead.

CATCH OF THE DAY

Broiled Lemon-Lime Tuna Steaks (this page)

Sautéed Spinach with Garlic

Chick-Pea, Tomato and Red Onion Salad

Chocolate Cream Pie

TUNA

A large, fatty saltwater fish, tuna is most familiar to Americans when it comes from a can. Fresh tuna, now more widely available, is strong-flavored, firm-textured and usually sold cut up into steaks. Broil, grill or sauté fresh tuna, being careful not to overcook the fish and dry out its flaky flesh.

HERBED FISH CAKES WITH MUSTARD-DILL SAUCE

A *tasty way to cook frozen fish fillets. Fresh flounder may be substituted for the frozen, and try the sauce with other fish or chicken, as well.*

Makes 8 fish cakes and 1¼ cups sauce. Recipe can be halved or doubled.

Nutrient Value Per Fish Cake: 270 calories, 15 g protein, 18 g fat, 13 g carbohydrate, 634 mg sodium, 81 mg cholesterol.
Nutrient Value Per 2 Tablespoons Sauce: 54 calories, 1 g protein, 5 g fat, 1 g carbohydrate, 79 mg sodium, 15 mg cholesterol.

Fish Cakes:
¼ cup (½ stick) *un*salted butter
¼ cup all-purpose flour
1 teaspoon dry mustard
1 cup half-and-half OR: milk
1 egg, slightly beaten
1 pound frozen flounder fillets, thawed and poached according to package directions, and flaked OR: leftover cooked, firm white fish, flaked
1 cup fresh bread crumbs (2 slices)
½ cup finely chopped celery
½ cup chopped chives
½ cup chopped watercress
2 teaspoons white wine vinegar
1 teaspoon salt
⅛ teaspoon pepper
½ cup seasoned bread crumbs
¼ cup vegetable oil

Mustard-Dill Sauce*:
2 tablespoons *un*salted butter
¼ cup finely chopped fresh dill
2 tablespoons dry white wine
1 cup half-and-half
1 tablespoon Dijon-style mustard
⅛ teaspoon white pepper

1. Prepare Fish Cakes: Melt butter in small saucepan over medium heat.

Whisk in flour and mustard until smooth; cook, stirring constantly, for 3 to 4 minutes or until thick. Gradually whisk in half-and-half; cook, stirring constantly, for 5 to 8 minutes or until thickened and bubbly. Remove from heat. Stir a little hot mixture into egg. Then stir egg mixture into half-and-half mixture.

2. Add flounder, fresh bread crumbs, celery, chives, watercress, vinegar, salt and pepper to half-and-half mixture; mix together until well blended. Cover and refrigerate for 2 hours or until well chilled and firm enough to shape into cakes.

3. Shape mixture into 8 equal cakes. Coat with seasoned bread crumbs; set aside.

4. Heat oil in large heavy skillet over medium heat. Add half the cakes; sauté 4 minutes or until golden brown. Turn and repeat with other side. Remove to plate and keep warm. Repeat with remaining cakes.

5. Prepare Mustard-Dill Sauce: Melt butter in small saucepan over medium-low heat. Add dill; cook 1 minute. Increase heat to medium. Add wine; boil 1 minute or until most of liquid has evaporated. Lower heat. Add half-and-half; simmer about 1 minute or until thickened. Stir in mustard and pepper; heat through, but do not boil. Serve with the fish cakes.

*Quick Sauces: Try these lower calorie/lower fat quick sauces. Mix a little bottled chili sauce with drained prepared horseradish and lemon juice; combine reduced-calorie sour cream with plain yogurt and pickle relish; or invent your own sauce.

Make-Ahead Tip: The fish cake mixture can be prepared and shaped into cakes several hours ahead and refrigerated, covered.

NEW ENGLAND SCALLOPED FISH CASSEROLE

Bake at 350° for 45 minutes.
Makes 4 servings.
Nutrient Value Per Serving: 499 calories, 33 g protein, 22 g fat, 44 g carbohydrate, 554 mg sodium, 102 mg cholesterol.

1 pound frozen cod or haddock fillets, thawed according to package directions
1 pound all-purpose potatoes, pared and quartered
½ pound leeks, green ends trimmed
2 tablespoons *un*salted butter
3 tablespoons all-purpose flour
¾ cup milk
½ teaspoon salt
¼ teaspoon ground white pepper
¾ cup shredded Gruyère cheese OR: Swiss cheese (3 ounces)
1 tablespoon dry sherry

Topping:
½ cup cracker crumbs (about 12 crackers)
1 tablespoon melted *un*salted butter
½ teaspoon sweet paprika

1. Lightly coat $13 \times 9 \times 2$-inch baking dish with nonstick vegetable-oil cooking spray. Cut fish into 8 pieces crosswise. Steam fish in steamer basket over 1 cup simmering water in covered saucepan for 8 minutes or until opaque. Cool. Flake with fork into prepared dish.
2. Meanwhile, slice potatoes. Slice leeks, rinsing pieces well. Add to steamer basket; cook 6 to 8 minutes or until tender. Scatter in baking dish with fish, reserving cooking liquid.

(continued)

CASSEROLE FOR A WINTER EVENING
Cod, leeks and potatoes flavored with cheese and sherry combine in this old-fashioned cracker-crumb-topped casserole. A good company dish for a cold evening. Serve with a green vegetable or salad.

NEW ENGLAND SCALLOPED FISH CASSEROLE
(*continued*)

3. Measure out ½ cup of cooking liquid, discarding remainder. Melt butter in steaming pan. Stir in flour until smooth; cook, stirring, 2 minutes. Remove from heat. Whisk in reserved cooking liquid, milk, salt and pepper; simmer, stirring, 4 minutes. Remove from heat. Stir in cheese and sherry. Spoon evenly over fish.
4. Preheat oven to moderate (350°).
5. Prepare Topping: Stir together crumbs, butter and paprika in small bowl; sprinkle over casserole.
6. Bake casserole, tented loosely with aluminum foil, in preheated moderate oven (350°) for 45 minutes or until bubbly and golden. Remove foil during last 20 minutes to brown. Serve hot.

Make-Ahead Tip: The casserole can be prepared a few hours ahead and refrigerated. Allow extra time for baking.
Microwave Directions (High Power Oven):
Place thawed fish in microwave-safe 2-quart casserole. Cover with lid. Microwave at 100% power 5 minutes. Remove from casserole. Flake into microwave-safe 13 × 9 × 2-inch baking dish. Add potatoes and leeks to casserole. Re-cover. Microwave at 100% power 10 minutes, stirring once. Lift out vegetables; scatter over fish. Measure liquid in casserole; add water if necessary to make ½ cup. Wipe out casserole. Place 3 tablespoons butter in casserole. Microwave, uncovered, at 100% power 1 to 1½ minutes to melt. Pour 1 tablespoon into cracker crumbs. Stir flour into 2 tablespoons butter in casserole until smooth. Gradually whisk in milk, cooking liquid, salt and pepper until smooth. Microwave, uncovered, at 100% power 4 minutes to full boiling, whisking once. Stir in cheese and sherry until well blended. Spoon over vegetables in baking dish. Sprinkle with crumb mixture and paprika. Microwave, uncovered, at 100% power 6 minutes, turning dish once. Let stand, covered, 2 minutes.

PROVINCETOWN FISH STEW MAKE-AHEAD TIP:
The stew can be made a day ahead, omitting the parsley, and refrigerated, covered. Gently reheat, stirring in the parsley.

PROVINCETOWN FISH STEW

LOW-CALORIE · LOW-CHOLESTEROL

A *rich stew made with frozen cod and linguiça, a Portuguese sausage. Serve over rice or orzo.*

Makes 4 servings.
Recipe can be halved or doubled.
Nutrient Value Per Serving: 287 calories, 28 g protein, 12 g fat, 16 g carbohydrate, 381 mg sodium, 49 mg cholesterol.

1 tablespoon olive oil OR: vegetable oil
1 red onion, chopped
1 sweet green pepper, cored, seeded and cut in squares
2 cloves garlic, finely chopped
3 ounces linguiça OR: chorizo sausage OR: pepperoni, cut in small cubes
¾ teaspoon leaf basil, crumbled
½ teaspoon ground cumin
⅛ teaspoon ground hot red pepper
1 can (28 ounces) whole tomatoes, in thick puree
1 pound frozen cod fillets, thawed according to package directions
½ cup chopped parsley

1. Heat oil in small Dutch oven or casserole over medium heat. Add onion and green pepper; cook 10 minutes or until softened. Add garlic; cook 1 minute. Add linguiça, basil, cumin and hot red pepper; cook 2 minutes. Add tomatoes; bring to boiling, stirring to break up tomatoes. Lower heat; simmer 15 to 20 minutes or until thickened.
2. Meanwhile, remove any bones from fish with tweezers. Cut into 1-inch chunks. Add fish and parsley to tomato mixture. Return to simmering; cook 5 minutes more or until fish flakes when tested with a fork.

CALIFORNIA TUNA SALAD

LOW-CALORIE · LOW-CHOLESTEROL

An old favorite spruced up with avocado, sweet red pepper and water chestnuts. Serve chilled over shredded lettuce for a light lunch or summer supper, or use as a sandwich filling. Try with cooked cubes of fresh tuna or shrimp.

Makes 4 servings.
Recipe can be halved or doubled.
Nutrient Value Per Serving: 316 calories, 26 g protein, 17 g fat, 16 g carbohydrate, 594 mg sodium, 35 mg cholesterol.

½ teaspoon grated lime rind
3 tablespoons fresh lime juice
2 tablespoons olive oil
2 teaspoons honey
½ teaspoon ground cumin
½ teaspoon salt
½ teaspoon liquid red-pepper seasoning
1 ripe avocado (about 12 ounces)
2 cans (6½ ounces each) tuna packed in
    water, drained
1 sweet red pepper, roasted, cored,
    seeded, peeled and cut into ½-inch
    squares *(see How-To, page 433)* OR:
    half of a 7-ounce jar roasted red
    peppers
½ of 8-ounce can water chestnuts, cut
    into cubes (½ cup)
2 tablespoons chopped cilantro OR:
    parsley

1. Whisk together lime rind and juice, olive oil, honey, cumin, salt and red-pepper seasoning in medium-size bowl until blended. Pit and peel avocado; cube. Add to dressing; toss to prevent discoloring.
2. Flake tuna into bowl with the avocado and dressing. Add red pepper, water chestnuts and cilantro to tuna; toss to combine. Serve chilled.

UPDATED TUNA NOODLE CASSEROLE

Bake at 375° for 30 minutes.
Makes 8 servings.
Nutrient Value Per Serving: 415 calories, 25 g protein, 17 g fat, 55 g carbohydrate, 612 mg sodium, 98 mg cholesterol.

1 package (12 ounces) wide egg noodles
¼ cup (½ stick) *un*salted butter
12 butter crackers, crumbed (½ cup)
1 medium-size onion, chopped
2 stalks celery, chopped
1 small sweet red pepper, cored, seeded and cut into squares
1 small sweet green pepper, cored, seeded and cut into squares
1 cup sliced mushrooms (about 4 ounces)
¼ cup all-purpose flour
1½ cups milk
1 cup cubed extra-sharp white Cheddar cheese (about 4 ounces)
1 large can (12½ ounces) tuna in water, drained and flaked
1 tablespoon chopped fresh dill OR: 1 teaspoon dried
1 teaspoon salt

1. Cook noodles according to package directions. Drain. Combine noodles with 1 tablespoon butter in $13 \times 9 \times 2$-inch baking dish until noodles are coated. Spread evenly in baking dish.
2. Preheat oven to moderate (375°).
3. Melt remaining 3 tablespoons butter in medium-size saucepan. Combine 1 tablespoon butter with crumbs in small bowl for topping.
4. Add onion, celery, red and green peppers and mushrooms to butter in saucepan; sauté for 10 minutes or until tender. Stir in flour until well combined; cook, stirring, 1 minute. Stir in milk until smooth. Bring mixture to boiling, stirring. Lower heat; simmer, stirring occasionally, 4 minutes. Stir in cheese cubes, tuna, dill and salt. Spoon over noodles. Sprinkle crumb topping lightly over casserole.
5. Bake in preheated moderate oven (375°) for 30 minutes or until heated through and bubbly. Serve hot.

Microwave Directions (High Power Oven):
Ingredient Changes: Add ½ teaspoon paprika; use ½ teaspoon dried dillweed instead of fresh dill.
Directions: Cook noodles as above. Place in microwave-safe $13 \times 9 \times 2$-inch baking dish with butter as directed. Place 3 tablespoons butter in microwave-safe 8-cup measure. Microwave, uncovered, at 100% power 1 to 1½ minutes to melt. Pour 1 tablespoon into crumbs. Stir onion, celery, red and green peppers, mushrooms and dill into measure. Microwave, uncovered, at 100% power 6 minutes, stirring once. Stir in flour. Gradually stir in milk. Microwave, uncovered, at 100% power 4½ to 5 minutes to full boiling, stirring once. Stir in cheese, tuna and salt. Assemble casserole; sprinkle with paprika. Microwave, uncovered, at 70% power 10 minutes. Let stand, covered, 5 minutes.

SUN-DRIED TOMATO SAUCE

LOW-CHOLESTEROL · QUICK

Serve with either mild or strong-flavored fish, fresh or frozen—especially delicious over grilled fish. It's even good over pasta or chicken.

Makes 1½ cups.
Recipe can be halved or doubled.
Nutrient Value Per ¼ Cup:
74 calories, 1 g protein, 5 g fat,
6 g carbohydrate, 329 mg sodium,
0 mg cholesterol.

1 tablespoon olive oil
1 medium-size onion, chopped
1 clove garlic, finely chopped
1 can (13⅓ ounces to 16 ounces) whole tomatoes
¼ cup drained oil-packed sun-dried tomatoes, chopped
½ teaspoon sugar
¼ to ½ teaspoon cracked black pepper
¼ cup loosely packed fresh basil leaves, thinly sliced
1 teaspoon balsamic vinegar OR: red wine vinegar

1. Heat oil in 2-quart saucepan over medium-high heat. Add onion; sauté 5 minutes or until softened. Add garlic; sauté 1 minute.
2. Add tomatoes with their liquid, sun-dried tomatoes, sugar and pepper, stirring to break up tomatoes. Bring to boiling. Lower heat; cover and simmer 20 minutes. Stir in basil and balsamic vinegar.

Make-Ahead Tip: The sauce can be prepared ahead without adding the basil and vinegar. Refrigerate, covered, for 1 or 2 days. Gently reheat and stir in the basil and vinegar.

RED PEPPER AND TOMATO SAUCE

LOW-CHOLESTEROL · QUICK

Perfect for fish or poultry. Blanching the garlic brings out its sweetness.

Makes 2⅔ cups.
Recipe can be halved or doubled.
Nutrient Value Per ¼ Cup: 52 calories,
1 g protein, 3 g fat, 6 g carbohydrate,
86 mg sodium, 0 mg cholesterol.

3 cloves garlic, peeled
2 slices white sandwich bread, toasted and torn into pieces
2 jars (7 ounces each) roasted red peppers, drained, rinsed and drained again
½ cup no-salt-added tomato sauce
2 tablespoons olive oil
2 tablespoons water
1 teaspoon sugar
¼ teaspoon salt
⅛ teaspoon ground hot red pepper
⅛ teaspoon black pepper

1. Drop garlic into small pot of boiling water; blanch 3 minutes. Drain. Transfer to food processor or blender. Add toast, roasted peppers, tomato sauce, olive oil, water, sugar, salt, ground red pepper and black pepper. Whirl until smooth.
2. Transfer mixture to medium-size saucepan. Bring to simmering over low heat. Serve.

Make-Ahead Tip: The sauce can be prepared up to 2 days ahead and refrigerated, covered. Reheat to serve.

MORE SAUCE IDEAS
For other sauces to accent fish, turn to the Sauces section (pages 462–464) in Chapter 10, Vegetables and Fruit.

MANGO SALSA

LOW-CHOLESTEROL · QUICK

Serve this colorful condiment with fish, pork or poultry.

Makes 1¾ cups.
Recipe can be halved or doubled.
Nutrient Value Per ¼ Cup:
41 calories, 0 g protein, 2 g fat,
6 g carbohydrate, 81 mg sodium,
0 mg cholesterol.

---

1 large mango, peeled, seeded and finely
    chopped (about 1 cup)
1 large sweet red pepper, halved, cored,
    seeded and finely chopped
¼ cup finely chopped shallots OR: white
    part green onion
1 tablespoon lemon juice
1 tablespoon olive oil
1 large clove garlic, finely chopped
¼ teaspoon grated lemon rind
¼ teaspoon salt
⅛ teaspoon liquid red-pepper seasoning

Combine mango, red pepper, shallots, lemon juice, olive oil, garlic, lemon rind, salt and red-pepper seasoning in medium-size bowl; toss together until well combined.

Make Ahead: Salsa can be made up to 1 day ahead and refrigerated, covered, until ready to serve. It's actually better if made ahead so the flavors have a chance to blend.

RED PEPPER MAYONNAISE

LOW-CHOLESTEROL · QUICK

Homemade roasted red peppers give this sauce a deep, smoky flavor. But if you don't have the time to roast your own (See How-To, page 433), buy jarred or canned. Be sure to rinse and drain them before using. Serve with strongly flavored fish or with poultry, or use in cold salads or as a sandwich topper.

Broil peppers for 15 minutes.
Makes 1 cup.
Recipe can be halved or doubled.
Nutrient Value Per Tablespoon:
32 calories, 0 g protein, 3 g fat,
2 g carbohydrate, 56 mg sodium,
2 mg cholesterol.

---

2 sweet red peppers (about 8 ounces
    each) OR: 1 jar (7 ounces) roasted
    red peppers, drained
¼ cup mayonnaise
3 tablespoons lowfat plain yogurt
¼ teaspoon salt

1. Preheat broiler. Place peppers on sheet of aluminum foil on broiler pan.
2. Broil 6 inches from heat source, turning, until blackened all over, about 15 minutes. Place in paper bag and close to soften.
3. When peppers are cool enough to handle, peel over sieve set in bowl so juice drips into bowl. Discard skin and seeds.
4. Transfer peppers and juices to food processor or blender. Whirl until smooth puree.
5. Whisk together mayonnaise, yogurt and salt in medium-size bowl. Stir in red pepper puree. Refrigerate, covered, until ready to use.

Make-Ahead Tip: Mayonnaise can be made up to 3 days ahead and refrigerated, covered.

BASIL MAYONNAISE

QUICK

Delicious on fish, broiled chicken or vegetables or as a salad dressing or sandwich spread. Cooking the garlic briefly in boiling water sweetens the flavor.

Makes 1⅓ cups.
Recipe can be halved or doubled.
Nutrient Value Per Tablespoon: 82 calories, 0 g protein, 8 g fat, 2 g carbohydrate, 66 mg sodium, 6 mg cholesterol.

2 cloves garlic, peeled
2 cups packed basil leaves
1 cup mayonnaise
2 teaspoons lemon juice
¾ teaspoon Dijon-style mustard

1. Drop garlic into small pot of boiling water; blanch 3 minutes. Drain; rinse under cold running water; drain again.
2. Combine garlic, basil, mayonnaise, lemon juice and mustard in food processor or blender. Whirl until smooth. Refrigerate, covered, until ready to use.

CILANTRO-LIME BUTTER

LOW-SODIUM · QUICK

Keep a ready supply in your freezer. Particularly good with swordfish, tuna and other strong-flavored fish, or try over grilled chicken or tossed with hot vegetables.

Makes ½ cup.
Recipe can be halved or doubled.
Nutrient Value Per Teaspoon: 34 calories, 0 g protein, 4 g fat, 0 g carbohydrate, 1 mg sodium, 10 mg cholesterol.

1 large lime
½ cup (1 stick) *un*salted butter, softened
¼ cup packed cilantro leaves, chopped

1. Grate enough lime rind to measure 1 teaspoon. Squeeze enough juice to measure 1 teaspoon; set aside.
2. Beat together butter, cilantro, lime rind and lime juice in small food processor or in small bowl with spoon until well blended.
3. Spoon butter onto piece of waxed paper. Use paper to help shape butter into 12-inch-long cylinder and then wrap. Refrigerate.

CITRUS-HERB BUTTER

LOW-SODIUM · QUICK

This butter is excellent tossed with warm vegetables as well as over fish. Try stuffing the butter under the skin of chicken for extra flavor (see page 250), or use as a spread for special sandwiches.

Makes ½ cup.
Recipe can be halved or doubled.
Nutrient Value Per Teaspoon: 34 calories, 0 g protein, 4 g fat, 0 g carbohydrate, 12 mg sodium, 10 mg cholesterol.

½ cup (1 stick) *un*salted butter, softened
¼ teaspoon grated lime rind
4 teaspoons lime juice
2 teaspoons orange juice
1½ teaspoons snipped chives
¾ teaspoon chopped fresh tarragon leaves OR: ¼ teaspoon dried
⅛ teaspoon salt
Pinch ground nutmeg

1. Beat together butter, lime rind, lime juice, orange juice, chives, tarragon, salt and nutmeg in small food processor or in small bowl with spoon until well blended.
2. Spoon onto sheet of waxed paper. Use paper to help shape butter into 12-inch-long cylinder and then wrap. Refrigerate.

BASIL MAYONNAISE MAKE-AHEAD TIP:
The mayonnaise can be made up to 3 days ahead and refrigerated, covered.

BUTTER MAKE-AHEAD TIP:
Refrigerate these butters for up to 1 week, or overwrap with aluminum foil and freeze for up to 1 month.

PERNOD AND FENNEL BUTTER

LOW-SODIUM · QUICK

Keep a ready supply in your freezer. Place a pat of the butter on fish for a finishing touch. Also good tossed with hot cooked green beans, peas and other vegetables.

Makes ½ cup.
Recipe can be halved or doubled.
Nutrient Value Per Teaspoon: 37 calories, 0 g protein, 4 g fat, 0 g carbohydrate, 1 mg sodium, 10 mg cholesterol.

½ cup (1 stick) *un*salted butter, softened
2 tablespoons Pernod (anise-flavored liqueur)
½ teaspoon fennel seeds, crushed

1. Beat together butter, Pernod, and fennel seeds in small food processor or in small bowl with spoon until well blended.
2. Spoon butter onto waxed paper. Use paper to help shape butter into 12-inch-long cylinder and then wrap. Refrigerate.

ROASTED RED PEPPER BUTTER

LOW-SODIUM · QUICK

This flavorful butter makes a quick and easy finish for fish and poultry, or even for spreading on roast beef or chicken salad sandwiches.

Makes ½ cup.
Recipe can be halved or doubled.
Nutrient Value Per Teaspoon: 34 calories, 0 g protein, 4 g fat, 0 g carbohydrate, 1 mg sodium, 10 mg cholesterol.

½ cup (1 stick) *un*salted butter, softened
2 tablespoons drained, finely chopped, jarred roasted red peppers
½ teaspoon finely chopped, seeded jalapeño pepper, fresh or canned

1. Beat together butter, roasted red pepper and pepper in small food processor or in small bowl with spoon until well blended.
2. Spoon butter onto piece of waxed paper. Use paper to help shape butter into 12-inch-long cylinder and then wrap. Refrigerate.

CURRY-CHIVE BUTTER

QUICK

A tasty accent to mackerel, bluefish and swordfish, and even mild-flavored fish. Place a pat on grilled chicken breasts or toss with your favorite hot cooked vegetables.

Makes ½ cup.
Recipe can be halved or doubled.
Nutrient Value Per Teaspoon: 34 calories, 0 g protein, 4 g fat, 0 g carbohydrate, 1 mg sodium, 10 mg cholesterol.

½ cup (1 stick) *un*salted butter, softened
¾ teaspoon curry powder
1 tablespoon chopped chives
1 teaspoon lemon juice

1. Heat 1 tablespoon butter in small saucepan over low heat. Add curry powder; cook 1 minute. Cover and refrigerate a few minutes until mixture cools.
2. Beat together remaining butter, chives, lemon juice and curry mixture in small food processor or in small bowl with spoon until well blended.
3. Spoon butter onto piece of waxed paper. Use paper to help shape butter into 12-inch-long cylinder and then wrap. Refrigerate.

PERNOD
Pernod is an anise- and herb-flavored liqueur, which complements the licorice-flavored fennel seeds in Pernod and Fennel Butter.

BUTTER MAKE-AHEAD TIP:
Refrigerate these butters for up to 1 week, or overwrap with aluminum foil and freeze for up to 1 month.

BAKED STUFFED CLAMS

LOW-CALORIE · LOW-SODIUM

Serve as an hors d'oeuvre with drinks, or an appetizer or first course. Our recipe is not overloaded with bread crumbs so the taste of the clams really comes through.

Broil for 3 to 5 minutes.
Makes 4 appetizer servings.
Recipe can be halved or doubled.
Nutrient Value Per Serving: 91 calories, 9 g protein, 4 g fat, 5 g carbohydrate, 85 mg sodium, 24 mg cholesterol.

16 littleneck clams, scrubbed
1 slice bacon, cut into ¼-inch pieces
1 medium-size sweet red pepper, cored, seeded and finely chopped
1 small onion, finely chopped
2 teaspoons finely chopped fresh thyme OR: ½ teaspoon dried
1 tablespoon plain bread crumbs

1. Place clams in single layer in large Dutch oven or saucepot with a little water in bottom. Cover. Heat clams over medium heat 6 to 8 minutes or until they just begin to open. Remove from heat. (Discard any unopened shells.)

2. When cool enough to handle, hold clams over bowl and, with knife, pry clams open. Scrape out clam meat and chop, reserving clam liquor. Reserve 16 clam shell halves.

3. Cook bacon in medium-size saucepan over medium heat until browned and crisp, stirring occasionally. With slotted spoon, remove bacon to paper toweling to drain. Cook pepper, onion and thyme in drippings in saucepan for 5 minutes, stirring occasionally. Remove from heat; cool slightly. Stir in chopped clams, 2 tablespoons reserved clam liquor, bread crumbs and bacon.

4. Divide clam mixture equally among reserved clam shells. Arrange stuffed clams on rack in broiler pan.

5. Broil 4 inches from heat in pre-heated broiler for 3 to 5 minutes or until browned and heated through. Serve hot.

Make-Ahead Tip: The clams can be prepared several hours ahead through Step 4 and refrigerated, covered.

OPENING CLAMS

To open an uncooked clam by hand, first wrap your hand in a clean kitchen towel for protection. Hold scrubbed raw clam in your palm, hinge down, and run a clam knife between the shell halves to cut the muscle that holds them together. Run the knife under the clam meat to release it from its bottom shell. Clams can also be opened by micro-waving, steaming on top of the stove, set-ting in a hot oven, or by grilling. Once a clam opens by any of these heating meth-ods, it is also fully cooked.

ABOUT CLAMS

Clams from the Atlan-tic and Pacific oceans are divided into hard-shell varieties such as littleneck, cherrystone and quahog or chow-der clams, and soft-shell varieties such as steamers and razors. Buy live clams, soak in salted water with a little cornmeal for several hours to remove sand, and scrub shells before cooking. Steam, stew or coat meat with crumbs and fry, but keep cooking time to a minimum or clams will become rubbery and hard to chew.

1¾ cups milk
½ teaspoon salt
⅛ teaspoon ground nutmeg
⅛ teaspoon pepper
1 cup frozen peas, thawed and drained
12 ounces lump crabmeat, picked over to
    remove bits of cartilage

1. Prepare Pie Dough: Stir together
flour, chives, paprika and salt in large
bowl. Cut in butter with pastry blender
or 2 knives until mixture resembles
coarse meal. Stir in yogurt and red pepper seasoning just until mixture comes
together. Transfer to lightly floured
work surface. With heel of hand, break
off pieces of dough, and then work back
together with heel until all the dough
has been worked and is together again.
Pat into a flat disk. Wrap in plastic
wrap and refrigerate several hours or
overnight.
2. Prepare Filling: Heat butter in large
skillet over low heat. Add onion; cover
and cook, stirring occasionally, until
soft, about 7 minutes. Add mushrooms;
cover and cook, stirring occasionally, 5
minutes or until lightly colored.
3. Stir in flour. Increase heat to
medium; cook, stirring, 1 minute. Stir
in milk, salt, nutmeg and pepper; cook,
stirring occasionally, until thickened,
about 5 minutes. Stir in peas and crab.
Pour into 9-inch pie plate. Set plate on
baking sheet.
4. Preheat oven to moderate (375°).
5. Roll pie dough out on lightly floured
surface with lightly floured rolling pin
into 12-inch round. Place over filling.
Fold overhanging dough under. Crimp
edges in decorative border. Cut a steam
vent in top.
6. Bake in preheated moderate oven
(375°) for 30 minutes or until crust is
golden and filling is bubbly.

Make-Ahead Tip: The dough can be prepared a day ahead, wrapped in plastic
wrap, and refrigerated, or overwrapped
in aluminum foil and frozen for up to 2
months. Thaw in the refrigerator. The
filling can be prepared a day ahead and
refrigerated, covered.

CRAB PIE

**GETTING THE MOST
FROM YOUR CRAB**
A delicious make-
ahead dish, Crab Pie
extends a small
amount of expensive
lump crabmeat to
serve eight. Serve
small portions for an
elegant first course.
Cooked lobster can
be substituted for the
crab.

Bake at 375° for 30 minutes.
Makes 8 servings.
Nutrient Value Per Serving: 312 calories,
15 g protein, 19 g fat, 22 g carbohydrate,
542 mg sodium, 93 mg cholesterol.

Pie Dough:
1 cup all-purpose flour
2 tablespoons snipped chives OR:
    chopped green onion tops
¼ teaspoon sweet paprika
¼ teaspoon salt
10 tablespoons (1¼ sticks) *un*salted
    butter, cut up
⅓ cup lowfat plain yogurt
¼ teaspoon liquid red-pepper seasoning

Filling:
1 tablespoon *un*salted butter
1 small onion, finely chopped
8 ounces mushrooms, trimmed and
    quartered or cut in eighths if large
3 tablespoons all-purpose flour

CRAB AND CORN CAKES

Makes 4 servings (4 crab cakes).
Recipe can be halved or doubled.
Nutrient Value Per Serving: 392 calories,
32 g protein, 16 g fat, 30 g carbohydrate,
558 mg sodium, 273 mg cholesterol.

2 teaspoons plus 2 tablespoons vegetable
    oil
1 medium-size sweet red pepper, cored,
    seeded and finely chopped
1 cup (5 ounces) frozen whole-kernel
    corn, thawed
1 pound lump crabmeat, picked over to
    remove bits of cartilage
2 tablespoons finely chopped chives OR:
    green onion tops
2 teaspoons lemon juice
¼ teaspoon salt
1½ teaspoons Dijon-style mustard
3 eggs, separated

¾ cup all-purpose flour
2 tablespoons cornmeal

1. Heat the 2 teaspoons oil in small
skillet over moderate heat. Add red
pepper; cook, stirring occasionally, until
soft, about 4 minutes. Add corn; cook 1
minute. Cool to room temperature.
Transfer to large bowl. Add crabmeat,
chives, lemon juice, salt, mustard and
egg yolks. Sprinkle ¼ cup flour over
mixture, tossing gently to combine.
Beat egg whites in second bowl until
soft peaks form. Fold into crab mixture.
Form into 4 equal patties.
2. Combine remaining flour and cornmeal on waxed paper. Dredge patties in
mixture. Transfer to plate and refrigerate, covered, 1 hour.
3. Heat remaining 2 tablespoons oil in
large skillet over moderate heat. Add
patties; cook until crisp and golden,
about 3 minutes. Turn over; cook 2 to
3 minutes.

CRAB
A sweet, lean, deli-
cate saltwater shell-
fish, crab dwells in the
shallow waters along
the Atlantic, Pacific
and Gulf coasts.
Hard-shell varieties
such as Dungeness
and stone crab are
best when steamed or
boiled. Soft-shell
crabs are East Coast
blue crabs that have
shed their shells and
are best when dusted
with flour and sautéed.

CRAB CAKES SERVING IDEAS
These are rich, yet
light. Serve with tartar
sauce, salsa or a mus-
tard sauce; coleslaw
as a side dish would
be ideal. Shape into
smaller cakes for
appetizer portions.

CRAB CAKES MAKE-AHEAD TIP:
Cakes can be assem-
bled 2 hours ahead
and refrigerated,
covered.

LOBSTER STEW WITH VEGETABLES

QUICK

Makes 4 servings.
Recipe can be halved or doubled.
Nutrient Value Per Serving: 370 calories, 27 g protein, 17 g fat, 22 g carbohydrate, 489 mg sodium, 143 mg cholesterol.

8 ounces all-purpose potatoes, pared and cut into ½-inch dice (1¼ cups)
2 carrots, pared and cut into 1½ × ¼-inch strips
6 ounces green beans, trimmed and cut diagonally into 1-inch pieces
1 leek, well washed, tough green removed, cut into ½-inch dice
¾ cup heavy cream
½ cup dry white wine
1 pound cooked lobster meat, cut into ½-inch-thick slices or chunks (about three 1¼-pound lobsters)
½ cup frozen peas, thawed
1 teaspoon chopped fresh tarragon OR: ¼ teaspoon dried
⅛ teaspoon ground hot red pepper
2 tablespoons snipped chives OR: finely chopped green onion tops

1. Cook potatoes in large pot of lightly salted water for 3 minutes. Add carrots and green beans; cook 4 minutes. Add leek; cook 30 seconds. Drain; rinse under cold water; drain again.
2. Combine cream and wine in large skillet. Bring to boiling. Reduce heat; simmer 4 minutes. Add potato, carrot, green beans, leek, lobster, peas, tarragon and ground red pepper. Return to simmer; simmer 4 minutes or until lobster is heated through and sauce coats lobster and vegetables. Stir in chives. Serve.

LOBSTER

Found in cold North Atlantic waters, lobster is a sweet, white-fleshed saltwater shellfish. Its dark brown armor turns bright orange when cooked and its meat quickly firms up. Lobster is usually simmered or steamed to keep the meat moist, but it can also be basted and baked, broiled or grilled.

LOBSTER FOR THE STEW

Purchase your pre-cooked lobster from an impeccable source and enjoy this dish for a special occasion. If you have the time and inclination, boil your own lobster and remove the meat for the recipe.

Mussels with Tarragon-Parsley Sauce

LOW-CALORIE · LOW-CHOLESTEROL

Be sure the mussels are absolutely fresh. Serve as a first course, or with a salad and crusty bread as a light dinner or lunch.

Makes 4 servings.
Recipe can be halved or doubled.
Nutrient Value Per Serving: 233 calories, 17 g protein, 10 g fat, 9 g carbohydrate, 391 mg sodium, 37 mg cholesterol.

Green Sauce:
1 cup packed parsley leaves
¼ cup sliced green onion (white and green part; 4 to 5 green onions)
3 tablespoons fresh tarragon leaves
1 tablespoon lemon juice
1 tablespoon olive oil
1 clove garlic

Mussels:
1 cup dry white wine
¼ cup packed parsley leaves
2 cloves garlic
1 tablespoon olive oil
3 sprigs tarragon leaves
4 pounds scrubbed and debearded mussels (40 large)

1. Prepare Green Sauce: Combine parsley, green onion, tarragon, lemon juice, olive oil and garlic in small food processor or blender. Whirl until smooth. Reserve in food processor.
2. Prepare Mussels: Combine wine, parsley, garlic, oil and tarragon leaves in Dutch oven or casserole. Bring to boiling over high heat. Working in 2 batches, add mussels. Cover and cook 3 minutes or until mussels open; uncover frequently and check mussels, removing them as they open and transferring with slotted spoon to large serving bowl or platter. (Discard unopened mussels.)

3. Strain mussel liquid through sieve lined with double-thickness cheese-cloth, over bowl. Add ½ cup strained liquid to green sauce in processor. Whirl until combined. Pour sauce over mussels. Serve hot, at room temperature or chilled.

Make-Ahead Tip: The sauce and mussels can be prepared earlier in the day and refrigerated separately, covered. Serve cold.

Scallops with Mushrooms and Dill

LOW-CALORIE · LOW-CHOLESTEROL
QUICK

Makes 4 servings.
Recipe can be halved or doubled.
Nutrient Value Per Serving: 272 calories, 21 g protein, 15 g fat, 10 g carbohydrate, 231 mg sodium, 64 mg cholesterol.

2 tablespoons olive oil OR: vegetable oil
4 ounces mushrooms, trimmed and thinly sliced (1½ cups)
1 pound sea scallops
3 tablespoons all-purpose flour
⅓ cup dry white wine
⅓ cup heavy cream
1 teaspoon Dijon-style mustard
3 tablespoons chopped fresh dill
½ teaspoon lemon juice

1. Heat 1 tablespoon oil in large skillet over moderately high heat. Add mushrooms; sauté until lightly browned, about 4 minutes. Remove with slotted spoon to bowl.
2. Add remaining oil to skillet. Toss scallops in flour to coat and add to skillet. Cook, tossing frequently, until lightly golden, 3 to 4 minutes. Remove scallops from skillet and reserve.
3. Add wine, cream, mustard, dill and mushrooms to skillet; cook, scraping up
(continued)

MUSSELS
These are full-flavored, lean, delicate saltwater shellfish. Choose live mussels with unbroken shells that are closed tight or stay closed when gently pressed. Pull off beard, scrub mussels clean and soak in salted water for 2 to 3 hours before steaming.

QUICK SCALLOP DISH
Need an elegant dish you can throw together effortlessly for company, with practically no preparation? Scallops with Mushrooms and Dill is it. Make sure the scallops are as fresh as possible, and serve with pasta or rice for "scooping up" the rich sauce.

SCALLOPS WITH MUSHROOMS AND DILL
(*continued*)

any bits from bottom, 3 to 4 minutes or until lightly thickened. Stir in lemon juice and scallops. Cook over low heat just until scallops are heated through, about 1 minute. Serve immediately.

SCALLOP ROLL

LOW-CHOLESTEROL · QUICK

Makes 4 servings (4 rolls).
Nutrient Value Per Serving: 371 calories, 24 g protein, 14 g fat, 38 g carbohydrate, 556 mg sodium, 40 mg cholesterol.

⅓ cup all-purpose flour
3 tablespoons dry bread crumbs
¼ teaspoon salt
⅛ teaspoon sweet paprika
1 pound sea scallops, cleaned, dried and halved widthwise if large
3 tablespoons corn oil
1 cup shredded lettuce *(optional)*
4 club or hot dog rolls
4 lemon wedges

1. Combine flour, bread crumbs, salt and paprika on sheet of waxed paper. Dredge scallops in flour mixture, shaking off excess.
2. Heat oil in large skillet over moderately high heat. Add scallops; cook, tossing frequently, until golden brown all over, 4 to 5 minutes. Place lettuce, if using, in rolls. Spoon scallops on top. Serve with lemon wedges.

SCALLOP ROLL
The kind of roll you'd find at the seaside. Delicious with our Red Pepper Mayonnaise *(see recipe, page 330).*

SCALLOPS
Sweet and mild-flavored, scallops are shellfish with a smooth, delicate texture. Bay scallops and calico scallops are the smaller varieties; sea scallops grow larger, up to 2 inches in diameter. All varieties are best when quickly steamed, sautéed or poached.

SHELLFISH FACTS
For information on buying and storing shellfish, see primer on page 296.

SHRIMP CARIBBEAN

LOW-CALORIE · QUICK

Makes 4 servings.
Nutrient Value Per Serving: 278 calories, 26 g protein, 15 g fat, 10 g carbohydrate, 246 mg sodium, 173 mg cholesterol.

2 tablespoons peanut oil OR: olive oil
¼ cup lime juice
1 tablespoon chili sauce
1 teaspoon sugar
1 cucumber (about 8 ounces), pared, halved lengthwise, seeded and sliced ¼ inch thick
1 pound large shrimp (21 to 25 per pound), peeled and deveined *(see How-To, page 340)*

⅛ teaspoon ground hot red pepper
⅓ cup flaked coconut
¼ cup shelled roasted peanuts

1. Whisk together 1 tablespoon oil, 2 tablespoons lime juice, chili sauce and ½ teaspoon sugar in small bowl.
2. Heat remaining tablespoon oil in large skillet over moderately high heat. Add cucumber; cook, stirring occasionally, for 4 minutes. Remove with slotted spoon to serving bowl.
3. Add shrimp to skillet; cook, stirring frequently, for 3 minutes or until almost done. Add remaining lime juice, sugar and the hot red pepper; cook 1 minute. Stir in coconut, peanuts and reserved chili sauce mixture. Toss in cucumbers; cook 1 minute. Serve.

CARIBBEAN COOKING
This unusual combination of shrimp and cooked cucumber works well. Serve with rice and noodles, or shredded lettuce.

SHRIMP CARIBBEAN MAKE-AHEAD TIP:
The dish can be made several hours ahead and refrigerated, covered. Serve at room temperature.

BROILED MARINATED SHRIMP

A simple make-ahead dish with lots of flavor that would be especially good with your favorite coleslaw. The shrimp cook quickly, so keep an eye on them.

Broil for 4 to 5 minutes.
Makes 4 servings.
Recipe can be halved or doubled.
Nutrient Value Per Serving: 194 calories, 19 g protein, 12 g fat, 2 g carbohydrate, 411 mg sodium, 140 mg cholesterol.

4 cloves garlic, crushed
3 tablespoons olive oil
¾ teaspoon leaf oregano, crumbled
½ teaspoon salt
⅛ teaspoon ground allspice
⅛ teaspoon ground hot red pepper
1 bay leaf, halved
1 pound large shrimp (21 to 25 per pound), peeled and deveined *(See How-To, at right.)*
1 tablespoon lemon juice

1. Combine garlic, olive oil, oregano, salt, allspice, ground red pepper and bay leaf in large bowl or food storage bag; mix well. Add shrimp; mix to coat. Refrigerate 4 hours, turning shrimp in marinade every 30 minutes. Add lemon juice during last 15 minutes of marinating and mix well.
2. Preheat broiler. Remove bay leaf from marinade.
3. Broil shrimp 4 inches from heat for 4 to 5 minutes, turning once during cooking, until cooked through. Serve hot or at room temperature. Discard any remaining marinade.

Make-Ahead Tip: The shrimp can be cooked several hours ahead and refrigerated, and then served at room temperature.

HOW TO SHELL AND DEVEIN SHRIMP
1. With kitchen shears, cut through shell along outer curve and into the shrimp about 1⁄16 inch to expose the thin, dark vein.

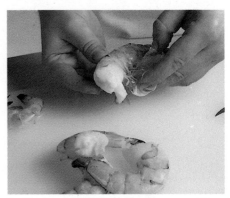

2. Peel back shell from the cut and gently separate shell, including tail, from the shrimp.

3. With tip of small paring knife, pull out thin vein and discard. Rinse the shrimp.

Blade Steaks with Artichoke Hearts
(page 352)

CHAPTER 9

MEATS

MEATS PRIMER

BEEF NOTES

- Choose cuts of beef with bright red color. The interior of ground meat and the exterior of vacuum-packed beef may be purplish-red because the meat is not exposed to air. The purple gives rise to red once the package is opened and the meat is exposed.
- Boneless cuts of beef provide 3 to 4 servings per pound. Bone-in roasts yield 2 to 3 servings per pound. Bony back ribs and short ribs yield 1 to 1½ servings per pound.
- Refrigerate cuts of fresh beef, well-wrapped, in the meat compartment or coldest part of the refrigerator for up to 4 days. Store ground beef up to 2 days. Freeze for longer storage. *(See Freezing Techniques and Storage Times, page 31.)*
- Marinate less tender cuts of beef, such as chuck, round or flank steaks, for a few hours or overnight before cooking to tenderize and add flavor. Pan-fry, slice and stir-fry, or broil 2 to 5 inches from heat, depending on thickness of steak.
- To roast larger cuts, such as rib, rib eye, tenderloin, rump and top round, place beef, fat side up, so the meat bastes itself as it cooks, in open roasting pan. Insert meat thermometer in center without touching bone or fatty portions, or test toward end of roasting time with an instant-read meat thermometer. Roast according to cut and weight. *(See Beef Roasting Timetable, this page.)* Large cuts of meat continue to cook after removal from oven, so remove when thermometer reaches 5° below desired doneness. Let stand 15 minutes before carving.

IS IT DONE YET?

- Check the internal temperature of beef roasts with a meat thermometer to determine if meat is cooked to desired doneness.
- Use an instant-read thermometer to gauge internal temperature towards the *end* of the minimum cooking time recommended for the weight of your roast. *(See Beef Roasting Timetable, this page.)* Unlike standard meat thermometers that remain in the roast from beginning to end of cooking time, thin-stemmed instant-read thermometers are inserted for only 10 seconds, then removed. They can be poked into different parts of a roast without leaving large holes from which juices can escape and they aren't left in the meat long enough to conduct heat into the center.
Rare: 140°
Medium-rare: 150°
Medium: 160°
Well-done: 170°
Ground beef: 160°-170°

- To see if a steak is done, make a small cut with a sharp knife and check the color of the interior.

THE LOWDOWN ON LEAN

Choosing leaner cuts of meat not only means less fat in your diet, it means increased amounts of essential nutrients such as iron, zinc and B vitamins, which are more highly concentrated in leaner meats.

Best beef bets: lean round, shoulder, rump or sirloin; ground round.

Best pork bets: center-cut lean ham, loin chops, pork tenderloin.

Best lamb bets: leg of lamb, loin chops, fore shanks.

Best veal bets: all cuts except ground veal (veal is generally lower in fat but higher in cholesterol than beef).

- Leaner cuts may be more expensive, so use less in stir-frys and main-dish salads. Serve smaller portions and extend with inexpensive sources of protein such as beans or tofu.
- The federal standard for lean meat is no more than 10% fat by

BEEF ROASTING TIMETABLE*

Cut & Weight	Approximate Total Cooking Time (in Hours)			Oven Temp
	Rare (140°)	Medium (160°)	Well Done (170°)	
Rib: Bone in				
4–6 lbs.	1¾–2½	2¼–3½	2¾–4	325°
6–8	2¼–3	2¾–3¾	3¼–4¼	325°
Rib Eye:				
4–6 lbs.	1¼–1¾	1½–2	1¾–2¼	350°
Sirloin Tip: Boneless				
3½–4 lbs.	2¼	2½	2¾	325°
6–8 lbs.	3–4	3–4¼	3¼–4½	325°
Tenderloin:				
Whole 4–6 lbs.	45–60 min.			425°
Half 2–3 lbs.	45–50 min.			425°

*Note: Temperature of roast will rise 5° during standing.

weight except for lean ground beef, which should be no more than 22.5% fat. State laws may vary from federal so the best way to judge is to read the label on packaged meat.

■ USDA grading of meat is determined by fat content and texture: PRIME: most tender; highest in fat. CHOICE: the most common grade of meat sold in supermarkets; moderately fatty. SELECT: the grade reserved for leaner meats.

■ Leaner cuts of meat require quick cooking at high temperatures (stir-fry, broil) or slow cooking at low temperatures (braise, stew, covered roast).

VEAL NOTES

■ Veal is favored for its lean meat and mild flavor. Choose veal cuts that are firm-textured and cream to pink in color. Store fresh veal, well wrapped, in the meat compartment or coldest part of the refrigerator for up to 2 days. Freeze for longer storage. *(See Freezing Techniques and Storage Times, page 31.)*

■ Boneless veal yields 3 to 4 servings per pound. Bone-in cuts such as leg round roast yield 2 to

3 servings per pound. Bony rib cuts provide 1 to 2 servings per pound.

■ All cuts of veal are cooked at low to medium temperatures to prevent the meat from toughening and drying out. Sauté thin cutlets or scaloppine, chops and ground veal patties; broil rib or loin chops; braise less tender, smaller cuts from the breast, foreshank, shoulder and round. Roast larger cuts of veal (2 or more pounds) from the loin, sirloin, rib, rump and shoulder.

■ To prepare veal for roasting, place meat, with any fat on top, so the meat bastes itself as it cooks, on rack in open roasting pan. Season well and insert meat thermometer into center of roast without touching bone or fat or test toward end of roasting time with an instant-read thermometer. Roast according to cut and weight. *(See Veal Roasting Timetable, this page.)*

■ Large roasts will continue to cook after removal from oven, so remove when thermometer registers 5° below desired doneness. Let roast stand 15 minutes before carving.

PORK NOTES

■ As with all meat, the number of servings of pork per pound depends on the cut and the cooking method. Generally, boneless chops and roasts provide 3 to 4 servings per pound. Bone-in roasts and meaty ribs yield 2 to 3 servings per pound. A pound of bony back ribs and spareribs may serve only 1.

■ Store fresh pork chops and roasts in plastic store packaging, or rewrapped in plastic wrap, in the meat compartment or coldest part of the refrigerator for up to 3 days. Ground pork keeps 1 to 2 days. Freeze pork for longer storage. *(See Freezing Techniques and Storage Times, page 31.)*

■ Pan-fry pork chops, tenderloin slices and pork patties that are less than 1 inch thick. Thicker chops and patties, as well as ribs, kabobs and whole tenderloins, can be broiled 4 to 5 inches from heat. Larger cuts (over 2 pounds) are roasted.

■ To roast pork, place fat-side up, so the meat bastes itself as it cooks, on rack in open roasting pan. Insert meat thermometer so bulb is centered in roast without touching fat or bone, or test toward end of roasting time with an instant-read meat thermometer. Roast according to cut and weight. *(See Pork Roasting Timetable, page 344.)*

■ Since pork is over 30% leaner than it was ten years ago, old cooking times and temperatures are obsolete and may result in tough, overcooked meat. The idea that pork must be cooked to a high internal temperature to prevent trichinosis disease is also outdated. The disease has been practically eradicated in the United States, and we now know that the organism is destroyed once meat reaches an internal temperature of 137°. As a result,

VEAL ROASTING TIMETABLE*

| Cut and Weight | Approximate Total Cooking Time (in Hours) | | Oven Temp |
	Medium (160°)	Well Done (170°)	
Rump or Round: Boneless			
2–3 lbs.	45 min.–1	55 min.–1¼	325°
Loin:			
Bone in 3–4 lbs.	1¾–2¼	2–2½	325°
Boneless 2–3 lbs.	40 min.–1	45 min.–1¼	325°
Shoulder: Boneless			
2½–3 lbs.	1¼–1¾	1½–2	325°

*Note: Temperature of roast will rise 5° during standing.

cooking pork to the recommended minimum internal temperature of 160° yields meat that is juicy and flavorful as well as thoroughly and safely cooked.

■ Large roasts will continue to cook after removal from oven, so remove when thermometer registers 5° less than desired doneness. Tent roast with aluminum foil and let stand 15 to 20 minutes before carving.

LAMB NOTES

■ Lamb is an especially tender meat because it is usually marketed when it is between six and eight months old. Since lamb is so young, very little marbling develops and most of the fat is found around the outside of the meat.

■ Boneless cuts of lamb yield 3 to 4 servings per pound. Bone-in roasts and chops provide 2 to 3 servings per pound. Bony riblets and neck meat yield 1 to 2 servings per pound.

■ Store all cuts of lamb in their original packaging in the meat compartment or coldest part of the refrigerator and use within 5 days. Use ground lamb within 2 days. Overwrap and freeze lamb for longer storage. *(See Freezing Techniques and Storage Times, page 31.)*

■ Cuts from the neck and breast are usually braised or stewed; chops less than 1 inch thick should be cooked in a skillet, while thicker chops are best broiled. Larger cuts from the rib, loin, shoulder, sirloin and leg are roasted.

■ To prepare lamb for roasting, place fat-side up, so the meat bastes itself as it cooks, in open roasting pan. Remove the parchment-like skin called the fell, if you wish, but leaving it on helps the larger cuts retain their shape and juiciness while cooking. Insert meat thermometer so bulb reaches center of meat

without touching bone or fat, or test toward end of roasting time with an instant-read meat thermometer. Roast lamb to rare, medium or well done, according to timetable for cut and weight. *(See Lamb Roasting Timetable, this page.)*

■ Larger cuts will continue to cook after the meat has been removed from the oven, so take a roast out when the thermometer reads 5° lower than desired doneness and allow meat to sit for 15 or 20 minutes before carving.

PORK ROASTING TIMETABLE*

Cut and Weight	Approximate Total Cooking Time (in Hours)		Oven Temp
	Medium (160°)	Well Done (170°)	
Center Loin: Bone in			
3–5 lbs.	1¼–2	1½–2½	325°
Center Loin: Boneless			
2–4 lbs.	45 min.–1½	1¼–2	325°
Whole Leg: Bone in			
12–16 lbs.		4¾–6	325°
Half Leg: Boneless			
3½ lbs.		2¼–2½	325°
Tenderloin			
½–1 lb.	20–25 min.	25–30 min.	425°

LAMB ROASTING TIMETABLE*

Cut and Weight	Approximate Total Cooking Time (in Hours)			Oven Temp
	Rare (140°)	Medium (160°)	Well Done (170°)	
Whole Leg: Bone in				
5–7 lbs.	1¾–2¾	2–3¼	2½–4	325°
7–9 lbs.	2¼–3	3–3¾	3½–4½	325°
Half Leg: Bone in				
Shank 3–4 lbs.	1½–1¾	1½–2	1¾–2¼	325°
Sirloin 3–4 lbs.	1¼–1¾	1¾–2½	2¼–3	325°
Leg: Boneless				
3–5 lbs.	1¼–2¼	1½–2½	1¾–3	325°
5–7 lbs.	2–3	2½–3½	3¼–4¼	325°
Rib (rack)				
1½–2 lbs.	45 min.	1	1¼	375°
2–3 lbs.	1	1¼	1½	375°

*Note: Temperature of roast will rise 5° during standing.

POT ROAST WITH VEGETABLES AND RED WINE

Bake at 350° for 2½ to 3 hours.
Makes 16 servings.
Nutrient Value Per Serving: 477 calories, 31 g protein, 30 g fat, 20 g carbohydrate, 433 mg sodium, 100 mg cholesterol.

Marinade:
4 cups dry red wine
2 cups sliced onions
½ cup sliced carrots
1 cup sliced celery
4 cloves garlic, sliced
1 teaspoon leaf thyme, crumbled
1 teaspoon leaf rosemary, crumbled
1 teaspoon black pepper
4 cloves
1 bay leaf
3 strips orange rind

1 rump roast of beef (5 pounds)
¼ pound slab bacon, cut into ½-inch slices
4 cups beef broth, homemade *(see recipe, page 118)* OR: canned
1 can (16 ounces) tomatoes, undrained
2 tablespoons tomato paste
2 pounds carrots, pared, halved lengthwise and quartered crosswise
3 pounds small white onions, peeled
2 tablespoons dry Madeira
2 tablespoons cornstarch
¼ cup heavy cream *(optional)*

1. Prepare Marinade: Combine wine, onion, carrot, celery, garlic, thyme, rosemary, pepper, cloves, bay leaf and orange rind in large bowl. Add meat. Cover and refrigerate overnight, turning occasionally.
2. To cook, preheat the oven to moderate (350°).
3. Drain meat and vegetables, reserving liquid, meat and vegetables separately. Pat meat dry with paper toweling.
(continued)

COME FOR DINNER
When rump roast goes on sale, buy a piece for this classic pot roast. Invite family and friends for dinner, or if serving a smaller crowd, you'll have wonderful leftovers to enjoy. Serve with buttered noodles, mashed potatoes or rice.

POT ROAST WITH VEGETABLES AND RED WINE (*continued*)

4. Place bacon in Dutch oven large enough to hold rump roast. Sauté over moderate heat until crisp. Transfer bacon with slotted spoon to a plate. Add meat to pot; brown on all sides, about 10 minutes. Remove meat. Add vegetables from marinade; cook, stirring, 5 minutes. Return meat to pot. Add marinade, broth, tomatoes and tomato paste. Bring to boiling over high heat. Cover pot.

5. Bake pot in preheated moderate oven (350°), covered, for 2½ to 3 hours or until meat is tender.

6. Remove meat from pot. Strain cooking liquid and discard solids; skim off fat. Return meat and strained liquid to pot. Add 2 pounds carrots, small onions, and reserved bacon pieces, if you wish. Simmer, covered, 20 to 25 minutes or until vegetables are tender.

7. Transfer meat and vegetables to large platter. Cover loosely with aluminum foil and keep warm. Boil cooking liquid to reduce to 4 cups, if necessary.

8. Combine Madeira, cornstarch and cream, if using, in small bowl. Bring liquid in casserole to boiling. Stir cornstarch mixture into pot liquid; cook until lightly thickened, 2 to 3 minutes. Lower heat; simmer sauce 5 minutes.

9. To serve: Slice meat and arrange on platter. Strain sauce into sauceboat. Spoon some of sauce over meat and vegetables. Pass remaining sauce.

Make-Ahead Tip: The meat, vegetables and cooking liquid can be prepared up to 2 days ahead through Step 6. Refrigerate, covered. Gently reheat sliced meat and vegetables with a little of the broth. Prepare the sauce in Step 8 just before serving.

THE HEAT IS ON

As is true with many Cajun and Creole dishes, Cajun Pot Roast is rather spicy. Vary the degree of spicy heat according to taste, but remember the seasoning will mellow during the long cooking time. Serve with rice, pasta or potatoes.

CAJUN POT ROAST MAKE-AHEAD TIP:

The dish can be made a day or two ahead and refrigerated, covered. Gently reheat the meat slices in the sauce.

SECONDS ON REQUEST

Carve just enough slices from a roast to serve everyone once; the remaining meat will stay juicy and warm if you wait until seconds are requested before carving.

CAJUN POT ROAST

Makes 12 servings.
Nutrient Value Per Serving: 414 calories, 30 g protein, 28 g fat, 10 g carbohydrate, 666 mg sodium, 106 mg cholesterol.

1 chuck roast of beef (4 pounds)
2 to 3 teaspoons ground hot red pepper, or to taste
2 to 3 teaspoons black pepper, or to taste
½ to 1 teaspoon salt, or to taste
2 tablespoons vegetable oil
2 tablespoons *un*salted butter
3 medium-size onions, chopped
1½ cups sliced celery (6 celery stalks)
1 large sweet green pepper, cored, seeded and diced
3 cloves garlic, finely chopped
3 tablespoons all-purpose flour
1½ cups tomato sauce
3 cups beef broth
1 can (16 ounces) whole tomatoes, undrained
1 teaspoon leaf thyme, crumbled
1 bay leaf

1. Pat roast dry with paper toweling. Rub with red pepper, black pepper and salt. Heat oil in Dutch oven or pot large enough to hold chuck roast, over moderate heat. Add meat; brown on all sides, about 10 to 15 minutes.

2. Transfer meat to plate. Pour off fat from pot. Add butter and heat. Add onion, celery, green pepper, and garlic; cook, stirring, over moderate heat for 5 to 7 minutes or until onion is golden. Stir flour into pot; cook, stirring, 2 minutes. Stir in tomato sauce, beef broth, tomatoes with their liquid, thyme and bay leaf. Add meat. Bring to boiling. Lower heat; simmer, covered, for 3 to 3½ hours or until meat is tender. Transfer meat to platter and keep warm. Skim fat from broth. Remove and discard bay leaf.

3. To serve: Slice meat and arrange on platter. Spoon some sauce over meat. Pass remaining sauce.

INDONESIAN POT ROAST WITH PEANUT SAUCE

For a richer flavor, refrigerate meat in the liquid mixture from Step 2 for several hours or overnight. Then proceed with Step 1. Use marinade for cooking liquid in Step 2.

Makes 12 servings.

Nutrient Value Per Serving: 415 calories, 33 g protein, 28 g fat, 7 g carbohydrate, 623 mg sodium, 92 mg cholesterol.

1 eye round roast of beef (4 pounds)
¼ teaspoon salt
⅛ teaspoon black pepper
3 tablespoons peanut oil or vegetable oil
3 medium-size onions, finely chopped
4 cloves garlic, finely chopped
3 cups beef broth
3 tablespoons soy sauce
2 tablespoons dark brown sugar
1 tablespoon finely chopped pared fresh
    ginger
1 teaspoon grated lemon rind
2 dried red chili peppers, seeded OR: ¼
    to ½ teaspoon crushed red pepper
    flakes
2 teaspoons ground coriander
2 teaspoons ground cumin
¼ teaspoon ground cloves
¼ teaspoon ground nutmeg

Peanut Sauce:

6 tablespoons creamy peanut butter, or to
    taste
3 cups beef cooking liquid
1 small onion, finely chopped
2 cloves garlic, finely chopped
1 teaspoon finely chopped pared fresh
    ginger

1. Pat meat dry with paper toweling. Season with salt and pepper. Heat 2 tablespoons oil in pot large enough to hold roast, over moderate heat. Add meat; brown on all sides, about 8 to 10 minutes. Transfer to platter. Pour off fat.
2. Add remaining oil to pot and heat.

Add onion and garlic; cook, stirring, until softened, about 5 minutes. Add broth, soy sauce, brown sugar, ginger, rind, chili pepper, coriander, cumin, cloves and nutmeg. Return meat to pot; simmer, covered, for 2½ to 3 hours or until meat is tender. Transfer to platter. Cover; keep warm.
3. Strain cooking liquid and discard solids. Skim off fat. Boil liquid until reduced to 3 cups.
4. Prepare Peanut Sauce: Stir together the peanut butter with a little cooking liquid in a bowl until a smooth liquid. Combine this with the remaining cooking liquid, onion, garlic and ginger in saucepan until smooth. Simmer 10 minutes.
5. To serve: Slice meat and arrange on platter. Spoon some sauce over. Serve remaining sauce separately.

INDONESIAN POT ROAST MAKE-AHEAD TIP:

The roast and cooking liquid can be prepared up to 2 days ahead and refrigerated, covered. Gently reheat slices of the meat in the cooking liquid. Then prepare sauce.

SERVING IDEAS

Serve with rice or Oriental noodles for soaking up the delicious Peanut Sauce. Garnish with finely chopped fresh coriander and crushed dry-roasted peanuts, if you wish.

New England Boiled Dinner (page 349)

NEW ENGLAND BOILED DINNER

A *cold-weather one-pot meal. Walnuts add texture to a traditional horseradish sauce. (Pictured on page 348.)*

Makes 12 servings.
Nutrient Value Per Serving: 407 calories, 31 g protein, 21 g fat, 24 g carbohydrate, 223 mg sodium, 105 mg cholesterol.

Beef:
1 fresh beef brisket (about 4¾ pounds)
12 cups water

Bouquet Garni:
1 tablespoon black peppercorns
2 whole cloves
1 bay leaf
1 teaspoon leaf thyme, crumbled
1 teaspoon mustard seeds

Vegetables:
1 small rutabaga (about 1 pound)
8 small red-skinned potatoes (about 1¼ pounds)
2 large parsnips (about ¾ pound)
6 medium-size carrots
1 bunch small beets (about 1½ pounds)
1 small head Savoy cabbage (about 1½ pounds) OR: green cabbage
8 small white onions

Horseradish Sauce with Walnuts:
½ cup heavy cream
¾ cup dairy sour cream
2 tablespoons bottled horseradish, drained
2 tablespoons chopped parsley
⅓ cup finely chopped toasted walnuts
½ teaspoon salt
⅛ teaspoon pepper

1. Prepare Beef: Trim excess fat from beef, leaving ¼-inch layer. Place beef and water in large Dutch oven.
2. Prepare Bouquet Garni: Tie peppercorns, cloves, bay leaf, thyme and mustard seeds in cheesecloth bag; add to pot. Bring to boiling. Lower heat; cover and simmer 2½ hours.

3. While beef is cooking, prepare Vegetables: Pare and cut rutabaga into 1½-inch pieces. Remove ½-inch strip of skin from around center of potatoes. Pare and cut parsnips diagonally into 1-inch-thick slices. Pare and cut carrots in half lengthwise; cut crosswise into 3-inch lengths. Trim beet greens, leaving 2 inches. Cut cabbage into wedges. Peel onions.
4. Add rutabaga to beef; simmer 10 minutes. Add onions; simmer another 10 minutes. Add potatoes, parsnips and carrots; simmer another 25 minutes.
5. While vegetables are cooking, prepare Horseradish Sauce: Beat cream in medium-size bowl until soft peaks form. Fold in sour cream, horseradish, parsley, walnuts, salt and pepper. Refrigerate until serving.
6. While other vegetables are cooking, cook beets in separate pot of boiling water until tender, about 25 minutes. Peel and keep warm.
7. After potatoes and other vegetables have simmered in Step 4, add cabbage to beef; simmer until cabbage is tender, about 15 minutes. Remove beef and vegetables to serving platter.
8. Slice brisket. Serve with hot broth and horseradish sauce.

BOILED DINNER MAKE-AHEAD TIP:
The recipe can be prepared up to 2 days ahead and refrigerated, covered. Slice the meat and gently reheat along with vegetables in broth.

BEFORE THE STORM

New England Boiled Dinner
(this page)

Horseradish Sauce with
Walnuts (this page)

Potato Onion Bread (39)

Green Salad with Creamy
Black Pepper Dressing
(183)

Pecan Poundcake (502)

MARINATED LONDON BROIL

Broiling time is for meat at room temperature. If meat is taken directly from the refrigerator, increase the cooking time by 1 to 2 minutes per side for rare meat. Serve the steak with grilled or roasted vegetables.

Broil 12 to 14 minutes.
Makes 6 servings.
Nutrient Value Per Serving: 303 calories, 31 g protein, 18 g fat, 3 g carbohydrate, 294 mg sodium, 89 mg cholesterol.

---

3 tablespoons reduced-sodium soy sauce
2 tablespoons dark brown sugar
2 tablespoons Dijon-style mustard
2 tablespoons Oriental sesame oil
1 small onion, chopped
1 teaspoon chopped, pared fresh ginger
2 large cloves of garlic, chopped
¼ teaspoon pepper
1 round steak for London broil (2 pounds), 1½ inches thick

1. Combine soy sauce, sugar, mustard, sesame oil, onion, ginger, garlic and pepper in blender. Whirl until combined.
2. Arrange steak in shallow baking dish. Cover with marinade. Refrigerate, covered, for at least 3 hours or overnight.
3. Broil steak in preheated broiler about 4 inches from heat for 6 to 7 minutes on each side for rare. Let meat stand 5 minutes before slicing.

Make-Ahead Tip: The meat can be marinated overnight in the refrigerator, covered. Or cook a day ahead and refrigerate, then slice and serve cold or at room temperature.

LONDON BROIL
Originally the term "London Broil" referred to flank steak. Today what is sold as London Broil in supermarkets can be any one of a number of cuts—top round, sirloin tip, etc. Here we have used a round steak, cut 1½ inches thick.

BALSAMIC FLANK STEAK

LOW-SODIUM · QUICK

Here's a dish with just 4 ingredients—ready in record time. Serve with stewed tomatoes and Italian flat beans.

Broil 8 minutes.
Makes 4 servings.
Nutrient Value Per Serving: 246 calories, 29 g protein, 15 g fat, 1 g carbohydrate, 161 mg sodium, 71 mg cholesterol.

1¼ pounds flank steak, trimmed
⅓ cup oil-based, bottled Italian dressing
3 tablespoons balsamic vinegar OR: red wine vinegar
¼ teaspoon pepper

1. Combine steak, dressing, vinegar and pepper in plastic food-storage bag. Secure with twist tie and marinate 10 minutes.
2. Meanwhile, preheat broiler.
3. Remove steak from marinade. Discard any excess marinade.
4. Broil steak 6 inches from heat for 4 minutes each side for medium-rare or to desired doneness. Let stand 5 minutes. Slice thinly across the grain.

QUICK-FIX FOR FOUR

Balsamic Flank Steak (this page)

Steamed New Potatoes

Three-Color Pepper Sauté (434)

Walnut-Stuffed Baked Apples

FLANK STEAK STUFFED WITH SWEET PEPPERS AND SPINACH

LOW-CALORIE · LOW-CHOLESTEROL

This can be served either hot or cold and the thin slices, with their spiral design, make an attractive presentation for a buffet.

Bake at 400° for 1 hour.
Makes 6 servings.
Nutrient Value Per Serving: 291 calories, 28 g protein, 15 g fat, 11 g carbohydrate, 440 mg sodium, 60 mg cholesterol.

1 medium-size sweet red pepper
1 medium-size sweet yellow pepper
1 package (10 ounces) frozen chopped
    spinach, thawed according to
    package directions
½ cup Italian-flavored dry bread crumbs
¼ cup grated Parmesan cheese
1 clove garlic, finely chopped
¼ cup pine nuts, toasted
1 egg white
1 flank steak (1½ pounds)

1. Broil peppers on broiler pan in pre-heated broiler 5 inches from heat, turn-ing occasionally, until all sides are blackened, about 15 minutes. Place in brown paper bag and seal. When cool enough to handle, core, seed and peel peppers (see How-To, page 433). Dice peppers and pat dry. Place in medium-size bowl.
2. Drain spinach and squeeze dry. Add to peppers. Add bread crumbs, Parme-san cheese, garlic, pine nuts and egg white; stir well until crumbs are evenly moistened.
3. Preheat oven to hot (400°).
4. Place flank steak on cutting board. With long, thin knife held horizontal to board, split steak in half lengthwise without cutting all the way through; open up like a book. Spread stuffing over steak, leaving 1-inch border. Roll

steak up fairly tightly from long side. Tie at 1-inch intervals with kitchen string. Place on rack in baking dish.
5. Roast in preheated hot oven (400°) for 1 hour. Remove from oven and let stand for 15 minutes. Slice crosswise into ½-inch-thick slices.

Make-Ahead Tip: Cook the steak a day ahead and refrigerate, covered. Serve cold or at room temperature.

SPICY FLANK STEAK WITH PAPRIKA

LOW-SODIUM

Vary the spiciness by adjusting the ground red pepper to taste. An onion-apricot relish adds a delicious accent.

Broil or grill for 8 to 10 minutes.
Makes 6 servings.
Nutrient Value Per Serving: 313 calories,
23 g protein, 20 g fat, 11 g carbohydrate,
118 mg sodium, 57 mg cholesterol.

SPICY FLANK STEAK MAKE-AHEAD TIP:
The meat can be marinated, covered, overnight in the refrigerator. The steak can be cooked a day ahead and then served cold or at room temperature.

4 cloves garlic, finely chopped
1 tablespoon ground cumin
1 tablespoon paprika
½ teaspoon ground ginger
½ teaspoon ground coriander
¼ to ½ teaspoon ground hot red pepper
½ teaspoon black pepper
¼ cup olive oil
2 tablespoons lemon juice
1 flank steak (1½ pounds)
1 large red onion, diced
¼ cup dried apricots, diced
1 tablespoon red wine vinegar
1 tablespoon honey
1 tablespoon chopped cilantro OR:
    parsley
⅛ teaspoon salt

1. Stir together garlic, cumin, paprika, ginger, coriander, ground red pepper, black pepper, olive oil and lemon juice in small bowl. Pour into large food storage bag. Add flank steak to bag; seal and turn steak to coat. Place bag in 13 × 9 × 2-inch baking dish. Refrigerate for at least 4 hours or overnight, turning the bag from time to time.
2. Preheat broiler. Remove steak from marinade; place on broiler-pan rack.
3. Scrape reserved marinade into medium-size skillet; heat over medium heat. Add onion and apricots; cook for 2 minutes. Stir in vinegar and honey. Reduce heat to low; cover and cook 5 minutes. Stir in cilantro and salt. Set onion relish aside.

4. Broil steak 4 inches from heat 4 to 5 minutes each side for medium-rare. Let stand 5 minutes. To serve, cut steak diagonally across grain into thin slices. Serve with onion relish.

BLADE STEAKS WITH ARTICHOKE HEARTS

QUICK

A quick dinner dish with vegetables that's meaty enough to stretch to six servings. (Pictured on page 341.)

Makes 4 servings.
Nutrient Value Per Serving: 520 calories,
31 g protein, 41 g fat, 6 g carbohydrate,
829 mg sodium, 130 mg cholesterol.

1 tablespoon olive oil
4 boneless beef chuck top blade steaks,
    each ¾ inch thick (about 1½
    pounds)
1 package (9 ounces) frozen artichoke
    hearts, thawed
1 teaspoon salt
1 teaspoon leaf thyme, crumbled
½ cup beef broth
½ pint cherry tomatoes, each cut in half
1 tablespoon *un*salted butter

1. Heat 1 teaspoon olive oil in large, heavy skillet over medium-high heat. Add half the steaks; brown on both sides, about 4 minutes for medium-rare or until desired doneness. Remove steaks to platter; keep warm. Repeat with remaining steaks and 1 teaspoon olive oil.
2. Add remaining 1 teaspoon olive oil to drippings in skillet. Add artichoke hearts, salt and thyme; cook 3 minutes, stirring constantly. Add beef broth and cherry tomatoes. Bring to boiling; boil 1 minute. Reduce heat to low; whisk in butter. Return steaks to skillet. Cover; heat through. Serve immediately.

STEAK AND SWEET PEPPER SAUTÉ

QUICK

An easy dinner main dish for every day or special enough for company.

Makes 4 servings.
Recipe can be halved or doubled.
Nutrient Value Per Serving: 310 calories, 35 g protein, 17 g fat, 4 g carbohydrate, 715 mg sodium, 100 mg cholesterol.

2 teaspoons olive oil
4 boneless rib eye steaks, each ½ inch thick (about 1½ pounds)
1 medium-size sweet red pepper, cored, seeded and cut into 1-inch pieces
1 medium-size sweet yellow pepper, cored, seeded and cut into 1-inch pieces

1 medium-size zucchini, cut lengthwise in half, then crosswise into ¼-inch-thick slices
1 teaspoon salt
½ teaspoon cracked black pepper
¼ cup beef broth
4 teaspoons balsamic vinegar OR: red wine vinegar

1. Heat 1½ teaspoons olive oil in large skillet over medium-high heat. Add half the steaks; cook until browned on both sides, about 4 minutes for medium-rare or until desired doneness. Remove steaks to platter; keep warm. Repeat with remaining steaks.
2. Add remaining ½ teaspoon olive oil to skillet. Add peppers, zucchini, salt and cracked black pepper; cook, stirring frequently, 5 minutes. Add beef broth and balsamic vinegar; bring to boiling, stirring up any browned bits from bottom of skillet. Pour sauce over steaks. Serve.

CUBE STEAKS WITH ONION RELISH

QUICK

The relish is a nice dress-up touch for these simply prepared steaks.

Makes 4 servings.
Recipe can be halved or doubled.
Nutrient Value Per Serving: 417 calories, 30 g protein, 28 g fat, 11 g carbohydrate, 352 mg sodium, 105 mg cholesterol.

1 pound onions
2 tablespoons *un*salted butter
2 teaspoons sugar
2 tablespoons red wine vinegar
½ teaspoon salt
¼ teaspoon pepper
1 tablespoon vegetable oil
4 cube chuck steaks (5 ounces each)

1. Cut onions into thin wedges. Heat butter in large skillet over medium heat. Add onion; sauté until browned, 10 to 15 minutes. Sprinkle with sugar. Stir in vinegar, salt and pepper. Remove relish to serving bowl.
2. Wipe skillet clean with paper toweling. Heat oil in skillet over medium-high heat. Add steaks in single layer; cook 1 minute each side or until cooked through. Serve with relish.

SPEEDY STEAK

Cube Steaks with Onion Relish (this page)

Egg Noodles with Poppy Seeds and Butter

Apple Pie

PEPPER FOR THE STEAK
For Steak with Pepper and Brandy Sauce we've used a combination of dried peppercorns—black, green and white. For a spicier hit, use Szechuan peppercorns. Serve with roast potatoes or garlic-mashed potatoes, along with grilled tomatoes.

STEAK WITH PEPPER AND BRANDY SAUCE

Makes 8 servings.
Recipe can be halved or doubled.
Nutrient Value Per Serving: 314 calories, 23 g protein, 21 g fat, 3 g carbohydrate, 235 mg sodium, 84 mg cholesterol.

1 teaspoon *each* black, white and green dried peppercorns OR: 1 tablespoon dried black peppercorns
1 boneless sirloin steak, about 1½ inches thick (about 2 pounds)
¼ teaspoon salt
1 tablespoon vegetable oil
2 tablespoons *un*salted butter
½ cup finely chopped shallot OR: white part green onion
1 tablespoon all-purpose flour
¼ cup Cognac OR: brandy
1 cup beef broth
¼ teaspoon Worcestershire sauce
2 tablespoons finely chopped parsley

1. Crush peppercorns in plastic bag with rolling pin, meat pounder or heavy bottle. Rub onto both sides of steak. Let steak marinate for at least 30 minutes; if longer, refrigerate. Season steak with salt.
2. Heat oil in large, heavy skillet over moderately high heat. Add steak; cook 5 to 6 minutes on each side for rare. Transfer to platter and keep warm.
3. Pour off fat from skillet. Add 1 tablespoon butter and shallot to skillet; cook over moderate heat, stirring, for 2 minutes. Stir in flour; cook, stirring, for 1 minute. Carefully add Cognac to avoid flaming; cook, stirring, for 1 minute. Add beef broth. Bring to boiling. Lower heat; simmer, stirring occasionally, 3 minutes. Stir in remaining tablespoon butter, Worcestershire sauce and parsley. Pour sauce over steak. Serve.

STEAK WITH ROASTED RED PEPPER AND MUSHROOM SAUCE

This is a dish for a special event. Any good-quality cut of steak can be used here—shell, sirloin or filet mignon. Serve the steaks with garlic-flavored mashed potatoes, pasta or a grain, and a salad.

Makes 4 servings.
Recipe can be halved or doubled.
Nutrient Value Per Serving: 412 calories, 28 g protein, 28 g fat, 13 g carbohydrate, 739 mg sodium, 97 mg cholesterol.

1 cup water
1 ounce dried shiitake mushrooms OR: other dried mushrooms
4 club steaks, 1 inch thick (each 4 to 5 ounces)
½ teaspoon salt
¼ teaspoon black pepper
2 tablespoons *un*salted butter
1 tablespoon vegetable oil
⅔ cup finely chopped shallot OR: white part green onion
1 clove garlic, finely chopped
¼ pound fresh shiitake mushrooms OR: cultivated mushrooms, sliced
½ cup dry white wine
1 can (13¾ ounces) beef broth
1 large sweet red pepper, roasted, peeled and sliced* OR: 7-ounce jar roasted red peppers, drained and sliced
1 tablespoon tomato paste
½ teaspoon leaf thyme, crumbled
¼ cup snipped fresh chives OR: green onion tops, for garnish *(optional)*

1. Bring water to boiling in small saucepan. Add dried mushrooms and remove from heat. Let stand 20 minutes. Drain mushrooms through sieve lined with double thickness of dampened paper toweling; reserve soaking liquid. Remove and discard any tough stems. Slice mushrooms.
2. Pat steaks dry with paper toweling.

Season with salt and pepper. Heat ½ tablespoon butter and the oil in large skillet over medium-high heat. Add steaks; cook 1½ to 2 minutes on each side for rare. Transfer steaks to platter.
3. Pour off fat from skillet. Heat remaining 1½ tablespoons butter in skillet over medium heat. Add shallot and garlic to skillet; cook, stirring, 1 minute. Add dried and fresh mushrooms; cook, stirring, 3 minutes. Add wine; boil 1 minute. Add broth, reserved mushroom soaking liquid, red pepper, tomato paste and thyme; simmer, stirring occasionally, 5 minutes.
4. Add steaks to skillet; simmer until heated through, 1 to 2 minutes. Sprinkle with chives, if you wish.

*Note: Broil pepper about 5 inches from heat, turning frequently, until charred on all sides, about 15 minutes. Place in paper bag and close. When cool enough to handle, core, seed and peel. *(See How-To, page 433.)*

STEAK WITH ROASTED RED PEPPER MAKE-AHEAD TIP:
The sauce can be prepared separately a day ahead and refrigerated, covered. Sauté steaks as directed. Heat sauce, add steaks and simmer until heated through.

BEEF AND RED PEPPER KABOBS WITH THAI SAUCE

LOW-CALORIE · LOW-CHOLESTEROL

Broil 6 to 8 minutes.
Makes 6 skewers (4 servings).
Recipe can be halved or doubled.
Nutrient Value Per Skewer: 203 calories,
17 g protein, 11 g fat, 23 g carbohydrate,
163 mg sodium, 46 mg cholesterol.

1 pound trimmed, lean boneless beef
   sirloin, cut into 1-inch cubes
½ cup dry white wine
2 tablespoons lemon juice
1 teaspoon leaf basil, crumbled
2 small sweet red peppers (5 to 6 ounces
   each), cored, seeded and cut into
   eighths
18 small mushrooms (8 ounces)

Peanut Sauce:
2 tablespoons chunky-style peanut butter
1 clove garlic, finely chopped
1 tablespoon reduced-sodium soy sauce
1 teaspoon sugar

1. Combine beef, wine, lemon juice and basil in sealable plastic bag or bowl; seal or cover. Refrigerate overnight.
2. To cook: Soak six 12-inch bamboo skewers in water. Preheat broiler.
3. Drain beef, reserving marinade. Thread beef, peppers and mushrooms alternately, just touching, on water-soaked skewers. Arrange on lightly greased broiler-pan rack.
4. Broil kabobs 4 inches from heat 6 to 8 minutes for medium-rare, turning once.
5. Meanwhile, prepare sauce: Combine peanut butter, garlic, soy sauce, sugar and the reserved marinade in small saucepan. Bring to boiling; boil 3 minutes. Pour over kabobs and serve.

KABOB SERVING IDEAS
Serves four as a main course, six as an appetizer. The sauce is a quickly cooked, spicy-sweet peanut butter mixture that can also be used to dress a crisp vegetable salad.

BEEF AND RED PEPPER KABOBS MAKE-AHEAD TIP:
The beef can be marinated the day before in the refrigerator.

BEEF AND VEGETABLE FAJITAS

LOW-FAT · LOW-CHOLESTEROL

A *delicious hot sandwich in a flour tortilla—easy to wrap your hand around.*

Broil 14 to 16 minutes.
Makes 4 servings.
Recipe can be halved or doubled.
Nutrient Value Per Serving: 481 calories,
30 g protein, 15 g fat, 56 g carbohydrate,
565 mg sodium, 56 mg cholesterol.

1 flank steak (1 pound)
1 Spanish onion, sliced
1 sweet red pepper, cored, seeded and
     sliced into strips
1 clove garlic, finely chopped
¼ cup lime juice
1 tablespoon olive oil
1 tablespoon balsamic vinegar OR: red
     wine vinegar
2 tablespoons chopped fresh cilantro OR:
     parsley
¼ teaspoon ground cumin
⅛ teaspoon salt
8 flour tortillas

1. Combine steak, onion and red pepper in shallow dish. Combine garlic, lime juice, oil, vinegar, cilantro, cumin and salt in small bowl; pour over steak and vegetables. Cover and refrigerate 1 to 2 hours.
2. Preheat broiler. Place steak on rack in broiler pan.
3. Broil steak 4 inches from heat for 2 to 3 minutes on each side. Add vegetables to broiler rack. Spoon remaining marinade over all. Broil, turning, 8 to 10 more minutes or until meat is desired doneness and vegetables are tender. Let meat stand 5 minutes. Cut meat diagonally across the grain into thin slices. Mound steak and vegetables into tortillas; fold tortillas over. Serve.

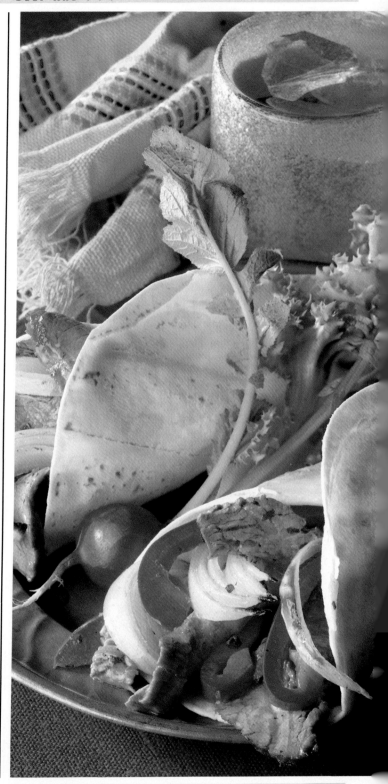

BEEF RIBS WITH MUSTARD AND HORSERADISH SAUCE

Make sure the short ribs are meaty. Serve this dish with mashed potatoes to soak up the rich sauce.

Makes 6 servings.
Recipe can be halved or doubled.
Nutrient Value Per Serving: 574 calories, 25 g protein, 50 g fat, 4 g carbohydrate, 280 mg sodium, 107 mg cholesterol.

---

1 tablespoon olive oil
4 pounds beef short ribs, cut into 3-inch pieces
1 large onion, chopped
1 large carrot, pared and chopped
3 cloves garlic, finely chopped
1 cup beef broth
½ cup dry red wine
½ cup water
1 teaspoon leaf marjoram, crumbled
1 teaspoon dry mustard
2 tablespoons Dijon-style mustard
1 tablespoon prepared horseradish
½ teaspoon pepper
1 tablespoon chopped parsley

1. Heat oil in Dutch oven or large pot over medium-high heat. Working in batches, brown ribs in pot. Remove ribs to platter as they brown.
2. Reduce heat to low. Pour off all but 1 tablespoon fat. Add onion and carrot; cook, covered, for 8 minutes. Add garlic; cook 1 minute. Add broth, wine, water, marjoram and dry mustard. Bring to boiling. Add ribs. Lower heat; cover and simmer for 2 hours or until ribs are tender. Remove ribs to serving dish and cover to keep hot.
3. Skim fat from sauce. Add Dijon-style mustard, horseradish and pepper. Bring to boiling; boil 5 minutes. Pour sauce over ribs. Sprinkle with parsley.

Make-Ahead Tip: The ribs can be prepared up to 2 days ahead and refrigerated, covered. Gently reheat in the sauce.

FANCY RIBS

Beef Ribs with Mustard and Horseradish Sauce (this page)

Yogurt Mashed Potatoes (439)

Steamed Carrots

Lemon Angel Food Cake (507)

STIR-FRY BEEF WITH BROCCOLI

LOW-CALORIE · LOW-CHOLESTEROL
QUICK

Serve with rice and it's dinner in no time at all.

Makes 4 servings.
Recipe can be halved or doubled.
Nutrient Value Per Serving: 273 calories, 26 g protein, 12 g fat, 17 g carbohydrate, 383 mg sodium, 51 mg cholesterol.

1 flank steak (about 14 ounces)
4 teaspoons reduced-sodium soy sauce
2 cloves garlic, finely chopped
¼ cup beef broth
1 head broccoli, separated into stalks and flowerets
2 carrots, pared and cut into 2 × ¼-inch strips
1 large onion, cut into eighths
1 teaspoon Oriental sesame oil
¼ teaspoon crushed red pepper flakes

1. Cut steak into thin strips; combine with soy sauce, garlic and 2 tablespoons broth.
2. Peel broccoli stalks; slice crosswise ½ inch thick. Cut flowerets into bite-size pieces.
3. Heat large nonstick skillet or wok over medium heat. Add beef with soy mixture; stir-fry 3 to 5 minutes until beef is almost cooked through. Remove with slotted spoon to platter, leaving any liquid in pan. Add broccoli, carrot and onion. Add remaining broth. Cover; cook 3 minutes. Add beef; stir-fry 1 to 2 minutes or until cooked through. Sprinkle on oil and pepper flakes. Serve.

MEAT PIE WITH PHYLLO CRUST

A spectacular presentation. For tips on working with phyllo dough, see our How-To, page 91.

Bake at 400° for 20 to 30 minutes.
Makes 8 servings.
Nutrient Value Per Serving: 515 calories, 26 g protein, 31 g fat, 32 g carbohydrate, 631 mg sodium, 89 mg cholesterol.

2 pounds boneless beef shoulder, cut into 1 inch cubes OR: packaged beef stew cubes
1 teaspoon salt
½ teaspoon pepper
3 tablespoons vegetable oil
½ pound carrots, pared and cut diagonally into ½-inch pieces
1 cup frozen pearl onions, thawed
2 tablespoons all-purpose flour
1 cup dry red wine
1 cup beef broth
1 bay leaf
1 teaspoon leaf rosemary, crumbled
½ pound potatoes, pared and cut into ¼-inch pieces
½ pound green beans, trimmed and cut into 2-inch pieces
12 sheets frozen phyllo dough, thawed according to package directions
3 tablespoons *un*salted butter, melted

1. Season beef cubes with salt and pepper. Heat 2 tablespoons oil in 5-quart Dutch oven or saucepan over medium-high heat. Working in 3 batches, add meat to pot and brown. Remove beef to bowl as it browns. Drain off drippings.
2. Heat ½ tablespoon oil in pot. Add carrots and pearl onions; cook, stirring occasionally, 5 minutes or until softened. With slotted spoon, remove carrots and onions to another bowl.
3. Add remaining ½ tablespoon oil to drippings in pot. Stir in flour; cook 1
(continued)

MEAT PIE WITH PHYLLO CRUST (*continued*)

**MEAT PIE
MAKE-AHEAD TIP:**
The meat filling can
be made a day
ahead and refriger-
ated, covered. Let
come to room tem-
perature before using.

minute, stirring constantly. Whisk in wine, beef broth, bay leaf and rosemary. Return beef to pot. Bring to boiling. Lower heat; simmer, covered, 1 hour. Return carrots and onions to pot. Stir in potatoes and green beans. Bring to boiling. Lower heat; simmer, covered, 10 minutes.

4. Preheat oven to hot (400°).

5. Meanwhile, arrange 1 sheet of phyllo on waxed paper, keeping remaining layers covered with damp towel to prevent drying out. Brush with some melted butter. Repeat to make 8 layers in all. Cover with damp dish towel.

6. Spoon beef mixture into 2-quart round baking dish at least 2¾ inches deep; remove and discard bay leaf.

Invert phyllo sheets onto baking dish; remove waxed paper. Fold overhang under. Cut a hole in center of phyllo. Brush top of phyllo with some melted butter. Arrange another sheet of phyllo on work surface; brush with some butter. Fold phyllo crosswise in half, then form a ruffle at edge and place on top of baking dish along outer edge. Repeat to make 3 ruffles in all. Brush remaining sheet of phyllo with butter. Fold phyllo lengthwise in half, then form a ruffle; place on top of baking dish around opening in phyllo crust. Brush phyllo ruffles with butter.

7. Bake in preheated hot oven (400°) for 20 to 30 minutes or until meat and vegetables are tender and phyllo is golden brown. Let stand 10 minutes before serving.

QUICK BEEF CURRY

LOW-CHOLESTEROL · QUICK

Makes 4 servings.
Recipe can be halved or doubled.
Nutrient Value Per Serving: 303 calories, 23 g protein, 19 g fat, 9 g carbohydrate, 250 mg sodium, 59 mg cholesterol.

1 flank steak (1 pound)
1 tablespoon reduced-sodium soy sauce
1 teaspoon sugar
1 tablespoon cornstarch
1 tablespoon cold water
2 tablespoons vegetable oil
1 medium-size onion, thinly sliced
1 stalk celery, thinly sliced
1 large carrot, pared and thinly sliced
2 cloves garlic, finely chopped
½ teaspoon ground cumin
½ teaspoon ground ginger
½ teaspoon ground turmeric
¼ teaspoon ground coriander
¼ teaspoon ground cinnamon
⅛ teaspoon ground hot red pepper
1 cup water

1. Cut flank steak lengthwise into thirds. Cut crosswise into ¼-inch-thick slices, or thicker for heartier curry. Place beef in medium-size bowl. Add soy sauce and sugar. Stir together cornstarch and cold water in small bowl until smooth. Add to beef with 1 tablespoon oil; toss to combine. Set aside.
2. Heat remaining oil in large skillet over medium heat. Add onion, celery and carrot; sauté 1 minute. Add garlic,
(continued)

QUICKER CURRY
For even quicker preparation, substitute 2 teaspoons curry powder for the individual spices. The separate spices do, however, make for a more interesting flavor.

CURRY CONDIMENTS
Serve with rice and condiments such as chutney, chopped peanuts, toasted coconut, chopped apples and raisins.

QUICK BEEF CURRY (*continued*)

cumin, ginger, turmeric, coriander, cinnamon, red pepper and water. Cover and cook 5 minutes.

3. Scatter beef slices over vegetables in skillet. Cover and cook 1 minute. Increase heat to high; cook, stirring, 2 minutes or until sauce thickens and beef loses its pink color. Serve.

HEARTY BEEF CHILI

LOW-CALORIE · LOW-CHOLESTEROL

We've used a leaner cut of beef for this chili to keep the fat down.

Makes 8 servings.
Recipe can be halved or doubled.
Nutrient Value Per Serving: 330 calories, 28 g protein, 16 g fat, 18 g carbohydrate, 516 mg sodium, 73 mg cholesterol.

2 pounds bottom round OR: round tip roast
1 large onion, finely chopped
3 large cloves garlic, finely chopped
2½ cups beef broth
2 fresh jalapeño peppers, halved, seeded and chopped
2 teaspoons chili powder
1 package (10 ounces) frozen corn kernels, thawed
1 can (15¼ ounces) red kidney beans

1. Cut meat into 1- to 1½-inch cubes. Combine meat, onion, garlic and ½ cup beef broth in medium-size saucepan. Cover and bring to boiling. Lower heat; simmer 15 minutes. Check once; add a little water, if necessary, to prevent drying out. Uncover saucepan. Cook over very high heat until meat lightly browns and most of liquid has evaporated, about 15 to 20 minutes.
2. Add remaining 2 cups broth, jalapeño peppers and chili powder. Bring to

boiling. Lower heat; simmer, covered, 1 to 1½ hours or until meat is tender.
3. Stir in corn and beans. Cook 2 minutes longer or until heated through.

Make-Ahead Tip: The chili can be made up to 2 days ahead and refrigerated, covered.

TREE-TRIMMING PARTY

Hearty Beef Chili (this page)

Pumpkin Cornbread (68)

Winter Root Salad with Honey-Mustard Dressing (155)

Spiced Oatmeal Date Cookies (512) with Ice Cream

SHEPHERD'S PIE WITH SQUASH AND POTATO TOPPING

Bake at 375° for 40 minutes.
Makes 8 servings.
Nutrient Value Per Serving: 524 calories, 21 g protein, 34 g fat, 36 g carbohydrate, 996 mg sodium, 127 mg cholesterol.

Squash and Potato Topping:
1 medium-size butternut squash (about 1½ pounds), halved lengthwise, seeded, pared and cut into 1-inch cubes
3 large baking potatoes (about 1½ pounds), pared and cut into 1-inch cubes
4 tablespoons *un*salted butter
½ cup heavy cream
¼ cup milk
1½ teaspoons salt
¼ teaspoon black pepper
¼ teaspoon ground nutmeg
⅛ teaspoon ground hot red pepper
1 egg
Paprika

Filling:
2 tablespoons vegetable oil
3 medium-size onions, chopped
2 cloves garlic, finely chopped
1½ pounds lean ground beef
1 tablespoon leaf basil, crumbled
1 tablespoon leaf oregano, crumbled
1 teaspoon ground cumin
1 teaspoon salt
½ teaspoon leaf thyme, crumbled
¼ teaspoon pepper
2 tablespoons all-purpose flour
1 can (28 ounces) Italian-style plum tomatoes, drained and cut up
1 pound green beans, trimmed and cut into ½-inch lengths

1. Prepare Topping: Drop squash and potatoes into large pot with enough cold, salted water to cover vegetables by 1 inch. Partially cover and bring to

boiling. Boil 15 minutes or until tender.
2. Drain squash and potatoes; return to pot. Add butter, cream, milk, salt, black pepper, nutmeg and red pepper. Mash with potato masher until fluffy. Cool slightly. Reserve egg and paprika.
3. Preheat oven to moderate (375°).
4. Prepare Filling: Heat oil in large skillet over medium heat. Add onion; sauté until softened, about 5 minutes. Add garlic; cook 1 minute. Remove to plate.
5. Crumble beef into skillet; cook over medium-high heat until browned, about 3 minutes. Stir in basil, oregano, cumin, salt, thyme, pepper, reserved onion mixture and the flour. Add tomatoes and green beans. Bring to boiling. Lower heat; cover and cook 10 minutes. Spoon into 13×9×2-inch glass baking dish.
6. Beat egg into squash-potato mixture. Spread evenly over filling, making decorative swirls or diamond grid pattern. Sprinkle with paprika.
7. Bake in preheated moderate oven (375°) for 40 minutes or until bubbly
(continued)

PIE VARIATION
Our version made with ground beef can also be made with lean ground pork, ground turkey, or more classically with ground lamb.

SHEPHERD'S PIE WITH SQUASH AND POTATO TOPPING

(*continued*)

and top is golden brown. Cool on wire rack at least 20 minutes before serving.

Microwave Directions for Topping (High Power Oven):

Ingredient Changes: Reduce salt to 1 teaspoon; reduce ground hot red pepper to few grains.

Directions: Prick whole squash several times with tines of fork. Place on double layer of paper toweling in microwave oven. Microwave, uncovered, at 100% power 10 to 12 minutes until soft. Halve and seed. Pierce potatoes with fork. Place, spoke-fashion, in microwave oven. Microwave, uncovered, at 100% power 12 to 13 minutes until soft. Remove flesh from squash with spoon; place in bowl. Peel potatoes; add to bowl. Mash as in Step 2.

ITALIAN MEATLOAF

The cottage cheese and mozzarella topping make this meat loaf especially rich.

Bake at 350° for 1 hour.
Makes 6 servings.
Nutrient Value Per Serving: 305 calories, 22 g protein, 20 g fat, 8 g carbohydrate, 496 mg sodium, 134 mg cholesterol.

12 ounces lean ground chuck
4 ounces ground pork OR: sausage
1 cup fresh soft bread crumbs
1 can (8 ounces) tomato sauce
2 eggs
1 teaspoon leaf oregano, crumbled
½ teaspoon leaf basil, crumbled
1 clove garlic, finely chopped
¾ cup lowfat cottage cheese
½ cup shredded part-skim mozzarella
    (2 ounces)

1. Preheat oven to moderate (350°). If serving from pan, grease 8½ × 3⅝ × 2⅝-inch loaf pan. Or to remove loaf from pan, line pan with heavy-duty aluminum foil, leaving 4-inch overhang all around. Grease foil.
2. Combine chuck, pork, bread crumbs, half the tomato sauce, 1 egg, oregano, basil and garlic in large bowl; mix well. Pack into prepared pan.
3. Combine cottage cheese, ¼ cup mozzarella and remaining egg in small bowl. Spread over meat. Top with remaining tomato sauce and mozzarella.
4. Bake in preheated moderate oven (350°) for 1 hour. Serve loaf directly from pan. Or, let cool at room temperature until topping is set, about 30 minutes. Lift loaf out of pan, using foil overhang as handles. Remove loaf from foil and serve.

Microwave Directions (High Power Oven):

Ingredient Changes: Reduce tomato sauce to ½ cup; oregano to ½ teaspoon.
Directions: Combine ground chuck, pork, bread crumbs, 6 tablespoons tomato sauce, 1 egg, oregano, basil and garlic in large bowl. Pack into microwave-safe 9-inch pie plate. Combine cottage cheese, ¼ cup mozzarella and remaining egg in small bowl. Spread over meat mixture. Top with remaining 2 tablespoons tomato sauce and ¼ cup mozzarella. Cover with waxed paper. Microwave at 100% power 5 minutes. Cover; let stand 5 minutes. Cut into wedges.

M-M-M MEATLOAF

Italian Meatloaf (this page)

Stewed Fennel with Tomato (420)

Roasted Potatoes with Peppers (440)

Sliced Pears with Raspberry Chocolate Sauce (537)

STUFFED TRICOLOR PEPPERS

Bake at 375° for 1 hour.
Makes 6 servings.
Recipe can be halved or doubled.
Nutrient Value Per Serving: 470 calories, 22 g protein, 27 g fat, 35 g carbohydrate, 754 mg sodium, 71 mg cholesterol.

2 medium-size sweet red peppers
2 medium-size sweet green peppers
2 medium-size sweet yellow peppers
1 tablespoon olive oil
1 large onion, finely chopped
1¼ pounds lean ground beef
¼ cup slivered almonds, toasted
¼ cup raisins
1½ cups cooked rice
½ cup sliced green olives
1 tablespoon chili powder
1 teaspoon paprika
1 teaspoon leaf oregano, crumbled
½ teaspoon salt
¼ teaspoon ground cinnamon
¼ teaspoon ground hot red pepper
1 can (28 ounces) crushed tomatoes
1 tablespoon brown sugar
1 tablespoon lemon juice
⅛ teaspoon black pepper

1. Bring large pot of water to boiling. Remove very tops of peppers, keeping any stems intact. Remove seeds and membranes from inside peppers. Blanch peppers and tops in boiling water for 5 minutes. Drain; rinse with cold water. Drain, cut-side down, on paper toweling. Set aside.
2. Heat oil in medium-size skillet over medium-low heat. Add onion; sauté until golden brown, about 10 minutes.
3. Combine onion, beef, almonds, raisins, rice, olives, chili powder, paprika, oregano, salt, cinnamon, ground red pepper and ¾ cup crushed tomatoes in large bowl. Fill peppers with beef mixture. Reserve pepper tops.
4. Preheat oven to moderate (375°). Place peppers in 2½-quart baking dish.

5. Stir together remaining crushed tomatoes, brown sugar, lemon juice and black pepper in small saucepan. Bring to boiling. Pour over peppers. Cover baking dish with aluminum foil.
6. Bake in preheated moderate oven (375°) for 30 minutes. Remove foil. Replace tops. Bake 30 minutes more or until filling is cooked through and peppers are tender.

Make-Ahead Tip: The filling can be made a day ahead and refrigerated, covered. Let come to room temperature before using.
Microwave Directions (High Power Oven): Scatter untoasted almonds over bottom of microwave-safe 12-inch shallow
(continued)

PEPPER FILLING
If red and yellow peppers are not available, use all green peppers. Don't let the length of the ingredient list intimidate you—many of the ingredients are spices that go into the Moroccan-style filling, which can also be used for stuffing other vegetables such as zucchini and eggplant.

STUFFED TRICOLOR PEPPERS
(*continued*)

baking dish. Microwave, uncovered, at 100% power 4 minutes to toast, stirring once. Remove and reserve. Combine oil and onion in same dish. Microwave, uncovered, at 100% power 4 minutes, stirring once. Transfer onions to bowl; mix filling as in Step 3. Divide filling into peppers. Evenly space peppers around edge of dish. Spoon crushed tomato mixture over and around peppers. Cover with microwave-safe plastic wrap, vented at one edge. Microwave at 100% power 10 minutes. Turn dish. Microwave at 70% power 15 minutes until peppers are tender and filling is cooked through, turning dish once.

LITTLE LASAGNA
These miniatures are great to make ahead and freeze. Serve right out of the pan (2 servings per pan) or unmold onto a serving plate for a more attractive presentation.

MINIATURE LASAGNA MAKE-AHEAD TIP:
The sauce can be prepared a day ahead through Step 2 and refrigerated, covered. The lasagna can be prepared ahead and refrigerated, covered, for up 2 days. Reheat in 350° until hot and bubbly, about 45 minutes. Or freeze the lasagna, tightly wrapped, for up to 1 month. Thaw overnight in the refrigerator and reheat as above.

MINIATURE LASAGNA

Bake at 350° for 45 to 50 minutes.
Makes 12 servings (each lasagna serves 2). Recipe can be halved or doubled.
Nutrient Value Per Serving: 563 calories, 32 g protein, 31 g fat, 39 g carbohydrate, 692 mg sodium, 107 mg cholesterol.

1 tablespoon olive oil
1 large onion, chopped
¼ pound mushrooms, chopped (1½ cups)
2 cloves garlic, finely chopped
1 pound lean ground beef
3 jars (7 ounces each) roasted red peppers, drained and chopped
1 can (16 ounces) whole tomatoes, in puree
½ cup chopped parsley
1 teaspoon leaf oregano, crumbled
1 teaspoon salt
½ teaspoon leaf basil, crumbled
½ teaspoon leaf thyme, crumbled
1 bay leaf
¼ teaspoon black pepper
18 lasagna noodles*

2 containers (15 ounces each) ricotta cheese
8 ounces fontina cheese, shredded (2 cups)
8 ounces mozzarella cheese, shredded (2 cups)
1 cup grated Parmesan cheese

1. Heat olive oil in large skillet over medium heat. Add onion, mushrooms and garlic; sauté 8 to 10 minutes or until softened. Using slotted spoon, transfer to medium-size bowl. Add beef to skillet; sauté until meat is no longer pink.
2. Add sautéed onion mixture, red peppers, tomatoes, parsley, oregano, salt, basil, thyme, bay leaf and black pepper to skillet. Bring to boiling. Lower heat; simmer about 1 hour and 15 minutes or until very thick. Remove and discard bay leaf.
3. Meanwhile, prepare lasagna noodles according to package directions.
4. Preheat oven to moderate (350°).
5. Assemble lasagna: Spoon about 2 tablespoons meat sauce into each of 6 individual 5½ × 3½ × 2-inch disposable aluminum-foil baking pans. Place 1 lasagna noodle in each pan, cutting lengthwise to fit. Spoon on ¼ cup more sauce. Top with about 2 tablespoons ricotta cheese. Sprinkle with about 2 tablespoons each of fontina and mozzarella cheeses and 1 tablespoon Parmesan. Repeat layering 2 more times, piecing together pieces of noodles to make the 5½-inch-long strips.
6. Bake in preheated moderate oven (350°) for 45 to 50 minutes or until hot and bubbly. Let stand for about 10 minutes before serving or unmolding.

*Note: For easier preparation, substitute 7 no-boil lasagna noodles (7 × 3½ inches) for regular noodles. Holding each noodle with pair of tongs, dip each into large pot of very hot water just to soften slightly in order to cut to size. Cut noodle to fit pan. Repeat as needed, piecing together pieces of noodles to make the 5½-inch-long strips.

ZITI WITH GROUND BEEF AND EGGPLANT

QUICK

Makes 4 servings.
Recipe can be halved or doubled.
Nutrient Value Per Serving: 592 calories, 23 g protein, 23 g fat, 73 g carbohydrate, 459 mg sodium, 34 mg cholesterol.

12 ounces ziti, penne or other long
    tubular pasta
½ pound lean ground beef
¼ cup olive oil
1 small eggplant (12 ounces), trimmed
    and cut into 1-inch cubes
1 medium-size onion, chopped
½ medium-size sweet red or yellow
    pepper, cored, seeded and chopped
1 clove garlic, crushed
2 large ripe tomatoes, cored and cut into
    ½-inch cubes
1 tablespoon chopped fresh basil OR: 1
    teaspoon dried
¾ teaspoon salt, or to taste
¼ teaspoon pepper, or to taste
Grated Parmesan cheese

1. Cook pasta according to package directions. Drain.
2. Meanwhile, sauté beef in large non-stick skillet over medium-high heat, breaking up clumps with spoon, until browned and no pink remains. With slotted spoon, remove beef to bowl. Drain fat from skillet.
3. Heat oil in same skillet over high heat. Add eggplant; cook, stirring constantly, until browned and cooked through, about 8 minutes. Add to beef.
4. Lower heat to medium-high. Add onion and sweet pepper to skillet; sauté until tender, 5 minutes. Add garlic; sauté 1 minute. Add beef-eggplant mixture and tomato; heat through. Stir in basil, salt and pepper. Remove garlic.
5. Toss mixture gently with pasta in large serving bowl. Serve with Parmesan.

BLUE CHEESE BURGERS

QUICK

Top these whoppers with lettuce, tomato and onion.

Makes 4 servings.
Recipe can be halved or doubled.
Nutrient Value Per Serving: 475 calories, 34 g protein, 27 g fat, 22 g carbohydrate, 573 mg sodium, 104 mg cholesterol.

1¼ pounds lean ground beef, such as
    round or sirloin
3 ounces blue cheese, crumbled
1 teaspoon vegetable oil
4 hamburger buns

1. Divide beef into 8 equal portions. Pat each portion into 4½- to 5-inch patty on waxed paper. Sprinkle cheese evenly on 4 patties, leaving ½-inch border. Top each one with another patty. Pinch edges together; press and shape each into 4-inch patty to seal.
2. Heat large, heavy skillet over medium-high heat. Lightly coat with oil. Add burgers; cook until browned, about 2 minutes each side. Serve on buns.

BLUE RIBBON BURGERS

Blue Cheese Burgers (this page)

Three-Bean Salad with Red Onion (154)

Blueberry-Peach Cobbler (527)

BEEF AND TOSTADA PIE

Bake at 450° for 15 minutes.
Makes 6 servings.
Nutrient Value Per Serving: 389 calories, 20 g protein, 23 g fat, 25 g carbohydrate, 785 mg sodium, 63 mg cholesterol.

12 ounces lean ground beef
1 large onion, chopped
1 clove garlic, finely chopped
2 tablespoons all-purpose flour
½ teaspoon ground cumin
½ teaspoon leaf oregano, crumbled
½ teaspoon salt
⅛ teaspoon pepper
1 can (16 ounces) whole tomatoes, in puree
1 can (4 ounces) chopped green chilies, undrained
8 tostada shells, broken into quarters OR: crisp-fried tortillas
1 can (16 ounces) pinto beans, drained and rinsed
1 cup shredded Cheddar cheese (4 ounces)

1. Position oven rack in upper third of oven. Preheat oven to very hot (450°).
2. Crumble beef into large, heavy skillet. Place over moderately high heat. Add onion and garlic; sauté until meat is no longer pink, 5 to 8 minutes. Carefully drain off fat. Add flour, cumin, oregano, salt and pepper; stir over medium heat for 1 minute. Add tomatoes and chilies, breaking up tomatoes with spoon; cook for 3 minutes or until thickened.
3. Arrange half the quartered tostada shells in 8-inch-square nonaluminum baking dish. Layer on half the beans, half the meat filling and half the cheese. Repeat with the remaining ingredients.
4. Bake in preheated very hot oven (450°) for 15 minutes or until heated through. Serve hot.

TOSTADA REPLACEMENT
If you can't find prepared tostada shells, substitute layers of large, unsalted tortilla chips. Garnish pie with lime slices.

VEAL CHOPS
Veal shoulder chops, available at the supermarket meat counter, are tender and relatively inexpensive. You can also use this recipe to prepare pork chops.

PIQUANT VEAL CHOPS

QUICK

Makes 4 servings.
Recipe can be halved or doubled.
Nutrient Value Per Serving: 361 calories, 32 g protein, 16 g fat, 16 g carbohydrate, 610 mg sodium, 129 mg cholesterol.

2 tablespoons olive oil
4 veal shoulder chops (7 ounces each)
¼ cup all-purpose flour
⅓ cup finely chopped shallots OR: white part of green onion
½ cup dry white wine
⅔ cup chicken broth
1 tablespoon catsup
2 teaspoons Dijon-style mustard
⅓ cup sliced gherkins

1. Heat oil in large skillet over moderate heat. Coat chops with flour, shaking off excess. Brown chops in skillet on both sides, about 5 minutes per side. Remove to a plate.
2. Reduce heat to low. Add shallots; sauté 2 minutes. Stir in wine; cook 4 minutes. Stir in broth, catsup, mustard and gherkins. Return chops to pan. Increase heat to moderate; cook 5 minutes or until chops are cooked through. Remove chops to serving platter. Bring sauce to boiling. Pour over chops. Serve.

QUICK CHOP

Piquant Veal Chops (this page)

Rice with Sweet Red Pepper

Lima Beans

Fruit Salad with Yogurt Topping

VEAL BUNDLES WITH MUSHROOM SAUCE

LOW-CALORIE · QUICK

An easy dish for a special dinner.

Makes 4 servings.
Recipe can be halved or doubled.
Nutrient Value Per Serving: 259 calories, 26 g protein, 14 g fat, 5 g carbohydrate, 463 mg sodium, 96 mg cholesterol.

1 pound veal cutlets or scaloppine, about 8 pieces, each ¼ inch thick
¼ cup packed flat-leaf Italian parsley leaves
2 tablespoons seasoned bread crumbs
2½ tablespoons olive oil
¼ pound mushrooms, sliced
1 tablespoon finely chopped shallots
    OR: white part of green onion
½ cup chicken broth
¼ cup dry white wine
¼ teaspoon salt
¼ teaspoon pepper
1 tablespoon *un*salted butter

1. Place veal cutlets on work surface. Arrange parsley leaves evenly on each veal cutlet. Sprinkle each veal cutlet with bread crumbs. Roll up each veal cutlet, jelly-roll style. Tie each bundle with kitchen twine in several places.
2. Heat 1 tablespoon oil in large skillet over medium-high heat. Add half the veal bundles; cook until browned on all sides and cooked through, about 5 minutes. Remove veal bundles to platter; keep warm. Repeat with remaining veal bundles and another tablespoon olive oil. Remove veal bundles to platter; keep warm.
3. Add remaining ½ tablespoon olive oil to drippings in skillet, heat. Add mushrooms and shallots; cook, stirring frequently, 5 minutes. Add chicken broth, white wine, salt and pepper. Bring to boiling over high heat; boil 1 minute. Return veal bundles to skillet.

Lower heat; cover and simmer 1 minute or until heated through. Remove skillet from heat. Whisk in butter.
4. To serve, remove twine. Slice each veal bundle diagonally in half. Spoon sauce over.

30-MINUTE VEAL MEAL

Veal Bundles with Mushroom Sauce (this page)

Sautéed Cherry Tomatoes with Basil (459)

Italian Bread

Strawberries and Cream with Amaretti Biscuits

MARINADES

Marinades, pungent mixtures that often contain oil and an acid such as wine, vinegar or citrus juice, add flavor and succulence to meats and frequently act as tenderizers for tougher cuts. Marinades can also be dry mixtures.

■ Smaller pieces of meat and scored steaks absorb marinade more quickly than larger cuts; the smaller the pieces or the deeper the score, the shorter the marinating time.

■ Use nonaluminum containers such as glass baking dishes or sealed plastic food storage bags for marinating; acids react with aluminum, discoloring the food and adding a disagreeable metallic flavor.

■ For marinating times of 30 minutes or less, cover the marinating meat or fish and let stand at cool room temperature. For longer marinating times, refrigerate the meat to prevent spoilage.

■ Reserve drained marinade for basting meat during cooking. To serve as a sauce, boil marinade for 2 to 3 minutes before using; *never* serve a marinade uncooked.

LEMON-SOY MARINADE

LOW-CALORIE · LOW-FAT
LOW-CHOLESTEROL · QUICK

Flavor beef, fish, pork or poultry with this piquant combination. Marinate beef or pork overnight, poultry up to 4 hours and fish up to 15 minutes. Use 1 recipe per pound of meat, poultry or fish.

Makes about 1 cup.
Recipe can be halved or doubled.
Nutrient Value Per Tablespoon:
8 calories, 0 g protein, 0 g fat,
1 g carbohydrate, 342 mg sodium,
0 mg cholesterol.

½ cup lemon juice (2 large lemons)
¼ cup soy sauce
3 tablespoons Dijon-style mustard
¼ teaspoon ground hot red pepper

Combine lemon juice, soy sauce, mustard and pepper in small glass measuring cup. Mix together until well combined.

Make-Ahead Tip: The marinade can be made up to 3 days ahead and refrigerated, covered.

LIME-GARLIC MARINADE

LOW-CALORIE · LOW-FAT
LOW-CHOLESTEROL · QUICK

Use this tangy citrus marinade to flavor beef, fish or poultry. Marinate beef and poultry for no more than 4 hours and fish for no more than 30 minutes. Use 1 recipe per pound of meat.

Makes ¼ cup.
Recipe can be doubled.
Nutrient Value Per Tablespoon:
7 calories, 0 g protein, 0 g fat,
2 g carbohydrate, 136 mg sodium,
0 mg cholesterol.

¼ cup fresh squeezed lime juice
2 cloves garlic, pressed
½ teaspoon ground coriander
¼ teaspoon salt
¼ teaspoon black pepper

Combine lime juice, garlic, coriander, salt and pepper in a small glass measuring cup. Mix together until well blended.

Make-Ahead Tip: The marinade can be made up to 3 days ahead and refrigerated, covered.

ITALIAN HERB RUB

QUICK

Rub this dry marinade on meat, such as lamb or pork, or poultry and refrigerate overnight. For fish, refrigerate up to 1 hour. Use 1 recipe per pound of meat.

Makes 4 teaspoons.
Recipe can be doubled.
Nutrient Value Per Serving: Insignificant

½ teaspoon leaf oregano, crumbled
¼ teaspoon leaf marjoram, crumbled
¼ teaspoon leaf thyme, crumbled
¼ teaspoon black pepper
1 clove garlic, finely chopped

Combine oregano, marjoram, thyme, pepper and garlic in small bowl. Mix until well blended.

Make-Ahead Tip: The rub can be made up to 2 days ahead and refrigerated, covered.

GLAZED PORK CHOPS WITH APPLES

QUICK

Makes 4 servings.
Recipe can be halved or doubled.
Nutrient Value Per Serving: 409 calories, 17 g protein, 23 g fat, 33 g carbohydrate, 275 mg sodium, 65 mg cholesterol.

2 teaspoons vegetable oil
4 thin pork chops, ½ inch thick (about 1 pound), trimmed
2 large Granny Smith apples
1 can (6 ounces) frozen unsweetened apple juice concentrate
2 teaspoons Dijon-style mustard
¼ teaspoon salt
⅛ teaspoon pepper

1. Heat oil in medium-size skillet over medium heat. Add chops; cook, turning occasionally, until cooked through, 8 to 10 minutes. Transfer to warm platter.
2. Pare, core and cut apples crosswise into rings about ¼ inch thick. After chops are removed from skillet, add rings to skillet; cook 2 to 3 minutes or until lightly browned. Add apple juice concentrate. Bring to boiling. Stir in mustard, salt and pepper. Spoon over chops.

GLAZED PORK CHOPS SERVING IDEAS
Serve with asparagus or sweet potatoes and stuffing.

PORK CHOPS AND SWEET PEPPERS WITH PASTA

LOW-CHOLESTEROL · QUICK

*H*ere's a whole dinner with meat, vegetable and pasta in a single dish.

Makes 4 servings.
Recipe can be halved or doubled.
Nutrient Value Per Serving: 601 calories, 27 g protein, 28 g fat, 59 g carbohydrate, 927 mg sodium, 65 mg cholesterol.

8 ounces penne, ziti or other short tubular pasta
2 tablespoons olive oil
4 thin center-cut pork chops, ½ inch thick (about 1 pound), trimmed
1 large onion, sliced into thin rings
1 large sweet red pepper, cored, seeded and cut into ¼-inch-wide strips
1 large sweet green pepper, cored, seeded and cut into ¼-inch-wide strips
1 clove garlic, finely chopped
1½ cups small mushrooms, quartered
½ cup dry white wine OR: red wine
2 teaspoons leaf basil, crumbled
1 can (16 ounces) whole tomatoes, in juice
2 teaspoons sugar
¼ teaspoon salt
¼ teaspoon pepper

1. Cook penne according to package directions until *al dente*, firm but tender. Drain; return to pot. Add 1 tablespoon oil; toss. Cover to keep warm.
2. Meanwhile, heat remaining oil in large, heavy skillet over moderately high heat. Add chops; sear on each side for 1 to 2 minutes or until lightly browned. Lower heat to moderate; pan-fry chops, turning frequently, 4 to 6 minutes until cooked through. Transfer chops to platter. Discard all but 1 tablespoon fat from skillet.
3. Add onion to skillet; sauté 3 minutes. Add sweet peppers; sauté 3 minutes. Add garlic; sauté 30 seconds. Add mushrooms, wine and basil; cover and cook 6 minutes or until peppers have softened. Add tomatoes, sugar, salt and pepper; simmer 3 minutes.
4. Return pork and juices from platter to skillet. Heat through, about 2 minutes. Serve over cooked penne.

Make-Ahead Tip: The sauce in Step 3 can be made a day ahead and refrigerated, covered.

MEXICAN PORK CHOPS WITH TOMATOES AND CORN

LOW-CHOLESTEROL · QUICK

Makes 4 servings.
Recipe can be halved or doubled.

Nutrient Value Per Serving: 355 calories, 30 g protein, 13 g fat, 33 g carbohydrate, 522 mg sodium, 72 mg cholesterol.

---

4 lean center-cut pork chops, ¾ inch thick (about 1½ pounds), trimmed
1 tablespoon vegetable oil
1 large onion, chopped
1 large clove garlic, finely chopped
1 medium-size sweet green pepper, cored, seeded and cut into ½-inch squares
½ medium-size sweet red pepper, cored, seeded and cut into ½-inch squares
2 tablespoons cornmeal OR: 1 tablespoon all-purpose flour
1 tablespoon chili powder
½ teaspoon leaf oregano, crumbled
½ teaspoon ground cumin
1 can (16 ounces) stewed tomatoes
1 package (10 ounces) frozen whole-kernel corn
¼ teaspoon salt
⅛ teaspoon pepper
1 lime, cut into 4 wedges

1. Trim excess fat from chops. Heat oil in heavy skillet, just large enough to hold chops in single layer, over moderately high heat. Carefully add chops and sear about 2 minutes. Turn and brown other side, about 2 minutes.

(continued)

MEXICAN PORK CHOPS SERVING IDEAS

Accompany with rice or noodles for soaking up the sauce. Garnish with a sprig of oregano.

MEXICAN PORK CHOPS WITH TOMATOES AND CORN *(continued)*

Cook about 4 minutes longer on each side, turning several times, until just cooked through. Remove to platter.

2. Add onion to skillet; sauté over moderately high heat until softened, about 3 minutes. Add garlic; sauté 1 minute. Add sweet peppers; sauté 2 to 3 minutes. Stir in cornmeal, chili powder, oregano and cumin; cook 30 seconds. Add tomatoes with their liquid; cook, stirring constantly, until sauce thickens and boils. Lower heat; simmer 3 to 4 minutes. Add corn; cook 2 minutes.

3. Return chops with juices from platter to skillet; spoon some sauce over chops. Heat just to serving temperature. Season with salt and pepper. Serve with lime wedges.

CURRIED PORK CHOPS

LOW-CHOLESTEROL · QUICK

Here's a quick idea for dinner. Serve with rice pilaf flecked with toasted slivered almonds and raisins.

Makes 4 servings.
Recipe can be halved or doubled.
Nutrient Value Per Serving: 279 calories, 17 g protein, 23 g fat, 1 g carbohydrate, 53 mg sodium, 65 mg cholesterol.

1½ teaspoons curry powder
¼ teaspoon ground cumin
⅛ teaspoon ground cinnamon
⅛ teaspoon ground hot red pepper
2 teaspoons vegetable oil
4 thin pork chops, ½ inch thick (about 1 pound), trimmed

1. Combine curry, cumin, cinnamon and red pepper in small bowl. Rub over chops.
2. Heat oil in large skillet. Add chops; cook, covered, over medium-high heat 3 minutes per side or until cooked through.

PORK CHOPS WITH MUSTARD-HONEY SAUCE SERVING IDEAS

This main course already has the vegetables in it. Just add potatoes or noodles and a green salad to make a filling meal.

PORK CHOPS WITH MUSTARD-HONEY SAUCE

LOW-CALORIE · QUICK

Makes 4 servings.
Recipe can be halved or doubled.
Nutrient Value Per Serving: 323 calories, 31 g protein, 13 g fat, 18 g carbohydrate, 494 mg sodium, 84 mg cholesterol.

¼ cup all-purpose flour
½ teaspoon salt
¼ teaspoon pepper
4 pork chops, 1 inch thick (1½ to 2 pounds), trimmed
1 tablespoon vegetable oil
1 large sweet red pepper, cored, seeded and cut into 1-inch pieces
2 large carrots, pared and cut into 3 × ⅛-inch sticks
1½ cups low-sodium beef broth
1 tablespoon Dijon-style mustard
1 tablespoon honey

1. Combine flour, salt and pepper in bag. Add chops to bag; shake to coat. Shake off excess flour; reserve flour mixture.
2. Heat oil in medium-size skillet over medium heat. Add chops; cook until golden on both sides, turning once, about 8 minutes. Transfer to serving plate. Discard all but 1 tablespoon fat from skillet, reserving the 1 tablespoon fat separately. Wipe out skillet with paper toweling.
3. Heat reserved fat in skillet over medium heat. Add red pepper and carrots; cook, stirring, 5 minutes or until softened. Add reserved flour mixture, stirring for 1 minute or until browned.
4. Stir in beef broth, mustard and honey; cook, stirring, until thickened, 1 to 2 minutes. Add pork chops and accumulated juices. Simmer, covered, 4 minutes or until chops are cooked through. Serve with sauce.

STUFFED PORK CHOPS WITH CITRUS GLAZE

Have your butcher make a deep pocket in the pork chops, or it's easy enough to do yourself. Garnish with citrus slices or curly lettuce, and serve with boiled new potatoes or mashed potatoes and vegetables.

Bake at 425° for 30 minutes.
Makes 4 servings.
Recipe can be halved or doubled.
Nutrient Value Per Serving: 612 calories, 38 g protein, 44 g fat, 13 g carbohydrate, 527 mg sodium, 140 mg cholesterol.

---

4 loin pork chops, 1 inch thick
    (1½ to 2 pounds), trimmed
1½ cups toasted bread cubes (¼ inch)
2 green onions, thinly sliced
2 tablespoons chopped parsley
2 cloves garlic, finely chopped
½ teaspoon salt
¼ teaspoon grated lemon rind
¼ teaspoon grated orange rind
¼ teaspoon leaf marjoram, crumbled
⅓ cup chicken broth
⅛ teaspoon pepper
2½ tablespoons orange juice
2 tablespoons lemon juice
1 tablespoon lime juice
1½ tablespoons sugar

WINTER COMFORT MEAL

Stuffed Pork Chops with Citrus Glaze (this page)

Gingered Red Cabbage (408)

Mashed Sweet and White Potatoes (440)

Chunky Red Applesauce with Cookies

1. Preheat oven to hot (425°). Lightly oil 11 × 7 × 1½-inch baking pan.
2. Cut deep pocket all the way to the bone in each pork chop.
3. Combine bread cubes, green onion, parsley, garlic, ¼ teaspoon salt, lemon rind, orange rind, marjoram and chicken broth in medium-size bowl. Stuff each chop with a generous 3 tablespoons of bread cube mixture. Sprinkle chops with remaining salt and the pepper. Transfer to prepared pan.
4. Stir together orange, lemon and lime juices and sugar in small bowl. Drizzle mixture over pork chops.
5. Bake in preheated hot oven (425°) for 30 minutes or until cooked through, turning chops over halfway through cooking.

STUFFED PORK CHOPS MAKE-AHEAD TIP:

The stuffing can be made up to a day ahead and refrigerated, covered. Let come to room temperature before using.

PORK CHOPS WITH CURRIED PEAR SAUCE

A *chutney-style sauce adds a sweet and spicy flavor to these baked chops.*

Bake at 375° for 35 minutes.
Makes 4 servings.
Recipe can be halved or doubled.
Nutrient Value Per Serving: 610 calories, 32 g protein, 39 g fat, 34 g carbohydrate, 447 mg sodium, 114 mg cholesterol.

1 firm ripe Bosc, Bartlett or Anjou pear, peeled, cored and cut into ¼-inch dice
¼ cup dried apricots (2 ounces), coarsely chopped
3 tablespoons dark seedless raisins
1 can (5½ ounces) pear nectar
¾ cup chicken broth
1 tablespoon lemon juice
2 teaspoons vegetable oil
4 loin pork chops, 1 inch thick (1½ to 2 pounds), trimmed
¼ teaspoon salt
⅛ teaspoon pepper
1 large onion, finely chopped
1 clove garlic, finely chopped
1 tablespoon curry powder
2 teaspoons all-purpose flour

1. Preheat oven to moderate (375°).
2. Combine pear, apricot, raisins, nectar, broth and lemon juice in small bowl. Set aside.
3. Heat 1 teaspoon oil in large nonstick skillet over medium heat. Add chops; cook 3 minutes on each side or until golden. Remove chops to 9 × 9 × 2-inch-square glass baking dish. Sprinkle with salt and pepper.
4. In same skillet, heat remaining 1 teaspoon oil. Add onion and garlic; sauté over medium-low heat 2 minutes. Combine curry powder and flour in small bowl. Sprinkle over onion mixture. Cook, stirring constantly, 2 minutes; mixture will be dry. Stir in fruit mixture with liquid. Bring to boiling, stirring up browned bits from bottom of skillet. Lower heat; simmer, stirring occasionally, 2 minutes. Spoon over chops in baking dish. Cover with aluminum foil.
5. Bake in preheated moderate oven (375°) for 20 minutes. Uncover and bake 15 minutes longer or until chops are cooked through.

SHREDDED PORK WITH CRISPY VEGETABLES

LOW-CALORIE · LOW-CHOLESTEROL
QUICK

This stir-fry keeps the fat down by using a small amount of oil for cooking and extending the meat with vegetables.

Makes 4 servings.
Recipe can be halved or doubled.
Nutrient Value Per Serving: 177 calories, 17 g protein, 8 g fat, 10 g carbohydrate, 366 mg sodium, 48 mg cholesterol.

10 ounces boneless pork cutlets, or scaloppine, from leg, loin or tenderloin
3 teaspoons grated pared fresh ginger
3 cloves garlic, very finely chopped
1 dried hot red chili pepper
1 medium-size yellow squash, halved lengthwise and each half cut crosswise into ¼-inch-thick slices (about 1¾ cups)
2 medium-size sweet red peppers, cored, seeded and cut into 1-inch squares (2 cups)
3 teaspoons vegetable oil
2 tablespoons reduced-sodium soy sauce
2 cups ½-inch-thick slices bok choy (Chinese cabbage)
2 teaspoons cornstarch
1 to 2 tablespoons balsamic vinegar OR: red wine vinegar
⅓ cup canned whole water chestnuts, rinsed and halved

1. Slice pork cutlets across grain into ¼-inch-thick slices. Cut each slice into 3-inch-long strips. Combine pork, 1 teaspoon ginger and one-third of the chopped garlic in small bowl.
2. Stir-fry chili pepper, remaining ginger and garlic, squash and sweet red pepper in 2 teaspoons oil in 12-inch nonstick skillet over medium heat for 5 minutes. (Add water if necessary to prevent sticking.) Add soy sauce; stir-

(continued)

SHREDDED PORK WITH CRISPY VEGETABLES
(*continued*)

fry 1 to 2 minutes or until vegetables are crisp-tender. Transfer vegetables to bowl; discard hot pepper.

3. Stir-fry pork in remaining 1 teaspoon oil in skillet over high heat for 3 to 4 minutes or until pork is no longer pink. Lower heat; return vegetables, along with bok choy, to pork in skillet.

4. Dissolve cornstarch in vinegar in small cup. Stir into skillet. Bring to boiling; cook, stirring, until sauce thickens, about 1 minute. Sprinkle with water chestnuts. Serve.

PRUNE-STUFFED LOIN OF PORK WITH GRAVY

LOW-CALORIE · LOW-FAT

The meat is simmered on top of the stove so the oven is free for any other tasks. If there are any leftovers, slice thinly for delicious sandwiches.

PRUNE-STUFFED LOIN MAKE-AHEAD TIP:
The pork can be pre-cooked a day ahead and refrigerated, covered. Gently reheat slices in the gravy, or serve the pork, sliced, without the gravy, at room temperature or chilled.

Makes 12 servings.
Nutrient Value Per Serving: 282 calories, 30 g protein, 10 g fat, 16 g carbohydrate, 647 mg sodium, 85 mg cholesterol.

1 boneless pork loin (4 to 4½ pounds)
1 tablespoon salt
¾ teaspoon white pepper
½ teaspoon ground ginger
20 or more pitted prunes
1 tablespoon *un*salted butter
1 medium-size onion, finely chopped
1½ cups prune juice
3 tablespoons all-purpose flour
3 tablespoons water

1. If loin is tied, untie it. Trim excess fat from meat. Wipe meat clean with paper toweling. Make a deep slice lengthwise down center of meat, without cutting through.

2. Combine salt, white pepper and gin-ger in small bowl. Rub all over meat. Arrange prunes down center of meat, leaving no space between prunes. Roll up meat tightly; tie at 2-inch intervals with kitchen twine.

3. Heat butter in large Dutch oven. Add onion; cook until softened, 5 to 10 minutes. Remove onion; reserve.

4. If pork doesn't fit in pot, cut in half. Brown meat on all sides, including ends. Return onion to pot. Add ½ cup prune juice to pot. Cover and simmer 45 minutes, basting meat occasionally.

5. Add remaining 1 cup prune juice to pot. Turn meat over. Continue simmer-ing, covered, until meat is tender and instant-read thermometer inserted in center registers 160°, another 20 to 30 minutes. Baste meat occasionally.

6. When meat is done, remove to plat-ter and keep warm.

7. Prepare gravy: Skim any fat from cooking liquid. Stir together flour and water in small cup until smooth. Stir in 4 to 5 tablespoons of cooking liquid until well blended. Stir mixture into cooking liquid in pot. Cook over medium-high heat, stirring occasionally, until gravy is reduced and thickened to desired consistency, 2 to 3 minutes; you should have about 1½ cups gravy.

8. Remove strings from meat. Thinly slice. Serve with gravy.

HARVEST MOON DINNER

Prune-Stuffed Loin of Pork with Gravy (this page)

Scalloped Parsnips with Cheese-Crumb Topping (429)

Baked Acorn Squash

Pumpkin Cheesecake (531)

SINGAPORE NOODLES WITH PORK AND VEGETABLES

LOW-FAT

This satisfying dish of noodles in broth has lots of flavor and texture.

Makes 4 servings.
Recipe can be halved or doubled.
Nutrient Value Per Serving: 397 calories, 24 g protein, 11 g fat, 51 g carbohydrate, 575 mg sodium, 90 mg cholesterol.

8 ounces medium-wide egg noodles
1 teaspoon Oriental sesame oil *(optional)*
3 teaspoons vegetable oil
8 ounces trimmed lean boneless pork
    loin, sliced thin and cut into ¼-inch
    strips
1 large onion, halved and cut into ¼-inch
    wedges
1 medium-size sweet red pepper, halved,
    cored, seeded and cut into
    ¼-inch-wide strips
1 tablespoon finely chopped or grated
    pared fresh ginger
1 clove garlic, finely chopped
1 teaspoon curry powder
3 small zucchini (about 5 ounces each),
    sliced ¼ inch thick
1½ cups chicken broth
1 tablespoon cornstarch
1 tablespoon reduced-sodium soy sauce
4 large green onions, sliced (½ cup)

1. Bring large pot of water to boiling. (Prepare other ingredients while waiting.) Add noodles to boiling water; cook following package directions. Drain. Return to pot; stir in Oriental sesame oil, if using. Cover pot.
2. Heat 2 teaspoons vegetable oil in large, heavy skillet or wok over moderately high heat. Add pork; stir-fry just until cooked through, about 2 minutes. Remove pork with slotted spoon to bowl. Add remaining teaspoon oil to skillet. Add onion and red pepper; stir-fry 2 minutes. Add ginger, garlic and curry; stir-fry 1 minute. Add zucchini; stir-fry 1 minute. Remove from heat.
3. Stir together a little chicken broth, cornstarch and soy sauce in small bowl until smooth. Stir in remaining broth. Add to vegetables. Cook over medium heat, stirring constantly, until sauce thickens and boils 1 minute. Add noodles, green onion and pork. Heat to serving temperature. Serve immediately.

Microwave Directions (High Power Oven):
Cook noodles as above. Combine 1 teaspoon of the oil, the onion, red pepper, ginger, garlic and curry in microwave-safe 10-inch square baking dish. Microwave, uncovered, at 100% power 3
(continued)

SINGAPORE NOODLES WITH PORK AND VEGETABLES (*continued*)

minutes, stirring once. Stir in zucchini. Microwave, uncovered, at 100% power 4 minutes, stirring once. Transfer to a bowl. Scatter meat over bottom of same dish. Pour on remaining 2 teaspoons oil. Microwave, uncovered, at 100% power 3 minutes. Reserve. Whisk together cornstarch and a little chicken broth in microwave-safe 4-cup measure until smooth. Stir in remaining chicken broth and soy sauce. Microwave, uncovered, at 100% power 4 minutes to a full boil, whisking once. Add vegetables, green onions, noodles and sauce to baking dish; stir well to blend. Microwave, uncovered, at 100% power 2 minutes to heat.

SINGAPORE SKILLET DINNER

Chilled Minted Peach Soup (137)

Singapore Noodles with Pork and Vegetables (379)

Coconut Custard

PORK MEDALLIONS WITH RED ONION RELISH

The natural sweetness of red onion complements the pork. Or serve the relish with other meats or as part of a vegetable platter.

Makes 4 servings.
Recipe can be halved or doubled.
Nutrient Value Per Serving: 634 calories, 21 g protein, 51 g fat, 23 g carbohydrate, 414 mg sodium, 83 mg cholesterol.

Red Onion Relish:
¼ cup olive oil
5 medium-size red onions (1½ pounds), halved and thinly sliced
1 teaspoon sugar
½ teaspoon salt
½ teaspoon leaf marjoram, crumbled
⅛ teaspoon ground allspice
1 cinnamon stick (2 inches)
1 bay leaf
¼ cup balsamic vinegar OR: red wine vinegar
2 tablespoons fresh orange juice

Pork:
⅓ cup all-purpose flour
⅛ teaspoon salt
⅛ teaspoon ground hot red pepper
1 pound fresh pork butt, sliced into 12 equal pieces and pounded ⅛ inch thick
3 tablespoons vegetable oil or corn oil

1. Prepare Relish: Heat oil in large, heavy skillet over medium-low heat. Add onion, sugar, salt, marjoram, all-spice, cinnamon and bay leaf. Cook, stirring occasionally, until onion is very soft, about 35 minutes. Add vinegar and orange juice; cook until liquid has almost evaporated, about 10 minutes longer. Remove bay leaf and cinnamon stick and discard. Set relish aside and keep warm.
2. Prepare Pork: Combine flour, salt and red pepper on sheet of waxed paper. Dredge pork in flour mixture, shaking off excess.
3. Heat oil in large skillet over medium-high heat. Add pork, working in batches if necessary; cook until golden brown and cooked through, 2 to 3 minutes per side. Transfer the pork to a serving plate, fanning the slices out. Spoon on relish.

Make-Ahead Tip: The Red Onion Relish can be made up to 2 days ahead and refrigerated, covered. Gently reheat.

APRICOT-STUFFED PORK TENDERLOIN

LOW-CALORIE · LOW-FAT

Bake at 400° for 40 to 50 minutes.
Makes 4 servings.
Nutrient Value Per Serving: 216 calories, 27 g protein, 4 g fat, 17 g carbohydrate, 265 mg sodium, 127 mg cholesterol.

¼ cup dried currants
¼ cup finely chopped dried apricots
2 tablespoons bourbon
1 tablespoon water
1 pound boneless pork tenderloin
1 cup fresh pumpernickel bread crumbs
¼ teaspoon salt
¼ teaspoon leaf rosemary, crumbled
⅛ teaspoon leaf sage, crumbled
⅛ teaspoon pepper
1 egg, lightly beaten

1. Preheat oven to hot (400°).
2. Soak currants and apricots in bourbon and water in small bowl until fruit are plumped.
3. Cut tenderloin lengthwise down center but not all the way through; open like a book. Pound between 2 sheets of waxed paper with bottom of heavy skillet until pork is an even ¼-inch thickness.
4. Add crumbs, salt, rosemary, sage, pepper and egg to fruit mixture. Spread stuffing lengthwise down center of pork, leaving ½ inch border at ends. Starting with long side, roll up, pushing in short ends as you roll. Secure roll with kitchen string every 2 inches. Place on rack in roasting pan.
5. Bake in preheated hot oven (400°) for 40 to 50 minutes or until meat is cooked through and stuffing is hot. Let stand 5 minutes. Remove string. Thinly slice.

Make-Ahead Tip: The tenderloin can be roasted a day ahead and refrigerated, covered. Serve at room temperature or cold.

ROAST PORK TENDERLOIN WITH PEPPERS AND ONIONS

LOW-CALORIE · LOW-CHOLESTEROL

Roast at 425° for 35 to 40 minutes.
Makes 8 servings.
Recipe can be halved or doubled.
Nutrient Value Per Serving: 199 calories, 23 g protein, 8 g fat, 8 g carbohydrate, 301 mg sodium, 67 mg cholesterol.

2 pork tenderloins (¾ to 1 pound each), trimmed
4 medium-size onions, halved
5 large cloves garlic, crushed
3 tablespoons olive oil
½ teaspoon leaf thyme, crumbled
2 large sweet red peppers, cored, seeded and cut lengthwise into 6 pieces
2 large sweet green peppers, cored, seeded and cut lengthwise into 6 pieces
¼ teaspoon salt
¼ teaspoon pepper
1 can (14½ ounces) reduced-sodium chicken broth
2 teaspoons Worcestershire sauce
1 teaspoon coarse-grain mustard
1 tablespoon cornstarch

1. Combine pork, onion, garlic, oil and thyme in large bowl. Add red and green peppers. Cover and refrigerate 2 to 3 hours, stirring occasionally. Let stand 30 minutes at a cool room temperature.
2. Preheat oven to hot (425°).
3. Season meat and vegetables with salt and pepper. Transfer just the vegetables and garlic to one flameproof large roasting pan or two 13×9×2-inch baking pans, dividing equally.
4. Roast vegetables in preheated hot oven (425°) for 15 minutes. Push vegetables to one side. Add pork, one tenderloin to each pan if using two pans. Continue to roast just until pork juices
(*continued*)

WHAT A TEAM!
Apricot-Stuffed Pork Tenderloin proves once again that dried fruits go well with pork, and the leftovers of this roast are delicious cold. Unlike our stove-top Prune-Stuffed Loin of Pork with Gravy (*page 378*), this is roasted in the oven.

ROAST PORK TENDERLOIN
A special recipe for a special dinner party. Pork tenderloins usually come two to a package.

ROAST PORK TENDERLOIN WITH PEPPERS AND ONIONS (*continued*)

run clear or until instant-read thermometer registers 160°, 20 to 25 minutes. Do not overcook.

5. Transfer meat and vegetables to platter; keep warm. Discard garlic. If there are any browned bits in roasting pan(s), place pan(s) over high heat. Add a little chicken broth and scrape up browned bits from bottom. Add to medium-size saucepan. Add chicken broth, reserving ¼ cup; add Worcester-shire and mustard. Boil 2 minutes.

6. Whisk together remaining ¼ cup broth and cornstarch in small bowl until smooth with no lumps. Slowly whisk cornstarch mixture into sauce. Boil 1 minute until thickened, whisking constantly. Strain through sieve into a bowl; you should have about 2 cups. Season with salt and pepper and additional mustard, if you wish.

7. To serve: Slice pork diagonally into thin medallions. Spoon sauce over and serve with vegetables.

HAM AND LIMA BEAN PIE WITH CORNMEAL CRUST

This dish takes a little work to prepare, but parts of the recipe can be done ahead to make things easier, and the finished pie is worth the effort. Serve as the centerpiece for a buffet, or make at holiday time.

Bake crust at 425° for 12 minutes; bake pie at 400° for 30 minutes.

Makes 8 servings.

Nutrient Value Per Serving: 685 calories, 18 g protein, 44 g fat, 54 g carbohydrate, 816 mg sodium, 141 mg cholesterol.

Filling:
¼ cup (½ stick) *un*salted butter
½ cup chopped green onion (white part only)
3 carrots, halved lengthwise and thinly sliced crosswise
1 stalk celery, halved lengthwise and thinly sliced crosswise
¼ cup all-purpose flour
2 teaspoons leaf thyme, crumbled
1 teaspoon ground allspice
¼ teaspoon pepper
1 cup beef broth
1 cup heavy cream
2 to 4 tablespoons bourbon *(optional)*
2 cups (scant ¾ pound) diced (¼ inch) cooked ham *(see note, page 384)*
1 package (10 ounces) frozen baby lima beans, thawed

Cornmeal Crust:
2 cups all-purpose flour
1 cup yellow cornmeal
¼ teaspoon salt
½ cup chopped green onion (green part only)
1 cup (2 sticks) *un*salted butter, cut in pieces
6 to 8 tablespoons water
Milk, for glaze

(continued)

HAM AND LIMA BEAN PIE WITH CORNMEAL CRUST (*continued*)

1. Prepare Filling: Heat butter in large saucepan. Add green onion, carrot and celery; sauté 1 minute. Cover and cook over medium heat until almost tender, about 6 minutes. Stir in flour, thyme, allspice and pepper; cook, stirring, 2 minutes. Stir in broth, cream and bourbon if using. Simmer, stirring, 5 minutes or until thickened. Remove from heat. Stir in ham and lima beans.
2. Preheat oven to hot (425°).
3. Prepare Crust: Combine flour, cornmeal and salt in medium-size bowl. Stir in green onion. Cut in butter until mixture is crumbly. Sprinkle on water, a tablespoon at a time, tossing with fork, until dough sticks together. Divide dough in half; dough will be very soft.
4. Roll out half of dough on lightly floured surface with floured rolling pin into 14-inch circle. Fit into 10-inch (2-quart) deep-dish pie plate or casserole. Form stand-up edge; crimp. Prick bottom all over with fork. Line with foil, covering crimped edge.
5. Bake in preheated hot oven (425°) for 8 minutes. Remove foil. Bake another 4 minutes. Remove dish to wire rack. Reduce oven temperature to 400°.
6. Roll out remaining dough on lightly floured surface into 12-inch circle. Cut into ¾-inch-wide strips.
7. Spoon ham filling into crust. Form lattice on top with dough strips, pinching strips to side of crust. Brush crust and lattice with milk. Place pie on baking sheet.
8. Bake in preheated hot oven (400°) for 30 minutes or until crust is browned and filling is bubbly. If crust browns too quickly, cover edges with aluminum foil. Let stand 15 minutes. Cut into wedges.

Note: Use a mild-flavored canned ham or lightly smoked or lightly cured ham from the deli.
Make-Ahead Tip: The filling and dough can be prepared a day ahead and refrigerated separately, covered.

CELEBRATE SPRING DINNER

Ham and Lima Bean Pie with Cornmeal Crust (383)

Asparagus with Mustard Dressing (397)

Citrus Layer Cake (507)

CURED HAM AND SMOKED PORK ROASTING TIMETABLE

Cut	Approximate Pound Weight	Oven Temperature	Internal Meat Temperature When Done	Total Roasting Time
Ham (cook before eating)				
Bone in, half	5 to 7 lbs.	325° F.	160° F.	2 to 2½ hours
Ham (fully cooked)				
Bone in, half	5 to 7 lbs.	325° F.	140° F.	1½ to 2¼ hours
Boneless, half	3 to 4 lbs.	325° F.	140° F.	1¼ to 1¾ hours
Arm Picnic Shoulder				
Bone in	5 to 8 lbs.	325° F.	170° F.	2½ to 4 hours
Shoulder				
Boneless roll	2 to 3 lbs.	325° F.	170° F.	1½ to 1¾ hours

BROILED HAM STEAKS WITH HONEY MUSTARD

LOW-CHOLESTEROL · QUICK

Broil 6 to 10 minutes.
Makes 6 servings.
Recipe can be doubled or halved.
Nutrient Value Per Serving: 305 calories,
21 g protein, 21 g fat, 6 g carbohydrate,
1,460 mg sodium, 75 mg cholesterol.

2 fully cooked ham steaks, ½ inch thick
    (about 10 ounces each)
¼ cup (½ stick) *un*salted butter, melted

3 tablespoons honey mustard OR: other
    flavored mustard
¼ cup dry bread crumbs
¼ cup grated Parmesan cheese

1. Pat ham steaks dry.
2. Combine 2 tablespoons butter and
mustard in small bowl. Combine crumbs
and Parmesan on waxed paper. Coat
ham with mustard mixture, then dip in
crumbs, pressing crumbs onto steaks.
Arrange on oiled broiler-pan rack. Drizzle with half the remaining butter.
3. Broil in preheated broiler 4 inches
from heat for 3 to 5 minutes on each
side or until golden brown. Drizzle second side with remaining butter before
broiling.

**HAM STEAKS
SERVING IDEAS**
A quick-cooking technique that turns an
old favorite into an
elegant entree. Serve
the ham steaks with
scalloped sweet potatoes and, for a dressier touch, glazed
mustard fruits, available in specialty food
shops.

**HONEY
MUSTARD—MAKE
YOUR OWN**
If honey mustard is
unavailable, simply
mix Dijon-style mustard with a little
brown sugar and
some cider vinegar.
Or experiment with a
shallot, green peppercorn or other flavored mustard.

BRATWURST, POTATOES AND APPLES

LOW-CHOLESTEROL

If you can't find bratwurst, use sweet Italian sausage for this very simple, tasty preparation. The sausage can be sliced or left whole.

Makes 4 servings.
Recipe can be halved or doubled.
Nutrient Value Per Serving: 450 calories, 17 g protein, 33 g fat, 21 g carbohydrate, 636 mg sodium, 68 mg cholesterol.

12 ounces all-purpose potatoes, pared and cut into ½-inch chunks (2 cups)
1 tablespoon vegetable oil
1 pound bratwurst, sliced ½ inch thick OR: sweet Italian sausage
1 large Granny Smith apple (8 ounces), pared, cored and thinly sliced (2 cups)

1. Cook potatoes in large pot of gently boiling water for 12 minutes. Drain. Rinse under cold running water. Drain well. Dry on paper toweling.
2. Heat oil in large skillet over moderately high heat. Add bratwurst; cook until browned all over, about 7 minutes. Add potatoes. Lower heat to moderate; cover and cook 10 minutes, shaking pan occasionally. Add apple; cover and cook 5 minutes longer or until apple is tender. Serve.

Microwave Directions (High Power Oven):
Ingredient Changes: Decrease oil to 1 teaspoon; add ¼ teaspoon paprika.
Directions: Combine potatoes and ½ cup water in microwave-safe 4-cup measure. Cover with microwave-safe plastic wrap, vented at one edge. Microwave at 100% power 6 minutes. Drain potatoes well; cover and reserve. Combine oil and bratwurst in microwave-safe 10-inch square baking dish with lid. Microwave, uncovered, at 100% power 4 minutes, stirring once. Stir in apple and potatoes; sprinkle with paprika. Cover with lid. Microwave at 100% power 5 minutes, stirring once.

SAUSAGE AND HOMINY CASSEROLE

Bake at 350° for 20 minutes.
Makes 4 servings.
Recipe can be halved or doubled.
Nutrient Value Per Serving: 582 calories,
29 g protein, 32 g fat, 43 g carbohydrate,
1,627 mg sodium, 90 mg cholesterol.

1 pound Italian-style sausages, sweet or
    hot or a combination
¼ cup water
1 large onion, chopped
2 cloves garlic, finely chopped
1 can (14½ ounces) tomatoes, in juice,
    undrained and broken up
2 tablespoons tomato paste
½ teaspoon leaf oregano, crumbled
½ teaspoon leaf thyme, crumbled
¼ teaspoon black pepper
2 cans (16 ounces each) hominy, drained
    and rinsed
1 cup Monterey Jack cheese, shredded
    (4 ounces)

1. Pierce each sausage twice with fork. Place in large skillet with water. Bring to boiling over medium-high heat; cover and cook 5 minutes. Remove sausage to paper toweling to drain. Empty skillet and wipe with paper toweling.
2. When cool enough to handle, cut sausages into ½-inch-thick slices. Add slices to same skillet; sauté until browned all over, about 5 minutes. Using slotted spoon, remove to paper toweling to drain. Drain all but 1 tablespoon fat from skillet and discard.
3. Reduce heat to medium. Add onion to skillet; sauté 3 minutes. Add garlic; sauté 2 minutes.
4. Return sausages to skillet. Add tomatoes with their liquid, tomato paste, oregano, thyme and pepper. Bring to boiling. Lower heat; simmer until thickened, about 30 minutes.
5. Preheat oven to moderate (350°).
6. Stir hominy into skillet. Scrape mix-

ture into 2-quart (11 × 7 × 2-inch) shallow baking dish.
7. Bake in preheated moderate oven (350°) for 15 minutes or until hot and bubbly. Sprinkle with cheese. Bake 5 minutes or until the cheese is melted.

Make-Ahead Tip: The entire recipe may be made 1 day ahead through Step 6. Refrigerate, covered. Let come to room temperature before baking.
Microwave Directions (High Power Oven):
Ingredient Changes: Drain tomatoes, saving liquid for another use.
Directions: Place pierced sausages in microwave-safe 9-inch square baking dish. Cover with paper toweling. Microwave at 100% power 6 minutes, rearranging sausages once. Remove sausages; slice. Drain drippings; do not wipe out dish. Add onion and garlic. Microwave, uncovered, at 100% power 4 minutes, stirring once. Mix in tomatoes, tomato paste, oregano, thyme and pepper. Add sausages and hominy. Cover with microwave-safe plastic wrap, vented at one edge. Microwave at 70% power 9 minutes. Remove plastic wrap; stir. Sprinkle with cheese. Microwave, uncovered, at 100% power 2 minutes.

COLD-WEATHER SUNDAY SUPPER

Sausage and Hominy Casserole (this page)

Green Salad with Citrus Dressing (179)

Poundcake with warm Winter Fruit Compote (529)

A SOUTHERN FAVORITE
The cooking technique here renders much of the fat out of the sausage in this Southern favorite. Serve for a brunch or a cold-weather Sunday supper. For a leaner variation, try with turkey sausages.

2 cups canned crushed tomatoes, in juice
⅓ cup dried apricots, quartered
    (2 ounces)
½ teaspoon leaf oregano, crumbled
¼ teaspoon ground cinnamon
2¼ cups lowfat milk
⅓ cup all-purpose flour
½ teaspoon salt
¼ teaspoon grated orange rind
⅛ teaspoon pepper
10 ounces ziti, cooked according to
    package directions
1 package (10 ounces) frozen chopped
    spinach, thawed and drained well
⅓ cup grated Parmesan cheese

1. Sauté onion and garlic in oil in large skillet over low heat until soft, about 10 minutes. Add lamb; increase heat to moderate; cook, stirring frequently, until no longer pink, about 5 minutes.
2. Add tomatoes with their liquid, apricots, oregano and cinnamon. Bring to boiling. Lower heat; simmer, covered, 10 minutes. Remove from heat.
3. Whisk milk into flour in medium-size saucepan; cook, stirring frequently, over moderate heat, for 5 minutes or until lightly thickened. Stir in salt, orange rind and pepper. Remove from heat.
4. Preheat oven to moderate (350°). Lightly grease 11 × 7 × 2-inch baking pan.
5. Spoon half the ziti into pan, all the meat mixture, all the spinach and half the sauce. Top with remaining ziti, sauce and Parmesan cheese. Cover loosely with aluminum foil.
6. Bake in preheated moderate oven (350°) for 25 minutes. Uncover and bake 20 minutes longer or until bubbly and lightly browned.

Make-Ahead Tip: The casserole can be assembled the day before and refrigerated, covered.

PASTITSIO WITH SPINACH AND DRIED APRICOTS

LOW-CHOLESTEROL

The dried apricots add a tart-sweet touch.

Bake at 350° for 45 minutes.
Makes 6 servings.
Nutrient Value Per Serving: 561 calories, 27 g protein, 24 g fat, 59 g carbohydrate, 525 mg sodium, 66 mg cholesterol.

1 large onion, chopped
3 cloves garlic, finely chopped
1 tablespoon olive oil
1 pound ground lamb

BRAISED LAMB SHANKS WITH VEGETABLES

Prepare this dish early in the day or the night before, and then reheat to have a hearty winter's meal on the table in minutes. The flavor improves with time.

Bake at 350° for 1 hour.
Makes 4 servings.
Recipe can be halved or doubled.
Nutrient Value Per Serving: 556 calories, 39 g protein, 29 g fat, 35 g carbohydrate, 418 mg sodium, 122 mg cholesterol.

1 tablespoon olive oil or vegetable oil
2 pounds meaty lamb shanks, cut into
    1½-inch-thick pieces*
¼ cup all-purpose flour
1 large onion, chopped
7 cloves garlic, peeled
2 teaspoons chopped pared fresh ginger
1 pound all-purpose potatoes, pared and
    cut in ¾-inch chunks
12 ounces white turnips, pared and cut in
    ½-inch chunks
6 ounces carrots (2 to 3), pared and cut
    diagonally into ¼-inch-thick slices
1 cup chicken broth
½ cup dry white wine
¾ teaspoon leaf rosemary, crumbled
¾ teaspoon grated lemon rind
⅛ teaspoon pepper

1. Preheat oven to moderate (350°).
2. Heat oil in ovenproof Dutch oven or pot over moderately high heat. Dredge lamb in flour. Working in batches, add lamb to oil; sauté until browned all over, about 5 minutes. Remove lamb to plate as it browns. Lower heat.
3. Add onion, garlic and ginger to pot; cook, uncovered, stirring occasionally, until softened, about 10 minutes.
4. Add potatoes, turnips, carrots, broth, white wine, rosemary, lemon rind, pepper and lamb. Bring to boiling. Cover.
5. Bake in preheated moderate oven (350°) for 1 hour or until meat is ten-

der. Transfer meat and vegetables to serving platter. Skim fat from sauce. Pour sauce over meat and vegetables. Serve.

*Note: Have your butcher saw the shanks into manageable pieces.
Make-Ahead Tip: The dish can be prepared a day ahead and refrigerated, covered. Remove fat from surface and gently reheat.

TARRAGON-GARLIC LAMB CHOPS

QUICK

For extra flavor, finely chop the garlic, spread it over the chops and let stand several hours, refrigerated, covered, before cooking. Discard the chopped garlic before cooking the chops.

Makes 4 servings.
Recipe can be halved or doubled.
Nutrient Value Per Serving: 366 calories, 27 g protein, 27 g fat, 1 g carbohydrate, 643 mg sodium, 113 mg cholesterol.

1¾ pounds thin-cut shoulder lamb chops (about 4 chops)
1 clove garlic, crushed
1 teaspoon salt
¼ teaspoon black pepper
1 tablespoon vegetable oil
2 tablespoons dry white wine
1 teaspoon leaf tarragon, crumbled
1 tablespoon *un*salted butter

1. Rub chops with garlic. Sprinkle with salt and pepper.
2. Heat oil in large, heavy skillet over medium-high heat. Add chops; sauté about 3 to 5 minutes on each side or until golden brown. Remove chops from skillet and keep warm. Remove skillet from heat.
3. Drain off fat from skillet, leaving any browned bits in bottom. Add wine and tarragon to skillet; stir with wooden spoon to loosen any browned bits from bottom. Stir in butter just until blended. Add lamb chops. Heat through, turning lamb once to coat with sauce. Serve.

RABBIT WITH ONION-MUSTARD SAUCE

Bake at 375° for 50 minutes.
Makes 6 servings.
Nutrient Value Per Serving: 403 calories, 37 g protein, 22 g fat, 13 g carbohydrate, 503 mg sodium, 99 mg cholesterol.

5 tablespoons olive oil or vegetable oil
4 large onions, halved and thinly sliced crosswise
1 rabbit (3 pounds), cut up (if frozen, thawed according to package directions)
¼ cup all-purpose flour
2 cups chicken broth
4 teaspoons Dijon-style mustard
½ teaspoon leaf rosemary, crumbled
¼ teaspoon ground ginger
2 teaspoons lemon juice
2 tablespoons snipped chives OR: green onion tops

1. Heat 2 tablespoons oil in ovenproof Dutch oven over moderate heat. Add onion; cook, stirring occasionally, until lightly golden, about 20 minutes.
2. Preheat oven to moderate (375°).
3. Meanwhile, heat 1½ tablespoons oil in large skillet over moderately high heat. Dredge rabbit in flour. Working in batches, add rabbit pieces to skillet; cook until browned, about 5 minutes per side, adding remaining oil as needed. Add to onion in Dutch oven. Add chicken broth, mustard, rosemary and ginger. Bring to boiling. Cover.
4. Bake in preheated moderate oven (375°) for 50 minutes or until tender.
5. Remove rabbit to platter. Bring sauce to boiling; boil 2 minutes, skimming any fat from surface. Stir in lemon juice and chives. Pour over rabbit.

Make-Ahead Tip: The dish can be made a day ahead and refrigerated, covered. Skim any fat from surface. Reheat gently, covered, in 350° oven, stirring occasionally.

RABBIT
Commercially raised rabbit can be found in specialty butcher shops and sometimes in the freezer case at the supermarket. It is usually sold cut up into ready-to-cook parts. If frozen, defrost in the refrigerator and cook within 2 days of thawing. Rabbit is lean and mild in flavor, with white meat that darkens when marinated and cooked. Smaller rabbits (less than 2 pounds) have more tender meat that can be broiled or roasted. When broiling or roasting, cook rabbit thoroughly, but avoid overcooking as its lean meat dries out quickly. Average-size rabbits (2½ to 3 pounds) are better suited to slower, moist-cooking methods and can be substituted for chicken in braised dishes or stews. Broth made from rabbit can be used as the base for a rich and flavorful soup.

VENISON STEAKS WITH CRANBERRY SAUCE

LOW-FAT · QUICK

*V*enison *is leaner than other red meat and is cooked rare to retain its own distinctive flavor. This sauce also goes well with pork.*

Makes 4 servings.
Recipe can be halved or doubled.
Nutrient Value Per Serving: 455 calories, 45 g protein, 12 g fat, 42 g carbohydrate, 621 mg sodium, 164 mg cholesterol.

1 tablespoon *un*salted butter
⅔ cup chopped shallots (about 6) OR: white part green onion
2 cloves garlic, crushed
3 tablespoons balsamic vinegar OR: red wine vinegar
1 bag (12 ounces) cranberries, picked over
½ cup sugar
4 strips (2 × ½ inch each) orange rind
½ vanilla bean, split lengthwise
3 cloves
2 cups chicken broth
1 tablespoon vegetable oil
4 boneless venison steaks from leg (6 to 7 ounces each)

1. Heat butter in large skillet over low heat. Add shallot and garlic; cook, stirring frequently, until softened, about 7 minutes. Add vinegar; cook until evaporated, about 3 minutes. Add cranber-

(continued)

VENISON
Venison is a catch-all term for deer, elk or caribou meat. Domestic farmed venison is available from specialty butchers, fresh or frozen, in cuts similar to beef and other meats. Venison is very lean and the meat toughens when overcooked. Loin steaks and chops are usually broiled; larger cuts, such as shoulder, rump or round roast, are best when braised and served pot-roast style. Pork fat is often mixed into ground venison meat to reduce toughness and enhance flavor. Freezing venison breaks down the muscle fiber and helps tenderize the meat; fresh venison benefits from the tenderizing effects of overnight marination.

VENISON STEAKS WITH CRANBERRY SAUCE
(*continued*)

ries, sugar, orange rind, vanilla bean and cloves. Increase heat to moderate; cook until sugar melts and berries begin to pop, about 5 minutes.

2. Add chicken broth; simmer gently for 10 minutes. Strain through fine-meshed sieve over bowl, pushing on solids to extract as much juice as possible. Discard solids.

3. Heat oil in large skillet over high heat. Add venison; cook 2 to 3 minutes per side until browned on outside and cooked to rare. Remove venison to serving plates; keep warm. Pour off fat from skillet. Add sauce; cook 2 minutes over high heat. Pour sauce over venison. Serve.

Make-Ahead Tip: The sauce can be made a day ahead and refrigerated, covered.

GROUND VENISON MEATLOAF

Since venison is leaner than other red meats, we've mixed in some ground pork for extra richness. Serve as a main course or in small slices, chilled, as an appetizer.

Bake at 350° for 1 hour.
Makes 8 servings.
Nutrient Value Per Serving: 311 calories, 28 g protein, 15 g fat, 13 g carbohydrate, 373 mg sodium, 131 mg cholesterol.

1 tablespoon vegetable oil
1 large onion, finely chopped
1½ pounds ground venison
¾ pound ground pork
½ cup soft fresh bread crumbs
⅓ cup milk
1 teaspoon salt
¾ teaspoon rubbed sage
½ teaspoon ground allspice
¼ teaspoon pepper

⅓ cup plum jam, finely chopped
2 tablespoons bourbon
1 egg

1. Preheat oven to moderate (350°). Lightly oil 9 × 5 × 3-inch loaf pan; set aside.

2. Heat oil in large skillet over low heat. Add onion; cook, stirring frequently, until softened, 7 to 10 minutes. Transfer to large bowl. Cool to room temperature. Add venison, pork, bread crumbs, milk, salt, sage, allspice, pepper, jam, bourbon and egg; mix well to combine.

3. Transfer mixture to prepared loaf pan. Pack down and smooth top with rubber spatula. Cover with aluminum foil.

4. Bake in preheated moderate oven (350°) for 1 hour or until firm and cooked through. Cool 10 minutes in pan. Carefully drain. Invert loaf onto serving platter. Serve hot, at room temperature, or chilled.

Make-Ahead Tip: The loaf can be prepared a day ahead and refrigerated, covered. Serve at room temperature or chilled.

WINTER SOLSTICE DINNER

Ground Venison Meatloaf
(this page)

Turnips with Pears (460)

Sautéed Spinach with Golden Raisins (447)

Walnut Tart (496)

Broiled Tomato Slices Provençale
(page 455)

VEGETABLES AND FRUIT

BRAISED ARTICHOKE WITH SWEET RED PEPPER

LOW-CALORIE · LOW-FAT · LOW-CHOLESTEROL

Serve with grilled or roasted meats, as part of a buffet or for lunch along with pasta and a loaf of crusty bread.

Makes 6 servings.
Recipe can be halved or doubled.
Nutrient Value Per Serving: 96 calories, 4 g protein, 3 g fat, 17 g carbohydrate, 374 mg sodium, 0 mg cholesterol.

6 large globe artichokes (about 12 ounces each)*
1 lemon, halved
1 tablespoon olive oil
1 sweet red pepper, cored, seeded and diced
1 large clove garlic, sliced
½ teaspoon salt
¼ teaspoon leaf sage, crumbled
½ cup chicken broth

1. Remove tough outer leaves from each artichoke by pulling each leaf out and down until it snaps off at base. Repeat until the tender, yellow-green leaves have been reached. With stainless steel knife, cut off 1 inch from top of each artichoke; discard. (If using the leaves for another use, such as steaming for a first course, to prevent discoloration, drop in bowl of water with a little lemon juice added.) Remove stem from each artichoke. Rub all cut surfaces of artichoke with cut lemon to prevent discoloration. With paring knife, trim dark green base from each artichoke bottom. Rub with cut lemon. With teaspoon, scrape out choke, the hairy center of each artichoke, and discard. Cut each artichoke bottom into thin wedges; place in lemon-water.
2. Heat oil in large, nonaluminum skillet over medium-high heat. Add red pepper and garlic; sauté 2 minutes. Drain artichokes. Add artichokes, salt, and sage to skillet; sauté 2 minutes. Add broth. Cover and simmer 20 minutes or until tender. Serve warm or at room temperature.

*Note: For an easier-to-prepare, but not quite as flavorful, alternative, substitute 1 package (10 ounces) frozen artichoke hearts, thawed, for the fresh, and reduce the salt to ¼ teaspoon.
Make-Ahead Tip: The dish can be made a few hours ahead and refrigerated, covered. Gently reheat.

JERUSALEM ARTICHOKE SAUTÉ

LOW-CALORIE · LOW-CHOLESTEROL
QUICK

Makes 4 servings.
Nutrient Value Per Serving: 96 calories,
2 g protein, 3 g fat, 15 g carbohydrate,
275 mg sodium, 0 mg cholesterol.

1 tablespoon vegetable oil
2 green onions, sliced
1 small sweet red pepper, cored, seeded
    and diced
1 package (16 ounces) Jerusalem
    artichokes, pared and cut into ¼-inch
    matchstick pieces
1 tablespoon chopped fresh mint OR: 1
    teaspoon dried
½ teaspoon salt
1 tablespoon lemon juice

1. Heat oil in large skillet over
medium-high heat. Add green onion
and red pepper; sauté 3 minutes or until
slightly softened.
2. Add Jerusalem artichokes, mint and
salt. Cook 3 minutes, stirring constantly. Stir in lemon juice.

**JERUSALEM
ARTICHOKES SERVING
IDEAS**
Jerusalem artichokes
have a flavor reminis-
cent of turnip and
water chestnuts. This
quick sauté is deli-
cious with roast
chicken or other
meats, or serve chilled
or at room tempera-
ture as an appetizer
or salad.

**JERUSALEM
ARTICHOKE
MAKE-AHEAD TIP:**
The recipe can be
prepared a day
ahead and refriger-
ated, covered. Serve
chilled or at room
temperature.

ARTICHOKES, JERUSALEM ARTICHOKES AND ASPARAGUS

ARTICHOKES

Although preparing fresh artichoke bottoms may seem tedious, there's the extra bonus of the leaves which can be steamed and served with a dipping sauce, such as mayonnaise with a little chopped garlic added. Just arrange half the leaves in a steamer basket. Place in a 5-quart Dutch oven with ½ inch boiling water, cover and steam 5 minutes or until tender. Repeat with remaining leaves and enjoy! **Globe Artichokes** A member of the thistle family, artichokes are **available** all year in some areas and at their peak throughout March, April and May. **Nutritionally,** artichokes are high in calcium, phosphorus, potassium and B vitamins.

- **Choose** young, tender artichokes with unspotted, tightly packed, olive-green leaves.
- **Store** artichokes in a plastic bag in the refrigerator for up to a few days.
- Tiny **baby artichokes** are sweet and tender enough to be served raw, with light vinaigrette dressing and shavings of Parmesan cheese. They can also be braised and served as a first course.
- To **prepare** a large or medium-size artichoke for cooking, see Braised Artichoke with Sweet Red Pepper *(page 394)*, but omit trimming the leaves 1½ inches from base.
- **Cook** artichokes by steaming or poaching until a leaf pulls out easily and the heart is tender when pierced with the tip of a knife: about 30 minutes in a covered saucepan on top of the stove. Don't use an aluminum, iron or carbon steel pot, as these metals may discolor the vegetable and impart a bitter flavor. Artichokes do particularly well in a microwave oven; follow manufacturer's instructions.

- **Serve** 1 large or medium-size artichoke or 3 to 4 baby-size per person.

JERUSALEM ARTICHOKES

This knobby root vegetable is **available** from mid-fall through early spring. Also known as sunchokes, Jerusalem artichokes are not artichokes at all, but do acquire a nutty, artichoke-like flavor when cooked. They resemble fresh ginger in appearance and have the texture of white potatoes. Jerusalem artichokes are **nutritionally** similar to legumes—high in protein, rich in iron and B vitamins.

- **Choose** the smoothest roots for easiest peeling. Avoid soft, wrinkled or dried-out vegetables.
- **Store** loosely covered in the refrigerator for up to 2 weeks.
- To **prepare** Jerusalem artichokes, scrub to remove all surface dirt, then cut off any dry, stringy portions and browned ends. Smooth-skinned chokes can be peeled with a swivel-bladed vegetable peeler, dropped into acidulated water (lemon water), then simmered until tender. For knobbier roots, simply trim off and discard the knobs to make the roots more manageable.
- **Cook** Jerusalem artichokes as you would potatoes. They can be roasted, pureed, served *au gratin* or diced into stew. They can also be served raw as a crisp addition to salads, as a dipping vegetable or a crunchy, low-calorie snack.
- Yields vary, since a very bumpy artichoke will require a lot of knob trimming. A pound will **serve** 2 to 4.

ASPARAGUS

Asparagus is **available** throughout March, April and May. **Nutritionally,** asparagus is low in calories and sodium, high in iron, vitamins A and C, and B vitamins.

- **Choose** medium-green, firm, straight spears with moist, unwrinkled stems and tight tips. Size and width do not affect taste but pencil-thin varieties have more tender stems that don't require peeling.
- If **storing** in the refrigerator for more than a few hours, or up to a day or two, wrap the bases of the spears in moist paper toweling, then place the bottoms in plastic bags.
- To **prepare,** gently rinse asparagus to remove any sand that lurks, particularly in the tips. Trim off tough bottoms. Economical cooks scrape the woody bases off with a vegetable peeler until they get to the tender centers; more extravagant ones snap off and discard the tougher portions. Either way, all of the spears should be about the same length for even cooking.
- To **cook,** simmer spears lying down in an inch or two of water in a large skillet until they are just tender, 3 to 5 minutes, depending on thickness of stem.
- Vertical asparagus steamers allow even cooking of tender tips and tougher stems. Stand the stalks upright in about 3 inches of boiling water; cover and cook for about 8 minutes.
- Cooked asparagus loses its sprightly green color when it's tossed with acidic dressings, so add vinaigrette or lemon juice just before serving.
- One pound of asparagus makes 2 first-course **servings** or 3 to 4 side-dish portions.

ASPARAGUS WITH MUSTARD DRESSING

LOW-CHOLESTEROL · QUICK

A *simple way to show off asparagus.*

Makes 8 servings.
Recipe can be halved or doubled.
Nutrient Value Per Serving: 76 calories,
2 g protein, 7 g fat, 3 g carbohydrate,
245 mg sodium, 0 mg cholesterol.

2 pounds fresh asparagus, trimmed and
  peeled
¾ teaspoon salt
¼ cup olive oil
2 tablespoons white wine vinegar
2 teaspoons Dijon-style mustard
1 clove garlic, finely chopped
¼ teaspoon sugar
Pinch pepper

1. Fill large skillet with enough water
to cover asparagus. Add ½ teaspoon
salt. Bring to boiling. Add asparagus.
Return to boiling. Lower heat; simmer
3 to 5 minutes or until crisp-tender and
knife tip can be inserted easily into
thick end.
2. Drain asparagus. Rinse with cold
water; drain. Arrange on platter.

SPRINGTIME SUPPER

**Tarragon-Garlic Lamb
Chops (390)**

**Asparagus with Mustard
Dressing (this page)**

Steamed New Potatoes

**Stewed Rhubarb with
Vanilla Ice Cream**

---

3. Combine olive oil, vinegar, mustard,
garlic, sugar, remaining ¼ teaspoon salt
and pepper in bowl. Pour over asparagus.

Make-Ahead Tip: The recipe can be prepared through Step 2 up to 2 hours
ahead and refrigerated, covered.

ASPARAGUS STIR-FRY

LOW-CHOLESTEROL · QUICK

A *delicious side dish for roast pork or
poultry, or arrange and serve as part of a
vegetable platter.*

Makes 4 servings.
Recipe can be halved or doubled.
Nutrient Value Per Serving: 60 calories,
2 g protein, 5 g fat, 2 g carbohydrate,
203 mg sodium, 0 mg cholesterol.

1½ tablespoons oil
1 pound asparagus, trimmed and cut
  diagonally into 1-inch lengths
¼ cup chicken broth OR: water
¼ teaspoon salt
¼ teaspoon pepper
Dash soy sauce OR: Oriental sesame oil

1. Heat oil in large nonstick skillet or
wok. Add asparagus; sauté 1 minute.
Add broth. Cover. Lower heat; cook
until tender, 3 to 5 minutes.
2. Drain. Season with salt, pepper and
soy sauce. Serve immediately.

FIBER FACTS
Dietary fiber is a non-digestible complex carbohydrate found *only* in plant foods. Fiber provides no calories because it cannot be absorbed into the body. For low-calorie sources of both *soluble* and *insoluble* dietary fiber, look to a variety of fresh fruit and vegetables.
■ *Soluble fiber* binds with fat and cholesterol, carries it out of the body and, to some extent, lowers blood cholesterol levels in the process.
■ Foods high in *soluble* fiber include: broccoli, Brussels sprouts, carrots, grapefruit, oranges, pears and prunes.
■ *Insoluble fiber* helps move food through the digestive tract more quickly, protecting against constipation and preventing prolonged exposure of intestinal tissue to possible cancer-causing agents in food.
■ Foods high in *insoluble* fiber include: peas, bean sprouts, pumpkin, corn, raspberries and dried figs.

CRANBERRY BEANS AND KALE

LOW-FAT • LOW-CHOLESTEROL • QUICK

Serve as a side dish with roasted lamb, ham or pork, or as a main dish with slices of crusty bread, and perhaps a glass of red wine. For variations, substitute Fresh spinach or Swiss chard for the kale, and frozen lima beans or black-eyed peas for the cranberry beans.

Makes 6 servings.
Recipe can be halved or doubled.
Nutrient Value Per Serving: 120 calories, 7 g protein, 3 g fat, 18 g carbohydrate, 430 mg sodium, 0 mg cholesterol.

1½ pounds fresh cranberry beans, unshelled (2¼ cups shelled)
1 clove garlic
4 whole cloves
1 bay leaf
1 tablespoon olive oil or vegetable oil
4 cups chopped kale OR: fresh spinach OR: Swiss chard
4 green onions, sliced
1 clove garlic, chopped
1 tablespoon slivered orange rind
½ teaspoon leaf tarragon, crumbled
½ cup orange juice
½ teaspoon cornstarch
1 teaspoon salt

1. Shell beans. Stud clove garlic with whole cloves. Fill medium-size skillet half full of water. Add studded garlic and bay leaf. Bring to boiling. Add beans. Lower heat; simmer 10 to 12 minutes or until tender. Drain; discard bay leaf and garlic.
2. Dry skillet. Add oil; heat over medium heat. Add kale, green onion, chopped garlic, orange rind and tarragon; cover and cook 4 minutes or until kale is wilted.
3. Meanwhile, stir together orange juice and cornstarch in small bowl. Add to skillet, along with cranberry beans and salt. Simmer 2 minutes. Spoon into serving dish and serve hot.

ON THE LAMB

Roast Leg of Lamb

Roasted Potatoes with Peppers (440)

Cranberry Beans and Kale
(this page)

Poached Pears with Raspberries (523)

GREEN BEANS WITH WATER CHESTNUTS

LOW-CALORIE · LOW-CHOLESTEROL
QUICK

Makes 4 servings.
Recipe can be halved or doubled.
Nutrient Value Per Serving: 65 calories,
2 g protein, 3 g fat, 8 g carbohydrate,
156 mg sodium, 0 mg cholesterol.

12 ounces green beans, trimmed
1 tablespoon vegetable oil
1 clove garlic, finely chopped
¼ cup sliced water chestnuts, chopped
1 tablespoon reduced-sodium soy sauce
⅛ teaspoon ground ginger

1. Cook green beans in small amount
boiling water in medium-size saucepan,
covered, until crisp-tender, 3 to 5 minutes. Drain. Dry saucepan.
2. Heat oil in same saucepan over
medium heat. Add garlic; sauté until
lightly browned, 1 to 2 minutes. Add
beans, water chestnuts, soy sauce and
ginger; heat through.

Make-Ahead Tip: Green beans can be
prepared up to 2 hours ahead and refrigerated, covered.

KABOB-IT

**Broiled Chicken Kabobs
with Oriental Marinade
(261)**

**Green Beans with Water
Chestnuts** (this page)

**Rice with Chopped Green
Onion**

**Orange Sherbet with
Toasted Coconut**

SHREDDED BEET AND APPLE

Shredding the beets before cooking allows
them to cook faster and absorb more flavor. To prevent staining, wear rubber
gloves when shredding the beets and shred
onto waxed paper. Serve with boiled beef,
roast duck or pork, as part of an appetizer
plate, or as a side salad. Tasty either warm
or at room temperature.

Makes 4 servings.
Recipe can be halved or doubled.
Nutrient Value Per Serving: 102 calories,
1 g protein, 6 g fat, 12 g carbohydrate,
193 mg sodium, 16 mg cholesterol.

1 pound fresh beets (1 pound without
 tops), peeled and shredded (3 cups)
1 large Granny Smith apple, pared and
 shredded (1 cup)
2 tablespoons *un*salted butter
¼ teaspoon salt
⅛ teaspoon leaf marjoram, crumbled
1⅔ cups water
1 teaspoon fresh lemon juice

1. Combine beets, apple, butter, salt,
marjoram and water in medium-size
saucepan. Bring to boiling. Lower heat;
simmer, covered, 20 minutes.
2. Uncover the saucepan. Increase heat
to high; cook 7 to 8 minutes or until
almost all liquid has evaporated and
beets are tender. Stir in lemon juice.
Serve warm or at room temperature.

Make-Ahead Tip: The recipe can be made
a day ahead and refrigerated, covered.
Gently reheat.

ROASTED BEETS

LOW-CHOLESTEROL

Bake at 400° for 1 hour.
Makes 4 servings.
Recipe can be halved or doubled.
Nutrient Value Per Serving: 105 calories, 2 g protein, 7 g fat, 10 g carbohydrate, 208 mg sodium, 0 mg cholesterol.

1¼ pounds fresh beets (4 to 5), tops trimmed and beets washed
2 tablespoons olive oil
1 tablespoon balsamic vinegar OR: red wine vinegar
1 tablespoon chopped fresh dill OR: ½ teaspoon chopped fresh rosemary leaves
¼ teaspoon salt

1. Preheat oven to hot (400°). Wrap each beet in aluminum foil; place on baking sheet.
2. Bake in preheated hot oven (400°) for 1 hour or until beets feel tender when pressed. Remove from oven.
3. When cool enough to handle, unwrap and peel off skin; using paper toweling or wearing rubber gloves will prevent staining. Quarter beets.
4. Combine oil, vinegar, dill and salt in small bowl. Add beets; toss to coat. Serve warm or at room temperature.

Microwave Directions (High Power Oven):
Place beets in microwave-safe 2-quart casserole with lid. Pour in ¼ cup water. Microwave, covered, at 100% power 14 minutes or until soft. Continue with Step 3.

BOK CHOY STRUDEL WITH MUSHROOMS AND ONIONS

*S*erve as an enticing first course, a side dish with poultry, meat or fish, or as a lunch dish with a green salad.

Bake at 375° for 25 minutes.
Makes 16 slices.
Nutrient Value Per Slice: 355 calories,
9 g protein, 17 g fat, 45 g carbohydrate,
308 mg sodium, 42 mg cholesterol.

½ ounce dried porcini OR: or other dried
　　mushrooms
5 tablespoons *un*salted butter
1 pound bok choy, thinly sliced (4 cups)
1 medium-size onion, chopped
1 large clove garlic, chopped
½ cup dry white wine
1 teaspoon honey
¼ teaspoon caraway seeds, crushed
1 tablespoon all-purpose flour
2 tablespoons reduced-calorie sour cream
8 phyllo leaves *(see How-To, page 91)*
¼ cup dried bread crumbs

1. Soak porcini mushrooms in boiling water to cover in small bowl for at least 20 minutes. Drain in sieve lined with damp paper toweling; rinse mushrooms to remove all grit. (Save the liquid for soup making.) Remove any tough stems; finely chop mushrooms.
2. Preheat oven to moderate (375°). Line jelly-roll pan with aluminum foil. Lightly spray with nonstick vegetable-oil cooking spray.
3. Melt butter in medium-size skillet over medium heat. Spoon 3 tablespoons into cup; reserve for phyllo. Add bok choy, onion, garlic, wine, honey and caraway seeds to remaining hot butter in skillet; cook 12 to 15 minutes or until bok choy is tender and liquid is evaporated. Stir in mushrooms and flour; cook 2 minutes, stirring occasion-ally. Remove from heat. Stir in sour cream. Cool to room temperature.
4. Meanwhile, lay out phyllo leaves on work surface; cover with waxed paper and damp toweling. Place one leaf on another sheet of waxed paper; brush lightly with reserved butter. Sprinkle lightly with about ½ tablespoon bread crumbs. Repeat layering with phyllo, butter and bread crumbs, ending with phyllo.
5. Spoon bok choy mixture down length of phyllo, 1 inch in from a long side. Roll up from long side, jelly-roll fashion, using waxed paper as guide. Place, seam-side down, on prepared baking sheet. Brush top of roll with butter.
6. Bake in preheated moderate oven (375°) for 25 minutes or until golden. Let stand 10 minutes. Slice crosswise into 16 equal slices.

BOK CHOY STRUDEL MAKE-AHEAD TIP: The filling can be prepared a day ahead and refrigerated, covered. Bring to room temperature before using. The strudel can be prepared up to 3 hours ahead and refrigerated, covered, then baked.

BEANS, BEETS AND BROCCOLI

BEANS

Green beans are **available** all year but are at their abundant best in late spring and summer. **Nutritionally,** green beans are high in Vitamin A.

- **Choose green beans** bright in color, smooth and blemish-free, and so crisp that they give a snap when bent. **Wax beans** should be bright yellow with no brown mottling. **Haricots verts** are thinner, more delicate and darker green than their more common green bean cousins. Trim tops, then steam or simmer whole.
- **Store** beans in plastic bags in the refrigerator and plan to cook them within a few days.
- To **prepare,** trim stem end from green or wax beans just before cooking. Keep beans whole, cut them into 1½-inch pieces, or "French" them by splitting them lengthwise.
- To **cook,** steam or simmer until just crisp-tender, 2 to 3 minutes. Drain well and serve at once or plunge into ice water to serve cold.
- **Cranberry beans** are shaped like green beans but are in fact legumes with plump, pink-mottled, inedible pods. Treat as you would other fresh legumes: Remove from the pods, cook in simmering water until almost tender, 10 to 12 minutes, then add seasonings.
- One pound of green or wax beans **serves** 4 to 5; 1 pound of cranberry beans in the pod serves 2; 1 pound of haricots verts serves 4 to 5.

BEETS

Ruby red beets peak in early spring but are **available** throughout the year. **Nutritionally,** the beet itself is high in potassium, low in sodium and a good source of Vitamin C. Beet greens are high in Vitamin A.

- **Choose** small, round beets with smooth, firm flesh, unmarred skins, and sprightly tops.
- To **store,** cut tops off 1 inch from beet root; refrigerate separately in plastic bags. The edible greens should be used within a day or two, while the beets keep for up to two weeks.
- To **prepare,** gently rub loose dirt from the beets, being careful not to puncture the skin or the beets will bleed into their cooking water. Leave beets unpeeled, with 1 inch of the stem and root ends attached.
- To **cook** beets, place in a large heavy saucepan with cold water to cover. Bring to boiling; lower the heat and simmer, uncovered, until the beets are barely tender, about 35 minutes for medium-small size. Drain and cool under cold running water. Or, individually wrap beets in aluminum foil, place on a rack in an oven dish and bake at 350° for about 1½ hours. Peel or rub off skin, slice and serve hot or cold.
- Cook young, tender beet greens as you would spinach, just in water that clings to the leaves, covered, over low heat, for just a few minutes or until barely wilted. Simmer older greens for 20 to 30 minutes to tenderize and remove bitterness.
- One and a half pounds beets **serves** 4; 1 pound of greens serves 2 to 3.

BROCCOLI

Broccoli is **available** all year, making it a staple vegetable in many households. **Nutritionally,** spears of fresh broccoli are densely packed with fiber, calcium, iron, Vitamin C and B vitamins.

- **Choose** bunches with tight, deep green or purple flowerets and firm stalks with no holes in the base. Avoid yellowing or flowering broccoli, as these are signs of deterioration and age.
- **Store** broccoli, unwashed, in a perforated plastic bag in the refrigerator for up to several days.
- To **prepare,** just before cooking or eating raw, wash well and trim off dry stem base and any wilted leaves
- To **cook** broccoli, cut flowerets into equal-size spears; pare tough stems with a swivel-bladed peeler or small, sharp knife for even cooking. Or, separate stems from flowerets. Reserve stems for another use or peel, slice crosswise and cook with flowerets. Steam, stir-fry or simmer flowerets and stems until bright green and crisp-tender. If cooking ahead to serve cold, plunge into ice water to stop cooking and preserve color.
- **Broccoli raab** (rapini) is a non-heading broccoli with an appealing bitter flavor. Choose bunches with firm stems, and with few buds or open yellow flowers. Store unwashed and loosely wrapped in plastic bag for several days. To cook, quickly steam or sauté with garlic in olive oil.
- Half pound broccoli yields about 4 cups cooked or 4 **servings.**

NOT-SO-BASIC BROCCOLI
A new way to serve broccoli: combine with grapefruit and garnish with crispy fried slivers of fresh ginger. Serve with rich meats and poultry.

GINGERED BROCCOLI AND GRAPEFRUIT

LOW-CHOLESTEROL · QUICK

Makes 6 servings.
Recipe can be halved or doubled.
Nutrient Value Per Serving: 112 calories, 4 g protein, 5 g fat, 16 g carbohydrate, 215 mg sodium, 0 mg cholesterol.

1 piece (2 × ½ inch) pared fresh ginger
1 large bunch broccoli (about 1¾ pounds)
2 tablespoons vegetable oil
½ teaspoon salt
¼ cup water
3 pink grapefruit, peeled, bitter white pith removed, sectioned and seeded

1. Cut ginger lengthwise into thin slices, then lengthwise into thin strips; set aside. Cut broccoli into flowerets; peel stems and diagonally slice.
2. Heat oil in 10-inch skillet over medium heat. Add ginger; cook 2 to 3 minutes or until golden brown. Remove ginger with slotted spoon to plate; reserve for garnish.
3. Add broccoli flowerets and stems and salt to skillet; stir to coat well with oil. Add water; cover and cook 5 minutes or until broccoli is crisp-tender.
4. Gently stir in grapefruit sections; cover and cook 2 minutes or until heated through. Spoon broccoli and grapefruit onto serving platter. Garnish with reserved ginger and serve.

Microwave Directions (High Power Oven):
Ingredient Changes: Decrease oil to 1 tablespoon; decrease the water to 2 tablespoons.
Directions: Combine ginger and oil in microwave-safe 3-quart casserole with lid. Microwave, uncovered, at 100% power 2 minutes, stirring once. Remove. Combine broccoli and water in same casserole. Microwave, covered, at 100% power 9 to 10 minutes until tender, stirring once. Drain. Add grapefruit and salt to broccoli. Microwave, uncovered, at 100% power 2 minutes. Sprinkle with reserved ginger.

BROCCOLI WITH GARLIC

LOW-CHOLESTEROL · QUICK

Broccoli and garlic—what could be better? Keep an eye on the garlic as it cooks so it doesn't overbrown.

Makes 4 servings.
Recipe can be halved or doubled.
Nutrient Value Per Serving: 75 calories, 3 g protein, 5 g fat, 6 g carbohydrate, 61 mg sodium, 0 mg cholesterol.

1 bunch broccoli (about 1½ pounds)
1½ tablespoons olive oil
1 clove garlic, finely chopped
Pinch salt
Pinch pepper

1. Bring large pot of water to boiling over high heat.
2. Peel broccoli stems. Cut stems lengthwise into long, thin strips so each has a floweret or two at top. Drop into boiling water. Cook 3 minutes or until just tender. Drain.
3. Heat oil in large, heavy skillet over medium heat. Add garlic; cook 1 minute or until lightly golden. Add broccoli; toss until coated and heated through. Sprinkle with salt and pepper and serve.

Make-Ahead Tip: The broccoli can be prepared up to 2 hours ahead through Step 2; run under cold water. When ready to serve, cook the broccoli as directed in Step 3.

SESAME BROCCOLI AND YELLOW PEPPERS

LOW-CALORIE · LOW-CHOLESTEROL
QUICK

The most difficult step in this recipe is toasting the sesame seeds. Serve with pork chops, chicken or steaks.

Makes 4 servings.
Recipe can be halved or doubled.
Nutrient Value Per Serving: 86 calories, 5 g protein, 4 g fat, 9 g carbohydrate, 258 mg sodium, 8 mg cholesterol.

1 tablespoon sesame seeds
4 cups broccoli flowerets (about 2 pounds)
1 small sweet yellow or red pepper, cored, seeded and cut into ¾-inch-thick slices
¼ cup chicken broth
1 tablespoon dry sherry *(optional)*
1 tablespoon *un*salted butter
1 teaspoon cider vinegar
1 teaspoon cornstarch
½ teaspoon finely chopped, pared fresh ginger
¼ teaspoon salt

1. Heat medium-size saucepan over medium heat. Add sesame seeds; toast, shaking pan, for 2 to 3 minutes or until golden brown. Transfer seeds to plate.
2. Fill saucepan with water. Bring to boiling. Add broccoli; cook 5 minutes or until crisp-tender. Add sweet pepper; stir for 30 seconds. Drain vegetables in colander. Transfer vegetables to serving bowl; cover to keep warm.
3. Meanwhile, whisk together broth, sherry if using, butter, vinegar, cornstarch, ginger and salt in saucepan. Bring to boiling, whisking constantly; cook 1 minute. Add vegetables; toss to coat. Transfer to serving bowl. Garnish with sesame seeds.

BRUSSELS SPROUTS WITH ROASTED CHESTNUTS

LOW-FAT

Roast chestnuts at 400° for 15 to 20 minutes.
Makes 6 servings.
Recipe can be halved or doubled.
Nutrient Value Per Serving: 542 calories,
10 g protein, 11 g fat, 104 g carbohydrate,
254 mg sodium, 16 mg cholesterol.

2 pounds unshelled chestnuts
2 pints (1½ pounds) fresh Brussels
sprouts, trimmed and X cut in stem
end
3 tablespoons *un*salted butter
½ teaspoon salt
¼ teaspoon black pepper

3 tablespoons snipped fresh chives OR:
finely chopped green onion tops

1. Preheat oven to hot (400°).
2. Cut an X into flat side of each chestnut. Arrange chestnuts in roasting pan.
3. Roast chestnuts in preheated hot oven (400°) for 15 to 20 minutes or until shells have split. When cool enough to handle, shell chestnuts and remove inner brown skin.
4. Meanwhile, cook sprouts in boiling salted water in large saucepan for 12 to 15 minutes or until tender. Drain sprouts; run under cold running water.
5. Melt butter in large skillet over moderate heat. Add Brussels sprouts, chestnuts and salt and pepper; cook mixture, stirring occasionally, until heated through, about 5 to 7 minutes. Sprinkle with chives. Serve.

INGREDIENT SUBSTITUTIONS
If fresh Brussels sprouts are unavailable, frozen may be substituted. Simply prepare the sprouts as directed on the package, omit Step 4, and proceed with the recipe. Vacuum-packed chestnuts also may be substituted for the fresh—use about 1½ pounds of shelled chestnuts.

BRUSSEL SPROUTS MAKE-AHEAD TIP:
The recipe can be prepared several hours ahead and refrigerated, covered. Gently reheat.

SWEET AND SOUR CABBAGE WITH APPLES AND RAISINS

LOW-FAT • LOW CHOLESTEROL

*B*est served the day after fixing, this cabbage dish goes well with chicken or pork. The sweetness comes from the brown sugar, apples and raisins, and the tartness from the cider vinegar.

Makes 6 servings (about 5 cups).
Recipe can be halved or doubled.
Nutrient Value Per Serving: 105 calories, 2 g protein, 2 g fat, 22 g carbohydrate, 307 mg sodium, 5 mg cholesterol.

1 tablespoon *un*salted butter
1 medium-size onion, thinly sliced
1 medium-size head red cabbage (1½ pounds), coarsely sliced
¼ cup cider vinegar
3 tablespoons dark brown sugar
3 tablespoons water
¾ teaspoon salt
⅛ teaspoon pepper
1 large red apple, pared, cored and sliced
¼ cup raisins

1. Heat butter in large saucepan over medium heat. Add onion; sauté until soft, about 5 minutes. Add cabbage, vinegar, sugar, water, salt and pepper. Bring to boiling. Lower heat; cover the saucepan and simmer 15 minutes, stirring occasionally.
2. Add apple and raisins to cabbage in saucepan. Cover and continue to simmer 15 minutes or until cabbage is tender, stirring occasionally. Serve.

Make-Ahead Tip: This cabbage dish can be prepared up to 2 days ahead and refrigerated, covered. Gently reheat.

CREAMY CABBAGE MAKE-AHEAD TIP:
Cabbage without the sauce can be steamed ahead and refrigerated, covered. Gently reheat cabbage and toss with the sauce just before serving.

CREAMY CABBAGE WITH CARAWAY

LOW-CALORIE • LOW-CHOLESTEROL

*S*erve with roast chicken or pork.

Makes 4 servings (about 3 cups).
Nutrient Value Per Serving: 90 calories, 4 g protein, 4 g fat, 13 g carbohydrate, 349 mg sodium, 9 mg cholesterol.

1 medium-size head green cabbage (about 1½ pounds), coarsely sliced
1 tablespoon *un*salted butter
3 green onions, trimmed and sliced
1 tablespoon all-purpose flour
½ teaspoon salt
¼ teaspoon caraway seeds
⅛ teaspoon pepper
½ cup lowfat (1%) milk

1. Heat 1 inch water to boiling in large saucepan. Add cabbage; return to boiling. Lower heat; cover and simmer 30 minutes or until cabbage is tender. Drain well.
2. Heat butter in small saucepan over medium heat. Add green onion; sauté until tender, about 5 minutes. Stir in flour, salt, caraway seeds and pepper until smooth; cook 1 minute. Gradually stir in milk until well blended; cook, stirring, until mixture bubbles and thickens slightly, about 2 minutes.
3. Toss cabbage with sauce in serving bowl and serve immediately.

"COMFORT FOOD" DINNER

Roast Chicken

Pan-Fried Potatoes

Creamy Cabbage with Caraway (this page)

Fudgy Brownies (521)

BRUSSELS SPROUTS, CABBAGE, CARROTS, CAULIFLOWER AND CELERY

BRUSSELS SPROUTS

These junior members of the cabbage family are **available** in all but the hot summer months and are most prolific in mid-winter. **Nutritionally,** Brussels sprouts are high in fiber and Vitamin C and contribute significant amounts of folic acid and Vitamin A.

- **Choose** smaller, more tender sprouts no more than 1 inch in diameter with tightly closed heads.
- **Store** sprouts, unwashed, in their supermarket container or a perforated plastic bag in the refrigerator for up to a few days.
- To **cook** sprouts: Trim stem end of sprouts and cut a deep "X" through the base to promote even cooking. Steam or simmer for 5 to 7 minutes.

CABBAGE

Ever-**available** head cabbage is at its best in the cooler months of fall and winter. Both red and green cabbage are **nutritionally** high in Vitamin C and trace minerals.

- **Choose** cabbages that are heavy in relation to size and free of deterioration or signs of infestation. Green cabbage whitens as it ages and is mildest when young.
- To **store** green or red cabbage, remove and discard any wilted outer leaves. Wrap loosely and refrigerate for up to 2 weeks. The more delicate, crinkly-leaved **Savoy** cabbage will hold for only a few days. Sturdy **Chinese or Napa** cabbage keeps for up to 1 month.
- Shred raw cabbage for salad or coleslaw. To **cook,** lightly braise, simmer or sauté chopped cabbage for a side dish. Cabbage's infamous stench is a result of overcooking, which also renders a mushy, watery vegetable.
- **Bok choy** is a cabbage of Chinese origin with crisp, white stalks and deep green leaves. It can be prepared in much the same way as green cabbage but can only be stored for a few days.
- One pound cabbage yields 3½ to 4½ cups shredded raw or 2 cups cooked; **serves** 4.

CARROTS

Carrots are **available** in bags or loose bunches, with or without their feathery greens attached, 12 months a year. **Nutritionally,** a single carrot provides a day's worth of Vitamin A.

- **Choose** small to medium-size, firm carrots with bright orange color. Avoid carrots that are limp and hairy. Young baby or finger carrots are the most tender of all. Large, older carrots tend to be tough, and are often bitter.
- Remove green fronds from carrots before **storing** (they draw strength from the vegetable). Store carrots in a perforated plastic bag in the refrigerator for up to 2 weeks.
- To **cook,** steam, simmer or stir-fry sliced carrots until just tender.
- One pound of carrots **serves** 4 to 6.

CAULIFLOWER

Winter-white heads of cauliflower are **available** all year round and are at their peak in October and November. Occasionally you may see a purple or green head. **Nutritionally** high in Vitamin C, fresh cauliflower is only 30 calories per cooked cup.

- **Choose** cream-colored, blemish-free heads with fresh green leaves. Sniff the head; old cauliflower has a strong, cabbagy smell.
- **Store** cauliflower, unwashed, in a perforated plastic bag in the refrigerator for a day or two.
- To **cook** cauliflower, cut into equal-size flowerets. The stems and leaves are edible and can be chopped and cooked. Briefly steam or braise until just tender.
- One pound of cauliflower yields approximately 1½ cups raw or cooked pieces or 4 **servings**.

CELERY

Celery is **seasonless** and never in short supply. **Nutritionally,** celery contains fair amounts of vitamins and minerals, but its greatest nutritional attribute is that it contributes so few calories to the diet.

- **Choose** tight, bright, pale to medium-green heads with compact outer shells and fresh-looking leaves. The greener it gets, the more intensely flavored celery becomes. Avoid celery that has cracked or limp stalks, frizzled leaves or brown spots. Celery hearts are lighter in color, more flavorful than the outer green stalks but not as crisp.
- To **store,** wrap whole bunches of celery in damp paper toweling and place in a plastic bag in the crisper section of the refrigerator for up to 2 weeks.
- To **prepare,** scrub stalks before using. Tough outer stalks are best for flavoring soups and stews unless peeled before using; pale inner stalks are less fibrous and good for eating raw.
- To **cook,** braise in broth and serve as a side dish to meat and poultry. For a fine finish, dust braised celery with grated Parmesan and run under the broiler until golden.
- Use chopped celery leaves to add flavor to soups, stews, sauces and salads or leave whole and use as a garnish.
- One medium-size stalk of celery makes about 1 cup of chopped pieces. One large head, trimmed and cooked, **serves** 3 to 4.

GINGERED RED CABBAGE

LOW-CHOLESTEROL

Serve with roast pork, duck or chicken.

Makes 8 servings.
Recipe can be halved or doubled.
Nutrient Value Per Serving: 110 calories,
2 g protein, 4 g fat, 19 g carbohydrate,
221 mg sodium, 0 mg cholesterol.

2 tablespoons olive oil
2 large onions, cut into 1-inch dice
2 large cloves garlic, finely chopped
2 medium-size semi-tart apples, such as
    McIntosh, pared, quartered, cored
    and diced
3 tablespoons finely chopped crystallized
    ginger
1 medium-size red cabbage (about 1½
    pounds), halved, cored and cut into
    large dice
¼ cup balsamic vinegar OR: red wine
    vinegar
¾ teaspoon salt
¼ teaspoon pepper
1 cinnamon stick, split lengthwise

1. Heat 1 tablespoon oil in large skillet
over medium-low heat. Add onion;
sauté until softened, about 10 minutes.
Add garlic; sauté 1 to 2 minutes or
until fragrant. Add apple and ginger;
cook 5 minutes.
2. Add cabbage, remaining tablespoon
oil, vinegar, salt, pepper and cinnamon
stick. Cover and cook 20 minutes or
until cabbage is tender but not mushy.
Discard cinnamon stick.

Make-Ahead Tip: The cabbage can be
prepared a day ahead and refrigerated,
covered. Gently reheat.

HONEYED CARROTS WITH GINGER AND ORANGE

LOW-FAT • LOW-CHOLESTEROL • QUICK

Serve with any of your favorite meat
dishes. You can substitute 2 to 3 teaspoons
of finely chopped fresh ginger for the crystallized ginger, and vary the amount of
honey according to taste.

Makes 4 servings.
Recipe can be halved or doubled.
Nutrient Value Per Serving: 146 calories,
1 g protein, 3 g fat, 30 g carbohydrate,
174 mg sodium, 8 mg cholesterol.

1 pound carrots, trimmed, pared and cut
    crosswise into 1-inch pieces
½ cup orange juice
1 strip (2 inches) lemon rind
3 tablespoons honey
1 tablespoon *un*salted butter
1 tablespoon crystallized ginger, finely
    chopped
1 teaspoon grated orange rind
¼ teaspoon salt
⅛ teaspoon black pepper

1. Combine carrots, orange juice,
lemon rind, honey, butter, crystallized
ginger, orange rind, salt and pepper in
large skillet with enough water to just
cover carrots. Bring water to boiling.
Lower heat; simmer, covered, for 6
minutes.
2. Uncover. Increase heat to moderately high; cook carrots, shaking pan
occasionally, until almost all liquid is
evaporated and carrots are nicely glazed,
10 to 15 minutes.

Make-Ahead Tip: The recipe can be prepared up to 1 hour ahead, and then
gently reheated.

STEAMED BABY CARROTS WITH LEMON-DILL BUTTER

LOW-CALORIE · LOW-CHOLESTEROL
QUICK

Good as an accompaniment to practically anything. Try with orange instead of the lemon, and chives or green onion tops for the dill.

Makes 6 servings.
Recipe can be halved or doubled.
Nutrient Value Per Serving: 83 calories, 1 g protein, 4 g fat, 11 g carbohydrate, 149 mg sodium, 10 mg cholesterol.

2 bags (12 ounces each) baby carrots, trimmed and pared
2 tablespoons *un*salted butter, softened
½ to 1 teaspoon grated lemon rind
2 to 3 teaspoons fresh lemon juice
2 tablespoons snipped fresh dill OR: 1½ teaspoons dried
¼ teaspoon salt
⅛ teaspoon black pepper

1. Cook carrots in steamer basket over simmering water in covered saucepan for 8 to 10 minutes or until tender.
2. Transfer carrots to bowl. Toss with butter, lemon rind, lemon juice, dill, salt and pepper. Serve immediately.

Microwave Directions to Cook Carrots (High Power Oven): Place carrots and ¼ cup water in microwave-safe 1½-quart casserole with lid. Microwave, covered, at 100% power 12 to 14 minutes until tender. Drain. Proceed with Step 2.

CURRIED CAULIFLOWER

LOW-CHOLESTEROL

Makes 6 servings.
Recipe can be halved or doubled.
Nutrient Value Per Serving: 130 calories, 3 g protein, 7 g fat, 14 g carbohydrate, 246 mg sodium, 0 mg cholesterol.

3 tablespoons vegetable oil
1 medium-size onion, finely chopped
2 teaspoons curry powder
1 teaspoon cumin seeds
1 teaspoon ground coriander
1/4 teaspoon ground turmeric
1 large clove garlic, finely chopped
2 teaspoons finely chopped pared fresh ginger
1 medium-size head cauliflower (about 2 pounds), separated into flowerets
1 large Russet potato (10 ounces), pared and cut into 1-inch pieces
1/4 teaspoon salt
1/8 teaspoon black pepper
1/8 teaspoon crushed red pepper flakes
2/3 to 1 cup chicken broth
1 teaspoon grated lemon rind
1 to 2 teaspoons fresh lemon juice, or to taste
2 tablespoons finely chopped fresh cilantro OR: parsley

1. Heat oil in large saucepan over moderate heat. Add onion; sauté for 3 minutes until softened. Add curry powder, cumin seeds, coriander, turmeric, garlic and ginger; cook, stirring, 1 minute.
2. Add cauliflower, potato, salt, black pepper and red pepper flakes; cook, stirring occasionally, for 4 minutes. Add 2/3 cup chicken broth and lemon rind. Bring to boiling. Lower heat; simmer, covered, stirring occasionally, for 20 to 25 minutes or until vegetables are tender. Add additional chicken broth if necessary.
3. Before serving, sprinkle with fresh lemon juice and cilantro.

Microwave Directions (High Power Oven):
Ingredient Changes: Decrease oil to 2 tablespoons; decrease both cumin seeds and coriander to 1/2 teaspoon; decrease ginger to 1 teaspoon; decrease black pepper to few grains; decrease chicken broth to 1/2 cup; decrease lemon rind to 1/2 teaspoon. Add 1 teaspoon cornstarch mixed with 1 tablespoon chicken broth.
Directions: Combine onion, oil, garlic and ginger in microwave-safe 3-quart casserole with lid. Microwave, uncovered, at 100% power 3 minutes. Add curry powder, cumin, coriander and turmeric. Microwave, uncovered, at 100% power 1 minute. Add cauliflower, potato, salt, black pepper, red pepper, broth and lemon rind. Microwave, covered, at 100% power 15 minutes or until potato is tender, stirring twice. Remove solids with slotted spoon to serving dish. Stir cornstarch mixture into cooking liquid. Microwave, covered, at 100% power 1 minute. Sprinkle with lemon juice and cilantro.

CRUSTY HERBED CAULIFLOWER

Bake at 400° for 20 minutes.
Makes 6 servings as a side dish.
Recipe can be halved or doubled.
Nutrient Value Per Serving: 137 calories,
6 g protein, 5 g fat, 19 g carbohydrate,
354 mg sodium, 77 mg cholesterol.

1 medium-size head cauliflower (about 2
    pounds)
2 eggs
½ teaspoon salt
¼ teaspoon black pepper
1 cup dry bread crumbs
½ cup fresh basil, chopped OR: 1
    tablespoon dried basil
¼ cup parsley leaves, chopped
3 tablespoons all-purpose flour
1 tablespoon *un*salted butter, melted

1. Cut cauliflower into medium-size
flowerets. Cook in steamer basket over
simmering water in covered saucepan
for 15 to 18 minutes or just until tender. Remove.
2. Meanwhile, beat together eggs, salt
and pepper in shallow pie plate. Toss
together bread crumbs, basil and parsley
in another shallow pie plate.
3. Preheat oven to hot (400°). Coat
baking sheet with nonstick vegetable-oil
cooking spray.
4. Place flour in bag. Add flowerets in
batches, shaking to coat.
5. Dip flowerets in egg mixture, then in
crumb mixture, turning to coat all
sides. Place on prepared baking sheet.
Drizzle with butter.
6. Bake in preheated hot oven (400°)
for 20 minutes or until golden and
crispy. Serve hot.

Make-Ahead Tip: The cauliflower can be
coated an hour ahead and placed on
waxed paper in refrigerator. Cook, drizzled with butter, as in Step 6 until hot.

SIMPLE FISH DINNER

Baked Cod

Rice with Corn Kernels

Crusty Herbed Cauliflower
(this page)

Fresh Fruit

**CRUSTY HERBED
CAULIFLOWER
SERVING IDEAS**
Delicious as a first
course or appetizer,
or as a side dish with
oven-baked fish.

STIR-FRIED CELERY WITH GARLIC AND GINGER

LOW-CHOLESTEROL · QUICK

An unusual side dish that takes just minutes to prepare. Add a little cooked chicken, beef or pork and you've created a main dish.

Makes 4 servings.
Recipe can be halved or doubled.
Nutrient Value Per Serving: 120 calories, 1 g protein, 11 g fat, 6 g carbohydrate, 444 mg sodium, 0 mg cholesterol.

1 bunch (1 pound) celery
2 tablespoons peanut oil OR: vegetable oil
2 green onions, finely chopped
2 cloves garlic, finely chopped
2 teaspoons finely chopped pared fresh ginger
½ teaspoon salt
⅓ cup chicken broth
1 tablespoon Oriental sesame oil
1 teaspoon sugar
1 teaspoon rice wine vinegar
¼ teaspoon chili oil, or to taste

1. Separate celery into stalks. If stalks are stringy, lightly peel with swivel-bladed vegetable peeler. Cut stalks into 2-inch lengths; cut lengthwise into ¼-inch-thick sticks.
2. Heat oil in large nonstick skillet over moderately high heat. Add green onion, garlic and ginger; cook, stirring, 1 minute. Add celery and salt; cook, stirring, 2 minutes. Add broth, sesame oil, sugar, vinegar and chili oil; cook, covered, 3 minutes or until celery is crisp-tender. Transfer mixture to serving plate. Serve the celery warm or at room temperature.

Make-Ahead Tip: The dish can be prepared a day ahead and refrigerated, covered. Gently reheat.
Microwave Directions (High Power Oven):
Ingredient Changes: Decrease ginger to 1 teaspoon; decrease salt to ¼ teaspoon; decrease broth to ¼ cup.
Directions: Combine oil, green onion, garlic and ginger in microwave-safe 2-quart casserole with lid. Microwave, uncovered, 1½ minutes. Stir in celery, salt, broth, sesame oil, sugar, vinegar and chili oil. Microwave, covered, at 100% power 6 to 8 minutes until celery is tender, stirring once.

BRAISED CELERY AND SWEET RED PEPPER

LOW-CHOLESTEROL · QUICK

Makes 4 servings.
Recipe can be halved or doubled.
Nutrient Value Per Serving: 58 calories,
1 g protein, 4 g fat, 6 g carbohydrate,
365 mg sodium, 0 mg cholesterol.

1 tablespoon olive oil
8 large stalks celery, cut into 2-inch
    lengths
1 small sweet red pepper, cored, seeded
    and cut into 1-inch squares
½ cup chicken broth
1 clove garlic, sliced
½ teaspoon leaf oregano, crumbled
¼ teaspoon salt
¼ teaspoon pepper

1. Heat oil in large, heavy skillet over
medium-high heat. Add celery; cook,
stirring occasionally, for 4 minutes. Add
red pepper, broth, garlic, oregano, salt
and pepper. Bring to a boil. Reduce
heat to low; cover and cook 6 minutes.
2. Increase heat to medium-high; cook,
uncovered, stirring occasionally, 4 to 6
minutes or until most of the liquid has
evaporated and the vegetables are tender and glazed.

WINTER BUFFET

**Indonesian Pot Roast with
Peanut Sauce (347)**

**Almond-Raisin Couscous
(222)**

**Braised Celery and Sweet
Red Pepper (this page)**

**Grated Carrot Salad with
Cilantro (152)**

**Lemon Angel Food Cake
(507)**

BAKED CELERY ROOT

LOW-CALORIE · LOW-CHOLESTEROL

Baking brings out the natural nuttiness
and sweet quality of the celery root. If you
find smaller celery roots, buy them and
decrease the cooking time accordingly.
Serve with roast meats and game, or as
part of an assorted appetizer plate.
(Pictured on page 414.)

Bake at 400° for 1 hour and 20 minutes.
Makes 4 servings.
Recipe can be halved or doubled.
Nutrient Value Per Serving: 86 calories,
2 g protein, 5 g fat, 11 g carbohydrate,
258 mg sodium, 12 mg cholesterol.

1 celery root or knob (1¼ pounds)
1½ tablespoons *un*salted butter
2 tablespoons water
¼ teaspoon salt
⅛ teaspoon sugar

1. Preheat oven to hot (400°). Wash
celery root. Wrap in aluminum foil.
Place on baking sheet.
2. Bake in preheated hot oven (400°)
for 1 hour and 20 minutes or until tender. (Timing will vary depending upon
size of celery root.) Cool the celery root
to room temperature.
3. When cool enough to handle, pare
celery root with small paring knife.
Halve and cut into 1-inch chunks.
4. Heat butter, water, salt and sugar in
medium-size skillet over moderate heat.
Add celery root; cook until heated
through and liquid has evaporated,
about 4 minutes. Serve.

Make-Ahead Tip: The celery root can be
baked a day ahead and refrigerated.
Don't pare until ready to use.
Microwave Directions (High Power Oven):
Ingredient Changes: Eliminate water.
Directions: Place celery root in
microwave-safe soufflé dish or casserole.
Microwave, covered, at 100% power 10
(continued)

**MORE THAN JUST
CHOPPED CELERY**
Braising whole stalks
is an example of
something you can
do with celery other
than chopping for
chicken salad. This
flavorful side dish
goes with practically
anything.

**BRAISED CELERY
MAKE-AHEAD TIP:**
The recipe can be
prepared a day
ahead and refriger-
ated, covered. Gently
reheat.

Baked Celery Root (page 413)

Corn Fritters (this page)

BAKED CELERY ROOT (*continued*)

to 12 minutes until soft, turning over after 6 minutes. Cool, pare and cut in chunks as above. Combine butter, salt and sugar in microwave-safe 9-inch pie plate. Microwave, uncovered, at 100% power 1 minute to melt. Stir in celery root. Microwave, uncovered, at 100% power 3 minutes, stirring once.

CORN FRITTERS

QUICK

The batter for these fritters is very light. Serve them with honey or maple syrup for breakfast, or as an accompaniment to roast pork or chicken. (Pictured at left.)

Makes 6 servings.
Recipe can be halved or doubled.
Nutrient Value Per Serving: 167 calories, 5 g protein, 10 g fat, 16 g carbohydrate, 239 mg sodium, 74 mg cholesterol.

⅓ cup all-purpose flour
½ teaspoon salt
¼ teaspoon baking powder
2 large eggs
½ cup milk
2 cups fresh corn OR: 1 package (10 ounces) frozen whole-kernel corn, thawed according to package directions and drained
Vegetable oil, for frying

1. Sift together flour, salt and baking powder into bowl. Add eggs and milk; whisk until smooth. Stir in corn.
2. Heat vegetable oil in deep-fat fryer or deep saucepan to 375°. Working in batches, carefully add batter in ⅛-cup measure to hot oil; do not crowd. Fry fritters for 1 to 2 minutes on each side or until golden brown, turning fritters over with slotted metal spatula.
3. Transfer fritters with spatula to tray lined with paper toweling. Serve hot or warm.

OLD-FASHIONED CORN PUDDING

This is some people's idea of true comfort food, flavored with a little mustard and a touch of hot pepper. Serve as a Sunday night supper accompanied with a simple green salad.

Bake at 350° for 1 hour.
Makes 8 side-dish servings, or 4 main-dish servings.
Nutrient Value Per Side-Dish Serving:
235 calories, 8 g protein, 13 g fat,
24 g carbohydrate, 408 mg sodium,
136 mg cholesterol.

2 tablespoons *un*salted butter
1 medium-size onion, finely chopped
1 medium-size sweet red pepper, cored, seeded and finely chopped
4 cups fresh corn kernels (3 to 4 ears)
    OR: 2 packages (10 ounces each) frozen whole kernel corn, thawed according to package directions and drained
¼ cup all-purpose flour
2 cups half-and-half
4 eggs, lightly beaten
1 tablespoon sugar
2 teaspoons Dijon-style mustard
1 teaspoon salt
½ teaspoon baking powder
¼ teaspoon ground hot red pepper

1. Preheat oven to moderate (350°). Butter 6-cup soufflé dish or other baking dish.
2. Heat butter in medium-size nonstick skillet over medium heat. Add onion and red pepper; sauté 5 minutes. Add corn; cook, stirring, 3 minutes.
3. Whisk together flour and ½ cup half-and-half in large bowl. Mix in remaining half-and-half, eggs, sugar, mustard, salt, baking powder and hot red pepper; stir in corn mixture. Transfer to prepared baking dish. Place baking dish in shallow pan on oven rack. Add enough hot water to pan to come halfway up sides of baking dish.

4. Bake pudding in preheated moderate oven (350°) for 1 hour or until set. If top begins to brown too quickly, cover with aluminum foil.

Microwave Directions (High Power Oven):
Combine onion, red pepper and butter in microwave-safe 1¼-quart casserole. Microwave, uncovered, at 100% power 4 minutes, stirring twice. Stir in corn and egg mixture. Microwave, uncovered, at 100% power 5 minutes. Gently push outer edges of mixture towards center. Microwave, uncovered, at 50% power 13 to 15 minutes until knife inserted in center comes out clean. Let stand, covered, for 5 minutes.

CELERY ROOT, CORN AND CUCUMBERS

CELERY ROOT

Crisp even when cooked, celery root (or celeriac) looks like a cross between fresh horseradish and turnips. **Available** usually from fall through early spring. **Nutritionally,** this root vegetable, like celery stalks, is very low in calories, and contains small amounts of B vitamins, iron and calcium. Raw or cooked, celery root has intense celery flavor that lends itself to a variety of foods from hot stews to cool salads. Its full flavor and substantial texture belie its low calorie count.

- **Choose** roots that are as smooth, firm and free of knobs as possible. Store in plastic bag in refrigerator for up to 1 month.
- To **prepare** for cooking, and for easier peeling and tender texture, parboil celery root: Place whole, unpeeled root in water to cover; simmer 20 to 30 minutes, or until crisp-tender. Cool, peel, slice and proceed with recipe.
- To **cook,** the whole root can be completely cooked in its skin by simmering for about 45 minutes. Peeled and sliced celery root cooks to crunchy tenderness in less than 10 minutes.
- Drop peeled, sliced, uncooked pieces of celery root in acidulated water as you cut them, to prevent discoloration. Raw celery root adds crunch to salads.
- One and a half pounds of celery root, raw or cooked, **serves** 4 to 6.

CORN

While **available** throughout the year, an abundance of fresh corn in the market sweetly signals the onset of summer. **Nutritionally,** corn is high in insoluble dietary fiber *(see Fiber Facts, page 397),* rich in complex carbohydrates and a source of Vitamins A and C, as well as essential minerals.

- **Choose** ears with fresh, green husks, moist silk and plump, even rows of corn kernels.
- Corn is best prepared as soon after picking as possible because the sooner it's used, the sweeter it will be. To **store,** if necessary, refrigerate corn, with the husks on, for up to 1 day.
- To **prepare,** remove the husks and silk just before cooking. To remove stubborn silk, hold each ear under cold running water; lightly run a vegetable brush along the rows between the kernels, moving toward the stem.
- To **cook** corn on the stove top, bring a large pot of water to boiling, adding a bit of sugar and milk, if desired, but no salt (it toughens corn). Slide husked ears of corn into the boiling water; don't crowd them. Cover and cook 2 to 3 minutes after the water returns to a boil. Alternatively, place ears of corn in water in large deep skillet or flameproof pan without crowding them. Cover and bring to boiling over moderately high heat. Remove skillet from heat. Drain and serve.
- To grill corn, pull husks back, leaving them attached at the stem. Remove the silk. Brush the corn with melted butter (or a flavored butter, pages 331–332); re-cover the ears with their husks, tying ends with string. Soak in cold water for 10 minutes. Grill over medium coals for 15 to 20 minutes, turning every 3 to 4 minutes. The husks will char but the corn kernels should stay bright. Carefully remove the husks, using oven mitts. (To grill ears in aluminum foil, proceed as above, wrapping the ears in heavy-duty aluminum foil. Grill them over hot coals, turning every 5 to 6 minutes.)
- To remove whole kernels from the cob, stand each ear of corn on its end in a shallow bowl; carefully slice underneath the kernels with a sharp, firm-bladed knife, using a steady downward motion to loosen the kernels and allow them to drop onto the plate.
- Each ear of corn provides about ½ cup of kernels, enough for ½ to 1 **serving,** depending on corn-loving capacity.

CUCUMBERS

Cucumbers are always **available** but are at their peak in summer months when we can best appreciate their cool, refreshing qualities.

- **Choose** firm, glossy, deep green cucumbers with no signs of mushiness, yellowing or withering that indicate age. Most cucumbers sold in supermarkets are waxed to protect against spoiling. Pare or wash well. "Burpless" and seedless varieties are available.
- To **store,** keep cucumbers refrigerated, unpeeled if possible, until cooking or serving time, or up to 4 days.
- To **prepare,** trim ends, peel and slice. Halve lengthwise and gently scrape out seeds with a spoon. Slice or dice as desired. Leave cucumber whole to slice into rounds; halve or quarter lengthwise before slicing for semicircles or triangles.
- Try **cooked** cucumber—it can be sautéed or stir-fried in less than 5 minutes.
- One large cucumber yields about 1½ cups of chopped, enough for 2 **servings.**

SWEET AND SOUR CUCUMBERS WITH RED ONION

LOW-CALORIE · LOW-CHOLESTEROL
QUICK

Makes 4 servings.
Recipe can be halved or doubled.
Nutrient Value Per Serving: 52 calories,
1 g protein, 2 g fat, 8 g carbohydrate,
155 mg sodium, 3 mg cholesterol.

2 large cucumbers (about 1½ pounds)
1 teaspoon olive oil
1 small red onion, chopped
2 tablespoons red wine vinegar
2 teaspoons sugar
1 tablespoon snipped chives OR: finely
    chopped green onion tops
1 teaspoon grated orange rind
1 teaspoon *un*salted butter
¼ teaspoon salt
⅛ teaspoon pepper

1. Pare and halve cucumbers lengthwise. Remove seeds. Cut halves in half lengthwise; cut crosswise into 1-inch-thick pieces.
2. Heat oil in medium-size skillet over medium heat. Add onion; sauté 2 minutes. Add cucumbers, vinegar and sugar; cook 3 minutes or until cucumbers are tender but still crisp. Stir in chives, orange rind, butter, salt and pepper.

SAUTÉED CUCUMBER

LOW-CALORIE · LOW-CHOLESTEROL
QUICK

Makes 6 servings.
Recipe can be halved or doubled.
Nutrient Value Per Serving: 58 calories,
2 g protein, 3 g fat, 7 g carbohydrate,
214 mg sodium, 0 mg cholesterol.

2 pounds cucumbers (2 to 3 large
    cucumbers)
1 tablespoon sesame seeds
1 tablespoon vegetable oil
1 green onion, diagonally sliced
1 tablespoon finely chopped pared fresh
    ginger
2 tablespoons reduced-sodium soy sauce
1 large carrot, pared and grated
¼ teaspoon lemon juice

1. Pare cucumbers lengthwise in alternating strips, leaving some peel on. Halve cucumbers lengthwise. Seed. Cut diagonally into ½-inch-thick pieces.
2. Toast sesame seeds in large skillet over low heat, stirring occasionally, 2 to 3 minutes. Remove sesame seeds to bowl; set aside.
3. Heat oil in same skillet over medium-high heat. Add green onion and ginger; sauté 1 minute. Add cucumber and soy sauce; cook, stirring frequently, 2 minutes or until slightly softened. Stir in carrot and lemon juice; heat through. Stir in sesame seeds. Serve warm or at room temperature.

Sautéed Cucumber (this page)

SERVING CUCUMBERS
Either of these cucumber recipes is a nice accent for roasted or grilled meats, sautéed liver, strong-flavored fish or the summer barbecue. Serve warm or at room temperature with roasted or grilled meats, or as part of a vegetable platter.

SWEET AND SOUR CUCUMBERS MAKE-AHEAD TIP:
Prepare a day ahead and refrigerate, covered. Gently reheat.

EGGPLANT WITH TOMATO AND CORIANDER

LOW-CALORIE · LOW-CHOLESTEROL

EGGPLANT WITH TOMATO SERVING IDEAS

An ideal accompaniment to roast lamb or broiled chicken, or serve on its own with the simple addition of warmed pita bread and a green salad. Add a spoon of this to liven up your usual green salad.

Broil for 20 minutes.

Makes 8 side-dish servings, or 4 main-dish servings. Recipe can be halved or doubled.

Nutrient Value Per Side-Dish Serving: 76 calories, 2 g protein, 4 g fat, 10 g carbohydrate, 345 mg sodium, 0 mg cholesterol.

2 medium-size eggplants (about 1¾ pounds), pricked several times
2 tablespoons vegetable oil
3 medium-size onions, finely chopped
1 tablespoon finely chopped garlic
1 tablespoon finely chopped pared fresh ginger
1 can (11½ ounces) whole tomatoes, in thick puree
1 teaspoon salt
1 teaspoon ground cumin
1 teaspoon ground coriander
½ teaspoon fennel seeds, crushed
¼ teaspoon pepper
3 tablespoons finely chopped fresh cilantro OR: parsley

1. Preheat broiler. Arrange eggplants on baking sheet lined with foil.

2. Broil eggplants 4 inches from heat, turning as they brown, for about 20 minutes or until eggplants are entirely browned and soft. Transfer to plate and let cool. Split eggplants. Scoop out flesh; chop. Discard skins.

3. Heat oil in medium-size saucepan over moderate heat. Add onion, garlic and ginger; sauté 3 minutes. Add eggplant; cook, stirring occasionally, 2 minutes. Add tomato, salt, cumin, coriander, fennel and pepper; simmer, covered, stirring occasionally, 15 minutes or until thick and almost all liquid is absorbed. Stir in cilantro. Serve hot, at room temperature or chilled.

Make-Ahead Tip: The recipe can be made a day ahead without the cilantro and refrigerated, covered. Stir in fresh cilantro just before serving.

Microwave Directions (High Power Oven):
Ingredient Changes: Reduce the garlic to 2 teaspoons.
Directions: Prick eggplants several times with a fork. Place on double thickness of paper toweling on floor of microwave oven. Microwave, uncovered, at 100% power 15 to 16 minutes until soft, turning over after 10 minutes. Place in shallow bowl to cool. Peel off skin; cut flesh into chunks. Combine onion, garlic, ginger and oil in microwave-safe 2-quart casserole with lid. Microwave, uncovered, at 100% power 4 minutes, stirring once. Mix in eggplant, tomatoes, salt, cumin, coriander, fennel seeds and pepper. Microwave, covered, at 100% power 7 minutes to simmering. Stir. Microwave, uncovered, at 100% power 5 minutes. Stir in cilantro.

EGGPLANT SANDWICHES WITH GOAT CHEESE

QUICK

*S*erve this versatile "sandwich" with grilled or roasted lamb or chicken, as part of an appetizer tray, as a lunch entree with a green salad—or even as a snack. Garnish with chives and strips of sweet red pepper.

Makes about 24 sandwiches.
Recipe can be halved or doubled.
Nutrient Value Per Sandwich: 70 calories,
3 g protein, 5 g fat, 3 g carbohydrate,
81 mg sodium, 16 mg cholesterol.

1 large eggplant (about 1¼ pounds)
¼ cup chopped pimiento
6 ounces mild goat cheese, crumbled
¼ cup snipped chives OR: finely chopped
    green onion tops
Pinch ground hot red pepper
½ cup dry bread crumbs
¼ cup grated Parmesan cheese
¾ teaspoon leaf basil, crumbled
1 egg
1 egg white
4 to 5 tablespoons olive oil OR: vegetable
    oil

1. Peel eggplant. Slice crosswise into ¼-inch-thick slices. (Keep slices paired together for sandwiches.) Drain pimiento; pat dry between layers of paper toweling.
2. Stir together goat cheese, chives, hot red pepper, pimiento and 1 table-spoon bread crumbs in small bowl.
3. Combine remaining bread crumbs, Parmesan cheese and basil in shallow pie plate. Beat together egg and egg white in second shallow pie plate.
4. Spread about 1 tablespoon cheese mixture on eggplant slice, mounding slightly in center; top with matching size slice, pressing to sandwich. Repeat with remaining eggplant slices and filling.
5. Dip each sandwich into beaten egg, then crumb mixture to coat; place on waxed paper.

6. Heat 1½ tablespoons oil in large nonstick skillet over medium-low heat. Add sandwiches in single layer; don't crowd skillet. Cook, covered, 8 to 10 minutes or until tender when pierced with fork, turning halfway through cooking. Repeat with remaining sandwiches and oil.

Make-Ahead Tip: The sandwiches can be prepared 4 hours ahead through Step 4 and refrigerated, covered.

1 large fennel bulb with stalks (about 1 pound)
1 tablespoon *un*salted butter
½ red onion, chopped
1 clove garlic, chopped
1 can (16 ounces) whole tomatoes, in thick puree, chopped
½ teaspoon sugar
¼ teaspoon grated lemon rind
¼ teaspoon fennel seeds, crushed
¼ teaspoon salt
⅛ teaspoon crushed red pepper flakes
1 bay leaf
1 tablespoon anise-flavored liqueur *(optional)*

1. Trim ends of fennel stalks, reserving feathery fronds for garnish. Cut fennel in half lengthwise; remove core. Cut crosswise into ½-inch pieces.

2. Heat butter in medium-size saucepan over medium heat. Add fennel and onion; sauté 8 minutes or until onion is softened. Add garlic; sauté for 1 minute.

3. Add tomato, sugar, lemon rind, fennel seeds, salt, red pepper flakes, bay leaf and liqueur, if using. Bring to simmering; simmer, covered, 20 to 25 minutes or until fennel is tender. Remove and discard bay leaf. Spoon into serving dish or individual ramekins or other dishes. Garnish with chopped fennel tops.

Make-Ahead Tip: The recipe can be made up to 2 days ahead and refrigerated, covered. Serve chilled or at room temperature or gently reheat in saucepan.

Microwave Directions (High Power Oven): Combine fennel, onion, garlic and butter in microwave-safe 1½-quart casserole with lid. Microwave, uncovered, at 100% power 5 minutes, stirring once. Stir in tomato, sugar, lemon rind, fennel seeds, salt, pepper flakes, bay leaf and liqueur. Microwave, covered, at 100% power 5 minutes. Stir. Microwave, uncovered, at 100% power 3 minutes until fennel is tender.

STEWED FENNEL WITH TOMATO

LOW-CALORIE · LOW-CHOLESTEROL

Serve hot with any variety of meats or poultry, or chilled as a relish with grilled fish or pork.

Makes 6 servings.
Recipe can be halved or doubled.
Nutrient Value Per Serving: 50 calories, 1 g protein, 2 g fat, 7 g carbohydrate, 274 mg sodium, 5 mg cholesterol.

Braised Fennel with Parmesan

LOW-CHOLESTEROL

Frequently used raw in salads, fennel develops a wonderful subtle flavor when cooked. Serve with roasted meats and poultry (especially duck), and stews and casseroles, or place on a brunch buffet as an unusual side dish.

Bake at 350° for 45 minutes; broil for 4 minutes.
Makes 4 servings.
Recipe can be halved or doubled.
Nutrient Value Per Serving: 82 calories, 5 g protein, 5 g fat, 5 g carbohydrate, 522 mg sodium, 12 mg cholesterol.

2 large fennel bulbs with stalks (about 2 pounds)
1 cup chicken broth
⅛ teaspoon pepper
¼ cup grated Parmesan cheese
1 tablespoon *un*salted butter, softened

1. Preheat oven to moderate (350°). Coat 9-inch round (2-quart) flameproof baking dish with nonstick vegetable-oil cooking spray.
2. Cut off fennel stalks; save stalks to slice for salads. Chop feathery fronds to equal 1 tablespoon. Halve fennel bulbs lengthwise. Remove core. Cut each half into 3 wedges.
3. Lay fennel wedges, cut-side down, in prepared baking dish. Pour chicken broth over. Sprinkle with pepper. Cover dish with aluminum foil.
4. Bake in preheated moderate oven (350°) for 45 minutes or until fennel is tender. Remove from oven.
5. Preheat broiler. Uncover fennel and sprinkle with Parmesan cheese and dot with butter.
6. Broil 2 inches from heat until top is browned, about 4 minutes. Sprinkle with reserved chopped feathery fronds.

Sautéed Mushrooms with Garlic Bread Crumbs

LOW-CHOLESTEROL · QUICK

If fresh shiitake mushrooms are not available, substitute an equal amount of regular domestic or button mushrooms.

Makes 4 servings.
Recipe can be halved or doubled.
Nutrient Value Per Serving: 152 calories, 4 g protein, 11 g fat, 12 g carbohydrate, 316 mg sodium, 0 mg cholesterol.

3 tablespoons olive oil
1 pound domestic (button) mushrooms, trimmed, cleaned well, and quartered or cut into sixths if very large
6 ounces fresh shiitake mushrooms, trimmed, cleaned well, and quartered
½ teaspoon salt
3 cloves garlic, finely chopped
3 tablespoons fine dry bread crumbs
3 tablespoons chopped parsley
2 tablespoons finely cut chives OR: finely chopped green onion tops

1. Heat 2 tablespoons oil in very large skillet over moderately high heat. Add half regular and half shiitake mushrooms; cook, tossing frequently, 3 to 4 minutes or until mushrooms begin to shrink.
2. Add remaining regular and shiitake mushrooms; sprinkle with salt. Reduce heat to low; cover and cook 8 to 10 minutes or until soft and juicy. Add garlic. Raise heat to moderately high; cook until all liquid has evaporated, about 4 minutes. Add remaining tablespoon oil, bread crumbs, parsley and chives; cook 2 minutes longer. Serve hot or at room temperature.

SAUTÉED MUSHROOMS MAKE-AHEAD TIP: This dish can be made earlier in the day and refrigerated, covered. Serve at room temperature or gently reheat.

SAUTÉED MUSHROOMS SERVING IDEAS Serve these sautéed mushrooms, either hot or at room temperature, as a side dish with anything—they are especially good with egg dishes, or as part of an appetizer plate. Keep in mind as an accompaniment for summer barbecues.

BRAISED FENNEL MAKE-AHEAD TIP: The dish can be baked ahead through Step 4 and refrigerated, covered, for up to one day. Gently reheat, covered, then proceed with Step 5.

BROILED MUSHROOM CAPS

LOW-CHOLESTEROL · QUICK

These are even better on the outdoor grill. Serve as a delicious accent to grilled or roasted meats and poultry, as well as egg dishes. Or cut up and toss with pasta. The flavored oil is the secret.

Broil for about 8 minutes.
Makes 4 servings.
Recipe can be halved or doubled.
Nutrient Value Per Serving: 112 calories, 1 g protein, 10 g fat, 5 g carbohydrate, 93 mg sodium, 0 mg cholesterol.

3 tablespoons olive oil
2 green onions, sliced
3 cloves garlic, sliced
¼ teaspoon crushed red pepper flakes
½ pound cremini mushrooms OR: other wide-cap, meaty mushrooms
1 tablespoon balsamic vinegar OR: red wine vinegar
½ teaspoon honey

1. Heat oil in small skillet over medium-low heat. Add green onion, garlic and red pepper flakes; sauté for 5 to 8 minutes or until garlic is golden; do not let garlic brown. Drain in small strainer over bowl, gently pressing solids to extract oil. Reserve oil; discard solids.
2. Meanwhile, preheat broiler. Trim tough stems from mushrooms. Brush caps with damp paper toweling to remove dirt. Toss mushroom caps in flavored oil. Arrange, rounded-side up, on broiler rack.
3. Stir together balsamic vinegar and honey in small dish.
4. Broil mushrooms 4 inches from heat for about 8 minutes, turning over halfway through cooking. Transfer caps to serving dish. Drizzle with balsamic vinegar mixture and sprinkle with salt. Serve hot or warm.

MUSHROOM-ONION RELISH

LOW-FAT · LOW-CHOLESTEROL · QUICK

A wonderful flavor accent with grilled or roasted meats, and especially tasty with sautéed liver. Spread on hamburgers and roast beef sandwiches, or spoon a little alongside your favorite egg dish. Serve hot, or at room temperature without the bacon.

Makes 4 servings.
Recipe can be halved or doubled.
Nutrient Value Per Serving: 29 calories, 2 g protein, 0 g fat, 6 g carbohydrate, 138 mg sodium, 0 mg cholesterol.

4 strips bacon*
½ pound shiitake mushrooms, cleaned well OR: other full-flavored mushrooms
1 large onion, halved and sliced crosswise
¼ teaspoon leaf thyme, crumbled
¼ teaspoon salt
1 tablespoon balsamic vinegar OR: red wine vinegar

1. If using bacon, cut into 1-inch pieces. Cook in skillet over medium-low heat for 6 to 8 minutes or until crispy and golden. Remove with slotted spoon to paper toweling to drain. Drain off all but 1 tablespoon fat from skillet.
2. Trim tough stems from mushrooms; thickly slice caps.
3. Heat fat in skillet. Add onion; cook, covered, 8 minutes or until softened. Add mushrooms, thyme and salt; cook, uncovered, 6 to 8 minutes or until mushrooms are tender. Remove from heat. Stir in balsamic vinegar. Spoon onto serving dish. Sprinkle with bacon, if using.

*****Note:** You may omit the bacon, and use 1 tablespoon olive or vegetable oil in Step 3.

MARINATED MUSHROOMS AND ARTICHOKE HEARTS

LOW-CHOLESTEROL

We've added artichoke hearts to give this make-ahead old favorite a new outlook. Or, omit the artichokes if you wish and add another package of mushrooms.

Makes 10 servings.
Recipe can be halved or doubled.
Nutrient Value Per Serving: 74 calories, 2 g protein, 6 g fat, 5 g carbohydrate, 127 mg sodium, 0 mg cholesterol.

1 cup water
½ onion, sliced
1 bay leaf
½ teaspoon black peppercorns
1 package (12 ounces) frozen artichoke
    hearts
1 package (12 ounces) button
    mushrooms, trimmed and wiped
    clean
½ cup red wine vinegar
¼ cup olive oil or vegetable oil
2 teaspoons fresh oregano, chopped
    OR: ½ teaspoon dried
1 teaspoon fresh thyme, chopped
    OR: ¼ teaspoon dried
1 teaspoon light brown sugar
½ teaspoon salt

1. Combine water, onion, bay leaf and peppercorns in medium-size nonaluminum saucepan. Bring to boiling. Add artichokes; cook, covered, 6 minutes.
2. Add mushrooms, vinegar, oil, oregano, thyme, brown sugar and salt to saucepan. Return to boiling. Lower heat; simmer 1 minute. Remove from heat.
3. Pour contents into nonaluminum bowl. Cool to room temperature. Cover and refrigerate for at least 8 hours or overnight. Remove and discard bay leaf. Serve cold.

Make-Ahead Tip: Recipe can be prepared several days ahead and refrigerated, covered. Let come to room temperature.
Microwave Directions (High Power Oven):
Ingredient Changes: Reduce water to ½ cup; use a small bay leaf.
Directions: Combine water, onion, bay leaf, peppercorns and artichokes in microwave-safe 1½-quart casserole with lid. Microwave, covered, at 100% power 8 minutes, stirring once. Add mushrooms, vinegar, oil, oregano, thyme, sugar and salt. Microwave, covered, at 100% power 4 minutes. Cool to room temperature. Cover and refrigerate as above.

SERVING IDEAS
Offer the Marinated Mushrooms and Artichoke Hearts as part of an appetizer platter or salad buffet, or serve with roasted meats and poultry—especially good with cold chicken for a picnic. Liven up a sandwich with a spoonful of this on the side.

EGGPLANT, FENNEL, OKRA AND PARSNIPS

EGGPLANT

Always **available** in good supply in any season, eggplants are **nutritionally** low in calories, high in complex carbohydrates and fiber, and contain small amounts of most essential vitamins and minerals.

- Whether you **choose** diminutive Japanese or Italian eggplants, large American or lanky Chinese specimens, freshness indicators are the same: green cap and stem; firm, taut skin with glossy, even color; heaviness for size; little if any scarring, pitting or bruising.
- **Store** eggplants in the refrigerator, covered, for 2 or 3 days.
- To **prepare,** the question is to peel or not to peel? If the eggplant is used as an edible container leave the peel on. If the eggplant is young and the skin thin and tender, leave it on. If the eggplant is mature, gently scrape away the skin with a swivel-bladed peeler.
- The bitterness that used to be a common trait in eggplants has been largely bred out of the vegetable. However, bitterness does occur and there's really no way to tell before the eggplant is cooked. If in doubt, salt it prior to cooking: Peel the eggplant or not, cut as desired, then sprinkle coarse salt lightly but evenly over all cut surfaces; let drain in a colander set over a bowl for at least 30 minutes. Pat dry with paper toweling to remove water and salt. Salting eggplant also removes excess liquid that might make a dish too watery and helps prevent the flesh from soaking up excess oil.
- To **cook** or prepare eggplant puree for dips or a side dish, bake the whole eggplant in its skin for 30 to 45 minutes or until the vegetable collapses and the flesh is very tender. Let cool, then gently scrape the flesh from the skin.
- For lower-calorie "fried" eggplant, brush a little oil over slices and broil until golden brown on each side.
- One large eggplant makes 4 **servings** when chopped or sliced. One medium-size eggplant makes two main-dish portions when generously stuffed. Very small eggplants provide individual servings.

FENNEL

Fennel, with its feathery cap and celery-like stalks, is **available** in late fall and through the winter months. Munch on its crisp licorice-flavored stems for a **nutritious** snack that's low in calories and high in Vitamin A.

- **Choose** whole, crisp white bulbs and stalks, avoiding any that have soft, wilted portions. The feathery fronds should be bright green and moist.
- To **store,** wrap fennel in a plastic bag and store in the refrigerator for a day or two.
- To **prepare** fennel, remove and discard any dry or pitted portions; remove and reserve the fronds for garnish or later use as an herb. Wash and dry the whole head; trim the stalks, removing any tough portions from the root end with a swivel-bladed vegetable peeler. Chop, slice or cut as desired.
- Fennel can be used raw in salad or an appetizer platter, or cooked and served as a vegetable side dish. To **cook,** prepare fennel as you would cooked celery: Braise in a small amount of liquid until the fennel is tender when pierced. Drop sliced raw fennel into acidulated water (water with a little lemon juice) to help prevent discoloration. Better yet, slice just before serving.
- One large or 2 medium-size heads, totaling about 1¼ pounds, **serves** 4.

OKRA

No one is neutral about okra—you either like its mucilaginous texture or you hate it. Okra is most plentiful and at its best during the **summer. Nutritionally,** it's high in calcium and a source of essential B vitamins and it contains only 3 or 4 calories per pod.

- **Choose** firm, plump, bright green pods up to 3 inches long. Longer, overgrown pods are less tender. Avoid okra that is turning soft and black along its ribs.
- If you must **store** okra, refrigerate unwashed for up to 1 day.
- To **cook,** steam, stew or stir-fry fresh okra.
- One pound of okra makes 3½ cups of slices or 4 to 6 **servings.**

PARSNIPS

Akin to the carrot, parsnips are a **winter** root vegetable with a sweet, nutty flavor when cooked. **Nutritionally,** parsnips contribute significant amounts of fiber, calcium, phosphorus, niacin and folic acid to the diet.

- **Choose** smooth, firm, well-shaped, medium-size roots; avoid parsnips that are overgrown and fibrous as they may be bitter.
- **Store** parsnips, unwashed, in a perforated plastic bag in the refrigerator for up to a week, longer if they remain firm and fresh.
- To **cook,** steam, simmer or sauté diced, peeled parsnips as a side dish, or add to hearty winter soups and stews. Well-cooked parsnips can be mashed or pureed.
- One pound of parsnips **serves** 4.

MUSHROOMS AND ONIONS

MUSHROOMS

Cultivated mushrooms like the common button found in every supermarket are **available** all year long, as are some of the more popular wild varieties such as shiitake and oyster mushrooms. **Nutritionally,** mushrooms are rich in essential trace minerals and provide a mere 9 calories for each ½ cup of raw slices.

■ **White button** mushrooms are plump and meaty but comparatively neutral in flavor. **Choose** firm mushrooms that are closed around the stem by a thin veil; avoid those that are bruised or broken. **Store,** unwashed, in a loosely closed paper bag in the refrigerator for up to one week.

■ **Chanterelles** are trumpet-shaped, orange to reddish-yellow mushrooms that are available in fresh form from summer through winter. Their delicate, nutty flavor has been compared to apricots and spices. **Store** at room temperature in a single layer, covered with damp cheesecloth, and use within one day. Sauté and serve with delicately flavored meats such as chicken or veal.

■ **Cremini** mushrooms are similar to white buttons but have a slightly meatier flavor. **Choose, store** and **use** the same as button mushrooms.

■ **Enoki** mushrooms are long-stemmed, white or cream colored, with tiny caps. They are mild in flavor and texture, and should be served raw or cooked no longer than one minute. Add to clear soups, stir-fries and salads. They will keep for up to one week in their packaging.

■ **Morels** have hollow, conical, spongy caps and vary widely in size. They are available in early spring and into summer and may be creamy or dark brown in color. Their aromatic flavor has been likened to hazelnuts or nutmeg. **Store** in a single layer in the refrigerator, covered with cheesecloth, for a day or two. Clean under cool running water just before cooking. Add to sauces or serve with poultry, veal, pasta or rice.

■ **Oyster** mushrooms are fan-shaped and cream-colored and vary in size. Look for dry, evenly colored, smooth mushrooms and use promptly. **Store** in clumps on a tray in the refrigerator, covered in dampened cheesecloth, for one or two days. Sauté or braise with butter and onions.

■ **Porcini** (cèpe, cep, bolete) mushrooms are shaped like the white button but have a more pungent flavor. They are often sold dried. Look for firm fresh porcini and **use** within one or two days.

■ **Shiitake** mushrooms are large and parasol-shaped, with a dark brown cap and creamy underside. They can grow up to 8 inches in diameter. Select firm, meaty mushrooms with a distinct aroma. **Store** in refrigerator for up to a few days, covered with moist cheesecloth. Add to sauces, soups and stir-fries or sauté and serve as a side dish or first course.

■ **Dried** mushrooms often have more flavor than fresh. To reconstitute dried mushrooms, rinse and then soak in hot water for 15 minutes to 1 hour, or until soft. Strain and reserve the soaking water (which may need to be strained again through layers of cheesecloth) to use as a flavor enhancer in soups and sauces. Discard tough mushroom stems.

ONIONS AND OTHERS

Onions, leeks, chives and garlic are all botanically related. Onions are **available** all year, although season as well as variety can affect the taste and strength of an onion, ranging from sweet and mild to robust and pungent. Generally, onions sold from February to August are sweeter than the onions of August to January. **Nutritionally,** onions contribute calcium and other essential minerals, as well as small amounts of B vitamins.

■ **Choose** onions that are clean and firm, with dry skin and no soft spots or sprouts. **Store** yellow, large white and red onions in a cool, dark place, such as a cellar, for up to several months. Discard any that soften or become overly aromatic. At normal room temperature, onions may last only a week or two.

■ **Yellow onions,** the strongest in flavor, are good for stews, soups, sauces and other slow-cooking foods because they survive long cooking without losing flavor.

■ **Jumbo Spanish, Bermuda, Sweet Vidalia, Maui and Walla Walla** onions are ivory or fawn-colored, juicy and sweet enough to eat raw. Slice for sandwiches and hamburgers or stuff and bake.

■ **Red onions** come in many sizes and strengths; most are sweet enough to eat raw. Substitute for yellow onions when a short cooking time is called for.

■ **White boiling onions** are mild in flavor and should be purchased small for longer storage. **Store** in the refrigerator or in a cool, dark place and use in creamed vegetable dishes or stews.

■ For more facts about onions, see pages 427 and 428.

OKRA SUCCOTASH

LOW-FAT · LOW-CHOLESTEROL

Makes 6 servings (about 4 cups).
Recipe can be halved or doubled.
Nutrient Value Per Serving: 127 calories,
5 g protein, 4 g fat, 19 g carbohydrate,
346 mg sodium, 10 mg cholesterol.

1 package (10 ounces) frozen lima beans
1 bay leaf
1 cup frozen whole-kernel corn
1 package (10 ounces) frozen okra
2 tablespoons *un*salted butter
3 shallots, chopped OR: 1 small red onion,
    chopped
1 teaspoon leaf marjoram, crumbled
¾ teaspoon salt
¼ teaspoon pepper
¼ cup chicken broth
1 tablespoon red wine vinegar

1. Cook lima beans with bay leaf in
saucepan according to package directions. Stir in corn. Drain into colander.
2. Rinse okra in another colander

under hot running water to thaw. Heat
butter in same saucepan over medium-
low heat. Add shallots and marjoram;
cook 6 minutes or until softened. Add
okra; cook, stirring, 5 minutes.
3. Stir in lima bean mixture, salt, pepper, broth and vinegar. Cook until
heated through. Remove and discard
bay leaf. Serve hot or warm.

Microwave Directions (High Power Oven):
Ingredient Changes: Use a small bay leaf;
reduce marjoram to ½ teaspoon.
Directions: Cook lima beans with bay
leaf in microwave-safe 2-quart casserole,
with lid, following package directions.
Stir in corn. Drain and place in bowl.
Place butter in same casserole. Microwave, uncovered, at 100% power 1
minute to melt. Add shallots and marjoram. Microwave, uncovered, at 100%
power 3 minutes. Add thawed okra and
broth. Microwave, covered, at 100%
power 4 minutes. Stir in lima bean mixture, salt, pepper and vinegar. Microwave, covered, at 100% power 2
minutes. Remove and discard bay leaf.
Serve hot or warm.

SUCCOTASH TWIST
We've made succo-
tash even better by
adding okra. For a
bonus, sprinkle with
sautéed buttered
bread crumbs. Serve
with baked ham or
sautéed ham slices,
pork chops, chicken
breasts, or broiled or
fried chicken.

VIDALIA ONION RINGS

LOW-CHOLESTEROL

Makes 6 servings.
Recipe can be halved or doubled.
Nutrient Value Per Serving: 132 calories,
2 g protein, 7 g fat, 15 g carbohydrate,
187 mg sodium, 0 mg cholesterol.

¾ cup all-purpose flour
½ teaspoon salt
¾ cup cold water
2 Vidalia OR: 1 Spanish onion (8 ounces
    total), sliced into ⅛-inch-thick rings
Vegetable oil, for frying
Coarse (kosher) salt *(optional)*

1. Combine flour and salt in medium-size bowl. Pour in water, whisking until blended and consistency of heavy cream. Separate onion slices into rings.
2. Heat 1 inch oil in Dutch oven or large deep skillet over medium-high heat until deep-fry thermometer registers 375°.
3. Drop 6 to 10 onion rings into batter, tossing with a fork to coat.
4. Drop rings individually into oil in single layer. Cook 2 to 3 minutes or until golden brown, turning once. Drain on paper toweling. Sprinkle with coarse salt, if you wish. Repeat with remaining onion rings.

SWEET ONION
Some people claim you can eat these sweet onions from Georgia out of hand as you would an apple, but we've never tried it. They also make delicious onion rings.

MORE ONIONS
▪ **Green onions,** sometimes called scallions, have small white bulbs and long, strongly-flavored, chive-like tops. **Store,** unwashed and trimmed of wilted, yellowing or slimy green parts, in a plastic bag in the refrigerator for up to 1 week. The white bulb can be sliced and cooked or eaten raw; chop the green top and use as a garnish.
▪ **Leeks,** part of the amaryllis family, look like large, thick green onions. They must be slit from top to bottom and well washed before cooking. **Store,** refrigerated, wrapped in plastic, for about 1 week. Sauté or braise, or add to soups.
▪ **Chives** are members of the lily family but are used to add mild onion flavor to salads, omelets and other raw and cooked dishes. Look for bright, deep green stalks; avoid chives that are slimy, yellowing or wilted. Wrap, unwashed, in damp paper toweling and place in plastic bag. **Store** for up to 1 week in the refrigerator.

WHOLE ROASTED ONIONS MAKE-AHEAD TIP:

The onions can be prepared up to 2 days ahead through Step 3, and refrigerated, covered. To serve, bring onion mixture to room temperature. Continue with Step 4.

■ **Garlic** is indispensable to its lovers, some of whom refer to it as "the Stinking Rose." Look for large, plump, firm bulbs; older, shriveled garlic can be disagreeably strong. Store garlic at room temperature in a ventilated container.

MEDITERRANEAN ONION RELISH

LOW-FAT • LOW-CHOLESTEROL

Serve as a relish with hamburgers or other charcoal-grilled meats and poultry, or as a tasty vegetable side dish.

Makes 3 cups.
Recipe can be halved or doubled.
Nutrient Value Per ¼ Cup: 68 calories, 1 g protein, 2 g fat, 10 g carbohydrate, 160 mg sodium, 0 mg cholesterol.

2 tablespoons olive oil OR: vegetable oil
1½ pounds Spanish onions, cut into slivers
1 tablespoon light brown sugar
1 can (16 ounces) whole tomatoes
¼ cup dry white wine OR: ¼ cup chicken broth
¼ cup raisins
1 tablespoon cider vinegar
½ teaspoon salt
¼ teaspoon fennel seeds, lightly crushed
⅛ teaspoon leaf thyme, crumbled

1. Heat oil in large, nonaluminum skillet over medium heat. Add onion; cook, stirring often, until lightly browned, about 10 minutes. Reduce heat to low. Add brown sugar; cook over low heat, stirring constantly, until sugar melts.
2. Break up tomatoes. Pour into skillet along with wine, raisins, vinegar, salt, fennel and thyme. Bring to boiling. Lower heat; cover and cook 10 minutes or until onions are tender. If relish is too thin, boil gently, uncovered, to reduce to a thicker consistency. Serve warm or chilled.

Make-Ahead Tip: The relish will keep refrigerated, covered, for up to 4 days.

WHOLE ROASTED ONIONS

LOW-CHOLESTEROL • LOW-SODIUM

Roasting makes these onions succulent. Have on hand to enhance a stew, or use as a simple side dish.

Roast at 375° for 40 to 45 minutes.
Makes 4 servings.
Recipe can be halved or doubled.
Nutrient Value Per Serving: 52 calories, 1 g protein, 3 g fat, 6 g carbohydrate, 71 mg sodium, 8 mg cholesterol.

12 ounces small (1½ inch) white onions, peeled (about 20)
1 tablespoon *un*salted butter
1 tablespoon snipped chives OR: slivered green onion tops
1½ teaspoons finely chopped flat-leaf Italian parsley
⅛ teaspoon salt

1. Preheat oven to moderate (375°).
2. Place onions, 5 or 6 at a time, in single line on sheet of foil. Roll foil up so that onions remain in single line; wrap tightly. Place on baking sheet.
3. Bake in preheated moderate oven (375°) for 40 to 45 minutes or until tender when pierced with knife through foil. When cool enough to handle, unwrap the onions.
4. Melt butter in skillet over low heat. Add onions, chives, parsley and salt. Cook until heated through.

STEAK AND ONIONS

Spicy Flank Steak with Paprika (352)

Honey-Baked Rutabaga (461)

Whole Roasted Onions (this page)

Fresh Berries with Cream

SCALLOPED PARSNIPS WITH CHEESE-CRUMB TOPPING

LOW-FAT · LOW-CHOLESTEROL

Even better than scalloped potatoes! Delicious with roast meats of all kinds. For a special touch, serve in individual ramekins.

Bake at 375° for 45 minutes.
Makes 8 servings.
Nutrient Value Per Serving: 138 calories, 4 g protein, 4 g fat, 22 g carbohydrate, 153 mg sodium, 12 mg cholesterol.

2 pounds parsnips, pared and sliced
1 medium-size onion, quartered and sliced
1 stalk celery, sliced
½ cup half-and-half
½ cup chicken broth
¼ teaspoon leaf thyme, crumbled
1 tablespoon all-purpose flour
½ cup lowfat milk
½ cup fresh bread crumbs
3 tablespoons grated Parmesan cheese
1 tablespoon melted *un*salted butter
½ teaspoon sweet Hungarian paprika

1. Steam parsnip, onion and celery in steamer basket over gently boiling water in covered saucepan for 15 minutes or just until tender. Spread vegetables evenly in 13 × 9 × 2-inch dish coated with nonstick vegetable-oil cooking spray.
2. Preheat oven to moderate (375°).
3. Combine half-and-half, broth and thyme. Pour over parsnips.
4. Bake, loosely tented with aluminum foil, in preheated moderate oven (375°) for 25 minutes.
5. Whisk together flour and a little milk in small bowl until smooth. Whisk in remaining milk. Pour over casserole. Toss together bread crumbs, Parmesan, butter and paprika in small bowl. Sprinkle over casserole.

6. Bake, uncovered, in preheated moderate oven (375°) for 20 minutes or until bubbly and golden.

Microwave Directions (High Power Oven):
Ingredient Changes: Reduce chicken broth to ¼ cup; increase paprika to 1 teaspoon.
Directions: Combine parsnips, onion, celery and chicken broth in microwave-safe 13 × 9 × 2-inch baking dish. Cover with plastic wrap, vented at one corner. Microwave at 100% power 10 to 12 minutes just until tender. Whisk together half-and-half, thyme, milk and flour in small bowl until smooth. Stir into parsnip mixture. Cover with paper toweling. Microwave at 100% power 8 minutes, stirring once. Sprinkle top with crumb mixture. Microwave, uncovered, at 100% power 3 minutes.

SCALLOPED PARSNIPS MAKE-AHEAD TIP:
The casserole can be prepared earlier in the day and refrigerated, covered. Bring to room temperature, and then reheat, covered, in moderate oven (350°).

PEAS, SWEET PEPPERS, SPINACH AND TURNIPS

PEAS AND PODS

Tiny, sweet peas are **available** in spring. **Nutritionally,** peas provide significant amounts of protein, iron, folic acid, Vitamin C and insoluble dietary fiber *(page 397)*.

- **Choose** smooth, plump pods filled with small, bright green peas. Taste a pea; it should be sweet, not bitter or starchy. If fresh peas are not really fresh, you're better off buying frozen. Store fresh peas in a plastic bag in the refrigerator for up to one week.
- To **prepare,** shell fresh peas just before cooking and serving.
- To serve cold or use later, **cook** or blanch the peas in boiling water for just a minute, then plunge into ice water.
- **Snow peas** and **sugar snap peas** have edible pods that are tender enough to be eaten raw. Snow peas have crisp, flat pods with tiny seeds and are often used in Oriental cooking. The sugar snap, a sweet cross between regular green peas and snow peas, has a plump pod filled with good-sized peas. Trim the stem ends of either and string the sides, if necessary. To cook, steam briefly or stir-fry just until bright green.
- One pound of pea pods yields 1 cup of peas or 2 **servings.** One pound of snow peas or sugar snaps yields 4 to 6 servings.

SWEET PEPPERS

Always in **season,** sweet peppers are especially high in Vitamin C and low in calories.

- **Choose** firm, smooth, glossy sweet peppers. Store, unwashed, in a plastic bag in the refrigerator for several days. Sweeter red, yellow and orange peppers deteriorate more quickly than green or purple peppers.
- **To cook,** sweet peppers can be steamed, sautéed, stir-fried, stewed, grilled or eaten raw in salads or as a snack. Roasted peppers have a sweet smoky flavor *(see How-To, page 433).*
- **Italian peppers** are sweet and pale green, with long, tapering bodies. They have more flavor than American sweet peppers and are most often used for frying.
- **Banana peppers** have elongated, bright yellow shells and come in varying sizes. They range in flavor from sweet to piquant.

SPINACH

Spinach is **available** all year, but best in cooler months. **Nutritionally** rich in vitamins and minerals, this leafy green vegetable is as good in a salad as it is cooked into a side dish.

- **Choose** fresh-smelling, fresh-looking leaves with a springy touch. If possible, buy loose bunches with stems intact rather than prepackaged spinach which, although free of most grit, often contains bruised leaves and many stems. Reject any spinach that's yellow or moldy.
- **Store** spinach, unwashed, in a plastic bag in the refrigerator for up to 2 days.
- To **prepare,** remove all traces of dirt by giving spinach a preliminary rinse under cool running water. Remove any tough stems or withered leaves. Place leaves in cool water in sink or large basin. Gently swish the leaves, then lift them from water, so any dirt that's released falls to the bottom of the sink. Continue swishing the leaves in clean batches of water, until no dirt accumulates in bottom of sink.
- The easiest way to **cook** spinach is by layering the leaves, with just the water that clings to them from washing, in a large deep saucepan with a tight-fitting lid. Cook over low heat just until the leaves begin to wilt, about 5 minutes per pound. Drain the spinach in a colander and season with finely chopped, sautéed garlic, if you wish.
- Two to 3 pounds of fresh spinach yields 2 cups of cooked, 2 to 4 **servings.**

TURNIPS

This winter root vegetable adds assertive flavor and a touch of sweetness to cold-weather soups and stews. **Rutabagas** (sometimes known as swedes or yellow turnips) are a type of large turnip with mustard-yellow flesh. **Nutritionally,** turnips and rutabagas are very low in calories—14 calories in ½ cup of cubes—and provide small amounts of most essential vitamins and minerals. Turnip greens are rich in Vitamins C and A, calcium, magnesium and other minerals.

- **Choose** small, firm **turnips** with smooth skin and with fresh green leaves intact, if possible. **Store** roots and greens in a plastic bag for up to a week in the refrigerator.
- **Choose rutabagas** that are heavy for their size, their exteriors marked with purple but relatively devoid of large bruises or soft spots. **Store** for up to a month in the refrigerator. Peel wax coating prior to washing, cutting and cooking.
- **In cooking,** white turnips are most often cubed and added to soups and stews but they can also be grated raw or cut into julienne sticks for salad. Rutabagas are usually mashed or pureed, but they are also delicious cubed and baked. Try mashing either into white potatoes.

SAUTÉED PEAS WITH WATER CHESTNUTS

LOW-CALORIE · LOW-CHOLESTEROL QUICK

Serve with chicken or fish.

Makes 6 servings.
Recipe can be halved or doubled.
Nutrient Value Per Serving: 92 calories,
3 g protein, 4 g fat, 12 g carbohydrate,
109 mg sodium, 0 mg cholesterol.

1 tablespoon sesame seeds
1 tablespoon vegetable oil
½ teaspoon Oriental sesame oil
3 green onions, trimmed and sliced
2 tablespoons slivered pared fresh ginger
1 package (10 ounces) frozen petit peas
1 can (8 ounces) water chestnuts, rinsed,
   drained and quartered
⅛ teaspoon crushed red pepper flakes
¼ cup chicken broth
1 teaspoon cornstarch
1 tablespoon rice wine vinegar
1 tablespoon sherry

1. Toast sesame seeds in dry skillet over
medium heat, stirring, until light brown
and fragrant, 2 to 3 minutes. Reserve
for garnish.
2. Heat vegetable oil and sesame oil in
medium-size skillet over medium heat.
Add green onion and ginger; sauté for 4
minutes or until softened.
3. Add peas, water chestnuts and red
pepper flakes; cook 6 minutes. Meanwhile, stir together chicken broth,
cornstarch, vinegar and sherry in small
bowl until smooth and blended.
4. Add cornstarch mixture to peas.
Bring to boiling; cook 2 minutes, stirring. Spoon into serving dish. Sprinkle
with toasted sesame seeds.

Microwave Directions (High Power Oven):
Ingredient Changes: Decrease ginger to

(continued)

SAUTÉED PEAS WITH WATER CHESTNUTS
(*continued*)

1 tablespoon. Increase the chicken broth to 6 tablespoons.

Directions: Spread sesame seeds on bottom of microwave-safe 1½-quart casserole with lid. Microwave, uncovered, at 100% power 4½ minutes to toast. Remove and reserve. Combine green onion, ginger and oils in same casserole. Microwave, uncovered, at 100% power 3 minutes. Add peas, water chestnuts and 2 tablespoons broth. Microwave, covered, at 100% power 10 to 11 minutes until peas are tender, stirring once. Whisk together remaining chicken broth, cornstarch, vinegar, sherry and pepper flakes until smooth. Stir into casserole. Microwave, covered, at 100% power 2 minutes. Sprinkle with sesame seeds.

SNOW PEA SAUTÉ

LOW-CALORIE · LOW-CHOLESTEROL
QUICK

Serve with chicken, pork or ham, or fish.

Makes 4 servings.
Recipe can be halved or doubled.
Nutrient Value Per Serving: 60 calories, 2 g protein, 3 g fat, 8 g carbohydrate, 277 mg sodium, 0 mg cholesterol.

2 teaspoons vegetable oil
1 large onion, chopped
½ teaspoon ground cumin
½ teaspoon paprika
½ teaspoon salt
⅛ teaspoon ground cinnamon
Pinch ground hot red pepper
½ pound snow peas, trimmed OR: frozen, thawed
1 teaspoon grated orange rind

1. Heat 1 teaspoon oil in large nonstick skillet over medium heat. Add onion, cumin, paprika, salt, cinnamon and hot red pepper; sauté until onion begins to brown, about 5 minutes.

2. Add snow peas and remaining teaspoon oil; sauté 3 minutes or just until cooked and still crisp. Remove from heat. Stir in orange rind. Serve immediately.

SUGAR SNAP PEAS WITH MINT

LOW-CALORIE · LOW-FAT
LOW-CHOLESTEROL · LOW-SODIUM
QUICK

Simple and quick to prepare. Serve hot or at room temperature. Delicious with lamb, chicken or fish.

Makes 4 servings.
Recipe can be halved or doubled.
Nutrient Value Per Serving: 76 calories, 3 g protein, 2 g fat, 11 g carbohydrate, 76 mg sodium, 0 mg cholesterol.

2 teaspoons olive oil
¾ pound sugar snap peas, trimmed OR: frozen, thawed
3 green onions, chopped
1 clove garlic, finely chopped
⅛ teaspoon salt
⅛ teaspoon pepper
1 tablespoon chopped fresh mint OR: 1 teaspoon dried

1. Heat oil in large skillet over medium heat. Add sugar snap peas, green onion, garlic, salt and pepper. Stir-fry 4 minutes or until peas are crisp-tender.

2. Remove from heat. Stir in mint.

MARINATED ROASTED PEPPERS

**LOW-CALORIE · LOW-FAT
LOW-CHOLESTEROL**

For an extra special flavor, roast the peppers over charcoal. Keep a supply of these peppers on hand to serve with grilled or broiled meats, to use as a sandwich topping, to throw into a salad, or arrange on an antipasti platter.

Broil for 15 minutes.
Makes 4 servings (2 cups).
Recipe can be halved or doubled.
Nutrient Value Per Serving: 25 calories, 1 g protein, 0 g fat, 6 g carbohydrate, 137 mg sodium, 0 mg cholesterol.

4 sweet peppers (red, orange, yellow and/or green)
2 tablespoons balsamic vinegar OR: red wine vinegar
¼ teaspoon salt
⅛ teaspoon ground hot red pepper

1. Preheat broiler. Place peppers on broiler-pan rack.
2. Broil peppers about 4 to 6 inches from heat, turning occasionally, until blackened all over, about 15 minutes. Place in a paper bag and seal. When cool enough to handle, core, seed, remove and discard skins. Cut peppers into strips.
3. Combine vinegar, salt and hot red pepper in small bowl. Add peppers. Cover and refrigerate overnight, stirring once.

Make-Ahead Tip: The peppers can be made up to 3 days ahead and refrigerated, covered. Serve as is at room temperature or use in other dishes.

HOW TO ROAST A PEPPER
1. Broil whole sweet peppers 4 to 6 inches from heat, turning with tongs, until charred on all sides, about 15 minutes.

2. Place peppers in paper bag and close. When peppers are cool enough to handle, halve, core and seed. Remove charred skins with paring knife and discard. Cut peppers into strips.

WHAT'S IN A NAME?
All eating peppers, sweet or hot, belong to the *capsicum* family, from the Latin word for box, *capsa*. Early botanists fancied that the shell resembled a box enclosing seeds.

THREE-COLOR PEPPER SAUTÉ

LOW-CHOLESTEROL · QUICK

THREE-COLOR PEPPER SAUTÉ SERVING IDEAS

Any color peppers can be used for this dish—it's a perfect accent for broiled or grilled steaks, sautéed chicken breasts, broiled pork chops or fish fillets. Add a touch of balsamic vinegar, and serve at room temperature or slightly chilled as a salad. Also delicious as a topping for an open-faced sandwich or grilled sausages tucked into a toasted roll.

Makes 4 servings.
Recipe can be halved or doubled.
Nutrient Value Per Serving: 41 calories, 1 g protein, 3 g fat, 4 g carbohydrate, 138 mg sodium, 0 mg cholesterol.

1 large sweet red pepper
1 large sweet green pepper
1 large sweet yellow pepper
2 teaspoons olive oil OR: vegetable oil
1 clove garlic, finely chopped
½ teaspoon leaf thyme, crumbled
¼ teaspoon salt
⅛ teaspoon black pepper
⅛ teaspoon crushed red pepper flakes

1. Core and seed the peppers. Quarter lengthwise and cut crosswise into ⅜-inch-thick slices.
2. Heat oil in large skillet over medium high heat. Add peppers; sauté for 2 minutes. Add garlic, thyme, salt, black pepper and red pepper flakes; sauté 3 minutes or until peppers are tender.

Make-Ahead Tip: The dish can be made up to one day ahead, refrigerated, covered, and then served chilled, at room temperature or reheated in a skillet.

PEPPERS WITH CHUTNEY AND MINT

LOW-CHOLESTEROL · QUICK

Serve hot or at room temperature with roasted meats and poultry, strong-flavored fish, and spicy casseroles and stews. Delicious as a sandwich topping for ham, roast beef or even egg salad sandwiches.

Makes 4 servings.
Recipe can be halved or doubled.
Nutrient Value Per Serving: 101 calories, 1 g protein, 6 g fat, 12 g carbohydrate, 294 mg sodium, 0 mg cholesterol.

1½ tablespoons olive oil OR: vegetable oil
2 large sweet green peppers, cored, seeded and slivered
1 large sweet red pepper, cored, seeded and slivered
½ red onion, slivered
2 cloves garlic, chopped
1 tablespoon chopped pared fresh ginger
½ teaspoon ground cumin
½ teaspoon salt
2 tablespoons chutney, chopped OR: orange marmalade, chopped
1 tablespoon dry sherry
2 tablespoons chopped fresh mint OR: 1½ teaspoons dried

1. Heat oil in medium-size skillet over medium heat. Add green and red peppers and onion; cook, covered, for 12 minutes or until softened. Stir in garlic, ginger, cumin and salt; cook, uncovered, 2 minutes.
2. Stir in chutney, sherry and mint. Cook, stirring, until heated through, about 2 minutes. Serve hot or at room temperature.

Make-Ahead Tip: The recipe can be prepared a day ahead and refrigerated, covered. Serve at room temperature or gently reheat in a skillet.

STUFFED PEPPER WEDGES

Bake at 350° for 35 minutes.
Makes 6 servings.
Recipe can be halved or doubled.
Nutrient Value Per Serving: 57 calories,
2 g protein, 4 g fat, 5 g carbohydrate,
136 mg sodium, 2 mg cholesterol.

3 teaspoons olive oil
1 large sweet red pepper
1 large sweet green pepper
1 large sweet yellow pepper
1 large tomato, seeded and diced
¼ cup Calamata olives, pitted and finely
    chopped OR: other black olives
2 cloves garlic, finely chopped
3 tablespoons grated Parmesan cheese
1 tablespoon capers, rinsed
1 tablespoon chopped parsley

1. Preheat oven to moderate (350°).
Grease $13 \times 9 \times 2$-inch baking dish with
1 teaspoon olive oil.
2. Halve, core and seed peppers. Cut
each half into 3 lengthwise wedges.
3. Combine tomato, olives, garlic, 2
tablespoons Parmesan, capers and parsley in small bowl. Divide mixture
among pepper wedges. Place pepper
wedges in prepared baking dish. Drizzle
with remaining 2 teaspoons oil.
4. Bake peppers in preheated moderate
(*continued*)

**PEPPER WEDGES
SERVING IDEAS**
Serve hot or at room
temperature, with
broiled steaks, grilled
chicken or fish, or as
an appetizer or part
of a salad plate.

JÍCAMA

Pronounced HEE-ka-mah, this pale brown root has easy-to-peel skin and crisp, juicy flesh with a slightly sweet, earthy flavor.
■ Available from early fall through late spring, jícama can be sliced, cubed or cut into sticks and served raw in Tex-Mex-style salads or as a low-calorie snack. It can also be sautéed or braised and served as a starchy side dish.

STUFFED PEPPER WEDGES (*continued*)

oven (350°) until tender, about 30 minutes. Sprinkle with remaining 1 tablespoon Parmesan cheese. Bake another 5 minutes. Serve immediately or at room temperature.

Make-Ahead Tip: The recipe can be prepared up to 2 days ahead and refrigerated, covered. Serve at room temperature or reheat.

Microwave Directions (High Power Oven):
Ingredient Changes: Reduce olive oil to 2 teaspoons.

Directions: Prepare peppers and stuffing as in recipe, using all the cheese. Stuff pepper wedges. Place in ungreased microwave-safe 13 × 9 × 2-inch baking dish. Cover with microwave-safe plastic wrap, vented at one edge. Microwave at 100% power 6 minutes, turning dish after 3 minutes.

RED PEPPER AND JÍCAMA

LOW-CALORIE · LOW-CHOLESTEROL
QUICK

Serve hot or warm as a side dish with roasted meats, as part of a salad selection, or on its own as a first course. If jícama is not available, substitute firm apple or water chestnuts. (*Pictured this page.*)

Makes 6 servings.
Recipe can be halved or doubled.
Nutrient Value Per Serving: 55 calories, 1 g protein, 3 g fat, 7 g carbohydrate, 362 mg sodium, 0 mg cholesterol.

½ cup chicken broth
½ teaspoon cornstarch
1 tablespoon oil
3 sweet red peppers (about 1 pound), cored, seeded and cut into thin strips
2 strips lemon rind (*optional*)
2 tablespoons chopped shallot OR: red onion
2 teaspoons chopped pared fresh ginger
¼ teaspoon ground cumin
3 green onions, cut lengthwise into slivers
½ small jícama (6 ounces), pared and cut into slivers
1 tablespoon lemon juice
¾ teaspoon salt

1. Stir together chicken broth and cornstarch in small bowl until smooth. Heat oil in large skillet over medium heat. Add peppers, lemon rind if using, shallot, ginger and cumin; cook, stirring, until peppers are slightly softened, about 8 minutes.
2. Stir cornstarch mixture. Add to skillet, along with green onion and jícama. Bring to boiling; cook 2 minutes or until jícama is tender but still crisp. Remove from heat. Stir in lemon juice and salt. Serve hot or warm.

Make-Ahead Tip: The recipe can be prepared a day ahead and refrigerated, covered. Gently reheat to serve.

STUFFED ANAHEIM PEPPERS

Makes 6 servings.
Recipe can be halved or doubled.
Nutrient Value Per Serving: 228 calories, 8 g protein, 14 g fat, 19 g carbohydrate, 402 mg sodium, 48 mg cholesterol.

Vegetable oil, for frying
6 Anaheim peppers (about 8 ounces) OR: green Italian frying peppers
3 tablespoons finely chopped dried apricot
2 tablespoons chopped blanched almonds
3-ounce chunk Monterey Jack cheese

Batter:
⅔ cup all-purpose flour
¾ teaspoon salt
½ teaspoon ground chili powder
½ teaspoon ground cumin
½ teaspoon baking powder
6 tablespoons beer OR: club soda
1 egg
2 tablespoons oil

All-purpose flour, for coating

1. Pour enough oil into medium-size skillet to reach 2-inch depth. Heat oil until it registers 375° on a deep-fat frying thermometer. Add peppers, 2 at a time, and fry until blistered, about 30 seconds, turning if needed. Transfer with slotted spoon to paper toweling to drain. Remove pan with oil from heat. Reserve for frying. When cool enough to handle, peel peppers.
2. Cut 3-inch lengthwise slit in one side of peppers, starting at stem end. Carefully cut out seed pod (do not remove stem); rinse pepper under water to remove all seeds; drain well. Combine apricots and almonds in small dish. Cut cheese into 3½ × ½ × ½-inch sticks.
3. Sprinkle apricot-almond mixture into peppers, spreading evenly down length of pepper. Place cheese sticks in peppers, dividing equally.
4. Prepare Batter: Stir together flour, salt, chili powder, cumin and baking powder in medium-size bowl until combined. Make well in center. Beat together beer, egg and oil in small bowl. Pour into well in dry ingredients. Stir together until combined.
5. Reheat oil to 375°.
6. Dredge stuffed peppers in flour, patting off excess. Dip each pepper into batter, holding by stem. (You can support peppers with icing spatula if necessary.) Working in 2 batches, fry peppers in hot oil for 1 to 2 minutes or until golden, turning if needed. Transfer with slotted spoon to paper toweling to drain. Serve hot or warm.

PICK-A-PEPPER DINNER

Stuffed Anaheim Peppers
(this page)

Red Pepper and Jícama
(436)

Strawberry-Raspberry Semifreddo (533)

ANAHEIM PEPPERS SERVING IDEAS
These peppers are best when freshly cooked and are well complemented by lemonade, beer, or plain or frozen margaritas. Or serve with roasted or grilled meats, or as a first course or part of an appetizer selection, with a salsa or sour cream sauce on the side.

MAKE-AHEAD TIP:
The peppers can be prepared several hours ahead through Step 3 and refrigerated, covered. Bring to room temperature and proceed with Step 4.

1½ teaspoons vinegar
¾ teaspoon salt
¼ teaspoon black pepper

1. Preheat oven to moderate (350°).
2. Heat 2 tablespoons butter in large, heavy skillet with ovenproof handle˙ over moderate heat. Add red pepper and oregano; sauté for about 3 minutes or until almost tender. Stir in carrot; sauté for about 2 minutes. Stir in corn; sauté for about 2 minutes. Remove to medium-size bowl. Reduce heat to low.
3. Add eggs to same medium-size bowl along with milk, vinegar, salt and pepper; beat slightly.
4. Swirl remaining 2 tablespoons butter over bottom and side of same skillet. Pour in egg mixture. Cook over low heat, stirring with flat side of fork, shaking pan back and forth, until frittata is firm on bottom and almost set on top, about 8 to 10 minutes. Remove from heat.
5. Bake in preheated moderate oven (350°) for 5 to 8 minutes or until eggs are set. Cut into wedges and serve.

˙Note: If handle is not ovenproof, wrap in aluminum foil.

SWEET RED PEPPER AND CORN FRITTATA

QUICK

WHAT'S A FRITTATA?
Nothing more than a large omelet, a frittata is ideal for a light supper, lunch or brunch.

Bake at 350° for 5 to 8 minutes.
Makes 6 servings.
Nutrient Value Per Serving: 190 calories, 8 g protein, 13 g fat, 11 g carbohydrate, 432 mg sodium, 234 mg cholesterol.

¼ cup (½ stick) *un*salted butter
1 large sweet red pepper, cored, seeded and cut into thin lengthwise strips, about 3 × ¼ inches
½ teaspoon leaf oregano, crumbled
1 large carrot, pared and cut into very thin, ½-inch-wide strips, using vegetable peeler (about 1¾ cups)
1 cup frozen whole-kernel corn, thawed and drained
6 eggs, slightly beaten
3 tablespoons milk

COME FOR BRUNCH

Blushing Beatrice (558)

Salsa Fresca (85) with Tortilla Chips

Sweet Red Pepper and Corn Frittata (this page)

Gruyère Cheese Bread, Toasted (41)

Spiced Pineapple (483)

Berries in Light Caramel Sauce (525) with Cookies

Frothy Mexi-Mocha Coffee (559)

YOGURT-MASHED POTATOES

LOW-FAT · LOW-CHOLESTEROL · QUICK

Yogurt fans will appreciate the tang.

Makes 4 servings.
Recipe can be halved or doubled.
Nutrient Value Per Serving: 201 calories,
7 g protein, 1 g fat, 41 g carbohydrate,
606 mg sodium, 3 mg cholesterol.

**2 pounds Russet potatoes, pared and cut
   into 1-inch cubes (about 5 cups)**
2½ teaspoons salt
1 cup lowfat plain yogurt OR: skim milk
**2 tablespoons *un*salted butter, melted
   (optional)**

1. Bring medium-size saucepan of water
to boiling. Add potatoes and salt. Cook
until fork-tender, 10 to 15 minutes.
Drain. Return to saucepan over very
low heat.
2. Add yogurt to potatoes. Mash potatoes with potato masher. Serve, or continue with Step 3 for browning top of
potatoes.
3. For an attractive presentation, spoon
potatoes into pastry bag fitted with decorative tip; pipe onto flameproof 9-inch
pie plate or similar shallow baking dish.
Or, spread potatoes in dish; form decorative design with fork. Drizzle with
melted butter, if you wish. Broil 3 to 6
minutes or until lightly browned, if you
wish.

CURRIED POTATOES

LOW-FAT · LOW-CHOLESTEROL · QUICK

Makes 6 servings.
Recipe can be halved or doubled.
Nutrient Value Per Serving: 108 calories,
3 g protein, 1 g fat, 23 g carbohydrate,
107 mg sodium, 0 mg cholesterol.

**3 large all-purpose potatoes (2 pounds),
   pared and cut into ¾-inch cubes**
1 teaspoon cumin seeds
1 teaspoon vegetable oil
1 small onion, finely chopped
1 clove garlic, finely chopped
**1 teaspoon finely chopped pared fresh
   ginger**
1 teaspoon curry powder
⅓ cup frozen peas
¼ teaspoon salt
⅛ teaspoon pepper

1. Bring medium-size saucepan of water
to boiling. Add potatoes to boiling
water. Cook just until tender, about 6
minutes. Drain.
2. Meanwhile, heat large nonstick skillet over medium heat. Add cumin
seeds; cook until toasted, about 4 minutes. Remove from skillet and reserve.
3. Heat oil in skillet. Add onion; sauté
until browned, about 3 minutes. Add
potatoes, cumin seeds, garlic, ginger,
curry powder, frozen peas, salt and pepper to skillet; sauté, turning potatoes
gently, 3 minutes. Heat through.

**CURRIED POTATOES
SERVING IDEAS**
A quick and different
way to dress up pota-
toes. Serve with sau-
téed chicken breasts
or pork chops. Deli-
cious at room temper-
ature, or even on a
picnic. *(Pictured on
this page.)*

**CURRIED POTATOES
MAKE-AHEAD TIP:**
The potatoes can be
prepared a day
ahead and refriger-
ated, covered. Serve
chilled, at room tem-
perature, or gently
reheated.

Curried Potatoes

ROASTED POTATOES WITH PEPPERS

LOW-CHOLESTEROL

This simple side dish is delicious with roast pork, leg of lamb and chicken.

Bake at 400° for 45 minutes.
Makes 4 servings.
Recipe can be halved or doubled.
Nutrient Value Per Serving: 245 calories, 4 g protein, 11 g fat, 34 g carbohydrate, 700 mg sodium, 0 mg cholesterol.

1½ pounds Russet potatoes, pared and quartered lengthwise
1 large sweet red pepper, halved, cored, seeded and cut into 8 wedges
1 large sweet green pepper, halved, cored, seeded and cut into 8 wedges
4 small onions, halved and quartered lengthwise
4 cloves garlic, chopped
3 tablespoons olive oil
1 teaspoon fresh rosemary leaves OR: 1 teaspoon dried rosemary, crumbled
1¼ teaspoons salt
¼ teaspoon black pepper
Fresh rosemary sprigs *(optional)*

1. Preheat oven to hot (400°).
2. Arrange potatoes and peppers alternately in spoke pattern in large shallow 12-inch-round baking dish or pie plate. Pile onions in center. Scatter garlic over top. Drizzle with olive oil. Sprinkle with rosemary, salt and pepper.
3. Bake in preheated hot oven (400°) until vegetables are lightly golden and tender, about 45 minutes. Garnish with rosemary sprigs, if you wish.

COOKING POTATOES FOR MASHED
For a special flavor, add 2 cloves of peeled garlic and a bay leaf to the potato cooking water. Remove bay leaf after draining potatoes.

MASHED SWEET AND WHITE POTATOES

LOW-CALORIE · LOW-FAT
LOW-CHOLESTEROL · QUICK

There is very little butter added to this dish, just a tablespoon at the end to round out and soften the flavor. Adding some of the cooking liquid to the mashed potatoes makes them "creamy" without adding heavy cream.

Makes 6 servings.
Recipe can be halved or doubled.
Nutrient Value Per Serving: 98 calories, 2 g protein, 2 g fat, 18 g carbohydrate, 191 mg sodium, 5 mg cholesterol.

2 cups water
12 ounces sweet potatoes, pared and thinly sliced
12 ounces all-purpose potatoes, pared and thinly sliced
1 small onion, grated (2 to 3 tablespoons)
3 cloves garlic, crushed
1 bay leaf
½ teaspoon salt
⅛ teaspoon grated nutmeg
1 tablespoon *un*salted butter

1. Bring water to boiling in medium-size saucepan. Add sweet potatoes, white potatoes, onion, garlic and bay leaf. Bring to boiling. Lower heat; simmer, partially covered, for 15 minutes or until potatoes are tender. Remove and discard bay leaf and garlic. Pour off liquid and reserve.
2. Mash potatoes with potato masher or pass through food mill. Stir in salt, nutmeg and butter. If mixture appears a little dry, add some of reserved cooking liquid. (The leftover potato cooking liquid can be used in soups or sauces or bread baking.)

SWEET POTATO AND APPLE CAKE

LOW-FAT · LOW-CHOLESTEROL

Bake at 400° for 1 hour and 15 minutes.
Makes 8 servings.
Nutrient Value Per Serving: 159 calories,
2 g protein, 2 g fat, 35 g carbohydrate,
161 mg sodium, 4 mg cholesterol.

3 large sweet potatoes (2 pounds)
2 Granny Smith apples
1 tablespoon *un*salted butter, melted
½ teaspoon salt
⅛ teaspoon pepper
2 tablespoons maple syrup

1. Preheat oven to hot (400°).
2. Spray 9-inch glass pie plate with
nonstick vegetable-oil cooking spray.
3. Pare and thinly slice sweet potatoes
about ⅛ inch thick. Pare and core
apples; thinly slice.
4. Lay one-third of sweet potato slices,
in circular pattern, overlapping, in pie
plate. Brush lightly with one-third
melted butter. Sprinkle with ¼ teaspoon salt and the pepper. Cover with
half the apple slices, overlapping. Drizzle with 1 tablespoon maple syrup.
Cover with one-third sweet potatoes.
Brush with one-third butter and sprinkle with remaining salt. Cover with
remaining apples. Drizzle with remaining maple syrup. Cover with remaining
sweet potatoes. Brush with remaining
butter. Cover dish with aluminum foil.
5. Bake in preheated hot oven (400°)
for 45 minutes. Uncover and bake until
potatoes are tender when pierced with
knife, about 30 minutes. Remove from
oven and let stand 5 minutes. Place
serving platter over pie plate; carefully
invert. Remove any sweet potato slices
that stick to dish, if necessary. Cut into
wedges to serve.

Microwave Directions (High Power Oven):
Ingredient Changes: Increase butter to
2 tablespoons.

Directions: Place butter in microwave-
safe 9-inch pie plate. Microwave,
uncovered, 1 to 1½ minutes to melt.
Reserve 1 tablespoon. Prepare sweet
potatoes and apples and layer in
microwave-safe pie plate as Step 4.
Cover with another microwave-safe pie
plate, inverted. Microwave at 100%
power 10 minutes. Uncover. Microwave, uncovered, at 100% power 3
minutes. Let stand, covered, 5 minutes.
Invert to serve as in Step 5.

SWEET POTATO AND APPLE CAKE SERVING IDEAS
Serve wedges of this
attractive pie with
roast turkey or other
poultry, ham, pork or
lamb. Perfect for a
buffet or holiday
dinner.

SAVORY SWEET POTATO PUDDING

LOW-FAT

Bake at 350° for 1 hour.
Makes 8 servings.
Nutrient Value Per Serving: 124 calories, 4 g protein, 3 g fat, 20 g carbohydrate, 253 mg sodium, 83 mg cholesterol.

3 cups water
1½ pounds sweet potatoes, pared, halved lengthwise and thinly sliced crosswise (3½ cups)
1 carrot, pared and thinly sliced
2 cloves garlic, thinly sliced
2 teaspoons finely chopped pared fresh ginger
1 teaspoon grated orange rind
¾ teaspoon salt
¼ teaspoon ground cardamom
⅛ teaspoon ground hot red pepper
¾ cup milk
3 eggs, slightly beaten

1. Bring water to boiling in medium-size saucepan. Add potato, carrot, garlic, ginger, orange rind and ¼ teaspoon salt. Bring to boiling. Lower heat; simmer, partially covered, for 15 minutes or until potato is tender. Drain, reserving liquid.
2. Preheat oven to moderate (350°). Coat 8 × 8 × 2-inch-square baking pan with nonstick vegetable-oil cooking spray.
3. Push potatoes through food mill, puree in food processor, or mash by hand. Transfer to large bowl. Add cardamom, hot red pepper, remaining ½ teaspoon salt, milk, eggs and ½ cup reserved cooking liquid; stir until well combined. Pour into prepared pan.
4. Bake in preheated moderate oven (350°) for 1 hour. Cool 10 minutes. Cut into rectangles and serve.

Microwave Directions (High Power Oven):
Ingredient Changes: Use small garlic cloves; reduce water to 1 cup.
Directions: Combine potatoes, carrot, garlic, ginger, orange rind and water in microwave-safe 8 × 8 × 2-inch-square baking dish. Cover with microwave-safe plastic wrap, vented at one edge. Microwave at 100% power 12 minutes. Carefully uncover. Drain as in Step 1 above, saving liquid. Combine potato mixture, salt, cardamom, red pepper, milk, eggs and ½ cup cooking liquid in food processor. Whirl until mixture is smooth. Wipe out baking dish; coat with nonstick vegetable-oil cooking spray. Pour potato mixture into dish. Microwave, uncovered, at 100% power 5 minutes, turning dish halfway through cooking. Microwave, uncovered, at 70% power 14 minutes, turning dish twice. Cover and let stand 10 minutes.

POTATOES AND SWEET POTATOES

russet

round red

all-purpose

round white

yam

Peruvian blue

sweet potato

Finnish butter

POTATOES

These days, potatoes come plain and fancy, and they are always **available.** Basic white varieties such as all-purpose boilers and bakers are making way for early red-skins, blue-fleshed Peruvians and buttery yellow Finnish potatoes. **Nutritionally,** most of the fiber, iron and other minerals are in or close to the skin.

- **Choose** potatoes that are heavy for their size, with firm, clean, smooth skins. Avoid those that are sprouting (a sign of age), bruised, mushy in spots or dappled with green (indicating the presence of a mildly toxic alkaloid called solanine that results from exposure to light).
- **Store** potatoes in a well-ventilated, dark, cool spot for up to 2 months. Avoid moist warm areas such as under the sink.
- **All-purpose** potatoes have thin, smooth, beige skin. They can be cut up and steamed, boiled, pan-fried or roasted alongside meat.
- Small, round **new potatoes, red or white,** are lower in starch than older potatoes, with a firmer texture and more delicate skin. They should be used within 2 weeks. Choose them for boiling,

roasting, grilling and using in potato salads.
- **Russet** potatoes are large and oblong, with coarse, dark skin. Inside, their cooked flesh is fluffy, producing outstanding mashed, baked or French-fried potatoes.
- **Peruvian Blues** have an otherworldly indigo color and intense potato flavor. Treat them as you would a new red or white.
- **Finnish Butter** potatoes are golden-fleshed and deeply flavored. Though their fat content is no higher than that of regular potatoes, they are rich enough to be enjoyed without adding butter or other fat.
- To **prepare** potatoes for boiling, scrub clean and peel or pare, or not, as you wish. If you do peel the potatoes, make thin peelings to preserve the nutrients close to the skin. To **cook,** drop into enough boiling water to cover; add salt if you wish. Cook until tender when pierced with a fork, usually about 20 minutes after boiling begins, depending on size.
- To bake potatoes, scrub them clean and leave their skins on. Potatoes wrapped in aluminum foil become steamed rather than baked. Rubbing the skin with oil

before baking adds chewiness.
- One pound potatoes equals 3 medium-size potatoes, about 3 cups peeled and sliced, or 2 cups French fries. One and a quarter pounds boiled potatoes will **serve** 4.

SWEET POTATOES

Sweet potatoes are **available** in their prime in late fall and early winter months. What is referred to as a yam in this country is usually a sweet potato with an adopted name. Orange and red sweets are rich in the beta carotene form of Vitamin A.

- **Choose** smooth-skinned potatoes with tapered ends and no bruises. Sweet potatoes vary in skin color from beige-brown to red-brown. Generally, the deeper the color of the flesh, the sweeter and more flavorful the potato. White-fleshed sweet potatoes have a flavor somewhere between white potatoes and orange sweet potatoes.
- To **cook,** sweet potatoes can be baked, mashed, sliced and fried or steamed.
- Three medium-size sweet potatoes weigh about 1 pound and will **serve** about 4.

POTATO PANCAKES
SERVING IDEAS
Serve these rich and
flavorful pancakes as
a side dish or for
lunch or brunch.

MAKE-AHEAD TIP:
The pancakes can be
made ahead and
refrigerated or fro-
zen. Reheat in pre-
heated moderate
oven (350°).

POTATO PANCAKES WITH CHIVES AND TARRAGON

LOW-CHOLESTEROL · QUICK

Makes 4 servings (4 patties).
Recipe can be halved or doubled.
Nutrient Value Per Serving: 150 calories,
2 g protein, 9 g fat, 17 g carbohydrate,
279 mg sodium, 0 mg cholesterol.

1 pound Russet potatoes, pared and
    shredded, but not rinsed (2½ cups)
2 tablespoons snipped chives OR: finely
    chopped green onion tops
1½ teaspoons chopped fresh tarragon
    OR: ½ teaspoon dried
½ teaspoon salt
⅛ teaspoon pepper
2½ tablespoons olive oil OR: vegetable oil

1. Combine potato, chives, tarragon,
salt and pepper in large bowl. Form into
4 equal patties, each about 3½ × ½-
inch, squeezing out liquid.
2. Heat oil in large skillet over moderately high heat. Add patties. Reduce
heat to moderate; cook 15 to 17 minutes, turning patties over every 5 minutes for even browning. Drain on paper
toweling. Serve as is or with a dollop of
lowfat plain yogurt or applesauce.

POTATO AND RED ONION FRITTATA

QUICK

Bake at 350° for 5 to 8 minutes.
Makes 6 servings.
Nutrient Value Per Serving: 188 calories,
8 g protein, 13 g fat, 10 g carbohydrate,
331 mg sodium, 234 mg cholesterol.

4 tablespoons (½ stick) *un*salted butter
½ pound red potatoes (3 small), thinly
    sliced
1 large red onion, chopped
½ teaspoon leaf rosemary, crumbled
1 clove garlic, finely chopped
6 eggs, slightly beaten
3 tablespoons milk
½ teaspoon salt
¼ teaspoon black pepper

1. Preheat oven to moderate (350°).
2. Heat 2 tablespoons butter in large
skillet with ovenproof handle* over
moderate heat. Add potatoes; sauté until golden, about 8 to 10 minutes, turning over once halfway through cooking.
Remove from skillet; set aside and keep
warm. Add onion and rosemary; sauté
for about 3 minutes. Add garlic; sauté
about 2 minutes. Remove to medium-
size bowl. Reduce heat to low.
3. Add eggs to onion mixture along
with milk, salt and pepper; beat.
4. Swirl remaining 2 tablespoons butter
over bottom and side of skillet. Pour in
egg mixture; cook over very low heat,
stirring with flat side of fork, shaking
pan back and forth, until frittata is firm
on bottom and almost set on top, 8 to
10 minutes. Remove from heat.
Arrange reserved potato over top.
5. Bake in preheated moderate oven
(350°) for 5 to 8 minutes or until eggs
are set and potato slices are heated
through. Cut into wedges.

*****Note:** If the skillet is not ovenproof,
wrap the handle with aluminum foil to
protect it.

WEEKEND BREAK

Potato and Red Onion
Frittata (this page)

Green Salad with
Horseradish Dressing (183)

FRITTATA SERVING IDEAS
The potato makes this
frittata especially
satisfying—equally
tasty at room temper-
ature or chilled. Cut
into small rectangles
for appetizer portions.

SPINACH PUDDING

LOW-CALORIE

Serve with fish, ham or poultry, or just on its own as a supper entree. Try the pudding in individual casseroles as a luncheon dish with crusty bread on the side. The dish also works well with well-drained frozen spinach.

Bake at 375° for 35 minutes.
Makes 8 servings.
Nutrient Value Per Serving: 98 calories, 9 g protein, 4 g fat, 7 g carbohydrate, 358 mg sodium, 38 mg cholesterol.

2 pounds fresh spinach
½ cup part-skim ricotta cheese
1 egg
1 egg white
½ cup fresh bread crumbs

1 tablespoon chopped fresh dill OR:
    ¾ teaspoon dried
¼ cup chopped green onion
    (2 medium-size)
1 cup lowfat milk
½ teaspoon salt
¼ teaspoon pepper
½ cup grated Parmesan cheese

1. Preheat oven to moderate (375°). Coat a shallow 2-quart baking dish with nonstick vegetable-oil cooking spray.
2. Stem and wash spinach. Working in batches if necessary, place spinach in large pot. Cook over high heat, stirring occasionally, until spinach wilts, about 2 minutes. Drain. When cool enough to handle, squeeze dry.
3. Finely chop spinach. Place in medium-size bowl. Add ricotta, whole egg, egg white, bread crumbs, dill, green onion, milk, salt, pepper and ¼ cup Parmesan cheese; stir well to combine. (This all can be done in a food processor.) Pour into prepared baking dish. Sprinkle top with remaining cheese.
4. Bake in preheated moderate oven (375°) for 35 minutes or until puffy and top is golden brown.

Microwave Directions (High Power Oven):
Place washed spinach in microwave-safe 13 × 9 × 2-inch baking dish; cover with another dish, inverted. Microwave at 100% power 5 minutes, stirring well after 3 minutes. Rinse, drain and squeeze as above. Place spinach in food processor. Whirl until finely chopped. Add ricotta, egg, egg white, dill, green onion, milk, salt, pepper and Parmesan cheese. Whirl until well mixed. Pour into microwave-safe 2-quart casserole. Microwave, uncovered, at 100% power 8 minutes, stirring outer portions towards center after 5 minutes and at end of cooking. Cover with paper toweling. Microwave at 70% power 5 minutes. Let stand, covered, 3 minutes.

SAUTÉED SPINACH WITH GOLDEN RAISINS

LOW-CHOLESTEROL · QUICK

Serve this sweet-and-sour spinach with fish, poultry, roast pork or your favorite egg dishes. If fresh spinach is unavailable, use frozen.

Makes 4 servings.
Recipe can be halved or doubled.
Nutrient Value Per Serving: 155 calories, 7 g protein, 9 g fat, 18 g carbohydrate, 405 mg sodium, 0 mg cholesterol.

2 pounds fresh spinach
1 tablespoon olive oil
2 cloves garlic, finely chopped
⅓ cup golden raisins
¼ cup pine nuts, toasted
1 tablespoon sherry wine vinegar OR: other vinegar
1 teaspoon sugar
½ teaspoon salt
⅛ teaspoon pepper

1. Stem and wash spinach. Working in batches if necessary, place spinach in large pot. Cook over high heat, stirring occasionally, until spinach wilts, about 2 minutes. Drain.
2. Heat oil in large skillet over high heat. Add garlic; stir until garlic browns lightly, about 15 seconds. Add spinach; cook for 1 minute.
3. Remove from heat. Stir in raisins, pine nuts, vinegar, sugar, salt and pepper. Serve immediately.

SAUTÉED YELLOW SQUASH WITH MUSTARD SEEDS

LOW-CHOLESTEROL · QUICK

This is especially good with poultry.

Makes 6 servings.
Recipe can be halved or doubled.
Nutrient Value Per Serving: 78 calories, 2 g protein, 6 g fat, 4 g carbohydrate, 207 mg sodium, 3 mg cholesterol.

2 tablespoons olive oil
3 green onions, chopped
2 teaspoons mustard seeds, crushed
1 pound yellow summer squash, cut lengthwise in half, then crosswise diagonally into ¼-inch-thick slices
½ teaspoon salt
1 ounce Jarlsberg cheese, shredded

1. Heat oil in large skillet over medium heat. Add green onion and mustard seeds; sauté 1 minute. Add yellow squash and salt; sauté 5 minutes or until tender. Sprinkle with cheese.
2. Reduce heat to low; cover and heat through until cheese melts. Serve hot.

SPICY CHICKEN LEGS

**Chicken Legs with
Ginger-Fennel Coating (248)**

Rice

**Sauteed Yellow Squash
with Mustard Seeds**
(this page)

Fruit Salad

SUMMER SQUASH WITH ROSEMARY

LOW-CHOLESTEROL · QUICK

Makes 6 servings.
Recipe can be halved or doubled.
Nutrient Value Per Serving: 70 calories, 2 g protein, 5 g fat, 7 g carbohydrate, 370 mg sodium, 0 mg cholesterol.

2 tablespoons olive oil
1 large onion, halved and thinly sliced crosswise (1 cup)
1 teaspoon leaf rosemary, crushed
2 cloves garlic, finely chopped
¾ pound yellow squash, coarsely shredded
¾ pound zucchini squash, coarsely shredded
1 teaspoon salt
¼ teaspoon black pepper

1. Heat olive oil in large skillet over medium heat. Add onion and rosemary; sauté for 5 minutes or until tender. Add garlic; sauté for 3 minutes. Add squashes; toss to coat with oil.
2. Cover and cook for 1 to 2 minutes, or just until tender. Season with salt and pepper.

Microwave Directions (High Power Oven):
Ingredient Changes: Reduce the oil to 1 tablespoon; reduce the rosemary to ½ teaspoon.
Directions: Combine oil, onion and rosemary in microwave-safe 2-quart casserole with lid. Microwave, uncovered, at 100% power 3 minutes, stirring once. Stir in squashes. Cover with lid. Microwave, covered, at 100% power 7 minutes until just tender, stirring once. Season with salt and pepper.

SAUTÉED ZUCCHINI SPEARS

LOW-CHOLESTEROL · QUICK

A *very quick side dish to serve with meats and barbecue dishes.*

Makes 4 servings.
Recipe can be halved or doubled.
Nutrient Value Per Serving: 63 calories, 2 g protein, 5 g fat, 5 g carbohydrate, 289 mg sodium, 0 mg cholesterol.

3 medium-size zucchini (1 pound)
1 tablespoon olive oil plus 1 teaspoon
½ teaspoon grated lemon rind
1 clove garlic, finely chopped
1 tablespoon dry bread crumbs
½ teaspoon salt
¼ teaspoon pepper

1. Halve zucchini lengthwise. Cut each half in half crosswise, then cut each piece lengthwise into 4 wedge-shaped sticks.
2. Heat the 1 tablespoon oil in large skillet. Add zucchini; sauté just until crisp-tender, 3 to 4 minutes. Remove zucchini to plate.
3. Heat the 1 teaspoon oil in skillet. Add lemon rind and garlic; sauté 30 seconds. Stir in bread crumbs and zucchini; sauté 15 seconds or until heated through. Transfer to serving platter. Season with salt and pepper. Serve immediately.

ZUCCHINI WITH LEMON

LOW-CHOLESTEROL · QUICK

Serve hot or at room temperature as a side dish with practically anything, or as part of a buffet table or appetizer plate. Save this recipe for summer barbecuing.

Broil for 5 to 6 minutes.
Makes 4 servings.
Recipe can be halved or doubled.
Nutrient Value Per Serving: 82 calories, 2 g protein, 7 g fat, 5 g carbohydrate, 140 mg sodium, 0 mg cholesterol.

1¼ pounds zucchini (2 medium-size), trimmed and cut lengthwise into ¼-inch-thick slices
2 tablespoons olive oil
2 cloves garlic, finely chopped
1 teaspoon finely chopped fresh rosemary OR: ½ teaspoon dried
½ teaspoon cracked black pepper
¼ teaspoon salt
Lemon wedges, for garnish

1. Preheat broiler.
2. Arrange zucchini slices in single layer in jelly-roll pan, overlapping slices to fit if necessary.
3. Combine olive oil, garlic, rosemary, and cracked black pepper in measuring cup. Brush zucchini slices with olive oil mixture.
4. Broil 6 inches from heat for 5 to 6 minutes or until tender. Sprinkle zucchini with salt. Arrange zucchini slices on platter. Serve with lemon wedges.

Make-Ahead Tip: The recipe can be prepared up to 2 hours ahead and served at room temperature.

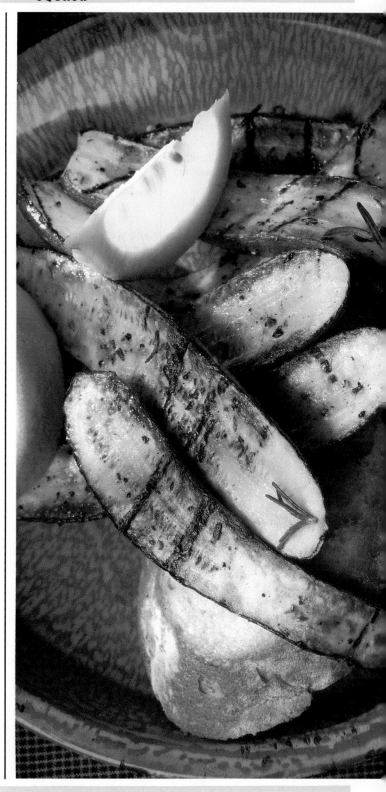

SQUASH

There's summer squash and there's winter squash, although both types are **available** year round. Tender-skinned summer squash includes **yellow squash, zucchini** and **pattypan.** Winter squash, rock-hard and covered with a durable and often inedible skin, includes **acorn, butternut** and **hubbard** varieties.

■ **Nutritionally,** summer squash is particularly low in calories; yellow and orange-fleshed winter varieties are excellent sources of the beta carotene form of Vitamin A.

■ **Choose summer squash** that is young, small, fresh and firm, with no blemishes or soft spots. **Store,** unwashed, in a plastic bag in the refrigerator, and plan on using within 4 days.

■ **Choose winter squash** that is firm and heavy for its size, indicating a meatier interior. The hard shell extends winter squash's **storing** qualities for up to three months or longer in a cool, dark, airy place.

■ **Green acorn** squash has a moist, nutty taste. It's at its most delectable in early winter. Look for dark green skin with orange spots. Cut the squash into rings; simmer in fruit juice, cinnamon and a knob of butter, or halve

Butternut
Spaghetti
yellow
Green Acorn
Buttercup

and stuff with dried fruits and nuts before baking. **Golden acorn** resembles the green variety in its moist texture, yet it is considerably sweeter.

■ **Golden nugget** squash is the size of an apple, making it ideal for single servings. Its bright orange color gives this squash the appearance of a diminutive pumpkin.

■ **Buttercup** squash has dark green skin flecked with gray and sports a turban-like top. Its flesh is sweet and smooth, with a slightly drier consistency than other winter squashes. For long keeping, choose a buttercup that still has its stem intact.

■ **Butternut** squash has a creamy, butter-like flavor. Look for pale, golden color and small size for optimum sweetness.

■ **Hubbard,** the behemoth of squashes, can weigh up to 20 pounds, so is sold in large packaged chunks rather than whole. Its sweet, nutty-flavored flesh is encased in a gray-green, blue-green or orange rind.

■ **Spaghetti** squash derives its name from its mildly flavored flesh, which fluffs up into long, spaghetti-like strands when cooked, the perfect foil for any sauce you'd use on pasta. There are several ways to prepare spaghetti squash. Try the following method, and turn to Spaghetti Squash with Pecans *(page 451)* and the How-To *(page 451).* Prick the squash all over with a long fork; place on a baking pan. Bake in a preheated moderate oven (375°) until tender when pierced with a fork, usually 45 minutes to 1 hour. Cut the squash in half; let stand until cool enough to handle. With a spoon, scoop out and discard the center portion of the seeds from the squash. Working with a fork around the edge toward the center, fluff up and scoop out the strands. Toss with your favorite sauce. One 3-pound spaghetti squash serves 6.

■ One pound of winter squash makes about 1 cup of puree. One pound of summer squash **serves** 4 as a side dish.

Hubbard
Golden Acorn
Pattypan
zucchini
Golden Nugget

SPAGHETTI SQUASH WITH PECANS

LOW-CHOLESTEROL

You may bake, steam or boil the spaghetti squash. While the cooking takes a while, it can be done a day ahead. Serve the spaghetti-like squash strands with poultry, pork or game.

Bake squash at 400° for 1 hour and 20 minutes; toast pecans at 400° for 5 to 7 minutes.

Makes 4 servings.

Nutrient Value Per Serving: 171 calories, 3 g protein, 11 g fat, 18 g carbohydrate, 393 mg sodium, 0 mg cholesterol.

1 spaghetti squash (2½ to 3 pounds)
⅓ cup pecans
1 tablespoon olive oil
5 cloves garlic, finely chopped (1 tablespoon)
1 tablespoon finely chopped pared fresh ginger
½ teaspoon salt
⅓ cup chicken broth OR: Vegetable Stock (*see recipe, page 116*)

1. Preheat oven to hot (400°). With fork or small paring knife, prick skin of squash all over. Wrap in aluminum foil and place on baking sheet.
2. Bake in preheated hot oven (400°) for 1 hour and 20 minutes or until soft to touch. Remove from oven and cool to room temperature.
3. Toast pecans on baking sheet in preheated hot oven (400°) for 5 to 7 minutes or until fragrant. Remove from oven and coarsely chop.
4. Halve squash, scoop out and discard seeds. Pull out spaghetti-like strands with fork.
5. Heat oil in large skillet over low heat. Add garlic and ginger; cook 2 minutes, stirring occasionally. Add squash strands and sprinkle with salt.

(continued)

ANOTHER WAY TO PREPARE SPAGHETTI SQUASH STRANDS

1. Cut uncooked spaghetti squash in half lengthwise. Scrape out seeds and fiber and discard.

2. Cook squash according to your favorite method: baking, grilling or microwaving. Scrape out the flesh with a spoon or fork into strands. Toss with a little oil or butter and serve, or use with your own pasta sauce recipe.

SPAGHETTI SQUASH MAKE-AHEAD TIP:
The recipe can be prepared a day ahead up through Step 4. Refrigerate the squash strands, covered. To serve, bring strands to room temperature and continue with Step 5.

SPAGHETTI SQUASH WITH PECANS
(*continued*)

Increase heat to moderate; cook 5 minutes longer, stirring occasionally. Stir in broth; cook 2 minutes. Add pecans; toss and serve.

Microwave Directions (High Power Oven):
Ingredient Changes: Chop pecans; reduce garlic to 3 cloves; reduce broth to ¼ cup.
Directions: Poke squash in several places with fork. Place on paper toweling in microwave oven. Microwave at 100% power 10 to 12 minutes until tender, turning squash over after 5 minutes. Halve, seed and remove flesh as in Step 4. Combine oil, garlic, ginger and pecans in microwave-safe 3-quart casserole. Microwave, uncovered, at 100% power 2 minutes. Stir in squash and broth. Microwave, uncovered, at 100% power 1½ minutes until hot.

BUTTERNUT SQUASH WITH PEAR AND GINGER

LOW-CHOLESTEROL · QUICK

Serve with spicy stews and casseroles and roasted meats, especially pork.

Makes 6 servings.
Recipe can be halved or doubled.
Nutrient Value Per Serving: 108 calories, 1 g protein, 4 g fat, 19 g carbohydrate, 222 mg sodium, 10 mg cholesterol.

2 tablespoons *un*salted butter
1 tablespoon finely chopped pared fresh ginger
1 butternut squash (about 2 pounds), pared, seeded and cut into 1-inch pieces
1 slightly underripe red or green pear, cored and cut into 1-inch pieces
½ teaspoon salt
⅛ teaspoon pepper

1. Heat butter in large skillet over medium heat. Add ginger; sauté for 1 minute. Add butternut squash; cover and cook, stirring occasionally, for 10 minutes or until almost tender.
2. Add pear; cover and cook 5 minutes or until squash and pear are tender. Season with salt and pepper

Microwave Directions (High Power Oven):
Combine ginger and butter in microwave-safe 2-quart casserole with lid. Microwave, uncovered, at 100% power 2 minutes. Stir in squash. Microwave, covered, at 100% power 9 minutes until almost tender. Stir in pear. Microwave, covered, at 100% power 3 minutes. Stir in salt and pepper.

FRUIT-STUFFED PUMPKIN HALVES

LOW-FAT · LOW-CHOLESTEROL

Bake at 350° for 60 to 70 minutes.
Makes 8 servings.
Recipe can be halved or doubled.
Nutrient Value Per Serving: 109 calories,
2 g protein, 3 g fat, 21 g carbohydrate,
170 mg sodium, 8 mg cholesterol.

1 medium-size pumpkin (3 to 4 pounds)
½ teaspoon salt
2 cups coarsely chopped pared apples
¾ cup fresh cranberries (3 ounces)
¼ cup firmly packed light brown sugar
¼ teaspoon ground nutmeg
¼ teaspoon ground cinnamon
2 tablespoons *un*salted butter, melted

1. Preheat oven to moderate (350°).
2. Cut pumpkin in half lengthwise;
remove and discard seeds. Place halves,
cut-side down, in shallow baking dish.
Add water to depth of 1 inch.
3. Bake in preheated moderate oven
(350°) for 30 minutes. Remove from
oven. Turn cut-side up. Sprinkle with
salt. Discard water.
4. Combine apple, cranberries, sugar,
nutmeg, cinnamon and butter in small
bowl. Spoon into pumpkin halves.
5. Bake, stuffed-side up, in preheated
moderate oven (350°) for 30 to 40 minutes or until pumpkin is tender. Cool
slightly. Cut each half into quarters.

HALVE IT YOUR WAY
A new way to serve
pumpkin as a side
dish for the holidays
or anytime. Consider
adding dried fruits,
such as raisins, apri-
cots and prunes. Per-
fect for a buffet table.

**PUMPKIN HALVES
MAKE-AHEAD TIP:**
The recipe can be
prepared several
hours ahead through
Step 3. To serve, con-
tinue with Step 4.

TOMATOES

red round

red plum

yellow cherry

red and yellow pear

yellow round

The sweetest tomatoes are **available** in their own regions throughout the summer growing months. **Nutritionally,** ripe tomatoes are a rich source of Vitamins C and A as well as essential minerals.

■ Tomatoes are at their best when they are vine-ripened to a deep red color. Most commercial tomatoes are picked at a turning stage from green to pink and never fully develop true tomato flavor.

■ **Yellow round** tomatoes are sweeter and less acidic than red varieties. **Red or yellow plum** tomatoes lend their meaty pulp to sauces and condiments, and tend to be more flavorful than other commercial varieties. **Red or yellow cherry** tomatoes are extra sweet, with a burst of juice in the mouth; toss them into salads, use as a garnish, or sauté and sprinkle with chopped herbs for a refreshing side dish. Tiny **red and yellow pear tomatoes** are

both flavorful and decorative. **Green tomatoes** are any variety of immature tomato; they're traditionally pickled, used to make relish, or dipped in cornmeal and fried.

■ For best results, **choose** unblemished tomatoes a few days before you plan to use them. Ripen on a counter rather than in a sunny window. You can speed up the process by placing tomatoes in a paper bag with a ripe apple. The apple emits a

Green tomatoes

natural gas that encourages ripening. Only cut tomatoes should be stored in the refrigerator.

■ Rinse tomatoes in tepid water just prior to using them, to remove all traces of fertilizers and pesticides.

■ **Cook** tomatoes in nonaluminum cookware, such as stainless steel or enamel pots or glass baking dishes, to avoid imparting a metallic taste.

■ To sweeten a pot of overly acidic tomato sauce, add a pinch of granulated sugar or a cupful of sautéed, chopped carrot and onion.

■ Tomatoes to be used for sauce can be frozen whole, and their skins will slide right off when they're thawed. (At 0° or less, the tomatoes will keep for 8 to 12 months.)

■ One pound of tomatoes yields 1½ cups of chopped tomatoes; one pint of cherry tomatoes makes 4 **servings.**

HOW TO PEEL AND SEED A TOMATO

A soup, sauce or other dish calling for chopped fresh tomato is sometimes much better without the tomato skins and seeds.

1. Drop tomatoes into large pot of boiling water for 30 to 60 seconds or until skins wrinkle slightly. Remove tomatoes from pot with slotted spoon. When tomatoes are cool enough to handle, remove skins with a paring knife.

2. Core the tomatoes and cut in half crosswise. Holding tomato over a bowl, scoop out seeds and pulp with a spoon. Reserve the pulp for soups or other uses, and then use the tomato as called for in your recipe.

BROILED TOMATO SLICES PROVENÇALE

LOW-CHOLESTEROL · QUICK

Broil for 5 to 7 minutes.
Makes 6 servings.
Recipe can be halved or doubled.
Nutrient Value Per Serving: 107 calories, 3 g protein, 7 g fat, 11 g carbohydrate, 315 mg sodium, 12 mg cholesterol.

4 large ripe tomatoes (about 2 pounds)
2 tablespoons *un*salted butter
¼ cup finely chopped onion
1 clove garlic, finely chopped
¾ cup soft bread crumbs
¾ cup canned pitted black olives, chopped
3 tablespoons chopped parsley
1 tablespoon grated Parmesan cheese
3 anchovy fillets, finely chopped
    (optional)

1. Preheat broiler.
2. Remove stem end and bottom of each tomato. Cut each tomato crosswise into 3 thick slices. Place tomatoes on large baking pan.
3. Heat butter in large skillet over medium heat. Add onion and garlic; sauté until soft, 2 to 3 minutes. Remove skillet from heat; stir in bread crumbs, olives, parsley, cheese and anchovies, if you wish.
4. Spoon an equal amount of bread crumb mixture on each tomato slice.
5. Broil 6 inches from heat until lightly browned, about 5 to 7 minutes. Serve hot or at room temperature.

SUMMER SNACK

Broiled Tomato Slices Provençale (this page)

Goat Cheese

Crusty Bread

Grapes

TOMATO PROVENÇALE SERVING IDEAS
This makes a great side dish with grilled or roasted meats, or an appetizer with warm crusty bread. If you're not particularly fond of anchovies, omit them. *(Pictured on page 393.)*

TOMATO PROVENÇALE MAKE-AHEAD TIP:
The recipe can be made up to 3 hours ahead and served at room temperature.

TOMATO AND ARUGULA BRUSCHETTA

QUICK

A *simple first course, light lunch sand-wich, or snack—basically a small open-faced sandwich on Italian bread with tomatoes, arugula, olive oil and grated Romano cheese.*

Bake at 400° for 10 minutes.
Makes 6 servings.
Recipe can be halved or doubled.
Nutrient Value Per Serving: 183 calories, 6 g protein, 7 g fat, 24 g carbohydrate, 322 mg sodium, 7 mg cholesterol.

1 bunch arugula (about 4 ounces), stems removed OR: watercress
2 tablespoons olive oil
1 loaf Italian bread (8 ounces), sliced diagonally into 1-inch-thick pieces
½ pound plum tomatoes, cored and sliced
⅓ cup coarsely shredded Romano cheese

1. Preheat oven to hot (400°).
2. From bunch of arugula, thinly slice enough leaves to measure ½ cup packed leaves. Reserve remaining leaves for garnish. Toss sliced arugula leaves with olive oil in small bowl. Spoon some arugula mixture on each slice of bread. Top with tomato slices; sprinkle with Romano cheese. Place bread on jelly-roll pan.
3. Bake in preheated hot oven (400°) for 10 minutes or until tomatoes are heated through and cheese is melted. Serve hot.

BROILED TOMATO AND MOZZARELLA CHEESE FANS

Broil for 6 to 8 minutes.
Makes 8 side-dish servings.
Recipe can be halved or doubled.
Nutrient Value Per Serving: 160 calories,
6 g protein, 13 g fat, 5 g carbohydrate,
182 mg sodium, 22 mg cholesterol.

¼ cup olive oil
1 tablespoon balsamic vinegar OR: red
    wine vinegar
1 clove garlic, crushed
½ teaspoon leaf basil, crumbled
¼ teaspoon leaf oregano, crumbled
¼ teaspoon salt
⅛ teaspoon crushed red pepper flakes
1 package (8 ounces) mozzarella cheese,
    cut into 12 slices
4 large ripe tomatoes (about 2 pounds),
    cored

1. Stir together oil, vinegar, garlic, basil, oregano, salt and pepper flakes in medium-size shallow dish. Add cheese slices, overlapping slices if necessary, and turning to coat completely with oil. Cover and refrigerate at least 30 minutes.

2. Preheat broiler.

3. Make 3 equally spaced vertical cuts in each tomato, starting from bottom and not cutting all the way through tomato. Insert a cheese slice into each cut. Place tomatoes in shallow flame-proof baking dish. Brush with any remaining marinade.

4. Broil tomatoes 6 inches from heat until cheese is melted and lightly browned and tomatoes are heated through, about 6 to 8 minutes. Pour any pan juices over tomatoes before serving.

Make-Ahead Tip: The tomatoes can be assembled ahead and refrigerated for up to 2 hours. Broil just before serving.

TOMATO AND MOZZARELLA FANS SERVING IDEAS
Equally good as a side dish or a light lunch. Use finely chopped fresh basil and oregano, if available.

BAKED TOMATOES AND ZUCCHINI

LOW-CHOLESTEROL · LOW-SODIUM
QUICK

Serve hot or at room temperature as a side dish, a first course or an appetizer, or even on its own as a salad with slices of crusty warm bread.

Bake at 425° for 20 to 25 minutes.
Makes 6 servings.
Recipe can be halved or doubled.
Nutrient Value Per Serving: 72 calories, 2 g protein, 6 g fat, 4 g carbohydrate, 100 mg sodium, 2 mg cholesterol.

1 pint cherry tomatoes, each cut in half
1 large zucchini (about ¾ pound), cut into ½-inch-thick slices
2 tablespoons olive oil
1 tablespoon chopped pitted oil-cured olives
1 teaspoon leaf thyme, crumbled
1 teaspoon finely chopped garlic
3 tablespoons grated Parmesan cheese

1. Preheat oven to hot (425°).
2. Arrange rows of tomatoes and zucchini alternately in 12 × 8 × 2-inch baking dish. Combine olive oil, olives, thyme and garlic in small bowl. Spoon olive oil mixture over vegetables. Sprinkle with Parmesan cheese.
3. Bake in preheated hot oven (425°) for 20 to 25 minutes or until vegetables are tender.

Make-Ahead Tip: The dish can be made up to 1 day ahead and refrigerated, covered. Gently reheat in preheated moderate oven (350°) or serve at room temperature.
Microwave Directions (High Power Oven):
Ingredient Changes: Reduce thyme to ½ teaspoon.
Directions: Overlap zucchini slices around edge of microwave-safe shallow round baking dish, about 12 inches in diameter. Place tomatoes in center. Spoon olive oil mixture over vegetables; sprinkle with cheese. Cover with paper toweling. Microwave at 100% power 5 to 6 minutes until zucchini is crisp-tender, turning dish once.

SAUTEED TOMATOES
SERVING IDEAS
Serve hot or at room
temperature with
grilled or roasted
meats or as an accent
to a sandwich platter.
This recipe specifies
balsamic vinegar, but
almost any variety of
vinegar would work
well in this dish.

SAUTÉED CHERRY TOMATOES WITH BASIL

LOW-CALORIE · LOW-FAT

LOW-CHOLESTEROL · LOW-SODIUM

QUICK

Makes 6 servings.
Recipe can be halved or doubled.
Nutrient Value Per Serving: 41 calories,
1 g protein, 2 g fat, 5 g carbohydrate,
96 mg sodium, 0 mg cholesterol.

1 tablespoon olive oil
1 small red onion, sliced
1 clove garlic, finely chopped

2 pints red and/or yellow cherry tomatoes
½ cup packed fresh basil leaves, sliced
¼ teaspoon salt
⅛ teaspoon black pepper
2 teaspoons balsamic vinegar OR: other
    vinegar

1. Heat oil in large skillet over medium
heat. Add onion and garlic; sauté until
tender, about 3 to 4 minutes. Add
cherry tomatoes, basil, salt and pepper;
cook, stirring, until skins of tomatoes
just start to wrinkle.
2. Add vinegar to skillet; heat through.

Make-Ahead Tip: The recipe can be made
up to 2 hours ahead and then gently
reheated or served at room temperature.

GREEN TOMATO CHUTNEY

**LOW-FAT · LOW-CHOLESTEROL
LOW-SODIUM**

A *good way to use up green tomatoes in the fall, especially if you are growing your own. Serve with roasted meats, hamburgers, curries, egg dishes or any other dish that strikes your fancy.*

Makes 3 cups.
Recipe can be halved or doubled.
Nutrient Value Per Tablespoon: 29 calories, 0 g protein, 0 g fat, 7 g carbohydrate, 5 mg sodium, 0 mg cholesterol.

2½ pounds green tomatoes, cored and cut into ½-inch pieces
1 sweet red pepper, cored, seeded and cut into ½-inch pieces (1 cup)
1 cup firmly packed brown sugar
1 cup cider vinegar
1 large shallot, sliced OR: 2 tablespoons chopped onion
½ cup dark raisins
2 tablespoons finely chopped pared fresh ginger
1 teaspoon crushed red pepper flakes
1 teaspoon mustard seeds

1. Combine green tomatoes, red pepper, brown sugar, vinegar, shallot, raisins, ginger, red pepper flakes and mustard seeds in Dutch oven or large pot. Bring to boiling; boil 20 to 25 minutes or until mixture thickens, stirring frequently.
2. Cool slightly. If not using immediately, spoon into clean, sterilized canning jars and refrigerate (*see Safe Storage for Unprocessed Canned Foods, at left*).

Make-Ahead Tip: The chutney can be prepared up to 2 weeks ahead and refrigerated in sterilized canning jars.

TURNIPS WITH PEARS

LOW-CHOLESTEROL · QUICK

The sweetness of the pears mellow the distinct turnip flavor. Serve with roast meats, poultry or duck.

Makes 4 servings.
Recipe can be halved or doubled.
Nutrient Value Per Serving: 133 calories, 2 g protein, 7 g fat, 17 g carbohydrate, 346 mg sodium, 3 mg cholesterol.

6 small turnips (1 pound), pared, halved lengthwise and cut crosswise into ¼-inch-thick slices
½ cup water
1 ripe pear (about 9 ounces), pared, halved, cored and cut crosswise into ¼-inch-thick slices
1 teaspoon grated lemon rind
1 teaspoon lemon juice
1 teaspoon finely chopped pared fresh ginger
⅓ cup walnuts, toasted and chopped
½ teaspoon salt
⅛ teaspoon pepper
1 teaspoon *un*salted butter

1. Combine turnips and water in large skillet. Bring to boiling over high heat. Cover and cook for 3 minutes or until turnips are tender.
2. Add pear to turnips. Reduce heat to medium-high; cook, uncovered, until liquid evaporates and mixture begins to brown, about 2 minutes.
3. Stir in lemon rind, lemon juice, ginger, walnuts, salt, pepper and butter until butter is melted. Serve.

Make-Ahead Tip: The recipe can be prepared a day ahead and refrigerated, covered. Gently reheat.

HONEY-BAKED RUTABAGA

LOW-CALORIE · LOW-FAT
LOW-CHOLESTEROL · LOW-SODIUM

At first glance these look like French fries, but they're really a healthful alternative. Try as an appetizer.

Bake at 375° for 45 minutes.
Makes 4 servings.
Recipe can be halved or doubled.
Nutrient Value Per Serving: 96 calories, 2 g protein, 3 g fat, 16 g carbohydrate, 59 mg sodium, 8 mg cholesterol.

1 rutabaga (1½ pounds)
1 tablespoon *un*salted butter, melted
1 tablespoon honey
⅛ teaspoon pepper

1. Preheat oven to moderate (375°). Coat jelly-roll pan with nonstick vegetable-oil cooking spray.
2. Pare rutabaga; cut into ½-inch slices. Cut slices into ½-inch-wide sticks. Stir together butter, honey and pepper in large bowl. Add rutabaga; toss together to mix. Place rutabaga on pan in single layer.
3. Bake in preheated moderate oven (375°) until tender and browned, about 45 minutes, turning sticks over after 30 minutes.

LIME AND HERB BUTTER

LOW-SODIUM · QUICK

This butter is excellent tossed with warm vegetables, or spread on toast. You can also stuff the butter under the skin of chicken (see How-To, page 250).

Makes ½ cup (1 stick) butter.
Recipe can be doubled.
Nutrient Value Per Teaspoon: 34 calories, 0 g protein, 4 g fat, 0 g carbohydrate, 12 mg sodium, 10 mg cholesterol.

½ cup (1 stick) *un*salted butter, at room temperature
¼ teaspoon grated lime rind
4 teaspoons lime juice
2 teaspoons orange juice
1½ teaspoons snipped chives OR: finely chopped green onion tops
¾ teaspoon fresh tarragon leaves, chopped OR: ¼ teaspoon dried
⅛ teaspoon salt
Pinch ground nutmeg

1. Combine butter, lime rind, lime juice, orange juice, chives, tarragon, salt and nutmeg in food processor or blender. Whirl until well combined, about 1 minute.
2. Spoon butter onto sheet of plastic wrap 12 inches long. Shape butter into log about 8 inches long. Roll up in plastic wrap and fold in the ends. Refrigerate.

Make-Ahead Tip: The butter can be made several days ahead and refrigerated, or overwrapped with aluminum foil and frozen for up to 1 month.

BLANCHING VEGETABLES

To prepare vegetables in advance, blanch, drain and rinse under cold running water to stop further cooking. Wrap and refrigerate. At serving time, drop blanched vegetables into boiling water for 30 seconds to reheat, then toss with flavored butter or one of our sauces on the following pages.

SWEET RED PEPPER SAUCE

LOW-CHOLESTEROL · QUICK

Delicious tossed with green vegetables, or spooned over fish or sautéed chicken breasts. Also good as a pasta sauce.

Makes 2 cups.
Recipe can be halved or doubled.
Nutrient Value Per ¼ Cup: 34 calories, 1 g protein, 2 g fat, 4 g carbohydrate, 125 mg sodium, 0 mg cholesterol.

1 tablespoon olive oil
2 large sweet red peppers (about 1 pound), cored, seeded and cut into 1-inch pieces
1 medium-size onion, sliced
1 clove garlic, sliced
½ teaspoon leaf thyme, crumbled
⅛ teaspoon black pepper
1 cup chicken broth

1. Heat oil in medium-size saucepan over medium heat. Add red pepper, onion, garlic, thyme and pepper; cook, stirring occasionally, 10 minutes or until red pepper is softened. Add chicken broth. Bring to boiling. Lower heat; cover and simmer for 15 minutes or until vegetables are very tender.
2. Pour pepper mixture into food processor or blender. Whirl until smooth puree. Serve hot.

Make-Ahead Tip: The sauce can be made up to 3 days ahead and refrigerated, covered. Gently reheat.

CHEDDAR AND RICOTTA CHEESE SAUCE

QUICK

*S*poon over broccoli, cauliflower, green beans, spinach or even sautéed chicken breasts.

Makes ¾ cup. Recipe can be doubled.
Nutrient Value Per Tablespoon: 30 calories, 2 g protein, 2 g fat, 1 g carbohydrate, 71 mg sodium, 7 mg cholesterol.

¼ cup part-skim ricotta cheese
2 teaspoons cornstarch
⅓ cup chicken broth
2 ounces shredded Cheddar cheese (½ cup)
1 tablespoon grated Parmesan cheese

1. Combine ricotta and cornstarch in blender. Whirl to blend. With motor running, slowly add chicken broth, blending until smooth.
2. Pour mixture into small saucepan. Add Cheddar and Parmesan cheeses. Cook over medium heat, stirring frequently, for 5 minutes or until mixture comes to simmer and is smooth; do not let boil. Serve hot.

TOMATO-GARLIC SAUCE

LOW-CALORIE · LOW-FAT
LOW-CHOLESTEROL · QUICK

*T*his sauce is ideal for dressing up fresh vegetables such as zucchini and green beans, as well as frozen vegetables. Add your favorite spices.

Makes 1 cup.
Recipe can be halved or doubled.
Nutrient Value Per Tablespoon: 7 calories, 0 g protein, 0 g fat, 2 g carbohydrate, 115 mg sodium, 0 mg cholesterol.

1 can (16 ounce) tomatoes, drained
2 cloves garlic, finely chopped
1 teaspoon all-purpose flour
1 teaspoon paprika
½ teaspoon salt
⅛ teaspoon pepper

1. Chop tomatoes. Combine tomatoes and any juices from chopping, garlic, flour, paprika, salt and pepper in small saucepan.
2. Bring to boiling over medium high heat. Lower heat; simmer 5 minutes. Serve hot or warm.

CREOLE SAUCE

LOW-CHOLESTEROL · QUICK

*L*iven up your favorite vegetables with this sauce. Drizzle over broiled or grilled hamburgers or strong-flavored fish such as tuna or bluefish.

Makes 2 cups.
Recipe can be halved or doubled.
Nutrient Value Per ¼ Cup: 31 calories, 1 g protein, 2 g fat, 3 g carbohydrate, 93 mg sodium, 0 mg cholesterol.

1 tablespoon vegetable oil
2 green onions, chopped
1 sweet green pepper, cored, seeded and chopped
1 stalk celery, chopped
1 clove garlic, finely chopped
1 can (14½ to 16 ounces) whole crushed tomatoes
½ teaspoon leaf thyme, crumbled
Pinch ground hot red pepper

1. Heat oil in medium-size saucepan over medium heat. Add green onion, pepper and celery; sauté 5 minutes or until softened. Add garlic; sauté 1 minute.
2. Add tomatoes with their liquid, thyme and red pepper. Cover and simmer 10 minutes. Serve hot.

SAUCE MAKE-AHEAD TIP:
All the sauces on this page can be made up to 2 days ahead and refrigerated, covered. Gently reheat without boiling.

CURRY SAUCE

LOW-CHOLESTEROL · LOW-SODIUM
QUICK

Spoon over poultry or vegetables.

Makes 2 cups.
Recipe can be halved or doubled.
Nutrient Value Per Tablespoon: 14 calories, 0 g protein, 1 g fat, 1 g carbohydrate, 37 mg sodium, 0 mg cholesterol.

2 tablespoons vegetable oil
1 carrot, pared and diced
1 stalk celery, diced
1 medium-size onion, diced
1 tablespoon all-purpose flour
2 teaspoons curry powder
1 cup chicken broth
1 cup skim milk

1. Heat oil in medium-size saucepan over medium heat. Add carrot, celery and onion; cook, stirring occasionally, for 5 minutes or until tender. Stir in flour and curry powder until smooth; cook 1 minute, stirring constantly.
2. Whisk in chicken broth and skim milk; cook, stirring constantly, until mixture boils and thickens slightly. Serve hot.

CITRUS AND GARLIC ACCENT

LOW-CHOLESTEROL · LOW-SODIUM
QUICK

A *piquant flavor enhancer that goes well with carrots, green beans, broccoli or zucchini. You just need a little. Or spoon over steaks, roast pork or sautéed chicken breasts.*

Makes about 1 tablespoon.
Recipe can be doubled.
Nutrient Value Per ¼ Teaspoon: 7 calories, 0 g protein, 1 g fat, 0 g carbohydrate, 48 mg sodium, 1 mg cholesterol.

CURRY AND LEMON-MUSTARD SAUCES MAKE-AHEAD TIP:
The sauces can be made a day ahead and refrigerated, covered. Gently reheat without boiling.

1 teaspoon *un*salted butter
1 teaspoon olive oil
2 cloves garlic, finely chopped
2 teaspoons grated lemon rind
1 tablespoon chopped parsley
¼ teaspoon salt
⅛ teaspoon pepper

1. Combine butter, oil and garlic in small saucepan. Cook over medium-low heat for 4 minutes; do not let garlic brown.
2. Stir in lemon rind, parsley, salt and pepper. To serve, toss with vegetables.

LEMON-MUSTARD SAUCE

LOW-CHOLESTEROL · QUICK

More *a flavoring than a sauce, this combination nicely accents fresh or frozen vegetables such as pearl onions, green beans, carrots and peas.*

Makes scant ¼ cup. Recipe can be doubled.
Nutrient Value Per Tablespoon: 28 calories, 0 g protein, 3 g fat, 1 g carbohydrate, 160 mg sodium, 3 mg cholesterol.

1 tablespoon Dijon-style mustard
1 tablespoon coarse-grained mustard
1 teaspoon *un*salted butter
1 teaspoon olive oil
2 teaspoons grated lemon rind
1 teaspoon lemon juice
⅛ teaspoon pepper

1. Combine both mustards, butter, olive oil, lemon rind, lemon juice and pepper in small saucepan.
2. Cook over low heat until butter melts and mixture is hot, stirring occasionally.

Make-Ahead Tip: The sauce can be made a day ahead and refrigerated, covered. Gently reheat.

From bottom: Honey-Raspberry Peaches (page 477); Spiced Pineapple (page 483); and Apples with Apricots and Prunes (page 466).

APPLES WITH APRICOTS AND PRUNES

LOW-FAT · LOW-SODIUM · QUICK

Makes about 4½ cups.
Recipe can be halved or doubled.
Nutrient Value Per ½ Cup: 90 calories,
0 g protein, 3 g fat, 17 g carbohydrate,
27 mg sodium, 7 mg cholesterol.

2 tablespoons *un*salted butter
1½ pounds Granny Smith apples (about
    3), cored and cut into thin wedges
1 tablespoon finely chopped pared fresh
    ginger
½ cup apple cider OR: apple juice
¼ cup pitted prunes, each cut in half
¼ cup dried apricots, each cut in half
1 teaspoon grated lemon rind

1. Heat butter in medium-size saucepan over medium heat. Add apples and ginger; cook, stirring occasionally, for 5 minutes.
2. Add apple cider, prunes, apricots and lemon rind. Bring to boiling over high heat. Lower heat; cover and simmer 5 to 10 minutes or until apples are tender. Serve hot or refrigerate. To store, see *Safe Storage for Unprocessed Canned Foods, page 460.*

Microwave Directions (High Power Oven):
Ingredient Changes: Reduce ginger to 2 teaspoons; add 1 teaspoon cornstarch.
Directions: Place butter in microwave-safe 3-quart casserole with lid. Microwave, uncovered, at 100% power 1 minute to melt. Add apples and ginger. Microwave, uncovered, at 100% power 4 minutes, stirring once. Stir together cider and cornstarch until smooth. Add to casserole with prunes, apricots and lemon rind. Microwave, uncovered, at 100% power 5 minutes until apples are tender, stirring once.

APPLE-CRANBERRY RELISH

LOW-FAT · LOW-CHOLESTEROL
LOW-SODIUM

Makes 5 to 6 cups.
Nutrient Value Per ¼ Cup: 79 calories,
0 g protein, 0 g fat, 20 g carbohydrate,
1 mg sodium, 0 mg cholesterol.

1¼ cups sugar
1 cup water
1 tablespoon finely chopped orange rind
1½ pounds Granny Smith apples (about 3
    apples), pared, cored and chopped
1 package (12 ounces) cranberries,
    coarsely chopped
1 tablespoon finely chopped crystallized
    ginger OR: ¼ teaspoon ground ginger
¼ teaspoon ground allspice
¼ teaspoon ground cinnamon
½ cup raisins

1. Combine sugar, water and rind in heavy medium-size saucepan. Bring to boiling. Lower heat; simmer until clear, about 2 minutes.
2. Add apple to saucepan. Simmer, stirring 5 minutes. Add cranberries, ginger, allspice and cinnamon. Simmer, stirring 7 to 8 minutes or until cranberries are soft. Stir in raisins.
3. Transfer relish to bowl. Let cool. Refrigerate overnight. If not using immediately, refrigerate in sterilized canning jars (*see Safe Storage for Unprocessed Canned Foods, page 460*).

Microwave Directions (High Power Oven):
Ingredient Changes: Reduce water to ¾ cup.
Directions: Combine sugar, water and orange rind in microwave-safe 8-cup measure. Cover with plastic wrap, vented at one edge. Microwave at 100% power 5 minutes, stirring once. Stir in apples, cranberries, ginger, allspice and cinnamon. Microwave, uncovered, at 100% power 10 minutes. Stir in raisins. Refrigerate as above.

APPLES WITH APRICOTS SERVING IDEAS
Serve this versatile condiment hot as a savory accompaniment to roasted meats and poultry and to egg dishes. It's even delicious cold as a topping for ice cream. *(Pictured on page 465.)*

APPLES WITH APRICOTS MAKE-AHEAD TIP:
This condiment will keep for up to 2 weeks, refrigerated, in sterilized canning jars.

RELISH MAKE-AHEAD TIP:
The relish will keep for up to 2 weeks, refrigerated, in sterilized canning jars.

RELISH SERVING IDEAS
Serve this relish *(pictured on page 481)* instead of the standard cranberry sauce for the holidays, or pair with grilled or roasted meats, especially pork, as well as poultry and game. Use as a sandwich spread to liven up turkey, ham or meatloaf. Feeling especially daring? Dab a little on ice cream.

SAUTÉED AVOCADO

QUICK

Serve these crunchy avocado slices as an appetizer with salsa, or with fish and tartar sauce. Half are coated with whole-wheat flour and the other half with cornmeal.

Makes 16 slices per avocado.
Recipe can be halved or doubled.
Nutrient Value Per Slice: 69 calories, 2 g protein, 5 g fat, 4 g carbohydrate, 25 mg sodium, 27 mg cholesterol.

3 tablespoons whole-wheat flour
½ teaspoon ground cumin
3 tablespoons yellow cornmeal
½ teaspoon chili powder
2 large firm, ripe avocados
Juice from 2 large limes
4 eggs, beaten
⅔ cup dry bread crumbs
⅔ cup vegetable oil

1. Combine whole-wheat flour and cumin on sheet of waxed paper. Combine cornmeal and chili powder on second sheet of waxed paper.
2. Halve, peel, pit and slice avocados into ¾-inch-thick slices. Sprinkle slices with lime juice. Dredge half the slices in flour mixture and half in cornmeal mixture. Dip slices into beaten eggs, then in the bread crumbs to coat.
3. Meanwhile, heat vegetable oil in large skillet over medium-high heat. Working in batches, pan-fry coated slices in hot oil about 15 seconds on each side or until golden brown. Transfer with slotted spoon to a large platter lined with paper toweling. Serve warm.

APPLES, AVOCADOS AND SUMMER BERRIES

APPLES

Thanks to their excellent keeping qualities and a wide range of local and commercial varieties, apples are **available** all year, though quality and quantity suffer somewhat in summer months. **Nutritionally,** apples are high in fiber and contain small amounts of most essential vitamins and minerals.

- **Choose** fresh, firm, well-colored apples. Handle carefully to avoid bruising and softening. **Store** apples in a plastic bag in the refrigerator.
- Three medium-size apples weigh about 1 pound. One pound of unpeeled apples **yields** 3 cups peeled, sliced or diced fruit.
- **McIntosh** is an all-purpose, thin-skinned apple used for cooking and eating out of hand. Its flavor ranges from tart to slightly sweet.
- **Granny Smith** apples are bright pale green in color, tart in flavor and crunchy in texture. They are ideal for cooking and baking.
- **Red or Golden Delicious** apples are sweet and mealy and best as an eating apple. Add to salads or eat out of hand as a snack.
- **Rome Beauty** apples are medium-large, greenish-yellow apples mottled with red. Hearty Rome Beauties are good keepers and excellent baking apples.
- Many varieties of apples are available in the areas where they are grown but are not sold commercially except to food processors. **Cortland** apples are crisp and slightly tangy hybrids of the McIntosh that are good for eating, baking and applesauce making. **Jonathan** apples are crisp, tart, juicy red cooking apples, often used for making pies and

tarts. **Empire** is another all-purpose McIntosh hybrid used for eating and cooking. **Newtown Pippin** is a medium-large, yellow-green cooking apple with crisp texture and tart flavor. Any local apples that you can buy will probably have better flavor than commercial varieties.

AVOCADO

The bland, nutty flavor and smooth, buttery texture of an avocado might fool you into thinking it's a vegetable. You'll find pebbly-skinned Haas avocados **available** from January through October and smooth-skinned varieties from November to May. Since avocados are rich in monounsaturated oils, their high fat content makes them higher in calories than other fruits. **Nutritionally,** however, these calories carry along with them a significant supply of Vitamins E and A.

- **Choose** firm avocados that yield slightly to pressure without being mushy. Avocados that are rock hard in the market may have been picked too soon and may begin to rot before they are ready to eat.
- To ripen an avocado, place in a loosely closed paper bag and store at room temperature for up to a few days. **Store** ripe avocados in the refrigerator.
- Slice a ripe avocado and serve in salads, as a side dish or mashed into a dip or spread. Avocados begin to brown quickly after they're cut; brush flesh with citrus juice to prevent darkening.

SUMMER BERRIES

June, July and August bring us abundant **availability** of fresh, sweet raspberries, blackberries

and blueberries. Market strawberries are at their best in the late spring months but are now sold throughout the year. The sweetest, most flavorful berries are often those you pick yourself. **Nutritionally,** berries are a good source of Vitamin C and fiber and a fair source of B vitamins.

- All berries are fragile and should be **stored** in the refrigerator, unwashed and loosely wrapped, and eaten as soon as possible.
- To freeze berries, arrange them in a single layer on a baking sheet. Freeze for about 2 hours or until solid. Pour into freezer bag, press air from bag, seal and use within 2 months.
- Use fresh berries to garnish fruit desserts and salads, flavor vinegar or to make tarts, jams, muffins, syrups or frozen desserts.
- Sweet **strawberries** have a deep red color and fresh green cap. Avoid unripe berries with white shoulders; they will not ripen any further off the vine. Wash berries before hulling and just before using to prevent water-log.
- Choose red, golden yellow or even white **raspberries** that are firm and unblemished, with no sign of mushiness or mildew.
- Look for clean, plump, firm **blueberries;** sort before using to remove any stem bits.
- **Cranberries** are only palatable when sweetened, which is why we usually find them in juice drinks, relishes, sugary sauces and baked into sweet breads.
- **Blackberries** are shiny, deeply colored berries that tend to be slightly sour.
- **Gooseberries** are rare, green sour berries that must be cooked before being eaten.

CRANBERRY CATSUP

LOW-FAT · LOW CHOLESTEROL

*S*erve *as a condiment with ham, pork, chicken or turkey, and experiment with it as a sandwich spread (pictured above).*

Makes about 1 cup.
Recipe can be doubled.
Nutrient Value Per Tablespoon: 62 calories, 0 g protein, 0 g fat, 16 g carbohydrate, 206 mg sodium, 0 mg cholesterol.

1 package (12 ounces) cranberries, fresh or frozen, thawed
1 medium-size onion, finely chopped
½ cup water
1 cinnamon stick, broken in half
½ teaspoon mustard seeds
½ teaspoon whole allspice
½ teaspoon whole black peppercorns
1 cup sugar
½ cup cider vinegar
1½ teaspoons salt

1. Bring cranberries, onion and water to boiling in large nonaluminum saucepan. Lower heat; cover and simmer 20 minutes.
2. Transfer cranberry mixture to blender or food processor, working in batches if necessary. Whirl until pureed. Return mixture to saucepan. Cook over medium heat until reduced to 1 cup.

(continued)

From left, clockwise: Cranberry Catsup (this page); Prune and Seckel Pear Chutney (page 477); and Pickled Blueberries (page 470).

CRANBERRY CATSUP MAKE-AHEAD TIP:
The catsup can be made up to 2 weeks ahead and refrigerated in sterilized canning jars.

CRANBERRY CATSUP (*continued*)

3. Tie cinnamon stick, mustard seeds, allspice and peppercorns in cheesecloth. Add to saucepan with sugar, vinegar and salt. Cook slowly over very low heat until mixture is very thick, stirring frequently. Remove spice bag. If not using immediately, spoon hot catsup into sterilized canning jars (*see Safe Storage for Unprocessed Canned Foods, page 460*). Refrigerate.

PICKLED BLUEBERRIES

LOW-FAT · LOW-CHOLESTEROL
LOW-SODIUM

Makes about 5 cups.
Recipe can be halved or doubled.
Nutrient Value Per ¼ Cup: 86 calories, 0 g protein, 0 g fat, 23 g carbohydrate, 2 mg sodium, 0 mg cholesterol.

1½ teaspoons mixed pickling spice
1¾ cups sugar
1½ cups cider vinegar
¾ cup water
1 cinnamon stick
2 pints blueberries, washed and
   picked over

1. Tie pickling spice in double-thickness cheesecloth bag.
2. Stir together spice bag, sugar, vinegar, water and cinnamon stick in large nonaluminum saucepan. Simmer, uncovered, 20 minutes.
3. Add blueberries; simmer 3 minutes or just until berries are softened. Pour mixture into large bowl. Cover and refrigerate overnight. To serve, remove spice bag and cinnamon stick and use slotted spoon to serve. If not using immediately, spoon into sterilized canning jars (*see Safe Storage for Unprocessed Canned Foods, page 460*). Refrigerate.

Microwave Directions (High Power Oven):
Ingredient Changes: Reduce sugar to 1¼ cups; reduce vinegar to ¾ cup; eliminate water.
Directions: Combine spice bag, sugar, vinegar and cinnamon stick in microwave-safe 8-cup measure. Cover with plastic wrap, vented at one edge. Microwave at 100% power 7 minutes, stirring once. Add blueberries. Microwave, uncovered, at 100% power 5 to 6 minutes just to boiling. Cool. Cover and refrigerate as in Step 3.

STRAWBERRY CHUTNEY

LOW-CALORIE · LOW-FAT
LOW-CHOLESTEROL · LOW-SODIUM

Makes 4 cups.
Recipe can be halved or doubled.
Nutrient Value Per Tablespoon: 21 calories, 0 g protein, 0 g fat, 5 g carbohydrate, 10 mg sodium, 0 mg cholesterol.

1½ pints strawberries, gently rinsed and
   hulled
1 large sweet red pepper, cored, seeded
   and cut into ½-inch dice
1 large tart apple such as Granny Smith,
   pared, cored and shredded
1 cup raisins
1 cup balsamic vinegar OR: red wine
   vinegar
¾ cup firmly packed light brown sugar
2½ teaspoons chopped pared fresh
   ginger
½ teaspoon ground allspice
¼ teaspoon salt
¼ teaspoon ground hot red pepper

1. Combine strawberries, sweet red pepper, apple, raisins, vinegar, brown sugar, ginger, allspice, salt and ground red pepper in large, heavy nonaluminum saucepan. Bring to boiling over medium heat. Gently boil, stirring frequently, until "glassy" and thickened, about 40 minutes. Refrigerate.
2. For longer storage, pour mixture into 4 sterilized ½-pint canning jars (*see Safe Storage for Unprocessed Canned Foods, page 460*). Refrigerate.

DRIED CHERRY AND ORANGE CONSERVE

LOW-FAT · LOW-CHOLESTEROL
LOW-SODIUM

Dried cherries are becoming increasingly popular. Serve this conserve as a flavor accent with roasted and grilled meats, poultry and game, or even spoon it on toast. (Pictured on page 481.)

Makes about 3 cups. Recipe can be doubled.
Nutrient Value Per Tablespoon: 60 calories, 0 g protein, 1 g fat, 15 g carbohydrate, 1 mg sodium, 0 mg cholesterol.

3 cups pitted dried red tart cherries
1 cup water
½ cup granulated sugar
⅓ cup firmly packed light brown sugar
2 tablespoons finely chopped orange rind
1 navel orange, peeled, bitter white pith removed and flesh cut into 1-inch cubes
2 teaspoons finely chopped lemon rind
¼ teaspoon ground allspice
¼ teaspoon ground cinnamon
½ cup pecans, toasted and coarsely chopped
⅓ cup orange juice
¼ cup lemon juice

1. Combine cherries, water, granulated sugar, brown sugar, orange rind, orange cubes, lemon rind, allspice and cinnamon in heavy, medium-size nonaluminum saucepan. Bring to boiling. Lower heat; simmer, stirring occasionally, for 5 minutes. Add pecans, orange juice and lemon juice; simmer 7 to 9 minutes or until thick.
2. Transfer conserve to bowl. Let cool. Refrigerate, covered, overnight. If not using within a day or two, spoon into sterilized canning jars (See Safe Storage for Unprocessed Canned Foods, page 460.)

Microwave Directions (High Power Oven):
Ingredient Changes: Reduce water to ½ cup.
Directions: Scatter pecans over bottom of microwave-safe 9-inch pie plate. Microwave, uncovered, at 100% power 4 minutes to toast, stirring once. Combine cherries, water, granulated sugar, brown sugar, cubed orange, orange rind, lemon rind, allspice, cinnamon, pecans, orange juice and lemon juice in microwave-safe 1½-quart casserole with lid. Microwave, covered, at 100% power 9 minutes to a full boil, stirring once. Stir. Microwave, uncovered, at 70% power 5 minutes.

CHERRY ONION RELISH

LOW-FAT · LOW-CHOLESTEROL

This relish is delicious with turkey, ham or pork, and barbecued foods.

Makes about 2 cups. Recipe can be doubled.
Nutrient Value Per Tablespoon: 34 calories, 0 g protein, 0 g fat, 8 g carbohydrate, 70 mg sodium, 0 mg cholesterol.

2 pounds cherries, stemmed, pitted and chopped
1 medium-size Spanish onion, diced
½ cup firmly packed light brown sugar
⅓ cup water
¼ cup cider vinegar
1 teaspoon salt
½ teaspoon grated fresh ginger

1. Place cherries, onion, sugar, water, vinegar, salt and ginger in large nonaluminum saucepan. Bring to boiling. Lower heat; simmer, uncovered, stirring occasionally, until thickened slightly, about 40 minutes.
2. Spoon mixture into bowl. Cool. Refrigerate, covered, until ready to serve. If not using immediately, spoon into sterilized jars (See Safe Storage for Unprocessed Canned Foods, page 460.)

CONSERVE MAKE-AHEAD TIP:
The conserve will keep for up to 2 weeks, refrigerated, in sterilized canning jars.

CHERRY ONION RELISH MAKE-AHEAD TIP:
The relish can be made up to 2 weeks ahead and refrigerated in sterilized canning jars.

ORANGE SALSA

LOW-CALORIE · LOW-FAT
LOW-CHOLESTEROL · QUICK

Try this salsa chilled or at room temperature in place of the more traditional tomato-based version. Delicious with Mexican food, lamb, pork or poultry, or even strongly flavored fish such as mackerel or bluefish. (Pictured on page 473.)

Makes 3 cups.
Recipe can be halved or doubled.
Nutrient Value Per ¼ Cup: 24 calories, 1 g protein, 0 g fat, 6 g carbohydrate, 93 mg sodium, 0 mg cholesterol.

¾ teaspoon grated orange rind
3 large navel oranges, peeled, bitter white pith removed and flesh finely chopped (3 cups)
1 medium-size tomato, peeled, seeded and finely chopped (1 cup)
1 small red onion, finely chopped
1 jalapeño pepper, seeded and finely chopped
1 clove garlic, finely chopped
2 tablespoons fresh cilantro, chopped OR: parsley
½ teaspoon lime juice
½ teaspoon salt
¼ teaspoon crushed red pepper flakes

1. Combine orange rind, chopped orange, tomato, onion, jalapeño pepper, garlic, cilantro, lime juice, salt and red pepper flakes in medium-size bowl.
2. Cover and chill until ready to serve, or serve at room temperature.

SPICED TANGERINES AND ORANGES

LOW-FAT · LOW-CHOLESTEROL
LOW-SODIUM

Serve this citrus combination during the holidays with your favorite baked ham or roast pork, poultry or lamb. Be daring and try it for breakfast or dessert. (Pictured on page 473.)

Makes 3½ cups.
Recipe can be halved or doubled.
Nutrient Value Per ½ Cup: 153 calories, 1 g protein, 0 g fat, 39 g carbohydrate, 2 mg sodium, 0 mg cholesterol.

6 tangerines
Water
1 cup water
1 cup sugar
⅓ cup balsamic vinegar OR: red wine vinegar
⅓ cup distilled white vinegar
2 tablespoons slivered pared fresh ginger
8 whole cloves
2 whole cinnamon sticks
1 navel orange, peeled, bitter white pith removed and flesh coarsely chopped

1. Place tangerines in large nonaluminum saucepan. Cover with water. Bring to boiling over medium-high heat. Cover and boil for 8 to 10 minutes or until skins can be easily pierced with fork. Drain; cut each tangerine into 8 wedges and cool slightly. Discard seeds. Coarsely chop and set aside.
2. In same saucepan, combine the 1 cup water, sugar, balsamic and white vinegars, ginger, cloves and cinnamon sticks. Bring to boiling. Add tangerines; return to boiling. Lower heat; simmer 10 minutes, stirring occasionally.
3. Add orange flesh; simmer 5 minutes or until heated through. Drain and cool. Cover and refrigerate or serve at room temperature.

From top: Melon Salsa (page 474); Spiced Tangerines and Oranges (page 472); and Orange Salsa (page 472).

Melon Salsa

LOW-CALORIE · LOW-FAT
LOW-CHOLESTEROL · QUICK

(Pictured on page 473.)

Makes about 4 cups
Recipe can be halved or doubled.
Nutrient Value Per ¼ Cup: 17 calories,
0 g protein, 0 g fat, 4 g carbohydrate,
72 mg sodium, 0 mg cholesterol.

1 cantaloupe (about 3 pounds)
1 sweet red pepper, cored, seeded and
    diced
1 small onion, diced
2 tablespoons chopped cilantro
2 tablespoons cider vinegar
½ teaspoon salt
⅛ teaspoon ground hot red pepper

1. Cut cantaloupe into quarters; remove and discard seeds. Remove fruit from rind; dice fruit.
2. Stir together cantaloupe, red pepper, onion, cilantro, vinegar, salt and ground red pepper in medium-size bowl. Cover and refrigerate until ready to serve.

Make-Ahead Tip: The salsa can be made a day ahead and refrigerated.

Curried Cantaloupe

QUICK

Makes 3 cups.
Recipe can be halved or doubled.
Nutrient Value Per Serving: 411 calories,
6 g protein, 25 g fat, 49 g carbohydrate,
825 mg sodium, 62 mg cholesterol.

2 tablespoons *un*salted butter
1 small onion, thinly sliced
1 teaspoon curry powder
¼ teaspoon ground coriander

1 medium-size cantaloupe, peeled, seeded
    and cubed
¼ teaspoon salt
⅛ teaspoon ground black pepper

1. Melt butter in large skillet over medium heat. Add onion; cook, stirring, until onion is tender. Add curry powder and coriander; cook, stirring, 1 minute.
2. Add melon; cook, stirring, until melon is soft, about 5 minutes. Season with salt and pepper.

Make-Ahead Tip: The recipe can be prepared a day ahead and refrigerated, covered. Serve chilled or at room temperature, or gently reheat.

Spiced Peaches

LOW-CALORIE · LOW-FAT
LOW-CHOLESTEROL · LOW-SODIUM

Makes 2½ to 3 cups.
Recipe can be halved or doubled.
Nutrient Value Per ¼ Cup: 51 calories,
0 g protein, 0 g fat, 14 g carbohydrate,
2 mg sodium, 0 mg cholesterol.

1½ pounds firm, ripe peaches
½ lemon, thinly sliced
¼ cup golden raisins
¼ cup cider vinegar
¼ cup firmly packed light brown sugar
2 whole allspice
1 whole stick cinnamon

1. Peel, pit and slice one-half of the peaches. Combine peaches, lemon slices, raisins, vinegar, brown sugar, allspice and cinnamon in medium-size nonaluminum saucepan. Bring to boiling. Lower heat; simmer 25 minutes.
2. Pit and slice remaining unpeeled peaches and add to mixture. Return to boiling. Lower heat; simmer 5 minutes. Serve warm, chilled or at room temperature.

Make-Ahead Tip: The peaches can be refrigerated for up to 1 week, covered.

CURRIED CANTALOUPE SERVING IDEAS
Serve with roast meats, poultry or broiled lamb or pork chops. Or serve as a condiment with a curried main dish. For an added touch, add 1 cup frozen peas to melon while cooking.

SPICED PEACHES SERVING IDEAS
Serve as an accent with roast lamb, pork, ham or poultry, and your favorite barbecued foods. Or try a little over vanilla ice cream for dessert. If using especially ripe peaches, you may wish to peel them since the skins may come off during cooking.

MELONS

Persian melon

Melons are sweetest in summer, although different varieties are **available** throughout the year. **Nutritionally,** all melons— particularly the orange-flesh varieties—are rich in Vitamin A.

■ **Choose** melon that's heavy for its size, with a fragrant stem end that gives under light pressure from your thumb. Melon should sound solid when lightly tapped.

■ Although a hard melon should soften if left on a sunny windowsill, it will never get any sweeter than on the day it was picked. Once a melon is cut open, it stops ripening altogether.

■ Puree overripe melon for use in cold fruit soups, sorbets and sauces.

■ **Cantaloupe**, sometimes referred to as muskmelon, has netted green-gray skin and orange flesh. Look for a melon with musky scent and a firm surface. The deeper the color of the flesh, the

sweeter the flavor.

■ **Casaba**, or winter melon, has a rough, hard rind that turns green or yellow-green when the melon is ripe. Some say its pale green, crisp flesh, tastes like that of a mango. Varieties include Golden Beauty, Canary and Santa Claus.

■ **Crenshaw**, a cross between can-

cantaloupe   crenshaw   honeydew

taloupe and casaba, is at its best when its skin develops blotchy shades of yellow-green or gold. The seed cavity is small, so you get a high proportion of tender, sweet, very juicy golden flesh.

■ **Honeydew** sports a smooth, hard, pale white to yellow rind over its 5- to 10-inch diameter surface. Its interior is usually bright green, although orange-flesh varieties are also available. Most varieties, particularly those with orange flesh, are sweeter

than cantaloupe. To pick a ripe honeydew, look for a melon that exudes a musky fragrance from its blossom end and has a smooth depression at its stem end. Allow the melon to soften for two days.

■ **Honeyloupe** is a new varietal cross between a cantaloupe and a honeydew, bred for sweetness.

Its warm orange flesh smells like flowers and honey. Look for one whose cream-colored skin has a blush of peach; a waxy appearance may indicate thin flavor and lack of sweetness.

■ **Persian melon's** netted skin goes from greenish to gray as it ripens, and its flesh becomes deep salmon orange. The best indications of good quality are sweet aroma and slight softness at the blossom end. One popular variety is the Sharlyn, with smooth, cantaloupe-like flesh and spicy undertones.

■ **Watermelons** vary in size from that of a cantaloupe to 30-pound monsters. The 6- to 10-pound Sugar Baby ripens early and is particularly sweet. New varieties include those with yellow or pink-red flesh (all have conventional mottled green rinds). Those labeled seedless actually contain small, white, and edible, seeds.

casaba

watermelon

honeyloupe

CITRUS FRUITS, PEACHES AND PLUMS

CITRUS STORIES

Oranges and grapefruits are **available** at their zesty best from late fall through the winter months. Lemons and limes never leave us—you can find them juicy and fresh throughout the year. Tangerines, mandarins, clementines and other tangerine hybrids appear in mid- to late fall through mid-winter. **Nutritionally,** all citrus is high in Vitamin C and even a small orange contains a full day's supply.

■ **Choose** citrus that's plump and heavy for its size. Skin color is not usually an indication of the quality of the fruit. Avoid citrus that is bruised or moldy. **Store** citrus fruit in the refrigerator.

■ **Valencias** are the most popular juice oranges. They have a thin orange or greenish skin. Store in the refrigerator but remove to room temperature for 30 minutes or so before juicing.

■ Seedless **navel** oranges have a sweet-tart flavor. Section and serve in salads or as a side dish to poultry.

■ **Blood oranges** are small with skin that ranges from orange to deep red. The flesh of a blood orange may be pure, deep red or pale orange mottled with crimson. The aftertaste of a blood orange is reminiscent of sweet berries or wine.

■ **Pink grapefruit** is usually sweeter than the **yellow-fleshed varieties,** but both can be juiced, sectioned, served with poultry or pork, made into ices and sherbet, or simply halved and broiled.

■ **Lemons** and **limes** are used for both juice and rind, the colorful outer layer of skin. To get the most juice from a lemon or lime, have the fruit at room temperature. Roll with gentle pressure over a flat work surface to break up the inner pulp before halving and juicing. Use a grater, swivel-blade vegetable peeler or citrus zester to remove the zest or outermost rind. Leave behind the bitter white pith that separates the rind from the fruit.

PEACHES AND NECTARINES

In season from late spring through early fall, peaches and nectarines are **available** at their most flavorful in late summer months. **Nutritionally** rich in complex carbohydrates, peaches and nectarines provide a variety of essential vitamins and minerals and are especially rich in potassium and Vitamin A.

■ **Look** for peaches and nectarines with strong aroma, since smell is the best sign of ripeness. A perfect peach is plump and round, vibrant and fresh-looking, with no hint of green; it should yield to gentle pressure and be neither hard as a rock nor mushy. Medium-size fruit are preferable to small or large ones. Pass on those that are bruised, blemished or shriveled, as well as those whose sticky exterior warns of infestation or mishandling.

■ Once ripe, peaches and nectarines should be consumed within a day or two.

■ To peel peaches or nectarines, start with perfectly ripe fruit. Immerse the fruit in boiling water for 30 seconds, then immediately plunge it into a bowl of ice water. The skin should pull off easily with the help of a paring knife.

■ Five or 6 peaches or nectarines usually weigh about 2 pounds.

■ **Yellow freestone** peaches, the most widely available, are easily pitted. **Cling** peaches have firmer flesh that "clings" to the pit, making it more difficult to remove.

■ **White peaches** have a greenish white flesh but similar flavor to orange-fleshed varieties.

■ **Nectarines** have a smooth, rather than fuzzy, skin, firmer flesh and lower juice content than peaches.

PLUMS

Plums are **available** in the summer, though some varieties make a brief appearance in mid-winter months. An average plum provides about 35 calories as well as small amounts of most essential vitamins and minerals.

■ **Choose** plump fruit with full color. Avoid plums with breaks in their skin, as well as those that are either rock-hard or overly soft. To test for ripeness, press plum gently with palm; it should yield slightly.

■ Plum varieties include tangy-sweet red **Casselman** and yellow-red **Laroda**; sweet reddish-blue **Roysum**; tart-sweet, deep-black **Friar** and green **Kelsey**. Small, black **Italian prune** plums, which come into season in late summer, are neither Italian nor dried and are wonderful for baking into tarts and pastries.

■ Soften firm, unripe plums in a loosely closed paper bag kept at room temperature for 3 to 4 days; check daily and **refrigerate** when ripe.

■ To freeze plums, halve or quarter them and remove stones, spread on a cookie sheet and freeze until firm, then place in freezer containers or plastic bags and return them to the freezer. Puree ripe plums and freeze in ice cube trays for later use as a frozen fruit snack.

■ One pound of fresh plums equals 6 medium-size pieces, 2½ cups sliced fruit, 2 cups diced fruit or 1¾ cups puree.

Honey-Raspberry Peaches

LOW-CALORIE · LOW-FAT
LOW-CHOLESTEROL · LOW-SODIUM

These peaches are just as good without the raspberry liqueur, but even this small amount rounds out the flavor very nicely. If using especially ripe peaches, you may wish to peel them since the skins may come off during cooking. Serve these peaches with any variety of roasted meats, especially pork, lamb and poultry. (Pictured on page 465.)

Makes 2½ to 3 cups.
Recipe can be halved or doubled.
Nutrient Value Per ¼ Cup: 42 calories, 0 g protein, 0 g fat, 11 g carbohydrate, 2 mg sodium, 0 mg cholesterol.

1½ cups dry white wine
2 tablespoons slivered pared fresh ginger
1½ pounds firm, ripe peaches, halved, pitted and thinly sliced
⅓ cup raspberry vinegar
3 tablespoons honey
2 tablespoons raspberry-flavored liqueur (optional)
2 tablespoons finely chopped red onion
½ teaspoon ground cinnamon

1. Combine white wine and ginger in large nonaluminum skillet. Bring to boiling. Lower heat; simmer until reduced by half, about 10 to 15 minutes.
2. Add peaches, vinegar, honey, liqueur if using, onion and cinnamon. Return to boiling. Lower heat; simmer 8 to 10 minutes or until peaches are just tender. Let stand for at least 30 minutes before serving. Serve warm, chilled or at room temperature.

Make-Ahead Tip: The peaches can be refrigerated for up to 1 week, covered.

Prune and Seckel Pear Chutney

LOW-FAT · LOW-CHOLESTEROL

Makes 6 cups.
Recipe can be halved or doubled.
Nutrient Value Per ¼ Cup: 84 calories, 1 g protein, 0 g fat, 21 g carbohydrate, 186 mg sodium, 0 mg cholesterol.

2 pounds Seckel pears, pared, cored and cut into 1-inch pieces
1 box (12 ounces) pitted prunes, coarsely chopped
1 medium-size yellow onion, finely chopped
3 cloves garlic, finely chopped
1⅔ cups white wine vinegar
⅔ cup firmly packed light brown sugar
1 tablespoon chopped pared fresh ginger
1 tablespoon yellow mustard seeds
2 teaspoons salt
½ teaspoon ground cinnamon
¼ teaspoon crushed red pepper flakes
¼ teaspoon ground cloves

1. Combine pears, prunes, onion, garlic, vinegar, sugar, ginger, mustard seeds, salt, cinnamon, pepper flakes and cloves in large, heavy nonaluminum saucepan. Simmer, stirring often, 45 minutes or until thick.
2. Transfer chutney to bowl. Let cool. Refrigerate, covered, overnight.

Microwave Directions (High Power Oven):
Ingredient Changes: Reduce vinegar to 1 cup; reduce salt to 1½ teaspoons.
Directions: Combine pears, prunes, onion, garlic, vinegar, sugar, ginger, mustard seeds, salt, cinnamon, pepper flakes and cloves in microwave-safe 2½-quart casserole with lid. Microwave, covered, at 100% power 10 minutes to boiling. Set lid slightly ajar. Microwave at 70% power 25 minutes until thick, stirring twice. Refrigerate as in Step 2.

CHUTNEY SERVING IDEAS
Serve with grilled or roasted meats and poultry, or as a side dish for stews and curries. (Pictured on page 469.)

CHUTNEY MAKE-AHEAD TIP:
The chutney can be refrigerated in sterilized jars for up to 3 weeks, covered (see Safe Storage for Unprocessed Canned Foods, page 460).

PEARS

A variety of pears, from the tiny Seckel to the long-necked Bosc, are **available** in season from early autumn through late spring and some varieties pop up during the summer months. **Nutritionally,** fresh pears are high in fiber, low in sodium and contribute small amounts of a wide variety of vitamins and minerals.

■ **Choose** underripe pears and allow them to ripen at home. Avoid pears with breaks in the skin, bruises or blemishes.

■ To ripen pears, **store** at room temperature just until they are soft at the stem end (softness at the bottom end may be a sign of interior rotting). Once ripe, pears should be refrigerated, unwashed, for 1 or 2 days.

■ Slightly underripe pears are preferable for poaching and baking, since they are less likely to fall apart when cooked.

■ Cooked pears retain their color without darkening.

■ Five pears weigh about 1½ pounds.

■ **Anjou** pears are all-purpose dessert pears. Large and plump, with thin yellow-green skin, a short neck and winelike flavor, they are in season from October to April.

■ **Bartlett** pears are perfect for cooking. In season from July to mid-October, they have red or yellow skin with a hint of green.

■ **Bosc** pears are large, russet-colored and long-necked, and have an aristocratic appearance. In season from October to February, their flavor is slightly tart, and their texture crisp, making them ideal for baking, poaching and sautéing.

■ **Comice** pears, pudgy with fragrant, buttery flesh, are in season from October through March. Their satiny flesh is delicious poached.

■ **Seckel** pears are small pears available from late August to December, and are used often in condiments and as garnishes. Their rich flavor has a spicy undertone.

Bartlett

Anjou

Seckel

Comice

Bosc

**CURRIED COMPOTE
SERVING IDEAS**
Makes a delicious
accompaniment to
pork or chicken, or
just serve over rice.
You can peel the
pears or not, before
cooking. Apples can
be substituted for the
pears.

**COMPOTE
MAKE-AHEAD TIP:**
The compote can be
made up to 2 days
ahead and refriger-
ated, covered. Gently
reheat.

CURRIED
HOT PEAR COMPOTE

LOW-CALORIE · LOW-FAT

LOW-CHOLESTEROL · LOW-SODIUM

QUICK

Makes about 4 cups.
Recipe can be halved or doubled.
Nutrient Value Per ¼ Cup: 63 calories,
0 g protein, 1 g fat, 14 g carbohydrate,
9 mg sodium, 2 mg cholesterol.

1 tablespoon *un*salted butter

1½ teaspoons curry powder

¼ cup apple jelly

2 tablespoons light brown sugar

4 ripe pears, cored and cut into large
    chunks

½ cup pitted prunes, halved

2 tablespoons water

1. Heat butter in large skillet over
medium heat. Add curry powder; cook,
stirring, 1 minute. Add apple jelly and
brown sugar; cook, stirring, until sugar
is dissolved.

2. Add pears, prunes and water to skillet; cover and simmer until pears are
tender, about 10 minutes, stirring occasionally. Serve warm.

Microwave Directions (High Power Oven):
Ingredient Changes: Use small pears;
eliminate water.
Directions: Combine butter and curry in
microwave-safe 1½-quart casserole with
lid. Microwave, uncovered, at 100%
power 1 minute. Stir in jelly and sugar.
Microwave, uncovered, at 100% power
1 minute. Add pears and prunes.
Microwave, covered, at 100% power 7
minutes until tender, stirring once.

GRAPES

Available year round, grapes are at their most plentiful from late summer through late autumn. They are generally classified as white grapes, which are actually yellow-green, or black grapes, which are actually reddish-blue or purple. At an average 3 calories per grape, they make a **nutritionally** perfect, sweet diet snack.

■ **Look** for grapes that are firmly attached to their stems, which should be green and resilient, not hard or dried out. The grapes should be vibrantly colored, with little or no white discoloration under the skin. Avoid grapes that are shriveled, excessively sticky (a sign of juice loss and mishandling), or soft and brown in spots.

■ **Store** grapes unwashed, loosely wrapped in paper toweling in a plastic bag in the refrigerator. At serving time, rinse grapes, drain on paper toweling and remove fruit from stems.

■ **Thompson Seedless** grapes, the largest selling grape in the United States, are pale green and firm, with mild flavor. Those that are yellow-green are the sweetest—perfect for eating out of hand or adding to salad.

■ **Red Flame Seedless** and other red varieties are at their sweetest when their red color predominates.

■ **Concord** grapes are deep blue-black, with tough skins. Although tasty eaten out of hand, this is predominantly a jam grape.

■ **Emperor** grapes are thin-skinned with red color and mildly sweet flavor; they have a relatively long shelf life, so they're frequently available.

■ **Ribier** grapes' mild flavor and long season have contributed to their popularity. This blue-black grape is round and quite large with tough skin.

■ **Champagne** grapes are not widely available, but when you do find these tiny treats, use them as garnishes for tarts or delicate out-of-hand nibbling.

PINEAPPLE DATE CONSERVE

LOW-FAT · LOW-CHOLESTEROL
LOW-SODIUM

Makes 4 cups.
Recipe can be halved or doubled.
Nutrient Value Per Tablespoon: 53 calories,
0 g protein, 1 g fat, 11 g carbohydrate,
0 mg sodium, 0 mg cholesterol.

1 large pineapple (about 4½ pounds)
2 cups sugar
½ cup unsweetened pineapple juice
1 cup pitted dates, chopped
1 cup chopped walnuts

1. Slice pineapple lengthwise into quarters through stem end to crown.

Remove each quarter of pineapple in one piece from rind. Cut out core from each quarter. (*See How-To, page 482.*) Cube pineapple into ¼-inch cubes.
2. Stir together pineapple and sugar in large nonaluminum saucepan. Cover; let stand 1 hour, stirring occasionally.
3. Add pineapple juice and dates to saucepan. Simmer, uncovered, until slightly thickened, about 30 minutes. Stir in walnuts.
4. Ladle into clean containers and cover. Cool on wire rack. Refrigerate.

Microwave Directions (High Power Oven):
Stir together pineapple and sugar in microwave-safe 2-quart casserole with lid. Let stand 1 hour, covered, stirring occasionally. Add juice and dates. Microwave, covered, at 100% power 11 to 12 minutes to boiling. Set lid ajar. Microwave at 70% power 25 minutes until slightly thickened, stirring twice.

PINEAPPLE DATE CONSERVE SERVING IDEAS
Dandy as a fruit spread or as a condiment with ham, chicken or pork. (Pictured below.)

PINEAPPLE DATE CONSERVE MAKE-AHEAD TIP:
The conserve can be refrigerated for up to 2 weeks, in sterilized canning jars (see Safe Storage for Unprocessed Canned Food, page 460).

From upper left, clockwise: Apple-Cranberry Relish (page 466); Dried Cherry and Orange Conserve (page 471); and Pineapple Date Conserve (this page).

PINEAPPLE

PINEAPPLES

Pineapples are most **abundant** during the spring and early summer months. Really ripe pineapples are often difficult to find. Since the fruit is very perishable when ripe, it is usually picked and shipped before reaching maturity. The more expensive air-shipped pineapple is ripened before harvesting so it usually has sweeter, more pronounced flavor. **Nutritionally,** pineapples are high in vitamin C and potassium.

■ Pleasing pineapple aroma is the best indication of ripeness, not whether you can pull out a leaf from the pineapple's crown. **Select** a pineapple heavy for its size, and with flesh that yields when gently squeezed. The crown should be vibrantly green, the base free of mold and stickiness, and the eyes protruding from the skin.

■ To help ripen a pineapple, place it in a perforated paper bag and let it stand at room temperature for a day or two. Once ripe, a whole pineapple should be **refrigerated** and used as soon as possible. Wrap sliced pineapple in plastic to minimize drying.

■ One pineapple serves 4.

■ The skin of a **Sugar Loaf** pineapple remains green even when the fruit is ripe. Its crown is characterized by long, broad leaves. **Red Spanish** pineapple, from Puerto Rico, has pale red skin and a multi-tufted crown. Less widely available, the **Cayenne** variety has a tall body and a single-tufted crown.

■ To cut up a pineapple, see our *How-To,* at right.

HOW TO CUT A PINEAPPLE INTO CHUNKS

1. Cut pineapple lengthwise into quarters through stem end to crown.

2. Cut the pineapple flesh of each quarter in one piece from the rind.

3. Cut out the core lengthwise.

4. Cut each quarter lengthwise in half, and then crosswise into chunks. Or cut the quarters into other desired shapes.

5. For an attractive presentation, reform the chunks into the whole piece and return to the rind.

SPICED PINEAPPLE

LOW-FAT · LOW-CHOLESTEROL
LOW-SODIUM

Serve warm or chilled with ham, chicken or pork, or your favorite barbecued foods. Also tasty over ice cream or pound cake. (Pictured on page 465.)

Makes 3½ cups.
Recipe can be halved or doubled.
Nutrient Value Per ¼ Cup: 85 calories, 0 g protein, 0 g fat, 22 g carbohydrate, 1 mg sodium, 0 mg cholesterol.

---

1 large pineapple (about 4½ pounds)
¾ cup sugar
½ cup unsweetened pineapple juice
½ cup cider vinegar
1 cinnamon stick
½ teaspoon whole cloves
⅛ teaspoon crushed red pepper flakes

1. Slice pineapple lengthwise into quarters through stem end to crown. Remove each quarter of pineapple in one piece from rind. Cut out core from each quarter. (See How-To, page 482.) Cut pineapple crosswise into ½-inch-thick pieces.
2. Stir together sugar, pineapple juice, vinegar, cinnamon stick, cloves and red pepper flakes in medium-size nonaluminum saucepan. Bring to boiling. Lower heat; simmer 15 minutes.
3. Add pineapple pieces to saucepan. Cover and simmer 10 minutes or until pineapple is tender. Pour into medium-size bowl. Serve warm or chilled.

Make-Ahead Tip: The pieces can be refrigerated for up to 3 days, covered.
Microwave Directions (High Power Oven):
Ingredient Changes: Eliminate pineapple juice.
Directions: Combine sugar, vinegar, cinnamon stick, cloves and red pepper flakes in microwave-safe 2-quart casserole with lid. Microwave, covered, at 100% power 4 minutes. Stir in pineapple. Microwave, covered, at 100% power 6 minutes, stirring once. Uncover and stir several times while cooling.

PLUM SAUCE

A sweet accompaniment to turkey, chicken or pork.

Makes 1½ cups.
Recipe can be halved or doubled.
Nutrient Value Per Serving: 29 calories, 0 g protein, 1 g fat, 4 g carbohydrate, 56 mg sodium, 3 mg cholesterol.

---

5 plums (1 pound)
2 tablespoons *un*salted butter
2 cloves garlic, finely chopped
¼ cup ruby port
1 tablespoon red wine vinegar
3 tablespoons sugar
½ teaspoon salt
¼ teaspoon pepper

1. Cut plums into eighths and pit. Heat butter in small saucepan over medium-low heat. Add garlic; sauté 1 minute. Add plums, port, red wine vinegar, sugar, salt and pepper. Bring to boiling. Lower heat; simmer, covered, for 12 minutes or until very tender.
2. Place in food processor or blender, working in batches if necessary. Whirl until smooth puree. Return to saucepan; simmer 5 minutes, stirring frequently.

Make-Ahead Tip: The sauce can be made up to 3 days ahead and refrigerated, covered. Gently reheat.

**PLUMS WITH PORT
SERVING IDEAS**
Spoon over ice cream
or use as a side dish
with ham or chicken.
Best when served
warm.

PLUMS WITH
PORT WINE

LOW-CALORIE · LOW-CHOLESTEROL

QUICK

Makes 4 servings.
Recipe can be halved or doubled.
Nutrient Value Per Serving: 133 calories,
1 g protein, 6 g fat, 16 g carbohydrate,
60 mg sodium, 16 mg cholesterol.

2 tablespoons *un*salted butter
6 plums (about 1 pound), pitted and
    quartered
¼ cup port wine
½ teaspoon grated orange rind
¼ teaspoon ground cinnamon

1. Melt butter in large skillet over
medium-high heat. Add plums; cook,
stirring, until lightly browned, about 5
minutes. Remove plums with slotted
spoon from skillet to heatproof bowl.
2. Add port wine, orange rind and cinnamon to drippings in skillet. Bring to
boiling. Pour over plums. Serve warm.

Microwave Directions (High Power Oven):
Combine butter and plums in
microwave-safe 2-quart casserole with
lid. Microwave, uncovered, at 100%
power 4 minutes, stirring once. Stir in
port wine, orange rind and cinnamon.
Microwave, covered, 1 to 1½ minutes
until plums are tender.
Note: This microwave version has more
liquid than if cooked on top of the
stove.

EXOTIC FRUITS

Fruit	Description	Peak Season	Storage and Use
Asian Pear (Apple Pear)	smooth yellow-green or russeted brown skin; round apple shape; mildly sweet, crisp, juicy flesh; hard when ripe	mid-summer to mid-winter	refrigerate for up to 1 week; eat raw (chilled) out of hand or slice into fruit salad; remains crisp when cooked and takes on more of a pear flavor
Blood Orange	smooth or dimpled orange skin, sometimes with a red blush; orange flesh flecked with ruby-red or all-red flesh; orange flavor with berry-like aftertaste; some varieties are seedless	winter to late spring	refrigerate for up to 1 week; eat out of hand, add to fruit salad, use as a garnish; juice; preserve in jelly or jam
Breadfruit	scaly green skin; heavy for size; starchy flesh	year round	use soon after purchase; more often served as a vegetable when green and hard; roast, boil, fry or steam like a potato; when ripe and soft, sieve or puree, chill and serve like pudding
Carambola (Starfruit)	deeply ribbed, glossy, waxy skin; green when unripe; yellow or white when ripe; tart or sweet citrusy flavor; resembles a 5-point star when sliced horizontally	fall to early winter	eat out of hand; slice into star shapes and add to fruit salad; sauté lightly and use to garnish meat dishes
Cherimoya (Custard Apple)	looks like a yellow-green pine cone with leathery, scaly skin; smooth, juicy, slightly mealy flesh; flavor like sweet custardy pineapple or mango	late fall to early winter	serve chilled; halve lengthwise and eat with spoon; puree or sieve, season with citrus juice and use as a sauce for other fruit; combine with berries and melon in a fruit salad
Clementine (Mandarin)	loose, glossy, bright orange skin; smaller and more flavorful than a tangerine	early winter	eat out of hand; section and use as a garnish or top with honey and mint; serve with poultry
Guava	round or pear-shaped, yellow-green fruit with flowery aroma and sweet or tart banana-berry flavor; white, yellow or red-fleshed	late fall to mid-summer	use quickly once ripe; puree or sieve and use in sauce for poultry or dessert; peel, seed and slice for fruit salad
Kiwifruit	small, egg-shaped fruit with furry brown skin and bright green flesh; juicy, acidic, sweet flavor; tiny, edible seeds	year round	ripen at room temperature, then refrigerate; halve crosswise and eat with spoon or peel, slice and serve with salad, poultry, ham or seafood
Kumquat	tiny, oval citrus with thin, edible orange skin; intense bittersweet orange flavor	late fall to late spring	store in refrigerator; blanch quickly in boiling water; halve lengthwise or crosswise; remove seeds; add to warm fruit compotes; garnish poultry dishes

(continued)

EXOTIC FRUITS

(continued)

Fruit	Description	Peak Season	Storage and Use
Lychee	brown, bark-like shell covers perfumy, slippery white fruit that clings to a large seed; rose-like flavor	mid-summer	store in refrigerator; easily cracked by hand; peel, halve and remove seed; combine with berries, mango, mandarins or other citrus; drizzle with honey, lemon or lime juice
Nopales (Cactus Leaves)	paddle-shaped green leaves; citrusy green-bean flavor; slippery texture (like okra)	early spring to late fall	refrigerate, wrapped in plastic; peel with swivel-bladed vegetable peeler; rinse off prickers under running tap water; add raw to salads; steam and sauté to use as side dish or add to omelets, salads, salsa; will thicken stews
Passion Fruit	small, egg-shaped fruit with purple-brown skin that wrinkles when ripe; tart, capsulated flesh encasing an edible seed	late winter to mid-summer	squeeze over fruit salad, ice cream, grilled seafood or poultry, other fruits; press through sieve to remove seeds; sweeten with sugar or honey
Plantain	large banana shape; skin is green when unripe; yellow when ripe and brown when very ripe; starchy flesh	year round	store at room temperature; bake, boil, grill or thinly slice and sauté
Prickly Pear (Cactus Fruit)	small, egg shaped fruit with tough green skin and mildly sweet, purple-red flesh	late summer to late spring	ripen at room temperature, then refrigerate; peel and slice into fruit salads or halve and eat with spoon
Pomegranate (Chinese Apple)	apple-like in appearance; leathery red skin encases clear red pulp and seeds that cling to rubbery white pith	fall to early winter	refrigerate up to 3 months; score skin and peel back with knife; remove fruit capsules; add to fruit salads, sprinkle over ice cream; sieve to remove seeds and press out juice
Quince	ivory-yellow skin; firm, dry, applelike flesh; must be cooked	late summer to early winter	refrigerate up to 2 months; peel, slice and bake, poach, stew or sauté; serve with roasted meat, poultry and game; use in preserves
Ugli Fruit	aptly named fruit that looks like a misshapen, mottled green or orange grapefruit; juicy, zesty-sweet, yellow-orange, segmented flesh	winter to late spring	refrigerate up to 1 month; eat out of hand; squeeze for juice; section and add to fruit or green salads

CHAPTER 11

Citrus Layer Cake (page 507)

DESSERTS

HOW TO MAKE A PIE (OR TART) CRUST

1. Stir together dry ingredients in a bowl. Cut in butter or other fat with pastry blender until mixture is crumbly.

2. Drizzle in water, a little at a time, tossing the flour mixture with a spoon or fork until the dough begins to mass together.

3. Shape dough into disk on floured surface. Flatten slightly. Chill until firm.

4. Roll disk out into circle with lightly floured rolling pin, rolling from the center outward and turning the dough as you work. As you roll to the edges, lift the rolling pin slightly to avoid making the edges too thin. Lift the dough occasionally to make sure it isn't sticking. Sprinkle with a little flour as needed to prevent sticking. Roll into a circle about 2 inches larger than the pie plate. Invert the pie plate onto the dough to properly measure.

5. Brush off excess flour from the dough with a brush.

(continued)

6. Roll half the dough circle loosely around on the rolling pin.

7. Lift the dough onto the pie plate, centering it over the plate. Unroll the dough onto the pie plate.

8. With your fingers, gently ease the dough into the bottom and up the sides of the plate. Don't stretch the dough at any time or it will shrink during baking. Trim overhang, allowing enough excess to form decorative edge (*see How-To, at right*).

HOW TO MAKE A DECORATIVE PIE CRUST EDGE

Fold edge of pie crust under. Then bring pastry up over pie plate rim. Pinch to form stand-up edge.

1. To make fluted edge: Place one index finger against stand-up edge. With index finger and thumb of other hand, pinch pastry against first index finger to make flute. Repeat around edge, leaving about ¼ inch between flutes.

2. To make rope edge: Press thumb at an angle into stand-up edge of pastry, and pinch pastry between thumb and knuckle of adjoining index finger. Place thumb in groove left by index finger and repeat all around the edge.

3. To make cutouts: Use small cookie cutter or truffle and aspic cutters to form decorative shapes. Attach shapes to top edge of crust.

BOURBON-SCENTED PEACH PIE

Bake at 375° for 1 hour and 15 minutes.
Makes 10 servings.

Nutrient Value Per Serving: 328 calories, 4 g protein, 14 g fat, 49 g carbohydrate, 171 mg sodium, 37 mg cholesterol.

Pastry:
1¼ cups whole-wheat flour
¾ cup all-purpose flour
¾ teaspoon salt
¾ cup (1½ sticks) chilled *un*salted
    butter, cut into pats
7 tablespoons cold water

Filling:
2½ pounds fresh peaches
½ cup granulated sugar
½ cup firmly packed light brown sugar
4 teaspoons quick tapioca
½ teaspoon ground cardamom
2 to 3 teaspoons bourbon
1 teaspoon grated lemon rind

1. Prepare Pastry: Combine whole-wheat and all-purpose flours, salt and butter in food processor. Whirl for about 40 seconds or until texture of coarse meal. Add water. Whirl just until mixture begins to mass together. (Or to prepare by hand, cut butter into dry ingredients with pastry blender; sprinkle water over top, tossing with fork, until mixture begins to mass together.) Divide pastry, making one portion slightly larger than the other. Wrap each in plastic wrap and chill at least 1 hour or until firm.

2. Meanwhile, prepare Filling: Bring large pot of water to boiling. Add peaches; blanch 30 seconds. Drain in colander. When cool enough to handle, peel. Pit and cut into wedges; place in large bowl. (You should have about 6 cups.)

3. Add granulated and brown sugars, tapioca, cardamom, bourbon and lemon rind to peaches; stir to combine. Let stand 15 minutes.

4. Preheat oven to moderate (375°).

5. Roll out larger portion of pastry on floured surface to 14-inch circle. Fit into 9-inch pie plate. Scrape filling into prepared shell. Place on foil-lined baking sheet.

6. Roll out top crust on floured surface to 12-inch circle. Place on top of pie. Fold overhang under; pinch to form stand-up edge; crimp to make decorative pattern. Cut slits in top crust for steam to escape. Tent with aluminum foil.

7. Bake in preheated moderate oven (375°) for 1 hour. Remove foil tent. Bake another 15 minutes or until filling is bubbly and crust is golden. Cool to room temperature. Serve.

CHOCOLATE-PRALINE PIE

This pie is terrific with or without the praline. Be sure to assemble the pie no more than an hour ahead since the praline has a tendency to begin to "weep."

Bake crust at 375° for 8 minutes.
Makes 10 servings.
Nutrient Value Per Serving: 406 calories, 6 g protein, 27 g fat, 39 g carbohydrate, 314 mg sodium, 90 mg cholesterol.

Praline:
½ cup sugar
¼ cup water
½ cup blanched slivered almonds

Chocolate Cookie Crust:
28 chocolate wafer cookies
6 tablespoons *un*salted butter, melted

Chocolate Filling:
3 tablespoons cornstarch
2 tablespoons sugar
¼ teaspoon salt
2 cups milk
4 squares (1 ounce each) semisweet chocolate, chopped
2 egg yolks
2 tablespoons *un*salted butter
1½ teaspoons grated orange rind

½ cup heavy cream, softly whipped

1. Prepare Praline (*see How-To, next page*): Grease baking sheet and metal spatula. Stir together sugar and water in small heavy saucepan. Bring to simmering over medium heat, washing down sides of pan with brush dipped in cold water; simmer, without stirring, until mixture turns an amber color, about 20 minutes. Watch carefully to make sure mixture does not turn too dark. Stir in almonds. Quickly pour praline onto prepared baking sheet. Using metal spatula, spread almond praline into a thin sheet; set aside.
2. Preheat oven to moderate (375°).
3. Prepare Chocolate Cookie Crust: Place chocolate wafer cookies in food processor or, working in batches, in blender. Whirl until cookies become fine crumbs. (You should have about 1½ cups.) Combine cookie crumbs and melted butter in 9-inch pie plate. Press cookie crumbs evenly over bottom and up side of pie plate.
4. Bake crust in preheated moderate oven (375°) for 8 minutes. Remove to wire rack to cool.
5. Prepare Chocolate Filling: Combine cornstarch, sugar and salt in heavy, medium-size saucepan. Stir in milk and chocolate. Cook, stirring constantly, over medium heat until mixture thickens and chocolate melts. Beat egg yolks lightly in medium-size bowl; stir in small amount of chocolate mixture. Pour yolk mixture back into chocolate mixture, stirring continuously to prevent lumping. Return saucepan to heat; cook over low heat, stirring constantly, about 2 minutes or until mixture is very thick; do not let boil or overcook. Remove saucepan from heat. Stir in butter and grated orange rind. Pour chocolate filling into metal bowl. Place plastic wrap directly on surface of filling. Refrigerate filling 2 hours or until chilled.
6. To assemble pie: About 1 hour before serving, crush half the praline. Spread crushed praline evenly over bottom of pie crust. Spoon chocolate filling into pie crust. Spoon whipped cream onto center of pie, spreading evenly out to edges. Break remaining praline into large pieces and use to garnish top of pie.

Make-Ahead Tip: The praline can be made 1 or 2 days ahead and stored in an airtight container in a cool dry place. To assemble the pie a day ahead, omit the crushed praline in the bottom of the crust, and garnish with the whipped cream and chunks of praline just before serving.

LEFTOVER PRALINE
Sprinkle any leftover praline over ice cream or whipped cream garnishes on other desserts.

HOW TO MAKE PRALINE

1. Simmer together sugar and water in heavy saucepan, without stirring, until mixture turns amber, about 20 minutes.

2. Stir nuts into saucepan. Quickly pour onto greased cookie sheet.

3. Using greased metal spatula, spread praline into thin sheet. Let cool.

4. Lift cooled praline from cookie sheet with metal spatula.

5. Break praline into small pieces. Use as directed in recipes.

APPLE PIE WITH STREUSEL TOPPING

LOW-CHOLESTEROL

Bake at 400° for 15 minutes; then at 350° for 45 to 55 minutes.
Makes 8 servings.
Nutrient Value Per Serving: 412 calories, 4 g protein, 20 g fat, 56 g carbohydrate, 210 mg sodium, 25 mg cholesterol.

Pastry:
1¼ cups all-purpose flour
½ teaspoon salt
¼ cup (½ stick) chilled *un*salted butter, cut into pats
¼ cup chilled solid vegetable shortening
3 to 4 tablespoons cold water

Filling:
2¾ pounds Granny Smith apples (about 4 large), pared, cored and thinly sliced
¼ cup firmly packed brown sugar
¼ cup granulated sugar
2 tablespoons all-purpose flour
1 teaspoon grated lemon rind
1 tablespoon lemon juice
½ teaspoon ground cinnamon

Streusel Topping:
½ cup all-purpose flour
½ cup firmly packed brown sugar
½ teaspoon ground cinnamon
¼ teaspoon ground ginger
¼ cup (½ stick) *un*salted butter, cut into pats
¾ cup walnuts, coarsely chopped

1. Prepare Pastry: Stir together flour and salt in medium-size bowl. Cut in butter and shortening with pastry blender until mixture resembles coarse meal. Sprinkle cold water, 1 tablespoon at a time, over mixture, tossing lightly with fork after each addition until pastry is just moist enough to hold together. Shape pastry into disk. Wrap in plastic wrap and chill 1 hour or until firm.
2. Preheat oven to hot (400°).
3. Roll pastry out on lightly floured surface with floured rolling pin into

11-inch circle. Transfer to 9-inch pie plate. Trim pastry, leaving 1-inch overhang. Fold overhang under; pinch to form stand-up edge; crimp.
4. Prepare Filling: Combine apples, sugars, flour, lemon rind, lemon juice and cinnamon in large bowl.
5. Prepare Topping: Combine flour, brown sugar, cinnamon and ginger in small bowl. Cut in butter until mixture is coarsely crumbled. Stir in walnuts.
6. Spoon filling evenly into pie shell. Spoon topping evenly over apples.
7. Bake pie in preheated hot oven (400°) for 15 minutes. Reduce oven temperature to 350°. Loosely cover topping with foil to prevent overbrowning. Bake 45 to 55 minutes or until apples are tender. Let stand 15 minutes.

FLAKY CRUST
This is our version of an old-fashioned pie with very thinly sliced apples and a flaky half-butter, half-shortening crust.

APPLE PIE MAKE-AHEAD TIP:
The pastry can be made 2 or 3 days ahead and refrigerated, well wrapped.

GINGERED PEAR AND CHERRY PIE

LOW-CHOLESTEROL

An old-fashioned pear pie, updated with dried cherries and a little crystallized ginger. Vary the amount of dried cherries to suit your own taste.

Bake at 400° for 15 minutes; then at 375° for 40 minutes.
Makes 8 servings.
Nutrient Value Per Serving: 278 calories, 3 g protein, 10 g fat, 46 g carbohydrate, 159 mg sodium, 13 mg cholesterol.

Gingered Pastry:

1¼ cups all-purpose flour
1 teaspoon ground ginger
½ teaspoon salt
¼ cup (½ stick) chilled *un*salted butter, cut into pats
¼ cup chilled solid vegetable shortening, in pieces
3 to 4 tablespoons cold water

Pear Filling:

6 pears, pared, cored and cut into ¼-inch-thick slices (3 pounds pears or about 7 cups sliced)
½ to 1 cup dried cherries
⅓ cup sugar
¼ cup all-purpose flour
2 tablespoons lemon juice
1 tablespoon finely chopped crystallized ginger

1 tablespoon milk
Sugar, for sprinkling

1. Prepare Pastry: Stir together flour, ginger and salt in medium-size bowl. Cut in butter and shortening with pastry blender until mixture resembles coarse meal. Sprinkle cold water, 1 tablespoon at a time, over mixture, tossing lightly with fork after each addition, until pastry is just moist enough to hold together. Shape pastry into disk. Wrap in plastic wrap and chill 1 hour or until firm.

GINGERED PEAR AND CHERRY PIE MAKE-AHEAD TIP:
Pastry can be made up to 3 days ahead and refrigerated, well wrapped.

2. Preheat oven to hot (400°).
3. Roll out two-thirds of pastry on lightly floured surface with floured rolling pin into 10-inch circle. Transfer pastry to 9-inch pie plate. Trim pastry even with edge of pie plate.
4. Roll any pastry trimmings and remaining one-third pastry into circle ¹⁄₁₆-inch thick. Using 3-inch leaf cookie cutter, cut out 15 leaves. Using a 2½-inch pear cookie cutter, cut out 8 pears.
5. Prepare Filling: Combine pears, dried cherries, sugar, flour, lemon juice and crystallized ginger in large bowl. Spoon filling evenly into pie shell. Press pastry leaves onto outer edge of pastry crust. Arrange pastry pears on filling in decorative design. Brush pastry leaves and pears with milk. Sprinkle pastry with some sugar.
6. Bake pie in preheated hot oven (400°) for 15 minutes. Reduce oven temperature to moderate (375°). Tent pie loosely with aluminum foil. Bake 40 minutes or until fruit is tender and pastry is golden brown.

SUMMER PIE-EATING CONTEST

Gingered Pear and Cherry Pie (this page)

Bourbon-Scented Peach Pie (490)

Apple Pie with Streusel Topping (493)

Assorted Ice Creams

Coffee, Tea and Club Soda

BERRY TART

LOW-CHOLESTEROL

Bake at 400° for 30 minutes.
Makes 10 servings.
Nutrient Value Per Serving: 244 calories,
3 g protein, 11 g fat, 34 g carbohydrate,
95 mg sodium, 25 mg cholesterol.

Nut Pastry:
1¼ cups all-purpose flour
¼ cup ground toasted almonds
2 tablespoons sugar
½ cup (1 stick) chilled *un*salted butter,
    cut into pats
3 to 4 tablespoons cold water

Berry Filling:
1 pint raspberries
½ pint blackberries
½ to ¾ cup sugar
3 tablespoons cornstarch
1 teaspoon finely chopped pared fresh
    ginger
½ teaspoon grated lime rind

1. Prepare Nut Pastry: Stir together
flour, almonds and sugar in medium-size
bowl. Cut in butter with pastry blender
until mixture resembles coarse meal.
Sprinkle cold water, 1 tablespoon at a
time, over mixture, tossing lightly with
fork just until pastry holds together.
Shape into disk. Wrap in plastic wrap
and chill 1 hour or until firm.
2. Preheat oven to hot (400°).
3. Roll two-thirds of pastry out on
floured surface with floured rolling pin
into 11-inch circle. Fit into 9-inch tart
pan with removable bottom. Fold pastry
over and press to reinforce side of tart.
4. Roll out remaining pastry into
8-inch circle. Make a lattice top (*see
How-To, at right*).
5. Prepare Filling: Combine raspberries,
blackberries, sugar, cornstarch, ginger,
and lime rind in large bowl. Spoon
berry filling into tart shell. Center largest pastry V's on fruit filling, with
points meeting in center and each V

covering a quarter of the pie. Trim
strips even with pastry edge if necessary;
pinch firmly to seal edge. Repeat with
remaining smaller pastry V's.
6. Bake in preheated hot oven (400°)
for 30 minutes or until filling is bubbly
and pastry is golden brown. Remove
to wire rack to cool. Remove side of
pan.

HOW TO MAKE A LATTICE TOP FOR A PIE
1. Roll out top crust into circle. Cut
into quarters. Cut each quarter into
three V's with sides about ¾ inch wide.

2. Center largest V's on top of pie filling, with points facing each other.
Repeat with smaller V's.

Walnut Filling:
2 cups heavy cream
1 cup sugar
2 eggs
2 cups walnut pieces
2 teaspoons vanilla

1. Prepare Pastry: Combine flour and salt in medium-size bowl. Cut in butter and shortening with pastry blender until mixture is crumbly. Sprinkle cold water, 1 tablespoon at a time, over mixture, tossing lightly with fork after each addition, until pastry is just moist enough to hold together. Shape pastry into disk. Wrap in plastic wrap and chill 1 hour or until firm.
2. Preheat oven to hot (400°).
3. Roll pastry out on lightly floured surface with lightly floured rolling pin into 11-inch circle. Fit into 9-inch tart pan with removable bottom. Fold overhang over and press to reinforce side of tart. Line pastry with aluminum foil. Fill with pie weights or dried beans.
4. Bake tart shell in preheated hot oven (400°) for 15 minutes. Remove foil and weights. Bake 5 to 10 minutes to brown. Do not turn oven off.
5. While tart shell is baking prepare Walnut Filling: Combine cream and sugar in medium-size, heavy saucepan. Simmer, stirring, for 30 to 35 minutes or until golden brown; raise heat slightly during last minutes. Do not let mixture boil over.
6. Lightly beat eggs in small bowl. Stir in small amount of hot cream mixture. Pour egg mixture into cream mixture in saucepan, stirring constantly to prevent lumping. Stir in walnuts and vanilla. Pour into tart shell.
7. Return to oven and bake at 400° for 20 minutes or until custard is nearly set and top is browned. Let cool on rack 15 minutes. Remove side of pan. Serve warm or at room temperature.

Make-Ahead Tip: The tart can be prepared a day ahead and refrigerated. Serve at room temperature.

WALNUT TART

FOR CHOCOHOLICS ONLY
For an even more extravagant dessert, brush 2 squares (1 ounce each) melted semisweet chocolate over the bottom of the partially baked tart shell.

Bake tart shell at 400° for 20 to 25 minutes; bake tart at 400° for 20 minutes.
Makes 10 servings.
Nutrient Value Per Serving: 556 calories, 7 g protein, 43 g fat, 38 g carbohydrate, 190 mg sodium, 120 mg cholesterol.

Pastry:
1¼ cups all-purpose flour
½ teaspoon salt
¼ cup (½ stick) chilled *un*salted butter, cut into pats
¼ cup chilled solid vegetable shortening
3 to 4 tablespoons cold water

Banana Chocolate Chip Loaf

Bake at 350° for 1 hour.
Makes 10 slices.
Nutrient Value Per Slice: 343 calories,
4 g protein, 18 g fat, 43 g carbohydrate,
135 mg sodium, 80 mg cholesterol.

2 cups cake flour
1½ teaspoons baking powder
¼ teaspoon salt
1 cup mashed ripe banana (about 2 large
    bananas)
2 tablespoons milk
¾ cup (1½ sticks) *un*salted butter
¾ cup sugar
2 eggs
1 teaspoon vanilla
½ cup miniature chocolate chips

1. Preheat oven to moderate (350°).
Grease and flour 9 × 5 × 3-inch loaf pan.
2. Stir together flour, baking powder
and salt in medium-size bowl. Beat
together banana and milk in another
medium-size bowl until smooth.
3. Beat butter in large bowl until
smooth and creamy. Gradually beat in
sugar until light and fluffy. Beat in eggs,
one at a time, beating well after each
addition. Beat in vanilla. Beat flour
mixture and banana mixture into butter
mixture. Stir in chocolate chips. Scrape
batter into prepared pan, spreading
evenly.
4. Bake in preheated moderate oven
(350°) for 1 hour or until wooden pick
inserted in center comes out clean.
Tent with aluminum foil if browning
too quickly. Cool loaf in pan on wire
rack for 15 minutes. Remove loaf from
pan to wire rack and cool completely.

**BANANA CHOCOLATE
CHIP LOAF
MAKE-AHEAD TIP:**
Wrap loaf in alumi-
num foil and store at
room temperature for
up to 3 days.

MEASURING
Measure dry ingredi-
ents such as flour and
sugar by lightly
spooning them into
the appropriate sized
dry measuring cup,
and leveling off any
excess by sweeping
the dull side of a
knife across the top.
Tapping the measur-
ing cup, packing it
down, or scooping up
ingredients with the
measuring cup will
result in an inaccurate
measurement. (See
page 9.)

LOWERING 25°
Our recipes assume
you use shiny, light
metal pans for bak-
ing. When baking in
glass, enamel or dark
metal pans, reduce
the oven temperature
by 25° to prevent the
cake from cooking
too quickly on the
outer edges and
browning too much.

CARROT CAKE

Bake at 350° for 45 to 50 minutes.
Makes 12 servings.
Nutrient Value Per Serving: 479 calories, 6 g protein, 27 g fat, 55 g carbohydrate, 477 mg sodium, 123 mg cholesterol.

2 cups all-purpose flour
1½ teaspoons ground cinnamon
1 teaspoon baking soda
1 teaspoon baking powder
¾ teaspoon salt
¼ teaspoon ground cloves
¼ teaspoon grated nutmeg
1¼ cups (2½ sticks) *un*salted butter, at room temperature
1 cup firmly packed light brown sugar
¾ cup granulated sugar
4 eggs
1 pound carrots, pared and shredded (about 4¼ cups)
1 cup chopped walnuts
⅓ cup golden raisins

1. Preheat oven to moderate (350°). Grease and flour 13 × 9 × 2-inch baking pan.
2. Stir together flour, cinnamon, baking soda, baking powder, salt, cloves and nutmeg in medium-size bowl.
3. Beat together butter, brown sugar and granulated sugar in large bowl until fluffy. Add eggs, one at a time, beating well after each addition. Beat in flour mixture until blended. Stir in carrots, walnuts and raisins. Spoon batter into prepared pan.
4. Bake in preheated moderate oven (350°) for 45 to 50 minutes or until wooden pick inserted in center of cake comes out clean. Cool in pan on wire rack 10 minutes. Remove from pan and cool completely on wire rack. Wrap and keep refrigerated.

Make-Ahead Tip: Cake can be refrigerated, covered, for up to 3 days.

HOMECOMING WEEKEND

Maple-Sesame Glazed Popcorn (100) and Garlic Pita Chips (96)

Tex-Mex Beef Stew with Corn (140)

Basmati Rice

Caesar Salad with Hard-Cooked Egg (148)

Garlic Bread

Carrot Cake (this page)

ORANGE POPPY SEED CAKE

Bake at 350° for 40 to 45 minutes.
Makes 16 servings.
Nutrient Value Per Serving: 450 calories,
4 g protein, 28 g fat, 47 g carbohydrate,
123 mg sodium, 123 mg cholesterol.

2 tablespoons poppy seeds
¼ cup milk
3 cups cake flour
2½ teaspoons baking powder
¼ teaspoon salt
1¼ cups (2½ sticks) *un*salted butter, at
    room temperature
1¾ cups sugar
4 eggs
1 tablespoon finely grated orange rind
2 teaspoons vanilla
¾ cup orange juice
Orange Glaze *(recipe follows)*

1. Soak poppy seeds in milk in bowl for
2 hours.
2. Preheat oven to moderate (350°).

Generously grease and flour 12-cup
Bundt pan.
3. Stir together flour, baking powder
and salt in medium-size bowl.
4. Beat butter in large bowl until
smooth. Gradually beat in sugar until
light and fluffy. Add eggs, one at a
time, beating well after each addition.
Beat in orange rind, vanilla and poppy
seed mixture. Beat in flour mixture and
orange juice alternately in 3 additions,
beginning and ending with flour. Scrape
batter into prepared pan.
5. Bake in preheated moderate oven
(350°) for 40 to 45 minutes or until
wooden pick inserted in center comes
out clean. Cool cake in pan on wire
rack for 15 minutes. Invert cake onto
rack and cool completely.
6. Place sheet of waxed paper under
cake rack. Pour Orange Glaze over
cake, allowing glaze to drip down sides.
Let set. Transfer to serving plate.

Orange Glaze: Combine 1 cup 10X (confectioners') sugar and 1 teaspoon finely
grated orange rind in small bowl. Whisk
in 3 to 4 tablespoons orange juice to
make good glazing consistency.

**POPPY SEED CAKE
SERVING IDEAS**
An old-fashioned
cake, ideal for a quiet
afternoon with a cup
of tea. Or cut a slice
for breakfast.

**POPPY SEED CAKE
MAKE-AHEAD TIP:**
Wrap cake well in
aluminum foil and
store at room temper-
ature for up to 3
days.

CREAMING
When creaming but-
ter and sugar
together, beat sugar
gradually into *soft-
ened* butter to be
sure it's absorbed.
Then beat on high
speed until mixture is
very light and fluffy in
texture, contains no
lumps and is almost
white in color. Stop
frequently to scrape
down the side of the
bowl. Creaming
incorporates air into
the butter to give the
cake a light, fine-
grained texture.

PEAR-CRANBERRY UPSIDE-DOWN CAKE

Serve warm or at room temperature, with a little whipped cream or even vanilla ice cream.

Bake at 350° for 35 to 40 minutes.
Makes 16 servings.
Nutrient Value Per Serving: 208 calories, 2 g protein, 9 g fat, 31 g carbohydrate, 217 mg sodium, 37 mg cholesterol.

Topping:
6 tablespoons *un*salted butter
½ cup firmly packed dark brown sugar
1 can (16 ounces) pear halves in light syrup, drained and halved lengthwise
1 cup fresh or frozen cranberries

Cake:
1½ cups all-purpose flour
¾ cup granulated sugar
2 teaspoons baking powder
½ teaspoon salt
⅔ cup milk
⅓ cup *un*salted butter, at room temperature
1 egg
2 teaspoons grated lemon rind
1 teaspoon vanilla

1. Preheat oven to moderate (350°).
2. Prepare Topping: Place butter in 9 × 9 × 2-inch-square baking pan. Place pan with butter in oven until butter melts. Stir in brown sugar. Arrange pears, rounded-side down, decoratively over sugar mixture in pan. Sprinkle cranberries between pears.
3. Prepare Cake: Stir together flour, sugar, baking powder and salt in large bowl. Beat in milk and butter until smooth. Beat in egg, lemon rind and vanilla until blended. Pour batter evenly over fruit in baking pan.
4. Bake in preheated moderate oven (350°) for 35 to 40 minutes or until wooden pick inserted in center of cake comes out clean. Cool cake in pan on wire rack 5 minutes. Loosen cake from sides of pan. Place serving platter on top of pan; invert cake onto platter, letting glaze drip down sides of cake. Serve warm or at room temperature.

Make-Ahead Tip: The cake can be made a day ahead and refrigerated. Warm in preheated slow oven (250°) or serve at room temperature.

LEMON PECAN TORTE

The rich, nutty-tasting cake layers are cushioned with a tart lemon-curd-like filling. There is little flour in this cake, and most of the lightness comes from the beaten egg whites. A special cake for your very special occasions.

Bake at 350° for 20 minutes.
**Makes 16 servings
(9-inch two-layer cake).**
Nutrient Value Per Serving: 341 calories, 5 g protein, 26 g fat, 26 g carbohydrate, 155 mg sodium, 135 mg cholesterol.

Lemon Filling:
¾ cup sugar
½ cup (1 stick) *un*salted butter
2 tablespoons grated lemon rind
¼ cup lemon juice
2 eggs, slightly beaten

Pecan Cake:
3 cups pecan halves, toasted
¼ cup all-purpose flour
1 teaspoon baking powder
¼ teaspoon salt
6 eggs, separated
¾ cup plus 1 tablespoon sugar

⅔ cup heavy cream

1. Prepare Lemon Filling: Stir together sugar, butter, lemon rind and juice in top of double boiler set over hot, not boiling, water until butter melts. Gradually and vigorously stir in eggs; cook, stirring constantly, until mixture is thickened and coats back of spoon, about 15 minutes (temperature should be 160°); do not boil. Strain, if necessary. Pour mixture into bowl; place plastic wrap directly on surface and refrigerate until well chilled.
2. Preheat oven to moderate (350°). Grease two 9-inch round cake pans (*see Note, next page*); line bottoms with waxed paper and grease paper.
3. Prepare Pecan Cake: Coarsely chop enough toasted pecans to measure 2

tablespoons; set aside. Place remaining pecans in food processor or blender. Whirl until finely ground. Stir together ground pecans, flour, baking powder and salt in small bowl.
4. Beat together egg yolks and the ¾ cup sugar in medium-size bowl until thick and lemon colored.
5. Beat egg whites in large bowl with clean beaters until soft peaks form. Gently fold egg whites with beaten yolks alternately with pecan mixture, beginning and ending with whites. Pour batter equally into prepared pans.
6. Bake in preheated moderate oven (350°) for 20 minutes or until cake springs back when lightly touched with finger. Cool cakes in pans on racks. Remove from pans; remove waxed paper. Cool on racks, 10 minutes.
7. To assemble: Place one cake layer on
(continued)

DIVIDING BATTER
The easiest way to divide cake batter evenly between pans is to use a measuring cup or ladle and go back and forth between pans.

MAKE-AHEAD TIP:
The filling can be made up to 2 days ahead and refrigerated, covered.

LEMON PECAN TORTE (*continued*)

serving platter. Spread one half of filling over surface. Top with second cake layer, then remaining filling.

8. Beat cream and 1 tablespoon sugar in bowl until stiff peaks form. Using pastry bag fitted with large star tip, pipe cream around top edge of cake. Sprinkle with reserved pecans.

Note: The cake can also be prepared with three 8-inch round cake pans. Bake layers for 15 minutes.

HOW TO CUT CAKE INTO LAYERS

1. Measure with ruler halfway up side of cake. Mark spot with wooden pick. Repeat all around side of cake.

2. Gently rest hand on top of cake to steady it. With a long, thin serrated knife, cut cake horizontally in half with a gentle sawing motion, using the wooden picks as a guide. Remove the picks when done.

PECAN POUND CAKE

Eat plain, *spoon fresh fruit over, or even toast for breakfast.*

Bake at 350° for 55 to 60 minutes.
Makes 10 servings.
Nutrient Value Per Serving: 403 calories, 5 g protein, 25 g fat, 41 g carbohydrate, 141 mg sodium, 88 mg cholesterol.

1¾ cups all-purpose flour
1½ teaspoons baking powder
½ teaspoon ground cinnamon
¼ teaspoon salt
¼ teaspoon ground ginger
¾ cup plus 2 tablespoons (1¾ sticks)
    *un*salted butter, at room temperature
1 cup granulated sugar
2 eggs
2 teaspoons vanilla
⅔ cup milk
1 cup chopped pecans
1 tablespoon 10X (confectioners') sugar

1. Preheat oven to moderate (350°). Grease and flour 9×5×3-inch loaf pan.
2. Stir together flour, baking powder, cinnamon, salt and ginger in medium-size bowl.
3. Beat the butter in large bowl until smooth. Gradually beat in sugar and beat until light and fluffy. Beat in eggs, one at a time, beating well after each addition. Beat in vanilla. Beat in flour mixture in three additions, alternating with milk, beginning and ending with flour mixture. Stir in pecans. Scrape batter into prepared pan.
4. Bake in preheated moderate oven (350°) for 55 to 60 minutes or until wooden pick inserted in center comes out clean. Tent with aluminum foil if cake begins to brown too much. Cool cake in pan on wire rack 15 minutes. Invert pan and cool cake completely on rack. To serve, dust with 10X sugar.

Make-Ahead Tip: Wrap well in aluminum foil and store at room temperature for up to 3 days.

CHOCOLATE RASPBERRY CAKE

Bake at 350° for 15 to 18 minutes.
Makes 12 servings (9-inch three-layer cake).
Nutrient Value Per Serving: 442 calories,
6 g protein, 26 g fat, 49 g carbohydrate,
133 mg sodium, 190 mg cholesterol.

¾ cup cake flour
1 cup sugar
½ cup unsweetened Dutch processed
    cocoa powder
¼ teaspoon salt
¼ teaspoon baking powder
8 eggs, separated
⅓ cup vegetable oil
1 teaspoon vanilla
1 cup seedless raspberry jam
Chocolate Whipped Cream Frosting *(see
    recipe, page 510)*

1. Preheat oven to moderate (350°).
Grease three 9-inch round cake pans.

Line bottoms with waxed paper circles.
Dust sides with flour; tap out excess.
2. Stir together ¾ cup flour, ¼ cup
sugar, cocoa powder, salt and baking
powder in medium-size bowl.
3. Beat together egg yolks, ½ cup sugar
and oil in large bowl until thick and
pale yellow. Beat in vanilla.
4. Beat egg whites with clean beaters in
medium-size bowl until foamy. Gradually add remaining ¼ cup sugar, 1
tablespoon at a time, beating until stiff,
but not dry, peaks form.
5. Sift one-third of flour mixture over
egg yolk mixture and add one-third of
egg whites; gently fold until combined.
Repeat with remaining flour mixture
and egg white mixture in 2 more additions. Divide batter equally among the
three pans.
6. Bake in preheated moderate oven
(350°) for 15 to 18 minutes or until
wooden pick inserted in centers comes
out clean. Loosen cakes from sides of
pans with thin knife. Immediately

(continued)

(continued)

**CHOCOLATE
RASPBERRY CAKE
MAKE-AHEAD TIP:**
The cake can be
made a day ahead
and refrigerated,
covered.

STORING CAKES
- Cover cut surfaces
with plastic wrap to
keep moist. Store in a
covered cake keeper
or invert a large bowl
over the cake plate.
- Cakes with butter,
cream, or cream
cheese frostings or
custard fillings should
be stored in the
refrigerator. Cakes
with sugar frostings
can be stored, cov-
ered, at room tem-
perature for up to
3 days.
- To freeze unfrosted
cake, tightly wrap
individual layers in
aluminum foil, freezer
wrap or a double
layer of plastic wrap.
Freeze for up to 4
months. Unfrosted
layers will thaw at
room temperature in
1 hour.

BAKING CAKE LAYERS

■ Bake single layers in center of oven in the middle of the oven rack. Good circulation is important when baking more than one layer—stagger pans on oven racks so they do not block heat circulation from one another.

■ A cake may fall if the oven door is opened too soon, if the oven is too hot, or if there is not enough flour in the batter.

■ A cake is done when the sides shrink back slightly from the side of the pan (except sponge and chiffon cakes, which cling tightly to the pan) or when the top springs back when lightly pressed with fingertips or when a cake tester or wooden pick inserted in the center of the cake comes out clean.

CAKE BATTER

When mixing flour and liquids into a cake batter, mix on low speed until they are just incorporated. Stir in any flour that remains around the edge of bowl by hand. Overbeating may result in a cake with a tough texture.

CHOCOLATE RASPBERRY CAKE (continued)

invert cakes onto wire racks to cool completely. Remove waxed paper.

7. Place one cake layer on serving plate. Spread top with half the raspberry jam. Spread about ⅔ cup frosting over jam. Stack second layer on top of first. Spread with remaining jam and about ⅔ cup frosting. Place third layer on top. Frost top and sides with remaining frosting. Refrigerate.

HOW TO TELL WHEN A CAKE IS DONE

1. Insert a wooden pick in the center of cake. If done, the pick should come out clean, with only a few crumbs attached, if any.

2. If the cake is not done, the wooden pick will be wet and covered with crumbs.

FROSTING A LAYER CAKE

Let the cake cool completely before frosting. Trim off any crisp edges and brush away any loose crumbs.

1. To keep the cake plate clean, cover the edges with strips of wax paper. Place the strips just slightly under the edge of the cake. Center the bottom cake layer, cut or flat side up, on the plate on top of paper. Spread filling over the layer, leaving a border all around the edge. Top with the second layer, top side up. Flat sides should face each other to prevent slipping. Swirl frosting up and down sides, swirling it up to make a slight ridge above the rim of the cake. Turn the cake plate as you work. When the sides are frosted, carefully slide out the paper. Touch up the bottom with more frosting, if needed.

2. Frost the top of the cake, swirling the frosting or spreading it smoothly. If the layers scoot around while frosting the cake, insert thin metal skewers or bamboo skewers through the layers to hold them together. When the cake is frosted, pull the skewers out and smooth over the holes.

PEANUT BUTTER CAKE

Bake at 350° for 25 to 30 minutes.
Makes 12 servings (9-inch two-layer cake).
Nutrient Value Per Serving: 640 calories,
12 g protein, 41 g fat, 59 g carbohydrate,
268 mg sodium, 103 mg cholesterol.

2 cups cake flour
2 teaspoons baking powder
¼ teaspoon salt
¾ cup (1½ sticks) *un*salted butter, at
    room temperature
1⅓ cups sugar
2 eggs
¾ cup creamy peanut butter
1 tablespoon vanilla

1 cup milk
Chocolate Frosting and Peanut Butter
    Filling *(recipe page 506)*
Chocolate Glaze *(recipe page 506)*

1. Preheat oven to moderate (350°).
Grease two 9-inch round cake pans.
Line bottoms with waxed paper circles.
Dust sides with flour, tapping out
excess.
2. Stir together 2 cups flour, baking
powder and salt in medium-size bowl.
3. Beat butter in large bowl until
smooth. Gradually beat in sugar until
light and fluffy. Beat in eggs, one at a
time, beating well after each addition.
Beat in peanut butter and vanilla. Beat
(continued)

PEANUT BUTTER CAKE (*continued*)

in flour mixture and milk, alternately in three additions, beginning and ending with flour. Scrape into prepared pans.

4. Bake in preheated moderate oven (350°) for 25 to 30 minutes or until wooden pick inserted in center comes out clean. Cool cakes in pans on wire rack for 15 minutes. Invert cakes onto wire rack and cool completely. Remove waxed paper.

5. Place one cake layer on serving plate. Spread top with Peanut Butter Filling. Place second layer on top. Frost top and sides with Chocolate Frosting. Pour Chocolate Glaze over top; tip plate in swirling motion so glaze drips down sides of cake.

Make-Ahead Tip: The cake can be made a day ahead and stored, covered, at room temperature.

CHOCOLATE FROSTING AND PEANUT BUTTER FILLING

Makes 12 servings.
Nutrient Value Per Serving:
258 calories, 6 g protein, 20 g fat,
19 g carbohydrate, 54 mg sodium,
34 mg cholesterol.

¾ cup (1½ sticks) *un*salted butter, at room temperature
1¼ cups 10X (confectioners') sugar
2 tablespoons milk
1 teaspoon vanilla
½ cup creamy peanut butter
½ cup Chocolate Glaze *(recipe follows)*

1. Prepare butter base for Filling and Frosting: Beat butter in large bowl until smooth. Gradually beat in 10X sugar until smooth. Add milk and vanilla; beat at high speed until very light and fluffy.

2. To prepare Peanut Butter Filling: Place ½ cup of butter mixture in small bowl. Stir in peanut butter.

3. To prepare Chocolate Frosting: Beat ½ cup cooled Chocolate Glaze into remaining butter mixture in large bowl.

KIDSTUFF BIRTHDAY PARTY

Fruit and Cheese Mini-Snacks (102)

Easy Mini-Pizzas (94)

Nutty Chicken Wings (257)

Peanut Butter Cake (505)

Vanilla Ice Cream with Chocolate Sauce (537) or Raspberry Vanilla Sauce (538)

CHOCOLATE GLAZE

Makes about 1 cup.
Nutrient Value Per Tablespoon: 70 calories,
1 g protein, 4 g fat, 7 g carbohydrate,
0 mg sodium, 1 mg cholesterol.

1 cup semisweet chocolate chips
⅓ cup water
2 tablespoons *un*salted butter, at room temperature
1 teaspoon vanilla

1. Melt chocolate with water, butter and vanilla in top of double boiler over hot, not boiling water. Stir until smooth. Cool completely.

2. Use ½ cup Glaze for Chocolate Frosting. Reserve the other ½ cup Glaze to pour over frosted Peanut Butter Cake. Gently reheat the glaze if it becomes too thick to pour.

CITRUS LAYER CAKE

Bake at 375° for 20 minutes.
Makes 12 servings (9-inch two-layer cakes).
Nutrient Value Per Serving: 413 calories,
4 g protein, 23 g fat, 48 g carbohydrate,
334 mg sodium, 77 mg cholesterol.

2⅓ cups cake flour
1 tablespoon baking powder
½ teaspoon salt
¼ teaspoon baking soda
½ cup (1 stick) *un*salted butter, at room
    temperature
1½ cups sugar
1 teaspoon vanilla
2 teaspoons grated orange rind
1 teaspoon grated lemon rind
¾ cup milk
2 tablespoons orange juice
1 tablespoon lemon juice
4 egg whites
Citrus Whipped Cream Frosting *(see
    recipe, page 510)*
Orange and lemon slices, for garnish
    (optional)

1. Preheat oven to moderate (375°).
Grease and flour two 9-inch round cake
pans.
2. Stir together 2⅓ cups flour, baking
powder, salt and baking soda in
medium-size bowl.
3. Beat together butter and 1 cup sugar
in large bowl until light and fluffy. Beat
in vanilla and orange and lemon rinds.
Alternately beat in flour mixture and
milk, beginning and ending with flour.
Beat in orange juice and lemon juice.
4. Beat egg whites in bowl with electric
mixer until foamy. Gradually add
remaining ½ cup sugar, beating until
stiff, but not dry, peaks form.
5. Gently fold beaten egg whites into
batter. Pour into prepared pans, dividing equally.
6. Bake in preheated moderate oven
(375°) for 20 minutes or until wooden
pick inserted in center of cakes comes
out clean. Cool cakes in pans on wire
racks 10 minutes. Remove cakes from

pans to racks to cool completely.
7. Fill and frost with Citrus Whipped
Cream Frosting. Garnish with orange
and lemon slices, if you wish.

Make-Ahead Tip: The cake layers can be
made a day ahead and stored, wrapped,
at room temperature. The entire cake
can be prepared a day ahead and refrigerated, covered.

LEMON ANGEL FOOD CAKE

LOW-FAT • LOW-CHOLESTEROL

Preheat oven to 375°; bake cake at 350° for
35 to 40 minutes.
Makes 10 servings.
Nutrient Value Per Serving: 169 calories,
5 g protein, 0 g fat, 37 g carbohydrate,
120 mg sodium, 0 mg cholesterol.

¾ cup cake flour
¼ teaspoon salt
1½ cups granulated sugar
12 egg whites
½ teaspoon cream of tartar
1 teaspoon finely grated lemon rind
½ teaspoon lemon extract
1 tablespoon 10X (confectioners') sugar

1. Preheat oven to moderate (375°).
Position rack in lower third of oven.
2. Sift together flour, salt and ¾ cup
sugar, twice.
3. Beat egg whites in large bowl until
foamy. Add cream of tartar; beat until
soft peaks form. Beat in remaining ¾
cup sugar, 1 tablespoon at a time. Beat
in lemon rind and extract. Continue
beating until stiff peaks form.
4. Resift one-third of flour mixture over
beaten whites; gently fold in just until
combined. Repeat twice more with
(continued)

HEAVEN SENT
Serve Lemon Angel
Food Cake with ice
cream or drizzle with
Raspberry Vanilla
Sauce (page 538).
Store egg yolks, cov-
ered with water, in
tightly covered clean
container in refrigera-
tor for up to 2 days.
Use yolks for scram-
bled eggs or omelets.

LEMON ANGEL FOOD CAKE (*continued*)

remaining flour mixture. Scrape batter into ungreased 10-inch tube pan; smooth top.

5. Place cake in oven. Reduce oven temperature to 350°. Bake for 35 to 40 minutes or until top is golden brown and cracks in top are dry. Invert cake pan and slip center tube over top of bottle so pan is elevated. Cool 1 hour. Gently remove cake from pan. Dust top with 10X sugar. At serving time use 2 forks to tear cake apart into "slices"; a knife will squish the cake down.

Make-Ahead Tip: The cake, well wrapped in aluminum foil, can be kept at room temperature for up to 2 days.

BANANA LAYER CAKE

Bake at 350° for 30 to 35 minutes.
Makes 12 servings (9-inch two-layer cake).
Nutrient Value Per Serving: 436 calories, 4 g protein, 27 g fat, 45 g carbohydrate, 264 mg sodium, 90 mg cholesterol.

2 cups cake flour
2 teaspoons baking powder
1 teaspoon baking soda
½ teaspoon salt
1¼ cups sugar
⅔ cup solid vegetable shortening
2 eggs
1 cup mashed ripe banana
1 teaspoon vanilla
⅓ cup buttermilk
2 cups heavy cream, whipped OR: Cream Cheese Frosting (*see recipe, page 509*) OR: Fudge Frosting (*see recipe; page 509*)
2 bananas, peeled and sliced

1. Preheat oven to moderate (350°). Grease and flour two 9-inch round cake pans.
2. Stir together flour, baking powder, baking soda and salt in medium-size bowl.
3. Beat together sugar and shortening in large bowl until well combined. Beat in eggs, mashed banana and vanilla. Beat in flour mixture. Then beat in buttermilk. Pour batter into prepared pans, dividing equally.
4. Bake in preheated moderate oven (350°) for 30 to 35 minutes or until wooden pick inserted in center of cakes comes out clean. Cool cakes in pans on wire racks 10 minutes. Remove cakes from pans to racks to cool completely.
5. Place one cake layer on serving plate. Cover with ⅔ cup whipped cream or frosting and half the banana slices. Top with second cake layer. Frost outside of cake with whipped cream or frosting. Decorate with remaining banana slices. If using frosting, chill or let stand until firm. Then garnish with banana slices.

Make-Ahead Tip: The cake layers can be made a day ahead and stored, wrapped, at room temperature. The assembled cake can be made a day ahead and refrigerated, covered.

CREAM CHEESE FROSTING

QUICK

A *traditional cream cheese frosting. Great on Carrot Cake (page 498) or Banana Layer Cake (page 508) or on pound cake.*

Makes about 2 cups. Enough to fill and frost 9-inch two-layer cake (12 servings). Recipe can be halved or doubled.
Nutrient Value Per Serving: 213 calories, 1 g protein, 7 g fat, 38 g carbohydrate, 80 mg sodium, 21 mg cholesterol.

1 package (8 ounces) cream cheese, softened
1 teaspoon milk
1 teaspoon vanilla
⅛ teaspoon salt
1 box (16 ounces) 10X (confectioners') sugar

1. Beat cream cheese in large bowl until smooth. Beat in milk, vanilla and salt.
2. Gradually beat in 10X sugar until the mixture is smooth.

FUDGE FROSTING

QUICK

A *quick and easy, rich and creamy fudge frosting prepared without using a candy thermometer.*

Makes 2 cups frosting. Enough to frost an 8- or 9-inch two-layer cake, or top of 13 × 9-inch cake (12 servings). Recipe can be halved or doubled.
Nutrient Value Per Serving: 264 calories, 2 g protein, 13 g fat, 39 g carbohydrate, 90 mg sodium, 23 mg cholesterol.

2 cups sugar
⅔ cup milk

½ cup (1 stick) *un*salted butter
4 squares (1 ounce each) unsweetened chocolate
2 tablespoons light corn syrup
1½ teaspoons vanilla

1. Combine sugar, milk, butter, chocolate and corn syrup in medium-size saucepan. Bring to boiling over medium heat; boil 1 minute, stirring constantly. Remove saucepan from heat. Stir in vanilla. Cool to lukewarm.
2. Beat mixture with electric mixer until good spreading consistency. (Mixture will thicken on standing.)

CARAMEL FROSTING

QUICK

An *easy frosting with a rich and buttery caramel flavor.*

Makes about 1⅓ cups frosting. Enough to frost top of 8-, 9- or 10-inch single-layer cake (8 servings). Recipe can be halved or doubled.
Nutrient Value Per Serving: 270 calories, 0 g protein, 9 g fat, 49 g carbohydrate, 90 mg sodium, 24 mg cholesterol.

1 cup firmly packed dark brown sugar
⅓ cup *un*salted butter
⅓ cup half-and-half
½ teaspoon vanilla
1½ cups 10X (confectioners') sugar

1. Combine brown sugar, butter and half-and-half in medium-size saucepan. Bring to boiling over medium heat; boil 2 minutes, stirring constantly. Remove saucepan from heat. Stir in vanilla. Cool to lukewarm.
2. Beat mixture with electric mixer, gradually adding 10X sugar until good spreading consistency. (Mixture will thicken on standing.)

CHOCOLATE WHIPPED CREAM FROSTING

LOW-SODIUM

A *rich frosting, good on practically anything.*

Makes about 3 cups. Enough to fill and frost 9-inch three-layer cake (12 servings).
Nutrient Value Per Serving: 167 calories, 1 g protein, 16 g fat, 6 g carbohydrate, 12 mg sodium, 48 mg cholesterol.

3 squares (1 ounce each) semisweet chocolate
2 tablespoons *un*salted butter
⅓ cup plus 1¼ cups heavy cream
2 tablespoons 10X (confectioners') sugar
1 teaspoon vanilla

1. Melt together chocolate, butter and the ⅓ cup heavy cream in top of double boiler over hot, not boiling water; stir until smooth. Cool completely.
2. Beat together the remaining 1¼ cups heavy cream, 10X sugar and vanilla in medium-size bowl just until soft peaks begin to form. Do not overbeat or frosting will become grainy.
3. Fold one-third of the whipped cream into the chocolate mixture just until combined. Fold the chocolate mixture into the remaining whipped cream just until combined.

CITRUS WHIPPED CREAM FROSTING

LOW-SODIUM

Delicious *on plain or chocolate cakes.*

Makes 4 cups. Enough to fill and frost 9-inch two-layer cake (12 servings).
Nutrient Value Per Serving: 154 calories, 1 g protein, 15 g fat, 5 g carbohydrate, 15 mg sodium, 54 mg cholesterol.

2 cups heavy cream
1 teaspoon grated orange rind
1 teaspoon grated lemon rind
½ teaspoon vanilla
¼ cup sugar

1. Beat together heavy cream, orange and lemon rinds, and vanilla in large bowl until soft peaks form.
2. Gradually beat in sugar until stiff peaks form.

HOLIDAY CAKE BUFFET

Citrus Layer Cake (507)

Chocolate Raspberry Cake (503)

Orange Poppy Seed Cake (499)

Carrot Cake (498)

Champagne, Coffee or Spiced Tea (560)

DOUBLE CHOCOLATE-CHUNK COOKIES

Bake at 375° for 10 to 12 minutes.
Makes about 2 dozen cookies.
Nutrient Value Per Cookie: 160 calories,
2 g protein, 10 g fat, 18 g carbohydrate,
83 mg sodium, 19 mg cholesterol.

6 squares (1 ounce each) semisweet
    chocolate
1¼ cups all-purpose flour
½ teaspoon baking soda
¼ teaspoon salt
½ cup (1 stick) *un*salted butter, at room
    temperature
½ cup firmly packed light brown sugar
½ cup granulated sugar
1 egg
1 teaspoon vanilla
1 cup coarsely chopped pecans

1. Preheat oven to moderate (375°).
2. Melt 1 square of chocolate in small saucepan. Cut remaining 5 squares chocolate into ½-inch chunks.
3. Stir together flour, baking soda and salt in small bowl.
4. Beat butter in large bowl until creamy. Gradually beat in brown sugar and granulated sugar until light and fluffy. Beat in egg and vanilla. Then beat in melted chocolate.
5. Beat flour, baking soda and salt into chocolate mixture until well blended. Stir in chocolate chunks and pecans.
6. Drop dough by rounded tablespoons, 2 inches apart, onto ungreased baking sheets.
7. Bake in preheated moderate oven (375°) for 10 to 12 minutes or until slightly browned around edge. Remove cookies from baking sheets to wire racks to cool.

A FAVORITE!
A good old-fashioned, slightly chewy cookie with lots of chocolate and chopped pecans. The double chocolate? There's chocolate in the batter itself and chunks of chocolate in the cookie. (Pictured below.)

DOUBLE CHOCOLATE-CHUNK COOKIES MAKE-AHEAD TIP:
Cookies can be stored in airtight container at room temperature for up to one week.

COOKIE BAKING TIPS
■ Cookies should be of a uniform thickness and size so they will bake in the same amount of time.
■ Use a cold cookie sheet to help cookies keep their shape.
■ Bake one cookie sheet at a time and be sure that the sheet fits in the oven with at least 1 inch of space around its edges for the proper heat circulation.
■ Unless the recipe directs otherwise, remove baked cookies from cookie sheet to wire rack immediately to prevent further baking.

Top, Banana Sandwich Cookies (page 518); bottom, Double Chocolate-Chunk Cookies (this page).

KITCHEN-SINK COOKIES

WHAT'S IN THE KITCHEN SINK?
We've mixed whole-wheat flour and old-fashioned oats with the all-purpose flour in these cookies. We've included raisins, nuts, coconut and apricots, but you can vary the add-ins to suit your own fancy. (Pictured on page 519.)

KITCHEN SINK COOKIES MAKE-AHEAD TIP:
Store in airtight container at room temperature for up to one week.

Bake at 350° for 12 minutes.
Makes 3 dozen cookies.
Nutrient Value Per Cookie: 123 calories, 2 g protein, 5 g fat, 18 g carbohydrate, 83 mg sodium, 19 mg cholesterol.

1 cup raisins
¾ cup water
1 cup all-purpose flour
¾ cup whole-wheat flour
½ cup old-fashioned oats (not quick-cooking)
½ teaspoon baking soda
½ teaspoon baking powder
½ teaspoon salt
½ cup (1 stick) *un*salted butter
1¼ cups firmly packed light brown sugar
2 eggs
1 teaspoon vanilla
½ cup chopped walnuts
½ cup chopped pecans
½ cup sweetened flaked coconut
½ cup dried apricots, finely chopped

1. Combine raisins and water in small saucepan. Bring to boiling. Lower heat and simmer for 5 minutes. Set aside to cool completely. The raisins should absorb most of the liquid.
2. Preheat oven to moderate (350°). Grease large baking sheets.
3. Combine all-purpose flour, whole-wheat flour, oats, baking soda, baking powder and salt in medium-size bowl.
4. Beat butter in large bowl until creamy. Gradually beat in light brown sugar until light and fluffy. Add eggs, one at a time, beating well after each addition. Mix in vanilla. Stir in dry ingredients until combined. Stir in walnuts, pecans, coconut, apricots and raisins along with unabsorbed liquid.
5. Drop dough by rounded tablespoonfuls, 3 inches apart, onto greased baking sheets.
6. Bake in preheated moderate oven (350°) for 12 minutes or until golden brown. Remove cookies from baking sheets to wire racks to cool.

SPICED OATMEAL DATE COOKIES

A slightly chewy cookie that's addictive. If you prefer raisins, substitute them for the dates. (Pictured on page 514.)

Bake at 350° for 15 minutes.
Makes about 3 dozen cookies.
Nutrient Value Per Cookie: 117 calories, 2 g protein, 4 g fat, 18 g carbohydrate, 89 mg sodium, 22 mg cholesterol.

1⅓ cups all-purpose flour
1¼ teaspoons baking soda
¾ teaspoon ground cinnamon
¼ teaspoon ground allspice
¼ teaspoon salt
¾ cup (1½ sticks) *un*salted butter, at room temperature
1¼ cups firmly packed light brown sugar
2 eggs
1 teaspoon vanilla
2¼ cups quick-cooking oats (not instant)
1 cup pitted dates, chopped

1. Preheat oven to moderate (350°).
2. Stir together flour, baking soda, cinnamon, allspice and salt in small bowl.
3. Beat butter in large bowl until creamy. Gradually beat in sugar until light and fluffy. Add eggs, one at a time, beating well after each addition. Beat in vanilla.
4. Gradually beat flour mixture into butter mixture until blended. Stir in oats and dates.
5. Drop dough by rounded tablespoonfuls, 2 inches apart, on ungreased baking sheets.
6. Bake in preheated moderate oven (350°) until golden for about 15 minutes. Remove cookies from baking sheets to wire racks to cool.

Make-Ahead Tip: Cookies can be stored in airtight container at room temperature for up to one week.

CARAMEL PECAN WAFERS

Crisp, buttery and rich. (Pictured on page 520.)

Bake at 375° for 8 to 10 minutes.
Makes about 5 dozen wafers.
Nutrient Value Per Wafer: 55 calories,
0 g protein, 3 g fat, 6 g carbohydrate,
41 mg sodium, 12 mg cholesterol.

---

1 cup (2 sticks) *un*salted butter, at room
    temperature
¾ cup firmly packed dark brown sugar
1 egg yolk
2 teaspoons vanilla
1⅓ cups all-purpose flour
¼ teaspoon salt
¼ cup pecans, toasted and finely
    chopped
¼ cup granulated sugar

1. Preheat oven to moderate (375°). Grease large baking sheets.
2. Beat butter in large bowl until creamy. Gradually beat in dark brown sugar until light and fluffy. Beat in egg yolk and vanilla. Stir in flour, salt and pecans.
3. Drop dough by teaspoonfuls, 3 inches apart, on prepared baking sheets. Dip bottom of a drinking glass in granulated sugar; press down dough into ¼-inch-thick circles, 1½ inches in diameter.
4. Bake in preheated moderate oven (375°) for 8 to 10 minutes or until edges brown. Cool 1 minute before carefully removing from baking sheets to wire racks. Cool completely.

Make-Ahead Tip: Wafers can be stored in airtight container at room temperature for up to one week.

DOUBLE-GINGER MOLASSES CRISPS

The double ginger—both fresh and ground. (Pictured on page 514.)

Bake at 375° for 7 to 8 minutes.
Makes about 5 dozen 2-inch cookies.
Nutrient Value Per Cookie: 34 calories,
0 g protein, 2 g fat, 7 g carbohydrate,
8 mg sodium, 4 mg cholesterol.

½ cup (1 stick) *un*salted butter, at room
    temperature
¾ cup firmly packed light brown sugar
¼ cup dark molasses
1 egg white
1 tablespoon grated pared fresh ginger
1 teaspoon ground ginger
½ teaspoon ground cinnamon
¼ teaspoon ground cloves
¼ teaspoon salt
2 cups all-purpose flour
1½ teaspoons baking soda
¼ cup granulated sugar

1. Preheat oven to moderate (375°).
2. Beat butter in small bowl until creamy. Gradually beat in brown sugar and molasses until fluffy. Add egg white, fresh ginger, ground ginger, cinnamon, cloves and salt; beat to blend.
3. Combine flour and baking soda in small bowl. Slowly add to butter mixture, beating on low speed just until combined.
4. Place sugar in small dish. Drop dough by rounded measuring teaspoonfuls into sugar; toss to coat. Place 1½ inches apart on ungreased baking sheets.
5. Bake in preheated moderate oven (375°) for 7 minutes for chewy cookies, or 8 minutes for crispy cookies. Remove cookies from sheets to racks to cool.

DOUBLE-GINGER MOLASSES CRISPS MAKE-AHEAD TIP:
Cookie dough can be made through Step 3 and refrigerated, covered, for up to 5 days before baking. Cookies can be stored in airtight container at room temperature for up to one week.

COOKIE STORAGE
■ Store cookies in an airtight box or tin to keep them crisp. Separate layers with sheets of wax paper or aluminum foil. If crisp cookies soften, place in a slow oven (300°) for a few minutes to make them crisp again.
■ Store soft cookies and crisp cookies separately. To keep soft cookies soft, place a slice of apple in the container to prevent them from drying out.

LEMON WAFERS

Drizzle cookies with melted chocolate if you'd like. (Pictured below.)

Lower right, clockwise: Lemon Wafers (this page); Double-Ginger Molasses Crisps (page 513); and Spiced Oatmeal Date Cookies (512).

Bake at 375° for 8 to 10 minutes.
Makes about 3 dozen wafers.
Nutrient Value Per Wafer: 57 calories, 1 g protein, 3 g fat, 8 g carbohydrate, 52 mg sodium, 13 mg cholesterol.

1¼ cups all-purpose flour
¾ teaspoon baking powder
¼ teaspoon salt
½ cup (1 stick) *un*salted butter, at room temperature
¾ cup sugar
1 egg
1 to 2 tablespoons grated lemon rind
½ teaspoon vanilla

1. Preheat oven to moderate (375°).
2. Stir together flour, baking powder and salt in medium-size bowl.
3. Beat butter in large bowl until creamy. Gradually beat in sugar until light and fluffy. Beat in egg, lemon rind and vanilla until smooth. Gradually beat flour mixture into butter mixture until well blended.
4. Drop dough by heaping teaspoonfuls, 2 inches apart, onto ungreased baking sheets.
5. Bake in preheated moderate oven (375°) for 8 to 10 minutes or until edges of cookies are lightly browned. Remove cookies from baking sheets to wire racks to cool.

Make-Ahead Tip: Store wafers in airtight container at room temperature for up to one week.

TAILGATE PICNIC

Chicken-Honey Mustard Spread (89) with Chili-Corn Madeleines (90)

Black Bean Soup (121)

Baked Ham and Brie Sandwich with Honey-Mustard (109)

Lemon Wafers (this page)

Maple Nut Rugelach

These really are best if served the same day they are prepared. Almonds or pecans would also work well. (Pictured at right.)

Bake at 350° for 15 to 20 minutes.
Makes 32 cookies.
Nutrient Value Per Cookie: 98 calories, 2 g protein, 6 g fat, 11 g carbohydrate, 49 mg sodium, 16 mg cholesterol.

Dough:
4 ounces (half 8-ounce package) cream cheese, softened
⅓ cup *un*salted butter, at room temperature
¼ cup sugar
2 tablespoons maple syrup
¼ teaspoon salt
1 egg yolk
1½ cups all-purpose flour

Filling:
1 cup finely ground walnuts
⅓ cup sugar
2 tablespoons maple syrup
⅛ teaspoon ground cinnamon

1 egg white
1 teaspoon water
1 teaspoon sugar

1. Prepare Dough: Beat together cream cheese, butter, sugar, maple syrup, salt and egg yolk in large bowl until smooth. Beat in flour just until blended. Shape dough into ball. Refrigerate, wrapped, until firm, about 2 hours.
2. Prepare Filling: Stir together walnuts, the ⅓ cup sugar, maple syrup and cinnamon in medium-size bowl.
3. Preheat oven to moderate (350°). Grease 2 large baking sheets.
4. Divide dough in half. Roll half of dough out on lightly floured surface
(continued)

Top, Fig Thumbprints (page 516); bottom, Maple Nut Rugelach (this page).

MAPLE NUT RUGELACH (*continued*)

with floured rolling pin to ⅛-inch thickness. Cut dough into 10-inch circle. Spread circle with half of the walnut mixture. Cut dough into 16 equal pie-shaped wedges. Starting with wide edge, roll up each wedge, jelly-roll fashion. Place cookies, point side down, on baking sheets. Repeat with remaining half of dough and filling.

5. Lightly beat egg white with water; brush over cookies. Sprinkle cookies with the 1 teaspoon sugar.

6. Bake in preheated moderate oven (350°) for 15 to 20 minutes or until lightly browned. Remove to wire racks to cool.

Make-Ahead Tip: Rugelach can be stored in airtight container at room temperature for up to 2 days.

FIG THUMBPRINTS

It is best to fill the cookies just before serving, either with our fig mixture or your favorite jam. (Pictured on page 515.)

Bake at 350° for 12 to 15 minutes.
Makes about 2½ dozen cookies.
Nutrient Value Per Cookie: 87 calories, 1 g protein, 5 g fat, 10 g carbohydrate, 71 mg sodium, 15 mg cholesterol.

Fig Filling:
Half 8-ounce package Calimyrna figs
2 tablespoons granulated sugar
2 teaspoons grated orange rind
¼ cup water
1 tablespoon orange juice
1 tablespoon brandy *(optional)*

Cookies:
½ cup (1 stick) *un*salted butter, at room temperature
⅓ cup firmly packed light brown sugar

1 egg
½ teaspoon vanilla
1¼ cups all-purpose flour
½ teaspoon salt
½ to ¾ cup ground walnuts

1. Prepare Filling: Place figs, sugar and orange rind in food processor. Whirl until pureed.

2. Place fig mixture, water, orange juice and brandy, if using, in small saucepan. Bring to boiling. Lower heat; simmer, uncovered, until thickened, about 5 minutes. Cool to room temperature.

3. Prepare Cookies: Beat butter in large bowl until creamy. Gradually beat in brown sugar until light and fluffy. Beat in egg and vanilla until blended. Stir in flour and salt just until dough holds together. Refrigerate dough until firm, about 30 minutes.

4. Preheat oven to moderate (350°)

5. Shape dough into 1-inch balls. Roll balls in walnuts to coat. Place 1 inch apart on ungreased baking sheets. With thumb, make indentation in center of each ball.

6. Bake in preheated moderate oven (350°) for 12 to 15 minutes or until lightly browned. Remove the cookies from the baking sheets to wire racks to cool completely.

7. Before serving, fill each cookie with Fig Filling.

Make-Ahead Tip: Cookies can be made ahead and stored, without filling, in airtight container at room temperature for up to one week. Filling can be made a few days ahead and refrigerated, covered. Fill cookies just before serving.

FREEZING COOKIES AND COOKIE DOUGH

■ Cookie dough and baked cookies can be frozen and stored for up to six months. Freeze baked cookies in an airtight box, separating layers with plastic wrap or aluminum foil. Wrap cookie dough in aluminum foil or a double layer of plastic wrap before freezing. Thaw cookies at room temperature for 10 minutes.

■ Thaw dough just until soft enough to use.

■ Rolled cookie dough can be frozen, already cut out into shapes, and transferred, still frozen, to cookie sheets or plastic freezer bags and stored in the freezer.

■ Freeze bar-cookie dough in the pan in which it is to be baked; cover with plastic wrap, then foil.

■ Thaw refrigerator cookie rolls just enough to slice.

**HAZELNUT
SHORTBREAD
SERVING IDEAS**
Tasty with sherbet
and ices, or with your
best brewed coffee.
The cake flour makes
for a slightly more
delicate shortbread.

MAKE-AHEAD TIP:
Shortbread can be
stored in airtight con-
tainer at room tem-
perature for up to
one week.

HAZELNUT SHORTBREAD

Bake at 325° for 30 to 35 minutes.
Makes 2 dozen shortbread wedges.
Nutrient Value Per Wedge: 164 calories,
2 g protein, 11 g fat, 15 g carbohydrate,
120 mg sodium, 26 mg cholesterol.

3 cups cake flour OR: all-purpose flour
¾ cup 10X (confectioners') sugar
½ cup hazelnuts, toasted and ground
¼ teaspoon salt
1¼ cups (2½ sticks) *un*salted butter, cut
  into small pieces
2 squares (1 ounce each) semisweet
  chocolate, melted *(optional)*

1. Preheat oven to slow (325°).
2. Stir together flour, 10X sugar, hazelnuts and salt in medium-size bowl.
3. Cut butter into flour mixture with
pastry blender until mixture resembles
coarse meal. Knead until mixture holds
together. Divide dough in half.
4. Place each half on ungreased baking
sheet. Pat each out into 9-inch circle;
crimp edges. Cut each circle into 12
equal wedges, but do not separate.
5. Bake in preheated slow oven (325°)
for 30 to 35 minutes or until golden
brown. Drizzle chocolate, if using, over
hot shortbread. Cool 10 minutes. Then
recut to separate wedges. Cool the
shortbread completely.

BANANA SANDWICH COOKIES

Bake at 350° for 15 minutes.
Makes about 35 sandwich cookies.
Nutrient Value Per Sandwich Cookie:
156 calories, 1 g protein, 8 g fat,
21 g carbohydrate, 85 mg sodium,
19 mg cholesterol.

Cookies:
1 cup (2 sticks) *un*salted butter, at room
    temperature
1 cup granulated sugar
1 teaspoon vanilla
2 medium-size ripe bananas (9 ounces),
    peeled and sliced
2½ cups all-purpose flour
¼ teaspoon salt
⅓ cup walnuts, finely chopped

Filling:
2 cups 10X (confectioners') sugar
¼ cup (½ stick) *un*salted butter, at room
    temperature
2 tablespoons cream cheese, softened
2 tablespoons dark rum OR: 1 tablespoon
    vanilla
⅛ teaspoon grated nutmeg

1. Preheat oven to moderate (350°).
Grease large baking sheets.
2. Prepare Cookies: Beat butter in large
bowl until creamy. Gradually beat in ¾
cup granulated sugar and vanilla until
light and fluffy. Add banana; beat on
medium speed for 1 minute. Beat in
flour and salt. Stir in walnuts.
3. Drop dough by scant teaspoonfuls,
2½ inches apart, onto prepared baking
sheets. Dip bottom of a drinking glass
in remaining ¼ cup sugar. Press down
dough into 2-inch circles.
4. Bake in preheated moderate oven
(350°) for 15 minutes or until edges are
golden brown. Remove cookies from
baking sheets to wire rack to cool.
5. Prepare Filling: Beat together 10X
sugar, butter, cream cheese, rum and
nutmeg in small bowl until smooth.
Sandwich cookies together.

CHOCOLATE PEANUT-BUTTER BARS

Bake at 375° for 10 to 15 minutes.
Makes about 2 dozen bars.
Nutrient Value Per Bar: 169 calories,
3 g protein, 11 g fat, 17 g carbohydrate,
109 mg sodium, 19 mg cholesterol.

1 package (8 ounces) semisweet
    chocolate squares
½ cup (1 stick) *un*salted butter, at room
    temperature
½ cup chunky peanut butter
⅓ cup firmly packed light brown sugar
⅓ cup granulated sugar
1 egg
½ teaspoon vanilla
1 cup all-purpose flour
½ teaspoon baking soda
¼ teaspoon salt
⅓ cup unsalted peanuts, chopped

1. Preheat oven to moderate (375°).
Grease 13 × 9 × 2-inch baking pan.
2. Cut 2 squares of chocolate into
coarse chunks.
3. Beat together butter, peanut butter,
brown sugar, granulated sugar, egg and
vanilla in large bowl until smooth. Stir
together flour, baking soda and salt in
medium-size bowl. Stir flour mixture
into butter mixture until blended. Stir
in chocolate chunks. Spread mixture in
prepared pan.
4. Bake in preheated moderate oven
(375°) for 10 to 15 minutes or until
golden brown. Remove from oven.
5. Chop remaining chocolate. Sprinkle
chocolate over hot cookies in pan.
Cover with aluminum foil and let stand
5 minutes or until chocolate is melted.
Remove foil; spread melted chocolate
evenly over surface of cookies. Sprinkle
with peanuts. Cool in pan on wire rack.
Cut into bars.

TO SANDWICH OR NOT?
You have a choice here: The banana cookies can be sandwiched together or left as singles and dusted with 10X sugar. (Pictured on page 511.)

BANANA SANDWICH COOKIES MAKE-AHEAD TIP:
Filled cookies can be refrigerated for up to 3 days, while single cookies can be stored in airtight container at room temperature for up to one week.

CHOCOLATE PEANUT-BUTTER BARS MAKE-AHEAD TIP:
The bars can be stored in airtight container at room temperature for up to 3 days. (Pictured on page 519.)

PEACH STREUSEL BARS

You can substitute your favorite preserves for the peach preserves. (Pictured at right.)

Bake at 375° for 40 minutes.
Makes 12 bars.
Nutrient Value Per Bar: 289 calories,
2 g protein, 12 g fat, 45 g carbohydrate,
169 mg sodium, 31 mg cholesterol.

2 cups all-purpose flour
½ cup firmly packed light brown sugar
1 teaspoon grated lemon rind
¼ teaspoon ground nutmeg
¼ teaspoon salt
¾ cup (1½ sticks) *un*salted butter
1 jar (12 ounces) peach preserves

1. Preheat oven to moderate (375°).
Grease $9 \times 9 \times 2$-inch square baking
pan.
2. Combine flour, sugar, lemon rind,
nutmeg and salt in large bowl. Cut in
butter with pastry blender until mixture
is crumbly. Set aside 1 cup. Pat remaining mixture evenly into prepared pan.
3. Spread preserves evenly over top of
dough in pan, leaving ¼-inch border all
around edges. Sprinkle with reserved
flour mixture.
4. Bake in preheated moderate oven
(375°) for 40 minutes or until lightly
browned. Cool in pan on wire rack.
Cut into 12 bars.

Make-Ahead Tip: Bars can be stored in
airtight container at room temperature
for up to one week.

**From top: Peach Streusel Bars
(this page); Chocolate Peanut-Butter
Bars (page 518); and Kitchen-Sink
Cookies (page 512).**

TOFFEE CRUNCH BARS

*P*ractically *any nut will taste good in this bar, including walnuts or almonds. (Pictured at left.)*

Bake at 350° for 30 minutes.
Makes 15 bars.
Nutrient Value Per Bar: 152 calories,
1 g protein, 11 g fat, 11 g carbohydrate,
64 mg sodium, 11 mg cholesterol.

3 bars (1.4 ounces each)
    chocolate-covered toffee bars
2 tablespoons sugar
½ teaspoon vanilla
1 cup all-purpose flour
⅓ cup *un*salted butter, at room
    temperature
⅓ cup coarsely chopped pecans

1. Preheat oven to moderate (350°). Grease 8 × 8 × 2-inch square baking pan.
2. Place one whole toffee bar in blender or food processor. Whirl until ground. Coarsely chop remaining bars.
3. Combine sugar and vanilla in medium-size bowl. Stir in ground toffee bar and flour. Cut in butter with pastry blender until mixture is crumbly. Press into prepared pan.
4. Bake in preheated moderate oven (350°) for 20 minutes or until lightly browned. Combine chopped toffee bars and pecans in small bowl. Sprinkle evenly over hot mixture in pan. Press down lightly with metal spatula. Bake 10 more minutes. While still hot, cut into bars. Cool in pan on wire rack.

Make-Ahead Tip: Bars can be stored in airtight container at room temperature for up to 3 days.

**Top, Caramel Pecan Wafers
(page 513); bottom, Toffee Crunch
Bars (this page).**

FUDGY BROWNIES

Bake at 350° for 30 minutes.
Makes 12 brownies.
Nutrient Value Per Brownie: 300 calories,
5 g protein, 20 g fat, 30 g carbohydrate,
95 mg sodium, 74 mg cholesterol.

4 squares (1 ounce each) unsweetened
    chocolate, coarsely chopped
½ cup (1 stick) *un*salted butter
1¼ cups sugar
3 eggs, slightly beaten
2 teaspoons vanilla
½ cup all-purpose flour
1 cup walnuts, chopped

1. Melt together chocolate and butter in top of double boiler over hot water. Cool for 15 minutes.

2. Preheat oven to moderate (350°). Line 9 × 9 × 2-inch-square baking pan with aluminum foil. Grease foil.

3. Stir sugar into chocolate mixture. Stir in eggs and vanilla. Stir in flour until blended. Pour into prepared pan, spreading evenly. Sprinkle with walnuts.

4. Bake in preheated moderate oven (350°) for 30 minutes. Cool completely in pan on wire rack. Refrigerate 30 minutes for easier cutting. Invert onto cutting surface. Peel off foil; turn over. Cut into squares.

**FUDGY BROWNIES
MAKE-AHEAD TIP:**
Brownies can be refrigerated, covered, for up to 3 days.

WATER BATH

Custards and puddings need an even, moderate heat to bake smooth and velvety, and to avoid overbaking and possible separation. To ensure this, the baking dish is placed in a larger dish of hot water which acts as an insulator and keeps the temperature uniform.

APPLE AND RAISIN BREAD PUDDING

It may be extravagant, but feel free to serve with a custard sauce, whipped cream or vanilla ice cream, or just drizzle with heavy cream. Try substituting pear for the apple, and golden raisins, chopped dried apricots or currants for the dark raisins.

Makes 8 servings.
Bake at 350° for 40 to 50 minutes.
Nutrient Value Per Serving: 367 calories, 10 g protein, 22 g fat, 33 g carbohydrate, 249 mg sodium, 166 mg cholesterol.

1 loaf (6 ounces) Italian or French bread, cut into ½-inch-thick slices (about 18 slices), lightly toasted
3 tablespoons *unsalted* butter, melted
½ cup raisins
1 small McIntosh apple, pared, cored and sliced
1 tablespoon lemon juice
3 eggs
⅓ cup granulated sugar
3 cups half-and-half
1 teaspoon vanilla
1 teaspoon grated lemon rind
½ teaspoon ground cinnamon
2 tablespoons *sifted* 10X (confectioners') sugar, for garnish

1. Butter 2½-quart shallow baking dish (11¾ × 7½ × 1¾ inches).
2. Arrange bread slices in bottom of dish, overlapping slices. Brush bread with butter. Sprinkle with the raisins.
3. Toss apple slices with lemon juice in small bowl. Scatter over bread in dish.
4. Beat eggs in large bowl until combined. Beat in sugar, a little at a time, until mixture is thick and yellow and falls in ribbon from beaters, 3 to 5 minutes. Stir in half-and-half, vanilla, lemon rind and cinnamon. Pour over bread; press down on bread to completely soak it in custard. Cover and let stand for 30 minutes.
5. Preheat oven to 350°.
6. Place baking dish in larger, shallow baking pan on oven rack. Add enough boiling water to larger pan to come halfway up sides of baking dish.
7. Bake in preheated moderate oven (350°) for 40 to 50 minutes or until pudding is set and puffed and knife inserted near center comes out clean. Tent with aluminum foil if browning too quickly. Let pudding cool to warm. Sprinkle with 10X sugar. Or serve chilled.

Make-Ahead Tip: The pudding can be prepared a day ahead and refrigerated, covered. Serve chilled.

PEAR GRATIN

LOW-SODIUM

A *classic dish—simple to prepare and full of pear flavor. Be sure to use firm, ripe pears. (Pictured on page 524.)*

Bake at 350° for 35 to 40 minutes.
Makes 4 servings.
Nutrient Value Per Serving: 224 calories, 1 g protein, 8 g fat, 40 g carbohydrate, 10 mg sodium, 27 mg cholesterol.

⅓ cup heavy cream
¼ cup maple syrup
1 tablespoon sugar
1½ teaspoons lemon juice
½ teaspoon vanilla
4 firm, ripe pears (6 ounces each)

1. Preheat oven to moderate (350°).
2. Whisk together cream, maple syrup, sugar, lemon juice and vanilla in small bowl. Pare, halve and core pears. Place pears, cut side down, on work surface. Slice thickly widthwise without cutting all the way through. Place, cut side down, in spoke-fashion in 9-inch round quiche dish or 10-inch pie plate. Pour cream mixture over.
3. Bake, uncovered, in preheated moderate oven (350°) for 35 to 40 minutes or until liquid is bubbly and pears are tender. * Serve warm.

*Note: If you find the dish too juicy after it is done, drain off juice into small saucepan and cook over high heat a few minutes until it is reduced and syrupy; pour over fruit.
Microwave Directions (High Power Oven):
Cut pears as above in Step 2. Place in microwave-safe 10-inch pie plate with narrow end of pears towards center. Pour cream mixture over pears. Cover with waxed paper. Microwave at 100% power 2½ minutes. Remove waxed paper; turn pie plate. Microwave at 100% power 2½ minutes until pears are tender.

POACHED PEARS WITH RASPBERRIES

LOW-FAT · LOW-CHOLESTEROL
LOW-SODIUM

The peppercorns give a little bite to our version of poached pears. Serve warm, at room temperature or chilled. (Pictured on page 524.)

Makes 6 servings.
Nutrient Value Per Serving: 154 calories, 1 g protein, 1 g fat, 39 g carbohydrate, 6 mg sodium, 0 mg cholesterol.

1 bottle (750 ml) white Zinfandel wine
⅓ cup sugar
1 tablespoon finely chopped pared fresh ginger
⅛ teaspoon whole black peppercorns, crushed
6 Bosc pears, pared and cored, with stems intact
½ cup raspberries, fresh or individually frozen, no syrup

1. Combine wine, sugar, ginger and peppercorns in Dutch oven or large saucepan. Bring to boiling over medium-high heat; cook 5 minutes or until sugar dissolves.
2. Stand pears upright in pan. Bring to boiling. Lower heat; cover and simmer 20 minutes or until pears are tender. Remove pears with slotted spoon to serving dish.
3. Bring poaching liquid to boiling over high heat; boil 5 minutes. Strain poaching liquid. Return strained poaching liquid to pan.
4. Add raspberries to poaching liquid. Heat over low heat. Spoon liquid over pears. Serve warm, at room temperature, or chilled.

POACHED PEARS MAKE-AHEAD TIP:
The pears and poaching liquid can be prepared a day ahead, without the raspberries. Refrigerate the pears in the poaching liquid, covered. Serve chilled with the raspberries in the liquid. Or gently reheat pears in liquid. Remove pears with slotted spoon to serving plate. Add raspberries to poaching liquid and proceed as in Step 4.

Poached Pears with Raspberries (page 523).

Nectarine and Cranberry Crisp (page 525).

Pear Gratin (page 523).

Berries in Caramel Sauce (page 525).

NECTARINE AND CRANBERRY CRISP

LOW-SODIUM

Bake at 375° for 40 minutes.
Makes 8 servings.
Nutrient Value Per Serving: 499 calories, 4 g protein, 26 g fat, 66 g carbohydrate, 11 mg sodium, 47 mg cholesterol.

Filling:
5 nectarines (about 1½ pounds), pared, pitted and sliced
1½ cups fresh or frozen cranberries, thawed
⅓ cup firmly packed light brown sugar
1 tablespoon *un*salted butter, cut into pieces
1 teaspoon grated lemon rind
1 tablespoon lemon juice
2 teaspoons all-purpose flour
½ teaspoon grated nutmeg

Crisp Topping:
½ cup all-purpose flour
½ cup old-fashioned rolled oats
⅓ cup firmly packed light brown sugar
⅓ cup granulated sugar
½ teaspoon ground cinnamon
½ cup (1 stick) *un*salted butter, cut into pieces
⅔ cup coarsely chopped pecans

1. Preheat oven to moderate (375°).
2. Prepare Filling: Combine nectarines, cranberries, brown sugar, butter, lemon rind and juice, flour and nutmeg in medium-size bowl. Transfer mixture to 10-inch pie plate.
3. Prepare Topping: Combine flour, oats, brown and granulated sugars, and cinnamon in small bowl. Cut in butter with pastry blender until mixture is crumbly. Add pecans. Sprinkle topping over nectarine mixture.
4. Bake in preheated moderate oven (375°) for 40 minutes or until top is golden brown. Serve warm, on its own, or with a drizzle of heavy cream, whipped cream or vanilla ice cream.

BERRIES IN CARAMEL SAUCE

QUICK

Makes 6 servings.
Recipe can be halved or doubled.
Nutrient Value Per Serving: 317 calories, 2 g protein, 19 g fat, 36 g carbohydrate, 32 mg sodium, 71 mg cholesterol.

⅔ cup sugar
¼ cup water
1 tablespoon lemon juice
1¼ cups heavy cream
½ cup milk
1 pint raspberries
1 pint blueberries

1. Stir together sugar, water and lemon juice in medium-size saucepan. Bring to boiling over moderate heat; cook without stirring until mixture is light amber colored, about 4 minutes; watch carefully so mixture doesn't become too dark.
2. Remove from heat. Carefully pour in 1 cup cream and the milk (mixture will sputter). Return to moderate heat. Cook, stirring, until caramel has dissolved and mixture reaches light coating consistency. Remove from heat. Toss in berries. Spoon into individual serving dishes. Drizzle remaining ¼ cup of cream over berries.

Microwave Directions (High Power Oven):
Ingredient Changes: Eliminate milk.
Directions: Combine sugar, water and lemon juice in microwave-safe 4-cup measure. Cover with microwave-safe plastic wrap, vented at one edge. Microwave at 100% power 7½ to 8 minutes until light amber. Stir in 1 cup cream. Microwave, uncovered, at 100% power 1 minute. Toss in berries and serve as above.

BERRIES SERVING IDEA
Use any combination of berries you like. Serve with crisp cookies on the side, or spoon the whole mixture over vanilla ice cream or a slice of plain cake. The caramel sauce is delicious on its own. (Pictured on page 524.)

CARAMEL SAUCE MAKE-AHEAD TIP:
The caramel sauce can be prepared a few days ahead and refrigerated, covered. Gently reheat in small saucepan.

CRISP CONCOCTIONS
Besides nectarines, you can partner cranberries with whatever fruit is in season— apples, peaches or pears. Serve with lightly whipped cream or ice cream.

NECTARINE AND CRANBERRY CRISP MAKE-AHEAD TIP:
The crisp can be assembled a few hours ahead and refrigerated. Allow extra baking time if taking directly from refrigerator. Already baked crisp can be reheated in a preheated moderate oven (350°) until warmed through. (Pictured on page 524.)

SUMMER BERRY PECAN SHORTCAKES

Bake at 425° for 12 to 15 minutes.
Makes 8 servings.
Nutrient Value Per Serving: 389 calories, 7 g protein, 17 g fat, 53 g carbohydrate, 327 mg sodium, 71 mg cholesterol.

Pecan Shortcakes:
2¼ cups all-purpose flour
2 tablespoons sugar
1 tablespoon baking powder
½ teaspoon salt
¼ cup (½ stick) *un*salted butter, cut into pieces
2 tablespoons vegetable shortening
½ cup plus 2 tablespoons chopped pecans
1 egg
½ to ⅔ cup milk

Egg Glaze:
1 egg mixed with 1 teaspoon water

Fruit:
3 pints berries, such as blueberries, strawberries, halved if large, or raspberries
¼ cup strained strawberry or raspberry preserves
1 teaspoon grated lemon rind
1 tablespoon lemon juice
2 tablespoons *sifted* 10X (confectioner's) sugar

1. Preheat oven to hot (425°).
2. Prepare Shortcakes: Stir together flour, sugar, baking powder and salt in medium-size bowl. Cut in butter and shortening with pastry blender until mixture resembles coarse meal. Add the ½ cup pecans. Beat together egg and ½ cup milk in small bowl. Add to flour mixture; stir until ball forms, adding more milk if necessary. Gently knead dough about 3 or 4 times until ingredients are well combined.
3. Pat dough out on lightly floured surface into ½-inch-thick round. Transfer to well-greased baking sheet. Brush with Egg Glaze. Sprinkle top with remaining 2 tablespoons pecans. Score top with large knife into 8 equal wedges, without cutting all the way through.
4. Bake shortcake in preheated hot oven (425°) for 12 to 15 minutes or until golden brown. Tent with aluminum foil if browning too quickly. Transfer to wire rack to cool to warm. Cut into wedges.
5. Meanwhile, prepare Fruit: Combine berries, preserves, lemon rind and lemon juice in large bowl. Cover and refrigerate for at least 30 minutes.
6. To serve: Split shortcake wedges in half horizontally. Spoon some of fruit mixture and juice over bottom half of each wedge. Place top half of wedge on fruit. Sprinkle with 10X sugar.

Make-Ahead Tip: The shortcake and fruit can be prepared several hours ahead and kept separate. Assemble just before serving.

BLUEBERRY-PEACH COBBLER

Serve the cobbler with whipped cream or ice cream, and vary the fruit according to seasonal availability.

Bake at 375° for 35 to 40 minutes.
Makes 8 servings.
Nutrient Value Per Serving: 400 calories, 6 g protein, 19 g fat, 52 g carbohydrate, 319 mg sodium, 86 mg cholesterol.

Fruit Filling:
1½ pounds (4 to 5) peaches, peeled, pitted and sliced
1 pint blueberries
⅓ cup sugar
½ teaspoon grated lemon rind
1 tablespoon lemon juice
2 teaspoons all-purpose flour

Pastry Topping:
2¼ cups all-purpose flour
2 tablespoons sugar
1 tablespoon baking powder
½ teaspoon salt
6 tablespoons *un*salted butter, cut into pieces
¾ to 1 cup heavy cream

Egg Glaze:
1 egg combined with 1 teaspoon water

1. Preheat oven to moderate (375°). Butter 2-quart baking dish no more than 2 inches deep.
2. Prepare Filling: Combine peaches, blueberries, sugar, lemon rind, lemon juice and flour in large bowl. Transfer to baking dish.
3. Prepare Topping: Stir together flour, 1 tablespoon sugar, baking powder and salt in medium-size bowl. Cut in butter with pastry blender until mixture resembles coarse meal. Stir in ¾ cup cream until mixture forms a ball, adding more cream if necessary. Gently knead 3 or 4 times until ingredients are well combined.
4. Roll dough out on lightly floured surface into round large enough to cover fruit. Transfer to baking dish. Crimp edges of dough. Brush dough with Egg Glaze. Sprinkle top with remaining 1 tablespoon sugar. Cut 3 steam vents in center of dough.
5. Bake in preheated moderate oven (375°) for 35 to 40 minutes or until filling is bubbling and crust is golden brown. Tent with aluminum foil if top begins to brown too quickly. Serve warm or at room temperature.

Make-Ahead Tip: The pastry can be prepared up to 2 days ahead and refrigerated, wrapped. The cobbler can be baked earlier in the day and kept at room temperature, covered. Reheat in preheated moderate oven (350°).

From left: Winter
Fruit Compote
(page 529); and
Summer Fruit
Compote
(this page).

COMPOTE SERVING IDEAS

Any seasonal combi-
nation of fruits would
work well in this
refreshing compote,
accented with mint.
Serve as a side dish
with roasted meats
and poultry, or on its
own as dessert, or
with yogurt, cottage
cheese or sherbet.

SUMMER FRUIT COMPOTE

LOW-CALORIE · LOW-FAT
LOW-CHOLESTEROL · LOW-SODIUM

Makes 10 servings (about 10 cups).
Recipe can be halved or doubled.
Nutrient Value Per Serving: 87 calories,
1 g protein, 1 g fat, 21 g carbohydrate,
5 mg sodium, 0 mg cholesterol.

2 peaches or nectarines, peeled, pitted
  and sliced
1 pint blueberries
1 pint strawberries, hulled
2 cups melon balls, such as cantaloupe,
  watermelon and honeydew
2 kiwifruit, peeled and sliced
½ pound Bing cherries, pitted
2 tablespoons honey
½ teaspoon grated orange rind
2 tablespoons orange juice
2 tablespoons finely chopped fresh mint
1 tablespoon lemon juice

1. Combine peaches, blueberries, strawberries, melon, kiwifruit and cherries in
large bowl.
2. Whisk together honey, orange rind,
orange juice, mint and lemon juice in
small bowl. Add dressing to fruit; toss
to combine. Cover and refrigerate for
30 minutes before serving.

Make-Ahead Tip: The compote can be
prepared several hours ahead and refrigerated, covered.

WINTER FRUIT COMPOTE

LOW-FAT · LOW-CHOLESTEROL
LOW-SODIUM

Makes 8 servings (about 7 cups).
Recipe can be halved or doubled.
Nutrient Value Per Serving: 293 calories,
1 g protein, 0 g fat, 76 g carbohydrate,
7 mg sodium, 0 mg cholesterol.

Poaching Liquid:
4 cups water
1½ cups sugar
2 strips (3 inches) orange rind
3 strips (2 inches) lemon rind
3 tablespoons orange juice
2 tablespoons lemon juice
1 stick cinnamon, cracked
1½ tablespoons finely chopped pared
    fresh ginger

Fruit:
2 Granny Smith apples, pared, cored and
    cut into thick slices
2 Bosc pears, pared, cored and cut into
    thick slices
1 cup dried apricots
1 cup raisins
1 teaspoon grated lemon rind
2 tablespoons lemon juice
1 tablespoon crystallized ginger, finely
    chopped

1. Prepare Poaching Liquid: Stir
together water, sugar, orange rind,
lemon rind, orange juice, lemon juice,
cinnamon and ginger in medium-size
saucepan to dissolve sugar. Bring to
boiling. Lower heat; simmer, uncovered, for 10 minutes.
2. Prepare Fruit: Add apples to poaching liquid in saucepan. Simmer, stirring, 2 minutes. Add pears; simmer 2 to
3 minutes or until fruit is just tender.
Stir in apricots and raisins. Let mixture
cool 30 minutes.
3. Strain fruit, reserving liquid. Discard
rinds and cinnamon. Transfer fruit to
heatproof bowl. Return poaching liquid
to saucepan. Boil over high heat until
reduced to 1 cup.

4. Pour syrup over fruit. Stir in lemon
rind, lemon juice and crystallized ginger. Refrigerate, covered, for at least 1
hour or overnight. Serve warm, at room
temperature or chilled.

Make-Ahead Tip: The compote can be
made several days ahead and refrigerated, covered. Gently reheat if serving
warm.
Microwave Directions (High Power Oven):
Ingredient Changes: For the poaching
liquid, use 2 cups hot tap water; reduce
fresh ginger to 2 teaspoons.
Directions: Combine hot water, sugar,
orange rind and juice, lemon rind and
juice, cinnamon stick and ginger in
microwave-safe 3-quart casserole with
lid. Microwave, covered, at 100%
power 7 minutes. Add apples. Microwave, covered, at 100% power 3 minutes. Add pears. Microwave, covered,
at 100% power 5 minutes until fruit is
tender. Stir in apricots and raisins. Let
mixture stand 30 minutes. Strain fruit
as in Step 3 above. Return poaching
liquid to casserole. Microwave, uncovered, at 100% power 18 minutes. Finish
as in Step 4 above.

"MIDNIGHT" SNACK

**Tomato and Sweet Red
Pepper Soup (134)**

Crackers

Winter Fruit Compote (this
page)

COMPOTE COMBO
Vary the dried fruit
combination accord-
ing to your own taste.
Serve the compote on
its own, or with a dol-
lop of sour cream or
yogurt, or spoon the
whole affair over
vanilla ice cream or
toasted slices of
pound cake. *(Pictured
on page 528.)*

CHOCOLATE-AMARETTO PUDDING

A rich, silky chocolate pudding—a little goes a long way.

Makes 8 servings.
Recipe can be halved or doubled.
Nutrient Value Per Serving: 568 calories, 4 g protein, 49 g fat, 32 g carbohydrate, 146 mg sodium, 133 mg cholesterol.

2 cups heavy cream
½ cup (1 stick) *un*salted butter
8 squares (1 ounce each) semisweet chocolate, chopped
1 cup coarsely crushed amaretti cookie crumbs (16 large cookies)
3 tablespoons amaretto liqueur (almond-flavored)
½ cup heavy cream, softly whipped, for garnish *(optional)*
Additional amaretti cookies, crushed, for garnish *(optional)*

1. Heat together heavy cream and butter in medium-size saucepan over medium heat until butter melts. Add chocolate, stirring constantly, until chocolate melts and mixture is smooth. Remove saucepan from heat. Stir in cookie crumbs and liqueur. Pour chocolate mixture into eight 4-ounce ramekins or small soufflé dishes. Cover and refrigerate 1 hour or until mixture is chilled and set.
2. To serve, garnish top of each ramekin with whipped cream and crushed cookies, if you wish.

Make-Ahead Tip: The cups can be made a day ahead, without the garnish, and refrigerated, covered.

CRANBERRY FOOL

LOW-SODIUM

This English-inspired dessert is a mixture of sweetened cooked fruit and whipped cream. Serve in stemmed glasses with cookies or as an attractive addition to a holiday table. (Pictured on book cover.)

Makes 6 servings.
Recipe can be doubled or halved.
Nutrient Value Per Serving: 234 calories, 1 g protein, 15 g fat, 26 g carbohydrate, 16 mg sodium, 54 mg cholesterol.

½ cup granulated sugar
¼ cup water
2 cups fresh or frozen cranberries
1 teaspoon grated orange rind
1 cup chilled heavy cream
3 tablespoons 10X (confectioner's) sugar

1. Combine granulated sugar and water in medium-size saucepan. Cook over moderate heat, stirring occasionally, until clear. Add cranberries; cook, stirring occasionally, for 7 to 8 minutes or cranberries have popped and are soft. Let mixture cool 5 minutes.
2. Transfer cranberries to food processor or blender. Whirl until smooth puree. Transfer mixture to medium-size bowl. Stir in orange rind. Refrigerate, covered, until cold, about 2 hours or overnight.
3. Beat cream with 10X sugar in chilled bowl until soft peaks form. Stir one-quarter of cream into cranberry puree. Fold in remaining cream. Spoon into stemmed glasses or dessert dishes. Or for a special presentation, layer the remaining cream with the cranberry puree in stemmed glasses.

Make-Ahead Tip: The puree can be prepared up to 2 days ahead and refrigerated, covered.

PUMPKIN CHEESECAKE

A rich, creamy cheesecake. Make this the day before you plan to serve it.

Bake at 325° for 1¼ hours.
Makes 10 servings.
Nutrient Value Per Serving: 463 calories, 11 g protein, 22 g fat, 58 g carbohydrate, 580 mg sodium, 140 mg cholesterol.

Crust:
1½ cups graham cracker crumbs (about 20 single-square crackers)
¼ cup granulated sugar
6 tablespoons *un*salted butter, melted
½ teaspoon ground cinnamon

Filling:
3 packages (8 ounces each) Neufchâtel cream cheese, softened
¾ cup firmly packed light brown sugar
¾ cup granulated sugar
5 eggs
1 can (16 ounces) solid-pack pumpkin puree (not pie filling)
1½ teaspoons ground cinnamon
½ teaspoon grated nutmeg
¼ teaspoon ground ginger
¼ teaspoon salt
10X (confectioners') sugar *(optional)*

1. Prepare Crust: Butter 9-inch spring-form pan. Combine crumbs, sugar, butter and cinnamon in small bowl. Press mixture over bottom and halfway up sides of pan. Chill at least 1 hour.
2. Preheat oven to slow (325°).
3. Prepare Filling: Beat cream cheese in large bowl until smooth. Beat in brown and granulated sugars until combined. Add eggs, one at a time, beating well after each addition. Beat in pumpkin puree, cinnamon, nutmeg, ginger and salt. Pour mixture into prepared pan.
4. Bake in preheated slow oven (325°) for 1¼ hours or until just set in center. Tent with foil if overbrowning.
5. Gently run thin knife around edge of pan. Cool cake in pan on wire rack. Refrigerate, covered, overnight.
6. To serve, remove side of pan. Sprinkle with *sifted* 10X sugar, if you wish.

PUMPKIN CHEESECAKE MAKE-AHEAD TIP:
The cake can be prepared up to 2 days ahead and refrigerated, covered.

CHOCOLATE SEMIFREDDO

LOW-SODIUM

(For more semifreddo recipes, see page 533.) Chocolate Semifreddo pictured at left.

Makes 6 servings.
Nutrient Value Per Serving: 362 calories, 7 g protein, 20 g fat, 38 g carbohydrate, 49 mg sodium, 46 mg cholesterol.

1 cup (6 ounces) semisweet chocolate morsels
¾ cup ricotta cheese
2 tablespoons sugar
1 tablespoon amaretto liqueur (almond flavored)
⅔ cup heavy cream
1½ cups (3 ounces) amaretti cookies, crushed

1. Melt chocolate in top of double boiler over simmering, not boiling water. Transfer to medium-size bowl. Cool to room temperature.
2. Combine ricotta, sugar and amaretto in food processor or blender. Whirl until smooth. Stir into chocolate mixture.
3. Beat cream in small bowl to soft peaks. Fold into chocolate mixture. Gently fold in crushed amaretti cookies. Spoon mixture into 6 individual ramekins or other dessert dishes. Cover with plastic wrap. Freeze at least 2 hours before serving.
4. To serve, remove to refrigerator 20 minutes before serving to soften.

Make-Ahead Tip: The recipe can be prepared up to 3 days ahead and frozen. To serve, proceed with Step 4.

From top: Banana Semifreddo (page 533); Strawberry-Raspberry Semifreddo (page 533); and Chocolate Semifreddo (this page).

STRAWBERRY-RASPBERRY SEMIFREDDO

LOW-SODIUM

A *cooling, semi-frozen mixture of straw-berries and raspberries, Italian in origin.*

Makes 8 servings.
Nutrient Value Per Serving: 191 calories, 1 g protein, 11 g fat, 24 g carbohydrate, 13 mg sodium, 41 mg cholesterol.

1 package (10 ounces) frozen
    strawberries, in light syrup
1 package (10 ounces) frozen
    raspberries, in light syrup
1 teaspoon vanilla
1 cup heavy cream
2 tablespoons honey

1. Pour strawberries with their syrup into food processor or blender. Whirl until smooth puree. Transfer to large bowl. Add raspberries with their syrup to food processor. Whirl until smooth puree. Push raspberry puree through fine-meshed sieve into strawberry mixture; discard seeds. Add vanilla.
2. Beat cream in medium-size bowl until foamy. Gradually beat in honey until soft peaks form. Gently fold into fruit mixture. Pour into plastic-wrap-lined 8½ × 3⅝ × 2⅜-inch loaf pan, or eight unlined 4-ounce ramekins. Cover with plastic wrap. Freeze at least 2 hours for ramekins, and 6 hours for loaf.
3. Remove individual ramekins or loaf from freezer 15 minutes before serving or until softened. To serve loaf, turn upside down onto serving platter. Carefully lift off mold and plastic wrap. Slice and serve.

Make-Ahead Tip: The semifreddo can be prepared up to 3 days ahead and frozen, covered. To serve, proceed with Step 3.

BANANA SEMIFREDDO

LOW-SODIUM

Toast almonds at 400° for 7 to 10 minutes.
Makes 8 servings (4 cups).
Recipe can be doubled.
Nutrient Value Per Serving: 239 calories, 3 g protein, 17 g fat, 20 g carbohydrate, 32 mg sodium, 41 mg cholesterol.

½ cup whole unblanched almonds
    (3 ounces)
1 pound ripe bananas, peeled and sliced
¼ cup firmly packed dark brown sugar
2 tablespoons dark rum
2 teaspoons lime juice
1 cup heavy cream
1 tablespoon granulated sugar
Pinch salt

1. Preheat oven to hot (400°).
2. Toast almonds on baking sheet in preheated hot oven (400°) for 7 to 10 minutes or until fragrant and crisp. Cool. Coarsely chop.
3. Combine bananas, brown sugar, rum and lime juice in food processor. Whirl until pureed. Transfer puree to large bowl. Beat cream in small bowl until frothy. Gradually beat in granulated sugar and salt until soft peaks form. Gently fold cream into banana mixture.
4. Reserve 2 tablespoons nuts for garnish. Fold remaining nuts into banana mixture. Spoon into 8 individual ramekins or dessert cups. Cover with plastic wrap and freeze 1½ hours or up to 3 days. (The longer the mixture is frozen the longer it will need to warm up slightly before serving.)
5. To serve: Remove from freezer and let stand for 30 minutes or until softened to smooth and creamy consistency. Sprinkle with reserved nuts.

Make-Ahead Tip: The recipe can be prepared up to 3 days ahead and frozen. To serve, proceed with Step 5.

WHAT ARE SEMIFREDDOS?
They're nothing more than a partially fro-zen mixture of fruit and heavy cream—an almost ice-cream-like custard. Garnish our Banana Semifreddo with toasted chopped almonds and our Chocolate Sauce *(see page 537).* For a large crowd, double the recipe and pre-pare in a loaf pan. To serve, cut into slices. *(Pictured on page 532.)*

DOUBLE CHOCOLATE GRANITA

GREAT GRANITA!
We've combined cocoa powder with semisweet chocolate in this coarse-grained ice. For a mocha ice, substitute espresso powder for the cocoa powder. Garnish with chocolate shavings or curls.

GRANITA MAKE-AHEAD TIP:
The granita can be prepared up to 3 days ahead and stored in freezer, covered. Let soften slightly before serving.

LOW-CALORIE · LOW-FAT
LOW-CHOLESTEROL · LOW-SODIUM

Makes 8 servings (4 cups).
Recipe can be doubled.
Nutrient Value Per ½ Cup: 116 calories,
1 g protein, 3 g fat, 24 g carbohydrate,
0 mg sodium, 0 mg cholesterol.

3 cups water
¾ cup sugar
¼ cup unsweetened cocoa powder
2 squares (1 ounce each) semisweet
    chocolate, chopped OR: morsels
½ teaspoon vanilla
¼ teaspoon ground cinnamon
Pinch grated nutmeg

1. Stir together water and sugar in medium-size saucepan to dissolve sugar. Bring to boiling over high heat; boil 1 minute without stirring. Remove from heat. Stir in cocoa powder, semisweet chocolate, vanilla, cinnamon and nutmeg until well combined and chocolate has melted.
2. Pour into 9 × 9 × 2-inch-square metal pan. Cover loosely with plastic wrap and place in freezer. As sides freeze, pull mixture in toward middle with spoon and return to freezer.
3. To serve, scrape out with an ice cream scoop. If frozen solid, let soften in refrigerator for 10 to 15 minutes.

HOW TO MAKE A GRANITA
1. Pour the granita mixture into a metal baking pan. Place in freezer. As the sides of the granita begin to freeze, pull the mixture with a spoon in from the sides toward the center to redistribute. Return to freezer.

2. When the granita is frozen, scoop out the large, icy crystals and serve.

PINEAPPLE-STRAWBERRY ICE

LOW-CALORIE · LOW-FAT
LOW-CHOLESTEROL · LOW-SODIUM

Makes 8 servings (about 5½ cups).
Recipe can be halved or doubled.
Nutrient Value Per Serving: 144 calories,
1 g protein, 1 g fat, 34 g carbohydrate,
36 mg sodium, 0 mg cholesterol.

1 cup water
⅔ cup sugar
2 vanilla beans, split
8 peppercorns
2 pints strawberries, washed, hulled and
    halved (4 cups)
4 cups fresh pineapple chunks (1½
    pounds) OR: 2 cans (20 ounces each)
    pineapple chunks, drained
2 tablespoons kirsch liqueur OR: other
    cherry-flavored liqueur
⅛ teaspoon salt

1. Stir together water and sugar in
medium-size saucepan to dissolve sugar.
Add vanilla beans and peppercorns.
Bring to boiling over medium heat; boil
4 minutes without stirring.
2. Add strawberries. Cover and cook
without stirring 4 minutes or until berries are soft. Push through sieve,
extracting as much liquid and pulp as
possible. Discard peppercorns.
3. Combine pineapple, kirsch, salt and
berry mixture in food processor or,
working in batches, in a blender. Whirl
until smooth. Pour into $9 \times 9 \times 2$-inch
metal pan. Cover with plastic wrap and
freeze, about 2 to 3 hours. When mixture starts to set around edges, pull set
edges in toward center with spoon and
freeze again.
4. Remove from freezer 15 minutes
before serving for easier scooping.

Make-Ahead Tip: The ice can be prepared up to 3 days ahead and frozen. To
serve, proceed with Step 4.

RASPBERRY-BLUEBERRY BUTTERMILK ICE

LOW-CALORIE · LOW-FAT
LOW-CHOLESTEROL

Makes 12 servings (6 cups).
Recipe can be halved or doubled.
Nutrient Value Per Serving: 96 calories,
2 g protein, 1 g fat, 21 g carbohydrate,
66 mg sodium, 2 mg cholesterol.

1 pint raspberries
1 pint blueberries
3 cups buttermilk
¾ cup sugar
2 teaspoons grated lemon rind

1. Combine raspberries and blueberries
in food processor or, working in batches,
in a blender. Whirl until fruit is pureed.
2. Strain fruit through sieve into large

(continued)

Pineapple-Strawberry
Ice (this page).

ICE CAPADES
Cool and refreshing,
this Pineapple-
Strawberry Ice works
well with either
canned or fresh pine-
apple, and the vanilla
and pepper add a
special lift.

VANILLA SUGAR
If you like, wash off
vanilla beans, let
them air dry and then
place them in your
sugar canister to
make vanilla-flavored
sugar.

Raspberry-Blueberry
Buttermilk Ice
(page 535).

RASPBERRY-BLUEBERRY BUTTERMILK ICE
(*continued*)

bowl; discard seeds. Add buttermilk, sugar and grated lemon rind, stirring to dissolve sugar. Pour fruit mixture into $13 \times 9 \times 2$-inch metal baking pan. Cover and freeze 3 to 4 hours or until mixture is partially frozen.

3. Spoon fruit mixture into food processor or, working in batches, a blender. Whirl until almost smooth, being careful not to overprocess and melt ice. Return fruit mixture to pan; cover and freeze until firm.

4. Remove from freezer 15 minutes before serving for easier scooping.

PRALINE ICE CREAM CAKE

Makes 12 servings.
Nutrient Value Per Serving: 509 calories, 7 g protein, 32 g fat, 51 g carbohydrate, 102 mg sodium, 112 mg cholesterol.

Almond Praline:
1 cup granulated sugar
⅓ cup water
1 cup slivered almonds

Cake:
1 pound cake (12 ounces), cut crosswise into ¼-inch-thick slices
1 pint chocolate ice cream, softened
1 pint strawberry ice cream, softened
1 pint vanilla ice cream, softened

1½ cups chilled heavy cream
3 tablespoons 10X (confectioners') sugar
¼ teaspoon vanilla

1. Prepare Praline (*see How-To, page 492*): Butter baking sheet and metal spatula. Stir together sugar and water in heavy saucepan to dissolve sugar. Bring to simmering over moderate heat, washing down sides of pan with brush dipped in water; simmer until liquid is golden brown, about 15 to 20 minutes. Watch carefully so mixture doesn't get too dark. Stir in almonds. Pour mixture onto prepared baking sheet; spread with spatula. Let praline cool until hard. Break into pieces. Place in food processor or, working in batches, in a blender. Whirl until coarsely ground. Transfer praline to airtight container. Store in cool dry place.

2. Prepare Cake: Lightly grease $9 \times 5 \times 3$-inch loaf pan; line with waxed paper. Arrange layer of cake on bottom of pan. Sprinkle with 2 to 3 tablespoons praline. Top praline with chocolate ice cream. Sprinkle with 2 to 3 tablespoons praline. Cover with another layer of cake. Continue to layer ice cream, praline and cake layer in same manner, ending with layer of cake. Cover with waxed paper. Freeze at least 4 hours or overnight.

3. To unmold: Run knife around inside of pan. Invert loaf pan onto platter. Gently rap pan on plate to unmold. Remove waxed paper. Return cake to freezer while preparing cream.

4. Beat together heavy cream, 10X sugar and vanilla in bowl until stiff peaks form. Spread over top and sides of cake. If you wish, transfer any remaining cream to pastry bag fitted with decorative tip and pipe borders onto cake. Sprinkle top of cake with some of the praline. Freeze for 1 to 2 hours more or until hard.

5. To serve: Let cake stand in refrigerator for 30 minutes or until slightly softened. Cut cake with serrated knife into slices.

CHOCOLATE SAUCE

QUICK

Makes 1 cup.
Nutrient Value Per Tablespoon: 70 calories, 1 g protein, 5 g fat, 8 g carbohydrate, 22 mg sodium, 6 mg cholesterol.

3 squares (1 ounce each) unsweetened chocolate
⅓ cup water
½ cup sugar
3 tablespoons *unsalted* butter
½ teaspoon vanilla

1. Heat together chocolate and water in small saucepan over low heat until chocolate is melted.
2. Stir in sugar until smooth. Bring to boiling; boil for 2 minutes, stirring constantly.
3. Remove saucepan from heat. Stir in butter and vanilla until butter is melted. Serve warm or at room temperature. Sauce will thicken slightly on standing.

Variations:
Bourbon Chocolate: Stir in 2 tablespoons bourbon with the butter and vanilla in Step 3.
Raspberry Chocolate: Stir in ¼ cup raspberry-flavored liqueur with the butter and vanilla in Step 3.
Mint Chocolate: Stir in 1 tablespoon mint-flavored liqueur with the butter and vanilla in Step 3.
Toasted Nut Chocolate: Stir in ⅓ cup chopped toasted almonds and 2 tablespoons almond-flavored liqueur with the butter and vanilla in Step 3.
Mocha Chocolate: Stir in 4 teaspoons instant coffee powder with the chocolate and water in Step 1.
Microwave Directions for Chocolate Sauce (High Power Oven): Ingredient Changes: Reduce water to ¼ cup.
Directions: Combine chocolate and water in microwave-safe 4-cup measure. Microwave, uncovered, at 100% power

1½ minutes. Stir until chocolate melts. Stir in sugar until blended. Microwave, uncovered, at 50% power 2 minutes, stirring once. Stir in butter and vanilla until butter is melted.
To reheat: Pour cold sauce into microwave-safe 2-cup bowl. Cover with microwave-safe plastic wrap, vented at one edge. Microwave at 100% power 1½ minutes.

PINEAPPLE SAUCE

LOW-CALORIE · LOW-FAT
LOW-CHOLESTEROL · LOW-SODIUM
QUICK

Makes 1⅓ cups.
Nutrient Value Per Tablespoon: 12 calories, 0 g protein, 0 g fat, 3 g carbohydrate, 1 mg sodium, 0 mg cholesterol.

1 can (8¼ ounces) crushed pineapple, in juice
½ cup water
2 tablespoons light brown sugar
1½ teaspoons cornstarch

1. Drain pineapple, reserving juice.
2. Stir together juice, water, sugar and cornstarch in small saucepan until blended. Add pineapple; cook over low heat until mixture comes to boiling; boil, stirring constantly, 1 minute until mixture thickens slightly. Cool to room temperature.

Microwave Directions (High Power Oven):
Ingredient Changes: Reduce water to ⅓ cup.
Directions: Drain pineapple juice into microwave-safe 4-cup measure. Whisk in sugar and cornstarch until smooth. Stir in water and pineapple. Microwave, uncovered, at 100% power 3½ minutes until mixture comes to full boil, stirring twice.

SAUCY SERVING IDEAS
Serve any of the sauces on this page over ice cream, fruit or pound cake.

CHOCOLATE SAUCE MAKE-AHEAD TIP:
The sauce can be made several weeks ahead and refrigerated, covered. To reheat, place in saucepan and gently heat over low heat until smooth.

PINEAPPLE SAUCE MAKE-AHEAD TIP:
The sauce can be made several weeks ahead and refrigerated.

MAPLE PRALINE SAUCE

QUICK

Makes ¾ cup.
Nutrient Value Per Tablespoon:
89 calories, 0 g protein, 7 g fat,
7 g carbohydrate, 41 mg sodium,
10 mg cholesterol.

¼ cup (½ stick) *un*salted butter
½ cup finely chopped pecans
¼ cup firmly packed dark brown sugar
3 tablespoons water
2 tablespoons maple syrup

1. Melt butter in small saucepan over low heat.
2. Add pecans; cook, stirring, until lightly browned. Gradually add sugar, stirring until smooth.
3. Stir in water and maple syrup. Bring to boiling; boil, stirring constantly, 1 minute. Serve warm.

MELON SAUCE

LOW-CALORIE · LOW-FAT
LOW-CHOLESTEROL · LOW-SODIUM
QUICK

Makes 1¼ cups.
Nutrient Value Per Tablespoon:
11 calories, 0 g protein, 0 g fat,
3 g carbohydrate, 2 mg sodium,
0 mg cholesterol.

1 cantaloupe (about 2 pounds)
2 tablespoons 10X (confectioners') sugar
¾ teaspoon grated lime rind
2 tablespoons lime juice

1. Cut melon in half; remove seeds. Remove fruit from skin; cut fruit into chunks.
2. Place fruit, sugar, lime rind and juice in food processor or, working in batches, in a blender. Whirl until smooth. Refrigerate until ready to serve. Stir before serving.

RASPBERRY VANILLA SAUCE

LOW-FAT · LOW-CHOLESTEROL
LOW-SODIUM · QUICK

Makes 1 generous cup.
Nutrient Value Per Tablespoon:
35 calories, 0 g protein, 0 g fat,
9 g carbohydrate, 2 mg sodium,
0 mg cholesterol.

½ cup sugar
¼ cup water
1 tablespoon orange juice
1½ cups (6 ounces) dry-pack frozen raspberries
1 tablespoon light corn syrup
¾ teaspoon vanilla

1. Combine sugar, water and orange juice in medium-size saucepan. Bring to boiling over medium heat; boil for 1 minute.
2. Add raspberries and corn syrup. Cover and cook 4 minutes or until raspberries are soft. Remove from heat.
3. Push through sieve into small bowl to remove seeds. Stir in vanilla.

Microwave Directions (High Power Oven):
Ingredient Changes: Reduce water to 2 tablespoons; use frozen raspberries, thawed.
Directions: Combine sugar, water and juice in microwave-safe 4-cup measure. Microwave, uncovered, at 100% power 2 minutes. Stir in raspberries and corn syrup. Cover with microwave-safe plastic wrap, vented at one edge. Microwave at 100% power 2 minutes. Sieve as above; stir in vanilla.

PRALINE SAUCE MAKE-AHEAD TIP:
The sauce can be made several weeks ahead and refrigerated, covered. Gently reheat in saucepan over low heat.

SERVING IDEAS
All the sauces here are terrific over ice cream or poundcake. Maple Praline Sauce is especially good served warm.

MELON SAUCE MAKE-AHEAD TIP:
The sauce can be made up to 2 days ahead and refrigerated, covered.

RASPBERRY VANILLA SAUCE MAKE-AHEAD TIP:
Sauce can be made up to 3 days ahead and refrigerated, covered. Serve cold or gently reheat in small saucepan.

PLUM PORT-WINE ICE

LOW-CALORIE · LOW-SODIUM
LOW-FAT · LOW-CHOLESTEROL

Makes 6 servings (3 cups).
Nutrient Value Per Serving: 134 calories,
1 g protein, 0 g fat, 28 g carbohydrate,
2 mg sodium, 0 mg cholesterol.

1 cup water
½ cup sugar
½ cup Port wine
1 pound ripe plums, pitted and quartered

1. Heat water, sugar and ¼ cup of the Port in small saucepan, stirring to dissolve sugar. Set syrup aside to cool completely.

2. Place plums and remaining ¼ cup Port in blender or food processor. Pour in cooled syrup. Whirl on low speed just to mix.

3. Transfer to ice cream maker; freeze according to manufacturer's directions. Transfer to freezer container. Freeze at least 8 hours. Or still-freeze in the freezer. (See Pineapple-Strawberry Ice, page 535.) Remove from freezer to refrigerator for 30 minutes before scooping and serving.

SENSIBLE DESSERTS
Beginning on this page, we've included a special collection of low-fat, low-calorie (and sometimes low-cholesterol) *Sensible Desserts.*

COCOA-MOCHA MOUSSE

LOW-CALORIE · LOW-FAT

LOW-CHOLESTEROL

NOT-SO-FORBIDDEN MOUSSE
Cocoa-Mocha Mousse is a rich, creamy dessert with fewer calories and less fat than traditional chocolate mousse.

Makes 6 servings.

Nutrient Value Per Serving: 150 calories, 8 g protein, 3 g fat, 23 g carbohydrate, 77 mg sodium, 8 mg cholesterol.

1 cup reduced-calorie ricotta cheese
¼ cup nonfat plain yogurt
1½ tablespoons unsweetened cocoa powder
½ cup sugar
½ cup water
1 envelope unflavored gelatin
½ teaspoon instant coffee granules
1 cup skim milk
1 tablespoon coffee-flavored liqueur OR: syrup
½ teaspoon vanilla
2 chocolate wafer cookies *(optional)*
Raspberries *(optional)*

1. Combine ricotta cheese, yogurt and cocoa powder in food processor or blender. Whirl 2 minutes until very smooth. Turn into medium-size bowl.
2. Combine sugar and water in small saucepan. Sprinkle gelatin over top and let stand 1 minute. Stir over medium-low heat until gelatin is completely dissolved, about 5 minutes. Stir in instant coffee granules. Blend coffee mixture with cheese mixture, along with milk, liqueur and vanilla. Refrigerate, stirring occasionally, until mixture mounds slightly when dropped from spoon, about 45 minutes.
3. Beat mixture with electric mixer at high speed for 2 minutes to aerate. Spoon into six 8-ounce ramekins or dessert cups. Refrigerate at least 3 hours before serving. Decorate with cut or crumbled chocolate wafers and raspberries, if you wish.

FROZEN BANANA-STRAWBERRY CREAM

LOW-CALORIE · LOW-FAT

LOW-CHOLESTEROL

Here's a dessert that's as rich and creamy as ice cream—without the calories and fat.

Makes 8 servings.

Nutrient Value Per Serving: 106 calories, 4 g protein, 1 g fat, 19 g carbohydrate, 128 mg sodium, 5 mg cholesterol.

1 pint strawberries, hulled and halved
1 banana, peeled and cut up
1 cup lowfat (1%) cottage cheese
½ cup reduced-calorie sour cream
⅓ cup honey
½ teaspoon vanilla

1. Combine berries, banana, cottage cheese, sour cream, honey and vanilla in food processor or blender. Whirl until very smooth, about 2 minutes, scraping down side as necessary.
2. Pour mixture into $9 \times 9 \times 2$-inch square baking pan. Freeze until edges are solid, about 30 minutes. Stir well. Freeze until mixture is just solid in center, about 2 hours; stir occasionally. To serve immediately, scoop or spoon into bowls.
3. To freeze for longer storage, pack into 1-quart freezer container; cover. To serve, remove from freezer to refrigerator for about 30 minutes. Remove from storage container to medium-size bowl; chop with knife into pieces small enough to fit in food processor. Place in processor. Pulse quickly with on-and-off motion until mixture softens slightly. Scoop or spoon into individual dessert bowls.

Spicy Apple Crepes with Maple Cream (page 542).

SPICY APPLE CREPES WITH MAPLE CREAM

LOW-CALORIE · LOW-FAT

(Pictured on page 541)

Makes 10 servings.
Nutrient Value Per Serving: 149 calories,
4 g protein, 1 g fat, 32 g carbohydrate,
98 mg sodium, 28 mg cholesterol.

Maple Cream *(recipe follows)*

Crepe Batter:
½ cup all-purpose flour
2 teaspoons sugar
⅛ teaspoon salt
¾ cup skim milk
1 egg

Filling:
2 tart cooking apples, such as Granny
  Smith
1 tablespoon lemon juice
½ cup apple cider OR: water
⅓ cup dark raisins OR: dried cherries
¼ cup sugar
½ teaspoon ground cinnamon
¼ teaspoon grated nutmeg
¼ cup red-currant OR: apple jelly

1. Prepare Maple Cream.
2. Prepare Crepe Batter: Combine
flour, sugar, salt, skim milk and egg in
blender or food processor. Whirl until
smooth. Pour into small bowl; set aside
30 minutes.
3. Prepare Filling: Pare, core and chop
apples into ¼-inch dice. Toss with
lemon juice in medium-size skillet. Stir
in cider, raisins, sugar, cinnamon and
nutmeg. Bring to boiling over medium-
high heat. Lower heat; simmer, stirring
occasionally, 10 minutes or until apples
are just tender. Stir in jelly; cook 5
minutes. Set aside and keep warm.
4. Prepare crepes: Lightly coat 8-inch
nonstick skillet with nonstick vegetable-
oil cooking spray. Heat skillet over
medium heat. Using scant 2 tablespoons
batter for each crepe, pour into center

of skillet, rotating skillet so batter
spreads to edges. Cook 30 seconds.
Loosen edge of crepe with spatula; flip
crepe over. Cook 15 seconds on other
side. Continue to make total of 10
crepes, stacking crepes between sheets
of waxed paper.
5. For each serving, place crepe on dessert plate. Spread 3 tablespoons filling
over one-half of crepe; fold crepe over.
Spoon 1½ tablespoons Maple Cream
over crepe. Serve hot or warm.

Maple Cream: Combine ½ cup lowfat
(1%) cottage cheese and ¼ cup nonfat
plain yogurt in food processor or
blender. Whirl for 2 minutes or until
very smooth, scraping down side of
bowl 2 times. Stir in ¼ cup maple
syrup. Refrigerate at least 30 minutes.

MELON AND BLUEBERRIES WITH YOGURT TOPPING

LOW-CALORIE · LOW-SODIUM
LOW-FAT · LOW-CHOLESTEROL · QUICK

*This brown-sugar-sweetened, vanilla-
scented yogurt topping turns any fruit combination into a creamy-rich dessert.*

Makes 4 servings.
Nutrient Value Per Serving: 93 calories,
3 g protein, 1 g fat, 20 g carbohydrate,
38 mg sodium, 2 mg cholesterol.

2 cups blueberries, washed
⅓ cantaloupe, pared, seeded and diced
⅔ cup plain yogurt
1 tablespoon light brown sugar
¼ teaspoon vanilla

1. Combine blueberries and cantaloupe
in a bowl. Spoon into 4 individual serving glasses.
2. Gently stir together yogurt, sugar
and vanilla in small bowl. Spoon over
fruit. Serve immediately.

BANANA-KIWI-STRAWBERRY TART

LOW-CALORIE · LOW-FAT
LOW-CHOLESTEROL

Bake pastry at 375° for 15 to 18 minutes; bake tart at 375° for 18 to 20 minutes.

Makes 6 servings.

Nutrient Value Per Serving: 145 calories, 5 g protein, 4 g fat, 23 g carbohydrate, 159 mg sodium, 11 mg cholesterol.

Pastry:
½ cup all-purpose flour
1 tablespoon light brown sugar
¼ teaspoon ground cinnamon
⅛ teaspoon salt
2 tablespoons chilled *un*salted butter
1 to 2 tablespoons ice water

Filling:
1 cup skim milk
3 egg whites
2 tablespoons sugar
Pinch salt
¼ teaspoon vanilla
4 slices banana (½ small banana)
1 kiwifruit, peeled and cut into 12 slices
1 cup strawberry slices

1. Prepare Pastry: Stir together flour, brown sugar, cinnamon and salt in medium-size bowl. Cut in butter with pastry blender until mixture resembles coarse meal. Sprinkle ice water over, tossing with fork just until evenly moistened. Shape into disk; wrap and refrigerate 30 minutes.

2. Prepare Filling: Heat milk in top of double boiler over simmering water (or in small nonstick saucepan over low

(continued)

BANANA-KIWI-STRAWBERRY TART
(*continued*)

TART MAKE-AHEAD TIP:

The pastry dough can be made several days ahead and refrigerated, well wrapped. The tart pan can be lined with the pastry and baked earlier in the day and the whole tart assembled, without the fruit topping, up to 8 hours before serving.

heat) just until bubbles form around edge of pan. Beat together egg whites, sugar and salt in small bowl. Beat spoonful of hot milk into egg mixture. Whisk egg mixture into milk in pan. Cook, stirring, over simmering water until mixture thickens slightly and coats a spoon, about 10 minutes; do not let boil. Remove from heat. Stir in vanilla. Cool to room temperature.

3. Preheat oven to moderate (375°). Lightly coat 8-inch tart pan with removable bottom with nonstick vegetable-oil cooking spray.

4. Roll out pastry on lightly floured surface with lightly floured rolling pin to 10-inch circle. Roll up pastry on rolling pin; transfer to pan. Fit pastry into pan; trim edge even with pan top. Pierce bottom in several places with fork.

5. Bake pastry in preheated moderate oven (375°) for 15 to 18 minutes or until golden brown. Remove to wire rack to cool completely.

6. Spoon custard into cooled pastry.

7. Bake in preheated moderate oven (375°) for 18 to 20 minutes. Remove to wire rack to cool to room temperature. Refrigerate up to 8 hours. Just before serving, arrange banana, kiwi and strawberry slices over custard.

RAISIN-OAT COOKIES

LOW-CALORIE · LOW-FAT

LOW-CHOLESTEROL

A *very lowfat cookie.*

Bake at 375° for 10 to 12 minutes.
Makes 4 dozen cookies.
Nutrient Value Per Cookie: 73 calories, 2 g protein, 1 g fat, 14 g carbohydrate, 59 mg sodium, 6 mg cholesterol.

1 cup all-purpose flour
¾ cup uncooked oat bran

½ teaspoon salt
½ teaspoon baking soda
½ cup (1 stick) reduced-calorie margarine, at room temperature
1 cup firmly packed light brown sugar
¼ cup granulated sugar
1 egg
½ cup nonfat plain yogurt
1 teaspoon grated orange rind
¼ cup orange juice
1 teaspoon vanilla
2½ cups old-fashioned rolled oats (not quick-cooking)
1 cup dark seedless raisins
½ cup hulled sunflower seeds *(optional)*

1. Preheat oven to moderate (375°). Lightly grease baking sheets.

2. Stir together flour, bran, salt and baking soda in small bowl.

3. Beat margarine in medium-size bowl until creamy. Gradually beat in brown and granulated sugars until fluffy. Beat in egg, yogurt, orange rind, juice and vanilla until blended. Beat in flour mixture. Stir in oats, raisins and sunflower seeds, if you wish.

4. Drop batter by level tablespoonfuls, 2 inches apart, onto greased baking sheets, flattening with back of spoon.

5. Bake in preheated moderate oven (375°) for 10 to 12 minutes or until lightly browned. Remove from baking sheets to racks to cool completely.

Make-Ahead Tip: Cookies can be stored in airtight container at room temperature for up to one week.

AFTER SCHOOL TREAT

Raisin-Oat Cookies (this page)

Summer Fruit Compote (528)

Milk

Spiced Lemonade (page 548)

CHAPTER 12

BEVERAGES FOR ALL OCCASIONS

APRICOT BUTTERMILK SMOOTHIE

LOW-FAT · LOW-CHOLESTEROL · QUICK

Cooling for a summer afternoon, rich enough for a snack.

From left: Apricot Buttermilk Smoothie and Chocolate Peppermint Frappé (both this page)

Makes 2 drinks.
Recipe can be halved or doubled.
Nutrient Value Per Drink: 229 calories, 7 g protein, 2 g fat, 49 g carbohydrate, 198 mg sodium, 7 mg cholesterol.

1 can (5½ ounces) chilled apricot nectar
8 dried apricot halves (about 1 ounce)
2 tablespoons sugar
1 tablespoon orange marmalade
1½ cups cold buttermilk

1. Combine apricot nectar, dried apricots, sugar and marmalade in blender. Whirl for 2 minutes or until smooth. Add buttermilk. Whirl until smooth.
2. Serve in tall glasses over ice.

CHOCOLATE PEPPERMINT FRAPPÉ

LOW-FAT · QUICK

A kid's favorite. Add a little peppermint-flavored liqueur, and it's for the grownups.

Makes 2 drinks.
Recipe can be halved or doubled.
Nutrient Value Per Drink: 273 calories, 8 g protein, 3 g fat, 57 g carbohydrate, 99 mg sodium, 9 mg cholesterol.

2 round peppermint candies (½ ounce)
½ pint frozen coffee yogurt OR: frozen chocolate yogurt
1 cup cold lowfat milk
¼ cup chocolate syrup
Peppermint sticks, for garnish *(optional)*

1. Place peppermint candies in blender. Whirl until pulverized. Add frozen yogurt, milk and chocolate syrup. Whirl until smooth.
2. Serve at once with peppermint sticks for garnish, if you wish.

From top: Raspberry Lime Rickey (page 548); Chocolate Cherry Fizz (page 548); and Melon Mint Cooler (this page).

MELON MINT COOLER

LOW-FAT · LOW-CHOLESTEROL
LOW-SODIUM · QUICK

A *little rum, vodka or gin transforms this into a party drink. (Pictured above.)*

Makes 2 drinks.
Recipe can be halved or doubled.
Nutrient Value Per Drink: 126 calories,
1 g protein, 0 g fat, 33 g carbohydrate,
15 mg sodium, 0 mg cholesterol.

3 cups honeydew cubes (about 10
    ounces, one-quarter of a melon)
2 tablespoons fresh lime juice
3 tablespoons superfine sugar
2 mint sprigs *(optional)*
2 lime slices *(optional)*

1. Combine honeydew, lime juice, sugar and mint sprigs, if using, in blender. Whirl 2 minutes or until smooth.
2. Serve in tall glasses over cracked ice. Garnish with lime slices and additional mint sprigs, if you wish.

RASPBERRY LIME RICKEY

LOW-FAT · LOW-CHOLESTEROL

LOW-SODIUM · QUICK

For a party version, add a little vodka, gin or rum. (Pictured on page 547.)

Makes 2 drinks.
Recipe can be halved or doubled.
Nutrient Value Per Drink: 117 calories,
0 g protein, 0 g fat, 31 g carbohydrate,
38 mg sodium, 0 mg cholesterol.

¼ cup raspberry puree or syrup (see
    sidebar)
¼ cup fresh lime juice (about 6 limes)
3 tablespoons superfine sugar
1½ cups club soda OR: seltzer water,
    chilled
Mint sprigs, for garnish *(optional)*

1. Stir raspberry puree, lime juice and sugar in bowl to dissolve sugar.
2. Divide into 2 highball glasses, filled with ice. Stir in club soda. Garnish with mint sprig, if you wish.

CHOCOLATE CHERRY FIZZ

LOW-FAT · LOW-CHOLESTEROL

LOW-SODIUM · QUICK

Our version of a soda parlor favorite. (Pictured on page 547.)

Makes 2 drinks.
Recipe can be halved or doubled.
Nutrient Value Per Drink: 253 calories,
2 g protein, 2 g fat, 63 g carbohydrate,
23 mg sodium, 0 mg cholesterol.

2 cups fresh sweet cherries, pitted OR:
    frozen dry-pack cherries, thawed
2 to 3 tablespoons chocolate syrup
2 teaspoons lemon juice
¼ cup superfine sugar
Club soda OR: seltzer water, chilled
Cherries on skewers OR: curled lemon
    rind *(optional)*

1. Combine cherries, chocolate syrup, lemon juice and sugar in blender. Whirl for 2 minutes or until smooth.
2. Pour into 2 tall glasses filled with ice. Top with soda and optional garnish.

SPICED LEMONADE

LOW-FAT · LOW-CHOLESTEROL

LOW-SODIUM

A touch of bourbon or rum would make this a little more adult. (Pictured on page 545.)

Makes 4 drinks.
Recipe can be halved or doubled.
Nutrient Value Per Drink: 223 calories,
0 g protein, 0 g fat, 59 g carbohydrate,
16 mg sodium, 0 mg cholesterol.

1 lemon
2 cups water
1 cup sugar
4 whole allspice
4 whole cloves
1 cinnamon stick
1 tablespoon chopped crystallized ginger
Pinch grated nutmeg
1 cup fresh lemon juice (about 8 lemons)
1 cup club soda OR: seltzer water, chilled
Mint sprigs, for garnish *(optional)*

1. Remove rind in pieces from lemon with swivel-bladed vegetable peeler; avoid any bitter white pith.
2. Combine water, sugar, lemon rind, allspice, cloves, cinnamon stick, crystallized ginger and nutmeg in small saucepan. Bring to simmering; simmer, covered, for 20 minutes. Strain into pitcher and chill; discard solids.
3. To serve, stir in lemon juice and club soda. Serve over crushed ice. Garnish with mint sprigs, if you wish.

HOMEMADE RASPBERRY PUREE
Place 1 package (10 ounces) raspberries in light syrup, thawed according to package directions, in blender. Whirl until smooth. Strain, discarding seeds, and use as directed at right.

LEMONADE MAKE-AHEAD TIP:
The syrup base in Step 2 can be made several days ahead and refrigerated, covered.

BERRY PEACHY FIZZ

QUICK

Summer cooler with a kick.

Makes 2 drinks.
Recipe can be halved or doubled.
Nutrient Value Per Serving: 163 calories,
0 g protein, 0 g fat, 29 g carbohydrate,
22 mg sodium, 0 mg cholesterol.

1 cup cranberry-blueberry cocktail drink
¼ cup peach-flavored liqueur
½ teaspoon fresh lime juice
½ to ¾ cup club soda OR: seltzer water,
   chilled
Fresh peach slices, for garnish *(optional)*

1. Fill tall glasses with cracked ice.
Chill in freezer.
2. Stir together cranberry-blueberry
cocktail drink, peach liqueur and lime
juice in 2-cup glass measuring cup.
3. To serve, divide drink mixture into
2 glasses. Top with club soda to taste;
stir to combine. Garnish with fresh
peach slices, if you wish.

Note: To serve "up," shake with crushed
ice and strain, then top with club soda.

PINEAPPLE PINK SUNSET

LOW-FAT · LOW-CHOLESTEROL
LOW-SODIUM · QUICK

Try a splash of rum, tequila or brandy.

Makes 2 drinks.
Recipe can be halved or doubled.
Nutrient Value Per Drink: 128 calories,
1 g protein, 0 g fat, 32 g carbohydrate,
17 mg sodium, 0 mg cholesterol.

1 cup apricot nectar
½ cup pineapple juice

1 teaspoon grenadine
8 dashes bitters
2 teaspoons superfine sugar
½ cup club soda OR: seltzer water,
   chilled
Pineapple wedges and fresh mint sprigs,
   for garnish *(optional)*

1. Fill 2 tall glasses with cracked ice.
Chill in freezer.
2. Stir together apricot nectar, pineapple juice, grenadine, bitters and sugar in
2-cup glass measuring cup.
3. To serve, divide drink mixture into
the glasses. Top off with club soda.
Garnish with pineapple wedges and
mint sprigs, if you wish.

**From left: Berry
Peachy Fizz and
Pineapple Pink
Sunset (both this
page).**

ORGANIZING THE BAR FOR A PARTY

Party Drink Guide Plan ahead, and your party's sure to be a success. The following are some basic tips for setting up a bar at home.

■ To guarantee you don't "run dry" before the party's over, follow our Wine and Liquor Buying Guide to figure out how much beverage to have on hand for the number of guests expected.

■ A basic bar includes Scotch whisky, rye, bourbon, gin, vodka and rum, plus mixers such as club soda, ginger ale, tonic water, lemon soda, cola, tomato juice, fruit juices and sweet-sour mix. Make sure you have plenty of nonalcoholic beverages as well for those who would prefer not to have a cocktail.

■ Check with your liquor store to see if they will take back unopened bottles of liquor and wine.

■ Have plenty of clean ice on hand. Buy bags of ice from a supermarket or distributor or start making cubes a few days in advance and collect in plastic storage bags.

■ If you don't have a built-in bar area, set up a sturdy table in an area where it won't block party traffic. For large crowds or small rooms, it may be more convenient to set up two bar areas, one at either end of the room, particularly if your guests are serving themselves. If possible, place the bar close to a sink and refrigerator —a kitchen island is ideal.

■ Stock up on all-purpose wine glasses, jumbo old-fashioned glasses and 8-ounce highballs. At a 2-hour party, each guest may use 2 to 3 glasses.

■ Check your local yellow pages for party equipment rental agencies that can provide glassware, tables, chairs, party-size coffee pots, or just about anything you need for a large get-together.

■ Depending on the types of drinks you plan to mix, some or all of the following bar equipment may be necessary:
  blender
  bottle opener
  cocktail shaker
  corkscrew
  cutting board
  juicer
  paring knife
  shot glass
  strainer
  ice bucket and tongs
  cocktail napkins and stirrers

■ Follow recipes exactly and always measure when mixing a drink. A standard jigger measures 1½ ounces.

■ Don't forget the finishing touches: lemon peel twists, lime wedges, orange wheels, olives, skewers of fresh fruit cubes.

■ Appetizers and snacks help your guests pace their drinking, so plan to serve a variety of snacks. Provide coffee and tea midway through and to the end of the party.

■ Don't let friends drink and drive. Call a cab or have someone drive home a person who has had one too many.

A Wine Guide When you don't know the wine preferences of each and every guest, the following guide to buying reds and whites can help you decide how much of each to have on hand for a party. Generally, white wine is more popular than red and, depending on the number of guests, you'll need at least twice as many bottles of white. Don't forget to include yourself when totaling the number of guests.

A WINE GUIDE

No. Of Guests	Bottles White (750 ml)		Bottles Red (750 ml)
4	2	+	1
6	2	+	2
10	4	+	2
12	6	+	2
30	9	+	4
40	13	+	6

Note: If you're using wine coolers, plan on two to three 6-packs for 8 to 12 guests, and at least 1 pound of ice per person.

WINE AND LIQUOR BUYING GUIDE

Bottle Size	Ounces	Number of Servings		
		Wine or Champagne (4 to 5-oz. servings)	Liquor (1½-oz. servings)	Cordials (1-oz. servings)
Split	6.4	1–2		
Pint	16.0		10–11	16
750 milliliter*	25.4	5–6	17	25
Fifth	25.6	5–6	17	25
Quart	32.0	8–10	21	32
Liter	33.8	8–10	22	33
Magnum	52.0	10–12		

* Standard size wine bottle

Seeing Red Margarita (page 552).

Super Watermelon Slush (page 552).

Blueberry Citrus Ice (page 553).

Ginger Julep (page 553).

SEEING RED MARGARITA

QUICK

A *delicious cherry version of a slush margarita. Use discretion when drinking. (Pictured on page 551.)*

Makes 4 jumbo or 6 regular drinks.
Recipe can be halved or doubled.
Nutrient Value Per Regular Drink:
191 calories, 0 g protein, 0 g fat, 19 g
carbohydrate, 1 mg sodium, 0 mg cholesterol.

1 cup fresh or frozen pitted sweet
    cherries
6 ounces tequila
4 ounces Triple Sec OR: other
    orange-flavored liqueur
¼ cup fresh lime juice
2 tablespoons superfine sugar
2 teaspoons grenadine
4 cups ice
Cherries or lime slices, for garnish
    (optional)

1. If using fresh cherries, freeze in single layer on baking sheet. Combine frozen cherries, tequila, Triple Sec, lime juice, sugar and grenadine in blender. Whirl 2 minutes or until smooth.
2. With machine running, drop in ice through small opening, stopping and scraping down side as needed.
3. If you wish, dip rims of chilled goblet glasses in lime juice; then dip in coarse salt to coat rims. Pour in margaritas. Garnish with fresh cherries or lime slices, if you wish. Serve immediately.

SUPER WATERMELON SLUSH

LOW-FAT · LOW-CHOLESTEROL
LOW-SODIUM

The *refreshing taste of watermelon in an icy liquid. For extra zap, add a splash of vodka, gin, rum, brandy or tequila. (Pictured on page 551.)*

Makes 2 drinks.
Recipe can be halved or doubled.
Nutrient Value Per Drink: 141 calories,
1 g protein, 1 g fat, 34 g carbohydrate,
13 mg sodium, 0 mg cholesterol.

2 cups watermelon cubes, seeded
    (about 8 ounces)
1 cup white grape juice
1 tablespoon fresh lemon juice
1 teaspoon superfine sugar, or to taste
Watermelon wedges and fresh mint
    leaves, for garnish *(optional)*

1. Chill saucer-like glasses in freezer.
2. Place watermelon cubes on waxed-paper-lined baking sheet; freeze until cubes are firm.
3. Combine grape juice, lemon juice, superfine sugar and 1 cup frozen watermelon cubes in blender. Whirl until smooth. With machine running, drop remaining 1 cup watermelon cubes through small opening in cover. Whirl until smooth, scraping down side with spatula as needed.
4. Pour immediately into chilled saucer-like glasses. Garnish with watermelon wedges and mint and serve with short straws, if you wish.

Make-Ahead Tip: Large batches of watermelon cubes can be frozen in plastic freezer bags up to 2 months ahead.

BLUEBERRY CITRUS ICE

QUICK

Makes 2 drinks.
Recipe can be halved or doubled.
Nutrient Value Per Drink: 167 calories,
1 g protein, 4 g fat, 25 g carbohydrate,
14 mg sodium, 11 mg cholesterol.

½ cup orange juice
¼ cup half-and-half
3 tablespoons Galliano liqueur
1 tablespoon superfine sugar
1 teaspoon fresh lemon juice
⅓ cup fresh or frozen blueberries
1 cup ice cubes
Skewered lemon and orange wedges, for
    garnish *(optional)*

1. Chill 2 tall glasses in freezer.
2. Combine orange juice, half-and-half,
Galliano, superfine sugar, lemon juice,
blueberries and ice in blender. Whirl
until smooth.
3. Serve in the chilled tall glasses with
optional garnishes.

GINGER JULEP

LOW-CALORIE · LOW-FAT
LOW-CHOLESTEROL · LOW-SODIUM
QUICK

Makes 2 drinks.
Recipe can be halved or doubled.
Nutrient Value Per Drink: 98 calories,
0 g protein, 0 g fat, 26 g carbohydrate,
9 mg sodium, 0 mg cholesterol.

½ cup water
¼ cup fresh lemon juice (2 lemons)
8 mint leaves
2 tablespoons superfine sugar
1 cup cold ginger ale
Fresh mint sprigs, for garnish *(optional)*

1. Fill 2 tall glasses with cracked ice
and chill in freezer.

2. Combine water, lemon juice, mint
leaves and sugar in blender. Whirl for
30 seconds. Strain through fine-meshed
sieve into glass measure. Refrigerate to
chill.
3. Divide drink mixture into glasses.
Top with ginger ale. Garnish with mint
sprigs, if you wish.

MAPLE CIDER TODDY

QUICK

Makes 8 drinks.
Recipe can be halved or doubled.
Nutrient Value Per Drink: 151 calories,
0 g protein, 0 g fat, 20 g carbohydrate,
5 mg sodium, 0 mg cholesterol.

4 cups apple cider
3 tablespoons maple syrup
½ vanilla bean, split
1 cinnamon stick
12 whole allspice berries
1 cup brandy OR: applejack
Apple slices and cinnamon sticks, for
    garnish *(optional)*

1. Combine cider, maple syrup, vanilla,
cinnamon and allspice in nonaluminum
saucepan. Simmer, covered, for 20 to
30 minutes; strain; discard solids.
Return liquid to saucepan.
2. To serve, stir in brandy. Ladle into
mugs or punch cups. Garnish with
apple and cinnamon, if you wish.

CITRUS ICE FOR KIDS
Blueberry Citrus Ice is
a delicious and fun
drink without the Gal-
liano. Try it at a fam-
ily get-together.
(Pictured on page
551.)

ON YOUR MARKS . . .
Serve Ginger Julep
for Derby Day. Add
bourbon for a version
more akin to the clas-
sic Mint Julep. (Pic-
tured on page 551.)

HOT TODDY
A warming drink for
in front of the fire.
Feature at holiday
season. (Pictured
below.)

Maple Cider Toddy
(this page).

RITE OF SPRING PUNCH

LOW-CALORIE · LOW-FAT
LOW-CHOLESTEROL · LOW-SODIUM

*W**e've incorporated the flavors of rhubarb and strawberries—the classic spring combination—into our spring punch. There are several options for spirited additions: white wine, champagne, tequila, rum, vodka or gin.*

Makes 20 servings.
Recipe can be halved or doubled.
Nutrient Value Per Serving: 78 calories, 1 g protein, 0 g fat, 20 g carbohydrate, 14 mg sodium, 0 mg cholesterol.

2 packages (10 ounces each) frozen strawberries in light syrup, thawed according to package directions
2 cups fresh or thawed, frozen sliced rhubarb
2 cups water
1 cinnamon stick
4 whole allspice berries
2 slices pared fresh ginger
4 cups orange juice
¼ cup grenadine
½ cup superfine sugar
4 to 6 cups club soda OR: seltzer water, chilled
Orange slices and whole strawberries, for garnish *(optional)*

1. Combine strawberries, rhubarb, water, cinnamon stick, allspice and ginger in small saucepan. Bring to simmering; simmer 15 minutes. Press through sieve with rubber spatula or back of spoon into bowl; discard solids. Refrigerate to chill.
2. Just before serving, stir together strawberry-rhubarb mixture, orange juice, grenadine and sugar in punch bowl to dissolve sugar. Slowly add club soda, pouring down side of bowl. Garnish with orange slices and whole strawberries, if you wish.

THE FINISHING TOUCH

For a spectacular presentation, float a fruited ice mold in your punch. To make the mold, pour ½-inch depth of water into a 4-cup ring mold that will fit into the punch bowl. Freeze for about 20 minutes. Arrange thinly sliced or diced fresh fruits of your choice in a decorative pattern over the frozen water. Pour ¾ cup very cold water over the fruit. Freeze for 15 minutes or until solid. Gradually add more water until the mold is filled. Freeze for 8 hours. To unmold, dip the mold in and out of a pan of hot water or allow to stand at room temperature for 5 minutes. Then invert the ring onto a cookie sheet. Slide the ring into a punch bowl no more than one-third full of punch.

SPRING PUNCH MAKE-AHEAD TIP:

The recipe can be prepared 2 days ahead through Step 1.

PEACH AND PASSION PUNCH

LOW-CALORIE · LOW-FAT
LOW-CHOLESTEROL · LOW-SODIUM
QUICK

*Y**our choice—with or without rum.*

Makes 16 servings.
Recipe can be halved or doubled.
Nutrient Value Per Serving: 65 calories, 0 g protein, 0 g fat, 16 g carbohydrate, 5 mg sodium, 0 mg cholesterol.

4 cups bottled guava passion fruit drink
1½ cups peach nectar
2 tablespoons fresh lime juice OR: lemon juice
1 package frozen raspberries in light syrup, thawed according to package directions
1½ cups club soda OR: seltzer, chilled *(optional)*
1½ cups rum *(optional)*

1. Stir together passion fruit drink, peach nectar and lime juice in pitcher until combined; refrigerate until chilled.
2. Chill punch bowl with ice cubes.
3. Just before serving, remove ice cubes from punch bowl. Pour passion fruit mixture into bowl. Gently stir in raspberries and their juice. Stir in club soda and rum, if you wish. Serve chilled.

Make-Ahead Tip: The recipe can be prepared a day ahead through Step 1.

Raspberry Champagne Punch (this page).

Caramel Eggnog (page 556).

RASPBERRY CHAMPAGNE PUNCH

A *ruby-red punch to celebrate any occasion any time of year.*

Makes 12 servings.
Recipe can be halved or doubled.
Nutrient Value Per Serving: 135 calories, 1 g protein, 0 g fat, 24 g carbohydrate, 6 mg sodium, 0 mg cholesterol.

2 packages (10 ounces each) frozen raspberries in light syrup, thawed according to package directions
1½ cups apricot nectar, chilled
1 cup white grape juice, chilled
¼ cup fresh lemon juice (about 2 lemons)
2 tablespoons honey
1 bottle champagne OR: sparkling white wine, chilled
Sliced lemons, fresh raspberries and mint sprigs, for garnish *(optional)*

1. Place raspberries in blender or food processor. Whirl until smooth. Strain through sieve into punch bowl; discard seeds.
2. Add apricot nectar, white grape juice, lemon juice and honey to the raspberries.
3. Just before serving, stir champagne into prepared raspberry mixture in punch bowl. Garnish with lemon slices, raspberries and mint sprigs, if you wish.

Make-Ahead Tip: The recipe can be prepared a day ahead through Step 2 and refrigerated, covered.

CARAMEL EGGNOG

With the increased concern about the use of uncooked eggs and possible salmonella, we've devised an eggnog with cooked eggs. For the holiday spirit, add dark rum or bourbon. (Pictured on page 555.)

Makes 10 servings.
Recipe can be halved or doubled.
Nutrient Value Per Serving: 236 calories, 7 g protein, 11 g fat, 27 g carbohydrate, 121 mg sodium, 156 mg cholesterol.

1 cup granulated sugar
2 tablespoons plus ¼ cup water
½ teaspoon lemon juice
6 eggs
4 cups lowfat milk
½ teaspoon vanilla
⅛ teaspoon grated nutmeg
⅛ teaspoon salt
¾ cup heavy cream
2 tablespoons almond- or
     hazelnut-flavored liqueur *(optional)*
1 tablespoon 10X (confectioners') sugar
Grated nutmeg and sliced almonds, for
     garnish *(optional)*

1. Combine granulated sugar, the 2 tablespoons water and the lemon juice in medium-size saucepan. Place remaining ¼ cup of water near stove. Bring sugar mixture to boiling over medium heat; cook 5 minutes or until dark amber in color. Remove from heat. Gradually and carefully add water to sugar mixture; it may spatter. Stir until caramel is dissolved.
2. Whisk together eggs and milk in a bowl. Stir into caramel mixture. Cook over medium-low heat for about 12 to 15 minutes or until mixture thickens and coats back of a spoon (160° on an instant-read thermometer). Immediately strain into clean bowl. Stir in vanilla, nutmeg and salt. Refrigerate, covered, until chilled.
3. Just before serving, beat together cream, liqueur, if using, and 10X sugar in small bowl until soft peaks form.

EGGNOG MAKE-AHEAD TIP:
The recipe can be prepared up to a day ahead through Step 2 and refrigerated, covered.

Pour chilled eggnog into serving bowl. Fold in whipped cream with a whisk. Sprinkle grated nutmeg and almonds on top, if you wish.

SPICED HOT GRAPE PUNCH

LOW-FAT · LOW-CHOLESTEROL
LOW-SODIUM · QUICK

Perfect for Christmas open-houses or any cold-weather get-together. For extra punch, add a little rum or bourbon.

Makes 16 servings.
Recipe can be halved or doubled.
Nutrient Value Per Serving: 70 calories, 0 g protein, 0 g fat, 18 g carbohydrate, 3 mg sodium, 0 mg cholesterol.

6 cups bottled purple grape juice*
2 cups Granny Smith apple juice (from
     concentrate) OR: regular apple juice
¼ cup fresh lemon juice (about 2
     lemons)
2 tablespoons dark brown sugar
3 slices pared fresh ginger, quarter-size
4 cardamom pods, lightly crushed
2 whole cloves
1 cinnamon stick
Red and green grapes, whole or cut in
     half, for garnish *(optional)*
Cinnamon sticks, for garnish *(optional)*

1. Combine grape juice, apple juice, lemon juice, brown sugar, ginger, cardamom, cloves and cinnamon stick in large nonaluminum saucepan. Bring just to simmering; simmer, covered, for 20 minutes. Strain to remove spices.
2. Serve hot in mugs. Garnish with grapes and cinnamon sticks.

*Note: A 12-ounce container frozen grape juice can be substituted. Prepare according to package directions.

ROSY SANGRÍA

Our version of the classic, with a special touch—herbal tea.

Makes 8 servings.
Recipe can be halved or doubled.
Nutrient Value Per Serving: 152 calories,
1 g protein, 0 g fat, 20 g carbohydrate,
12 mg sodium, 0 mg cholesterol.

1 cup water
½ cup sugar
3 lemon slices
3 whole cloves
1 cinnamon stick
4 blackberry or cranberry herbal tea bags
1 bottle (750 ml.) white Zinfandel wine
2 to 4 tablespoons brandy
½ pint strawberries, trimmed

¼ pound fresh sweet cherries, pitted
1 orange, cut into 1-inch chunks
1 cup club soda OR: seltzer

1. Combine water, sugar, lemon, cloves and cinnamon stick in small saucepan. Bring just to simmering; simmer 10 minutes. Remove from heat. Add tea bags; let steep 5 minutes. Remove solids and discard. Refrigerate tea mixture to chill.
2. Stir together tea mixture, wine and brandy in large pitcher. Add strawberries, cherries and orange. Refrigerate, covered, 4 to 48 hours.
3. Just before serving, stir in club soda. Serve sangría in chilled glasses, spooning in some of the fruit with the wine.

Make-Ahead Tip: Recipe can be prepared through Step 1 up to 5 days ahead.

BLUSHING BEATRICE

QUICK

A beautiful color—hence the name.

Makes 1 drink. Recipe can be doubled.
Nutrient Value Per Drink: 160 calories,
0 g protein, 0 g fat, 27 g carbohydrate,
11 mg sodium, 0 mg cholesterol.

1 can (5½ ounces) pear nectar, chilled
¼ to ½ cup white Zinfandel, chilled
1 teaspoon cassis liqueur (black currant)
   (optional)
½ teaspoon grenadine

1. Combine pear nectar, Zinfandel, cassis, if using, and grenadine in tall glass.
2. Add cracked ice and serve cold.

WINE AND CHEESE PARTY TIPS

Serving Guide

■ Plan to serve about ¼ pound cheese per person. *(For serving suggestions, see Cheese Choices, pages 171–172.)*
■ Serve cheese at room temperature for best flavor. Take soft cheese out of the refrigerator half an hour ahead; hard cheese one to two hours ahead. To prevent the cheese from drying out, leave it in its wrapper until serving time.
■ Serve cheese on wooden boards, marble cheese servers or platters with cutting knives and slicers. Separate strong-flavored cheeses from mild varieties and surround each with assorted crackers, breads, fruits and vegetables.
■ Cut fruit into bite-size wedges shortly before serving. Sprinkle pear, apple, peach or nectarine wedges with lemon juice to prevent discoloration. Separate grapes into small bunches. Cut juicy fruits such as melon and pineapple into cubes and serve with picks. Cover tightly with plastic wrap and refrigerate until serving time.

■ Crisp, raw vegetables such as sweet red pepper, cucumber and fennel are perfect partners for cheese. Cut into thin strips and sticks. *(See How to Julienne, page 34.)*
■ Refrigerate white and rosé wines just until chilled, for 1 or 2 hours before serving. Chill light red wines only slightly, if you wish, and serve full-bodied reds at room temperature. Open bottles of red wine in advance to allow for "breathing" time.
■ Chill white wine glasses on a tray in the refrigerator or freezer before using.
■ After the party, store leftover cheeses, individually wrapped in airtight plastic wrap, in the coldest part of the refrigerator. Recork and refrigerate the wine on its side. Use up all leftovers as soon as possible.

FROTHY MEXI-MOCHA COFFEE

LOW-SODIUM · QUICK

Rich enough to be a dessert.

Makes 2 drinks.
Recipe can be halved or doubled.
Nutrient Value Per Drink: 393 calories,
2 g protein, 14 g fat, 72 g carbohydrate,
33 mg sodium, 11 mg cholesterol.

½ cup lightly packed light brown sugar
2 ounces semisweet chocolate, chopped
½ strip orange rind (2 × ¼ inch)
¼ teaspoon ground cinnamon
⅛ teaspoon ground allspice
1½ cups hot strong coffee

¼ cup half-and-half, warmed
Orange rind and cinnamon sticks, for
      garnish *(optional)*
Chocolate-covered coffee beans *(optional)*

1. Combine sugar, chocolate, orange
rind, cinnamon and allspice in blender.
Whirl until finely chopped.
2. Add coffee to blender. Whirl for 1
to 2 minutes or until smooth and chocolate is melted, scraping down side if
needed. Pour into saucepan. Gently
heat. Combine in blender with warmed
half-and-half. Whirl until frothy.
Strain; discard solids.
3. Serve in cappuccino cups. Garnish
with orange rind and cinnamon sticks,
and chocolate covered coffee beans, if
you wish.

SPICED TEA

LOW-CALORIE · LOW-FAT

LOW-CHOLESTEROL · LOW-SODIUM

QUICK

A restorative brew, for after dinner, in the afternoon, or whenever you may feel like a little pampering. Pleasantly seasoned with ginger, cumin and allspice and sweetened with honey and dates.

Makes 4 drinks.
Recipe can be doubled or halved.
Nutrient Value Per Drink: 57 calories,
0 g protein, 0 g fat, 15 g carbohydrate,
3 mg sodium, 0 mg cholesterol.

---

4 cups water
2 tablespoons honey
4 slices pared fresh ginger, quarter-size
2 strips fresh lemon rind (2 × ¼-inch)
1 cinnamon stick
2 whole allspice berries
4 pitted dried dates, chopped
2 mild-flavored tea bags (non-herbal)

1. Combine water, honey, ginger, lemon rind, cinnamon and allspice in medium-size nonaluminum saucepan. Bring to simmering; cover and simmer 20 minutes. Add tea bags. Remove from heat. Steep 3 minutes.
2. Strain into cups and serve hot.

TEA FOR TWO

Buttermilk Scones with
Currants (78)

Maple Nut Rugelach (515)

Spiced Tea (this page)

TIPS FOR MAKING PERFECT TEA

■ To warm the tea-pot, fill with boiling water, then drain before adding tea.
■ Use freshly boiled water to make a pot of tea. Start with cold tap water, bring to a full rolling boil, remove from heat and pour over tea.
■ Use 1 teaspoon of loose tea or 1 tea bag for each cup of water.
■ Allow tea to steep 3 to 5 minutes; remove tea bags before serving. (Loose tea leaves will settle to the bottom of the pot; pour carefully.)
■ When making iced tea, use 50 percent more tea to allow for dilution from melting ice.
■ Once refrigerated, tea may turn murky or cloudy. The flavor is not affected, and the clear appearance can be restored by adding a little boiling water. To prevent cloudiness, store freshly made tea at room temperture until ready to serve.

CAPPUCCINO BRANDY SHAKE

QUICK

A rich after-dinner drink for coffee lovers.

Makes 2 drinks.
Recipe can be halved or doubled.
Nutrient Value Per Drink: 317 calories,
9 g protein, 8 g fat, 43 g carbohydrate,
117 mg sodium, 10 mg cholesterol.

Lemon slice
3 tablespoons grated semisweet chocolate
1 cup lowfat milk
1 cup frozen vanilla yogurt
¼ cup coffee-flavored brandy
1 teaspoon fresh lemon juice
1 teaspoon instant espresso powder
¼ teaspoon ground cinnamon
Shaved chocolate and ground cinnamon,
    for garnish *(optional)*

1. Rub rim of 2 saucer-like glasses with cut lemon. Dip in grated chocolate. Chill in freezer.
2. Combine milk, frozen yogurt, brandy, lemon juice, espresso powder and cinnamon in blender. Whirl until smooth.
3. Pour into chilled glasses. Sprinkle with shaved chocolate and cinnamon, if you wish.

CHAPTER 13

Barbecued Coconut Shrimp (page 564).

COOKING ON THE GRILL

BARBECUE PRIMER

HOW HOT IS HOT?

To check the temperature of your fire, *briefly* hold your hand, palm down, about 5 inches above coals, counting the seconds before you pull your hand away:

5 seconds—medium-low fire
4 seconds—medium fire
3 seconds—medium-hot fire
2 seconds—hot!

BARBECUE SAFETY
Preparing the Grill

- Read the manufacturer's instructions for your grill and follow them carefully.
- Check previously used equipment to ensure it is in proper working order, i.e., vents free from foreign material. On gas models, check to see there are no leaking connections.
- Situate the barbecue grill so that the operator's back is to the wind.
- Place the grill on a level, noncombustible surface and allow at least an 18-inch clearance on all sides to maintain sufficient supply and circulation of air. Don't set up under a tree.
- Keep a fire extinguisher handy in case of accidents.
- Cut all excess fat from meats to eliminate the risk of flare-ups.
- If using starter fluid, reseal after use and place it at a safe distance from the grill and all flames.
- Do not lean over the grill when lighting the coals or cooking.
- Never add liquid starter after coals are lighted.
- When lighting a gas model, be sure the cover remains open until the burner is burning smoothly.

Using Your Grill

- Never wear loose clothing when working with a barbecue. Loose clothing can present a potential fire hazard.

- Wear barbecue mitts when adjusting hot vents and, of course, whenever using the grill.
- Use long-handled tongs or spatula when turning food on the grill.
- If flare-ups do occur, remove the food to the side of the grill until the flames have died down.
- Keep young children and all animals away from the hot grill.

The End of a Successful Barbecue

- Do not dispose of coals until they have cooled completely.
- Make sure all burner control valves are switched off and, if applicable, gas supplies discontinued.
- Clean the barbecue grill once it has cooled down and store in a dry place.

A GUIDE TO GREAT GRILLING

Use the following guide for a no-fail, no-burn barbecue.

- Store charcoal in a cool, dry place, tightly closed in its original package. Charcoal is difficult to light if it gets wet or absorbs a lot of moisture from the air.
- Heap the charcoal in the center of the grill and set aflame. Or use a special metal "chimney" to start coals, following manufacturer's directions. With this device, coals are ready in about 15 minutes, and no special starting fluid is required.
- To start the fire, use charcoal starter or an electric starter. Chemical charcoal starter may cause "off" flavors in food; the electric starter imparts no odor. If you're using liquid starter, wait for 2 minutes before igniting so the starter can soak in properly, or follow the manufacturer's instructions. Block or solid starters are also very good.

- Start a charcoal fire at least 30 to 40 minutes before you want to begin cooking, to allow the coals to burn and become covered with a gray ash. The heat then will be radiant and cook the food gradually without burning.
- Once the coals are hot, separate them into an even layer on the bottom of the grill. For long cooking times, add charcoal from time to time.
- Sprinkle the charcoal with fresh herbs, such as marjoram, rosemary, thyme or mint, or dried herbs that have been soaked in water, such as bay leaf or fennel, to give grilled food a subtle flavor.
- Brush the grill rack, before placing over the fire, with vegetable oil or coat with nonstick vegetable-oil cooking spray just before cooking to prevent food from sticking.
- When grilling fatty foods, make a drip pan of aluminum foil and place directly under food to prevent flare-ups from dripping fat. Arrange coals around pan.
- To maintain an even temperature, place the grill in a sheltered place, away from drafts, but not under a tree or too near a building. On windy days, cover the grill with a hood or dome or a tent of aluminum foil.
- The last glowing embers can be used to keep coffee hot, toast marshmallows or pound cake, heat fudge or sauce for ice cream, warm cookies, rolls and pie, or grill orange or pineapple slices.

Marvelous Micro-Grilling Use your microwave oven to help speed up barbecue cooking time. Follow microwave oven manufacturer's instructions for precooking chicken, sausage, spareribs and "hard" vegetables such as potatoes and carrots.

GRILLED QUESADILLAS

LOW-CHOLESTEROL · QUICK

Grill tortillas for 30 seconds, quesadillas for 3 minutes; or broil quesadillas for 3 to 5 minutes.
Makes 8 servings.
Recipe can be halved or doubled.
Nutrient Value Per Serving: 503 calories, 17 protein, 32 g fat, 39 carbohydrate, 974 sodium, 49 g cholesterol.

Vegetable Filling:
1½ cups chopped cooked broccoli
1 cup shredded Cheddar cheese (4 ounces)
1 can (4 ounces) chopped green chilies, drained
⅓ cup finely chopped green onion
2 tablespoons finely chopped cilantro OR: parsley
½ teaspoon salt

Sausage Filling:
1 tablespoon olive oil
1 medium-size yellow onion, finely chopped
2 sweet red peppers, roasted *(see How-To, page 433)*, peeled, seeded and chopped (⅔ cup chopped) OR: ⅔ cup chopped, bottled, roasted red pepper
1 clove garlic, finely chopped
1 teaspoon ground cumin
½ teaspoon salt
½ pound sweet Italian sausage, casing removed and meat crumbled
1 cup shredded Monterey Jack cheese (4 ounces)
2 tablespoons finely chopped fresh cilantro OR: parsley
1 tablespoon finely chopped pickled jalapeño pepper OR: 3 or 4 dashes liquid red-pepper seasoning

10 corn tortillas (7 inches)
6 flour tortillas (10 inches)
Oil for brushing grill and tortillas

1. Prepare Vegetable Filling: Combine broccoli, Cheddar cheese, chilies, green onion, cilantro and salt in small bowl. Cover and refrigerate until ready to use.
2. Prepare Sausage Filling: Heat oil in medium-size skillet over medium heat. Add onion and red pepper; cook, stirring occasionally, for 10 minutes or until softened. Add garlic, cumin and salt; cook 2 minutes. Scrape into medium-size bowl. Add sausage to skillet; cook until no longer pink, about 6 minutes. Transfer to bowl. Add Monterey Jack cheese, cilantro and jalapeño pepper to bowl. Cover and refrigerate until ready to use.
3. Prepare grill or preheat broiler. Oil grid or baking sheet.

(continued)

ASSORTED FILLINGS
Here are two fillings for quesadillas—one vegetable and one meat. However, almost any vegetable/cheese/chili or meat/cheese/chili combination will work. Serve the quesadillas with a fresh salsa, guacamole or taco sauce.

GRILLED QUESADILLAS (*continued*)

4. Brush both sides of tortillas with oil. Grill 5 inches above medium coals for 15 seconds on each side or until blistered and softened. Or, cook tortillas in nonstick skillet over moderately high heat as above.
5. Prepare Vegetable Quesadillas: Arrange ½ cup of Vegetable Filling along one side of each flour tortilla; fold over other side to enclose filling and form turnover. Brush both sides of folded tortillas with oil.
6. To grill: Grill 5 inches above medium coals for 1½ minutes on each side or until crisp and filling is heated through. Transfer quesadillas to platter.
7. To broil: Broil quesadillas on prepared baking sheet 5 inches from heat for 1½ to 2½ minutes on each side.
8. Prepare Sausage Quesadillas: Arrange ⅓ cup Sausage Filling along one side of each corn tortilla; fold over other side to enclose filling and form turnover. Brush both sides of tortillas with oil. Cook as in Step 6 or 7. Serve with salsa, guacamole or taco sauce, if you wish.

QUESADILLAS MAKE-AHEAD TIP:
The fillings can be made a day ahead and refrigerated, covered.

BARBECUED COCONUT SHRIMP

Try *as a main course. (Pictured on page 561.)*

Toast coconut at 400° for 6 minutes. Grill shrimp and banana for 6 minutes; or broil for 6 to 7 minutes.
Makes 21 to 25 pieces (appetizer servings). Recipe can be halved or doubled.
Nutrient Value Per Piece: 39 calories, 3 g protein, 2 g fat, 3 g carbohydrate, 78 mg sodium, 24 mg cholesterol.

¾ cup flaked coconut
1 medium-size banana
2 pieces pared fresh ginger, quarter-size
1 clove garlic, peeled

2 tablespoons lime juice
1 tablespoon peanut oil OR: corn oil
½ teaspoon ground turmeric
½ teaspoon salt
⅛ teaspoon ground hot red pepper
1 pound large (21 to 25) shrimp, shelled and deveined

1. Preheat oven to hot (400°).
2. Toast coconut on baking sheet in preheated hot oven (400°) for 6 minutes or until golden brown; stir occasionally. Reserve ¼ cup; transfer remainder to food processor or blender.
3. Add one-third of banana, the ginger, garlic, lime juice, oil, turmeric, salt and ground red pepper to processor. Whirl until smooth. Transfer to bowl.
4. Mix shrimp with banana-coconut mixture to coat. Refrigerate 2 hours.
5. Prepare grill or preheat broiler.
6. Slice remaining banana ½ inch thick. Toss shrimp and banana with remaining ¼ cup toasted coconut.
7. To grill: Grill shrimp and banana in grill basket (or thread on skewers) 4 inches above medium coals for 6 minutes or until shrimp are firm-tender, turning once.
8. To broil: Broil shrimp and banana on sheet of aluminum foil 4 inches from heat for 6 to 7 minutes or until shrimp are firm-tender, turning once.

INTERNATIONAL GRILL

Hummus with Vegetable Sticks

Pita Bread

Barbecued Coconut Shrimp
(this page)

Green Salad with Ginger-Sesame Dressing
(179)

Blueberries and Strawberries

GRILLED PEPPERS WITH CORN AND CHEESE

QUICK

Grill for 7 minutes; or broil for 10 minutes.
Makes 4 servings.
Recipe can be halved or doubled.
Nutrient Value Per Serving: 175 calories,
9 g protein, 12 g fat, 11 g carbohydrate,
296 mg sodium, 25 mg cholesterol.

2 large sweet red peppers (8 ounces
    each), cored, seeded and halved
    lengthwise
2 teaspoons vegetable oil OR: olive oil
¾ cup fresh whole-kernel corn OR:
    frozen, thawed and drained
½ cup firmly packed cilantro leaves,
    chopped OR: parsley
4 ounces Monterey Jack cheese, cut into
    ½-inch cubes
1 tablespoon lime juice OR: orange juice
¼ teaspoon salt
¼ teaspoon ground coriander

1. Prepare grill or preheat broiler. Oil
grid or broiler-pan rack.
2. Brush peppers with oil. Combine
corn, cilantro, cheese, lime juice, salt
and ground coriander in small bowl.
3. To grill: Grill peppers, rounded-side
down, 4 inches over medium coals for 3
minutes or until lightly charred and
softened. Fill each pepper with corn
mixture. Grill, covered with dome, 4
minutes or until cheese is melted and
peppers are hot.
4. To broil: Broil peppers, cut-side
down, 6 inches from heat for 5 minutes
or until lightly charred and softened.
Fill each pepper with corn mixture.
Broil for 5 minutes or until cheese is
melted and peppers are hot.

Make-Ahead Tip: The peppers can be
cooked and then filled up to 3 hours
ahead and refrigerated, covered. Grill or
broil with filling just before serving.

GRILLED PITAS WITH CHICK-PEAS

LOW-CHOLESTEROL

Grill for 3 to 4 minutes; or broil for 8 minutes.
Makes 4 main-dish servings or 16 appetizers.
Recipe can be halved or doubled.
Nutrient Value Per Serving: 442 calories, 12 g protein, 16 g fat, 64 g carbohydrate, 669 mg sodium, 0 mg cholesterol.

1 small bunch escarole (8 ounces), coarsely chopped or sliced (4 cups)
3 cloves garlic, finely chopped
2 ripe tomatoes (6 ounces each), seeded and cut into ½-inch chunks
¼ cup golden raisins
2 tablespoons chopped parsley
1½ tablespoons chopped fresh mint
    OR: 1 teaspoon dried
1 can (19 ounces) chick-peas, drained, rinsed and drained
4 tablespoons olive oil
2 tablespoons water
2 tablespoons lemon juice
¼ teaspoon salt
4 large pitas (6 to 7 inches each)

1. Prepare grill or preheat broiler. Oil grid or broiler-pan rack.
2. Blanch escarole in large pot boiling water 1 minute. Drain; rinse under cold water; drain and dry well.
3. Combine escarole, garlic, tomatoes, raisins, parsley and mint in bowl; reserve. Combine ¾ cup chick-peas, 2 tablespoons oil, the water and 1 tablespoon lemon juice in food processor or blender. Whirl until smooth, about 30 seconds, scraping down side as needed. Add to escarole mixture along with remaining chick-peas, 1 tablespoon oil, lemon juice and salt.
4. Open one end of each pita; spoon escarole mixture into pita. Brush each pita with remaining oil.
5. To grill: Grill pitas 5 inches from medium coals, uncovered, until lightly browned, crisped and heated through, 1½ to 2 minutes each side.
6. To broil: Broil pitas 6 inches from heat until browned, crisped and heated through, about 4 minutes each side.

PITA BREAD SERVING IDEAS
Delicious as an appetizer, or for lunch.

PITA BREAD MAKE-AHEAD TIP:
The filling can be made 2 days ahead and refrigerated, covered, but fill the pitas just before serving.

GRILLED STUFFED CHICKEN BREASTS WITH FENNEL

The chicken can be served on the bone, or for a more dramatic presentation, removed from the bone and cut into thin slices. Also delicious as picnic food at room temperature or chilled. Try the fennel with other grilled meats, as part of a vegetable platter or as a first course.

Grill chicken for about 16 minutes, fennel for about 12 minutes; or broil chicken for 12 to 16 minutes, fennel for 12 to 15 minutes.

Makes 4 servings.
Recipe can be halved or doubled.

Nutrient Value Per Serving: 628 calories, 60 g protein, 38 g fat, 8 g carbohydrate, 967 mg sodium, 184 mg cholesterol.

Stuffing:

3 tablespoons *un*salted butter
⅔ cup finely chopped onion
½ cup finely chopped fresh fennel
1 clove garlic, finely chopped
⅓ cup chopped prosciutto (1 ounce)
2 tablespoons grated Parmesan cheese
2 tablespoons dry bread crumbs
1 tablespoon snipped feathery fennel top
⅛ teaspoon salt
⅛ teaspoon pepper

2 large whole chicken breasts (about 1½ pounds each), split and pocket cut out along breastbone side of each half
2 tablespoons olive oil
½ teaspoon salt
¼ teaspoon pepper

Grilled Fennel:

1 large fresh fennel bulb (about 1¼ pounds), trimmed and quartered lengthwise
2 tablespoons olive oil
¼ teaspoon salt
⅛ teaspoon pepper

1. Prepare grill or preheat broiler. Oil grid or broiler-pan rack.

2. Prepare Stuffing: Heat butter in medium-size skillet over moderate heat. Add onion and fennel; cook, stirring occasionally, for 5 minutes. Add garlic; cook, stirring, for 1 minute. Transfer vegetables to bowl; add prosciutto, Parmesan, bread crumbs, fennel top and salt and pepper.

3. Pat chicken dry with paper toweling. Spoon stuffing into chicken pockets; close with wooden pick or metal poultry skewer. Brush chicken with olive oil; sprinkle with salt and pepper.

4. Prepare Fennel: Brush fennel with oil; season with salt and pepper.

5. To grill: Arrange chicken, skin-side down, in center of grid 5 inches above hot coals. Arrange fennel around outside of grid. Cover the grill with dome. Grill the fennel turning occasionally, for about 12 minutes or until tender; grill the chicken for about 16 minutes or until cooked through and no longer pink near bone.

6. To broil: Broil 4 inches from heat; chicken for 12 to 16 minutes or until
(continued)

STUFFED CHICKEN BREASTS MAKE-AHEAD TIP: The stuffing can be prepared several hours ahead and refrigerated in a bowl, covered. The chicken can be cooked several hours ahead and refrigerated, covered. Serve chilled or at room temperature.

GRILLED STUFFED CHICKEN BREASTS
WITH FENNEL *(continued)*

no longer pink near bone, turning once; fennel for 12 to 15 minutes or until tender, turning frequently and brushing with oil as needed.

7. To serve: Remove picks or skewers from chicken and serve with fennel. Leave chicken on bone, or remove and cut into thin slices.

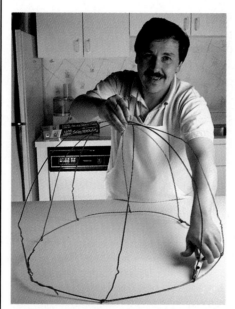

HOW TO MAKE A GRILL DOME COVER

When a recipe calls for a covered grill, an open-style grill may be used by constructing your own dome from a wire coat hanger frame and covering it with heavy-duty aluminum foil.

1. Untwist the hooks of several hangers and open hangers out into straight pieces. With pliers, twist together the ends of 2 or 3 hanger pieces to make a base ring the size of your grill. Use 4 more straightened hangers to fashion a dome: Bend one hanger into a semicircle. Use pliers to attach ends to base at opposite points of the ring. Repeat with remaining hangers, spacing evenly around the ring and crossing at the center top. Snip the hook from another hanger to use as a top handle. Use pliers to attach.

2. Starting at base ring, wrap sheets of foil over top center of dome, down to opposite side of base ring. Use several sheets of foil and repeat wrapping until dome is completely covered. Snip a hole at the top and pull the hanger handle through.

3. Lightly press foil, molding to dome frame. Tuck foil under base ring, crimping tightly to secure.

GRILLED CHICKEN WITH PEARS

Mixed greens and blue cheese salad are delightful accompaniments. Or serve the grilled pears as an appetizer with blue cheese.

Grill for 30 minutes; or broil for 30 minutes.
Makes 4 servings.
Recipe can be halved or doubled.
Nutrient Value Per Serving: 464 calories, 33 g protein, 31 g fat, 13 g carbohydrate, 245 mg sodium, 116 mg cholesterol.

4 whole chicken legs (about 8 ounces each)
2 ripe Bosc or Anjou pears, halved lengthwise and cored
½ cup olive oil
½ cup balsamic vinegar OR: red wine vinegar
2 teaspoons finely chopped fresh rosemary OR: ½ teaspoon dried
2 cloves garlic, crushed
½ teaspoon salt
¼ teaspoon ground black pepper
Fresh rosemary, for garnish *(optional)*

1. Place chicken and pears in 3-quart casserole or bowl. Stir together oil, vinegar, rosemary, garlic, salt and pepper until well blended. Pour over chicken and pears; gently toss to coat well. Cover casserole and refrigerate overnight, stirring occasionally.
2. Prepare grill or preheat broiler. Oil grid or broiler-pan rack. Pour marinade into small saucepan. Boil 10 minutes.
3. To grill: Grill chicken, skin side up, on grid 5 inches above medium-hot coals, covered with dome with vents half open, for 20 minutes. Turn chicken over halfway through cooking and baste with marinade. Add pears, cut-side up, to grill. Continue to grill, covered, 10 minutes, turning chicken and pears over halfway through and basting with marinade. When cooked, the chicken should no longer be pink near bone and pears should be heated through and tender.
4. To broil: Broil chicken, skin-side down, 7 to 9 inches from heat, for 20 minutes, brushing occasionally with marinade. Add pears, cut-side up, to broiler pan. Turn chicken over. Broil another 10 minutes, brushing with marinade, until chicken is no longer pink near bone and pears are heated through and tender.
5. Garnish with fresh rosemary, if you wish.

Make-Ahead Tip: The chicken can be marinated, covered, in the refrigerator a day ahead. The chicken can also be cooked a day ahead and refrigerated, covered, and served chilled.

GRILLED CORNISH HENS WITH CITRUS

The citrus oil is also delicious with chicken, pork chops or swordfish.

Grill for 25 minutes; or broil for 18 to 20 minutes.
Makes 4 servings.
Recipe can be halved or doubled.
Nutrient Value Per Serving: 464 calories, 35 g protein, 31 g fat, 11 g carbohydrate, 378 mg sodium, 110 mg cholesterol.

¼ cup corn oil OR: canola oil
4 strips orange rind (3 × ¼ inch each)
3 strips lemon rind (3 × ¼ inch each)
3 strips lime rind (2 × ¼ inch each)
2 strips grapefruit rind (1 × ½ inch each)
½ teaspoon ground cinnamon
⅛ teaspoon ground allspice
⅔ cup orange juice
1 tablespoon lemon juice
1 tablespoon lime juice
1 teaspoon grenadine
1 grapefruit, peeled and bitter white pith removed*, and flesh sliced crosswise into ½-inch-thick rounds
2 Cornish game hens (1¼ pounds each), split down backbone
½ teaspoon salt

1. Heat oil in small skillet over low heat. Add orange, lemon, lime and grapefruit rinds, cinnamon and allspice; remove from heat. Let stand 2 hours. Remove and discard rinds. Transfer oil to small bowl.
2. Combine orange, lemon and lime juices in small skillet. Cook, uncovered, over moderately high heat until syrupy and reduced to 3 tablespoons, about 6 minutes. Stir juice into citrus oil along with the grenadine.
3. Prepare grill or preheat broiler. Oil grid or broiler-pan rack.
4. Brush grapefruit slices with 2 tablespoons citrus oil; reserve. Brush hens with half of the remaining oil; sprinkle with salt.
5. To grill: Grill hens, skin-side down, 5 inches above medium-hot fire, covered with dome, for 25 minutes or until no longer pink near bone; turn hens over about 4 times, brushing with remaining oil. During last 5 minutes of grilling time, place grapefruit rounds alongside hens. Grill, covered.
6. To broil: Broil hens, skin-side down, 6 inches from heat for 10 minutes. Turn skin-side up and brush with remaining oil. Broil 8 to 10 minutes or until no longer pink near bone. During last 5 minutes of broiling time, place grapefruit rounds on broiler pan.
7. Serve hens with grapefruit rounds.

*Note: Leave outer membrane on grapefruit slices intact so slices hold together during cooking.
Make-Ahead Tip: The citrus oil can be prepared several days ahead. The hens can be grilled ahead and served at room temperature. If preparing hens several hours ahead, refrigerate, covered.

BARBECUED BRISKET WITH RANCHERO SAUCE

*O*ur Ranchero Sauce is a tomato-y barbecue sauce with garlic, Worcestershire and
herbs. Although the brisket requires some
attention while on the grill, the results are
well worth it.

Grill 14 to 20 minutes, then grill, wrapped, 2
to 2½ hours; or broil 14 to 20 minutes, and
then roast, wrapped, at 400° for 2 to 2½
hours.
Makes 12 servings.
Nutrient Value Per Serving: 475 calories,
27 g protein, 37 g fat, 7 g carbohydrate,
909 mg sodium, 104 mg cholesterol.

Dry Rub:
1 tablespoon salt
1 teaspoon black pepper
1 teaspoon ground hot red pepper
1 teaspoon leaf oregano, crumbled
1 teaspoon ground cumin

1 fresh beef brisket (about 4 pounds),
    trimmed
2 cloves garlic, sliced

Ranchero Sauce:
2 tablespoons vegetable oil OR: olive oil
1 medium-size onion, chopped
1 stalk celery, chopped
2 cloves garlic, finely chopped
2 teaspoons chili powder
1 teaspoon ground cumin
½ teaspoon leaf oregano, crumbled
1 can (15 ounces) tomato sauce
1 can (14½ ounces) tomatoes, chopped,
    with liquid
1 tablespoon Worcestershire sauce
2 teaspoons brown sugar
Bay leaf
2 tablespoons finely chopped cilantro OR:
    parsley

1. Prepare grill or preheat oven to hot
(400°). Oil grid or broiler-pan rack.
2. Prepare Dry Rub: Combine salt,
black pepper, hot red pepper, oregano
and cumin in small bowl. Pat brisket
dry with paper toweling. Cut small slits
all over brisket; push garlic in slits. Rub
brisket with dry mixture.
3. To grill: Grill brisket on oiled grid 5
inches above medium-hot coals, covered with dome, 7 to 10 minutes on
each side or until browned.
4. Remove brisket from grid. Carefully
remove grid from grill. Scoop coals to
side of grill; no coals should be directly
under the center of the grill where the
meat will be. Replace grid. Carefully
wrap brisket in heavy-duty aluminum-
foil packet. Place packet on grid. Cover
with dome. Cook over medium coals
until tender, about 2 to 2½ hours, re-
placing and banking coals as necessary.
After 1½ hours, listen for juices sizzling
in foil packet. If you don't hear sizzling,
carefully unwrap and rewrap in new aluminum foil, adding 1 to 2 tablespoons
water to meat. Continue cooking.
5. To broil: Broil brisket 3 inches from
heat for 7 to 10 minutes on each side or
until browned. Then bake, wrapped, in
preheated hot oven (400°) for 2 to 2½
hours or until tender, checking after
1½ hours as in Step 4 above.
6. Meanwhile, prepare Ranchero Sauce:
Heat oil in medium-size saucepan. Add
onion and celery; cook over moderate
heat, stirring, for 5 to 7 minutes or
until onion is golden. Add garlic, chili
powder, cumin and oregano; cook, stirring, for 1 minute. Add tomato sauce,
tomatoes with liquid, Worcestershire
sauce, brown sugar and bay leaf. Bring
to boiling. Lower heat; simmer, stirring
occasionally, for 20 minutes.
7. Remove brisket packet from grid or
oven. Carefully open and transfer brisket to carving board. Pour accumulated
cooking juices from brisket into sauce.
Skim any fat from sauce. Remove bay
leaf. Stir in cilantro.
8. Slice meat and serve with sauce.

Make-Ahead Tip: The brisket can be
cooked a day ahead and refrigerated,
covered. Serve cold or at room temperature with heated sauce.

THE MYSTIQUE OF MESQUITE
Mesquite is one of the
wide variety of foods
that add special fla-
vor to outdoor-
cooked meals. Long
used as a charcoal in
Texas, where the
shrub wood grows
profusely, mesquite
imparts a pungent
taste, so pair with full-
flavored foods such
as pork, beef, lamb,
sausages and
stronger-flavored fish
such as salmon and
bluefish. Mesquite is
commercially avail-
able in two forms—
charcoal and wood
chips. The former is
used interchangeably
with charcoal bri-
quets. Mesquite char-
coal produces a
hotter fire than the
standard briquets, so
raise the cooking grid
accordingly. Mesquite
wood chips, on the
other hand, burn
slowly and should
always be used in
conjunction with char-
coal briquets. Soak a
handful of chips for at
least 30 minutes, and
then add directly to
the coals. Watch the
grill carefully, since
mesquite charcoal has
a tendency to snap
and send sparks
flying.
    For other flavors,
experiment with hick-
ory, apple or cherry
wood chips. Use
according to package
directions.

2 dried ancho chilies (2 ounces), or other
  mild dried chilies
2 cups hot water
1 can (13¾ ounces) beef broth
1 can (14½ ounces) tomatoes, undrained
¼ cup white wine vinegar
1 medium-size onion, sliced
2 cloves garlic, chopped
6 whole peppercorns
4 whole cloves
1 small cinnamon stick, cracked
1 teaspoon cumin seeds
1 teaspoon leaf oregano, crumbled
2 tablespoons sugar
4 pounds short ribs, cut into 6- to 8-inch
  lengths

1. Soak chilies in the hot water in
small bowl for 15 minutes or until soft.
2. Strain soaking liquid into large pot.
Stem, seed and chop chilies. Add chilies, broth, tomatoes, vinegar, onion,
garlic, peppercorns, cloves, cinnamon,
cumin seeds, oregano, sugar and short
ribs to casserole. Bring to boiling.
Lower heat; simmer, covered, for 1 to
1½ hours or until meat is tender.
3. Transfer meat to plate. Remove cinnamon stick and discard. Skim fat from
liquid and discard. Strain liquid, reserving solids and liquid separately. Remove
ribs to a platter. Working in batches if
necessary, add tomato and other solids
from cooking broth to food processor or
blender. Whirl until pureed, adding any
liquid as necessary. Combine puree and
reserved liquid in pot.
4. Boil, uncovered, stirring occasionally, until thickened and reduced to
about 3 cups, about 30 minutes.
5. Prepare grill or preheat broiler.
Spoon some sauce over ribs.
6. To grill: Grill ribs 5 inches above
medium-hot coals, covered with dome,
for 8 to 10 minutes or until crisp, basting and turning.
7. To broil: Broil ribs 4 inches from
heat for 8 to 10 minutes or until crisp,
basting and turning.
8. Serve remaining sauce separately.

BARBECUED RIBS WITH ANCHO CHILI SAUCE

The ancho chilies add a subtle, hot smoky
taste to the sauce, but you can substitute
any dried chili. Serve with our Grilled
Cheddar Grits (page 584). Any leftover
sauce can be used for grilling other meats
or poultry.

Grill or broil for 8 to 10 minutes.
Makes 8 servings.
Recipe can be halved or doubled.
Nutrient Value Per Serving: 459 calories,
17 g protein, 41 g fat, 5 g carbohydrate,
231 mg sodium, 84 mg cholesterol.

BURGERS WITH BULGUR AND CASHEWS

Grill for 5 to 7 minutes; or broil for 7 to 10 minutes.
Makes 5 burgers.
Nutrient Value Per Burger: 298 calories, 18 g protein, 19 g fat, 16 g carbohydrate, 170 mg sodium, 87 mg cholesterol.

⅓ cup bulgur
¼ cup (¾ ounce) chopped sun-dried
    tomatoes (dry pack)
1 cup boiling water
¾ pound lean ground beef
¾ cup chopped cashews (3 ounces)
2 green onions, chopped
1 egg
¼ teaspoon salt
¼ teaspoon ground black pepper
5 split hard rolls or buns

1. Soak bulgur and sun-dried tomatoes in boiling water in small saucepan off heat for 20 to 30 minutes. Drain in sieve, pressing out any excess liquid if necessary. Place in large bowl.
2. Prepare grill or preheat broiler.
3. Add ground beef, cashews, green onion, egg, salt and pepper to bulgur mixture; stir until well blended. Shape into five 5-ounce patties, about 3½ inches in diameter.
4. To grill: Place burgers on grid 5 inches above hot coals. Grill, uncovered, 5 to 7 minutes or until desired doneness, turning halfway through cooking.
5. To broil: Broil 3 inches from heat for 7 to 10 minutes or until desired doneness, turning once halfway through cooking.
6. Serve on split hard rolls with condiments.

CHANGE-OF-PACE BURGER
Bulgur Cashew Burgers have a deliciously nutty taste, making them a surprising alternative to regular burgers.

BULGUR BURGER MAKE-AHEAD TIP:
Burgers can be assembled up to 6 hours ahead and refrigerated, covered. Bring to room temperature.

SPICY GRILLED PORK TENDERLOIN

LOW-CALORIE · LOW-FAT

LOW-CHOLESTEROL

Serve thinly sliced with a citrus salad or a salad from our Salads and Dressings chapter (page 143).

Grill for 10 minutes; or broil for 10 to 12 minutes.

Makes 3 servings.

Recipe can be doubled.

Nutrient Value Per Serving: 166 calories, 25 g protein, 3 g fat, 9 g carbohydrate, 772 mg sodium, 73 mg cholesterol.

PORK TENDERLOIN MAKE-AHEAD TIP:

Pork can be marinated, covered, several hours ahead in the refrigerator. The pork can also be cooked ahead and refrigerated, covered. Serve chilled or at room temperature.

¼ cup soy sauce

3 tablespoons brown sugar

1 teaspoon ground cumin

1 teaspoon dried mustard

½ teaspoon sweet paprika

5 cloves garlic, sliced

2 tablespoons chopped cilantro OR: parsley

1 pork tenderloin (about 12 ounces), trimmed

1. Combine soy sauce, sugar, cumin, mustard, paprika, garlic and cilantro in plastic food-storage bag. Fold under thin end(s) of tenderloin to make an even thickness; tie end(s) with kitchen string. Add tenderloin to bag. Push out all air; seal. Refrigerate and let marinate for 30 to 60 minutes.

2. Prepare grill or preheat broiler. Oil grid or broiler-pan rack.

3. To grill: Grill tenderloin 5 inches above hot coals, covered with dome, 10 minutes or until instant-read thermometer registers 160°; turn over halfway through grilling, basting with marinade. Let stand 5 minutes.

4. To broil: Broil tenderloin 3 inches from heat for 10 to 12 minutes or until instant-read thermometer registers 160°; turn over halfway through cooking, basting with marinade. Let stand 5 minutes.

5. Thinly slice crosswise. Discard any leftover marinade.

SATURDAY BARBECUE

Spicy Grilled Pork Tenderloin (this page)

Citrus Salad with Honey-Poppy Seed Dressing (184)

Grilled Sweet Peppers

Fresh Fruit

GRILLED STUFFED PORK ROAST

Grill for 1½ hours; or roast at 350° for 1¾ hours.
Makes 10 servings.
Nutrient Value Per Serving: 385 calories, 25 g protein, 23 g fat, 16 g carbohydrate, 117 mg sodium, 84 mg cholesterol.

Stuffing:
⅓ cup ruby port
2 teaspoons brown sugar
¼ teaspoon ground cardamom
½ cup dried cherries, pitted
½ cup dried apricot halves, slivered
½ cup chopped pistachios OR: whole

Basting Sauce:
½ cup ruby port
1 can (5½ ounces) apricot nectar
1 tablespoon red wine vinegar
¼ teaspoon ground cardamom
¼ teaspoon salt
1 tablespoon finely chopped fresh sage
    OR: 1 teaspoon dried
¼ teaspoon ground black pepper

1 pork roast (about 3½ pounds), chine
    bone removed

1. Prepare grill or preheat oven to moderate (350°). Oil grid or broiler-pan rack.
2. Prepare Stuffing: Heat port, brown sugar and cardamom in small saucepan to boiling. Remove from heat. Add cherries and apricots, pressing down into port. Let stand 15 minutes. Stir in pistachios.
3. Meanwhile prepare Sauce: Combine port, nectar, vinegar, cardamom and salt in small saucepan. Bring to boiling. Lower heat; simmer until reduced to ⅓ cup, about 10 minutes. Stir in sage and pepper.
4. Trim any excess fat from pork. Using long, narrow sharp knife, make horizontal slit from one end into center of roast; twist knife to make opening. Repeat from other end.

5. Stir stuffing to combine. Push into slits, working from both ends. Use narrow handle end of wooden spoon to help distribute stuffing into middle of roast.
6. To grill: Pour 1 cup water into rectangular metal pan. Move coals to side of grill and place pan in center under grid. Grill pork roast 5 inches above medium-hot coals over pan, covered with dome, for 1½ hours or until instant-read thermometer registers 160°. Replace and bank coals as necessary. Coals will cool down to medium-low. Baste roast occasionally with basting sauce during the last 15 to 20 minutes. Let roast stand 10 minutes before carving.
7. To broil: Pour 1 cup water into bottom of broiler pan. Place roast on broiler pan rack. Roast in preheated moderate oven (350°) for 1¾ hours or until instant-read thermometer registers 160°. Baste roast with sauce during last 30 minutes of cooking, brushing every 10 minutes. Let roast stand 10 minutes before carving.

PORK ROAST SERVING IDEAS
Warm or at room temperature, the roast can be accompanied by wild rice. Or try it chilled, sliced, for a picnic.

PORK ROAST MAKE-AHEAD TIP:
Roast can be stuffed up to 3 hours ahead and refrigerated, covered. Basting sauce can be prepared a day ahead and refrigerated, covered. Reheat. You can also cook the pork roast a day ahead and refrigerate, covered. Slice and serve chilled.

GRILLED LAMB KABOBS WITH PAPAYA

Grill lamb for 8 to 12 minutes, papaya for 2 minutes; broil lamb for 8 to 12 minutes, papaya for 2 minutes.

Makes 6 servings.

Recipe can be halved or doubled.

Nutrient Value Per Serving: 478 calories, 37 g protein, 30 g fat, 15 g carbohydrate, 169 mg sodium, 135 mg cholesterol.

Marinade:

¼ cup olive oil
2 tablespoons lemon juice
1 tablespoon finely chopped pared fresh ginger
1 tablespoon finely chopped garlic
2 teaspoons Dijon-style mustard
1 teaspoon leaf rosemary, crumbled
¼ teaspoon salt
¼ teaspoon pepper

2½ pounds boneless leg of lamb, cut into 2-inch pieces

Sauce:

1 ripe papaya (1 pound), peeled, halved and seeded
1 teaspoon grated orange rind
⅓ cup orange juice
1 tablespoon lemon juice
2 teaspoons finely chopped pared fresh ginger
2 teaspoons honey, or to taste

1 ripe papaya (1 pound), peeled, cut lengthwise into sixths and seeded
1 tablespoon lemon juice
1 teaspoon finely chopped pared fresh ginger
1 tablespoon *un*salted butter, melted

1. Prepare Marinade: Combine olive oil, lemon juice, ginger, garlic, mustard, rosemary, salt and pepper in medium-size bowl. Add lamb; toss to coat. Refrigerate, covered, for 2 hours or overnight.

2. Prepare Sauce: Cut papaya into cubes. Transfer to food processor. Add orange rind and juice, lemon juice, ginger and honey. Whirl until smooth puree; you should have about 1⅔ cups. Transfer to small bowl and refrigerate, covered, until ready to serve.

3. Combine papaya slices, lemon juice and ginger in medium-size bowl. Cover and refrigerate until ready to serve.

4. Prepare grill or preheat broiler.

5. Thread meat on 6 skewers. Thread papaya slices lengthwise on 2 skewers; brush with butter.

6. To grill: Grill kabobs, turning occasionally, 5 inches above medium-hot coals, covered with dome, for 8 to 12 minutes for medium-rare. Add papaya slices; grill, covered, 1 minute each side or until heated through.

7. To broil: Broil kabobs, turning, 4 inches from heat for 8 to 12 minutes for medium-rare. Add papaya slices; broil 1 minute each side or until papaya is heated through.

8. Arrange skewer on each of 6 plates, along with 2 tablespoons sauce and 1 slice grilled papaya. Pass extra sauce.

GRILLED SWORDFISH STEAKS

LOW-CALORIE · LOW-FAT
LOW-CHOLESTEROL

*D*ouble the marinade and set aside half to use as a dipping sauce.

Grill or broil for 6 minutes.
Makes 4 servings.
Recipe can be halved or doubled.
Nutrient Value Per Serving: 161 calories, 20 g protein, 4 g fat, 9 g carbohydrate, 350 mg sodium, 39 mg cholesterol.

2 tablespoons molasses
1 tablespoon soy sauce
1 teaspoon honey
¾ teaspoon lemon juice
⅛ teaspoon ground ginger
4 swordfish steaks (4 to 5 ounces each, from two 8-ounce steaks, halved)
¼ teaspoon coarsely ground pepper
1 teaspoon sesame seeds

1. Stir together molasses, soy, honey, lemon juice and ginger in small bowl. Spoon half the marinade onto platter or baking dish. Place fish on top. Spoon remaining half of marinade over fish. Refrigerate, covered, 1 hour.
2. Prepare grill or preheat broiler. Oil grid or broiler pan rack.
3. To grill: Place fish on grid 5 inches above hot coals. Grill, covered with dome, 3 minutes on each side or until fish is lightly glazed and flakes easily when tested with a fork.
4. To broil: Broil fish on broiler pan rack 4 inches from heat for 3 minutes on each side or until fish is lightly glazed and easily flakes when tested with a fork.
5. To serve, sprinkle pepper and sesame seeds over fish.

GRILLED MACKEREL WITH PEACH-GINGER CHUTNEY

*T*he chutney cooks along with the fish and makes a delicious sauce. Try the chutney with oily fish such as bluefish, with poultry, such as Cornish hens, or with pork.

Grill 20 minutes: or broil 20 minutes.
Makes 4 servings.
Recipe can be halved or doubled.
Nutrient Value Per Serving: 447 calories, 35 g protein, 26 g fat, 18 g carbohydrate, 442 mg sodium, 129 mg cholesterol.

Peach Ginger Chutney:
12 ounces ripe peaches
¼ cup sherry wine vinegar
3 tablespoons sugar
3 cloves garlic, finely chopped
3 pieces fresh ginger, each size of quarter, pared and finely chopped
½ teaspoon chopped, seeded, fresh jalapeño pepper
½ teaspoon salt
½ teaspoon ground hot red pepper

2 mackerel (1½ pounds each), boned

1. Prepare Chutney: Blanch peaches in large pot boiling water for 1 minute. Remove peaches with slotted spoon from water. Run under cold water. Peel. Remove pit; chop peaches into ½-inch chunks. Transfer to medium-size bowl. Add vinegar, sugar, garlic, ginger, jalapeño, salt and ground red pepper.
2. Prepare grill or preheat broiler.
3. Place one mackerel on lightly oiled sheet of aluminum foil, large enough to come over fish and enclose it. Spoon half the peach mixture around fish. Pull 2 long sides of foil up and fold edges over 3 times to seal and make tight packet. Fold ends over. (*See How-To, page 614*). Repeat with remaining fish and peach mixture.

(continued)

GRILLED MACKEREL WITH PEACH-GINGER CHUTNEY (*continued*)

4. To grill: Place packets, seam-side down, on grid 5 inches from medium coals. Grill, covered with dome, 15 minutes, turning over after 10 minutes. Carefully open packets to expose fish and chutney. Grill, covered, for 5 minutes or until fish flakes when tested with a fork.

5. To broil: Broil packets 6 inches from heat for 15 minutes. Carefully open packets. Broil 5 minutes or until fish flakes easily when tested with a fork.

6. Serve the fish with the chutney.

Make-Ahead Tip: The chutney can be made up to 2 hours ahead.

GRILLED SALMON PINWHEELS

LOW-CALORIE

An *elegant dish for a special barbecue party.*

Grill for 5 to 6 minutes; or broil for 8 to 10 minutes.
Makes 4 servings.
Recipe can be halved or doubled.
Nutrient Value Per Serving: 300 calories, 44 g protein, 12 g fat, 1 g carbohydrate, 285 mg sodium, 117 mg cholesterol.

Basting Sauce:
1 small shallot OR: ¼ small red onion
¼ cup fresh parsley leaves
1 tablespoon chopped fresh dill OR: ½ teaspoon dried
2 tablespoons lemon juice
1 tablespoon lime juice
1 tablespoon olive oil OR: vegetable oil
¼ teaspoon salt
6 drops liquid red-pepper seasoning

1 pound piece salmon fillet, cut from thick end
2 sole fillets (about 1 pound)

1. If using 8 wooden skewers rather than metal, soak in water for 1 hour.

2. Prepare Basting Sauce: Combine shallot, parsley, dill, lemon and lime juice, oil, salt and red-pepper seasoning in blender. Whirl for 2 minutes or until smooth. Scrape into small bowl.

3. Cut salmon *crosswise* into eight ½-inch-thick pieces. Cut sole fillets *lengthwise* into 8 strips.

4. Prepare grill or preheat broiler. Oil grid or broiler-pan rack.

5. Lay one salmon and one sole strip on top of each other. Roll up, pinwheel fashion. Push wooden pick through end into pinwheel to secure the ends of the sole. Repeat with remaining fish.

6. Thread 2 skewers, parallel and leaving about ¾-inch space between the skewers, through 2 fish pinwheels. Place each skewer on small strip of aluminum foil. Brush with basting sauce.

7. To grill: Grill fish pinwheels 5 inches above medium-hot fire, uncovered, for 5 to 6 minutes or until cooked through, turning once and basting with sauce. Use large spatula to help turn pinwheels.

8. To broil: Broil fish pinwheels 3 inches from heat for 8 to 10 minutes or until cooked through, turning once and basting with sauce. Use large spatula to help turn skewers.

GRILLED SALMON WITH HORSERADISH BUTTER

Try *the butter with other fish, or grilled hamburgers or steaks.*

Grill vegetable packet for 20 minutes, salmon for 10 minutes; or broil vegetable packet for 30 minutes, salmon for 10 minutes.

Makes 4 servings.

Recipe can be halved or doubled.

Nutrient Value Per Serving: 394 calories, 34 g protein, 26 g fat, 4 g carbohydrate, 374 mg sodium, 135 mg cholesterol.

⅓ cup *un*salted butter, at room
    temperature
2 tablespoons prepared horseradish
1 teaspoon grated lemon rind
¼ teaspoon cracked black pepper
2 sweet red peppers, cored, seeded and
    cut into thin strips
2 large shallots, sliced
1 clove garlic, finely chopped
4 salmon steaks (about 6 ounces each, 1
    inch thick)
1 tablespoon vegetable oil
¼ teaspoon salt

1. Prepare grill or preheat broiler.
2. Stir together butter, horseradish, lemon rind and black pepper in small bowl.
3. Place red peppers, shallots and garlic on large piece of heavy-duty aluminum foil. Dot with 2 tablespoons horseradish butter. Pull long sides of foil up and fold edges together 3 times to seal. Fold each end over 2 or 3 times to seal as well. (*See How-To, page 588.*)
4. To grill: Grill vegetable packet 5 inches above medium-hot coals, covered with dome, for 20 minutes; turning over once. Brush salmon on both sides with oil; place on grid for last 10 minutes of cooking time for vegetables. Sprinkle salt over salmon. Grill salmon, covered, 5 minutes on each side or until cooked through.
5. To broil: Broil vegetable packet 4 inches from heat for 30 minutes, turning over once. Brush salmon with oil and sprinkle with salt. During last 10 minutes of cooking time for vegetables, place salmon on broiler pan rack. Broil 5 minutes on each side.
6. Serve salmon with remaining horseradish butter and vegetables with their drippings.

GRILLING VEGETABLES AND FRUITS

Simple Side Dishes

Fresh vegetable and fruit side dishes add flavor and variety to an outdoor dinner. Such choices as grilled eggplant, tomato, mushroom and pepper kabobs, pineapple spears and sliced peaches are easy to prepare, fresh and naturally delicious.

The following tips will help you take advantage of a good barbecue fire. Remember that you have less control over the heat than if you were cooking on an indoor stove. Be watchful, particularly of delicate vegetables or fruit to make sure they don't overcook.

Foil-Wrapped Vegetables

This is a simple, easy way to prepare vegetables for grilling. They may be cooked alone or in combination. Wash the vegetables, but do not dry. The excess moisture helps steam-cook most vegetables. Place up to 4 servings of the vegetables on a sheet of heavy-duty aluminum foil. Dot with butter, margarine or olive oil for extra flavor, if you wish; very little is needed since the vegetables will steam in their own juices. Experiment with different fresh seasonal herbs, such as fresh basil with zucchini and carrots; fresh tarragon with mushrooms; fresh thyme with green beans. Wrap the vegetables tightly in foil (see How-To, page 588) and place 4 to 6 inches above medium-hot coals. Shift the packets occasionally and turn over so the vegetables cook evenly. Most vegetables are done if tender when pierced with a two-tined fork.

Cooking times for foil-wrapped vegetables will vary depending on the size of the packets and the size of the vegetables.

When cooking vegetables in combination, try to keep their sizes and density uniform.

Vegetable Kabobs

Cooking vegetables on separate skewers, without meat, makes for more easily controlled cooking.

Wash and cut vegetables into 1-inch lengths or pieces. Alternately thread vegetables that have about the same cooking times on metal skewers or wooden skewers that have been soaked in water. Grill 4 to 6 inches above low to medium-low coals. Cook, turning often, and brush with a basting sauce if you wish (see pages 590–591).

Roasting Vegetables on the Grill

Corn on the cob, potatoes, yams and onions may be grilled in their own natural wrapping.

Corn Pull the husks back, remove the silk, then brush the corn generously with melted butter or margarine or other basting sauce. Replace the husks and secure with wooden picks, twist ties or wet kitchen string. Grill 4 to 6 inches above medium coals for 15 to 20 minutes, turning occasionally. The husks will char but the corn kernels will be golden. Remember to remove wooden picks before serving.

Potatoes and Yams Wash, then prick with a two-tined fork to allow steam to escape. Grill 4 to 6 inches above medium-hot coals. Grill, shifting several times, for about 1 hour or until the potatoes are soft when squeezed. The skins will become brown and crunchy.

Onions Prick large mild yellow onions with a two-tined fork. Do not peel. Place the onions, wrapped in heavy-duty aluminum foil, 4 to 6 inches above medium-hot coals. Grill, shifting

several times, about 35 to 45 minutes or until the onions are soft when squeezed. Before serving, remove the skins.

Direct Grilling

Potatoes, eggplant, zucchini and other similar vegetables become crispy and flavorful when grilled on a sheet of heavy-duty aluminum foil or a small-meshed grill rack placed directly on top of the grill rack.

Cut vegetables lengthwise, about ¼ inch thick. Brush both sides with butter, margarine or oil, or a flavored marinade (see pages 590–591). Sprinkle with salt and pepper to taste (add chopped fresh herbs for extra flavor). Place on heavy-duty foil or grill rack sprayed with non-stick vegetable-oil cooking spray. Grill 4 to 6 inches above medium-hot coals, turning occasionally, until desired doneness.

Foil-Wrapped Fruit

For an unusual accompaniment to grilled meat, poultry or seafood, or as a light dessert, try foil-wrapped fruit. Simply cut fruit, place on a sheet of heavy-duty aluminum foil and dot with butter. Sweeten with granulated sugar, brown sugar or honey and sprinkle with ground cinnamon, ginger or nutmeg (or a combination) and add a splash of lemon juice for extra flavor, if you wish. Seal (see How-To, page 588) and place the foil-wrapped package on the grill rack 4 to 6 inches above medium-hot coals. Cook, shifting the packet often and turning over, for 5 to 15 minutes, depending on the fruit, or until heated through.

Fruits best suited to foil cooking are apples, bananas, peaches, nectarines, pears, pineapples, grapefruit, oranges and rhubarb.

GRILLED CHILI CORN IN HUSKS

A *tasty switch from the usual corn-on-the-cob. This recipe can also be prepared in heavy-duty aluminum foil packets (see How-To, page 588).*

Grill or broil 30 minutes.
Makes 4 servings.
Recipe can be halved or doubled.
Nutrient Value Per Serving: 118 calories, 2 g protein, 8 g fat, 13 g carbohydrate, 291 mg sodium, 16 mg cholesterol.

4 ears corn with husks
2 tablespoons *un*salted butter, melted
1 clove garlic, finely chopped
2 teaspoons chili powder
½ teaspoon ground cumin
¼ teaspoon salt
⅛ teaspoon ground hot red pepper
1 large tomato, cored and diced
1 small sweet green pepper, cored, seeded and diced
¼ cup pitted ripe olives, sliced
2 tablespoons finely chopped onion

1. Prepare grill or preheat broiler. Oil grid or broiler-pan rack.
2. Pull husks back from each ear of corn; remove silk and ears of corn, leaving husks attached to stems. Place husks in 3 inches of boiling water in Dutch oven or large saucepan. Lower heat; cover and simmer 5 minutes. Remove husks to paper toweling to drain. Cool until easy to handle.
3. Cut 2 ears of corn into ¾-inch pieces (reserve remaining 2 ears corn for use another day).
4. Stir together melted butter, garlic, chili powder, cumin, salt and hot red pepper in large bowl. Add corn pieces, tomato, green pepper, olives and onion.
5. Into each of the 4 corn husks, place equal amount of corn mixture. Close up husks, being sure mixture is covered completely. Tie open end securely with string that has been soaked in water.

6. To grill: Grill husks 5 inches above medium coals, covered with dome, for 30 minutes, turning once or twice so husks don't become too browned.
7. To broil: Broil husks 7 to 9 inches from heat for 30 minutes, turning occasionally.
8. Serve hot or warm. Let each diner open their own husk.

Make-Ahead Tip: Recipe can be prepared several hours ahead through Step 5 and refrigerate, covered with damp paper toweling.

GRILLED TOMATO PARMESAN SANDWICHES

Serve these as a vegetable dish or appetizer, with grilled bread.

Grill for 6 minutes; or broil for 5 minutes.
Makes 6 servings.
Recipe can be halved or doubled.
Nutrient Value Per Serving: 86 calories,
3 g protein, 7 g fat, 4 g carbohydrate,
301 mg sodium, 5 mg cholesterol.

4 firm ripe tomatoes (5 ounces each)
6 thin slices (¼ ounce each) Parmesan
    cheese
6 fresh sage leaves OR: 1¼ teaspoons
    dried
2 tablespoons olive oil
½ teaspoon salt

1. Prepare grill or preheat broiler. Oil grid or broiler-pan rack.
2. Trim off and discard stem end of tomatoes. Slice each tomato into 3 thick slices. Lay piece of cheese and sage leaf on top of each of 6 slices. Drizzle with oil and sprinkle with salt. Place 6 remaining slices on top.*
3. To grill: Grill tomato sandwiches 5 inches above hot coals, uncovered, 3 minutes on each side or until heated through and cheese is melted.
4. To broil: Broil 6 inches from heat for 3 minutes. Turn over and broil 2 minutes or until browned and cheese is melted.
5. Garnish with additional sage leaves, if you wish.

***Note:** For four lunch-size portions, reassemble slices into whole tomato and grill.

GRILLED SPAGHETTI SQUASH WITH FRESH TOMATO SAUCE

LOW-CHOLESTEROL

This recipe is a vegetable alternative to pasta. Add seasonal fresh vegetables as a sauce and it becomes spaghetti squash primavera. You can also serve the squash strands plain, tossed with a little butter or olive oil, with grilled meats or poultry. (See How-To, page 451.)

Grill for 35 to 45 minutes; or bake at 375° for 1¼ to 1½ hours.

Makes 6 servings. Recipe can be doubled.

Nutrient Value Per Serving: 193 calories, 4 g protein, 13 g fat, 19 g carbohydrate, 466 mg sodium, 3 mg cholesterol.

1 spaghetti squash (about 3 pounds)
2 cloves garlic, finely chopped
½ teaspoon salt
¼ teaspoon leaf basil, crumbled
¼ teaspoon leaf thyme, crumbled
⅛ teaspoon black pepper
2 teaspoons olive oil

Fresh Tomato and Basil Sauce:

2 pounds tomatoes, peeled, seeded and
    chopped (2 cups chopped)
2 cloves garlic, finely chopped
¼ cup olive oil
½ teaspoon salt
⅛ teaspoon black pepper
⅓ cup finely chopped fresh basil
¼ cup grated Parmesan cheese
1 tablespoon finely chopped fresh basil,
    for garnish

1. Prepare grill or preheat oven to moderate (375°).
2. Halve spaghetti squash; scoop out and discard seeds and loose strings. Sprinkle cut sides of squash with garlic, salt, basil, thyme, pepper and olive oil. Wrap each half in double thickness of aluminum foil.
3. To grill: Grill squash 5 inches above

medium-hot coals, covered with dome, turning often, until tender, 35 to 45 minutes. (Or bury squash halves in coals; cook, turning often, for 35 to 45 minutes or until tender.) Fold back foil during last 15 minutes of cooking time to enhance flavor of squash.
4. To bake: Bake squash in preheated moderate oven (375°), turning often, until tender, 1¼ to 1½ hours.
5. Prepare Sauce: Combine tomatoes, garlic, olive oil, salt, pepper, basil and Parmesan in bowl. Set aside.
6. Completely unwrap squash; scrape out flesh with fork or spoon onto large platter. Spoon sauce over squash; toss to combine. Garnish with basil.

Make-Ahead Tip: Squash can be prepared a day ahead through Step 4. Scrape out strands as directed in Step 6 and refrigerate, covered. To serve, gently reheat squash strands in skillet, sprinkling with a little water. Prepare sauce as in Step 5. Serve as in Step 6.

GRILLED CHEDDAR GRITS

Serve these as a side dish to grilled meats or poultry, or for an alfresco breakfast with sausage patties, apple rings and a drizzle of maple syrup.

Grill or broil for 6 to 10 minutes.
Makes 8 servings.
Nutrient Value Per Serving: 210 calories, 4 g protein, 16 g fat, 12 g carbohydrate, 228 mg sodium, 21 mg cholesterol.

3 cups water
¾ cup grits (not quick-cooking)
½ teaspoon salt
3 tablespoons *un*salted butter
⅔ cup finely chopped green onion
   (4 green onions)
½ cup grated Cheddar cheese (2 ounces)
¼ cup grated Parmesan cheese
⅛ teaspoon ground hot red pepper
Vegetable oil for brushing grill and grits

1. Bring the water to boiling in medium-size saucepan over moderate heat. Add grits and salt in stream, stirring, until mixture is well combined. Simmer grits, covered, stirring occasionally, over low heat for 15 to 20 minutes or until very thick.
2. Transfer grits to bowl. Add butter, green onion, Cheddar, Parmesan and hot red pepper; stir to combine. Transfer mixture to buttered 8 × 8 × 2-inch square baking pan, smoothing surface; rap pan against hard surface to level. Chill grits, covered, for 1 to 2 hours or until cold and solid.
3. Prepare grill or preheat broiler. Oil grid or broiler-pan rack.
4. Dip bottom of baking pan in hot water for 1 minute. Invert pan onto cutting board; remove pan. Cut grits into 8 equal triangles (divide square into eighths through center). Brush both sides of grits cakes with oil.
5. To grill: Grill 5 inches above medium-hot coals, uncovered, 3 to 5 minutes on each side or until golden brown and crisp.
6. To broil: Broil 4 inches from heat for 3 to 5 minutes on each side or until golden brown and crisp.

Make-Ahead Tip: The grits can be prepared in the pan a day ahead and refrigerated, covered.

GRILLED VEGETABLE SALAD WITH CHEESE CROUTONS

Grill vegetables for 15 to 25 minutes; or broil for 8 to 10 minutes.

Makes 4 main-dish or 6 side-dish servings. Recipe can be halved or doubled.

Nutrient Value Per Main-Dish Serving (without croutons): 209 calories, 5 g protein, 13 g fat, 18 g carbohydrate, 414 mg sodium, 0 mg cholesterol.

Herb Marinade/Dressing:

¼ cup red wine vinegar
¼ cup chopped fresh mixed herbs, such as basil, marjoram and thyme
2 teaspoons Dijon-style mustard
1 clove garlic, finely chopped
½ teaspoon salt
¼ teaspoon pepper
¼ cup olive oil
¼ cup reduced-sodium chicken broth

Grilled Vegetables:

6 baby carrots, trimmed and cut in half if large
1 sweet red pepper, cored, seeded and cut lengthwise into 6 pieces
1 sweet yellow pepper, cored, seeded and cut lengthwise into 6 pieces
¼ pound wild mushrooms OR: white domestic mushrooms, trimmed
3 plum tomatoes, halved crosswise
1 bunch green onions, trimmed
1 zucchini, cut lengthwise into eighths, then crosswise into 2-inch lengths
1 yellow summer squash, cut lengthwise into eighths, then crosswise into 2-inch lengths

6 cups mixed greens, such as spinach, curly endive and watercress
Grilled Cheese Croutons *(recipe follows)*

1. Prepare Marinade/Dressing: Whisk together vinegar, herbs, mustard, garlic, salt and pepper until blended in small bowl. Gradually whisk in oil and chicken broth until blended. Set aside.

2. Prepare Grilled Vegetables: Arrange carrots, red and yellow peppers, mushrooms, tomato halves, green onions, zucchini and yellow squash in large nonaluminum baking dish. Pour marinade over; toss gently to coat. Set aside until ready to grill or up to 1 hour.
3. Prepare grill or preheat broiler.
4. To grill: Make 2 trays from heavy-duty aluminum foil by folding foil over for double strength and folding up sides. Punch small holes in bottom of trays. Arrange carrots, red and yellow pepper and mushrooms on one foil tray. Arrange tomatoes, green onions, zucchini and yellow squash on other tray. Place foil trays of vegetables on grid 5 inches above medium-hot coals. Grill, covered with dome, for 15 to 25 minutes, turning occasionally and brushing with Marinade, and removing smaller and softer vegetables as they cook.

(continued)

CRAZY ABOUT CROUTONS

The croutons are so good, they can be served on their own as a first course or even as a snack.

GRILLED VEGETABLE SALAD WITH CHEESE CROUTONS (*continued*)

Reserve remaining Marinade in baking dish for brushing vegetables during cooking and dressing.

5. To broil: Oil broiler-pan rack. Arrange vegetables in single layer on rack, working in batches if necessary. Broil 6 inches from heat for 8 to 10 minutes, turning once and brushing with marinade, and removing smaller or softer vegetables as they cook. Reserve remaining marinade for dressing.

6. Serve warm grilled vegetables over crisp greens with Grilled Cheese Croutons on side. Drizzle remaining marinade over vegetables.

GRILLED CHEESE CROUTONS:

Nutrient Value Per Crouton: 106 calories, 4 g protein, 2 g fat, 18 g carbohydrate, 200 mg sodium, 6 mg cholesterol.

Cut twelve 1-inch-thick slices Italian bread. Grill or broil until lightly toasted on one side. Remove from grill or broiler. Sprinkle toasted sides with ½ cup grated Gruyère cheese, dividing evenly among croutons. Return to grill or broiler, cheese-side up, to toast bottoms of croutons and melt cheese.

GRILLED RICE SQUARES

LOW-FAT · LOW-CHOLESTEROL

Grill for 12 to 14 minutes; or broil for 12 minutes.
Makes 12 servings.
Nutrient Value Per Serving: 173 calories, 3 g protein, 1 g fat, 37 g carbohydrate, 173 mg sodium, 0 mg cholesterol.

4¾ cups water
½ cup rice wine vinegar OR: white wine vinegar
2 tablespoons honey
2 teaspoons Oriental sesame oil
2½ cups long-grain enriched white rice
2 carrots, pared and shredded (1 cup)
2 green onions, sliced

Basting Sauce:
2 tablespoons tamari OR: soy sauce
1 tablespoon lemon juice
1 tablespoon honey
½ teaspoon Oriental sesame oil

1. Line 9×9×2-inch square pan with plastic wrap. Bring water, vinegar, honey and sesame oil to boiling in large saucepan. Stir in rice. Lower heat; simmer, covered, 15 minutes. Stir in carrot and green onion; cook, covered, 10 minutes or until liquid is absorbed and rice is tender. Cool.

2. Spoon rice mixture into prepared pan, spreading level. Cover with plastic wrap. Place another 9×9×2-inch pan or 8×8×2-inch pan on top and press down to compact rice and make level. Refrigerate, covered, at least 4 hours, or until firm enough to cut.

3. Prepare grill or preheat broiler. Oil grid or broiler-pan rack.

4. Invert rice onto cutting board; remove pan. Remove plastic wrap. Cut into 16 squares.

5. Prepare Basting Sauce: Combine tamari, lemon juice, honey and sesame oil in small dish. Brush rice squares with basting sauce.

6. To grill: Grill squares 5 inches above medium-hot coals, uncovered, 6 to 7 minutes on each side or until lightly spotted, brushing occasionally with sauce.

7. To broil: Broil squares 6 inches from heat for 6 minutes on each side or until lightly spotted, brushing occasionally with sauce.

8. Serve hot or cold.

Make-Ahead Tip: The rice can be prepared in the pan up to 2 days ahead and refrigerated, covered.

RICE SQUARES SERVING IDEAS
Offer Rice Squares, flavored with honey and Oriental sesame oil, with grilled chicken or strongly flavored fish. (Pictured on page 589.)

GRILLED POTATOES WITH GARLIC

LOW-CHOLESTEROL

If you love roasted garlic, throw a few extra cloves onto the grill.

Grill for 25 to 30 minutes; or roast at 450° for 30 to 40 minutes.
Makes 4 servings.
Nutrient Value Per Serving: 272 calories, 4 g protein, 14 g fat, 33 g carbohydrate, 363 mg sodium, 0 mg cholesterol.

1½ **pounds small red new potatoes, scrubbed**
4 **large cloves garlic, unpeeled**
4 **tablespoons olive oil**
½ **teaspoon salt**
4 **sprigs fresh rosemary**
1 **tablespoon white wine vinegar**
2 **teaspoons Dijon-style mustard**
¼ **teaspoon pepper**
2 **green onions, thinly sliced**

1. Prepare grill or preheat oven to very hot (450°). Make tray from heavy-duty aluminum foil by folding foil over for double strength and folding up sides; oil tray.
2. Cut potatoes into pieces no larger than 1½ inches. Combine potatoes, garlic cloves, 1 tablespoon oil and ¼ teaspoon salt in medium-size bowl; toss until potatoes are well coated. Spoon potato mixture into foil tray, keeping potatoes in single layer. Top with rosemary sprigs.
3. To grill: Grill potatoes 5 inches above medium-hot coals, covered with dome, turning occasionally, for 25 to 30 minutes or until tender and crisply browned.
4. To roast: Roast potatoes in preheated very hot oven (450°), stirring occasionally, for 30 to 40 minutes or until tender and browned.
5. Meanwhile, whisk together vinegar, mustard, remaining ¼ teaspoon salt and pepper in medium-size bowl. Gradually whisk in remaining 3 tablespoons oil. Discard woody rosemary stems from grilling tray. Squeeze grilled garlic cloves from skins into dressing in bowl. Mash slightly into dressing.
6. Add potatoes and green onions to dressing; toss gently to coat. Serve warm.

Make-Ahead Tip: The potatoes can be prepared up to 2 hours ahead and served warm or at room temperature.

SPICY GRILLED ONIONS

LOW-CHOLESTEROL

Serve this with grilled meat, poultry or fish or as part of a vegetable platter. Good hot or at room temperature.

Grill or broil for 30 minutes.
Makes 4 servings.
Recipe can be halved or doubled.
Nutrient Value Per Serving: 162 calories, 2 g protein, 11 g fat, 16 g carbohydrate, 139 mg sodium, 0 mg cholesterol.

---

3 tablespoons olive oil
1 tablespoon sugar
2 teaspoons leaf oregano, crumbled
¼ teaspoon salt
¼ teaspoon ground coriander
¼ teaspoon ground cumin
⅛ teaspoon ground cloves
1½ pounds red onions, sliced into
    ½-inch-thick rounds

1. Whisk together oil, sugar, oregano, salt, coriander, cumin and cloves in medium-size bowl. Add onion. Cover and marinate 1 hour at room temperature.
2. Prepare grill or preheat broiler.
3. Place onion and marinade on sheet of heavy-duty aluminum foil. Pull long sides of foil up and over; bring edges together and fold over 3 times. Fold each short end over 3 times to form tightly sealed package. (*See How-To, at right.*)
4. To grill: Grill packet 5 inches above medium coals, covered with dome, for 30 minutes or until tender, turning 1 or 2 times.
5. To broil: Broil packet 6 inches from heat for about 30 minutes or until tender, turning 1 or 2 times.
6. Serve warm or at room temperature.

Make-Ahead Tip: Onions can be cooked ahead and served at room temperature. Store in refrigerator, wrapped.

HOW TO COOK VEGETABLES (OR FISH) IN FOIL PACKETS

1. Place small, uniform pieces of vegetables on a rectangular piece of aluminum foil. Fold long sides of foil up and over vegetables. Fold long edges together three times to seal.

2. Fold the short ends over three times to form a tightly sealed packet. Grill or transfer to a baking sheet and cook as directed.

GRILLED ORANGE AND ONION KABOBS

LOW-CALORIE · LOW-FAT
LOW-CHOLESTEROL · LOW-SODIUM

Delicious with grilled meats, or serve on its own as a salad. (Pictured at right.)

Grill for 8 minutes; or broil for 10 to 12 minutes.
Makes 4 servings.
Recipe can be halved or doubled.
Nutrient Value Per Serving: 89 calories, 1 g protein, 0 g fat, 22 g carbohydrate, 47 mg sodium, 0 mg cholesterol.

2 navel oranges
2 red onions, peeled
2 tablespoons brown sugar
4 teaspoons orange marmalade
1 teaspoon distilled white vinegar OR:
    cider vinegar
½ teaspoon soy sauce

1. Bring large saucepan of water to boiling. Add whole oranges; cover and cook 10 minutes.
2. Meanwhile, cut onions crosswise in half. Skewer each half crosswise with wooden pick to keep from separating.
3. Add onions to oranges in boiling water; cover and cook 10 minutes or until wooden pick is easily inserted in orange. Pour off water. Let oranges and onions stand until cool enough to handle.
4. Cut each orange into 4 wedges. Cut onion halves in half. Thread 2 orange pieces and 2 onion pieces alternately on each of 4 metal skewers or soaked wooden skewers, piercing oranges lengthwise and onions crosswise.
5. Prepare grill or preheat broiler. Oil grid or broiler-pan rack.
6. Stir together brown sugar, marmalade, vinegar and soy sauce in small dish. Brush skewers with brown sugar mixture.

7. To grill: Grill skewers 5 inches from hot coals, uncovered, until lightly browned, about 8 minutes; turn and baste twice.
8. To broil: Broil skewers 3 inches from heat for 10 to 12 minutes or until lightly browned, basting and turning twice.
9. Serve hot or warm.

Make-Ahead Tip: The oranges and onions can be prepared a day ahead and refrigerated, covered.

From left: Grilled Rice Squares (page 586) and Grilled Orange and Onion Kabobs (this page).

CHILI MARINADE

Works with beef, chicken or pork. Adjust the spice level to suit your own taste.

Makes 1 cup.
Recipe can be halved or doubled.
Nutrient Value Per Tablespoon:
67 calories, 0 g protein, 7 g fat, 1 g carbohydrate, 199 mg sodium, 0 mg cholesterol.

**MARINADE
MAKE-AHEAD TIP:**
These marinades can be made up to 3 days ahead and refrigerated, covered.

1 tablespoon cumin seeds
3 large cloves garlic, finely chopped
1 small onion, finely chopped
½ to 1 tablespoon chili powder
1 teaspoon leaf oregano, crumbled
¼ to ½ teaspoon crushed red pepper flakes
3 tablespoons soy sauce
1 tablespoon lime juice
½ cup olive oil

1. Toast cumin seeds in small skillet over medium-low heat, shaking skillet occasionally, until lightly browned, about 2 minutes.
2. Crush cumin seeds. Combine cumin seeds, garlic, onion, chili powder, oregano, red pepper flakes, soy sauce, lime juice and oil in small bowl.
3. Use to marinate foods, refrigerated for up to 1 hour, depending on your "hotness" level. Fish should be marinated for no more than 30 minutes.

CHICKEN LEG GRILL

**Grilled Chicken Legs with
Orange Spice Marinade**
(this page)

Grilled Potatoes with Garlic
(587)

**Tossed Green Salad with
Curried Yogurt Dressing**
(178)

**Grilled Maple-Macadamia
Stuffed Pears** (592)

ORANGE SPICE MARINADE

LOW-SODIUM

Good with pork, beef, chicken or fish.

Makes 2¼ cups.
Recipe can be halved or doubled.
Nutrient Value Per Tablespoon: 26 calories, 0 g protein, 2 g fat, 2 g carbohydrate, 0 mg sodium, 0 mg cholesterol.

3 large cloves garlic, finely chopped
1 tablespoon finely chopped pared fresh ginger
1 medium-size onion, thinly sliced
1 tablespoon grated orange rind
1 cup fresh orange juice (2 or 3 oranges)
⅓ cup olive oil
2 tablespoons honey
1 tablespoon lemon juice
½ teaspoon ground cumin
½ teaspoon ground coriander
½ teaspoon ground cinnamon
½ teaspoon leaf oregano, crumbled
¼ teaspoon ground cardamom
¼ teaspoon pepper

1. Combine garlic, ginger, onion, orange rind and juice, oil, honey, lemon juice, cumin, coriander, cinnamon, oregano, cardamom and pepper in small bowl.
2. Use to marinate foods, refrigerated, for up to 4 hours. Fish should be marinated no more than 30 minutes.

PLUM CHUTNEY GLAZE

LOW-CALORIE · LOW-FAT
LOW-CHOLESTEROL · LOW-SODIUM

Pungent and spicy, this glaze makes lamb chops, spareribs and pork chops taste extra-special, whether grilled, broiled or roasted. Give as a gift or a thank you.

Makes 4 cups.
Recipe can be halved or doubled.
Nutrient Value Per Tablespoon: 13 calories, 0 g protein, 0 g fat, 3 g carbohydrate, 1 mg sodium, 0 mg cholesterol.

1 large red onion, peeled and chopped
1 large sweet green pepper, cored, seeded and chopped
1 navel orange, peeled, sectioned and chopped
1 large tomato, cored and chopped
1 clove garlic, finely chopped
½ cup lime juice
1 jar (10 to 12 ounces) plum jam
1 tablespoon pumpkin pie spice

1. Combine onion, green pepper, orange, tomato, garlic and lime juice in large, heavy nonaluminum saucepan. Slowly bring to boiling, stirring often. Lower heat; simmer 45 minutes, stirring often.
2. Stir in plum jam and pumpkin pie spice; simmer 15 minutes, stirring often.
3. Use to brush on grilled foods for the last 10 to 15 minutes of cooking.

Make-Ahead Tip: The glaze can be refrigerated, tightly covered, for up to one week.

BARBECUE SAUCE

LOW-FAT · LOW-CHOLESTEROL

Doesn't take much time to make your own. Also delicious as a basting sauce or a dipping sauce. If used for the latter, be sure the sauce has not been used to marinate raw meat.

Makes about 3 cups.
Recipe can be halved or doubled.
Nutrient Value Per Tablespoon: 24 calories, 0 g protein, 0 g fat, 5 g carbohydrate, 216 mg sodium, 0 mg cholesterol.

1 tablespoon vegetable oil
1 small onion, finely chopped
3 large cloves garlic, finely chopped
1 bottle (12 ounces) chili sauce
1½ cups catsup
¼ cup steak sauce
2 tablespoons Worcestershire sauce
2 tablespoons red wine vinegar
½ teaspoon liquid red-pepper seasoning
2 tablespoons light brown sugar
1 tablespoon dry mustard
½ teaspoon pepper

1. Heat oil in small saucepan over medium heat. Add onion and garlic; sauté for 2 minutes.
2. Stir in chili sauce, catsup, steak sauce, Worcestershire sauce, vinegar, red-pepper seasoning, brown sugar, dry mustard and pepper. Simmer 15 minutes, stirring frequently.
3. Use as a marinade, marinating beef for 1 hour, or chicken for 30 minutes.

Make-Ahead Tip: The sauce can be made up to 3 days ahead and refrigerated, covered.

GRILLED MAPLE-MACADAMIA STUFFED PEARS

LOW-FAT · LOW-CHOLESTEROL · LOW-SODIUM

A *delicious dessert, with a surprise inside.*

Grill for 8 minutes; or broil for 9 minutes.
Makes 4 servings.
Recipe can be halved or doubled.
Nutrient Value Per Serving: 204 calories,
2 g protein, 9 g fat, 34 g carbohydrate,
48 mg sodium, 4 mg cholesterol.

¼ cup macadamia nuts
3 tablespoons maple syrup
2 tablespoons shredded coconut
2 tablespoons Neufchâtel OR: cream
    cheese
⅛ teaspoon vanilla
4 medium-ripe Anjou pears (about 1¼
    pounds)
½ lemon

**GRILED PEARS
MAKE-AHEAD TIP:**
The filling can be pre-
pared a day ahead
and refrigerated, cov-
ered. Bring to room
temperature before
using.

1. Prepare grill or preheat broiler. Oil
grid or broiler pan rack.
2. Reserve 4 large whole nuts. Chop
remaining nuts and place in small bowl.
Add maple syrup, coconut, cream
cheese and vanilla to bowl; stir with
spoon until blended.
3. Pare pears whole; rub well with cut
side of lemon to prevent discoloring.
With melon baller or small paring knife
and working up from bottom of pear,
scoop out core and leave cavity for
macadamia filling. Spoon macadamia
mixture into pears. Push whole macadamia nut into bottom to keep filling in
pear.
4. To grill: Grill pears on their sides, 5
inches above low coals, covered with
dome, for 8 minutes or until heated
through, turning every 2 or 3 minutes.
5. To broil: Broil pears 3 inches from
heat for about 9 minutes or until heated
through, turning every 2 or 3 minutes.
6. Stand pears upright on dessert plates.
Serve plain or with Maple Praline
Sauce or Raspberry Vanilla Sauce (*see
page 538*).

GRILLED PINEAPPLE SANDWICHES

LOW-CHOLESTEROL

A *delicious dessert sandwich that takes just minutes to grill.*

Grill for 6 minutes; or broil for 10 minutes.
Makes 4 sandwiches.
Recipe can be halved or doubled.
Nutrient Value Per Sandwich: 211 calories,
3 g protein, 9 g fat, 34 g carbohydrate,
85 mg sodium, 7 mg cholesterol.

⅓ cup toasted hazelnuts, skinned
4 tablespoons light brown sugar
⅓ cup chopped pitted dates
¼ cup Neufchâtel cheese OR: cream
  cheese
2 teaspoons orange juice
8 slices (¼ inch thick) fresh pineapple,
  with core

1. Combine nuts and 2 tablespoons sugar in food processor. Whirl until nuts are chopped. Add dates. Whirl until finely chopped. Add cream cheese. Whirl until blended, scraping down side as needed. (The nuts and dates can be finely chopped with the sugar by hand, and then blended with the cream cheese in a bowl with a wooden spoon.)
2. Prepare grill or preheat broiler. Oil grid or broiler-pan rack.
3. Stir together remaining 2 tablespoons brown sugar and orange juice in small dish.
4. Cut four ½-inch slits in center core of each pineapple slice. Spoon nut mixture on 4 slices, dividing evenly. Spread evenly over slices, leaving ¼-inch border. Top with remaining pineapple slices, pressing lightly to stick. Brush top of sandwiches with brown sugar mixture.
5. To grill: Grill sandwiches 5 inches above medium coals, covered with dome, 3 minutes on each side or until

lightly browned and filling is hot; brush with brown sugar mixture after turning over.
6. To broil: Broil 3 inches from heat for 5 minutes on each side or until lightly browned and filling is hot; brush with brown sugar mixture after turning over.
7. Let sandwiches stand 10 minutes. Serve with wafer cookies, if you wish.

Make-Ahead Tip: The nut filling can be made up to 4 days ahead and refrigerated, covered.

GRILLED DESSERT FOCACCIA WITH GRILLED FRUIT MELANGE

LOW-FAT

Grill fruit for 6 to 8 minutes, focaccia for 3 minutes; or broil fruit for 8 to 12 minutes, focaccia for 3 to 4 minutes.

Makes 12 servings.

Recipe can be halved or doubled.

Nutrient Value Per Serving: 216 calories, 5 g protein, 4 g fat, 40 g carbohydrate, 129 mg sodium, 42 mg cholesterol.

Dough:
¼ cup firmly packed light brown sugar
⅓ cup warm water (105° to 115°)
1 package active dry yeast
½ cup milk
2 eggs
½ teaspoon salt
2 tablespoons *un*salted butter, melted
1 tablespoon grated lemon rind
3 to 3¼ cups all-purpose flour

Fruit Topping:
2 tablespoons brown sugar
2 teaspoons orange juice
½ pineapple, cut into spears *(see How-To, page 482)*
2 nectarines, halved and pitted
1 cup fresh or frozen pitted cherries, thawed
1 tablespoon orange-flavored liqueur

1. Prepare Dough: Combine 1 teaspoon brown sugar and warm water in 1-cup measure. Sprinkle yeast over water; stir to dissolve yeast. Let stand 10 minutes or until foamy.

2. Combine remaining sugar, milk, eggs, salt, butter, lemon rind and yeast mixture in large bowl. Beat in 1½ cups flour on low speed for 2 minutes. Stir in enough remaining flour to make soft dough; dough *must* be soft for light, puffy focaccia. Use just enough flour to make handling easy.

3. Turn dough out onto floured board. Knead until smooth and elastic, about 5 minutes. Place in lightly oiled bowl; turn to coat. Cover with plastic wrap. Let rise in warm place, away from drafts, until doubled in bulk, about 45 to 60 minutes.

4. Prepare grill or preheat broiler. Oil broiler-pan rack. Do not oil grill grid.

5. Meanwhile, prepare Fruit Topping: Stir together brown sugar and orange juice in small dish. Brush pineapple and nectarines with brown sugar mixture.

6. To grill: Place nectarines, skin side up, and pineapple 5 inches above medium-hot coals, uncovered. Grill nectarines for 6 minutes and pineapple for 8 minutes, or until lightly browned and heated through, turning once and then basting.

7. To broil: Broil nectarines and pineapple 3 inches from heat, nectarines for 8 minutes, and pineapple for 12 minutes, or until heated through and lightly browned, turning and basting halfway though cooking.

8. When cool enough to handle, cut nectarines and pineapple into cubes. Combine with cherries and liqueur in medium-size bowl.

9. Punch dough down. Roll into 12-inch log on floured surface. Cut into 12 even pieces. Flatten each piece into 3- or 4-inch disk. Let rest 10 minutes.

10. To grill: Slide disks onto grid 5 inches above medium-hot coals, uncovered. Grill 3 minutes or until puffed and browned, watching closely and turning over halfway through cooking.

11. To broil: Broil disks 3 inches from heat for 3 to 4 minutes or until puffed and browned.

12. To serve, spoon fruit mixture over hot focaccias. Top with dollop of whipped cream, if you wish.

Make-Ahead Tip: Dough can be made a day ahead and refrigerated, covered. Bring to room temperature. Fruits can be grilled and tossed together up to 4 hours ahead.

CHAPTER 14

Turkey Enchiladas (page 604).

MICROWAVE MAGIC

MICROWAVE PRIMER

How Do Microwave Ovens Work?
Microwaves reflect off the sides, top and bottom of the oven cavity, penetrating the cookware and causing the water molecules in food to vibrate (about 450 million times per second), which results in friction. The friction, in turn, creates heat and it is this internal heat that cooks the food.

Hot Spots Even though microwave technology has advanced in recent years, many microwave ovens still cook with hot spots or areas of unevenly concentrated microwaves.

Try this test to locate hot spots: Microwave a pastry shell without rotating during cooking time. If you see darker areas interspersed throughout the cooked dough, these are the hot spots.

To prevent food from cooking unevenly, you usually have to rotate the dish. Wind-up turntables or carousels save you the trouble of opening the oven door and turning the dish manually.

Some ovens feature built-in carousels. Before you buy one, make sure the larger dishes you plan to use will fit on the tray as it rotates.

What's Your Wattage?
Countertop ovens (by far the most popular type, as opposed to under-the-cabinet or others) come in a complete selection from full size to subcompact models. Ovens with output wattages or cooking power from 600 watts and up are considered high power ovens. These models cook faster and are the best choice for cooking rather than just reheating. Ovens with less than 600 watts are considered low power ovens.

If you don't know your oven wattage, check with the manufacturer, or look in the use and care manual or on the oven's nameplate, located on the side, the back or inside the oven door. Or try the following test.

Combine 1 cup water with ice in a 2-cup measure. Stir for 2 minutes or until the ice stops melting and the water is very cold. Remove the ice. Pour 1 cup of the cold water into a microwave-safe glass measure. Place in center of cold (not used for a while) microwave oven. Microwave at high or full power (100%) until the water begins to boil. If the water boils in less than 3½ minutes, you have a high power oven; if in more than 3½ minutes, the oven is low power. Most recipes are developed for high power ovens. If yours is low power, experiment with small increments of additional cooking time when trying a recipe, or seek out a microwave cookbook with low-wattage recipes or adaptations.

For Owners of New Ovens Only
Most microwave oven manufacturers are now using the IEC-705 standard (or 1 liter test) to determine the output wattage of their ovens. This test can give a higher wattage number than the tests used previously. As a result, new model ovens may be rated up to 100 watts higher than before. What this means is that an oven rated with 600 watts of cooking power may really cook like a 500 watt oven. At the same time, some companies have redesigned their ovens to actually make them more powerful.

If all this seems confusing, remember that *you* are the best judge of how your microwave oven works. Many factors, not just cooking wattage, affect the speed of cooking, such as the amount of food and the voltage in your home and its steadiness. So get in the habit of checking the food at several points through the cooking to get a feel for how fast your oven cooks. For high power ovens, check the food at the minimum time indicated in the recipe. For a low power oven, start checking at the middle of the cooking time range.

Take Cover!
When deciding whether or not to cover during cooking, the principles used in conventional cooking also apply to cooking in the microwave oven. Use a cover when you need to retain moist heat or stop evaporation, or when the food should make a lot of juice or sauce. A cover also has the advantage of holding in heat and distributing it more evenly throughout the dish. Different covers give different results during microwave cooking.

Lids and **plastic wrap** form a tight cover to hold in moisture and speed cooking. Be sure to only use plastic wrap recommended for microwaving. In most cases, vent the dish by folding back a corner of the plastic wrap to allow steam to escape during cooking. Don't let the plastic touch high fat or high sugar foods while heating. When uncovering, remove wrap away from your hands and face to avoid steam burns.

Waxed paper makes a loose cover that holds in heat, yet allows some steam to escape for crisper-textured foods.

Paper toweling is best for absorbing grease and moisture from foods. Use it for covering bacon and wrapping bread and baked goods to avoid sogginess when heating. Plain white paper toweling is best; recycled toweling may contain impurities or bits of metal that may ignite in the oven.

A Clean Machine

- Baking soda safely cleans all the spatters and spills that can accumulate in a microwave oven. Just mix 2 tablespoons of baking soda with 2 cups of warm water, and sponge down the interior.
- For stubborn stains, sprinkle on dry baking soda, rub lightly with a small sponge, rinse and buff dry.
- Baking soda is an effective and safe cleanser; unlike many cleaning powders and liquids, it won't scratch or erode the delicate interior of the microwave.
- To neutralize food odors, leave a small dish of baking soda inside the microwave oven. Remember to *remove* the baking soda before using the oven.

Is It Microwave Safe?

Here's a quick test to see if cookware you already have can be used in your microwave oven.

Place a microwave-safe glass measure with ½ cup water in the microwave oven. Set the dish to be tested near the cup, but not touching. Microwave at high or full power (100%) for 1 minute. If the dish is cool or slightly warm to the touch, it is safe for microwaving. If the dish is hot, it should not be used in the microwave.

Microwave Techniques

- Thicker, larger pieces of meat, fish, vegetables and other foods take longer to cook in the microwave oven than smaller pieces of food.
- For even cooking, it's particularly important to cut each ingredient into uniform pieces.
- If possible, arrange ingredients in single layer so they are not touching; they'll cook even faster.

- Food placed on the outside of the cooking dish receives more microwave energy and therefore cooks faster than food in the center of the dish.
- In most cases, food cooks most evenly if arranged in a ring near the outer edge of the dish. Zucchini sticks and other oblong-shaped foods can be set on the dish to resemble wheel spokes.
- Thicker or slower-cooking parts, such as the meaty ends of drumsticks or the stems of broccoli, should face the outer edge of the dish.
- The lower energy received in the center of the dish is an advantage when you are cooking ingredients with varying cooking times. Put quick-cooking snow peas, for instance, in the center of the dish and arrange pieces of chicken around the perimeter.

Factors Affecting Cooking Time

Quantity The more food in the microwave oven, the longer the cooking time. Conventional ovens have thermostats to keep the temperature constant inside the oven no matter how you load up the shelves. Whether you are baking 2 or 22 potatoes, the oven will maintain a more or less steady temperature, and the cooking time won't vary by much. In contrast, the microwave oven has only a certain amount of energy it can put out when it's operating at full power. If you cook one apple, for instance, all the microwave energy will be directed to that one apple. If you cook two apples instead, the oven will put out the same amount of energy, but that energy will get divided between the two apples. Each apple will then absorb less energy per minute while it's in the microwave, so the cooking time will be longer.

Shape Food in small, uniform pieces cooks faster and more evenly, and thin pieces cook faster than thicker.

Starting temperature The colder the food, the longer the cooking time.

Composition Foods high in fat and sugar attract the microwaves, so they cook faster. Foods with high moisture content such as vegetables do well in the microwave.

Density Denser foods such as a potato or squash take longer to cook than more open, porous foods such as a cupcake.

Taking the Chill Off: Defrosting

It is a myth that microwave ovens are good *only* for defrosting and reheating, but it is true that they perform these functions well.

- Some ovens come with programmed defrost functions, which set time and temperature based on the weight of the food to be defrosted. If your oven is without such a program, use a low setting or follow the manufacturer's directions.
- When defrosting food, check it frequently—after the food defrosts, it will begin to cook.
- For even thawing, remove store wrapping and trays.
- Elevate roasts, steaks and chops on a rack to hold them out of their juices.
- Stir vegetables, casseroles and saucy foods halfway through defrosting. Turn over or rotate foods that can't be stirred.
- Separate or pull pieces apart that are thawed and remove them from the oven.
- Defrost roasts and poultry just until they can be pierced in the center with a skewer.

VEGETABLE QUESADILLAS

QUICK

A delicious appetizer or snack. Feel free to substitute your favorite vegetables.

Makes 12 servings.
Nutrient Value Per Serving: 134 calories, 6 g protein, 7 g fat, 14 g carbohydrate, 265 mg sodium, 12 mg cholesterol.

1 sweet red pepper, cored, seeded and thinly sliced
1 large leek, rinsed well and thinly sliced
1 fresh jalapeño pepper, seeded and chopped
1 clove garlic, chopped
1 teaspoon olive oil OR: vegetable oil
¾ teaspoon chili powder
½ teaspoon ground cumin
¼ teaspoon salt
1 tablespoon chopped cilantro OR: parsley
12 flour tortillas (6 inch)
1½ cups shredded Monterey Jack cheese (6 ounces)
Cilantro, for garnish (optional)

1. Combine sweet pepper, leek, jalapeño, garlic, olive oil, chili powder, cumin and salt in microwave-safe 1-quart baking dish or 9-inch pie plate. Cover with waxed paper. Microwave at 100% power for 6 minutes or until vegetables are tender. Stir in cilantro.
2. Spoon 2 tablespoons of the vegetable mixture evenly over each of 6 tortillas. Sprinkle ¼ cup cheese evenly over each tortilla. Top each with remaining plain tortillas.
3. Stack tortilla "sandwiches," with a piece of paper toweling between each sandwich, on microwave-safe plate. Microwave, uncovered, at 100% power for 2 minutes or until heated through. Remove the pieces of paper toweling. Cut stack into equal wedges. Garnish with cilantro, if you wish.

Make-Ahead Tip: The stack can be assembled up to 3 hours before serving and refrigerated, covered. Reheat at 100% power. Cut into wedges.

STIRRING THINGS UP
The center of a dish receives less microwave energy than the outside, so many dishes require stirring during the cooking time to redistribute the food from the cooler center to the warmer outside. Many liquids also benefit from stirring to prevent lumps. It's easy to open the door and stir the dish without removing it from the oven. Just remember that the dish itself is likely to be very hot.

BUTTERNUT SQUASH SOUP WITH MAPLE SYRUP

You can substitute any winter squash, such as acorn, for the butternut. Add chunks of leftover cooked chicken or ham to create a main-dish soup.

Makes 6 servings.
Nutrient Value Per Serving: 165 calories, 3 g protein, 7 g fat, 25 g carbohydrate, 567 mg sodium, 17 mg cholesterol.

1 carrot, pared and sliced
1 red onion, cut into 8 wedges
1 stalk celery, sliced
2 tablespoons *un*salted butter
1½ pounds butternut squash
1 can (about 14¼ ounces)
    reduced-sodium chicken broth
¼ cup maple syrup
1 teaspoon salt
¼ teaspoon ground allspice

Pinch ground hot red pepper
3 tablespoons reduced-fat sour cream
Green Onion Cream *(recipe follows)*

1. Combine carrot, onion, celery and butter in microwave-safe 3-quart casserole with lid. Microwave, covered, at 100% power for 5 minutes.
2. Meanwhile, peel, seed and cut squash into ¾-inch cubes.
3. Add squash cubes, chicken broth, maple syrup, salt, allspice and ground hot red pepper to casserole. Microwave, covered, at 100% power for 16 minutes or until tender.
4. Remove solids with slotted spoon and place in food processor or blender, along with sour cream. Whirl until pureed, adding a little cooking liquid if needed. Stir puree into cooking liquid in casserole. Spoon into bowls. Drizzle with Green Onion Cream.

Green Onion Cream: Place ½ cup parsley and 1 cup sliced green onion in food processor or blender. Whirl until finely chopped. Add ¼ cup reduced-fat sour cream. Whirl until smooth.

SQUASH SOUP MAKE-AHEAD TIP:
The soup can be made a day ahead without the addition of the sour cream and the garnish, and refrigerated, covered. Bring to room temperature. Reheat, covered, at 70% power. Stir in sour cream and garnish with Green Onion Cream.

PEANUT AND CHICKEN SOUP

LOW-CALORIE

A *variation of a favorite Southern soup—serve as a first course or a main dish.*

Makes 6 servings.
Nutrient Value Per Serving: 238 calories, 17 g protein, 14 g fat, 14 g carbohydrate, 528 mg sodium, 23 mg cholesterol.

1¼ cups lowfat milk
½ cup smooth peanut butter
3 tablespoons all-purpose flour
1 teaspoon grated pared fresh ginger
1 fresh jalapeño pepper, seeded OR: ½ pickled jalapeño pepper, seeded
1 tablespoon tamari OR: soy sauce
2 green onions, quartered
1 tablespoon chopped cilantro OR: parsley
1 can (14¼ ounces) reduced-sodium chicken broth
¾ cup frozen whole-kernel corn
1 cup shredded cooked chicken
2 tablespoons plain yogurt, for garnish

1. Combine milk, peanut butter, flour, ginger, jalapeño, tamari, green onion and ½ tablespoon cilantro in blender. Whirl until smooth. Pour into microwave-safe 2-quart casserole with lid. Stir in chicken broth and corn.
2. Microwave, covered, at 100% power 10 minutes, whisking halfway through cooking. Stir in chicken. Microwave, covered, at 100% power 2 minutes or until heated through.
3. Spoon into bowls. Garnish with dollops of yogurt and additional cilantro and corn kernels, if you wish.

Make-Ahead Tip: Soup can be made a day ahead through Step 7 and refrigerated, covered. Bring to room temperature. Reheat, covered, at 70% power.

RISOTTO WITH HAM AND PEAS

LOW-CALORIE · LOW-FAT
LOW-CHOLESTEROL · QUICK

Our version requires no stirring, unlike its famous Italian counterpart. The rice should be tender but firm, not mushy, and bathed in a creamy liquid. Italian arborio rice should be used for best results.

Makes 6 servings.
Nutrient Value Per Serving: 218 calories, 10 g protein, 5 g fat, 30 g carbohydrate, 762 mg sodium, 20 mg cholesterol.

2 cloves garlic, chopped
2 shallots, chopped OR: ¼ cup chopped red onion
2 tablespoons *unsalted* butter *(optional)*
1 can (13¾ ounces) chicken broth
1 cup uncooked arborio rice
⅓ cup white wine
½ teaspoon salt
¼ teaspoon leaf thyme, crumbled
1 to 1½ cups water
½ cup frozen peas, thawed
½ cup slivered or chopped baked ham (2 ounces)
6 drops liquid red-pepper seasoning
½ cup shredded Italian fontina cheese OR: provolone cheese (2 ounces)
¼ cup grated Parmesan cheese

1. Combine garlic, shallots, butter, if using, broth, rice, wine, salt and thyme in microwave-safe 2-quart casserole or soufflé dish. Cover with microwave-safe plastic wrap, vented at one edge. Microwave at 100% power 15 minutes.
2. Stir in 1 cup water. Microwave, covered, at 100% power 5 minutes. Stir in peas, ham and red-pepper seasoning. Re-cover. Let stand 5 minutes.
3. If needed, stir in remaining water until risotto is creamy. Stir in fontina and Parmesan.

STANDING TIME

When food is removed from a microwave oven, it continues to cook because the heat generated in the outer layers continues to penetrate inward to the center by conduction. With some foods, the time it takes to carry them to the table is enough for proper heat redistribution. Dense foods may continue to cook for 15 to 20 minutes after they have come out of the oven. Many microwave recipes account for this by recommending a specific standing time after cooking. During this period, cover the dish to retain heat and set the dish directly on a heatproof surface. Some foods, including cakes and bar cookies, won't look quite right until they have some standing time.

SPAGHETTI CARBONARA

LOW-FAT · QUICK

Makes 4 servings.

Nutrient Value Per Serving: 356 calories, 16 g protein, 12 g fat, 44 g carbohydrate, 268 mg sodium, 128 mg cholesterol.

8 ounces spaghetti
4 ounces sliced bacon, cut up
2 eggs
½ cup half-and-half
¼ cup grated Parmesan cheese
2 tablespoons chopped parsley
½ teaspoon pepper

1. Cook spaghetti following package directions. Drain.

2. While spaghetti is cooking, scatter bacon pieces in two layers between doubled sheets of paper toweling on microwave-safe dinner plate. Microwave at 100% power 5 minutes.

3. Slightly beat the eggs in a microwave-safe 2-cup measure. Whisk in the half-and half. Microwave, uncovered, at 50% power 2½ minutes, whisking after 1½ minutes.

4. Transfer cooked spaghetti to serving bowl. Sprinkle top with bacon, cheese, parsley and pepper. Pour sauce over. Toss gently to blend ingredients. Taste for salt and serve.

CARBONARA, PRONTO!
While the spaghetti is cooking, the microwave oven makes short work of the egg sauce and bacon.

LASAGNA WITH VEGETABLES

Makes 6 servings.

Nutrient Value Per Serving: 465 calories, 23 g protein, 29 g fat, 30 g carbohydrate, 1,138 mg sodium, 89 mg cholesterol.

1 medium-size zucchini (7 ounces), thinly sliced
1 small eggplant (8 ounces), cut into ½-inch cubes
1 medium-size sweet red pepper (5 ounces), cored, seeded and thinly sliced
1 medium-size sweet yellow pepper (5 ounces), cored, seeded and thinly sliced
¼ pound mushrooms, thinly sliced
1 container (15 ounces) whole-milk ricotta cheese
3 tablespoons chopped sun-dried tomatoes, packed in oil
1 teaspoon leaf oregano, crumbled
1 teaspoon leaf basil, crumbled
½ teaspoon salt
⅛ teaspoon pepper
1¾ cups bottled marinara sauce
⅓ cup heavy cream
2 large cloves garlic, finely chopped
6 no-cook lasagna sheets
½ pound whole-milk mozzarella cheese, shredded
½ cup grated Parmesan cheese

1. Place zucchini, eggplant, red and yellow peppers, and mushrooms in microwave-safe 11¾ × 7½ × 1¾-inch baking dish; stir to combine. Cover dish tightly with microwave-safe plastic wrap. Microwave at 100% power 10 minutes or until vegetables are tender, turning dish halfway through cooking. Carefully pierce plastic wrap to release steam. Carefully remove plastic wrap. Drain vegetables in colander.
2. Combine ricotta, sun-dried tomatoes, oregano, basil, salt and pepper in medium-size bowl.

3. Combine marinara sauce, cream and garlic in small bowl.
4. Spread ⅓ cup sauce over bottom of microwave-safe 8 × 8 × 2-inch square baking dish. Top with 1 pasta sheet. Cover evenly with one-third vegetables. Sprinkle with one-quarter of the mozzarella cheese. Spread evenly with ¼ cup sauce. Top with pasta sheet. Spread with half the ricotta mixture. Sprinkle with one-third Parmesan cheese. Spread with ¼ cup sauce. Repeat vegetable layers twice more, with a ricotta layer in between. Top with remaining pasta sheet. Spread remaining sauce over top.
5. Cover dish tightly with microwave-safe plastic wrap. Microwave at 100% power for 5 minutes. Turn dish. Microwave at 50% power for 5 minutes. Turn dish. Microwave at 100% for 5 minutes. Carefully pierce plastic wrap to release steam. Carefully remove plastic wrap. Sprinkle top with remaining mozzarella and Parmesan cheese. Microwave, uncovered, at 100% power for 2 minutes. Cover dish with aluminum foil. Let stand 10 minutes before serving.

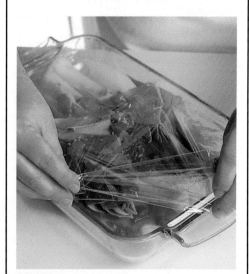

VENTING
Microwave-safe plastic wrap is used to cover dishes to hold in moisture and speed cooking during microwaving. In most cases, vent the dish at one corner to allow the steam to escape during the cooking.

BASQUE CHICKEN

LOW-CALORIE · QUICK

This dish has so much flavor you would never suspect it was quickly cooked in a microwave oven. Serve with rice or hunks of crusty bread.

Makes 4 servings.

Nutrient Value Per Serving: 284 calories, 34 g protein, 10 g fat, 14 g carbohydrate, 850 mg sodium, 79 mg cholesterol.

---

1 large onion, thinly sliced
1 large sweet red pepper, cored, seeded and cut in ½-inch-thick slices
2 cloves garlic, finely chopped
2 tablespoons olive oil
1 large sweet yellow pepper, cored, seeded and cut in ½-inch-thick slices
1 can (14½ ounces) tomatoes
2 tablespoons tomato paste
2 teaspoons cornstarch
1 pound boneless, skinned chicken breasts
¼ pound smoked or baked ham, cut in ¾-inch dice
¾ teaspoon leaf basil, crumbled
¼ teaspoon leaf thyme, crumbled
¼ teaspoon salt
⅛ teaspoon pepper
1 tablespoon chopped parsley

1. Combine onion, peppers, garlic and oil in microwave-safe 3-quart casserole with cover. Microwave, covered, at 100% power 8 minutes or until onion and pepper are tender, stirring once.
2. Drain tomatoes, reserving ½ cup liquid. Coarsely chop tomatoes. Stir tomato paste and cornstarch into reserved tomato liquid until smooth. Cut chicken breasts into 1½-inch pieces. Stir tomatoes, tomato-cornstarch mixture, chicken, ham, basil, thyme, salt and pepper into onion mixture. Microwave, covered, at 100% power for 5 minutes or until chicken is cooked
(*continued*)

BASQUE CHICKEN (*continued*)

through, stirring after 3 minutes. Sprinkle with parsley.

Make-Ahead Tip: The recipe can be prepared up to 2 days ahead and refrigerated, covered. Bring to room temperature. Reheat, covered, at 100% power, stirring once or twice.

```
MICROWAVE MAGNIFIQUE

Basque Chicken (603)

Rice

Praline Cheesecake (620)
```

TURKEY ENCHILADAS

LOW-CALORIE · LOW-CHOLESTEROL QUICK

A *good way to use up leftover turkey. Serve with rice, colored and flavored with ground turmeric. (Pictured on page 595.)*

Makes 10 servings.
Nutrient Value Per Serving: 217 calories, 15 g protein, 9 g fat, 20 g carbohydrate, 445 mg sodium, 37 mg cholesterol.

¼ cup hulled pumpkin seeds
1½ cups lowfat milk
3 tablespoons all-purpose flour
¼ teaspoon salt
2 cups cooked, cubed turkey (8 ounces)
1 can (3½ ounces) whole mild green chilies, rinsed and sliced
¼ cup chopped cilantro OR: parsley
1½ cups shredded jalapeño Jack cheese OR: plain Monterey Jack cheese

1 can (8 ounces) no-salt-added tomato sauce
¼ cup bottled medium or hot salsa
10 flour tortillas (6 inch)

1. Place pumpkin seeds on piece of paper toweling on floor of microwave oven. Microwave, uncovered, at 100% power 3 minutes, stirring halfway through cooking. Remove and set aside.
2. Whisk together 3 tablespoons milk and flour in microwave-safe 4-cup measure until smooth. Stir in remaining milk and salt. Microwave, uncovered, at 100% power 3 minutes or until boiling and thickened, stirring twice during cooking. Stir in turkey, chilies, 2 tablespoons cilantro and 1 cup cheese until well blended.
3. Stir together tomato sauce and salsa in small bowl. Spoon about ¼ cup sauce into bottom of microwave-safe 13 × 9 × 2-inch baking dish.
4. Wrap tortillas in damp paper toweling. Microwave at 100% power 45 seconds or until warmed.
5. Keeping remaining tortillas covered, spoon about ¼ cup of the turkey mixture down the center of a tortilla. Roll up and place, seam-side down, in prepared baking dish. Repeat with remaining tortillas and filling. Spoon remaining sauce over tortillas. Cover with waxed paper.
6. Microwave at 100% power for 15 minutes or until heated through in center. Sprinkle on remaining ½ cup cheese and pumpkin seeds. Let stand 5 minutes. Serve hot.

Make-Ahead Tip: The enchiladas can be prepared up to 3 hours ahead without the final addition of the cheese and pumpkin seeds in Step 6, and refrigerated, covered. To serve, bring to room temperature. Reheat, covered, at 70% power until heated through.

CRANBERRY-GLAZED PORK LOIN

LOW-CALORIE · LOW-CHOLESTEROL

Special enough for a festive get-together. (Pictured at right.)

Makes 6 servings.
Nutrient Value Per Serving: 346 calories, 21 g protein, 17 g fat, 22 g carbohydrate, 454 mg sodium, 73 mg cholesterol.

½ cup cranberry juice
2 teaspoons cornstarch
⅓ cup honey
⅓ cup dry sherry
¼ cup reduced-sodium soy sauce
2 tablespoons red wine vinegar
1 tablespoon grated pared fresh ginger
2 cloves garlic, chopped
¼ teaspoon Chinese five-spice powder
　　OR: ¼ teaspoon ground cloves
1 boneless pork loin (1½ pounds)

1. Stir together the cranberry juice and the cornstarch in microwave-safe 11 × 7 × 2-inch baking dish. Stir in honey, sherry, soy sauce, vinegar, ginger, garlic and five-spice powder until blended. Microwave, uncovered, at 100% for 3 minutes or until thickened, stirring halfway through cooking.
2. Add pork loin to sauce; turn to coat. Cover with waxed paper. Microwave at 70% power for 25 minutes or until internal temperature registers 160° on instant-read meat thermometer; turn meat over halfway through cooking and baste with sauce. Remove meat to cutting board. Let stand 10 minutes before slicing. Pour sauce from baking dish into small bowl; cover while meat is resting. Stir sauce and serve on side.

Pork Tenderloin Variation: Substitute 2 pork tenderloins (about 1¼ pounds total) for pork loin in Step 1. Tuck pointed ends of tenderloin under to get
(continued)

Cranberry-Glazed Pork Loin (this page).

Corned Beef and Potato Casserole (page 606).

CRANBERRY-GLAZED PORK LOIN (*continued*)

an even thickness. Microwave, covered with wax paper, at 70% power 17 to 20 minutes or until internal temperature registers 160° on instant-read thermometer, basting with sauce halfway through. Continue as above.

Make-Ahead Tip: The pork loin and the tenderloin variation can be cooked ahead and refrigerated, covered. Serve cold or at room temperature by itself, or with the sauce, warmed.

CORNED BEEF AND POTATO CASSEROLE

QUICK COMPANY DISH

A casserole that's perfect to make when friends drop in. Just pick up some sliced corned beef at your deli—you probably will already have the remaining ingredients at home. (Pictured on page 605.)

Makes 4 servings.

Nutrient Value Per Serving: 419 calories, 19 g protein, 22 g fat, 37 g carbohydrate, 1,373 mg sodium, 115 mg cholesterol.

2 large baking potatoes (1¼ pounds)
1 egg
⅛ teaspoon salt plus ½ teaspoon
⅛ teaspoon pepper plus ¼ teaspoon
½ cup sliced green onion
1 small sweet red pepper, cored, seeded and chopped
2 tablespoons vegetable oil
8 cups coarsely shredded green cabbage (1¼-pound head)
½ teaspoon caraway seeds
2 teaspoons vinegar
8 ounces sliced corned beef, finely chopped (1½ cups)
¼ cup packaged bread crumbs
½ teaspoon paprika
Mustard Sauce (*recipe follows*)

1. Prick potatoes several times with fork. Place on paper toweling in microwave oven. Microwave at 100% power 8½ to 9½ minutes until soft, turning 2 or 3 times. Peel and mash in medium-size bowl. Mix in the ⅛ teaspoon *each* of salt and pepper. Reserve.

2. Combine green onion, sweet red pepper and oil in microwave-safe baking dish, about 12 × 8 inches. Cover with waxed paper. Microwave at 100% power 4 minutes. Spoon about half the mixture into bowl with potatoes. Reserve. Stir cabbage and caraway seeds into remaining green onion mixture in baking dish. Re-cover. Microwave at 100% power 6 minutes, stirring once. Stir in vinegar, the remaining ½ teaspoon salt and ¼ teaspoon pepper.

3. Mix corned beef into potato mixture until ingredients are well blended. Shape into 6 or 8 equal-size patties, about 2½ inches in diameter. Combine bread crumbs and paprika on piece of waxed paper. Dip patties into crumb mixture to coat both sides. Place on top of cabbage in baking dish.

4. Microwave, uncovered, at 70% power 6 minutes, turning dish once. Let stand, covered, while preparing Mustard Sauce. Serve casserole with sauce.

Mustard Sauce: Whisk together 1 tablespoon cornstarch, ¾ cup reduced-sodium chicken broth and ¼ cup grainy mustard in microwave-safe 2-cup measure until smooth. Microwave, uncovered, at 100% power 4 minutes to full boil, whisking once. Whisk in ¼ cup half-and-half.

Make-Ahead Tip: The dish can be prepared through Step 3 several hours ahead and refrigerated, covered. To serve, bring to room temperature and then proceed with Step 4.

MICROWAVE CASSEROLE MAGIC

Corned Beef and Potato Casserole (this page)

Peas and Carrots

Rye Bread

Coconut Custard Rice Pudding (618)

COD WITH VEGETABLES AND MINT

LOW-CALORIE · LOW-FAT
LOW-CHOLESTEROL · QUICK

Makes 4 servings.
Nutrient Value Per Serving: 227 calories,
32 g protein, 7 g fat, 8 g carbohydrate,
416 mg sodium, 89 mg cholesterol.

1 medium-size onion, thinly sliced
2 cloves garlic, finely chopped
2 tablespoons *un*salted butter
2 large carrots, pared and shredded
1 small zucchini, shredded
2 tablespoons capers, drained and rinsed
2 teaspoons grated lemon rind
2 tablespoons chopped fresh mint OR: 1
    teaspoon dried
1 tablespoon chopped parsley
¼ teaspoon salt
⅛ teaspoon pepper
1½ pounds cod fillet (1 inch thick)
1 tablespoon lemon juice

1. Combine onion, garlic and butter in
microwave-safe 10 × 10-inch baking dish
with lid. Microwave, covered, at 100%
power for 4 minutes, stirring once halfway through cooking. Stir in carrot and
zucchini. Microwave, covered, at 100%
power for 2 minutes.
2. Stir in capers, 1 teaspoon lemon
rind, 1 tablespoon mint, the parsley,
salt and pepper. Cut cod into 4 equal
pieces. Place fish in dish, thickest part
toward outside edge of dish. Sprinkle
fish with lemon juice. Microwave, covered, at 100% power 9 minutes or until
fish flakes when tested with fork; turn
dish after 3 minutes and 6 minutes.
Sprinkle fish with remaining lemon rind
and mint.

MICROWAVING MEAT AND FISH

MICROWAVING POULTRY

Chicken and turkey pieces microwave much better than a whole bird. Moist-cooking methods, such as braising, poaching or steaming, work very well in the microwave oven.

■ Place dark meat pieces, thighs and drumsticks, toward the edge of the dish, and white meat breasts and wings toward the center.

■ If you're preparing a batch of all drumsticks, all wings or all thighs, arrange them spoke-style in a round dish, with the thicker parts facing out.

■ In a rectangular dish, line up the parts, alternating thick and thin ends. Cover the dish tightly with microwave-safe plastic wrap. When done, carefully pierce the plastic to release the steam, then carefully uncover.

MEATY ISSUES

The microwave oven will never replace the backyard grill for making delicious burgers, but it does a good job of cooking chili, meatloaf and similar dishes that use ground beef and pork in combination with other ingredients.

Beef

■ For "unground" beef, the microwave is best for stewing and braising. Recipes for these types of dishes usually use less liquid than their conventional counterparts, since there is little evaporation during microwave cooking. To cook steak or roast beef, conventional dry heat methods work best.

■ When browning meat, do so on the stove top or with a microwave browning tray.

■ To microwave stews and braises for the most tender results, start the dish on full power. Once the liquid boils, lower the power to maintain the simmer.

Pork

Microwaved pork has the same strengths and limitations as beef.

■ Use the microwave oven for stews and braises and small pieces of boneless pork cooked with a glaze, such as a tenderloin, but save the browned roasts for the conventional oven.

■ When cooking several pork chops, arrange them in a ring, with the meatiest portions toward the edge of the dish. Use a browning tray, or cover the chops loosely with waxed paper or with microwave-safe paper toweling.

SEAFOOD: A MICROWAVE SUCCESS STORY

Both fish and shellfish cook quickly and stay moist in the microwave oven.

Shellfish

■ Arrange clams, mussels or shrimp in a ring in a microwave-safe shallow round dish. Cover and microwave at full power. Cook clams and mussels just until their shells open.

■ Shrimp are done as soon as the flesh turns opaque; if you're preparing them unpeeled, cook them until the shells turn bright pink. Scallops do best arranged in a ring in a shallow dish, covered, and microwaved at half or 50% power.

Fish

To cook several fish fillets, arrange them spoke-style, with the thicker ends toward the outside of the dish. Cover with a lid or plastic wrap. If cooking a single fillet, double over the thin end so the fish cooks evenly.

Thin fillets, because of their greater surface area, cook more quickly than an equal weight of thicker fillets.

■ Fish steaks usually take slightly longer to cook than fillets; arrange them with the thinner portions toward the center of the plate. If you don't have a carousel, rotate the dish once or twice during cooking. Start with the minimum recommended cooking time, test for doneness (fish should be barely opaque and flake easily with a fork) and add cooking time in half-minute increments.

SCALLOPS AND FENNEL IN BROTH WITH ORANGE

LOW-CALORIE • LOW-FAT
LOW-CHOLESTEROL • QUICK

A *delicate dish that spotlights the flavor of the scallops. Serve with crusty bread.*

Makes 4 servings (about 8 cups).
Nutrient Value Per Serving: 191 calories, 21 g protein, 5 g fat, 15 g carbohydrate, 793 mg sodium, 38 mg cholesterol.

2 carrots, pared and cut into slivers
1 small leek (4 ounces), well rinsed and cut into 2-inch slivers
½ bulb fennel, cored and thinly sliced
2 cloves garlic, chopped
1 tablespoon olive oil
4 cups hot tap water
2 fish bouillon cubes OR: fish bouillon granules to season 4 cups water
2 strips orange rind
1 tablespoon Pernod (licorice-flavored liqueur)
1 pound sea scallops
⅓ cup slivered fresh basil leaves

1. Combine carrot, leek, fennel, garlic and olive oil in microwave-safe 2½-quart casserole with lid. Microwave, covered, at 100% power 6 minutes or until tender-crisp.
2. Add water, bouillon, orange rind and liqueur to casserole. Microwave, covered, at 100% power 12 to 15 minutes or until the mixture comes to simmering.
3. Meanwhile, halve scallops horizontally into rounds. Stir into broth, along with basil. Let stand, covered, 3 minutes or until scallops are opaque in center. Serve immediately.

TWICE-BAKED YOGURT POTATOES

LOW-FAT • LOW-CHOLESTEROL • QUICK

Twice-baked potatoes in no time at all, flavored with the tang of yogurt.

Makes 4 servings.
Nutrient Value Per Serving: 103 calories, 4 g protein, 1 g fat, 21 g carbohydrate, 191 mg sodium, 3 mg cholesterol.

2 large (8 ounces each) baking potatoes
⅓ cup lowfat plain yogurt
1 tablespoon chopped chives OR: green onion tops
¼ teaspoon salt
3 drops liquid red-pepper seasoning
1½ tablespoons grated Parmesan cheese

1. Pierce potatoes with fork. Place in microwave-safe 10-inch pie plate. Microwave, uncovered, at 100% power 10 minutes or until fork-tender, turning twice. Cut in half lengthwise. When cool enough to handle, scrape out potato into medium-size bowl.
2. Add yogurt, chives, salt, red-pepper seasoning and 1 tablespoon Parmesan to potatoes. Mash with back of spoon until smooth. Spoon back into potato shells. Sprinkle tops with remaining Parmesan. Arrange in pie plate. Cover with microwave-safe plastic wrap, vented at one edge.
3. Microwave at 100% power 3 minutes or until heated through. Serve hot.

Make-Ahead Tip: The potatoes can be prepared a day ahead up through Step 2 and refrigerated, covered. Let the potatoes come to room temperature and proceed with Step 3.

FROM CONVENTIONAL TO MICROWAVE
Many conventional recipes can be successfully converted for microwave cooking. Here are some general guidelines:
■ Moist foods convert well to microwaving.
■ Look for a microwave recipe similar to the one you want to convert and use it as a guide.
■ Recipes that serve up to 8 work best.
■ Reduce or omit fats; use two-thirds of liquids since little evaporation occurs during microwaving.
■ When converting casseroles, substitute instant or quick cooking ingredients for longer cooking ones. Cut vegetables into smaller pieces than normally called for.
■ Use less salt or less highly flavored seasonings.
■ Cut back cooking time by one-third to one-fourth of the conventional recipe time.
■ Use lower power levels for less tender meat and more delicate foods.

MARMALADE BEETS

LOW-CALORIE • LOW-FAT
LOW-CHOLESTEROL

A *colorful addition to a salad plate, barbe-cued foods or roasted meats.*

Makes 2 cups.
Nutrient Value Per ¼ Cup: 89 calories,
1 g protein, 0 g fat, 22 g carbohydrate,
124 mg sodium, 0 mg cholesterol.

APPLESAUCE MAKE-AHEAD TIP:
The applesauce can be made several days ahead and refrigerated, covered.

2 pounds fresh beets, scrubbed and
    trimmed
⅓ cup orange marmalade
½ cup fresh orange juice
2 tablespoons sugar
½ teaspoon grated pared fresh ginger
¼ teaspoon salt
2 tablespoons cold water
2 teaspoons cornstarch
1 tablespoon red wine vinegar

1. Place beets in microwave-safe 2-quart casserole. Cover with microwave-safe plastic wrap, vented at one edge. Microwave at 100% power 20 minutes or until fork-tender. When cool enough to handle, peel under running water. Halve and slice beets.
2. Stir together marmalade, orange juice, sugar, ginger and salt in microwave-safe 1-quart serving bowl. Microwave, uncovered, at 100% power for 2 minutes or until boiling.
3. Meanwhile, stir together water and cornstarch in small bowl. Stir into orange mixture. Microwave, uncovered, at 100% power 1 minute or until the mixture is thickened.
4. Stir in sliced beets and vinegar. Cover and refrigerate until chilled. Serve cold or at room temperature.

Make-Ahead Tip: The beets can be prepared up to 2 days ahead and refrigerated, covered.

RASPBERRY APPLESAUCE

LOW-FAT • LOW-CHOLESTEROL
LOW-SODIUM

One *of the best applesauces we've ever had—very gentle, subtle flavor.*

Makes 4½ cups.
Nutrient Value Per ½ Cup: 109 calories,
0 g protein, 0 g fat, 28 g carbohydrate,
1 mg sodium, 0 mg cholesterol.

2 pounds cooking apples, such as
    Northern Spy (about 4 large)
¾ pound Bartlett or Bosc pears (about
    2 large)
1 cup fresh or dry-pack frozen
    raspberries
4 to 5 tablespoons honey
½ teaspoon ground cinnamon
¼ teaspoon ground cloves
Pinch ground hot red pepper

1. Quarter apples and pears. Combine apples, pears, raspberries, honey, cinnamon, cloves and red pepper in microwave-safe 3-quart casserole with lid.
2. Microwave, covered, at 100% power 20 minutes or until fruits are tender. Pass through food mill. Refrigerate until chilled. Serve cold or at room temperature.

**LOVIN' FROM THE
(MICROWAVE) OVEN**

Broiled Pork Chops

Raspberry Applesauce (this
page)

Twice-Baked Yogurt
Potatoes (609)

Green Beans

Black Bottom Pie (617)

BRAISED LEEKS WITH TOMATO ORANGE SAUCE

LOW-FAT · LOW-CHOLESTEROL

*S*erve *with your favorite roasted meat, or at room temperature as a first course.*

Makes 4 servings.
Nutrient Value Per Serving: 144 calories, 4 g protein, 3 g fat, 28 g carbohydrate, 500 mg sodium, 6 mg cholesterol.

4 large leeks (about 2 pounds), trimmed
1 can (14½ ounces) no-salt-added tomatoes, in juice
1 cup orange juice
¾ cup chicken broth
¼ cup dry white wine
3 cloves garlic, crushed
½ teaspoon leaf basil, crumbled
½ teaspoon salt
¼ teaspoon fennel seeds, crushed
⅛ teaspoon black pepper
2 teaspoons cornstarch
¼ cup half-and-half

1. Split leeks lengthwise to within ½ inch of root end. Rinse well under running water to remove all sand. Place in microwave-safe 13 × 9 × 2-inch baking dish, alternating root and top ends.
2. Drain tomatoes and chop. Add to baking dish, along with orange juice, broth, wine, garlic, basil, salt, fennel and pepper. Cover with microwave-safe plastic wrap, vented at one corner.
3. Microwave at 100% power 15 minutes. Turn leeks over. Re-cover. Microwave at 100% power 10 to 15 minutes or until fork-tender. Transfer leeks to serving plate, leaving liquid in dish. Cover leeks to keep warm.
4. Stir together cornstarch and half-and-half in small bowl until blended. Stir into mixture in baking dish. Cover tightly with microwave-safe plastic wrap. Microwave at 100% power 5 minutes. Carefully pierce plastic wrap to release steam. Carefully uncover. Whisk to blend. Spoon sauce over leeks. Serve hot or at room temperature.

Braised Fennel Variation: Substitute 3 large fennel bulbs (about 1½ pounds) for leeks. Trim stalk ends and cut each bulb into 8 wedges, trimming off root. Arrange in single layer in microwave-safe 13 × 9 × 2-inch baking dish. Proceed as directed in Step 2.
Make-Ahead Tip: This recipe and its variation can be prepared a day ahead and refrigerated, covered. Reheat, covered, at 100% power. Or serve the leeks at room temperature.

VEGETABLE BAKE WITH CHEDDAR

Makes 6 servings.
Nutrient Value Per Serving: 180 calories, 10 g protein, 9 g fat, 14 g carbohydrate, 332 mg sodium, 94 mg cholesterol.

VEGETABLE BAKE SERVING IDEAS
Offer with a salad for a light lunch or supper, or as a side casserole with roasted meats. You can vary the vegetables depending on what you have on hand. (Pictured on page 613.)

MAKE IT SNAPPY
Microwaved vegetables cook in little or no water, so their flavors remain intense, their colors stay vibrant and their textures do not become mushy. Water-soluble vitamins, robbed by the cooking liquid when vegetables boil conventionally, are retained by microwave cooking.

1 pound broccoli
1 large sweet red pepper
1 medium-size zucchini
1 large carrot
1 clove garlic, finely chopped
4 slices white bread
1 cup shredded Cheddar cheese (4 ounces)
2 large eggs
½ cup milk
¼ teaspoon salt
⅛ teaspoon pepper

1. Cut flowerets from broccoli stalks. Reserve stalks for another use. If flowerets are large, cut in half. Core and seed red pepper; cut into ¾-inch pieces. Cut zucchini into ¾-inch pieces. Pare and shred carrot.
2. Place broccoli, red pepper, zucchini, carrot and garlic in microwave-safe 2-quart round baking dish with cover; stir. Microwave, covered, at 100% power 4 minutes or until partially cooked, turning dish halfway through cooking.
3. Remove vegetables to colander to drain. Cut bread into ½-inch cubes. Place bread cubes evenly in bottom of baking dish. Cover with half the vegetables. Sprinkle with half the cheese. Cover with remaining vegetables and cheese. Beat eggs in small bowl; add milk, salt and pepper and beat to combine. Pour custard around edge of dish.
4. Microwave, covered, at 100% power 4 minutes, turning dish halfway through cooking. Microwave, uncovered, at 50% power 4 minutes. Turn dish. Microwave, uncovered, at 100% power 2 minutes. Let stand 2 minutes before serving.

BRAISED RED CABBAGE

LOW-CALORIE · LOW-CHOLESTEROL
QUICK

A new twist on an old favorite, and it only takes 12 minutes in the microwave oven. Serve with pork, beef or duck. (Pictured on page 613.)

Makes 6 servings.
Nutrient Value Per Serving: 80 calories, 2 g protein, 4 g fat, 11 g carbohydrate, 323 mg sodium, 10 mg cholesterol.

1 small head red cabbage (1¼ pounds)
2 tablespoons *un*salted butter
1 tablespoon light brown sugar
2 tablespoons red wine vinegar
¾ teaspoon salt
⅛ teaspoon pepper
1 large navel orange
2 tablespoons chopped parsley
1 teaspoon mustard seeds

1. Quarter and core cabbage. Slice thinly. Place butter in microwave-safe 3-quart baking dish with lid. Add cabbage, sugar, vinegar, salt and pepper; stir to combine. Microwave, covered, at 100% power 10 minutes or until cabbage is tender, stirring halfway through cooking.
2. While cabbage is cooking, grate 2 teaspoons orange rind. Peel and section orange. Coarsely chop orange. Stir orange rind, chopped orange, parsley and mustard seeds into cabbage. Microwave, covered, at 100% power for 2 minutes.

Make-Ahead Tip: The recipe can be prepared a day ahead and refrigerated, covered. Reheat, covered, at 100% power.

Vegetable Bake with Cheddar (page 612).

Spaghetti Squash with Fontina (page 614).

Braised Red Cabbage (page 612).

Lentils with Carrot and Red Pepper (page 614).

SPAGHETTI SQUASH WITH FONTINA

Makes 8 servings.

Nutrient Value Per Serving: 202 calories, 6 g protein, 15 g fat, 12 g carbohydrate, 308 mg sodium, 34 mg cholesterol.

1 large spaghetti squash (3½ pounds), halved lengthwise
2 tablespoons *un*salted butter
1 large clove garlic, finely chopped
¼ cup heavy cream
½ cup walnuts, chopped
¼ pound fontina cheese, shredded (1 cup)
½ teaspoon salt
¼ teaspoon pepper
3 tablespoons chopped parsley

1. Cut squash lengthwise in half; scoop out seeds. Place, cut-sides down, in microwave-safe 13×9×2-inch baking dish. Microwave, uncovered, at 100% power 10 minutes. Rotate squash in dish. Microwave, uncovered, 10 minutes or until squash is tender but not mushy. Turn squash cut side up and let stand until cool enough to handle.
2. Place butter and garlic in microwave-safe 2-quart round baking dish. Microwave, uncovered, at 100% power 4 minutes or until garlic is golden. Remove squash strands with fork and add to garlic-butter. Add heavy cream, walnuts, fontina cheese, salt, pepper and 2 tablespoons parsley. Stir to combine.
3. Microwave, uncovered, at 100% power 6 minutes or until squash is hot, turning dish halfway through cooking. Sprinkle with remaining parsley before serving.

Make-Ahead Tip: The spaghetti squash can be cooked a day ahead and refrigerated, covered. To serve, bring squash to room temperature and proceed with Step 2.

LENTILS WITH CARROT AND RED PEPPER

LOW-CHOLESTEROL

Makes 8 servings.

Nutrient Value Per Serving: 205 calories, 10 g protein, 9 g fat, 23 g carbohydrate, 410 mg sodium, 10 mg cholesterol.

¼ pound thick-sliced bacon
½ pound dried lentils, picked over and rinsed
2 large cloves garlic, finely chopped
1 medium-size onion, chopped
1 large stalk celery, cut into ½-inch dice
2 large carrots, pared and cut into ½-inch dice
1 small sweet red pepper, cored, seeded and cut into ½-inch dice
½ teaspoon leaf thyme, crumbled
⅛ teaspoon pepper
1 cup chicken broth
1 cup water
1 can (8 ounces) tomato sauce

1. Cut bacon crosswise into ½-inch pieces. Place in microwave-safe 3-quart casserole dish with lid. Microwave, covered, at 100% power 5 minutes.
2. Add lentils, garlic, onion, celery, carrot, red pepper, thyme, pepper and chicken broth to bacon; stir to combine. Microwave, covered, at 100% power 10 minutes. Stir in water and tomato sauce. Microwave, covered, at 100% power 20 minutes or until lentils are tender but not soft, stirring halfway through cooking. Let stand, covered, 10 minutes.

Make-Ahead Tip: The dish can be prepared a day ahead and refrigerated, covered. Bring to room temperature. Reheat, covered, at 100% power, stirring once or twice.

PLANTAIN AND PINEAPPLE CASSEROLE

LOW-FAT · LOW-CHOLESTEROL · QUICK

A *good way to try plantains if you've never had them. Serve with ham or pork and barbecued foods.*

Makes 6 servings.

Nutrient Value Per Serving: 120 calories, 1 g protein, 0 g fat, 31 g carbohydrate, 278 mg sodium, 0 mg cholesterol.

2 ripe black plantains (1 pound)
1 can (8 ounces) pineapple tidbits, packed in juice
3 carrots (8 ounces), shredded
⅔ cup reduced-sodium chicken broth
1½ tablespoons honey
½ teaspoon salt
¼ teaspoon ground cinnamon
Pinch ground cloves

2 tablespoons lemon juice
½ teaspoon cornstarch

1. Peel and quarter plantains lengthwise; thickly slice crosswise. Set aside.

2. Drain pineapple tidbits, reserving liquid. Place ⅓ cup pineapple liquid in microwave-safe 2-quart casserole with lid. Stir in carrot, chicken broth, honey, salt, cinnamon and cloves.

3. Microwave, covered, at 100% power 5 minutes. Stir in plantains and ½ cup pineapple tidbits. Microwave, covered, at 100% power 4 to 5 minutes until plantains are tender.

4. Stir together lemon juice and cornstarch in small bowl. Stir into casserole. Microwave, uncovered, at 100% power 1 minute. Serve warm or at room temperature.

Make-Ahead Tip: The casserole can be made a day ahead and refrigerated, covered. Bring to room temperature. Reheat, covered, at 100% power.

MICROWAVE COOKING CHART FOR FRESH VEGETABLES

Vegetable	Quantity	Water	Preparation Tips	Cooking Time	Standing Time
Artichoke	1 medium-size	¼ cup	Turn upside down in small dish or custard cup. Cover with plastic wrap.	5–7 min. Stem should be fork tender.	5 min. covered.
Asparagus Spears	1 pound	3 Tbs.	Snap off tough ends. Arrange buds toward center of dish, cover with plastic wrap.	5 min.	5 min. covered.
Beans (green, wax)	1 pound	½ cup	Snap ends and pull off strings. Cover with plastic wrap or lid.	12–15 min. Stir every 5 min.	5 min. covered.
Beets	6	1½ cups	Wash. *(Do not peel.)* Cover with lid or plastic wrap.	14–16 min. Turn after 7 min.	5 min. covered. Let cool, peel.
Broccoli Spears	1½ pounds	—	Place buds toward center of plate. Cover with lid or plastic wrap.	8–10 min. Rotate dish or plate after 5 min.	4 min. covered.
Brussels Sprouts	1 pound	2 Tbs.	Cover with lid or plastic wrap.	6–7 min. Stir after 3 min.	3–5 min. covered. Stem ends should be fork tender.

(continued)

(*continued*)

MICROWAVE COOKING CHART FOR FRESH VEGETABLES

Vegetable	Quantity	Water	Preparation Tips	Cooking Time	Standing Time
Cabbage	1 pound	2 Tbs.	Discard wilted outer leaves. Cover with lid or plastic wrap.	4–6 min. (shredded) 6–8 min. (wedges) Stir or turn ½ way through cooking.	3 min. covered.
Carrots	1 pound	¼ cup	Slice in uniform size or leave whole. Cover with lid or plastic wrap.	6–7 min. (slices) 8–9 min. (whole) Stir or rotate ½ way through cooking.	5 min. covered.
Cauliflower	1½ pounds	2 Tbs.	Remove outer leaves. Trim stem end. Separate flowerets or leave head whole. Cover with lid or plastic wrap.	6–8 min. (flowerets) 10–11 min. (whole) Stir or rotate head ½ way through cooking.	4–5 min. covered.
Corn on the Cob	1 ear	—	Secure husk closed with string. (Or shuck and cover in dish.) Place on paper toweling on microwave floor.	3–4 min. per ear. Turn each ½ way through cooking.	2–3 min. per ear.
Greens (kale & mustard)	1¼ pounds	—	Rinse and coarsely chop. Cover with lid or plastic wrap.	7–8 min. Stir after 3 min.	2 min. covered.
Mushrooms	1 pound	2 Tbs. *or* 2 Tbs. butter	Cut to even shapes. Cover with waxed paper.	4–6 min. Stir after 2 min.	2 min. covered.
Onions	1 pound	—	Quarter, slice or leave whole. Cover with waxed paper.	4–6 min. Stir after 2 min.	5 min. covered.
Peas	2½ pounds (3 cups shelled)	¼ cup	Shell and rinse. Cover with lid or plastic wrap.	9–13 min. Stir after 5 min.	5 min. covered.
Potatoes (baking, sweet potatoes, yams)	1	—	Pierce skin on 4 sides with fork. Place on paper toweling on microwave floor. Arrange 1 on floor; 2 side by side; 4 or more in spoke fashion.	4–5 min. Add 2–3 min. per potato. Turn each ½ way through cooking.	5–10 min. covered. Should give to slight pressure.
Spinach	1 pound	—	Rinse; shake excess water. Cover with lid or plastic wrap.	5–7 min. Stir after 3 min.	2 min. covered.
Squash (winter)	1 medium-size	—	Cut and remove seeds. Place on plate with hollow side up. Cover with plastic wrap.	10–12 min. Rotate after 5 min.	5 min. covered.
Squash (summer)	1 pound	2 Tbs.	Cover with lid or plastic wrap.	6–7 min. Stir after 3 min.	3 min. covered.
Turnips	1 pound	3 Tbs.	Cut into cubes. Cover with lid or plastic wrap.	7–9 min. Stir after 3 min.	3 min. covered.

BLACK BOTTOM PIE

There's a double "black bottom" in this pie—a dark chocolate wafer crust as well as the bottom layer of chocolate filling. Drizzle melted semisweet chocolate across the top, if you wish.

Makes 8 servings.

Nutrient Value Per Serving: 348 calories, 6 g protein, 15 g fat, 49 g carbohydrate, 233 mg sodium, 100 mg cholesterol.

Crumb Crust:
2 tablespoons *un*salted butter
1½ cups chocolate wafer crumbs
    (two-thirds 9-ounce package)
2 tablespoons sugar

Filling:
3 cups milk
⅔ cup sugar
3 tablespoons cornstarch
⅛ teaspoon salt
3 egg yolks
3 squares (1 ounce each) semisweet
    chocolate, chopped
½ teaspoon vanilla
1 tablespoon bourbon

1. To prepare Crust: Place butter in microwave-safe 9-inch pie plate. Microwave, uncovered, at 100% power 1½ to 2 minutes to melt. Mix in crumbs and sugar until well blended. Press into even layer over bottom and up sides of plate. Microwave, uncovered, at 100% power 1½ minutes.

2. To prepare Filling: Whisk together ½ cup milk, 3 tablespoons sugar and cornstarch in small bowl until smooth. Reserve. Pour remaining milk, sugar and salt into microwave-safe 8-cup measure. Microwave, uncovered, at 100% power 6 to 7 minutes to simmering. Whisk a little hot mixture into sugar-cornstarch mixture. Stir sugar-cornstarch mixture into measure. Microwave, uncovered, at 100% power 3 to 4 minutes to full boiling, stirring once. Beat egg yolks slightly in small

bowl; whisk in a little hot mixture. Stir into remaining hot mixture.

3. Remove 1½ cups to small bowl. Add chocolate and vanilla. Stir until melted. Pour into crumb crust. Quick-chill in freezer 10 minutes. Stir bourbon into remaining filling. Spoon on top of chocolate.

4. Cover lightly and refrigerate 4 to 6 hours.

Make-Ahead Tip: The pie can be prepared a day ahead and refrigerated, lightly covered.

Coconut Custard Rice Pudding (this page).

COCONUT CUSTARD RICE PUDDING

An easy, make-ahead rice pudding. (Pictured at left.)

Makes 6 servings.

Nutrient Value Per Serving: 284 calories, 6 g protein, 5 g fat, 55 g carbohydrate, 154 mg sodium, 47 mg cholesterol.

2½ cups water
¾ cup uncooked long-grain white rice
⅓ cup sugar
1 tablespoon cornstarch
¼ teaspoon salt
3 tablespoons honey
1 egg
2 cups milk
¾ teaspoon vanilla
1 teaspoon grated orange rind OR: lemon rind
½ cup golden raisins OR: dried pitted cherries
⅓ cup shredded sweetened coconut
Ground cinnamon *(optional)*

1. Combine water and rice in microwave-safe 3-quart baking dish or soufflé dish. Cover with waxed paper. Microwave at 100% power for 10 minutes, stirring once. Microwave at 50% power for 10 minutes or until rice is tender, stirring once.
2. Meanwhile, stir together sugar, cornstarch and salt in medium-size bowl. Beat in honey, egg and 1 cup milk until smooth. Stir into cooked rice, along with vanilla, orange rind and raisins. Re-cover with waxed paper.
3. Microwave at 100% power 6 minutes or until thickened, stirring halfway through cooking. Stir in remaining 1 cup milk and coconut. Cover and refrigerate until chilled.
4. Spoon into dessert dishes and sprinkle with ground cinnamon, if you wish.

Make-Ahead Tip: The pudding can be made a day ahead and refrigerated.

Apple Butter Date Bars (page 619).

APPLE BUTTER DATE BARS

LOW-CHOLESTEROL • LOW-SODIUM

Offer as a dessert with coffee, nibble on as a snack, or pack into lunch boxes. (Pictured on page 618.)

Makes 16 bars.
Nutrient Value Per Bar: 175 calories, 2 g protein, 8 g fat, 26 g carbohydrate, 37 mg sodium, 16 mg cholesterol.

¾ cup apple butter
¾ cup chopped dates
1 tablespoon honey
¼ teaspoon ground cinnamon
¼ teaspoon ground ginger
1 teaspoon vanilla
¾ cup whole-wheat flour
⅓ cup firmly packed dark brown sugar
¼ teaspoon salt
½ cup (1 stick) chilled *un*salted butter, cut into pieces
1 cup old-fashioned rolled oats OR: quick-cooking oats (not instant)
⅓ cup chopped walnuts

1. Stir together apple butter, dates, honey, cinnamon and ginger in microwave-safe 4-cup measure. Microwave, uncovered, at 100% power for 4 minutes or until thickened. Stir in vanilla. Set aside.
2. Combine whole-wheat flour, brown sugar and salt in food processor. Whirl until blended. Add butter. Whirl until mixture resembles coarse meal. Add oats. Whirl just to combine. (Or, combine by hand in a bowl.)
3. Remove ¾ cup of oat mixture and reserve. Scrape remaining mixture into microwave-safe 8½ × 8½ × 2-inch square baking dish. Press level across bottom of dish, and push ¼ inch up side of dish. Microwave, uncovered, at 100% power 4 minutes, turning dish halfway through cooking. Cool on wire rack 5 minutes.

4. Spoon apple butter mixture over crust and spread level. Sprinkle with reserved oat mixture and the walnuts. Microwave, uncovered, at 100% power 4 minutes, turning halfway through cooking. Cool completely on wire rack. Cut into 16 bars.

PEANUT BRITTLE

LOW-CHOLESTEROL • QUICK

A very good version that's not as sweet as some others.

Makes about ¾ pound.
Nutrient Value Per ¼ Cup: 192 calories, 3 g protein, 8 g fat, 29 g carbohydrate, 121 mg sodium, 5 mg cholesterol.

½ cup firmly packed light brown sugar
½ cup granulated sugar
½ cup light corn syrup
1 cup *un*salted peanuts
2 tablespoons *un*salted butter
¼ teaspoon salt
¾ teaspoon baking soda
½ teaspoon vanilla

1. Spray back of cookie sheet and icing spatula with nonstick vegetable-oil cooking spray. Stir together brown sugar, granulated sugar and corn syrup in microwave-safe 2-quart casserole or glass measure. Microwave, uncovered, at 100% power for 4 minutes; sugars will begin to dissolve.
2. Stir in peanuts, butter and salt until blended. (Insert microwave thermometer, if using.) Microwave, uncovered, at 100% power 5½ to 6 minutes or until temperature reaches 300° (hard-crack stage).
3. Quickly stir in baking soda and vanilla. Pour onto prepared sheet, spreading with spatula. Cool until firm. Break into small pieces. Store in airtight containers.

DATE BARS MAKE-AHEAD TIP:
The bars can be made up to 5 days ahead and refrigerated, covered.

KIDS AND THE MICROWAVE OVEN
■ Make it a rule that your children must always ask permission to use the microwave oven.
■ Get children in the habit of setting the oven to the minimum amount of time and checking for doneness. Explain about standing time.
■ Explain that, although a microwave oven doesn't get hot, what's inside does. Demonstrate how to use a potholder, and make it clear that food should be allowed to cool slightly before being tasted.
■ Show children the proper way to remove a lid or plastic wrap after cooking: lifting the cover away from their hands and faces to avoid burns from hot steam.
■ Another rule: Cleaning up after cooking is mandatory.

PEANUT BRITTLE MAKE-AHEAD TIP:
The brittle can be stored for up to 2 weeks in an airtight container.

PRALINE CHEESECAKE

A *delicious cheesecake with a shortbread
crust, from the microwave oven. The praline can be used for other desserts—scatter
over ice cream or a whipped-cream-topped
piece of pie or cobbler, or whatever else
suits your taste.*

Makes 12 servings.
Nutrient Value Per Serving: 454 calories,
7 g protein, 32 g fat, 36 g carbohydrate,
199 mg sodium, 134 mg cholesterol.

Praline:
1 cup pecans OR: whole blanched
　　almonds
1 cup firmly packed light brown sugar
2 tablespoons water
½ teaspoon lemon juice

Cheesecake:
4 tablespoons (½ stick) *un*salted butter
1 cup shortbread crumbs (from about
　　14 cookies)
¾ cup wheatmeal biscuit crumbs (from
　　about 6 crackers) OR: graham
　　cracker crumbs
2 tablespoons granulated sugar
2 packages (8 ounces each) cream
　　cheese
4 eggs
1½ teaspoons vanilla
1 tablespoon cornstarch
Grated rind of 1 lemon
1 container (8 ounces) dairy sour cream
8 whole pecans, for garnish

1. Prepare Praline: Place nuts on sheet
of paper toweling on microwave oven
floor. Microwave, uncovered, at 100%
power 5 minutes or until fragrant, stirring once during cooking; set aside.
2. Combine brown sugar, water and
lemon juice in microwave-safe 4-cup
measure. Microwave, uncovered, at
100% power for 8 to 9 minutes or until
amber. Stir in nuts; spread with metal
spatula onto greased baking sheet. Cool
on wire rack. Break praline into pieces.
Place in processor or, working in

batches, in blender. Whirl until finely
chopped. Store in airtight container.
3. Prepare Cheesecake: Place butter in
microwave-safe 8 × 2-inch round cake
dish or 10-inch pie plate. Microwave,
uncovered, at 100% power 1 minute or
until melted. Stir in shortbread crumbs,
wheatmeal crumbs and sugar until
blended. Spread level across bottom of
dish, and press with sheet of plastic
wrap halfway up side of dish. Microwave, uncovered, at 100% power 2
minutes.
4. To soften cream cheese, place in
microwave-safe large bowl. Microwave,
uncovered, at 100% power 1 minute
and 30 seconds. Add 1¼ cups praline,
eggs, vanilla, cornstarch and lemon rind
to cream cheese. Beat for 1 minute or
until smooth. Beat in sour cream at low
speed just until combined.
5. Microwave, uncovered, at 100%
power 5 minutes or until thickened and
texture of sour cream, whisking mixture
twice during cooking. Pour into prepared pan. Arrange 8 pecan halves on
top, if you wish. Sprinkle top with 2
tablespoons praline.
6. Microwave, uncovered, at 100%
power for 7 to 8 minutes or until almost
set in center, turning halfway through
cooking. Cool on wire rack. Refrigerate
at least 4 hours or overnight.

Make-Ahead Tip: The praline can be
made up to 2 weeks ahead and stored in
airtight container. The cake can be
made a day ahead and refrigerated,
covered.

CHAPTER 15

NO TIME TO COOK

**DINNER FROM
THE DELI**

(previous page) You won't need a single skillet to prepare this party fare. It's a new look for deli favorites that takes no more than a spooning from store carton to your own stylish crockery, and a little garnishing. Sprinkle macaroni salad with chopped sun-dried tomatoes, top fruit salad with a handful of trail mix, and serve together chunks of sweet red pepper and marinated artichoke hearts for nibbling. Impress your guests by serving their deli vegetable salad in edible containers—quick-to-core, colorful sweet peppers take the place of salad bowls. The finishing touch: an assortment of rolls, flatbread and breadsticks.

Today, more and more of us have less time to shop and cook. But we still want to prepare meals for our families and friends, and we enjoy entertaining when our busy schedules permit.

In this chapter we show you how to take advantage of the delicatessen, frozen food case, and refrigerated prepared food section of your supermarket for no-effort dinner ideas. Convenience foods can be dressed up just by transferring them to fancier serving plates and adding a few personalized touches.

We also offer suggestions about stocking your pantry and freezer, time-saving kitchen equipment, and strategies for beating the breakfast crunch.

DINNER FROM THE DELI

Try the following for quick-fix buffets, or a fast dinner.

■ **Macaroni and potato salads:** Present them on a bed of mixed lettuce greens; sprinkle with shredded carrot or zucchini and top with chopped fresh chives or parsley, sliced green onions or olives, or slivered sun-dried tomatoes.

■ **Deli meat platters:** Add color and flavor with bottled roasted red peppers, green and ripe olives, marinated artichoke hearts, hot peppers, pickles, hearts of palm, thinly sliced red onion or a bowl of salsa.

■ **The best of bread:** Serve an assortment of dinner rolls, sliced breads, breadsticks and flatbreads with cold cuts and salads, and little crocks of prepared flavored butters and cheese spreads.

Or, a single loaf of bread can make a family meal! Slice a loaf of Italian or French bread lengthwise; top each half with sliced roast turkey, marinated vegetables and shredded mozzarella cheese. Broil or bake just long enough to warm through and melt the cheese. Serve open-face, garnished with chopped parsley.

■ **Prepared tuna, egg or vegetable salads:** They look great, taste delicious in hollowed-out raw vegetables: sweet peppers, tomatoes, zucchini boats.

■ **Dessert from the deli:** Combine deli rice pudding or fruit salad with dried fruit-and-nuts trail mix for an on-the-spot after-dinner sweet. Spoon into individual glasses and garnish with a dollop of sour cream, whipped cream or vanilla yogurt.

TORTILLAS: RAPID WRAP-UPS

Corn or flour tortillas from the refrigerated food section and packaged taco shells require no more than a quick warm-up and can be wrapped around everything from main courses to desserts.

■ **Build a burrito** with heated, mashed canned beans and shredded cheese folded into a warm flour tortilla. Serve with prepared salsa and/or prepared frozen guacamole.

■ **Create Oriental pancakes** with tortillas to wrap up quickly cooked frozen stir-fry combinations.

■ **Spoon prepared chili or "sloppy Joe" fillings** into a warm tortilla roll.

■ **Make an open-faced tostada sandwich** by placing a corn tortilla in a hot oven for a few minutes; top with chili and cheese, mashed beans and prepared salsa; or pile on finely chopped and shredded salad bar vegetables. Fill a crisp, packaged taco shell with any of the same.

■ **Create a dessert crepe** with a warm flour tortilla filled with fruit salad. Drizzle with pourable fruit topping.

QUICK FIXES FROM THE FREEZER

Add fresh foods to frozen entrees and canned soups for the taste and appearance of homemade.

■ **Stir-fry a frozen vegetable medley with** sautéed sliced meat or poultry. Season with soy sauce, Oriental sesame oil and rice wine vinegar.

■ **Start with split pea soup** from the freezer case; stir in chopped ham and grated carrot while the soup is heating up. For a touch of the exotic, flavor with curry powder, ground cumin or crushed fennel seeds. Float a slice of lemon on each serving.

- **Top cooked frozen potatoes** with grated cheese; sprinkle with chopped fresh chives or dill. Or top with canned chili or microwave-cooked vegetables.
- **Make a main-dish salad** from the freezer: Combine thawed, cooked black-eyed peas, chopped spinach or kale, corn kernels and diced sweet pepper. Toss with slivered ham and bottled vinaigrette dressing.
- **Take a frozen pie shell,** thaw it, and fill with leftover meat and vegetables, or steamed chopped vegetables from the salad bar and precooked meat from the deli; add **ready-to-pour quiche batter** and pop in the oven.

PASTA PRONTO

- **Fresh prepared pasta** cooks more quickly than dried; top it with **no-cook sauces** made from fresh vegetables (tomato, onion, sweet pepper, garlic) finely chopped in a food processor. Season sauce with anchovies and pure olive oil. Add chunks of drained canned tuna or salmon and pass the grated cheese.
- **Spruce up bottled pasta sauces** with sautéed onions, mushrooms, peppers or summer squash and fresh herbs. Serve with **frozen or fresh-prepared ravioli, linguine or tortellini.**
- **Think cheese and pasta.** Toss hot cooked spaghetti or linguine with crumbled blue cheese, gorgonzola, goat or feta cheese and a little of the pasta cooking water for a quick, creamy sauce. Top with sun-dried tomatoes, sliced imported olives, fresh chives, parsley or basil.
- **Instant primavera sauce** is easy to do: Steam raw salad-bar vegetables and toss with olive oil and Parmesan cheese.
- **Bottled vinaigrette dressing** goes wonderfully well with cooked cavatelli or tortellini. Add cherry tomato halves, fresh herbs or thinly sliced crunchy vegetables such as fennel, celery or jícama. Serve warm or at room temperature or make ahead and refrigerate to serve as a cold salad or first course.

FROM SHELF TO PLATE

Especially good for quick, special touches.
- **Have instant side dishes on hand.** Stock up on prepared chutneys, relishes, marinated vegetables, stuffed grape leaves, bottled salsa, pickled peppers.
- **Turn pasta salad mix into a main dish.** Pair pasta with canned tuna or salmon, cooked meat from the deli section or refrigerated food case, hard-cooked eggs or cubes of cheese.
- **Go with fast-fix grains.** Try couscous, instant white or brown rice, quick-cooking barley and grits.
- **Sauté quick-to-make patties.** Combine instant mashed potatoes with chopped deli corned beef, pastrami or ham.

SPEEDY SOUPS

Prepare quick "homemade" soup with store-bought bases.
- **Begin with dehydrated noodle soup mix.** Add shredded fresh coleslaw mix, frozen snow peas or spinach and cubes of firm tofu.

WRAP-UPS

(pictured above) Here's dinner in a flash: toast corn tortillas or crisp taco shells, fill with prepared chili or "sloppy Joe" mixture and top with ready-grated cheese. For a vegetarian version, toss mixed vegetables from the same salad bar with bottled salad dressing, drizzle with melted cheese and accent with a few pumpkin seeds. Then try tortilla for dessert! Mixed fruit from the salad bar, wrapped in a warm flour tortilla and topped with fruit sauce and nuts, takes Tex-Mex to the finish.

■ **Start with broth from a can.** Toss in vegetables from the salad bar, meat from the deli, seasoning from your cupboard.

■ **Bring fresh flavor to canned and frozen soups.** Add grated nutmeg or a drop of sherry to cream of mushroom; chili powder or hot sauce to creamy Cheddar cheese soup; chopped fresh basil or dill to tomato; a squeeze of lemon to chicken and rice; ground cumin to black bean soup; shredded mozzarella to onion soup; grated Parmesan to minestrone.

SAUCE IT!

Create instant sauces and toppings.

■ **Use pesto, salsa, hot pepper jelly or crumbled goat cheese** to top steamed vegetables, baked potatoes, broiled seafood.

■ **Thicken apple or cranberry juice with cornstarch,** add raisins, simmer until thickened and serve over ham steaks or pork chops.

■ **Make simple dessert sauces** by puréeing soft fresh fruit and berries or thawed frozen fruit with a little fruit juice or liqueur. Use it to top ice cream, cake or poached fruit.

DESSERTS: SHORT & SWEET

Upgrade ready-made desserts.

■ **Dress up a poundcake or sponge ring** with a dusting of 10X (confectioners') sugar or a drizzle of bottled dessert sauce and mint sprigs for garnish.

■ **Sandwich ice cream** between layers of thawed poundcake. Slice poundcake lengthwise; spread on softened ice cream; return to the freezer to firm up. Slice and serve with chocolate syrup or thawed frozen fruit and sprinkle with chopped nuts.

■ **Split a plain cake layer** into two rounds, sandwich together with fruit spread or jam, drizzle with melted chocolate and garnish with fresh berries.

■ **Serve yogurt parfaits** in elegant wine glasses. Swirl layers of vanilla or lemon yogurt with sliced fruit and chopped nuts in stemmed glasses and serve.

■ **Create instant sorbets** by freezing fruit juice in ice cube trays, or drained, canned fruit in freezer containers; pulse in food processor.

■ **Glamorize prepared applesauce** with sliced fresh fruit and a swirl of cream.

■ **Take two chocolate wafer cookies** and sandwich slightly softened ice cream or frozen yogurt in between. Freeze until ready to serve. Eat out of hand as a snack or serve on dessert plates with hot chocolate sauce.

■ **Toast frozen waffles** and use as a base for ice cream desserts. Top with syrup, fruit and nuts.

"EMERGENCY" RATIONS

Keep in a supply of "emergency" foods—enough to make a meal or a snack when you can't cook or shop. See "Stocking the Pantry," page 19, for guidelines.

■ **Stock the freezer with unsauced frozen pasta entrees**—stuffed shells, tortellini, cavatelli, ravioli. Keep the go-withs on your pantry shelf: bottled sauces, roasted peppers, artichokes, olives, capers and canned tuna or salmon.

■ **Store dry milk powder,** evaporated milk and shelf-stable milk in aseptic (sterilized) packaging in the pantry.

■ **Keep dehydrated foods on hand:** dried fruits, sun-dried tomatoes, soup and sauce mixes, beans, instant potatoes, a variety of dried herbs and spices.

■ **Keep cake, muffin, pastry and bread mixes** at the ready. Prepare them with reconstituted dry milk and frozen egg substitutes, or jazz them up with dried fruits and spices.

MORNING GLORIES

Hasty mornings preclude breakfast time, and that's too bad because this eye-opening meal is the most important one of the day. A breakfast high in carbohydrates and protein, but low in fat, will fuel the morning's activities and set the day on a high energy course. Here are some suggestions for quick starts:

■ **Make a better bagel:** Fill a toasted split bagel with part-skim ricotta cheese or lowfat cottage cheese instead of cream cheese. The night before, flavor the cheese with a savory blend of chopped fresh vegetables such as green onion, sweet pepper and celery. Or go the sweet route and add plumped raisins, wheat germ and a pinch of ground spice, such as cinnamon or cloves.

■ **Bake muffins on the weekend** and refrigerate them. Warm the muffins in a microwave for just-baked taste.

■ **Whip up a yogurt and fruit smoothie:** Combine ¾ cup lowfat yogurt, ¼ cup skim milk and 3 ice cubes in the blender.

Add your choice of peeled, sliced fruit such as bananas, strawberries, raspberries or peaches. Add a teaspoon of sugar or honey, if you wish, and whirl until smooth and thick.

■ **Microwave hot cereals**: they're ready in less than 5 minutes and there's no messy pot to clean.

■ **Prepare pancake and waffle batter** the night before, for easy morning skilletry. Or cook the pancakes, cool them, then wrap and freeze with waxed paper between them to prevent sticking. Reheat in the microwave or toaster oven.

■ **Make fresh juice combinations** and refrigerate in big pitchers. Use as quickly as possible for best nutritional value.

■ **Serve dried fruit compotes** (warm or chilled): add cut-up fresh fruit, then top with a generous dollop of plain, lemon or vanilla yogurt and a dusting of ground cinnamon.

QUICK-COOKING EQUIPMENT

A **microwave oven** has many uses, from quick thawing to reheating to fast cooking. Remember, the more food you put in a microwave oven, the slower the cooking—so if you're baking six potatoes, for example, you might do just as well with a conventional oven, if time is your only consideration.

■ A **food processor** chops, shreds, slices, grates, grinds and purees, and kneads bread, in record time.

■ A **mini chopper** saves time grating hard cheeses, mincing garlic or chopping small amounts of most foods.

■ A **blender** pulverizes dry ingredients such as nuts and purees soft, liquidy ingredients in no time.

■ A **hand-held mixer** is easier to store than a stand mixer and will whip heavy cream and eggs faster than a whisk or rotary beater.

■ Although the action is slow in a **slow-cooker,** you can set it up and forget it until you're ready to eat. Also, it's a wonderful way to tenderize tougher cuts of meat.

WHEN YOU FIND TIME

In one good "cookathon," you can prepare enough food for at least a week's worth of meals.

■ **Plan to cook freezable main dishes** like stews and casseroles, and round out the menu with simple salads, canned and frozen side dishes and prepared desserts. Devise more interesting vegetable side dishes to go with simple broiled meat, poultry or fish entrees that don't require much preparation. (*See some of our quick vegetable sautés in Chapter 10.*)

■ **Make a menu plan** for a given number of days, gather recipes and build a shopping list around them. Group similar items together on the list to save time in the supermarket. Remember to include a variety of beverages, snacks, breads, baked goods and condiments.

■ **Prepare often-used ingredients in quantity** to make quantity cooking go more quickly. Skim over the recipes you've chosen for the week and look for similar ingredients. You can save time by chopping enough vegetables, grating enough cheese or measuring out dry ingredients all at the same time to use in a number of recipes, rather than starting from scratch with each individual recipe.

■ **Make up mixes of dry ingredients** for pancakes, waffles, quick breads and muffins. Measure ingredients directly into food storage bags; label the bag with directions for completing the recipe.

TOO BUSY TO CLEAN

Short of hired help, a busy cook's best friend may be the dishwasher, especially when you're feeding a large crowd or cooking in quantity to save time later on. While many people believe in the "wash as you go" school of thought, it's more economical and certainly quicker to load a dishwasher to capacity, turn it on and forget it than to clean up by hand. Other clever cleaning ideas:

■ Cover work surface with flattened grocery bags or old newspaper. Trim and peel produce or shellfish directly over paper. When you're done, gather up paper and trimmings and discard (or carry out to the compost heap).

■ Use quick-to-clean equipment like plastic cutting boards and nonstick cookware, and don't use more equipment than you need—the same spoon can stir the sauce *and* the vegetables, with a quick rinse in between.

■ Pop dirty dishes/utensils in the dishwasher and put away items as you work to avoid a kitchen full of overwhelming clutter.

■ Save cleaning time by lining broiling and roasting pans with aluminum foil.

■ Whenever possible, serve food in the same container in which it was cooked.

■ To save space and the time it takes to find the right container for food storage, refrigerate or freeze food in heavy-duty plastic storage bags (which can usually be washed and used again).

INDEX

(SOME OF THE RECIPES IN THIS INDEX ALSO APPEAR IN A SPECIAL INDEX FOR HEALTHFUL RECIPES, WHICH BEGINS ON PAGE 644.)

▲ = MICROWAVE; • = QUICK

▲ = MICROWAVE; • = QUICK

▲ = MICROWAVE; • = QUICK

▲ = MICROWAVE; • = QUICK

▲ = MICROWAVE; • = QUICK

▲ = MICROWAVE; • = QUICK

▲ = MICROWAVE; • = QUICK

▲ = MICROWAVE; • = QUICK

634

▲ = MICROWAVE; • = QUICK

▲ = MICROWAVE;　• = QUICK

▲ = MICROWAVE; • = QUICK

▲ = MICROWAVE; • = QUICK

▲ = MICROWAVE; • = QUICK

▲ = MICROWAVE; • = QUICK

▲ = MICROWAVE; • = QUICK

▲ = MICROWAVE; • = QUICK

▲ = MICROWAVE; • = QUICK